Bahrain 1975/76–2020

Contemporary Archive of the Islamic World

VOLUME 6

The titles published in this series are listed at *brill.com/caiw*

Bahrain 1975/76–2020

Edited by

Anthony Axon
Susan Hewitt

BRILL

LEIDEN | BOSTON

The Library of Congress Cataloging-in-Publication Data is available online at https://catalog.loc.gov
LC record available at https://lccn.loc.gov/2023946124

Typeface for the Latin, Greek, and Cyrillic scripts: "Brill". See and download: brill.com/brill-typeface.

ISSN 2589-8124
ISBN 978-90-04-68632-8 (hardback)
ISBN 978-90-04-68633-5 (e-book)
DOI 10.1163/9789004686335

Copyright 2023 by Koninklijke Brill NV, Leiden, The Netherlands.
Koninklijke Brill NV incorporates the imprints Brill, Brill Nijhoff, Brill Schöningh, Brill Fink, Brill mentis, Brill Wageningen Academic, Vandenhoeck & Ruprecht, Böhlau and V&R unipress.
All rights reserved. No part of this publication may be reproduced, translated, stored in a retrieval system, or transmitted in any form or by any means, electronic, mechanical, photocopying, recording or otherwise, without prior written permission from the publisher. Requests for re-use and/or translations must be addressed to Koninklijke Brill NV via brill.com or copyright.com.

This book is printed on acid-free paper and produced in a sustainable manner.

Contents

Preface XI
Acronyms XIV
Map XVIII
Introduction XIX
1975/76 1

>Independence – National Assembly – Elections – Military Ties with UK and US – Arab/Israeli War – Aluminium Bahrain – Traditional Industries Waning – Education – Well Developed Banking and Telecommunication Services – Pearling – Financial Policy – *Entrepôt* Trade

1977 6

>Boom Conditions – Constitution – Off-Shore Banking Licences – Concorde – National Assembly Dissolved – 'Good Neighbour' Policy – Qatar Relations Strained – Arab Shipbuilding and Repair Yard – Oil Revenue Increase – Social Spending – Infrastructure – Low-Cost Housing – Banking

1978/79 18

>Causeway from Saudi Arabia – OAPEC – Abu Safah Oilfield – Early Social Development – Development Bonds – BAPCO – Caltex – ALBA – Khuff Strata – Monetary Authority – Commercial Banking – Offshore Banking – Entrepôt Business – Gulf Air – Education – ASRY – Hotel Industry

1980 34

>Success as a Service Centre – Causeway Optimism – The British Connection – Iranian Claims – State of Emergency – The Importance of Oil – Saudi Generosity Towards Its Poorer Neighbour – Gas Offers Brighter Picture – ALBA a Commercial Success – ASRY Drydock – Supremacy as a Financial Centre – Islamic Banking – 1980 to See Upward Economic Turn – Political and Social Pressures from a Sophisticated Multi-National Community

1981 47

>Winds of Change – Camp David Accords – OPEC – Natural Gas Liquids Exports – BANAGAS – APICORP – Offshore Banking Units – Industrial Expansion – Economic Slowdown – Isa Town

1982/83 54

Instability in the Gulf – Iranian Agression – Support for President Saddam Hussein – Demonstrations by Shi'a – Israeli Invasion of Lebanon – Gulf Rapid Deployment Force – European Initiative – Arab Shipbuilding and Repair Yard – Offshore Banking Sector – Agriculture – Causeway to Saudi Arabia – Four Year Development Plan 1981–85

1984 66

Shi'a Muslims – Gulf Co-operation Council – Historical Role – al-Khalifa Rule – National Assembly – Constitution – Housing Programmes – ALBA Expansion – Hamad Town – Bahraini-isation – Tourism – Inter-Gulf Trade – No Feast or Famine – A Fully Fledged Financial Market – Refinery Losses

1985 82

Iran/Iraq War: Escalation But No Panic – A Time-Zone Midway Between Europe and the Far East – Decline of Bahrain's Role as a Service Centre for Saudi Arabia – Exempt Companies – Meagre Oil Resources Dwindling – Iran Relinquishes Longstanding Claims to Bahrain – Viability of Bahrain Depends on Saudi Goodwill – Small Number of Dissenters – The Economy Loses its Buoyancy – Major Activity is in the Gas Field – Search For New Outlets Becomes a Matter of Survival – Aluminium Price Recession – 'No More Heavy Industry, Let Us Digest What We Have'

1986 97

Shi'a Disaffection – Aluminium Bahrain – Gulf Co-operation Council – Expatriates – State-run and Quasi State-run Operations – Migration From Iran – Weekly Majlis – Four-Year Development Plan – Banking Recession – 'Low Risk, Low Reward' Strategy

1987 110

Conflict With Qatar – Hostages Taken – Peninsula Shield – Oil Production Rises (Slightly) – Spending Slashed – Retrenchment – Housing Provision – Overdue Debts – Shifting Patterns of Employment – Averting Unemployment – Emerging Labour Force

1988 121

Transformation Under Way – Coup Attempt – Inter-Gulf Trade – Dwindling Oil Reserves – Increased Commercial Sophistication – Over Manned Bureaucracy – Major Projects Held Back – Five-Year Development Plan

CONTENTS   VII

1989   130
Improved Security – US Navy – Royal Navy – Sense of Insecurity –
Income Tax Rejected – Debt Provisions – Industry's Mixed
Messages – Post-War Business Boom?

1990   136
Upswing in Gulf Business – Contacts With Iran Increased –
Relationship With Washington – Economic Challenges – Stock –
Unemployment – Negligible Debt – High Reserves

1991/92   144
Military Upheaval – Economic Uncertainty – Iranian Threats –
Financial Sector Viability – Construction Projects – Water –
Transition and Trial

1993/94   151
Border Problems – Budget Problems – Human Resources –
Foreign Companies Law – New National Assembly Planned –
Open Skies Policy – Plunging Aluminium Prices – Stock Market
Expansion

1995   156
Exports and Imports Gap – Hawar Islands Dispute – Oil
Exploration Prevented – The Importance of ALBA – GCC Export
Success – Banking Centre of the Gulf – Tourism a Billion Dollar
Industry – Regional Headquarter Choice

1996   163
Shi'a Protests – Sunni-Dominated Régime – GCC Support –
Zubara – Development Schemes Delayed and Cancelled –
Aluminium Production Cut – Stock Market Integration – Oil
Reserves – Developing Downstream Industries

1997   168
Unrest – Organised Protest – Executions – Urban Terrorism –
Hawar Dispute – Development Loans – Islamic Banking –
Development Projects – Gas Reserves

1998   173
Demand for Greater Representation – Consultative Council –
Political Violence – Execution of Dissidents – Relations with
Iran Improve, but not with Qatar – Stock Market Opens –
Important Regional Centre for Islamic Banking – Surplus
Trade Balance – Employment Opportunities

1999   178
Shi'a Demands – Human Rights Abuses – Unemployment – Hard Line Policy – Utilities Problems – Local Loans to Government – Offshore Exploration

2000   183
Improved Prospects – Political Reform Falters – Policy Changes – Worsening Living Standards – Ruling Family Divisions – Oil Revenues Climb – Tight Monetary Policies – Political Unrest Vulnerability

2001–02   188
New Emir – Political System Liberalisation – National Assembly – Respect for Human Rights – Hawar Resolution in Sight – Rising Unemployment – Financial Services – Stock Exchange – Tele-Density

2003/04   195
Municipal and National Elections – Political Liberalisation – 2002 Constitution – Social Issues – Terrorist Threats – Protests – Overt and Covert Support for Washington – Entrenched Economic Elite – Bahraini-isation – Telecommunications Liberalisation

2005/06   200
Bi-Cameral Parliament – Dominance of Conservative Islamists – Monetary Union – Key Structural Areas – Inter-Generational Equity – Customs Union – Cosmopolitan Living Environment

2007   208
Offshore Banking – Awali Production Declines – Financial Sector Triples – Draft Labour Law – Monetary Agency – Democratic Credentials – Election Boycott

2008   214
Moves to Modernise – Left at the Post – Corruption – Threat of Instability – Enhanced Due Diligence – Unemployment Benefits – Robust Economic Performance – Shi'a Unemployment – New Offshore Licensing Round

2009   220
Backwater – National Action Charter – Gentle Reform Process – Hydrocarbons Decline – Safe Haven Investment Location – From Emir to King – Potential New Oil Reserves

2010   227
Rankings – Foreign Influences – Dense Population – Religious Balance Tilts – Societies – Islamic Finance Centre – Iranian Suspicions – Regenerating Oil Production

CONTENTS IX

2011/12   232

Gulf Staging Post – Iranian Interference – Rumblings of Dissent – Violent Periods – Saudi Troop Reinforcements – Royal Family Wrong-Footed – An Uprising, Not a Revolution – A Deepening Human Rights Crisis – Decency and Tolerance? – The World's Newest Pariah State

2013   237

Military Tribunal Convictions – Vindictiveness – Reform Agenda – Continuing Unrest – Job Creation – Key Challenge – Fiscal Unsustainability – Decline in Bank Assets

2014   244

Imprisoned Human Rights Defenders – 'Honest and Open Discussions' – HRW Criticism – No Willingness to Change – *Annus Horribilis* – Bond Issue – Fiscal Improvement

2015   249

Government's Maladroit Actions – Reconciliation Talks – Bahrain Independent Commission of Inquiry (BICI) – 'Foreign Interference' – Moderate Economic Growth – New Crown Prince Out Manoeuvered? – First to Produce Oil, First to Cease Oil Production?

2016   256

Heavy-Handed Response to Street Protests – al-Wefaq Election Boycott – iPhones for Voters – Bahrain Joins the Yemen Coalition – GDP Growth, Low Unemployment – Vision 2030: Competitiveness, Integrity and Sustainability – New Pipeline Planned – Prison Riots – Torture Allegations

2017   262

Iran's Territorial Ambitions – List of 68 Terrorist Groups – Lebanese Residents Deported – Economic Vulnerabilities Rise – Fiscal Deficit Remains High – GCC Funding – Economic Malaise and Uncertainty.

2018   268

Early Social Development – Pearling Prosperity – Confused and Sullen Aquiesence – Bahraini Doctors and Lawyers – One-sided Stalemate – First Executions for Twenty Years – Shared Grievances – Khalij al-Bahrain – Political and Social Uncertainties – Hesitant Investment Climate

2019   276

Attempts to Redress the Religious Imbalance – Frustrated Demands – Perceived Instability – Astride Three Middle East Fault Lines – Friends in the West – ALBA Expansion

2020   284

Human Rights – Banking Reforms – FinTech: High Hopes – Oil Price Plunges – Diversification Again – New Discoveries – New Pipeline – Asset Rich, Cash Poor

The Islamic Calendar   295

Arabic Naming Practice   300

Notes   302

Timeline   407

Bibliography   414

Country Profile   416

Index   431

Preface

In the early 1970s the founders of World of Information identified the need for a comprehensive but readily accessible source of information on the countries of the Middle East. The 'oil shock' rises in the price of a barrel of oil saw queues grow at petrol stations across Europe and North America. The world's fragile dependency on a handful of little-known Middle Eastern countries had become plain to see. This vulnerability was not matched for some time by an increase in regional coverage on the part of the traditional news media.

Thus the *Middle East Review* was launched, rapidly establishing itself as an objective, affordable information source. Published from leafy Saffron Walden some 100km north of London and just south of the university city of Cambridge, the *Middle East Review* appeared annually. It soon established itself internationally, with subscribers in over 100 countries and a strong bookshop presence throughout the Middle East, from Beirut to Bahrain, Khartoum to Kuwait.

This volume re-publishes the *Middle East Review*'s annual appraisals of Bahrain, the background to the country's formation, its economy and its nascent politics. At the time of the discovery of oil deposits in 1932, Bahrain was a relatively 'mature' state, its schools and hospitals placing it well ahead of its neighbours in developmental terms. For much of the twentieth century Bahrain's relationship with the United Kingdom certainly had shades of colonialism. Following the Second World War its relationship with Britain endured, while its near neighbour Saudi Arabia found itself in the US sphere of influence. During the conflict British concerns had been focussed on preventing any German presence establishing itself in the Gulf, or forming alliances with the larger, more established, states to the north, or more critically, with Iran.

International press coverage of the onset of the Arab Spring in 2011 was initially focussed on Tunisia, followed by Egypt and Libya. Coverage of events in Bahrain was less widespread, for the most part slipping under the world's radar. This was surprising as the Gulf State's upheavals were equally, or even more, dramatic. Bahrain's population comprised a Shi'a majority ruled by a Sunni minority. Its relationship with Shi'a Iran was closer that of any other Gulf State, and the rumblings against the political *status quo* lent themselves to what became a volatile, even violent state of affairs in February 2011. Although many commentators saw the Bahrain uprisings as a straightforward clash between Sunni and Shi's, this superficial interpretation failed to take into account the often complex political ambitions of Bahrain's educated work force. Such was the volatile climate of opinion throughout the Arab World in 2011, that ambitions soon translated into protests. On 14 February Bahrain's so-called 'Day of Rage' saw organised, largely peaceful protests initially put down by police tear gas, followed by shots resulting in a number of deaths. One month later the Gulf Co-operation Council (GCC) despatched its Peninsula Shield Force representing the GCC member states (excluding Oman), largely comprising Saudi motorised troops, into Bahrain via the Causeway. The Bahrain government declared a State of National Safety in March; it was lifted by King Hamad on 1 June. The late Robert Fisk writing in the London *Independent* noted that the Saudis 'never received an invitation. They simply invaded and received a post-dated invitation.'

This state of affairs, and the lukewarm support the intervention drew from Kuwait and Qatar, marked a shift in Gulf perceptions. The GCC's hitherto unchallenged unity had been replaced by doubts and differences. A few years later, those differences became even more apparent when, in 2017, Bahrain, alongside its principal regional ally, Saudi Arabia, severed diplomatic ties with Qatar. Fellow GCC members, joined by Egypt, followed suit. By early 2021 it appeared that the differences with Qatar had been quietly resolved. Bahrain paid little more than lip service to the Saudi lead (and UAE supported) Operation Decisive Storm against the Houthi-led and Iranian backed coalition. The overt calm that had characterised Bahrain for most of its post-independence history disguised myriad political and social tensions that have been swept under the carpet. By 2011 those tensions began to reveal themselves, aggravated by the Government's inept and often disproportionate response.

Our thanks are due to countless people without whom the *Middle East Review*, from which these articles are extracted, would probably not have been published for so many years. Their help extended to research and documentation, editing and proof reading, not to mention providing commercial and moral support, guidance and generous hospitality. With apologies to those we have inadvertently left out, and to those who may have been unaware of their valuable input, we would like to mention:

Alan Asbridge, Marion Board, Dan Bindman, Kathleen Bishtawi, Daniel Brett, James Buchan, James Buxton, Rennie Campbell, Dick Carrington, Nicholas Childs, Naomi Collet, Roger Cooper, Louise Denver, David Docherty, Michael Field, Carol Filby, Mary Frings, Liselotte Fussner, Graham Hancock, Bob Jiggins, Richard Johns, Ali Kamel, Michel Kaikati, Warwick Knowles, Chris Kutschera, David Ledger, Alan Mackie, Simon Martin, Anthony McDermott, Tony Morbin, Lewis Moreland, Michael Morris, Marianne Morse, Zaki Nusseibeh, Bobbie Reynolds, Michael Ritchie, David Shirreff, Sara Searight,

PREFACE

Pamela Ann Smith, Alan Taylor, Doina Thomas, Fumihiro Tanaka and Ken Whittingham.

Finally, thanks are also due to the staff and members of the organisations that allowed us to use their facilities in preparing this book, and the *Middle East Review*. These include: the Cambridge City Library, various departments of Cambridge University and the Cambridge University Library. The Middle East Association (London), the Hong Kong Foreign Correspondents Club and the Tokyo Foreign Press Club.

Acronyms

ABC	Arab Banking Corporation
ADHRB	Americans for Democracy and Human Rights in Bahrain
AISCO	Arab Iron and Steel Company
ALBA	Aluminium Bahrain
AML/CFT	Anti-Money Laundering/Countering Financing of Terrorism
APICORP	Arab Petroleum Investments Corporation
ARAMCO	Saudi Arabian Oil Company
ARIC	Arabia Insurance Company
ARIG	Arab Insurance Group
ASRY	Arab Shipbuilding and Repair Yard Company
AUB	Ahli United Bank
AWACS	Airborne Warning And Control System
AWS	Amazon Web Services
BAB	Bahrain Association of Banks
BAII	Banque Arabe et Internationale de l'Investissement
BALCO	Bahrain Saudi Aluminium Marketing Company
BALEXCO	Bahrain Aluminium Extrusion Company
BANAGAS	Bahrain National Gas Company
BANOCO	Bahrain National Oil Company
BANZ	Bahrain National Cold Storage and Warehousing Company
BAPCO	Bahrain Petroleum Company
BASREC	Bahrain Ship Repair and Engineering Company
BATELCO	Bahrain Telecommunications Company
BBK	Bank of Bahrain and Kuwait
BBME	British Bank of the Middle East
BCHR	Bahrain Centre for Human Rights
BD	Bahrain dinar
BDF	Bahrain Defence Force
BFB	Bahrain FinTech Bay
BHRF	Bahrain Human Rights Forum
BHRO	Bahrain Human Rights Observatory
BHRS	Bahrain Human Rights Society
BIB	Bahrain International Bank
BICI	Bahrain Independent Commission of Inquiry (Bassiouni Commission)
BIPD	Bahrain Institute for Political Development
BIRD	Bahrain Institute for Rights and Democracy

BKIG	Bahraini Kuwaiti Investment Group
BMA	Bahrain Monetary Agency
BMB	Bahrain Middle East Bank
BNGEC	Bahrain National Gas Expansion Company
BOAC	British Overseas Airways Corporation
BP	British Petroleum
BPA	Bahrain Press Association
BRAVO	Bahrain Rehabilitation and Anti-Violence Organisation
BSE	Bahrain Stock Exchange
BTS	Bahrain Transparency Society
BW	Bahrain Watch
CBB	Central Bank of Bahrain
CIS	Commonwealth of Independent States
CSO	Central Statistical Organisation
DIFC	Dubai International Financial Centre
EBOHR	European Bahrain Organisation for Human Rights
EC	Exempt Company
EDB	Economic Development Board
EEC	European Economic Community
EIA	(US) Energy Information Administration
EWA	Electricity and Water Authority
FAO	UN Food and Agriculture Organisation
FBP	Fiscal Balance Programme
FDI	Foreign Direct Investment
FRAB	Banque Franco-Arabe
FSAP	Financial Sector Assessment Programme
FTB	FinTech Bay (aka Bahrain FinTech Bay)
GARMCO	Gulf Aluminium Rolling Mill Company
GATS	General Agreement on Trade in Services
GCC	Gulf Co-operation Council
GCHR	Gulf Centre for Human Rights
GDP	Gross Domestic Product
GFH	Gulf Finance House
GIB	Gulf International Bank
GIC	Gulf Investment Corporation
GIIC	Gulf Industrial Investment Company
GISFC	Global Islamic and Sustainable FinTech Centre
GNP	Gross National Product
GOIC	Gulf Organisation for Industrial Consulting
GPIC	Gulf Petrochemicals Industries Corporation

HOCC	Heavy Oil Conversion Company
HRW	Human Rights Watch
IBL	Investment Banking Licence
ICJ	International Court of Justice
IDB	Islamic Development Bank
IDC	Industrial Development Centre
IDD	International Direct Dialing
IFLB	Islamic Front for the Liberation of Bahrain
IHT	International Herald Tribune
IIF	Institute for International Finance
IMF	International Monetary Fund
IS	Islamic State
ISIL	Islamic State of Iraq and the Levant
ISIS	Islamic State in Iraq and Syria
IRGC	Islamic Revolutionary Guard Corps
JGC	Japan Gas Corporation
KUFPEC	Kuwait Foreign Petroleum Exploration Company
LNG	Liquefied Natural Gas
LPG	Liquefied Petroleum Gas
MEA	Middle East Airlines
MEFG	Middle East Financial Group
MENA	Middle East and North Africa
MFN	Most Favoured Nation
MIA	Ministry of Information Affairs
MTBE	Methyl Butyl Tertiary Ether
MWHB	Military Wing of Hezbollah Bahrain
NAFTA	North American Free Trade Agreement
NBK	National Bank of Kuwait
NED	National Endowment for Democracy
NGL	Natural Gas Liquids
NIHR	National Institute for Human Rights
NOGA	National Oil and Gas Authority
NUC	National Union Committee
OAPEC	Organisation of Arab Petroleum Exporting Countries
OBU	Offshore Banking Unit
OGJ	Oil and Gas Journal
OPEC	Organisation of the Petroleum Exporting Countries
PDRY	People's Democratic Republic of Yemen
PFLOAG	Popular Front for the Liberation of the Occupied Arabian Gulf
PLO	Palestine Liberation Organisation

ACRONYMS XVII

RAF	Royal Air Force
RBA	Royal Bahraini Army
RBAF	Royal Bahraini Air Force
RDF	Rapid Deployment Force
RNBF	Royal Bahrain Naval Force
SaA	Saraya al-Ashtar
SABIC	Saudi Basic Industries Corporation
SAMA	Saudi Arabian Monetary Authority
SDB	Sacred Defence Bahrain
TAIB	Trans-Arabian Investment Bank
TAIC	The Arab Investment Company
UBAF	Union des Banques Arabes et Francaises
UGB	United Gulf Bank
UGI	United Gulf Investments
UGIC	United Gulf Industries Corporation
ULCC	Ultra Large Crude Carrier
UNHCR	United Nations Human Rights Council
VAT	Value Added Tax
VLCC	Very Large Crude Carrier
VRS	Voluntary Retirement Scheme
WTI	West Texas Intermediate
WTO	World Trade Organisation

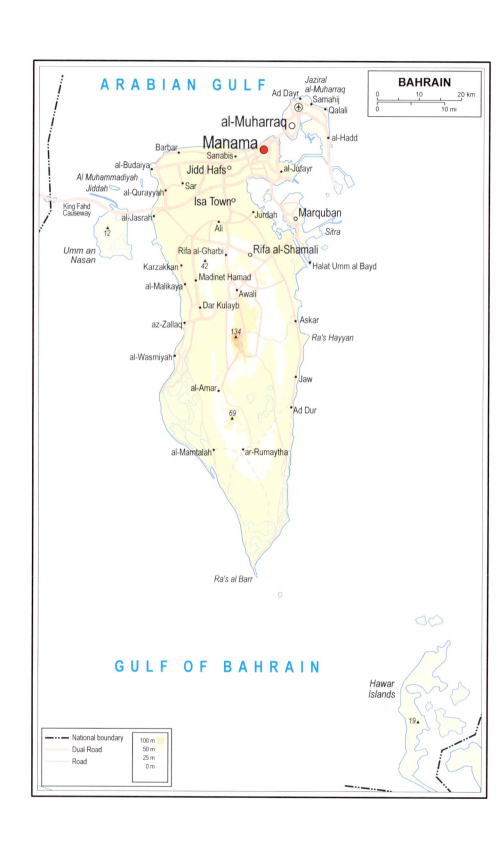

Introduction

Bahrain has roots deep in the past, going back some 5,000 years, during which time it has been home to three civilisations, those of Dilmun, Tylos, and Awal. It became known as 'the Land of Immortality' or the 'Paradise', names attributed to its abundance of fresh water springs and palm tree fields. Bahrain was also a vital link between civilisations, such as the Phoenicians in the Levant, Mesopotamia, in what was to become Iraq, and Egypt's Nile Valley. Archaeological excavations have confirmed its place as a commercial *entrepôt* and a sea transit point between east and west.

Although by the twenty-first century Bahrain, in terms of its depleted oil reserves, was seen by many as the Gulf States' 'poor relation', for centuries it had been seen as the region's most developed and (in the absence of hydrocarbons) most wealthy territory. It was, for example, recognised as the centre of the all-important pearling industry. Bahrain can also be proud of the fact that it was the first territory outside the mainland of the Arabian Peninsula to accept and embrace Islam. In the seventh century (the eighth year of the Islamic calendar) the prophet Mohammed's envoy, Al-Ala al-Hadhrami, arrived in Bahrain in 628 AD with a letter from Mohammad to the ruler of Bahrain, Al-Mundhir ibn Sawa At-Tameemi, inviting him to accept Islam. The ruler consulted with the heads of the tribes and most of them agreed to accept the Prophet's invitation and consequently embraced Islam. Previously, the inhabitants of Qatar and Bahrain had worshipped idol gods, but such was the attraction of Islam, the new faith soon spread through the region that is now Bahrain and Qatar. By the end of the seventh century Islam was established throughout the region. Such was his success, Al-Ala al-Hadhrami was appointed by Mohammed as his representative in Bahrain to collect the Jizyar (tax paid by non-Muslims). Al-Ala was also the ruler of the region from 633 until his death in 635.

Following the death of Prophet Mohammed, Bahrain came under the political control of the Umayyad and Abbasid dynasties and over the centuries that followed, Bahrain came under the control of a number of Arab and Persian dynasties. Even the Portuguese ruled the islands for 80 years in the fifteenth century. Conquerors, mercantile people, adventurers, slavers, extreme religious groups and soldiers of fortune, all walked these lands and came in search of the treasures of Bahrain.

What might be termed the modern era of Bahrain began in 1783, following the island state's conquest by Ahmed al-Fateh, and has been ruled by the al-Khalifa family since. Sheikh Isa bin Salman al-Khalifa came into power on 16 December 1961, and was considered one of the pioneer Arab leaders that built their countries based on justice and stability. He consolidated the Arabism and independence of the country with the support of the Bahrainis, who voted in a poll organised under the United Nations confirming that Bahrain was (and with some reservations) remains, an independent Arab state ruled by the al-Khalifa. Bahrain was declared fully independent from the United Kingdom on 15 August 1971, and of the British protectorate on 16 December of the same year. During the era of the modern state, Bahrain issued its first constitution in 1973.

When Hamad bin Isa al-Khalifa assumed power as Hakim in 1999, Bahrain entered a new era of reform and development, becoming a constitutional monarchy in 2002, in line with the National Action Charter and the amended constitution. On the positive side of the balance sheet, Bahrain has thus made pioneering achievements in development, as well as advanced and continuous political and democratic reforms, and positive developments within laws and constitutional institutions, which gave Bahrain a prominent position regionally and internationally.

However, on the negative side is a sadly unpublished aspect of Bahrain's political development. It is perhaps best reflected by the island Kingdom's impressive number of non-governmental human rights associations, groupings, and pressure groups – not to mention political 'parties' and coalitions. There are, for example, four bodies with a title beginning with 'Bahrain Human Rights'; these include The Bahrain Human Rights Forum, the Bahrain Human Rights Observatory, the Bahrain Human Rights Society and the Bahrain Human Rights Watch. Not to be outdone, the Bahraini government has established not only a Ministry for Human Rights, but also a National Institution of Human Rights (NIHR).

Following the 2011 uprising (inspired by the Arab Spring movement) which saw street protests and their often violent suppression, few countries would have promptly appointed an Independent Commission of Inquiry (BICI) headed by a distinguished neutral – in the case of Bahrain, the Egyptian Cherif Bassiouni. But for Bahrain a high priority was that of maintaining where possible, good relations with its allies – not only those in the Middle East headed by Saudi Arabia, but also in Europe where Bahrain's government, that is to say its Royal Family, saw the United Kingdom as a natural ally with whom it shared a number of values.

1975/76

Independence – National Assembly – Elections – Military Ties with UK and US – Arab/Israeli War – Aluminium Bahrain – Traditional Industries Waning – Education – Well Developed Banking and Telecommunication Services – Pearling – Financial Policy – *Entrepôt* Trade

Bahrain became an independent state in August 1971. This date officially marked the end of the special political and military treaties with the British government under which Britain had been responsible for the islands' defence and foreign affairs. The declaration of independence was superseded by several important events, namely the decision in 1970 of Iran to relinquish its historical claim to the group of islands (the state of Bahrain consists of a group of 33 low-lying islands) and the decision of the Bahraini government to opt out of the United Arab Emirates (UAE) in spite of the efforts of the Saudi-Kuwaiti Mediation Mission. As an independent Arab state, Bahrain became a member of the United Nations and the Arab League shortly afterwards.

The state of Bahrain is ruled by Sheikh Isa bin Salman bin Hamad al-Khalifa who is the tenth of his line in succession since Sheikh Ahmed bin Mohammed al-Khalifa assumed sovereignty over the islands in 1783. The ruling establishment has been essentially autocratic in its power but benevolent and liberal in practice. Prior to 1970 the administration of the government had been undertaken by appointed officials who were in turn advised by nominated councils and committees, while the towns were administered by elected municipal councils. In January 1970 a Council of State was formed and given complete executive powers by the Ruler, although he continued to retain sovereign powers. The state's first elections were held in December 1972, in order to elect 22 of the 44-seat Constituent Assembly (the rest were appointed), whose first task was to deliberate on a draft constitution of the state. Bahrain's first constitution was published in June 1973, which provides for equality, freedom of speech and religious belief. It introduces a democratic style government in its call for the formation of a National Assembly composed of the members of the cabinet and 30 members elected by popular vote to represent Bahrain's eight constituencies. Elections to the first National Assembly were held in December 1973, and the Assembly was convened for the first time in mid-December.

Politically, the state of Bahrain still maintains close trade and military ties with Britain, and to a lesser extent with the United States of America (US) under a formal agreement with Washington whereby the US Navy is entitled to use facilities in Bahrain. These relations were strained by the October 1973 Arab/Israeli war but the US navy continued to use the facilities for a twelve-month period following official termination of the agreement by Bahrain. At the same time, Bahrain espouses all the political ideals of the Arab world in respect of its adherence to the claims of the Arab League and support for the Palestinian cause. As an independent entity with small resources, Bahrain has attempted in the last two years to reduce its vulnerability by cementing closer economic and political relations with its powerful neighbours, namely Saudi Arabia and Kuwait, and has striven to establish close trade links with the UAE and Qatar.

The Economy

Bahrain's 33 islands lie some 30km off the east coast of Saudi Arabia, covering a total area of 785sq km. The census of April 1971 showed that the total population of the Bahrain islands had reached 216,000, with an estimated growth rate of 3.3 per cent per annum. The state is divided into eight administrative districts with Manama, the capital, accounting for half the population, followed by Muharraq – the second largest island – with an estimated population of 50,000. Bahrain enjoys a mixed free enterprise system, with the government playing an active role in the development of the economy through the extension of basic infrastructure and participation in large local projects. Apart from agriculture and fishing, Bahrain's prosperity depended in the past on its trade and pearl diving (pearling) before oil was discovered in 1932. Pearl diving was killed off, as elsewhere in the Gulf, by Japan's cultivated pearls and, more importantly, by the advent of oil.

While petroleum has and will continue to be of crucial importance, not the least because it provides over half the government's revenue, development of the economy has been recently directed towards making Bahrain a regional centre, both for business in general and the provision of services for the Gulf oil industry in particular.

Bahrain has the most developed banking andtelecommunication services in the Gulf, the highest level of education in the area, and the most prosperous merchant community. The prosperity brought by the discovery of oil has brought with it, however, its attendant pressures, namely those of urbanisation and sharply rising consumer demand. Although no figures exist on consumer prices, it is believed that the cost of living has risen very sharply in recent years as a result of demand outstripping supply of goods. The problem has moreover been accentuated by shortages of labour with Bahrainis accounting for approximately 65 per cent of the economically active population. The economy remains heavily dependent on foreign unskilled labour (Indo-Pakistani and

Iranian) as well as professional and technical expertise, and inflation is still a problem to be tackled.

In early 1974, the government introduced subsidies on sugar, flour and meat, and later on rice, in an attempt to combat the rise in food prices.

Production

Bahrain has no agriculture to speak of. By far the greatest expanse is sterile desert, with only 10 per cent in the north and north-western periphery of the islands under vegetation due to the presence of water springs. Of this area two-thirds are under date palm trees and the rest is devoted to vegetables, forage and fruits. Although the government has been trying to encourage agricultural development in conjunction with the United Nations Food and Agriculture Organisation (FAO), the prospects are not very encouraging in view of two basic problems: that of salinity and the dwindling proportion of farm labour, which is being increasingly attracted to higher wages in the cities. Fishing, however, remains an important activity, and has been recently expanded by the establishment in 1965 of the Bahrain Fishing Company (40 per cent the British Ross Group, 60 per cent Bahraini) which catches and freezes prawns for export on a considerable scale. Plans are in hand for the purchase of 300 Friesian cattle from Australia to establish a local dairy industry. Experiments are also to be carried out with sheep farming.

The major industry in the country is oil production and refining. Traditional industries such as boat-building, pearl fishing and weaving have tended to decline with the advent of oil. As in many developing countries, the first non-petroleum-orientated industries were comparatively unsophisticated ones requiring little expertise such as the manufacture of building materials, textiles and soft drinks. The major industrial development, however, started with the establishment of Bahrain's aluminium smelter – Aluminium Bahrain (ALBA) – completed in 1972 and making use of Bahrain's considerable supplies of natural gas. Output is estimated to be running at 120,000 tons a year, mostly for export, and the government is pressing ahead with ancillary industries based on the smelter for the manufacture of aluminium powder, and an aluminium extraction plant. The government seems committed to a policy of industrial diversification and other projects being considered by the development bureau include a water desalination plant on the island of Sitra.

Bahrain is the oldest oil-producing state in the Gulf; the first strike was in 1932 and commercial production began in 1934, by the Bahrain Petroleum Company (BAPCO) (established by the Standard Oil Company in 1928) from the Awali oilfield. Reserves are relatively small (estimated at 375 million barrels at end 1972) and prospecting has so far been disappointing. It is estimated that known oil reserves can only be exploited for about another 20 years. Production has been stable for a number of years but in 1972 fell by 6–7 per cent to 25.5 million barrels due to government conservation restrictions. Although production is expected to continue to fall, revenues are expected to increase significantly as a result of the recent upward adjustments of the posted price. The BAPCO refinery (the second largest in the Middle East) treats both Bahraini and Saudi Arabian crude, and processed 94 million barrels of crude oil and other stocks in 1971. An important development has been the discovery of substantial gas reserves which are now being examined, and part of which are used by the ALBA aluminium smelter.

As a member of the Organisation of the Petroleum Exporting Countries (OPEC) and the Organisation of Arab Petroleum Exporting Countries (OAPEC), Bahrain has joined the other Arab countries in enforcing the oil embargo on the Western world, and at the same time it is a signatory to the higher posted prices negotiated by OPEC.

Transport and Communications

Bahrain has a well-developed network of roads, many of them dual carriageways and there are over 15,000 motor vehicles in the state. Bahrain is the first aviation centre of the Gulf and its airport is the first in the world to be built specifically to take jumbo-jets and receives more than 300 flights a week. Telephones, telex and cable services both within the state and those linking Bahrain with other countries have been developed greatly, the latest and most important project being the station for satellite communications. A deep-water harbour at Mina Salman provides docking facilities for six ocean-going vessels, and extensive warehousing facilities. The port also includes a large free transit area with ample sheds and mechanical handling facilities. The oil port on Sitra Island is presently being expanded to take tankers up to 100,000dwt. The proposed OAPEC dry dock, to be operated by a consortium of Portuguese and Japanese ship-repairers, is also to be located in Bahrain.

Finance

For some two decades, Bahrain's principal sources of income have remained basically the same with about 60 per cent of the state's income deriving from oil revenues. Additional income is chiefly derived from customs receipts and land registration fees. In 1968 the first indirect tax was introduced in the form of a duty on petrol. The government's financial policy has been to direct the major portion of its income to public and social services. The total estimated receipts and expenditures in the 1973 budget amounted to BD32.5 million, an increase of 23 per cent over the 1972 budget. The major allocations of total expenditure were earmarked for development projects followed closely by education and housing. Monetary affairs of the state are controlled by the Bahrain Currency Board (established in 1964). The Bahrain dinar is backed by short-term British government securities and cash reserves with the Bank of England. Total currency in circulation stood at BD23.28 million by the end-September 1972. Bahrain has no income or profit taxation.

Given the government's limited resources, additional impetus for industrial development, and particularly with respect to foreign participation in local projects, has been provided in the form of the free repatriation of funds, the absence of any exchange control, and customs concessions on imports of capital equipment.

Foreign Trade

The geographical position of the islands has had an important effect in making Bahrain the centre of a substantial *entrepôt* trade. This has also been enhanced by the rapid industrial development and by the provision of modern and adequate facilities such as sea- and air-ports to handle the increasing volume of trade to the Gulf area. Despite keen competition by Dubai in recent years, Bahrain's exports and re-exports (mostly the latter) have kept a steady pace, with half of them going to Saudi Arabia. The latest figures available relate to 1973 and show that the total value of imports reached BD128.0 million compared with BD100.1 million in 1972. Principal imports are machinery and transport equipment, foodstuffs and consumer goods. Exports were unchanged at BD32.0 million. As with other developing nations, the principal imports were accounted for by capital equipment. Bahrain's main supplier remains Britain followed closely by Japan, the USA and China, while her customers are mainly Saudi Arabia and the Gulf states.

Despite what appears to be an enormous trade gap, Bahrain with its issued currency more than covered by gold and foreign exchange, has no balance-of-payments problems. There is a sizeable trade in gold. Mina Salman port is a free zone; duties on actual imports are 5 per cent *ad valorem* on foodstuffs and necessities, 10 per cent on non-essentials, 35 per cent on tobacco and 50 per cent on liquor. On transit goods there is a small storage charge only. As a concession the government waives the import duty on capital equipment imported for the purpose of establishing a new industry. Local businesses are often willing to enter into partnership with foreign companies.

At present, Bahrain has no import or export controls except for a short list of prohibited items including firearms and cultured pearls. As in other Arab countries, the provisions of the Israeli and Rhodesian boycotts are enforced.

1977

Boom Conditions – Constitution – Off-Shore Banking Licences – Concorde – National Assembly Dissolved – 'Good Neighbour' Policy – Qatar Relations Strained – Arab Shipbuilding and Repair Yard – Oil Revenue Increase – Social Spending – Infrastructure – Low-Cost Housing – Banking

The steady planned progress which has been the unswerving policy of Bahrain's development experts over the past few decades is serving it well in the boom conditions affecting all Gulf states since the dramatic oil revenue increases of the 1973 energy crisis.

Bahrain's income is tiny compared with that of the giants of the oil industry which surround it on the mainland, but the island seems set fair to retain its position as a regional commercial, communications and servicing centre. To these facilities must now be added a strong bid to become a world financial centre with the decision taken in 1975 by the Bahrain Monetary Agency (BMA) to offer limited licences to international banks to undertake off-shore banking from offices located there.

Already 32 such licences have been issued and taken up by so many leading names from the USA, Canada and Europe that the venture is now scarcely likely to be challenged seriously by any other Gulf state. The issue of offshore banking licences has been described as possibly the most significant decision taken in Bahrain during the past few years.

In the early part of 1976 Bahrain has also enjoyed much publicity following its choice by British Airways as the destination of its first Concorde supersonic passenger flights. The arrival of the first flight in January became front page news in the international press and publicity was gratifyingly enhanced by full page advertising booked by British Airways itself in the same newspapers. Bahrain suddenly found itself in the centre of a world spotlight, and the focus of much inquiry.

Politics

Bahrain became independent in August 1971 after more than a century of a special relationship with the United Kingdom based on a series of treaties and agreements which dated back to 1853. Two important events had preceded independence. In 1970 Iran agreed to relinquish its historic claim to Bahrain, relieving Bahrain's main anxiety as to its future following British withdrawal.

Bahrain also decided not to join a proposed federation of nine lower Gulf States after varying ambitions among them had proved irreconcilable. After independence Bahrain became a member of the Arab League and of the United Nations and many of the latter's subsidiary organisations. (Bahrain is too small an oil producer to qualify for membership of the Organisation of the Petroleum Exporting Countries (OPEC), but is a member of the Organisation of Arab Petroleum Exporting Countries (OAPEC) and is benefiting greatly by that organisation's decision to choose Bahrain as the site of its first downstream operation, the building of a dry dock and repair yard for super-tankers.)

Bahrain's Head of State is HH the Emir Sheikh Isa bin Salman bin Hamad al-Khalifa, now 42 and in the fifteenth year of his rule. He is the tenth in line of succession since Sheikh Ahmed bin Mohammed al-Khalifa assumed sovereignty over the islands in 1782. Heir Apparent is Sheikh Hamad bin Isa bin Salman al-Khalifa, the present Minister of Defence. The ruling establishment is regarded as autocratic in its power but in most cases liberal and benevolent in practice.

In January 1970 a Council of State was formed and given complete executive powers by the Emir although he continued to retain sovereign powers. Prior to that date, administration had been exercised by appointed officials advised by nominated councils and committees. Towns were administered by elected municipal councils.

The state's first elections were held in December 1972, to elect 22 members by popular vote to a 44 seat Constituent Assembly (the remainder being appointed) whose task was to deliberate a draft constitution of the state. This constitution was published on 2 June 1973. It contains 108 Articles and provides for equality and freedom of speech and religious belief. It introduces a democratic style government in its call for a National Assembly composed of the members of the cabinet and 30 members elected by the people from eight constituencies.

Elections to the first National Assembly – in which 85 per cent of all-male suffrage turned out to vote – were held 7–8 December 1973 and it was first convened on 16 December that year. Unfortunately this experiment in democracy, taken far in advance of any other southern Gulf State, has proved premature, if not abortive.

By August 1975 unfamiliarity with committee procedures, unconstructive argument by elected members, combined with blocking tactics against the government by certain factions, had led to a huge pile of unapproved Bills. In boom conditions development progress was being brought to a standstill. To break the impasse, in August 1975 Sheikh Isa dissolved the Assembly by Emiri decree. The Prime Minister, Sheikh Khalifa bin Salman al-Khalifa, stated at the time: 'We dissolved the National Assembly to give us time... to find a better more workable solution for an institution which was not truly representative of the people. We are still a democratic country.' The months following the dissolution saw a spate of delayed government measures on welfare, security and commercial development brought into operation.

Foreign Relations

In foreign relations Bahrain still maintains close ties with the United Kingdom of Great Britain and Northern Ireland (UK) and to a lesser extent with the United States of America (US) under a formal agreement with Washington whereby the US navy is entitled to use limited facilities in Bahrain. These relations were strained by the Arab-Israeli war of October 1973 (and the agreement was even formally terminated by the Bahrain government) but the US navy continues to use the facility which it has enjoyed for well over 25 years. Future tenure is likely to depend on the US pursuing a more even handed policy in the Arab-Israeli conflict. Relations with France have warmed following an official visit paid by the Emir to Paris early in 1976.

Bahrain stands firmly for Arab solidarity and pursues a 'good neighbour' policy with the countries that surround her – though relations with Qatar have traditionally been strained as a result of long standing territorial and family disputes. Friendship is close with Saudi Arabia, Kuwait and Abu Dhabi all of which have in recent years given Bahrain substantial financial support either by direct grant or by 'soft loans'. The Palestine Liberation Organisation (PLO) has established offices in Manama. Outside the Arab World, there are no diplomatic ties with Iron Curtain countries although trade is exchanged between them.

Human Resources

Bahrain enjoys a mixed free enterprise system with the government playing a major role in development of the economy through the extension of basic infrastructure and participation in local projects.

Prior to the discovery of oil in 1932 Bahrain's prosperity had been built up on its trade and its pearling industry. Until recently, with the expansion of Dubai's port, Bahrain's position as the Gulf's premier *entrepôt* was unchallenged. To its central Gulf position it could add the advantages of a naturally sheltered harbour and abundant fresh water which bubbles up from the springs in the north and north-west of the island and clothes the coastline there in heavy vegetation. In ancient times the combination of shelter and fresh water existed nowhere else on the long and hazardous voyage between Mesopotamia and Sind. It was an essential calling point for mariners. archaeological evidence has shown that a lively trading post existed there as long as 5,000 years ago.

Bahrain also possessed the most prolific pearling banks and by the turn of this century prosperous merchant communities had grown up both in Manama and Muharraq whose wealth was based on pearls and trade. The economy suffered an abrupt reverse in the late 1920s when Western markets suddenly became bombarded by Japanese cultured pearls, but the situation was retrieved with the advent of oil.

While petroleum has since been, and for some years to come will continue to be, crucial to the economy not least because it provides well over half the government's revenue, recent policies have been directed towards making Bahrain a business centre and to provide services for the Gulf oil industry in particular.

For well over 50 years it has been a matter of considerable pride (and much publicity) in Bahrain that modern education for both boys and girls is entirely free at all levels (including higher education abroad) and that it has consistently been a major item in successive budgets.

From a single boys' school started in 1919, facilities have grown so that today the state has 160 schools and just over 60,000 attending pupils of whom nearly half are girls. This policy has added much to the responsibilities of government because young Bahrainis expect more from the state. Emphasis is now strongly on vocational training. The government remains the largest employer in its civil and related services and light industry, business and commerce is expanding, but reasonable employment for middle-class young Bahrainis remains a problem.

At the lower end of the scale, there is a labour shortage and the economy is becoming increasingly dependent on foreign unskilled labour (Indo-Pakistanis, Afghans and Iranians).

Increasing prosperity, especially over the past two years, has brought attendant pressures of urbanisation and sharply rising consumer demand. Imported world inflation is a further unwelcome factor as are increased freight charges. Bahrain, like all other Gulf states, needs to import most necessities of life. The cost of living has spiralled sharply.

No official figures for consumer prices exist, but independent sources put the rise in cost of living at at least 20 per cent in each of the past two years. For an expatriate, if vastly increased residential and office rents are added, the figure is much higher.

In 1974, government introduced subsidies on sugar, flour, meat and vegetable oil and later on rice in an attempt to combat food price rises. It has also purchased three trawlers and opened its own retail fish shop to cut out middle-man profiteering in fish. Charges for electricity supply to households have been slashed by 50 per cent.

Food Production

Bahrain has little agriculture to speak of. Two-thirds of the main island are sterile desert. The fertile northern fringe consists of about 30,000 acres chiefly under date palms, alfalfa and vegetables, and fruits, especially dates. This area is, however, being alarmingly cut into by developers for where land becomes available it is being snapped up for conversion into up-market residential housing estates. The ambition of only ten years ago to make Bahrain self-sufficient in all vegetables for some months of the year and self-sufficient in some other vegetables for all the year now seems far from attainment and may not be revived until 1983 when nine million gallons of re-cycled water daily from Bahrain's planned sewerage system is promised for crop growing.

Meanwhile, studies have been completed for a large-scale poultry farm at Hamala capable of producing 15 million eggs a year for home consumption – a third of Bahrain's needs. Also near Hamala, sheep rearing on a limited scale is progressing from a flock of 300 Awasi ewes imported from Saudi Arabia in 1975. A pilot scheme is in operation for a national dairy farm on Muharraq for which 300 Australian-bred Friesians are to be imported. The intention is to market a full range of dairy products, but success depends on the capability to produce enough fodder to support the cows.

Fishing remains an important activity and, apart from the government's trawling venture, this sector was expanded in 1965 by the establishment of the Bahrain Fishing Company (40 per cent Ross Seafoods (Gulf) Ltd; 60 per cent Bahraini). The company produces processed Gulf prawns – among the world's best – for luxury markets overseas. Fishing by traditional methods using traps and nets is still practised in coastal villages and building of wooden dhows for local trading countries.

Cottage-type industries such as weaving, pottery and ornamental carving are dying away as labour is drawn from villages to industry.

Oil

The state's major industry is oil production and refining. Oil was first struck here in 1932 and was considered a miracle at the time for it was the first strike to be made on the Arabian side of the Gulf. The yield, however, has been small by any standards and beginning with 9,600 barrels per day (bpd) in 1934, rose to a peak of 76,000bpd in 1972 and has since been in gentle decline to its present level of 55,000bpd. The life of the field allowing for a steady fall in production is now estimated at 20 years.

From its beginning, the oil industry has been run by the Bahrain Petroleum Company (BAPCO) owned by the Caltex partnership of Standard Oil of California and Texaco. The National Assembly ratified a participation agreement in

June 1975 for the government to take a direct 60 per cent interest in oil and natural gas production. The government has also announced its intention of acquiring the remaining 40 per cent of BAPCO's operations and has now formed its own National Oil Company to prepare for future developments. The agreement does not, however, cover BAPCO's refinery which is the company's most valuable asset and which maintains an output of 250,000bpd, the bulk being crude being carried by pipeline from Saudi Arabia.

Oil revenues have shown an astonishing increase over the past two years as a result of the quadrupling of prices at the end of 1973. Revenues for 1976 are expected to reach BD131 million, while those for 1975 were BD111 million. (In both years BD50 million was expected from Abu Safah, an offshore oilfield whose yield Bahrain shares with Saudi Arabia.) Figures for the years 1976 and 1975 should be compared with the year 1972/73 when oil revenues were a mere BD10.2 million. Going further back in history it might be mentioned that the years between 1936 and 1956 yielded a total of BD12 million for the entire period.

After the government, BAPCO remains Bahrain's largest employer with nearly 4,000 persons on its books. Ninety per cent of employees are Bahraini. Through the years BAPCO has contributed greatly to a general rise in living standards not only as an employer but by creating sub-contracting businesses and spending millions of dinars in buying as much of its requirements as possible through Bahraini merchants. BAPCO was also the pioneer of vocational training here. Training includes on-the-job instruction, academic tuition at colleges in Bahrain and overseas and specialised courses at it own training school.

An important discovery has been the presence of substantial reserves of natural gas. Some 250 million cubic feet a day are being produced from BAPCO's 15 gas wells to help meet the island's increasing power requirements. About 40 per cent of the daily total is consumed by the Aluminium Bahrain Company's smelter which operates the world's largest gas turbine power station.

Aluminium Bahrain (ALBA)

Bahrain's second major industry is the aluminium smelter Aluminium Bahrain (ALBA). This began production in 1972, the company having been formed in 1968 by a consortium of six international companies, themselves users of aluminium, plus the government who originally held 19 per cent of the shares. The companies chose Bahrain as the smelter location because of what seemed then a limitless supply of cheap power in the form of natural gas and because it was well placed geographically in relation to the source of alumina – Western Australia – as well as to destinations of the finished product.

The government welcomed the project for three main reasons. It was diversification from petroleum-based industry; it would create employment at a time when this was a critical problem; it would again spread wealth among subcontractors and their employees, and among the merchant community by local purchases.

Investment to date has been BD105 million, output runs rather over the planned capacity of 120,000 tonnes annually in a normal year, and the workforce numbers 2,600 of whom 2,400 are Bahrainis. Like BAPCO, ALBA lays great stress on the training of young Bahrainis. Half a million dinars are spent yearly on this purpose, and in 1976 an apprentice scheme has been launched with the opening of a new training complex, part of an additional BD500,000 investment.

ALBA has also given an industrial relations lead to other Gulf companies by introducing joint management-employee consultations which give the latter an active part in decision making. A Plant Council meets every two months for a frank exchange of views with management.

An important policy change took place early 1976 with the appointment of a commercial marketing manager. Thus ALBA became a more fully integrated company, instead of relying on shareholders to sell metal themselves.

Over the years the government has been gradually buying out other shareholders so that as of May 1976 the breakdown of shareholdings was: Bahrain government 77.9 per cent, Kaiser Aluminium Bahrain 17 per cent and Breton Investments 5.1 per cent. The present preponderant government shareholding is seen by some observers as a move designed to protect the work force from temporary lay-offs during times of depressed prices.

Principal buyers from ALBA have been Japan, China, Europe and South and North America. Late in 1975 Iraq placed an order for 14,000 tonnes, the first Arab country to become a substantial purchaser.

Satellite industries have not sprung up around ALBA to the extent that was first hoped. An aluminium atomiser plant is in operation and an extrusion plant is now being built by Alusuisse on nearby Sitra island and will commence operation in 1977. There are also plans for a rolling mill.

Dry Dock

Bahrain has one further heavy industry now in the process of development. This is the Arab Shipbuilding and Repair Yard (ASRY), the first downstream venture to be undertaken by OAPEC with seven members participating.

OAPEC's Ministerial Council decided to proceed with this project, which will be centred round a dry dock capable of receiving VLCCs of up to 450,000 tons, in 1970. Various possible Gulf sites were inspected and Bahrain finally chosen not only for its location in the heart of the world's major crude loading area, but because of its more advanced infrastructure and its then considerable reservoir of skilled manpower. In fact, this reservoir has been much depleted by boom conditions, and a major factor which in 1975 caused ASRY's management to award the contract (worth US$150 million) for the actual building of the dock to the South Korean firm of Hyundai, is that the latter undertook to provide its own skilled work force of 1,200 men and build accommodation for them at the dock site itself.

Hyundai began work on the dock in October 1975, after the site, a 450,000sq metres artificial island and a 7km long causeway leading to it, has been raised from the sea by the Dutch dredging and reclamation firm, FALCO. The dock will be managed by Lisnave Shipyards SA of Portugal, the largest and most experienced VLCC repair yard in Europe.

The dock and the necessary ancillaries are expected to employ about 3,000 Arab nationals, not necessarily Bahrainis. Complete 'Arabisation' of the workforce is hoped for in about 15 years. Prospects for the dock eventually becoming viable are by no means assured, but seem reasonable.

Infrastructure and Social Spending

Early in 1975 the then Ministry of Development and Engineering Services found itself having to come to terms with two new problems. First, further drilling of gas wells to cater for ALBA and the new powerhouse and desalination plant at Sitra have shown that while the gas reservoir is immense, its extent had been over-estimated. From data now available, reserves are now estimated more realistically at between eight and 11 trillion cubic feet. This has caused the government to veer away from further heavy industries which could be wasteful of gas and to hold present commitments – especially expanding public utilities – as priorities.

Secondly, a report prepared by demographers engaged for the purpose estimated that Bahrain's population will more than double to about 580,000 by the end of the century. The combination of these two new factors has made Bahrain's planners decide to concentrate on civil engineering projects to consolidate and improve living standards and enhance the quality of life for the inhabitants of the islands.

Power generating capacity is gradually to be expanded from its present 200MW to a projected 2,000MW by the year 2000. The desalination plant linked to the Sitra powerhouse will eventually be producing 20 million gallons daily which will be blended into the existing natural water system. Laying of comprehensive sewerage system is to begin late this year. The first stage of the project is estimated at BD30 million.

An accelerated government housing scheme is to see 1,000 low-cost houses built yearly. The programme has been generously assisted by Saudi Arabia's

King Khalid, who on his first visit here in March 1976 donated BD40 million towards the cost.

With the present strong emphasis on vocational training, the Gulf Technical College (founded in 1968 as a joint venture between Bahrain, Abu Dhabi and Britain) and which now has 1,100 students, is to have added to it a new Business Administration faculty which is to cost BD1 million. Work is also to start shortly on a junior technical college, for 1,500 students, for which Saudi Arabia has donated BD13 million. Training schools for the dry dock, the State Electricity Department and the hotel and catering industry are government initiatives, while in addition to BAPCO and ALBA, Gulf Air and Cable and Wireless have their own training programmes.

To cope with greatly increased sea traffic the port – Mina Salman – is to have six further berths added to the present six. The first two are to be ready in 1977.

To promote commercial activity the area round the port has always been a free-zone. Adjacent to it is an industrial zone reclaimed from shallow sea. The initial reclaimed area of eight million square feet has already been leased or reserved and a further 15 million square feet is to be added. A two mile causeway across the sea has been completed to link Mina Salman to Sitra and the east coast heavy industrial area, saving a long detour through the interior of the island.

The shallow off-shore shelf which surrounds Bahrain is also being utilised to relieve congestion in Manama. About one-third of the capital now stands on recently reclaimed land and upon it new hotels, office blocks and department stores are springing up together with a new and greatly expanded municipal meat, vegetable, fruit and fish market complex. The reclaimed land has also enabled a double-lane fast ring road to be built within a few hundred yards of the cluttered town centre.

The government is also spending considerably on improving recreational facilities for lower- and middle-class Bahrainis and a BD6 million cultural centre is planned. Joint ventures between foreign companies and private interests here are planning up-market residential enclaves with marinas, swimming pools and other amenities for upper class Bahrainis and the expanding expatriate community.

A further result of King Khaled's visit has been an announcement that Saudi Arabia is to go ahead in the near future with a 30km causeway to connect Bahrain to the mainland. The cost is estimated to be US$250 million. The advantages to Bahrain of the causeway will be considerable. There will be an inevitable spin off from the huge sums being spent on Saudi Arabia's Eastern Province. Bahrain will benefit by handling more Saudi Arabian imports and by being directly linked with the trans-Arabian highway system and beyond, through Turkey, to the trans-European system. The island will most likely also receive increased invisible earnings from the larger numbers of Saudis who will come across at weekends. Bahrain is the first aviation centre of the Gulf and its airport, the first in the world purpose-built to take jumbo jets, is now used by 16 major airlines on scheduled international flights. Nearly 500,000 passengers used the airport in the first six months of last year.

Extensions and improvements to the terminal building now allow six jumbo jets to be serviced simultaneously, four through articulated air-bridges and two from the ground. A third phase of expansion begins at the end of this year with the provision of a cargo apron for the largest freight carriers and storage facilities to form a major depôt for redistribution of cargo round the Gulf.

Maintenance workshops are unrivalled in the region – in part a legacy from the British Royal Air Force (RAF) who shared the airport until 1971. Good facilities were a major factor in deciding British Airways to choose Bahrain as the destination for its first passenger carrying Concorde.

Bahrain is also the headquarters of Gulf Air (owned jointly by the governments of Bahrain, Qatar, Abu Dhabi and Oman). On 1 April 1976 Gulf Air added Tristars to its fleet of VC10s for long distance international routes.

Bahrain has excellent international telecommunications, a matter of prime interest to many foreign companies recently established there and not least to the holders of off-shore banking licences. The Gulf's first satellite earth station was opened in Bahrain in 1969. There is an efficient and extensive internal telephone network. Bahrain's television station, the first colour service in the Gulf, came into operation in 1973 and is now government-owned.

Oil revenues, rent on government property and customs receipts are the main sources of state income. In 1968 a first indirect tax was introduced in the form of a duty on petrol. There are no corporate, withholding or personal taxes. Government's financial policy has been to direct the main portion of its income to public and social services, and this particularly so in 1976.

The revenue from the budget for 1976 is estimated at BD181.2 million (1975: BD134.2 million) and expenditure at BD191.2 million (1975: BD130 million). The deficit of BD10 million is being met from reserves.

Banking

Control of the state's monetary affairs is in the hands of the Bahrain Monetary Agency (BMA) which was established in December 1973 to assume all powers and duties normally exercised by a central bank. The BMA became fully effective on 1 January 1975, when commercial banks moved their clearing settlement accounts to the Agency from the National Bank of Bahrain (50 per cent government owned).

Bahrain has 18 fully licensed commercial banks which continue to fulfil their traditional role of serving the day-to-day needs of the public and financing trade. Direction of lending in December 1975 showed no percentage upsets over the figures for recent years with trade (39.5 per cent), construction (26.35 per cent) and manufacturing (15.75 per cent) being the main borrowers.

When the BMA launched its Offshore Banking Unit (OBU) scheme in October 1975, it was aware that the local banks were not particularly interested in participating as principals in the main euro-currency market. The large depositors of funds – governments, their agencies and others – went direct to the European and American markets. The BMA considered that while it remains a logical development that Arab banks and institutions will intermediate between the depositors of 'petrodollars' and the eventual borrowers, the degree to which they can accept the credit and liquidity risks, and the expertise available, must for some time be limited.

The BMA has therefore offered banks the opportunity of opening branches in Bahrain for the purpose of undertaking non-resident business, and, in particular, of creating a market in the Gulf itself capable of handling the investment of the surplus funds of the region. It was made clear that the Bahrain branches must be full dealing centres and not just a name in the books used from elsewhere. The Agency went out of its way to attract leading international banks, recognising that these are the banks already used by the oil exporters to handle their funds, and able by strength and experience to do so. Branch status rather than local incorporation was insisted on to ensure credibility in the market.

In advertising its move, the BMA stressed that on top of the many attractions Bahrain had to offer as a regional centre must be added the crucial factor that it is located in a time zone, allied working hours, that fits neatly between Singapore and London.

Fifteen OBU licences (each costing US$25,000 annually) were issued in November 1975 and by the end of the first quarter of 1976 the total had reached 32. That the service is attractive is suggested by the fact that US$1.5 billion had been handled by the end of 1975. It is forecast that this figure will rise to US$10 billion by the end of 1976.

Trade

Despite keen competition from Dubai, Bahrain remains the centre of substantial *entrepôt* trade. The non-oil export position has been much enhanced by the output of the aluminium smelter. Exports and re-exports rose in 1975 to a value of BD83.9 million against BD71.1 million in 1974.

Boom conditions (plus inflation) have resulted in imports rising in value to BD229.5 million in 1975 as compared to BD176 million in 1974. The UK, which in

1974 lost its traditional role as chief supplier to the US, has now regained its top position with an estimated 17 per cent of the 1975 market. The US has dropped to second place with 15 per cent, followed by Japan with 12 per cent and China with 7 per cent. Principal imports in 1975 were machinery and transport equipment, manufactured goods, food and live animals.

Duties on actual imports are 5 per cent *ad valorem* on foodstuffs and other necessities, 10 per cent on non-essentials, 35 per cent on tobacco and 50 per cent on liquor. On transit goods there is a small storage charge only. As a concession the government waives import duty on capital equipment imported for the purpose of establishing a new industry.

Local businesses are often willing to enter into partnership with foreign companies, but new company and agency laws introduced in 1975 now, in broad terms, restrict foreign participation to 49 per cent.

1978/79

Causeway from Saudi Arabia – OAPEC – Abu Safah Oilfield – Early Social Development – Development Bonds – BAPCO – Caltex – ALBA – Khuff Strata – Monetary Authority – Commercial Banking – Offshore Banking – Entrepôt Business – Gulf Air – Education – ASRY – Hotel Industry

Bahrain, the smallest and poorest of the independent Gulf oil states, has decided that its future lies in becoming the service centre of the wealthy region. Its definition of 'service' is a wide one, ranging from light industries complementary to the heavier ones planned by its neighbours, to sophisticated financial skills that will use their riches, and leisure facilities, for the entertainment of their citizens. The plan is so to integrate the Bahrain economy with those of its neighbours, that when its main plank, the oil revenues, shrinks into insignificance in the foreseeable future, the whole will remain afloat. The physical expression of this integration will be the US$800 million plus, 24 kilometre causeway linking Bahrain with Saudi Arabia.

It is expected that sometime during 1978 bids will be invited for the construction of this causeway. If a contractor is chosen before the end of the year it is hoped that the planned four-lane causeway will be finished by the early 1980s. And so will end a 4,000 year history as a physically and, perhaps, politically independent trading state.

The decision to build the causeway is an historic one, and one whose impact will only be fully assessed in retrospect. No one has formally projected the possible effects of this umbilical link with mainland Arabia, whether easy-going Bahrain will be converted by the more austere Saudi, Wahhabi, influence, or whether it will become one vast dormitory town for the Western expatriates at present living and working in the Kingdom's Eastern Province. Or whether, indeed, to quote an enthusiastic and chauvinist Bahraini 'the causeway will make Bahrain the capital of the Eastern Province.' A more sober assessment is that the causeway will merely turn an already strong family, political and financial relationship into a physical one.

The final cost of the causeway could go as high as a billion dollars if all the landworks and other associated onshore facilities – such as the township for 5,000 in Bahrain – are included. And Saudi Arabia has said that it will bear the entire cost – thus effectively making a gift worth around US$4,000 per man, woman and child of Bahraini nationality in Bahrain. The magnitude of this gift

© KONINKLIJKE BRILL NV, LEIDEN, 2023 | DOI:10.1163/9789004686335_004

underlines emphatically the close relationship between the immensely wealthy young Kingdom and the relatively poor and small island Emirate of Bahrain.

Need for More Revenues

The link with Saudi Arabia is all important to Bahrain and Bahrainis are not ashamed of it. Every important decision taken by the Emirate since it severed the treaty relationship with Britain in 1971, has been supported by Saudi finance and Saudi influence. Saudi influence reportedly swayed the member states of the Organisation of Arab Petroleum Exporting Countries (OAPEC) to decide in favour of Bahrain as the site for their first major industrial venture, the drydock Arab Shipbuilding and Repair Yard Company (ASRY). It was a decision of the late King Faisal II (Faisal bin Abdul-Aziz al-Saud) of Saudi Arabia to share the revenues of the Abu Safah oilfield which lies in the straits between the two countries that prevents Bahrain's oil income sinking into insignificance.

Bahrain is only poor when compared with its oil producing neighbours. Oil revenues amount to about US$1,600 per capita and account for around 60 per cent of total government revenues. Also Bahrain is the oldest of the Arabian Peninsula oil producers, exporting commercial quantities of oil since the early 1930s. This early 'oil wealth' enabled the country to invest in basic infrastructure on a gradual basis. So Bahrain had roads, schools, a health service, telephones and so on many years before its neighbours.

However there were disadvantages to this early social development – much of the infrastructure needed modernising by the mid-1970s when Bahrain, with its limited oil income, could not afford the price. The government initially took a cautious view of spending after the 1974 oil price rise, but the island's needs became too compelling by 1975–76 and the budget went into deficit – admittedly a minute deficit – for those two years. The difference between its income expenditure was made up by soft loans largely from Saudi Arabia and Kuwait.

The main needs were for a better and greater housing stock and better power and transport services. The Bahrain population is growing at about 4 per cent per annum and the tendency to Western style, nuclear family living is growing. So each newly married couple wants its own accommodation instead of living with the husband's parents in traditional Arab style. The peak of capital expenditure will come during 1978 as Bahrain completes major road, sewage and power networks. By 1979 it is planned that recurrent expenditure should be greater than capital expenditure.

While Bahrain has been able to depend a great deal on Saudi and Kuwaiti aid for its projects, it has also been seeking ways of raising finance domestically.

The cost of many of the government services have increased noticeably during the past two years, the price of electricity, for example, has been put on a consumption related tariff which is rather nearer the cost of production in the upper price range. Business registration fees are now an annual payment on a graduating scale rather than a token outlay once a corporate lifetime.

The most adventurous revenue raising exercise has been the government's launch of development bonds in the autumn of 1977. This was the first time any Gulf government had borrowed domestically. There were a number of reasons for the creation of the bonds: first, the need to test out additional sources of finance for the government, second, to mop up excess liquidity in the banking system, and third to provide a secure domestic investment for the growing pension and other institutional funds in the island. The first US$25 million of bonds were received by local institutions and the government is considering widening the market for the second tranche. It is also considering development bonds as a means of financing revenue generating projects. And though it has never been overtly stated, the possibility of going to the international capital markets must be at the back of government's collective mind.

Oil Industry

In the short term, oil revenues both from the island's own oilfield and from Abu Safah will provide the mainstay of government revenues. It is envisaged in the 1978–79 budgets that 1978 will be the peak year for oil revenues, though this is dependent on future OPEC price moves. (Although Bahrain is too small a producer to belong to OPEC, it is a member of the Organisation of Arab Petroleum Exporting Countries (OAPEC) and follows the Saudi oil policy line). In March of 1978 Bahrain finally completed the 100 per cent take-over of its oil producing operation with the consequent shift in emphasis. As senior government officials pointed out, what is good for Caltex (the concessionaire through the Bahrain Petroleum Company (BAPCO)) with its many sources of oil may not always be equally good for Bahrain with only one source. The oil refinery, however, was left out of the take-over plans for purely financial reasons, according to Bahrain government sources. (The same has applied in Saudi Arabia to Aramco's Ras Tanura refinery.)

Bahrain's refinery, managed by BAPCO, a subsidiary of Caltex, opened in 1963 and has a rated capacity of 250,000 barrels a day. It is the oldest refinery on the west side of the Gulf and had always been excepted from the Bahrain government's plans for nationalisation of its hydrocarbon resources, though the government has the right to take it over. Defensive maintenance costs for the refinery – that is continual repairs – are running at about US$25 million a year and BAPCO has spent considerable sums in recent years upgrading the plant.

A low sulphur fuel oil unit was commissioned in the course of 1974 at a cost of around US$60 million following on a considerable rehabilitation programme after a serious tank fire in 1972. A new power station which will cost just under US$20 million is under construction. Repairs to the loading berth at Sitra island have opened the terminal to bigger tankers, up to 110,000 tons deadweight (dwt). The average daily crude run from the Bahrain (Awali) oilfield to the refinery during 1974 was marginally lower at 58,000 barrels than during 1976. The bulk of the refinery's throughput comes piped undersea and across land from Saudi Arabia.

The government took a 60 per cent stake in its oil resources as late as 1975 and did not set up its own national oil company, the Bahrain National Oil Company (BANOCO), until late 1976. Early in 1978 the government's ownership was raised to 100 per cent of all crude output, local marketing of refined products, and non-associated gas output of around 330 million cubic feet a day. It is an indication of the small scale of Bahrain's oil operations that the change from 60 to 100 per cent ownership will only add around US$4 million to Bahrain's oil income. But for Bahrain, faced with a steadily declining output from present known reserves and the possibility of no oil at all by the year 2,000, every additional dollar counts.

This need for even marginal income has also stimulated a renewed exploration programme on- and off-shore in Bahraini territory. Its purpose is not so much to find new oilfields as to determine more exactly the parameters of the existing Awali oilfield. Recently a Caltex reservoir study team visited the island to evaluate the field and look into the various methods of recovery being used. The oilmen in Bahrain are actively studying tertiary methods of recovery; for Bahrain, a reduced profit per barrel owing to higher production costs is better than no profit at all.

Gas Project

Consistent with its policy of maximising the return from its dwindling hydrocarbon resources, is Bahrain's intention to build a US$90 million gas-gathering and processing natural gas liquids (NGL) facility for the associated gas, even though this gas may only be produced for another 20 years or so. The contract, which was won by the Japan Gasoline Corporation, was awarded early in 1978 and the plant is supposed to be on stream by 1980. The basic feedstock gas is the 100 million cubic feet a day of associated gas from the Awali oilfield which is currently being vented or flared. The intention is to produce around 280,000 tons of propane, butane and natural gasoline annually, mostly for export, with the light residue gases being used locally for power generation or possibly conversion into fertiliser. While the marketing arrangements were not finalised by

May 1978, the government was sufficiently confident to predict that it should be able to repay the loan raised within four to five years – despite all the other NGL plants being built in the region. It is cautious about giving estimates of possible sales value but some have suggested it could be as high as US$33 million – depending on world prices.

The residue gases could well be used to supply as much as three-quarters of Bahrain's aluminium smelter's power needs, thus saving some 85 million cubic feet a day of non-associated gas. Reserves of non-associated gas in Bahrain are on a more generous scale than oil and are estimated to be around 9 trillion cubic feet. Current production of this non-associated gas from the Khuff strata is of the order of 330 million cubic feet a day. At present about a third is used for power for Aluminium Bahrain (ALBA), a quarter injected into the oil wells, about 20 per cent is used by the refinery and the rest is used for domestic electricity generation.

The products of the associated gas will be marketed by a new company which will be associated with BANOCO. Its proposed capital is US$20 million and both Caltex and the Arab Petroleum Investments Corporation (APICORP) (the OAPEC investment company) will have a 12.5 per cent share. The money for the project has been raised by the Gulf International Bank (GIB), owned by seven Arab states including Bahrain. GIB is an offshore bank headquartered in Bahrain and while the offshore banks are not supposed to deal with commercial institutions trading in the island, the government is prepared to make specific exceptions.

ALBA – *Reorganisation*

Another such exception is Aluminium Bahrain (ALBA) whose working capital needs used to be funded through London. But now the smelter's promissory notes are bid for by the domestic and offshore banks that showed themselves keen to take on the company's paper. The competitive bidding has considerably reduced the cost of finance for ALBA which, now in its seventh year, is embarking on a cost-cutting exercise, prior to possible expansion of the plant.

The idea of setting up an aluminium smelter in an Arab state, and more particularly in Bahrain, was first mooted by a group of aluminium users in 1968. The idea was to use Bahrain's natural gas as a cheap fuel for the plant. By 1971 the plant was in operation, capable of producing up to 120,000 tons of aluminium a year and buying its gas at a reported nine cents per barrel equivalent. The smelter negotiated a long term contract with an Australian alumina producer which is still advantageous, although re-negotiated recently.

Over the past years changes in the world market for aluminium have persuaded some of ALBA's original shareholders to sell out. By January 1976 the

1978/79 23

Bahrain government had increased its shareholding in the smelter to 77.9 per cent. The other two remaining shareholders are Kaiser Aluminium (US) 17 per cent and Breton Investments (Netherlands) with 5.1 per cent. This change in ownership persuaded the Bahrain government to start marketing its own share of the metal rather than allowing it to be sold by the Amalgamated Metal Corporation as its agents.

Finished metal production in 1977 was 121,356 tonnes, marginally above the plant's rated capacity. The market value of the output has been estimated to be US$125 million though there is a considerable stockpile awaiting better world prices – the change to largely government ownership having enabled the company to stockpile in times of poor world prices. At present it is company policy to sell only spot metal. At the end of 1977 the stockpile was 50,000 tonnes – the same as at the beginning so the smelter did manage to sell its entire annual output. Japan continues to be the single biggest importer of Bahraini aluminium though the regional market is now of growing importance. In 1977 the Far East as a whole took 88,000 tonnes of metal (compared to 93,000 in 1976) and the Arab world took 22,000 tonnes, a threefold increase over the previous year.

1978 is to be a crucial year for ALBA, which is undergoing some reorganisation of management and is going to have to take a decision on the proposed US$77 million expansion plan. A crucial factor will be the assessment of other regional states' aluminium plants, particularly Iran's Dulsais, and that planned by Saudi Arabia. The addition of a further potroom should add 35,000 tonnes to capacity within the present infrastructure of the plant. The expansion would demand an extra four turbines at the power station to boost generating capacity to 373MW and some more minor modifications to the cast house and the carbon plant. Plans for a joint production facility with BAPCO to produce green coke, however, have been shelved, as have plans for a rolling mill, given the plans of neighbouring countries.

There have been serious increases in the costs of ALBA's raw materials, particularly for petroleum coke which has quadrupled in price since ALBA started production and which is likely to double again in the next four years. The most serious cost pressure, however, has been staffing, in particular expatriate salaries. The company estimates that it costs about BD22.000 to keep one Western expatriate in Bahrain – and it used to employ around 200. The beginning of 1978 saw 50 of these declared redundant, for many of the jobs had been directly dependant on the initial start up problems of the smelter which was using a never before combined mixture of technologies.

It is commonly accepted that ALBA is over-manned and the new general manager aims to cut the present workforce down from 2,600 to under 2,000. Natural wastage should take care of the Bahraini side, thus neatly avoiding any possible political repercussions of local redundancies. It is ironic for one of the original aims of the smelter was to generate employment for Bahrainis who are increasing in number at a rate of around 4 per cent a year. But new developments in service industries have changed the labour market.

The profitability or otherwise of ALBA is subject to some argument with other smelters pointing accusingly at ALBA's cheap fuel. In the boom year of 1974 when aluminium prices were last at a world high, the value of ALBA's output was around US$113 million. Subtract from that the imported raw material costs, and the added value works out at US$82.5 million. In 1977 the same sums produced an added value of just under US$80 million on the production's value of US$128 million. Net foreign exchange earnings – important to Bahrain which needs to diversify its source of foreign exchange away from oil revenues – are slightly less than the added value figure because about 5 per cent of ALBA's production is now sold locally.

On that basis, the rough net foreign exchange income generated by ALBA is around US$73.6 million, or US$294.40 per capita. This compares quite favourably with the foreign exchange earnings from Bahrain's own oil resources which work out at around US$790 per capita. Even that 5 per cent of aluminium that is sold domestically will, at one remove, be generating further foreign exchange for the island as the two principal aluminium using industries are both geared to export.

The first spin-off plant produces aluminium powder used in paint, metallic inks and explosives. Bahrain Atomisers International, as it is now known, was set up near ALBA in 1973 and has a production capacity of 3,000 tonnes annually. The majority shareholder is the Bahrain government with 58 per cent and the remainder is held by Breton Investments (one of the original smelter shareholders). The second plant is an extrusions factory, Bahrain Aluminium Extrusion Co (BALEXCO), which is wholly government owned though constructed and managed by Alusuisse of Switzerland. Its planned capacity is 3,000 tons with hopes of reaching 2,500 by the end of 1978.

Even the Bahrain private sector is now venturing to go into aluminium processing. The first wholly privately owned company to use ALBA billet will be Midal Cables, a joint venture between the Australian Olex Cables Company and the Bahraini merchant family A A Zayani – best known as the Gulf agent for Rolls-Royce cars. The new cables plant in Bahrain will eventually take about 12,000 tonnes of billet from ALBA. The plant will consist of a complex casting and rolling mill with a range of wire drawing and stranding equipment. However, the government is now cautious about further industrialisation and is likely to permit only export minded industries complementary to the plans of Saudi Arabia and possibly of Iran.

Bahrain Monetary Agency

In a way Aluminium Bahrain could be said to be the father of Bahrain's best known service industry, the offshore banking market. The smelter was built by British Smelter Constructions with a considerable amount of export credit backing from the British government. British Smelter Constructions' bankers, Williams & Glyn, sent a man to Bahrain to oversee the financing of the project, Alan Moore. The first chairman of ALBA was Bahrain's then finance minister, Sayed Mahmoud al-Alawi, for the investment, over US$100 million, was an ambitious project for Bahrain at the time – virtually a year's oil revenues. Sayed Mahmoud later invited Mr Moore to stay in Bahrain and set up the Bahrain Monetary Agency (BMA) to regulate the domestic banking market.

In the course of regulating the domestic banking market, setting the level of interest free balances to be kept with the BMA, monitoring the interest rates and supervising foreign exchange business, Mr Moore was also able partially to restructure the financing of ALBA, to the benefit of both the local banks and the smelter. In 1975 the BMA organised the issue by ALBA of promissory notes in dinars, for periods of one to six months, which are available for competitive monthly tender. The offshore banks may bid with the domestic banks for similar dollar notes, which have proved extremely popular with both categories of banker.

Basically the BMA has responsibility for the note issue, it is the government's banker, it manages the country's investment portfolio, it regulates the banks and controls the money supply. It was, for example, the government's sole agent and advisor on the 1977 bond issue. The Agency reports direct to the Bahraini cabinet and both the Prime Minister, Sheikh Khalifa bin Sulman al-Khalifa, brother of the Ruler, and the new Finance Minister, Ibrahim Abdul-Karim, are on the board as chairman and deputy respectively. Since October 1977 a Bahraini, Abdulla Saif, has been director general of the BMA; he joined at the same time as Alan Moore, who now has the title 'advisor to the board'.

Commercial Banking

In the domestic market there are nineteen banks reporting to the BMA. In early 1978, the nineteenth, the Al-Ahlia Bank, had only just been formed, licensed and signed a technical assistance agreement with the Bank of America (which also has an offshore branch in Bahrain). Despite the generally low level of business during 1977, the year when the oil boom bust throughout the Gulf, it was not a bad year for Bahrain's commercial banks. The two major banks with local shareholdings, the National Bank of Bahrain which is a government/private sector venture, and the Bank of Bahrain and Kuwait (BBK), a 50/50 joint venture with Bahraini and Kuwait interests, both experienced reasonable profits in 1977.

During that year the National Bank of Bahrain made a net profit of around US$7.25 million, an increase of just over 11 per cent on 1976. BBK, a much smaller bank, turned in net profits of US$4.5 million, an increase of just under 42 per cent on the previous year. The total assets of the National Bank of Bahrain increased by just under 17 per cent while advances increased by just under 2 per cent – advances the previous year had topped 70 per cent. The comparable percentages for BBK are just over 25 per cent growth in total assets and 43 per cent in advances.

1977 was very much a year of consolidation for the National Bank of Bahrain, which had suffered a fairly traumatic 1976 when business completely outstripped its administrative resources. The reorganisation of staffing-up of the bank was virtually complete at the end of 1978. The growth during 1977/78 for the bank was entirely natural, but in 1979 it plans to start vigorous marketing for new business which should give the Al-Ahlia Bank a tough start to its business life.

Although 1977 was primarily a year of reorganisation for the National Bank of Bahrain, it also moved into the local and international money markets, participating in the dollar bond issue for Eurofima, the Bahraini dinar bond issues for Pemex (the Mexican state oil company), for the Philippine government and for the Bahrain government's own development bonds – the first ever Gulf gilts. The bank is also planning to apply for an offshore licence before the end of 1978.

The most noticeable change in the retail banking picture over the past couple of years has been the emergence of the construction sector as the principal borrower in Bahrain. Until 1975 trade dominated the lending picture, largely because Bahrain, like all other Gulf states, has to import virtually everything it needs other than oil. But the post oil price rise construction boom peaked in Bahrain during 1976, with builders accounting for virtually a third of all bank lending. During 1977, in spite of the business slowdown, construction's share of the lending rose to 40 per cent of the total, as opposed to a quarter for trade. At the beginning of 1978 bank lending was still slow and letter of credit business was looking but a shadow of even the reduced 1977 figure. Local commentators reckon that business in Bahrain was not likely to pick up until the end of 1978 – unless the causeway contract is awarded earlier.

Offshore Banking

It is generally believed in Bahrain that the offshore banking concept developed from the nature of business being booked by one of Bahrain's foreign retail banks. Whatever actually stimulated the idea in October 1975, the world's banks welcomed it with open arms and by the end of November that year about 15 of the major world banks had applied for offshore banking licences. The package that the BMA placed before the bankers was the opportunity to open up a full branch, with no necessity to involve a local partner, with virtually no prospect of nationalisation, on an island without corporate or personal taxes or exchange control. The only area of banking forbidden to them would be personal or corporate current accounts and other forms of financing for local companies or individuals – with exceptions (such as ALBA and the BANOCO gas project financing) at the BMA's discretion. The sudden shift in world wealth after the 1973 quadrupling of the oil price had focused bankers' minds on a region then US$60 billion better off, and in particular on the chronic-surplus states of Saudi Arabia, Kuwait, Abu Dhabi and Qatar, who all had more money than they could use.

The theory supporting the offshore banking concept was that the world could bear another money market and, because of the shift in wealth, that it should be in the Arab world. The factors supporting Bahrain as its home were largely the result of its early affluence. The island's oil income from the mid-1930's on had been invested in infrastructure, communications, and education. So when the bankers started to assess the island, they discovered a state that was located in time zone terms between Britain and Singapore, that boasted good telephone and air communications and a large, relatively well educated, relatively sophisticated indigenous population. Bahrain's traditions as an *entrepôt* centre had also accustomed its people to foreigners.

At the end of 1977 there were 33 fully-fledged offshore banking units (OBUs) in operation which between them had amassed assets amounting to US$15.7 billion. By the end of the first quarter of 1978, when the market was just 2 years old, the assets had risen to US$17.5 billion and 37 banks were in business – with a further six licence holders busy setting up and a comfortable rate of new enquiries. An analysis by the BMA of the audited figures of the banks in operation at the end of 1977 showed that most of them made profits, in total thought to amount to about US$75 million. The three or four who did not make profits had not been in business long enough. In many cases the fees and commissions alone covered the OBUs operating expenses which turned out to be less than originally forecast at around US$500,000 each.

While it was the lure of possible petrodollar surplus deposits that first brought the bankers to Bahrain, once ensconced they discovered that the scope for commercial business was much greater than they had anticipated, particularly in local currency lending. This was directly due to the less sophisticated non-restrictive banking practised in the wealthier neighbour states.

Preliminary studies of the first quarter 1978 figures show that deposits from Arab countries increased by just under 15 per cent to US$9.5 billion. Loans to Arab countries were also up at US$7.8 billion and dealings in Arab currencies were up to US$4.5 billion, principally in Kuwaiti dinars and Saudi riyals. A conspicuous Saudi riyal deal was the SR300 million raised for the Saudi company, REDEC. It was a floating rate five year loan at 2 per cent over Saudi interbank offered rates of 1 per cent – whichever was the greater, a proviso which, according to one offshore banker, indicated the relative youth of the market. However, an acknowledgement of the growing importance of Saudi riyal business was the decision by the BMA to develop a central riyal clearing facility (this is also a reflection on communications with Jeddah and Riyadh).

Most of the world's major banks now have an offshore unit in Bahrain and the new inquiries are coming from the smaller regional banks. The main Arab consortium banks, Banque Arabe et Internationale de l'Investissement (BAII), Union des Banques Arabes et Françaises (UBAF), EuropeaArabBank and the Banque Franco-Arabe (FRAB), are all present in Bahrain. BAII has taken a noticeable lead in syndicated lending. It was lead manager for the REDEC loan as well as for the biggest Bahraini dinar bond issue to date – the BD15 million for Pemex. UBAF early in 1978 launched the first floating rate dollar denominated certificates of deposit in the Bahrain market through the agency of Merrill Lynch International.

FRAB-Bank and the new Gulf Riyadh Bank have both taken advantage of Bahrain's extension of the offshore banking concept and incorporated themselves as Bahraini exempt companies (see below). Merrill Lynch International is to take out an investment banking licence (IBL) to further its Gulf business. The IBL licence was devised by the BMA for merchant banking activities and one of the earliest takers was the British merchant bank Kleinwort Benson (which has considerable business in the Arab world) who will also incorporate an exempt company. A feature of the last half of 1977 was the increasing muscle of the Gulf International Bank (GIB), set up in late 1976 and jointly owned by Saudi Arabia, Kuwait, the United Arab Emirates, Qatar, Oman, Iraq and Bahrain. The bank's authorised capital is US$100 million, paid up is US$70 million. It is either lead manager or co-manager in the syndicated loans raised for the United Arab Shipping Company, the BANOCO (for the associated gas project) and Gulf Air. While the bank has an admitted advantage over others in its parentage for certain kinds of business, it also feels it has a responsibility towards the Arab world and the development of its financial institutions.

The sudden influx of a large number of mostly Western expatriates during 1975/76 put something of a strain on Bahrain's infrastructure resources. The telecommunications bore up well but there was an acute shortage of domestic and office accommodation of suitable quality. Prices rocketed during 1976 and only broke in the summer of 1977. (Bahraini landlords and hoteliers who over-reacted and over-invested in response to this upsurge in demand are now looking to the causeway as the beginning of their salvation).

The advent of all these people, however, produced a further injection of foreign exchange into the Bahrain economy, some of which will admittedly have been spent in bringing in more foreign goods, though a great deal went on fixed assets such as housing. The banks estimate that they spend between US$18–US$19 million in Bahrain, some of it on salaries for Bahrainis, who have taken rather enthusiastically to banking.

Exempt Companies

Following on the success of the offshore banking idea, the Bahrain government launched the notion of exempt companies in October 1977. It did not take off as rapidly as the banking licence but its implications need to be assessed very thoroughly by the commercial companies at whom it is aimed. The basic idea is that any company trading in the area can incorporate in Bahrain, without a majority Bahraini shareholding, providing it fulfils certain obligations as to capital and financial reporting and does not trade in Bahrain itself. The government has not promoted this possibility as extensively as that of offshore banking was marketed, because it does not wish to devalue the status of Bahrain into just another tax haven. For this reason the exempt companies will have to maintain an office and some staff in Bahrain, have a minimum capital of US$5 million and meet once a year on the island. The government's face is firmly set against brass plate operations. The offshore implications for commercial companies are being further studied and the government is looking into the advantages and disadvantages of establishing a free industrial zone near Bahrain's main port, Mina Salman.

Transport Service Industries

There are already a number of service industries established on the present industrial area near Mina Salman. The American oil installation service company, Brown & Root, for example, has an engineering workshop there and sends its engineers from Bahrain to service oil installations throughout the Gulf. The Bahrain Ship Repair Company (BASREC) has been established there since 1963 and has built up for itself a reputation for at-sea repairs and maintenance of larger ships that can be accommodated on its two 240 feet long slipways. The Bahrain Slipway Company, owned by Gray Mackenzie, is older still.

The Bahrain government and port authorities are gradually coming round to the idea that they should increase the *entrepôt* business of the port, which at present runs at about a third of imports. In the near future two food importing and distributing companies will set up near the port. One is a US$50 million joint venture between the Bahrain government and the New Zealand government (though in New Zealand it is hoped to sell shares to interested companies), and the other is a joint Bahraini private sector/government project. Both companies are planning to import foodstuffs in bulk, break-bulk and repackage in Bahrain and re-export the resulting goods.

With the *entrepôt* business in mind the Bahrain port authorities started on the physical expansion of the port in 1975 and all works should be completed by the end of 1978. The expansion plan, which cost around US$150 million, included the construction of six more permanent berths, bringing the port's total capacity to 16, which will be able to take vessels up to 50,000 tons dwt. A new container terminal at Sitra Island is also to be built with an additional storage capacity of 150,000 square yards. Mina Salman itself will offer roll-on/roll-off facilities also. At the turn of 1977 Mina Salman was handling an average of 125,000 shipping tons a month. Major lines using the port include the P&O Group, Maersk, Hansa, Hellenic, Barber, Willine and Pacific International, The Australian company Blue Port, part of the conglomerate Blue Star, has made Bahrain its major port of call for cold store goods intended for distribution throughout the Gulf, and to encourage more cold store traffic the port was installing further facilities in 1978.

Bahrain's major transport link with the other Gulf states is through the regional airline, Gulf Air, which is headquartered at the island's airport on Muharraq, the second biggest island of the Emirate of Bahrain. The airline, which is owned by Qatar, the UAE, Bahrain and Oman, and with which most Gulf residents have a running love/hate relationship, calls at all major Gulf cities at least once daily. And linking the island with the world outside are 26 major international air carriers, including Pan Am, TWA, British Airways, Qantas (for whom it is a transit stop on the Australia-Europe route) KLM and Middle East Airlines (MEA), which has daily flights to Beirut. Gulf Air, together with Saudia, runs an airbridge link into Saudi Arabia with flights every two hours to Dhahran.

Gulf Air operates from Bahrain for both historic and practical reasons. The airline grew out of the tiny Gulf Aviation Company (in which British Airways had a stake) which started life with a once a week service between Bahrain and Sharjah, then the two major centres of British influence in the Gulf. It became Gulf Air as known today in 1974 when Bahrain had the best airport facilities of any of the Gulf states. The Bahrain government has consistently since then improved all the airport facilities, and the air traffic control for the Eastern Gulf section is handled from Bahrain.

Bahrain's airport and Gulf Air together are now major employers in Bahrain. And the need to find employment for the increasing number of educated Bahrainis must also have been at the back of the owning states' minds when Gulf Air started to expand. While the airline does not yet employ Bahraini air stewardesses it does employ Bahraini secretaries and junior managers. And the majority of ground handling staff at the airport are Bahrainis.

Surprisingly Bahrainis have also taken to the hotel and catering training centre with some enthusiasm – this is unusual given Gulf Arab attitudes to service.

Concern to find employment for the Bahrainis presently at school (roughly half the population is under 20) and so prevent social unrest is a pre-occupation of both the Bahrain government and its neighbours. The post oil price rise boom temporarily mopped up the problem, but now, with the back of the boom broken and more school leavers joining the 100,000 strong labour force, the question has become urgent again. Associated with this is the current questioning of the quality of Bahraini education – does it produce employables? And the Bahrain government has embarked on a massive sports education programme with American help, taking the gamble of creating football hooligans as preferable to political hooligans.

ASRY Dry Dock

The aluminium smelter was the first planned attempt to provide jobs for Bahrainis and, in employing some 2,000 Bahrainis it now indirectly supports about 1 per cent of the population. (The average Bahraini head of family has six or seven dependants). The latest, and probably last, large scale industrial source of employment is the OAPEC owned dry dock company, the Arab Shipbuilding and Repair Yard. While the geographic and hydrological reasons for basing it on Bahrain were sufficient in themselves to justify the decision, there is no doubt that the possibility of an Arab work force also appealed to OAPEC, which wants to see Arabs acquire industrial skills.

Bahrainis early in 1978 accounted for about a third of the yard's 1,400 strong workforce. The training school established in the yard is taking in a small number of graduates but the skilled, heavy work is being done mostly by Asian expatriates. Both ASRY and ALBA point out that it is only in times of economic hardship that people go into heavy industry. The boom of the past couple of years has permitted more Bahrainis to set up their own small businesses (being a nation of small shopkeepers is something the Bahrainis have taken over from the British) or go into the more pleasant and more highly rewarded clerical jobs in banking or government.

But another hoped-for benefit to Bahrain from hosting the dry dock is in industrial spin-off through sub-contracting, as well as purchasing through local agents. In its early months of operations ASRY did subcontract some engineering work to local companies.

Both the small ship repair yards established on the island, the Bahrain Slipway (located on the causeway to Muharraq) and BASREC, have done work for ASRY and there is other engineering capability available in the island – such as the General Electric apparatus servicing company, Middle East Engineering Ltd, which is GE's regional company.

When the ASRY project was first conceived the world shipping pattern was very different to the tanker slump that was in its fourth year in 1978. Then in 1968, the Suez Canal was closed and tankers were getting ever bigger, outgrowing the drydock capacity of Europe and the Far East. The ASRY yard is ideally located in that it is sited half way up the Gulf and is able to receive gas free tankers in an area where around 80 per cent of tanker traffic originates. Most of the Arab oil loading ports are in the Gulf.

ASRY, though it started life on a competitive basis with the other ship repair yards round the world, should have a captive market in the growing Arab tanker and general shipping fleet. At the end of the first quarter of 1978 the yard had docked 14 Very Large Crude Carriers (VLCC) and carried out 13 other repairs at its jetties. The VLCCs included two tankers owned by the Arab Maritime Petroleum Transport Company. The wealth of its seven shareholders should support ASRY's efforts to remain price competitive on a still falling market. The company, at present ship repair rates, is unlikely to make money in the foreseeable future, and indeed, given the volume of goods it needs to import to carry out its business, is initially unlikely to contribute positively to Bahrain's balance of payments problems.

Hotels, and the Leisure Industry

However, there is no doubt that the siting of ASRY in Bahrain was a tremendous morale boost for the island and a firm sign of the other states' concern for the stability and health of Bahrain. In the past three years, as the island has been modernising its infrastructure to keep up its image as a service centre for the Gulf, the other Gulf states have pitched in with aid to varying degrees to help pay for it all. The current electricity production and transmission plans, for example, are funded by considerable loans from the Saudi Development Fund and the Kuwait Fund for Arab Economic Development. Money from other Arab states, particularly from Saudi Arabia and Kuwait, is visible in the private sector also. The Kuwaitis are heavily involved in Bahrain's growing hotel accommodation and the mushrooming office blocks.

The next couple of years are likely to be tough for Bahrain's hotel industry, for from a total of around 500 decent first class hotel beds during 1975 the island should have about 3,000 by 1980 – and unless business picks up in the Gulf generally, most of those beds will remain empty. Bahrain's hoteliers are now making conscious efforts to attract holidaymakers from the Gulf region itself, whether Arab or expatriate. At least two of the smaller hotels are actively marketing cut rate weekend packages to ARAMCO employees in the Eastern Province of Saudi Arabia.

In choosing to be a service centre for the Gulf states and Saudi Arabia, Bahrain has chosen to walk a tightrope between the industrialised West and the more conservative states of Arabia. Nowhere will the difficulties of this balancing act be more apparent than in its hotel and catering industries. The obvious question after the causeway is – will Bahrain go dry? It is generally understood that Saudi Arabia will not force Bahrain to abandon its attitude to alcohol, provided it remains as discreet as at present.

1980

Success as a Service Centre – Causeway Optimism – The British Connection – Iranian Claims – State of Emergency – The Importance of Oil – Saudi Generosity Towards Its Poorer Neighbour – Gas Offers Brighter Picture – ALBA a Commercial Success – ASRY Drydock – Supremacy as a Financial Centre – Islamic Banking – 1980 to See Upward Economic Turn – Political and Social Pressures from a Sophisticated Multi-National Community

Despite public confidence, many Bahrainis are undergoing twinges of uncertainty about their future. Their dilemma is either to increase co-operation with the other states of the region, particularly Saudi Arabia, which will inevitably involve some loss of political independence, or to see their present prosperity gradually decline as the oil wells run dry.

It is really not a choice at all, since the government is firmly committed to linking the island's destiny to that of its neighbours, by turning it into a service centre to complement their completely different types of economic development. The more astute members of Bahrain's ruling élite in both government and business realised that the 1974–75 boom would be short lived and so took steps to cushion the effects of the recession before it came. These effects were therefore less personal than elsewhere in the region. Already substantial progress has been made in diversification along political lines.

Nevertheless, many Bahrainis have not yet come to terms with what this will entail. Nostalgia for national childhood under British tutelage, when the decision making could be left to the grown-ups, is not uncommon, and despite the general increase in living standards there are many at the lower end of the income scale who have not benefited from the boom years and hanker after the old days. Life was slower and simpler then, but perhaps more enjoyable.

Causeway to Saudi Arabia

The biggest physical expression of the new Bahrain has yet to take shape, but is already casting its shadow over almost all social and economic thinking. It is the 25 kilometre causeway that by the middle of the next decade is planned to link Bahrain and the Arabian mainland. Although there had been sceptisism in many quarters that this mammoth project would ever start, 1979 saw a flurry of activity, and by mid-year work was nearing completion on the pre-qualification of tenderers. Invitations to tender were to be issued shortly afterwards, with the rest of the year devoted to their preparation and evaluation. According to this timetable, the contract – one of the largest civil works of all time – would be awarded by early 1980, with construction taking less than five years.

The effects of this physical union between a fertile archipelago graced by an ancient civilisation and a desert country that has suddenly acquired enormous wealth and power are difficult to foresee. Economically, there will be huge benefits for Bahrain, both during the construction stage of the causeway, when local firms are likely to win large volumes of sub-contracting work, and afterwards when Bahrain's economy will be in direct contact with one of the richest and fastest developing regions of the world. The benefits to Saudi Arabia, which is footing the entire bill (currently estimated at US$800 million–US$1 billion), are less obvious.

Although there are some tangible advantages in being able to tap Bahrain's relatively better trained labour force and to give residents of Saudi Arabia's Eastern Province better access to leisure facilities (including liquor) not available in the Kingdom, the main motivation is political. The Saudis do not want to see economic depression in Bahrain give rise to potentially contagious instability (Bahrain's record of political activity is second only to Aden's among the countries of Eastern Arabia), and the causeway is simply one of many efforts to prevent this happening. Others are the regular support for budget deficits, and co-operation in Bahrain's dry dock and aluminium projects. The special relationship between Saudi Arabia and Bahrain, strengthened by the ties of kinship between the two ruling families, is unique in a region where relations between neighbours are generally less than cordial.

History

To the student of Bahrain's history, close links with another more powerful state should come as nothing new, for the islands' fresh water springs, lush vegetation, rich pearl beds and mercantile tradition have always attracted the attention of powerful outsiders. The earliest records show the civilisation of Dilmun, as Bahrain was known, as an important *entrepôt* between Mesopotamia and the Indus Valley peoples some 5,000 years ago. The islands were successively conquered or controlled by the Sumerians, Assyrians, Babylonians, Achaemenian Persians, Greeks, Sasanian Persians, various Arab dynasties, Portuguese, Safavid Persians and Omanis. Even the present ruling family, the al-Khalifa, came from Kuwait via Qatar, which they later abandoned. But no sooner had they consolidated their control, fighting off invasions from Omanis, Persians, Turks and Wahhabis from the Arabian mainland, than the British established a quasi-colonial presence which was to last 150 years. Full independence from Britain was proclaimed in 1970.

With such a history, Bahrain is refreshingly free from folk-memories of conquest and empire, its proudest memories being of the Dilmun period, when it was reputed to be a terrestrial paradise visited by the Sumerian hero Gilgamesh in his search for immortality.

Foundations of Prosperity

The British connection, especially after the Second World War, when the defence and foreign affairs of Kuwait, Qatar, the Trucial States and Oman were administered from Bahrain, gave the islands valuable prestige and even more valuable infrastructure. Bahrain was lucky with its oil, too. The first successful oil strike in an Arab country was made in Bahrain (in 1932) just in time to prevent the total collapse of the economy that might have occurred, as it did in Qatar, when Japanese cultured pearls put an end to the main industry. The advantages of this privileged youth meant that Bahrain enjoyed for decades the best education, health and telecommunications services in the region. Although massive spending by its neighbours has closed the gap, Bahrain is still ahead on most counts.

Early prosperity meant that as late as 1970, when discussions of the post-independent form of the nine states of the Lower Gulf were coming to a head, Bahrain opted out of the proposed federation of all nine on the grounds that its population, then over half that of the total, entitled it to political representation appropriate to its numerical supremacy in whatever government structure was agreed upon.

Less than a decade later it is still the largest individually, but with the massive influx of foreign workers into the United Arab Emirates (UAE), Bahrain's population, thought to be approaching 400,000 is only about a quarter of the total population of the nine. Bahrain, like Qatar, therefore opted for single-state independence.

A second question-mark over Bahrain was the long-standing claim to sovereignty by Iran, based on long periods of colonisation and the substantial number of Bahrainis of Iranian origin (and Shi'a faith). Although this claim was more a Pahlavi sop to Iranian chauvinism, designed to focus public opinion on to a 'safe' subject, it had to be taken seriously. In 1970 a special representative of the UN Secretary General visited the islands in an attempt to discover the populace's wishes without the dangerous precedent of a referendum. There were sighs of relief when the verdict was that most Bahrainis wanted independent status as an Arab state, and the Shah accepted this.

He nevertheless felt obliged to placate Iranian chauvinism through another dormant claim, and a year later annexed Abu Musa and The Tumbs, Gulf islands of far lesser importance.

Political Evolution

Even well before independence, Bahrain had its moments of uncertainty and unrest. Although its economy and administration were soundly established by the early fifties (thanks in no small measure to the efforts by Sir Charles Belgrave, who for three decades served as administrative adviser to successive Rulers) the traditional system of government was no longer universally acceptable. Trouble began in 1954 with agitation for reform in social fields and complaints by the large Shi'a community that they were discriminated against by the Sunni-dominated judiciary and police force. This led to the creation of councils, partly elected and partly appointed, and two years later the Ruler appointed an Advisory Council, the forerunner to today's Council of Ministers. But later, in 1956, coinciding with the Suez crisis, serious rioting broke out. A state of emergency was proclaimed, British troops were used to restore order, and several leaders were jailed or exiled.

The political history of Bahrain for the next 20 years can be seen in terms of demands for change, expressed with varying degrees of force, to which the establishment has usually responded with concessions somewhat less than the demands. The unrest, frequently expressed in the form of localised strikes against major employers, reached a new peak in August 1975, when the National Assembly, composed of both appointed and elected members (with a strong leftist bias among the latter) was suspended after less than two years of life. Since then, perhaps because of the years of economic boom and the ability of the government after the 1973 oil price increases, to improve workers' welfare, there has been general stability but it would be naïve to assume that militancy in the Bahrain labour force is played out or that the political energies unleashed during the short period of parliamentary experimentation will not re-emerge one day in some form or other.

Yet, for the time being, partly no doubt because of the efficiency of the Special Branch, Bahrain is undergoing a period of political calm. Even the Iranian Revolution, which might have been expected to set off reactions among Shi'a Bahrainis, produced nothing more serious than one brief demonstration.

Family Strength in the Gulf Community

The closure of the National Assembly, with even less talk of a re-opening than occurred when Kuwait took a similar step a year later, passed off quietly, leaving Bahrain with a system of government that is far more democratic in practice than in theory. The position of the Ruler is not unlike that of the chairman of a loosely-run, paternalistic family business. The business has expanded rapidly in recent years, necessitating a number of outsiders being brought on to the board, and a host of consultants and advisors have their say. The original workers enjoy generous bonus schemes, have little say in how the business should be run, but are welcome to drop in at the chairman's office whenever they like and tell him their problems, while much of the skilled and dirty work is contracted out. The last word, however, is still with the chairman, tenth in line since the firm was founded and at 47 looking set for many years to come, unless some unwelcome merger or take-over bid should succeed.

Bahrain is often portrayed as the poor member of the Gulf Club, a somewhat misleading impression. It is more accurate to describe it as the second least affluent (in terms of GNP and considering the UAE as a single unit) in an extremely wealthy neighbourhood. It is richer than some of its neighbours in terms of infrastructure, both for the historic reasons already mentioned, and because its compact size and relatively small population make it easier to complete such projects. Its wealth is more evenly distributed than is the case with most of the others and there is little ostentation or degradation at the two ends of the income scale.

Of the Gulf States, Bahrain is one of the two non-members of the Organisation of the Petroleum Exporting Countries (OPEC) (the other being Oman), although it is a member of the Organisation of Arab Petroleum Exporting Countries (OAPEC), the parallel body of purely Arab oil exporters. Nevertheless, oil is still vital to the economy, accounting as it does for 57 per cent of budgeted government revenue for 1979 (and in view of the price increases during the year, probably closer to 70 per cent in practice). The oil industry is also the state's largest employer.

Oil as the Economic Foundation

After British oil interests had expressed a lack of interest, the Bahrain oil concession was awarded to the Standard Oil Company of California, which jointly with Texaco (as Caltex), formed the Bahrain Petroleum Company (BAPCO) to operate the concession. BAPCO, which in 1980 celebrates its golden anniversary, commenced drilling in 1931 and made its first commercial discovery the following year. Production began in 1934 and by 1936 a small refinery was in operation.

But the Bahrain Oilfield, located in the centre of the main island, is small by Middle Eastern standards. With 233 producing wells it is fully developed and production is declining at 4.00 per cent annually. By 1978 production had dropped to 55,000 barrels per day (bpd) from a peak of 70,000bpd. At this rate of decline the proved reserves of about 300 million barrels will be completely depleted by about the end of the century unless costly tertiary recovery operations are introduced. Already secondary recovery methods are in use, including gas injection and the only well-pumping in the Middle East.

In 1978 BAPCO commissioned a study of possible means of increasing ultimate oil recovery, which – though expensive in themselves – are made more viable by higher oil prices. Although prospects of making new discoveries in Bahrain's territorial land or waters are not considered promising, drilling continues into deeper zones, and there are plans for offshore exploration.

Meanwhile, Bahrain obtains the maximum value added from its production. Not only is all its crude oil refined, for local consumption and export as products, but also the BAPCO refinery processes some 190,000bpd of crude oil from Saudi Arabia, which is piped from the mainland and provides Bahrain with additional revenue from taxes. The refinery, which is relatively expensive to run because of its age, has a capacity of about 250,000bpd, one of the largest in the Middle East.

A further source of oil revenue comes from the Abu Safah off-shore oilfield, which in 1978 brought in some US$210 million, slightly more than earnings from the Bahrain oilfield. Abu Safah lies in non-delineated water and the decision made by the late King Faisal (of Saudi Arabia) to divide this revenue 50:50 was considered another example of Saudi Arabian generosity towards its poorer neighbour.

In 1974 the State acquired a 60 per cent participation share in BAPCO's operations, which was expected to increase to 100 per cent during 1979. The government's shareholding is vested in the Bahrain National Oil Co (BANOCO). Established in 1976, BANOCO has also taken over the marketing and distribution of oil products in Bahrain, although the BAPCO refinery is still completely Caltex-owned.

Gas Prospects Higher

Gas is second only to oil in its importance to Bahrain's economy, and here reserves present a much brighter picture. Gas occurs both in association with crude oil and as separate accumulations in the deep Khuff Zone, production from which has been rising steadily to its current level of about 360 million cubic feet per day, the equivalent in terms of thermal energy of 60,000bpd of oil. About 30 per cent of gas output is injected into the oil-producing reservoir for pressure maintenance, and 22 per cent is used in the refinery. Of the balance, 16 per cent is delivered to power and desalination plants and 32 per cent goes to the aluminium smelter. Reserves of Khuff gas are currently estimated at some 10 billion cubic feet, the energy equivalent of 1.6 billion barrels of oil, over five times that of remaining oil reserves.

Associated gas from the Bahrain oilfield is not at present utilised, but a major project to produce natural gas liquids will soon be operational, as the US$90 million gas gathering and processing facility was expected to be mechanically complete by the autumn of 1979. It will process the 100 million cubic feet of gas now being vented into some 280,000 tonnes of propane, butane and naphtha a year, which Caltex has already contracted to purchase in full. The tail gas will be used to supplement Khuff production or perhaps later to produce fertiliser. Although the life of the project is limited by that of the oilfield and cannot be expected to exceed 20 years, the project is still considered worthwhile since the entire capital cost can be amortised over a five year period.

ALBA Reaches Commercial Success

It is also gas that enables Bahrain to have one of the first and most successful metallurgical industries in the Middle East, Aluminium Bahrain (ALBA). Bahrain was first mooted as the site of an aluminium smelter in the late 1960s, when a group of major aluminium users formed a consortium to ensure the provision of part of their own supplies, previously purchased on the open market or by contract with producers.

Aluminium is obtained by electrolytic reduction of alumina, pure oxide of aluminium, itself produced by chemical separation from naturally occurring bauxite. This involves large quantities of cheap energy, or energy that can be costed cheaply, such as Bahrain's natural gas, for which at the time no alternative market existed without huge capital investment. Although the exact price at which ALBA buys gas has never been published, it has clearly been set to ensure the smelter's commercial success.

Unfortunately, the plant came into operation in 1971 at the start of a long depression in the market price of aluminium, which is only now showing signs of ending. Costs rose rapidly, so losses were inevitable. This led to most of the other shareholders in the original consortium selling out to the Bahrain government, which could afford to take a longer, and less commercial, view. By 1979 the government owned 77.9 per cent with Kaiser Aluminium of the US holding 17 per cent and Breton Investments of West Germany 5.1 per cent. In July 1979 the Bahrain government sold 20 per cent of the equity to SABIC, a Saudi government holding company.

That coincided with a remarkable rise in spot prices for aluminium ingot and a cost cutting exercise by ALBA that makes the project a commercial success at last. But Saudi Arabia is not buying into ALBA purely as an investment. The plan is that once SABIC has learned from its participation in Bahrain, it will build a smelter of its own, at Jubail, in which Bahrain will have a share of the equity. ALBA's expertise should be an important factor in ensuring the success of the new plant.

Meanwhile, ALBA is going ahead with a long-standing plan to expand capacity by early 1982 from the present level of 120,000 tons of aluminium to 162,000 tons by the addition of a new generating plant and potrooms, at a cost of some US$130 million. The existing power station, with a capacity of 300 megawatts, was the largest gas turbine station in the world when commissioned, and it generates more power than the peak daily demand of the entire state.

Like BAPCO, ALBA is a major employer, and about 70 per cent of its 2,100 workers are Bahrainis. The turnover of labour has been quite high, but the skills acquired continue to benefit the economy as a whole. As part of the cost-cutting programme 500 jobs were cut in 1978 and 200 in 1979 although natural wastage and the phasing out of expatriate workers cushioned the effect on the local labour market.

The ALBA smelter also produces valuable industrial spin-offs, the most important to date being an aluminium powder plant (Bahrain Atomisers) with an annual capacity of 3,000 tons of powder, which is used in the paint and explosives industries, an extrusion plant (BALEXO) with a capacity of 3,000 tons, and an aluminium cable plant (Midal Cables) which opened in 1978. These mainly export-oriented operations face an uphill struggle in a highly competitive world market where they must pay the full rate for their raw materials yet incur higher than average labour costs.

Arab Shipbuilding and Repair Yard Company
Bahrain's other large industrial project is the Arab Shipbuilding and Repair Yard Company (ASRY), the first 'downstream' investment of OAPEC. Saudi Arabia, Kuwait, the UAE, Qatar and Bahrain each own 18.84 per cent of the equity, Iraq has 4.7 per cent and Libya 1.1 per cent. Magnificently equipped as the first yard in the world purpose-built to handle VLCC's, ASRY received its first tanker in 1978. Built at a cost of US$340 million, it is capable of drydocking tankers up to 500,000dwt, the largest now afloat. ASRY is operated by the Portuguese shipyard Lisnave Shipyards SA and has an impressive training school.

Despite its healthy order-book, from a wide range of tanker-owners as well as its own stockholders, the depressed state of the tanker industry means that it is unlikely to make a profit. But its owners see its role not just as a commercial venture, but as an important channel for the transfer of technology to the Arab world, one which Bahrain obviously benefits from most of all. In the long run, it is felt that ASRY's strategic position at the centre of the Gulf and the desire of the OAPEC members to move their oil industries downstream makes the original investment a viable one, although the competition from Dubai's even larger drydock is unfortunate. Given the fact that its rival is now complete, ASRY feels that it would be sensible for the two facilities to co-operate rather than compete, which can only harm them both, but it is still waiting for a response from Dubai Drydocks.

Financial Centre of the Gulf

Although Bahrain's concept of its role as is a service centre to complement its neighbours' economies is large enough to include such major industrial projects as aluminium smelting and the drydocking of super tankers, it is in the more usual sense of the term that its expertise is having the greatest regional impact. Since 1975 it has firmly established itself as the Middle East's No 1 financial centre, taking over and elaborating on Beirut's former role and compensating for its shortage of indigenous capital by providing the skills to utilise the abundant surpluses of its neighbours.

The master-stroke in establishing Bahrain's supremacy as a financial centre came in September 1975 when the Bahrain Monetary Agency, the state's central bank in all but name, introduced a new licence that permitted international banks to conduct foreign currency business with non-residents through offshore banking units (OBU's) in Bahrain. OBU's are not taxed, but pay an annual licence fee of about US$25,000. Many major banks responded to this idea and by July 1979, when a moratorium on the issue of new licences was introduced, 53 OBU's had been licensed. A further five were stuck in the pipeline when the ban came. By the end of 1978 total assets and liabilities of the OBUs exceeded US$23 billion, roughly the same as that of the offshore banks in Singapore, which have been going several years longer. Much of their trade is denominated in regional currencies, particularly Kuwaiti dinars and Saudi Arabian riyals, thus underlining Bahrain's growing importance to its neighbours' economies.

Bahrain's position roughly midway between the nearest major money markets of Singapore and London is an additional benefit, since its business hours, plus 'working weekends' (Saturday and Sunday are not holidays in Bahrain), provide a welcome flexibility. According to the BMA, the average OBU has assets of about US$450 million, annual expenses of US$1 million and a profit of slightly more than that. Bahrain benefits not only from the US$3.1 million in licence fees, but from the US$50 million in operating costs, which represent a substantial boost to the balance of payments and the local economy as a whole.

Not all is plain sailing in the world of OBUs, however. Bahrain's success has triggered off some antagonism from Kuwaiti and Saudi Arabian banks, which felt that the bankers of Bahrain were profiting at their expense, and from the UAE, particularly Dubai, where plans for offshore banking were scuppered by the advent of the OBUs. The rapid growth of OBUs, as reflected in their assets, began to slow down in 1978 and in the first quarter of 1979 total assets fell by almost 5 per cent. The BMA expressed no surprise at this, saying that a level had been reached where further growth was unlikely, and the instability of the dollar had affected markets. The moratorium on new banks was widely seen as a step towards stabilising the position, and with the growth of Gulf currency assets still strong the higher prices for OPEC oil should generate new growth as these funds trickle through to the private sector, since the OBUs are concerned primarily with private sector, not public sector, surpluses.

The success of the OBU concept encouraged the BMA in 1978 to introduce an investment banking licences (IBL), and at the same time a new form of company registration, the exempt company (EC), was introduced. Six IBLs had been issued by mid-1979 and 20 ECs registered, the latter designed for firms requiring a regional headquarters based in Bahrain as distinct from a normal trading corporation. But just as the 'instant bank' was discouraged from applying for an OBU licence, so the Bahrain government has sought to deter 'brass plate' firms from setting up, and an EC must establish a properly staffed headquarters office in Bahrain. ECs are exempt from the normal rule that locally registered corporations must be at least 50 per cent locally owned, a rule that applies in most of the Gulf. They pay an annual fee of US$6,250 (US$26,000 in the case of public companies), but no income tax.

Apart from its OBUs and IBLs, Bahrain has a number of other financial institutions, including 19 commercial banks and 28 representative offices, many of which were thought to be testing the water before applying for OBU licences. The commercial banks have weathered the two year recession well. Having been largely responsible for the property boom of 1974–76 there is some poetic justice in the fact that they still carry on their books a number of doubtful loans for construction projects. Some of which are never likely to be repaid. The banks' policy, like that of the UAE banks where a similar situation prevails, is not to foreclose for fear of setting off a chain reaction that might affect even their sounder customers (in some cases good and bad loans are booked to the same individuals). Construction, still a depressed industry with the main building projects now complete and little more to come, still accounts for more than 40 per cent of the banks' loan portfolios, followed by trade (22 per cent) and then manufacturing as a poor third (13 per cent). With import and re-export business also slowing up and the adverse effects of the Iranian revolution, it is a testimony to the bankers' prudence that overall profits of the commercial banks in 1978 were held to the level of the previous year (US$26.5 million).

Prospects for the Banking Sector

Business among the 19 commercial banks is by no means evenly distributed. Two Bahraini banks – the National Bank of Bahrain and the Bank of Bahrain and Kuwait – were responsible in 1978 for 55 per cent of total assets, 49 per cent of all loans and 44 per cent of all profits, while the performance of the remainder, including four Arab, three British, three American and two Iranian banks varied considerably, with one US bank turning in a loss for the third year running. A third local bank, al-Ahli Commercial Bank started operations late in 1978. With its 22,000 shareholders and management contract with Bank of America, it is likely to move quickly up the performance league. A fourth locally incorporated bank was expected to open its doors towards the end of 1979. This is the Bahrain Islamic Bank, to be run on Islamic lines involving the sharing of profits (and losses) with its customers rather than the charging of interest. The only other commercial venture of this kind in the region, including Iran, is the Dubai Islamic Bank, which has a minority holding in the new bank.

Bahrain's banking community is expecting 1980 to mark the start of a new upward turn in the economy. Factors behind this optimism include the anticipated letting of the causeway contract, the establishment of a government housing bank in 1979, tentative steps by the private sector into sensible light industrial projects, and higher oil prices (although Bahrain, which has always followed Saudi Arabia's lead in oil matters, will benefit less from the price rises). Meanwhile 1979 was expected to be an improvement on 1978, with bank lending up about 10 per cent over the previous year and liquidity some 15 per cent higher, according to BMA forecasts.

With port, airport, road and hotel capacity adequate for the next few years, even assuming a period of modest growth, few large-scale construction projects are on the drawing board. The main new work is likely to be in low cost housing, for which the housing bank is especially designed, and related projects such as sewerage. Over 5,000 government houses have been built in the past three years but this high rate of growth must be kept up for several more years if the shortage is to be eliminated. Many of the existing facilities on the islands, such as roads, the suq and the older residential areas are badly in need of renovation or replacement, and new investment is tending in this direction rather than towards brand-new projects. Old houses, often with interior courtyards and gardens, once modernised and re-decorated, are much in demand among the more imaginative of the expatriate community, while hundreds of villas built in the boom years stand empty. Rents have certainly lowered from the extremely high peak of 1977, but still represent a major item of expenditure for the foreign firm employing expatriate labour.

Repercussions From the Causeway

The causeway project will have numerous physical spinoffs for Bahrain. The route will start some six kilometres south of al-Khobar on the mainland and cross Umm Nasan island, close to Bahrain island. There are plans for a construction camp for 5,000 workers at the Bahrain end, which would later become a permanent township, and new access roads will be required to bring the traffic across the north of the island to the capital area. The causeway itself is almost a misnomer, since the length of bridgework will exceed that of embankment. This is both to provide navigational channels for the limited local shipping (the main bridge will be almost 100 feet above water) and to prevent the silting that would soon occur if tides were prevented from sweeping through. It is not clear whether the construction headquarters will be in Bahrain or Saudi Arabia. Bahraini businessmen obviously hope that the decision will be in their favour, but similar pressure will come from the Saudi Arabian side, which is of course paying the bill.

It remains a mystery why, despite the obvious advantages of linking the two countries, there is still no regular ferry boat or hydro-foil service. At present, apart from an air shuttle between Bahrain and Dhahran, with the disadvantages of cost and lengthy check-in, there is only a slow and uncomfortable dhow service once a day in each direction. The cost and trouble of shipping a car by dhow makes the often-criticised English Channel car-ferries look like a well-run charitable service, and it is extraordinary that no entrepreneur has yet developed this obvious market. It should also be said that unless the customs and immigration services of both countries streamline their present procedures the four lane causeway will produce nothing but monumental traffic jams, and if visa regulations are not simplified few potential visitors will find sufficient inducement to make the journey for pleasure's sake.

The shortage of hotel rooms at the start of the boom set off a speculative wave of hotel construction, particularly in the luxury category. Because of the long lead-times with such projects, many of these rooms were only completed after the bubble had burst, and more again are on the brink of completion. The effect is that the 800 such rooms will double during 1980. While hoteliers are grateful for the business brought to Bahrain by the regular programme of business exhibitions now being held, they are counting on the causeway project, from the tendering stage and through to the hoped-for week-end and holiday business from Saudi Arabia after completion, to compensate for the past two lean years. The current low room occupancy rates are being felt throughout the range of hotels, and when existing projects are completed it seems likely that a number of hotels will go out of business, notably those without the advantages of international room-marketing support or where inefficiency combines with high prices. But despite the present cut-throat competition, which is likely before it gets better (room rates have stopped rising but have not yet fallen) many hoteliers are confident that the long term prospects are good. The availability of liquor and night-life is undoubtedly an attraction to residents in neighbouring countries, and this factor alone is a major impetus to Bahrain's hotel and restaurant trade.

Communications Key to Service Centre Success

Bahrain has first class air services. The Bahrain International Airport on Muharraq island, linked to central Manama by causeway, is the busiest in the region, and is served by some two dozen airlines, including Gulf Air, which is partly owned by the Bahrain government and has its headquarters there. Becoming the first destination for British Airways' Concorde flights was a great boost for Bahrain's prestige as a communications centre.

Mina Salman, only a year or two ago as congested as any other Gulf port, has settled down to an efficiently run operation. A US$160 million expansion, completed in 1979, increased the number of berths from six to sixteen, and in 1980 a new access channel will enable ships up to 1,000 feet in length to use the ultra-modern container port, which the authorities hope will lead to a renewed upsurge in Bahrain's traditional importance as an *entrepôt*.

Good telecommunications are perhaps the most important element of Bahrain's infrastructure if its service centre strategy is to succeed, and here Bahrain has always given the regional Jones's something to keep up with. The first earth satellite station in the Gulf was commissioned in 1968, and the system has been steadily improved, with automatic telex switching introduced in 1974, and more recently, a facsimile transmission system. A second earth station was scheduled for completion in 1979. This will be beamed at an Atlantic Ocean satellite, putting Bahrain in direct contact with North America. At present such traffic is routed via Europe, to which the station is linked via an Indian Ocean satellite. Cable and Wireless, which operates all telecommunications services for the government, including a successful training college, plans to spend US$425 million over the next five years to meet the rapid increase in demand.

The task which Bahrain's planners have set, modest though it may appear to outsiders, is fraught with problems of many kinds, some of which are not within the control of those affected. The financial constraints, which are likely to become more severe year by year, are only one aspect, and indeed the planning discipline imposed by these constraints is already proving beneficial. Political and social pressures, both from within the islands relatively sophisticated multi-national community and from outside, may prove more vexatious, and the formula for success does require a large measure of an ingredient usually in short-supply in the Gulf – the sincere co-operation of neighbours. The special relationship that is developing with Saudi Arabia and the goodwill of Kuwait are perhaps the most hopeful omens for Bahrain's future.

1981

Winds of Change – Camp David Accords – OPEC – Natural Gas Liquids Exports – BANAGAS – APICORP – Offshore Banking Units – Industrial Expansion – Economic Slowdown – Isa Town

Bahrain, like most of the other Arab Gulf states, is sensing the winds of change. The turbulent events of 1979 – the signature of the Camp David Accords between Egypt and Israel; the revolution in Iran and the Soviet invasion of Afghanistan – have each left a permanent mark on the country's foreign and domestic policies. And while the period from mid-1979 to mid-1980 represented an attempt to come to terms with these dramatic developments, the next year is expected to witness some profound changes in the country's internal and external policies as the government seeks to balance a rise of nationalist and Islamic feeling at home with the need to continue its alliances with the US and Western Europe.

Islamic Feeling

The Camp David Accords were seen by much of the population of Bahrain as yet another example of 'imperial' interests overcoming the Arab world's need for independence and self-reliance. While no doubt many would welcome a permanent settlement to the endemic conflict with Israel, they see the treaty as a capitulation, on Sadat's part, to the US and Israel.

By the summer of 1979 the continuing agitation in Iran, following the declaration of an Islamic Republic and the consolidation of power by the Ayatollah Khomeini, added still more fuel to the flames. Bahrain's population is estimated to contain up to two-thirds Shi'a Muslims so the Ayatollah enjoys a large measure of support in the country.

In addition there was the question of Iran's renewed claims to Bahrain, which were first mooted by the Shah in 1971 at the time Bahrain became independent from Britain.

Mediation by leaders of the Palestine Liberation Organisation (PLO) in the autumn of 1979 seemed at first to have improved the strained relations between Bahrain and Iran. By the end of the year, however, the resignation of the civilian government in Tehran, the taking of the American hostages at the embassy, and the increasing power of the clergy again led to a revival of Iranian claims to the islands.

© KONINKLIJKE BRILL NV, LEIDEN, 2023 | DOI:10.1163/9789004686335_006

Foreign Policy Reassessed

Caught between an increasingly militant Islamic population on the one hand, and a history of development along Western lines on the other, the ruling family has been facing an acute dilemma. While it would like to retain close links with the US and Britain, particularly because of the growing Soviet threat to the area, it must also avoid antagonising the country's Shi'a majority. This has meant that Bahrain has come to rely more on its neighbours for support while at the same time seeking new sources of arms and advanced military equipment.

In the autumn of 1979 the government began serious talks with the Saudis, the United Arab Emirates, Qatar and Oman aimed at forging an alliance designed to prevent the spread of super-power influence in the Gulf. But the plan foundered over differences between the various regimes and Iraq, and was further troubled in the first half of 1980 by Oman's determination to go it alone and to increase its ties with the US.

Having already opened discussions with France on the provision of advanced weaponry and training facilities for its armed forces, the government moved further to cement its links with Paris in the absence of a broader consensus on Gulf security. In May 1980 the two countries signed a huge agreement under which France promised to supply missile-launching patrol boats, anti-submarine corvettes and sophisticated radar and electronics equipment, as well as advisers to help train the armed forces.

The agreement followed a highly successful tour of the Gulf in March 1980 by the French president, Giscard d'Estaing, during which he pledged France's support for a new initiative on the Middle East and the recognition of an independent state for the Palestinians. Significantly, the agreement was signed in Riyadh: the Saudis agreed to provide a substantial part of the US$700 million needed to finance the arms sales. Still more of these trilateral' agreements', covering the supply of industrial and consumer goods as well as weapons, can be expected in the next year.

Oil Earnings Rise

Bahrain's economic future looks considerably brighter than it did in 1979–80 when the country experienced a slowdown in construction and investment as a result of the completion of several basic infrastructural projects. Part of the recovery stems from the dramatic rise in oil prices which boosted Bahrain's earnings from crude oil exports to BD772.5 million in 1979 compared with only BD585.5 million in 1978. Although Bahrain is not a member of OPEC, it generally follows the organisation's pricing policies and as a result oil earnings could rise by another 30 per cent or so by the end of 1980.

Although oil was discovered in Bahrain in 1932, production at the onshore Jebel al-Dukhan oilfield on the main island has been declining in recent years necessitating the installation of costly secondary and tertiary recovery programmes. However, the loss is being made up in part by increased output from the offshore Abu Safah field which Bahrain shares with Saudi Arabia. Even so, production in 1979 averaged 51,350 barrels per day (bpd) compared with almost 66,000 bpd in 1974.

In December 1979 the state-owned Bahrain National Oil Company (BANOCO) took over full control of the country's oil production. Previously the Bahrain Petroleum Company (BAPCO), a subsidiary of Caltex and Socal of the US, held 40 per cent of production and exploration rights. At the time of the takeover the government said BAPCO would remain as operator for the oilfields and that it would be allowed to retain control of the 250,000 bpd oil refinery at Sitra. However, in the spring of 1980 there were reports that BANOCO had told the two American firms that it would, in the long term, be looking for a majority shareholding in the refinery. Pressure from Saudi Arabia, which provides some of the oil processed at the refinery, could add weight to BANOCO's arguments.

Bahrain is also benefiting from an increase in the output of non-associated gas produced from the offshore Khuff Zone as well as from the production of gas found in association with oil ('associated gas').

Total production in 1979 increased to 141,762m cu feet compared to 131,153 million cu feet in 1978. Altogether the country's gas reserves are estimated to total 9,000 billion cu feet. While this is not large by Middle Eastern standards, the gas is re-injected into the oilfields to improve recovery rates and also provides sufficient energy to fuel the country's aluminium smelter and to generate electricity and desalinate water, thereby reducing local consumption of the more costly crude oils.

Exports of natural gas liquids (NGL) started in March 1980 after the completion late in the previous year of a new US$100 million liquefaction plant built by the Japan Gasoline Corporation. By May 1980 it was running at about 80 per cent of capacity, which totals 280,000 tons of NGL a year or about 125,000 tons of naphtha, 80,000 tons of propane and 75,000 tons of butane. It is run by the Bahrain National Gas Company (BANAGAS) which was set up in April 1979 as a joint venture between BANOCO (75 per cent), Caltex (12.5 per cent) and the Arab Petroleum Investments Corporation (APICORP) (12.5 per cent).

BANOCO is also due to provide feedstock for two new petrochemical plants to be built at Sitra by the Bahrain-Kuwait Petrochemicals Industries Corporation. The two plants, which will produce 1,000 tons of ammonia and an equal amount of methanol each day, are expected to cost some US$375 million. Production should begin at the end of 1982 or early in 1983.

In the longer term the government is hoping that a new exploration programme, which was launched in 1980 with funds provided by Kuwait and Saudi Arabia, will produce some promising new finds of either oil or gas. However most informed observers say that while some new hydrocarbons may still remain undiscovered, any new fields are likely to be small and of use primarily to the local market.

Caution in Offshore Banking Sector

Despite a substantial rise in assets reported in 1979 by Bahrain's offshore banking units (OBU's) most bankers are treading a cautious path during 1980–81 in the midst of international economic recession. The sector, which dates its origin to October 1975 when Bahrain decided to permit the establishment of offshore units, now counts more than 53 licensees, including several new arrivals from the Far East.

While trading in Saudi riyals and other Gulf currencies has risen considerably and now accounts for about 20 per cent of total assets, dealers are concerned about this market as a result of the Saudi's strenuous efforts to prevent speculation in the riyal and to avoid it becoming an international currency. In March 1980 some OBUs lost up to US$200,000 each when the Saudis unexpectedly revalued their currency when most had predicted a devaluation.

Other problems stem from the relatively high interest rates prevailing in Europe, Saudi Arabia's decision to denominate its contracts in dollars rather than in riyals, fears about US intentions in the area and proposals by neighbouring governments to stem the inflow of speculative funds to Bahrain. Thus although total assets at the end of March 1980 stood at US$29.1 billion, this was about US$1 million less than the record total reached in January 1980. However the slowdown has been welcomed; the phenomenal increases which saw the sector grow to the size of Singapore's in 18 months, could not continue and a steadier rate of growth will help to stabilise investment.

Onshore bankers continue to be worried about the huge outflow of capital from Bahrain which resulted in a net drain from the commercial banking system of BD42.5 million. Although in part this outflow reflected the unusually high interest rates obtaining in the US and Europe in the latter part of 1979, the outflows continued despite the rapid fall in US rates early in 1980. A more basic problem is that Bahrain, like its neighbours, regulates interest and foreign exchange rates but does not enact controls on foreign exchange. As long as local rates remain low and currencies in the Gulf maintain their value against the dollar, high dollar interest rates will result in sizeable outflows. The same is true to a certain extent for the pound sterling. Although the worst fears have eased because of the US action in lowering rates, officials at the Bahrain Monetary

1981 51

Agency (BMA) are still pressing for a rise in local rates –which currently stand at 10.5 per cent – to counter the outflow.

Causeway to Start

After several long delays, progress on plans to construct a huge new causeway to Saudi Arabia are now proceeding on schedule. Bids from the list of pre-qualified companies, which included 21 international consortia, were received at the end of June 1980 and the contract was expected to be awarded later in the year. Front runners in the bidding were a Bahraini company, headed by Hamed Zayani, which submitted a tender in association with a Saudi company, Bin Laden, and two other firms from West Germany and Japan, as well as Balfour Beatty of the UK which is part of a joint UK-Japanese venture.

The causeway will be 25 km long stretching over four high span bridges. Because of the delays due to the re-examination of technical specifications work is not now expected to be completed before 1984. However the project, which is to cost US$1 billion and which is being financed by Saudi Arabia, is already helping to further Bahrain's plans to become a major service centre for the Gulf. Investors are pouring funds into new hotel and housing projects, tourism, communications and light industry.

Industrial Expansion Planned

Although some traditional crafts and industries from Bahrain's pre-oil days still remain, most of the country's industrial output is derived from either hydrocarbon related industries or from the aluminium industry. Aluminium Bahrain (ALBA) began production in 1972 and output is now running about five per cent above the smelter's original capacity of 120,000 tons a year. Most of the production, in the form of ingots, is exported to Saudi Arabia, Kuwait and Dubai as well as to other developing countries. The firm is now owned jointly by the government (57.9 per cent), Saudi Arabia's SABIC (20 per cent), Kaiser Aluminium Bahrain (17 per cent) and Breton of West Germany (5.1 per cent).

The smelter is currently being expanded to raise capacity to 165,000 tons a year. Finance for the project, which is expected to cost US$120 million, was raised through an international loan syndicated by Gulf International Bank and National Westminster of the UK. This should help to increase the company's profits which, in 1979, totalled US$50 million – five times more than the figure recorded in 1978, thanks in part to the company's new-found ability to export its products free of contractual commitments to its shareholders.

Along with the smelter Bahrain has seen the opening of several related industries in recent years. These now include an aluminium powder plant, and factories to produce extruded products as well as aluminium cables. Plans by the government to build a 40,000-tons-per-year aluminium rolling mill in partnership with Saudi Arabia were announced late in 1979 but, at time of writing, the financing for the plant has still to be arranged.

Bahrain is also the site of the huge Arab Shipbuilding and Repair Yard (ASRY), the drydock complex built by members of OAPEC. Since it was opened in November 1977 it has handled some 300 tankers, including several in the ultra large crude carrier (ULCC) class. Although capacity utilised in 1978 was 87 per cent, the 1979 figure saw a decline due to the poor state of the international tanker market. Despite this, earnings have improved as the initial operating expenditure, running in and labour training costs have declined. Although some observers fear the yard may suffer as a result of the opening in 1979 of an even bigger yard in Dubai, ASRY's excellent reputation and sound management, under Lisnave Shipyards SA of Portugal, should give it a substantial competitive edge.

Transport and Communications Improving

The country's transport and communications facilities, already considered to be the best in the Gulf, are undergoing still further improvement and expansion. A major plan to develop a new international airport is being drawn up by British Airports International; the existing field on Muharraq Island handled over two million passengers in 1978, almost double the 1975 figure. The locally-based airline, Gulf Air, which is jointly owned by Bahrain, Qatar, the UAE and Oman, expects to show increased profits in 1980 as a result of the completion of a major expansion programme that included the purchase of new Lockheed TriStars and Boeing 737s. Bahrain also is the stop-over point for British Airways' Concorde service to Singapore.

The country's telephone and telex system has been modernised, and this together with its earth satellite station, gives it the capacity to handle direct transmissions to most parts of the world. Sitra Island was linked to the national telephone network in 1979 and the waiting list for telephones on the main island was expected to diminish in 1980 as a result of the installation of new lines and of a computerised central exchange in Manama.

Social Services and Education

Bahrain's early lead in oil production has enabled it to establish an advanced system of social services, which includes free medical and educational facilities for Bahraini citizens. A new 500-bed general hospital was opened in 1978, and another military hospital was completed during 1979.

Low-cost housing is provided for 8,000 residents at Isa Town. Although the government has announced plans to build another low-cost housing project, possibly in an entirely new town to be located in the centre of Bahrain, there is still no sign that progress is being made on raising the necessary finance.

While the slowdown in the economy during 1979 helped to improve the prospects for such projects insofar as land prices began to recede from the dizzying heights they had reached during the boom years, private speculation remains the order of the day.

Bahrain's student body numbers 65,000 and is growing at the rate of 3,000 a year. In addition, in 1979, the government ordered all companies to introduce training schemes for workers or face a four per cent levy on their expatriate payrolls. Most of the larger firms already operate such schemes and so will escape the levy; however smaller firms in the hotel, catering and trade sectors will be badly affected.

Other government plans, announced in the spring of 1980, call for more representation of workers in company managements.

1982/83

Instability in the Gulf – Iranian Agression – Support for President Saddam Hussein – Demonstrations by Shi'a – Israeli Invasion of Lebanon – Gulf Rapid Deployment Force – European Initiative – Arab Shipbuilding and Repair Yard – Offshore Banking Sector – Agriculture – Causeway to Saudi Arabia – Four Year Development Plan 1981–85

The tiny island kingdom of Bahrain is facing one of its most difficult years yet. Having weathered the storms of the past two-and-a-half years, which brought the Soviet invasion of Afghanistan, the Iran/Iraq War and Israel's violent attacks on Lebanon, Iraq and the Palestinians, it is now looking for ways to increase its defence and security in a time of widespread instability regionally and internationally.

Foremost among Bahrain's concerns is the continuing instability in the Gulf region and the effect this could have on its own population, more than half of which is Shi'a Muslim in belief. The lack of a long-term political settlement on the issue of Palestinian rights and the future of the territories occupied by Israel is another major concern, as is the apparent inability of the Arab states as a whole to draw up a unified approach to the issue. The worldwide economic recession, which has seen oil prices fall in real value and which led to a drop in demand for petroleum products, is also affecting the country's economy and its ability to plan knowledgeably for the future.

Iranian Aggression Provokes Concern
The decision by Iran to send its troops across the border into Iraq in July 1982 provoked widespread concern in Bahrain about the future intentions of the militant Islamic regime in Tehran. Bahrain, like its other neighbours in the Gulf, strongly supported the regime of president Saddam Hussein of Iraq in private, although its public statements were more equivocal.

The ruling al-Khalifa family, which is Sunni Muslim in belief, has not forgotten that Iran, under the former Shah, claimed Bahrain as part of its own territory. These claims were revived in 1979 by the Ayatollah Sadiq Rohani, a leading member of the Ayatollah Ruhollah Khomeini government, who also voiced highly critical comments about the rulers in Bahrain. No formal renouncement of these claims has been forthcoming from Tehran in the years since, and its actions against Baghdad are seen as another demonstration that it will not be content until it has spread its version of revolutionary Islam throughout the Gulf.

The concern about Iran's intentions had been mounting even before the invasion of Iraq. The failure of Saddam Hussein's troops to achieve a decisive victory early in the Iran/Iraq War, which broke out in September 1980 when Iraqi troops crossed the border, was surprising enough. Even more so was the total rout of Iraqi troops at the decisive battle of Khorramshahr in May 1982 and the huge losses suffered by Iraq during the fighting. Efforts by Jordan and some of Bahrain's neighbours in the Gulf to enlist the aid of Egyptian troops to help bolster the Iraqi frontline were rejected by president Hosni Mubarak later that month and the Gulf states were left with little alternative but to try to stop further fighting through diplomatic means.

At a meeting of its partners in the Gulf Co-operation Council (GCC) held in the Saudi summer capital of Taif in July, Bahrain called upon the Iranian regime to 'spare the region any escalation in the conflict' which it said could only produce chaos and instability that would benefit foreign powers rather than those in the region.

It also supported a resolution passed by the United Nations (UN) Security Council in early July calling on Iran to accept a ceasefire with Iraq and to accept UN observers along the border. However, Iran's total rejection of such pleas for moderation and its insistence on calling for the overthrow of the Ba'athist regime in Baghdad meant that such diplomatic efforts had little effect on the worsening situation.

Internal Troubles Feared

The turmoil in the northern part of the Gulf also led to heightened concern about the internal situation in Bahrain. While many of the country's Shi'a Muslims have shared in the prosperity which Bahrain has enjoyed since the oil price revolution of the early 1970s, a significant portion of the population remains discontented with the existing form of government and is known to feel that Shi'as suffer from national, economic and social discrimination. Exhortations by the Iranian regime to rebel, and inflammatory comments by leading Shi'a clergymen broadcast across the Gulf to Bahrain on Tehran Radio during the fighting between Iran and Iraq, did nothing to ease the concern felt in ruling circles in Manama.

Nor have these exhortations fallen on deaf ears. Demonstrations by Shi'a Muslims broke out in Bahrain in April 1980 against the execution in Iraq of a leading Shi'a clergyman, the Ayatollah Mohammed Baqr al-Sadr. Trouble erupted again in December 1980 during the Shi'a religious festival of Muharram and some demonstrators were heard to shout pro-Khomeini slogans. Their leaders were rounded up and gaoled, and this action helped to further the discontent.

While the situation remained relatively calm throughout most of 1981, the discovery in December of an alleged *coup d'état* to overthrow the monarchy demonstrated the degree to which Shi'a sentiments must be taken seriously. After a secret trial and conviction of 73 Shi'a Muslims three months later, the government claimed that it had nipped such discontent in the bud. However, the fact that the 73 included 60 Bahrainis of mainly Arab, rather than Iranian, origin, was seen by many outside observers as proof that the regime does not enjoy the widespread support it claimed. The additional fact that the plotters included 13 Saudis, an Omani and a Kuwaiti, was also taken as a sign that the conspiracy enjoyed the support of dissidents elsewhere in the Gulf and that they may have received training abroad. By the middle of 1982 few doubted that more trouble could be expected in Bahrain in the future, especially if the Iranians scored more military successes in Iraq.

Israeli Action Condemned

Another major cause of concern stemmed from the Israeli invasion of Lebanon in June 1982 and the failure to achieve a just settlement of the Palestinian problem. The Israeli action, which led to the deaths of thousands of Lebanese and Palestinians and the destruction of half of the country, brought renewed criticism of the Gulf regimes from Palestinians and other Arabs for what was seen as their failure to act decisively to force an early Israeli withdrawal. While Bahrain, together with its five other partners in the Gulf Co-operation Council, condemned the Israeli invasion and called in July for the United Nations Security Council to enact economic sanctions against Israel, many Arabs both inside and outside the country were reported to feel that Bahrain could have done more to help the Palestinians and to restore Lebanese sovereignty. Their criticisms were echoed by some of the more radical Arab regimes in the area, such as Syria and Libya, which wanted Bahrain and its Gulf partners to halt oil supplies to those states, mainly the United States of America (US), which support Israel.

Signs that Arab radicals, including some Palestinians, were joining the Iranians in calling for the overthrow of those Gulf monarchies which failed to take direct action against Western supporters of Israel led some members of the government in Manama to argue that only by disassociating itself from the United States could further dissension be avoided. However, others close to the ruling family were said to feel that only by reinforcing its ties with Saudi Arabia and indirectly with the US could Bahrain's defence and internal security be assured. By the middle of 1982 it appeared that those who favoured a stronger public stance against Israel and against United States support for Menachem Begin's regime were getting the upper hand.

Palestinian Rights Supported

Behind the scenes Bahraini diplomats were also working strenuously for a long-term resolution to the Palestinian problem and for an Israeli withdrawal from the territories it occupied in 1967. Overtures were made to Egypt after the assassination of President Anwar Sadat in October 1981 in the hopes that a more comprehensive peace settlement than that envisaged in the Camp David accords could be achieved with the support of Sadat's successor, President Mubarak.

However, Egypt's apparent inability to act after the Israeli invasion of Lebanon in June 1982 did not bode well for attempts to open the way for its return to the Arab fold. While many within the ruling circles in Bahrain strongly support President Mubarak and his attempt to restore relations with the Arab world and to press the Israelis to grant the Palestinians a larger degree of autonomy in the West Bank and Gaza, they fear that a closer rapprochement between Manama and Cairo without firmer action to resolve the Palestinian problem could only lead to greater opposition from those who criticise Egypt for retaining its diplomatic ties with Israel. Closer links between the two countries would also give Iran a greater excuse to interfere in Bahrain.

One way out of the dilemma appears to centre on proposals made by the former Saudi Crown Prince Fahd al-Saud before he became King in June 1982. The proposals, which were announced in August 1981, call for an Israeli withdrawal from all the Arab territories occupied in 1967, the establishment of an independent Palestinian state with Jerusalem as its capital and the right of all states in the region to live in peace. Bahrain endorsed the proposals later that year, but objections by Syria and other 'rejectionist' states in the Arab world effectively put an end to them for the time being. They were resurrected again in July 1982 after the Israeli invasion of Lebanon when it was also hoped that a change in United States policy might lead to their implementation. Meanwhile Bahrain with its other Gulf partners continued to provide financial aid to the Palestinians and to take symbolic action against Israeli repression in the West Bank and Gaza. In April 1982 airports and telecommunications in Bahrain and in the area were closed for one day to protest against an attack on the Al-Aqsa Mosque in Jerusalem and the arrest of Islamic leaders in the West Bank.

European Aid Enlisted but Ambivalence Towards the US

Talks were also held throughout the second half of the year on ways to revive the so-called 'European initiative' on resolving the Palestinian problem and on ways to increase the defence and security of the Gulf states. Although Bahrain had been disappointed by the lack of progress on the initiative during the earlier part of the year, the government was said to have been encouraged by the strong stand taken by Britain, France and other members of the European Economic Community (EEC) against the Israeli invasion of Lebanon and by EEC efforts to include Palestinians in negotiations to resolve the conflict. Closer relations with Britain in particular followed a visit made by the British Prime Minister Margaret Thatcher to Bahrain in September 1981 and another made by the Bahraini Foreign Minister to Britain in July 1982.

Although Bahrain and five other Gulf states in July 1982 condemned the US action in vetoing resolutions calling for an Israeli withdrawal from the Lebanon, the outbreak of renewed fighting in the Gulf led to pressure from within the government to improve relations. Such thinking stems from Bahrain's own military weakness: its armed forces have only a handful of helicopters and 14 coastal patrol craft plus an armoured-car squadron, and would be unable to withstand any attack on the country from Iran. The agreement of the United States to provide Saudi Arabia with advanced AWACS radar equipped aircraft and the extension of their cover to Bahrain in 1982 helped to alleviate fears that the country would have no warning of imminent danger, but the need for increased defence continues. The government has decided that the US can help, along with Britain and other Western powers. Earlier in the year it ordered a number of F-5 fighter jets from the US, as well as 60 air-to-air missiles as part of a major programme to improve its air force. And, in an interview with a London magazine in May, Prime Minister Sheikh Khalifa bin Salman al-Khalifa, reiterated his country's view that the US had a role to play in the area. He said that while he favoured the formation of a Gulf deployment force, he thought the US could play a role in the area using diplomatic, rather than military, means. 'This doesn't mean having American marines, or whatever here,' he added, 'but political assistance to peace-loving countries of the region would help a lot.'

The appointment of George Schultz, who is on good terms with Gulf rulers, to US Secretary of State in July 1982 after the resignation of General Alexander Haig is also seen as boding well for closer links between Washington and Manama as well as between the US and other states in the Gulf. However, Bahrain will seek to ensure that such links are not used as an excuse for increasing superpower rivalries in the area or as evidence supporting Iranian accusations that the US has a free hand in the region.

Gulf Partnership Widens

Meanwhile the broad alliance of the Gulf monarchies under the umbrella of the Gulf Co-operation Council is deepening, to include closer co-ordination on defence and security affairs as well as on economic matters. The Council, which was set up in January 1981 as a result of discussions held at the Third Islamic Summit Conference in Riyadh, groups Bahrain, Qatar, the United Arab Emirates, Oman, Kuwait and Saudi Arabia.

Two summit meetings were held subsequently during 1981, one in Abu Dhabi in May and another in Riyadh in November. They produced co-ordinated action to help resolve the dispute between Iran and Iraq and between Oman and South Yemen (PDRY) as well as joint measures on increasing military co-operation. In 1982 measures to provide financial aid to Iraq were agreed, as were actions aimed at obtaining an Israeli withdrawal from the Lebanon. Additional measures to set up a Gulf-wide Rapid Deployment Force (RDF) which would be run by the GCC member-states themselves were expected to be agreed later in the year. The agreement had been delayed by disagreement among the states over how they should be related to the Rapid Deployment Force set up by the US.

On the economic front the council agreed to make both Bahrain and Oman centres for industrialisation in the Gulf and to set up joint-ventures which would utilise the area's oil and gas wealth more productively. Measures to establish a common market and to abolish customs tariffs on domestic products as well as to remove restrictions on trade and travel between member-states, to promote co-operation in agricultural development and to encourage co-ordinated investment policies were also agreed at a meeting of the Gulf Co-operation Council's finance ministers held in Riyadh in June 1982.

Bahrain is already the centre for several joint industrial ventures sponsored by the Gulf states, including the Arab Shipbuilding and Repair Yard Company (ASRY), the Gulf Petrochemical Industries Corporation (GPIC), the Arab Iron and Steel Company (AISCO), the Gulf Aluminium Rolling Mill Company (GARMCO) and the Heavy Oil Conversion Company. The huge Arab Insurance Group (ARIG), which is capitalised at US\$3 billion, opened its doors in Bahrain in October 1981 and, together with two of the Arab world's largest banks, the Arab Banking Corporation (ABC) and the Gulf International Bank (GIB) has helped to make Bahrain a financial centre for the Gulf as well.

Still other projects could be established in Bahrain in the near future as a result of the Council's agreement in January 1982 to set up a joint Gulf Investment Corporation (GIC) and, one month later, to form a ministerial committee to co-ordinate activities in oil and gas exploration, production, refining, pricing, transport and storage. The GIC, which is to receive US\$3 billion from the GCC council members, is part of the GCC's efforts to establish a Gulf common market, and there have been some suggestions that it may be headquartered in Bahrain.

Expenditure Rises

The government has increased the amount it planned to spend over the two-year period from 1 January 1982 to the end of 1983 by almost 60 per cent, compared to the previous two-year period. Expenditure during the 1982/83 period is to total US$3.2 billion, compared to only US$2 billion for 1980/81. Capital spending will account for half the total planned expenditure, or about US$1.6 billion. The remainder is to be used primarily for administrative expenses, including salary increases for government employees.

The increased budget is part of a major four-year plan which is expected to cost a total of US$6.1 billion by the end of 1985. Priority will be given to expanding the country's infrastructure and to improving social services as well as local industries. Projects envisaged include raising power generation from 487 megawatts (MW) to 917MW; increasing the capacity of desalination water plants from five million gallons per day (gpd) to 45 million gpd; the installation of 350 kilometres of new sewerage lines; the construction of a new runway and terminal building at Bahrain International Airport and two container berths at the port of Mina Salman; the building of 22 new schools and the provision of US$75 million for home building loans.

Oil Earnings Increase

Revenue to fund the spending programme will come largely from the export of oil and refined petroleum. Earnings on the oil account in 1981 totalled 523.7 Bahraini dinars (BD) or about US$1,393 million, 15 per cent more than in 1980. Exports of crude oil and refined petroleum products in 1981 totalled BD1,458.8 million, compared with BD1,206.6 million a year earlier, while imports of crude oil cost BD935.1 million in 1981, up from BD750 million in 1980.

While there are some doubts that Bahrain's oil earnings will continue to rise, given the world recession and the falling value of crude oil exports, its ability to withstand economic pressures is enhanced by the location of one of the Gulf's largest refineries in the country. The complex, which is 60 per cent owned by the government, processed a record level of 259,000 barrels per day (bpd) on average in 1981, including some 200,000bpd of crude oil imported from Saudi Arabia. The fighting in the Iran/Iraq War, which led to the destruction of a large part of the huge Abadan refining complex in Iran, coupled with rising demand for petroleum products throughout the Gulf states, has helped Bahrain to maintain its earnings from the oil sector and should continue to do so even though other crude oil producers are experiencing falling revenues from their exports.

Like those other producers, however, Bahrain will also find that it cannot expect the increased revenue from its crude oil exports that it has enjoyed in the past, barring a major change in world oil demand over the next year. Furthermore, production at the country's small Jebel al-Dukhan oilfield has been declining by about 5.0 per cent a year and more than half of the country's exports now come from the offshore Abu Safah oilfield which Bahrain shares with Saudi Arabia.

To the extent that Bahrain's refinery relies on imported crude, however, any decline in the value or volume of crude oil exports may be recovered from the falling cost of crude oil brought from Saudi Arabia.

Bahrain is also becoming an increasingly important producer of non-associated gas, which exists offshore in the Khuff Zone. Reserves are estimated to total nine trillion cu feet. While some of the gas is used to fuel power facilities, the oil refinery and the aluminium smelter, and other amounts are used to enhance the recovery of crude oil, an increasing amount of the gas is being exported by the Bahrain National Gas Company (BANAGAS), which opened a natural gas liquids plant in Bahrain in December 1979. By the end of August 1981 it had produced 680,206 barrels of propane, 528,865 barrels of butane and 757,018 barrels of naphtha, most of which is exported to Japan and to the other Gulf States.

Bahrain will also benefit from the construction of two major hydrocarbon facilities which are being set up in the country with the aid of Saudi Arabia and Kuwait. The first, to be located on Sitra Island near the existing refinery, will produce 1,000 tonnes of methanol and 1,000 tonnes of ammonia a day. Production is expected to begin in 1985. It will be owned by the Gulf Petrochemical Industries Company (GPIC), a joint-venture in which Bahrain will have 40 per cent of the equity, the remainder being shared by Saudi Arabia and Kuwait. The second facility, a US$600 million fuel oil cracker plant, will process 80,000 barrels of heavy fuel a day when operation begins, by 1985. A contract for feasibility studies for the complex was awarded by the Heavy Oil Conversion Company (HOCC) at the end of 1981. HOCC was set up to run the company by Bahrain, Saudi Arabia and Kuwait. Each will have the same shareholdings as they do in GPIC.

Integrated Industries Go Ahead

In addition to these two plants, Bahrain is rapidly becoming a centre for industrial joint ventures which reflect the willingness of all the Gulf States to avoid duplication of facilities and to integrate their manufacturing and production plants.

Kobe Steel of Japan was named at the end of 1981 as prime contractor for the construction of a new pelletising plant to be run by the Arab Iron and Steel Company (AISCO). The plant, which will be located east of the dry dock, will also have its own 100MW power plant and a 3,000 cubic metres per day desalination complex as well as a separate deep-water jetty offshore. Production is expected to total some four million tonnes of pellets a year. Partners in AISCO include the Kuwait Foreign Trading, Contracting and Investment Company, Kuwait Metal Pipes and the Amman-based Arab Mining Company. Several private shareholders from the Gulf are also taking part.

Another joint-venture now under way is the GARMCO, which is planning to set up a 40,000 tonnes-a-year aluminium rolling mill in North Sitra. A US firm was awarded a contract to survey the site in early 1982. Saudi Arabia, Iraq, Kuwait and Bahrain each have a 20 per cent share in GARMCO, while Oman and Qatar will have 10 per cent each. Operations are expected to begin by the end of 1986, using feedstock provided by the country's aluminium smelter. The smelter, which is run by Aluminium Bahrain (ALBA) was completed in 1972. Production in 1981 totalled 141,000 tonnes but could have risen to 170,000 tonnes by the end of 1982 as a result of the installation of a new potline at the works. Output in 1980 totalled 125,954 tonnes, even though the plant's official capacity at the time totalled only 120,000 tonnes a year.

Despite the utilisation of all its capacity, the fall in demand and the build-up of stocks produced a trading loss during the first quarter of 1982 amounting to US$4.5 million, the first time since 1975 that the books went into the red. Profits in 1981 totalled US$13.2 million. ALBA's shareholders include the government of Bahrain (57.9 per cent), Kaiser Aluminium Bahrain (17 per cent), Breton Investments (5.1 per cent) and the Saudi Arabian Basic Industries Corporation (SABIC) (20 per cent).

One of the most successful joint ventures to be set up in Bahrain is the Arab Shipbuilding and Repair Yard Company, which accepted its first vessel in November 1977. Managed by a Portuguese firm, Lisnave Shipyards SA, the yard has experienced occupancy rates of 90 per cent a year or more since then and in 1981 recorded a rate of 94 per cent. The yard, which is owned by the governments of Bahrain, Iraq, Kuwait, Libya, Qatar, Saudi Arabia and the United Arab Emirates (UAE), is capable of handling very large crude carriers (VLCCs) of up to 500,000 tonnes. Plans to open a second dock to handle smaller vessels are being discussed as is a proposal that the yard also take on the management of the dry dock in Dubai which opened in 1979 but has not been in operational use. In 1981 ASRY also announced plans to fabricate steel for desalination plants at its yard using labour employed on the site. ASRY holds 15 per cent of the shares in the Kuwait Desalination Plant Company which designs and markets such facilities worldwide.

Bahrain is also the site of several smaller industries, including several producing aluminium products such as cables and aluminium powder. Plans are under way to encourage the establishment of other light industries producing building materials, processed foods and wood products for export to Saudi Arabia and other parts of the Gulf. Some of these will be located at a new site north of Sitra being set up by the Bahrain Light Industry Company, a state-owned firm.

Industrial production in Bahrain should benefit greatly from the construction of the huge new causeway linking the country to Saudi Arabia. A contract for the 25-kilometre link was awarded to a Dutch firm in 1981 and by mid-1982 local contractors were also benefiting as demand for building materials, labour, catering facilities and transport equipment rose to help meet the project's needs. The causeway is expected to cost US$564 million. When it is opened, in late 1984 or early 1985, it will enable Saudis to travel to Bahrain for both business and leisure, a fact which some Bahrainis fear could change the country's social and cultural traditions.

Banking Assets Rise Again

Bahrain is also the site of a large offshore banking sector which now is almost as large as that of Singapore. Assets of the offshore banking units (OBUs) rose to a record US$55.6 billion at the end of the first quarter of 1982, US$4.9 billion more than the amount recorded at the end of December 1981. Bankers said at the time that the increase reflected the good performance of two large banks in particular, the Arab Banking Corporation and the Gulf International Bank, and see the figures as a sign that the decline in world oil prices is not affecting Bahrain's strength as a financial centre. The rise also occurred despite the reports of an attempted coup in the country, a fact which the government sees as an endorsement of its decision to act swiftly.

In 1982 the Bahrain Monetary Agency (BMA), the equivalent of a central bank, announced that it would grant fewer OBU licences during the year and would give priority to institutions from the Middle East, Latin America and the Far East as part of a plan to spread the sector's geographic representation. By the end of the first quarter of 1982 some 65 OBUs had received licences to operate in Bahrain.

The BMA also announced at the beginning of the year that it had imposed a 12-month ban on the formation of new publicly owned OBUs and investment companies. The move follows several spectacular share issues which occurred when the BMA allowed Bahraini investors to participate in public issues of shares for the offshore sector.

One of the first such issues, made by the Bahrain International Bank in early 1982, was 280 times oversubscribed. Subsequent issues, by the Bahrain and Kuwait Investment Company and the Bank of Bahrain and the Middle East were oversubscribed by factors of 350 and 1,800 respectively. The moratorium should help to curb this 'share fever' and alleviate fears that excessive speculation could detract from Bahrain's reputation as a well regulated financial centre.

The country's banking sector has also been expanding to include operations in gold dealing and commodity trading, although BMA officials expect these operations to remain secondary to that of commercial and offshore banking. The insurance sector is also growing rapidly. The Arab Insurance Group, a joint-venture of the governments of Kuwait, Libya and the United Arab Emirates (UAE), opened its doors in October 1981 with a total capital of US$3 billion, a figure which makes it almost a rival of the huge Lloyds of London syndicate.

The Group was started in response to Lloyds' decision to declare the Gulf a war-risk area, a move that was taken even before the outbreak of the Iran/Iraq War in September 1980. A smaller company, Al-Ahlia Saudi Insurance, began operations in 1982 in Bahrain with a total capital of US$15 million. The company, which is a joint venture between Saudi, Bahraini and Hong Kong interests, intends to open branch offices in Jeddah, Riyadh and Dammam.

Agriculture Emphasised

The new Four Year Development Plan 1981–55 [Ed: later extended by two years] is placing greater emphasis on increasing agricultural production in the country. Although Bahrain in the past was self-sufficient in food, changes in diet, rising disposable incomes, industrialisation and the influx of immigrant labour have led to a huge rise in the cost of imported food. Total spending on agriculture over the period from January 1982 to the end of 1985 is to reach BD26 million, about US$70 million. Overall production is to rise to 16 per cent of domestic food requirements, 10 per cent more than current output.

Government programmes call for the construction of a new date-processing plant in 1983, the building of workshops to produce and maintain agricultural machinery and works to expand the country's drainage system. Subsidies will be provided for chicken feed and farmers will be given free greenhouses as part of an experimental programme involving ten farms to grow crops out of season. Already land for the production of vegetables has been increased from 450 hectares in 1979 to more than 540 hectares. Vegetable production has risen from 6,400 tonnes in 1979 to 7,200 tonnes a year. Egg production now accounts for about 80 per cent of local demand, compared with only 10 per cent in 1976. Under the new plan, egg production should fully meet local needs by 1985, while vegetable production should account for 75 per cent of domestic demand.

Milk production is also expected to rise to provide about 30 per cent of local demand while Livestock and fishing are also getting renewed attention under the plan. Desalinated water will be used to increase cattle, sheep and goat herds and new breeds are to be introduced.

Although the country's fishing industry, once a mainstay of the economy, has declined as labour has been attracted to other sectors and as catches have fallen, the government is providing new incentives for fishermen to modernise their equipment. There is also discussion on ways to revive the Bahrain Fishing Company, which was closed in 1979.

1984

Shi'a Muslims – Gulf Co-operation Council – Historical Role – al-Khalifa Rule – National Assembly – Constitution – Housing Programmes – ALBA Expansion – Hamad Town – Bahraini-isation – Tourism – Inter-Gulf Trade – No Feast or Famine – A Fully Fledged Financial Market – Refinery Losses

Bahrain is an island emirate situated just 15 miles from the coast of Saudi Arabia. Politically it is characterised by a laissez-faire administration which contains its 60 per cent Shi'a Muslim population by giving them greater licence to participate in the country's affairs than any other Arabian Gulf State.

It is potentially the poorest of the six states of the Gulf Co-operation Council (GCC), with the least mineral resources. Although Bahrain was the first Gulf country to exploit its oil – the first well in the Gulf was spudded in at Jebel al-Dukhan on 16 October 1931 – it will be the first Gulf state to run out of oil, estimated to finally dry up within 45 years. Socially, however, Bahrain is perhaps the richest of the Arabian Gulf states. It was the first to boast a school in 1919 and has the lowest illiteracy quotient in the Gulf with more than 60 per cent of its indigenous 250,000 population able to read and write. Women play a vital role in the labour force, comprising 11 per cent of the total and continuing to increase their share by an average of 4 per cent a year.

Bahrain is also known throughout the Middle East as the most advanced of all the Gulf states by dint of its historical role as a trading nation. It is acknowledged as the commercial centre of the region, with a well developed merchant class and associated legal structure of internationally acceptable commercial and company laws. In line with an early understanding that to survive as an entity in its own right Bahrain had to be forward-looking, it encouraged a free-enterprise economy welcoming participation from all comers, both private and public, foreign as well as Arab. It was the first Gulf state to concentrate on diversifying its economy from oil and, aware that its greatest resource, relative to the rest of the Gulf, was in fact human, Bahrain has placed much emphasis on manpower development since the first apprenticeship programmes were launched 30 years ago.

Commercial Banking Structure

Bahrain was also the first Gulf state to realise that something needed to be done with the huge amounts of money that were flowing into the region after the first oil-price rise in the 1970s. Bahrain already boasted the best developed commercial banking structure in the region and with characteristic imagination developed its financial sector, opening the first offshore banking unit (OBU) in the Middle East in 1976 and reaching for the giddy heights of today where the volume of business handled by this burgeoning sector has outstripped Singapore and is on a par with Hong Kong.

In the words of the internationally known Bahraini Minister of Industry and Development, Yusuf al-Shirawi: 'Our country does not believe in too tight a control. As long as we maintain a reasonable balance between our labour resource and materials and growth we will keep the developmental kettle boiling... We have been working in this way for 30 years – not because of vision, but from lack of money.'

In December of 1983 Bahrain celebrated its 200th year of al-Khalifa rule. His Highness Sheikh Isa bin Salman al-Khalifa, the present Emir of the State of Bahrain succeeded his father, Sheikh Salman bin Hamad bin Isa al-Khalifa on 2 November 1961. The Emir's own son, Sheikh Hamad bin Isa bin Salman al-Khalifa is Crown Prince and Commander-in-Chief of the Bahrain Defence Force.

It was only 13 years ago, in 1971, that the present Emir declared total independence from Britain and Bahrain was admitted to the League of Arab States (generally known as the Arab League). Eventually a cabinet was formed under the Emir's brother, the Prime Minister Sheikh Khalifa bin Salman al-Khalifa, which now has 15 ministers of whom only five are drawn from the royal family. And, unique in the Gulf, five of Bahrain's cabinet ministers are Shi'a Muslims.

In the early years of independence Bahrain experimented with a National Assembly – prior to this all government ministers were of the Sunni Muslim sect, the ruling sect in the Arabian Gulf although not predominant in Bahrain or the Eastern Province of Saudi Arabia. The Shi'a Muslim sect is the ruling party in Iran and is also the predominant sect in Iraq, and as such is thought to pose a threat to Sunni political stability in the region.

Bahrain's National Assembly came about as a result of internal pressures for the unrepresented Shi'a majority to have a voice in the government. It lasted for approximately three years when it was disbanded by the Emir on the grounds that it was unproductive – too many dissenters took the floor making it impossible to agree on policy decisions. To placate those whom the speakers in the National Assembly represented, it became an unwritten policy that the new governing body of Bahrain would have a third of its number made up of Shi'as and the rest Sunnis.

The National Assembly was first formed on Bahrain's National Day, 16 December 1972, authorised six months earlier by Emiri decree. The assembly consisted of 22 members elected by universal secret suffrage, plus eight members nominated by decree and the then 12 cabinet ministers who were *ex officio*. Its first duty was to approve a draft Constitution for the country.

The Constitution was carefully discussed twice a week for 45 meetings until June 1973, when the National Assembly finally approved it. The Emir ratified the Constitution in December 1973. It laid down the political and legal foundations of the state, defining Bahrain as an Arab Islamic state, independent and fully sovereign. Its rule would be hereditary, passed from the Emir to his eldest son unless the Emir should decide during his lifetime to appoint another of his sons as his successor. Bahrain's system of government was described in the document as democratic, in which sovereignty would reside with the people, beginning with the right of election. In the 109 articles of the Constitution provision was made for legislative powers being vested in the Emir and the National Assembly, with the executive powers vested in the Emir, the cabinet and the ministers, and the judicial power required to be passed first by the Assembly before ratification by the Emir. Election Day was fixed as 7 December and for these elections Bahrain was divided into eight constituencies. The Constitution was modelled on that of Kuwait's 1962 Constitution and was the first step towards establishing a democratic system of government in the Lower Gulf.

In 1975, however, this courting of democracy in Bahrain was renounced. Acquiescence in the closure of the National Assembly in those early oil-boom days can be partly explained by the economic growth that swept even the less privileged along in its flood. In the present boom days, however, the government has to tread more carefully, planning assiduously to keep growth on a par with the needs of the populace. The Labour Minister has pledged to create some 40,000 jobs over the next decade and offer incentives for the national workforce to attain the necessary levels of education to achieve required technical and professional skills.

Bahrain is forging ahead with its housing programmes, a large slice of the national budget allotted to meeting the demand of 330 applicants for housing a month. The first residents moved into Bahrain's US$1 billion new Hamad Town in 1983; construction continues to keep pace with the target of 1,600 houses and 1,000 private plots a year of the 17,000 dwellings projected.

Bulk of Budget Goes to Social Development

The Ministry of Finance was very careful with the 1983 budget, investing 17 per cent more in expenditures over 1982 before the anticipated cutbacks of 1984. Of the US$1.4 billion 1983 budget, some US$850 million was allocated to recurrent expenditure of which housing, education including manpower training, water, works and power take the greatest chunk. This was an increase of 24 per cent over 1982. Before the expected economic crunch Bahrain is determined to maintain its commitment to placating its potentially volatile population, defusing any political dissatisfactions that might emerge.

The Bahraini people are conscious of the material wellbeing of their brothers in neighbouring states. And although Bahrain is largely tax-free (income, sales, capital gains, or estates) , and provides free education and medical services and a housing programme with rentals fixed at no more than 25 per cent of the householders' income, the cost of essential services, power, water and fuel are less subsidised by the state than in Qatar, Saudi Arabia, Kuwait, Oman or the United Arab Emirates (UAE).

Such disparities of wealth in the region are, through the aegis of the GCC, being gradually eroded. The aim of the GCC is to bring the six member-states into an equal economic line by supporting development projects in the less oil-rich states and cutting back on subsidies in the more wealthy. However, before the advent of the GCC, Bahrain had developed bi-lateral relations with both Kuwait and Saudi Arabia, offering diversification opportunities and a better developed workforce and facilities in return for much needed investment. The now commonplace concept of the joint venture was begun in Bahrain.

Bahrain's 1965 census painted a gloomy picture of a stagnant oil market with impending unemployment and redundancies and the prospect of 45,000 school leavers about to enter the market. The country's present prime minister, at that time Minister of Finance, decided that the time had come to industrialise Bahrain and in 1968 a proposed aluminium smelter was the project finally selected. A consortium of nine shareholders, with the major share taken by the Bahrain government, formed Aluminium Bahrain (ALBA). Production began in 1971 and the last shareholding transaction took place in 1979 as part of a funding operation for ALBA's expansion with the government upping its share to 57.9 per cent, the Saudi government coming in with 20 per cent and two of the original holders, Kaiser Aluminium and Breton Investments, with 17 and 5.1 per cent respectively.

In the first 10 years of its growth, ALBA had a significant impact on Bahrain's economy. It fulfilled its original mandate to begin the industrialisation of the island; of the 2,000 employees of the company 76 per cent of the workforce is now Bahraini, and in 1981 ALBA was the source of income for approximately 6 per cent of the country's population.

ALBA has also led directly to the formation of several other important industrial and commercial operations in Bahrain. Chief among these are the Bahrain Saudi Aluminium Marketing Company (BALCO), the smelter's marketing arm, Bahrain Aluminium Extrusion Company (BALEXCO), producing aluminium extrusions, Bahrain Atomisers International, ALBA's first spin-off industry which converts molten aluminium to high-quality aluminium powder for export to

Europe, and the predominantly Arab joint-venture Midal Cables which was the first Gulf factory to produce stranded aluminium power transmission and distribution cables for the Gulf markets.

ALBA's history has not been easy. It was created to fill a vacuum in Bahrain's economy and in spite of a lack of raw materials, a small market, competition and the 'dumping' habit of the industrialised world (primarily in Japan, a major single customer of ALBA's) and an untrained and high-cost labour force, the smelter has succeeded. Says ALBA's present chairman and Minister for Industry and Development: 'It was largely due to our abundant supplies of natural gas and eagerness.' Certainly the world aluminium market has not helped ALBA's expansion, with prices during 1979 and 1981 halving from a peak of well over US$2,000 a ton to US$1,200.

ALBA *Still Expanding*

Nevertheless, the company continues to expand. Almost 10 years to the day after the plant was inaugurated, an additional potroom was commissioned which is now operational and has brought the total annual rated capacity of the plant to 170,000 metric tons (mt) of aluminium bars. Capital was raised primarily from local sources, with the Saudi government stepping in as a shareholder, from a private loan of US$70 million arranged by the Gulf International Bank, and service contracts placed within Bahrain which accounted for an additional US$16 million.

The regional consensus in the Gulf has been most supportive of ALBA. It has been left to get on with the business of production and Bahraini-isation of its workforce, the marketing headaches being handled exclusively by the shareholders, the largest of which, Saudi Arabia and Bahrain, have their own marketing company BALCO. BALCO is run entirely on commercial lines with no subsidies even in the regional marketing, having to compete with an international market in the throes of glut and recession. It has proved itself, recording a net profit of US$6.2 million in 1981 despite stinging bank interest rates and stockpile losses. BALCO is committed to market 135,000 tons a year of ALBA's production and the Gulf markets absorb only a maximum of 40 per cent of this.

BALCO's outgoing managing director, Sandy Ross MacDonald, says: 'We have been facing the music that the oil industry is mobilised for, for two years now. In oil terms what the aluminium industry would be talking about is trying to hold the price at US$16 a barrel, not US$30.'

Now that the aluminium industry is established in the region – with hindsight, it is questionable whether it would have been – the Gulf Ministers of Industry have mobilised to inject as much vitality into it as possible, through downstream projects. In 1983 an agreement was signed between Kobe Steel of

Japan and seven (six GCC states plus Iraq) Gulf state shareholders of the Gulf Aluminium Rolling Mill Company (GARMCO) to build an aluminium rolling mill with a 40,000 ton capacity. ALBA will provide much of GARMCO's feedstock and the region will absorb 80 per cent of its production. With Gulf demand for aluminium rolled products forecast in the region of 240,000 tons per annum over the next decade, the US$106 million plant is anticipated to be a cost-effective exercise.

In the meantime BALEXCO's board of directors has approved a US$666,000 modernisation and expansion plan for the aluminium extrusion and anodising plant. The scheme will increase production by 25 per cent to reach 6,000 tons a year and meet the current full order books from Bahraini and Gulf customers.

The five-year-old Midal Cables, another industry spawned by ALBA, also records continued expansion, with plans going ahead for a new plant to make copper and wire cable. An insulated cable production capability is on the drawing board and the present consumption of 12 per cent of ALBA's production a year is expected to increase at least to 15 per cent. Midal Cables is the largest private sector company in Bahrain and has pushed ahead with the country's policy of training and employing Bahrainis. More than 80 per cent of its 18,000mt production of conductors is exported, mostly to the Gulf Co-operation Council countries, and with the coming of the Bahrain-Saudi causeway present shipping costs will be slashed, enabling the company to operate at the plant's full capacity of 20,000mt.

For Midal Cables it costs almost as much to ship a ton of cable to neighbouring Kuwait as it does to Japan. The coming of the causeway will therefore give a huge boost to Midal and to the manufacturing companies that are growing from the basic industries.

The 1983 International Monetary Fund (IMF) report on the economy of Bahrain praised the government for increasing its non-oil revenue and encouraging the private sector to participate in building up the basic projects and the Gulf Co-operation Council's joint projects sited in Bahrain. A GCC Industrial Ministers' meeting envisaged Bahrain, the Eastern Province of Saudi Arabia and Qatar being linked in the 1990s as an industrial area for the region, with five major industries – cement, iron, aluminium, petrochemicals and fertilisers – being co-ordinated and jointly funded. Over the next two years, two of these industrial projects worth US$2 billion will be established in Bahrain and Oman, and an industrial bank will be formed co-operatively to handle the finances.

Causeway to Open in 1986
The markets for these schemes will initially be the GCC member-states before extending to cover the rest of the Middle East. Consequently the causeway link

between Bahrain and Saudi Arabia will be of vital importance in rationalising marketing costs. The 25 kilometre, two-lane dual-carriageway will take a projected 31,000 vehicles a day. Link roads on both sides of the Gulf are already under construction in preparation for the target opening in January 1986. And from the Eastern Province on the Saudi side, Western Europe is only 5,000 kilometres away; a journey to Bahrain from France, Germany or Britain would take just over a week. Despite the crippling capital costs of the venture, awarded to the Amsterveen-based firm Ballast Nedam for US$564 million – which at US$30,000 a metre makes the Saudi-Bahrain causeway the most expensive civil engineering project of its type in the world – the Bahrain government believes the eventual halving of transport costs and the industrial boost it will give the island will quickly make the causeway cost-effective.

Already many of the island's construction companies are reaping benefits from road network contracts and the Bahraini company Bramco Group has grossed US$19 million for the supply of between 3,000 and 3,500 tons of quarried rock a day over 24 months. Bramco, with Swiss company, IMF AG, also formed a joint-venture and won the US$7.8 million contract to supply 450,000 tons of aggregate from two quarries in the UAE for the 584 concrete piles required to support the bridging structures. Main contractors Ballast Nedam are happy at the speed and efficiency of the work they have sub-contracted locally; the causeway contract holds severe penalty clauses if extended over the 1986 target date.

Apart from the obvious industrial advantages of the causeway to Bahrain, it will also directly benefit the consumers. Under Secretary at Bahrain's Ministry of Development and Industry Sheikh Isa bin Abdullah al-Khalifa says: 'The biggest boost will be to poorer and middle income families, for whom I think we have to build a better future.' Sheikh Isa envisages the prices of consumer goods such as food and cars to become much cheaper. Says his boss, Yusuf Shirawi: 'Because we are next door to a huge economically active partner we will be able to share their bulk orders and help balance the shortages for which small Third World countries like Bahrain have become notorious.'

The causeway will also bring tourist revenue to the island. The present over-subscribed hotel market, with the island's eight luxury hotels struggling to fill their 3,000-plus rooms, is looking at the causeway with high hopes. Bahrain has always had a resort reputation for Gulf tourist traffic; there were over 200,000 visitors designated solely as tourists in 1982, mostly from Gulf and Middle East states. The road link should give this industry a substantial shot in the arm. Additionally, the many airlines that operate to and from Bahrain are looking to handle extra traffic in 1986, spreading their destination service to the rest of the world for the whole Gulf region.

The causeway is also being used by GCC appointees to encourage a greater private sector participation in industry. It is the carrot that will open up the regional markets to the traditional trader mentality of Bahrain's merchants, to encourage them to overcome their pattern of demanding a quick return of capital outlay rather than a longer one.

Says Sheikh Isa bin Abdullah al-Khalifa: 'I believe the private sector has to play a bigger part in the future of the island.' He goes on to stress that his own, not the government's, opinion is that it is time for more participation from private individuals. 'We are neither a communist nor a capitalist-based society. We like to believe that we are somewhere in between and encourage individual and group participation in industry.

It has been proven too many times in the past that bureaucracy gets in the way of running businesses economically and state-controlled industries are notorious for their unprofitability. The private sector has to invest in the industrial future of the country. If a project such as the Gulf Aluminium Rolling Mill can be set up by private investors, then there is no reason why other equally large projects cannot be.'

Schemes to Encourage Private Interest

There are various schemes to encourage such private interest. The Directorate for Customs and Ports in Bahrain does not charge any import duty on what is classified as capital equipment. A GCC article of economic agreement introduced in early 1983 abolished all customs duties on locally manufactured goods between member-states in an effort to boost inter-Gulf trade and encourage greater industrial co-operation between the private sectors in the states. A unified customs levy on all imported goods was scheduled to be imposed in September 1983. This will set a 4–20 per cent levy on taxable goods and also break down all imports into three categories: protected goods, tariff-free goods and customs goods. For states like Bahrain with customs duties formerly starting at 5 per cent on food products and building materials and up to 10 per cent on electronic and electrical goods, the lower levy will mean lower prices on some goods. And such a parity on imports into the whole region will inevitably bind the Gulf states closer and eventually work to the advantage of smaller states such as Bahrain.

The immediate concern of Bahraini businessmen and private investors is that by lifting tariffs between the Gulf states, their own small market will be flooded by the bigger production capacities of their neighbours. There are protection clauses for a phasing in of the economic agreement, and the Bahrain government, in an effort to protect the developing manufacturing industries, has long had an industrial strategy that is beginning to pay dividends.

Of the 16 industrial sites at present catering for the diversity of small and large industries on the island, there are within them specific areas allocated as zones free from customs duty. These are primarily for manufacturing industries where part of the assembly of the finished product is carried out in Bahrain. They also cater for offshore businesses.

The first of these industrial zones was started near Bahrain's major port, Mina Salman, in the 1960s and it now has 85 units. The leading manufacturer of building materials in Bahrain, the al-Zamil Group, was one of the first local manufacturers to take advantage of the government's industrial zone incentives. It is these small nest industries which are labour-intensive and have a built-in expansion capacity that Bahrain's government goes all out to encourage. The al-Zamil Group now boasts three factories in Mina Salman, producing marble tiles, nails and screws and aluminium building materials. Its first step towards switching from a major trading family into a manufacturer was taken with the advent of the aluminium industries in the Gulf. The Group is now the major supplier and producers of aluminium doors, windows, frames partitions, balustrades and shop fronts. They are also distributors and agents for aluminium machinery, fittings, nails and accessories. They have responded to the new demand and produce automatic doors and ladders.

The Group went into marble production in 1974. This factory now cuts, polishes and installs around 3,000 square metres of marble each month. The al-Zamil nails and screws factory set up in 1979 is now producing at a record five tons a day, giving the factory an export capacity. It is this type of indigenous local industry that the Bahrain government is encouraging as the key to diversified industrial development. And the industries in their turn are looking to the causeway for the impetus they need for expanded markets. The design of the causeway allows for extra road lanes as well as a rail link. Saudi Arabia in the meantime has a huge container depot in its Eastern Province managed by a leading Bahraini merchant family, Kanoo, which is capable of handling containers to feed the whole of the Arabian peninsula by both road and the modern rail network that criss-crosses Saudi Arabia with trains that reach speeds of 120mph between Riyadh and Jeddah.

The authorities assure the island's businessmen and private industrialists through an active Chamber of Commerce that Bahrain's more specialised capability will continue to protect them from producers in neighbouring markets. As opposed to seeing the causeway as a threat which will bring goods from neighbouring countries, the authorities regard it as a means of linking up with neighbours to get cheaper raw materials from outside the region.

Moreover, the island's Minister of Industry and Development periodically addresses this group of private investors, keeping them up to date with GCC's

1984 75

plans for Bahrain whereby the injection of GCC funds into further industrial joint-ventures to be sited in Bahrain will continue to stimulate the economy.

Port is Being Extended

Bahrain's modern container port, Mina Salman, is in process of being extended. The lengthening of the terminal and an extra 2,000 ton storage facility for cargo are in line with the port's authorities' estimates for 90 per cent of their traffic in 1990 to be containerised.

Although the increase of container handling has levelled to a maximum 7 per cent growth factor a year, the causeway again is expected to stimulate further trans-shipment traffic. This traffic accounts for just over 20 per cent of the work at Mina Salman. Imports in 1982 rose by 35 per cent to 1.4 million tons over 1981. However, exports fell dramatically by 49 per cent to 100,814 tons. The increase in imports helped Mina Salman to become one of the success stories of the nation as the world recession hit most of Bahrain's other big revenue pullers. Only five years ago ships often had to wait up to 50 days before being unloaded, a combination of the construction boom demand and the inadequate handling and docking facilities. The government was forced to take action and spent around US$132.6 million on a development programme that has given Bahrain one of the region's most modern and efficient ports. The port control room is now fully computerised, so that a vessel carrying 350 containers can be unloaded and the units stacked in pre-designated areas within eight hours. In 1982 the port boasted a throughput of 2.6 million tons. The fall in exports was credited to the drop in scrap and sulphur exports, which is expected to pick up again by early 1984 with the greater move of aluminium anticipated.

Of Bahrain's exports, manufactured goods, which include aluminium, rank second in the commodity table. They are outstripped by mineral fuels, lubricants and related minerals, which include refined oil exports, by US$3.6 billion. However, figures available up to the third quarter of 1982 show revenue derived for oil exports alone at US$2.4 billion, down by US$0.4 billion on the previous year. Altogether Bahrain recorded a 20 per cent fall in revenues in 1982 from exports of refined oil and its products over 1981.

When oil receipts go down, earnings obviously also drop and balance of payment experts at Bahrain Monetary Agency worry about meeting the import bill. To make up for the poor performance of 1982, the government cut its expenditures on imports by 18 per cent. Much of this trade picture revolves around oil. The country's oil production from its own fields stands at only 42,000 barrels a day; in the heyday of its refinery Bahrain imported six times this amount from Saudi Arabia to meet the Bahrain Petroleum Company's (BAPCO) refining capacity of 250,000 barrels per day (bpd).

The current import figure from Saudi Arabia is well below 150,000bpd, putting the average handling capability for the BAPCO refinery throughout the last quarter of 1982 and into the first two quarters of 1983 at a maximum of 175,000bpd and often much less at around half that. Buying less crude in from Saudi Arabia lessens the impact of fewer exports, but the refinery's profits from not running at its maximum capacity are accordingly severely slashed. The refinery's profit margin used to run at around US$3 to US$4 per barrel, but with the new oil prices this has been halved to give refineries like BAPCO a US$4 per barrel loss. So from a reasonable profit to a substantial loss the outlook with even the present turn around in prices is still bleak for the refining industries.

BAPCO was in the fortunate position of having scheduled a US$36 million light isomet plant project (LIP) for the first part of 1983, coinciding with the worst discrepancies in crude/refined prices. This project necessitated a shutdown in three of the refinery's major plants, so that the refinery was unable to process more than 100,000bpd and for some months the supply of crude from Saudi Arabia dried up altogether. The purpose of the LIP project was to reduce BAPCO's production of lower priced heavy fuel oils by around 6 per cent and increase the production of diesel and low-sulphur fuels. However, further catastrophe struck early in 1983 when a refinery fire damaged the hydro-desulphurising plant, causing damage estimated at US$3.4 million in physical repair bills alone.

All these factors together have enforced a fresh look at the operational cutbacks, originally estimated not to exceed 5 per cent than would have otherwise been spent and to leave the company's workforce unaffected. In effect this meant savings of US$1 million a month in the early part of 1983 and US$2 million from June. Bahrain Petroleum Company's chief executive Don Hepburn said, 'The oil industry is traditionally cyclical, ultimately there is no feast or famine, we just have to wait it out.'

Employment Levels Affected

However, for BAPCO's workforce a famine is in the offing. The official employment figures for 1982 and into 1983 were 4,300 people on the payroll of which 80 per cent were Bahraini. This made BAPCO the largest employer on the island. However, throughout 1982 and 1983 the expatriate workforce suffered drastic layoffs – initially recorded as non-renewal of contracts for the operations force of employees seconded from the Caltex Petroleum Corporation who as of 1981 relinquished their 100 per cent holding in the refinery to take a 40/60 cut with the state of Bahrain which now holds the major share.

The non-renewals of contract were throughout followed by large-scale expatriate redundancies, so that the 900 expatriates who made up BAPCO's

workforce in 1981 were reduced to a maximum of 500 by early 1983, with the redundancies and non-renewal of contracts being aimed at the expensive UK and
US employees, continuing throughout the year.

In fact the Bahrain refinery, one of the largest in the world, was operated by
500 people, and since it is government policy to Bahrainise the refinery it is
conceivable that from 1984 the expatriate labour force on the BAPCO payroll
could be less than 100. But what is worrying the government and the Bahraini
workforce at BAPCO is that the need to rationalise costs may well necessitate a
major layoff of Bahrainis as well. BAPCO's support services, that is, the oil-town-
ship's utilities – electricity, water, telephones and generating plants – as well as
the leisure complex club, the hospital, the school, and all their associated services are in line for private enterprise take-overs. These services employ a substantial proportion of Bahrainis. If budget cutbacks do necessitate their lay-off,
there is the possibility of some Bahrainis being re-employed by the private enterprises that will take over these areas, but leaving others out of work.

Those employed on the operational side, however, could be absorbed by the
marketing arm of Bahrain National Oil Company (BANOCO), and Bahrain National Gas Company (BANAGAS) the national company for the production and
distribution of Bahrain's substantial natural gas resource. But only so many of
these Bahrainis could be so absorbed. The heady days of jobs at all costs helped
those costs to soar out of all proportion. The expensive expatriate workforce is
being axed in every section of the oil refinery and there are bound to be
Bahraini casualties too. The government, in an effort to soften the blow will put
its most creative manpower schemes to work and in the meantime keep the
impending lay-offs at as low a profile as possible until viable alternatives arise.

The huge losses the refinery is suffering simply have to be rationalised.
BAPCO's chief executive gave a cut-off date of April 1983 before the world situation forced the company to take action. Unfortunately that time was reached
with little alleviation from the world market. And the capital outlays needed to
upgrade the quality of the refinery's end products require time to make any real
difference to the books.

BAPCO produces 90 grades of product. It is conceivable that production will
be rationalised to as few as six. The government could also buy in the Saudi
crude at subsidised levels. This was not the case when the refinery was operated as a purely commercial venture by the Caltex Petroleum Corporation, but
now with Bahrain having the substantial share in the refining operation it may
be able to use some GCC muscle to achieve more favourable purchase prices
from the Saudis.

With a production of 100,000bpd, that is, 60,000 barrels purchased from the
Saudis and of course nothing but extraction overheads for the 40,000 barrels of

Bahraini crude, the refinery can make a profit of up to US$4 a barrel usually, however, it just reaches break-even.

Heavy Oil Conversion Company

To counteract this grim picture which refinery executives expect to continue into 1984, Bahrain's government is pursuing an expansionist policy within the context of the GCC. The next major heavy industry planned for Bahrain will be associated with the refinery – a US$1.8 billion heavy oil conversion cracker which will be able to take up some of BAPCO's slack workforce. Sheikh Isa bin Abdullah al-Khalifa, Under Secretary at the Ministry for Development and Industry and chairman of the proposed Heavy Oil Conversion Company (HOCC), said: 'The results of the feasibility study show that the project will be very profitable.' It will be the biggest project that Bahrain has undertaken and could become one of the island's biggest sources of revenue. It will include a distillation unit to produce fuel oil and a hydrocracker to refine this product even further into more expensive products such as diesel, kerosene and naphtha.

Saudi Arabia, which is a shareholder in the project with Kuwait and Bahrain, has agreed to supply 80,000 barrels a day of heavy crude, US$4 a barrel cheaper than Saudi Arabian light. This will come from fields not yet tapped in the peninsula. The feasibility study was completed mid-1983 by the US consultancy company C E Lummus who based their projections on the use of the latest energy-saving techniques to convert the heavy oil into light saleable products at the top end of the market. HOCC will have an 80,000 to 110,000 barrel-a-day capacity, 30,000 to be supplied by Bahrain's own refinery. So through a strategic plan that will link the old with the new, Bahrain is set to save its present teetering oil industry and provide additional opportunities for its well-trained indigenous workforce.

Under construction at present is another downstream industry from the oil fields. The Gulf Petrochemical Industries Company (GPIC) awarded an US$80 million lump sum contract to the Italian firm Snamprogetti to build a twin ammonia and methanol plant that will cost the Bahraini, Kuwaiti and Saudi shareholders between US$350 and US$400 million.

GPIC is a prime example of the new-wave of Arab projects. It has been managed from the start by Bahrainis. Dr Tawfeq al-Moayyed is GPIC's vice chairman and chief executive. He has tried to ensure that the project will be economically viable from the word go. The construction contract was tightly specified by the Bahrainis, broken down into equipment procurement agreements, purchasing agreements, subcontracting and labour agreements and ultimately pitched at the Arab banks for financing agreements of a flexible package of loans and export credit guarantees all of which are designed to allow Bahrain's economy and its labour force to reap the maximum benefit from the project. Gone are the days of easy contract awards. If foreign firms wish to win the contracts, which are still substantial, they have to refine their bids and trim their profit margins, for the Gulf principals know what they want and how to get it.

A similar heavy industry venture to be sited in Bahrain is the Arab Iron and Steel Company (AISCO) pelletisating plant. The construction deal for this US$345 million pelletisation plant was akin to a tight game of poker in which the original bids were whittled down by 35 per cent over a year from the time the two international giants Hitachi and Kobe Steel of Japan were first invited to tender for the job. As well as a turnkey plant with an initial production of 4.0 million tons of pellets a year, the contract specified that the construction firm undertake to train the Bahrainis and Gulf nationals who will make up 70 per cent of the workforce.

The aluminium rolling mill is the fourth big industrial project to be planned for Bahrain; work was begun on its construction by Kobe in the summer of 1983. This mill is another joint venture of the Arabian Gulf states, including Iraq and excluding the UAE. The US$106 million dollar mill is scheduled to come on stream with 40,000 tons of rolled aluminium products in 1985. Together the steel pelletisation plant and the petrochemical plant will create some 650 jobs, of which at least 70 per cent are reserved for Bahrainis.

Minister of Development and Industry, Yusuf Shirawi says, 'When the Bahrain cabinet directed the Ministry of Finance to unleash these major development schemes, we asked them to hold them until at least 1983, so that we could beat inflation and not deplete our carefully nurtured human and other resources.'

In the meantime the mainstay of Bahrain's economy is still its depleting oil industry, which through a US$16 million seismic programme for offshore exploration will be boosted for a further 50 years. Such programmes with a 10 per cent improvement in technology every two to three years will, it is believed, help spin out the life of Bahrain's oil industry.

OBUs Represent 25 Countries

After the substantial rise in oil prices in 1973, liquidity became abundant in the Gulf oil producing countries. And Bahrain in its traditional role as a service centre responded to the regional situation. With relatively well developed communications – growing from a hand-cranked telephone and 12 lines in 1932 to a digital exchange with 73,000 lines five decades later – Bahrain developed a sophisticated banking sector well placed between the time zones of the money markets of the East and the West to handle the substantial sums of money that were looking for placement.

In 1983 Bahrain had in the short span of seven years created an offshore banking sector boasting 65 OBUs representing 25 different countries. In the first quarter of 1983 the assets and liabilities of these units had reached US$60 billion. In August 1982 the assets and liabilities of the OBUs stood at US$61.1 billion but had taken a fall of US$2 billion by December 1982 due to the squeeze on liquidity and less inter-bank business. Such business accounts for around 16 per cent of the OBU dealings and is likely to have been more pronounced throughout 1983 with interest rates coming down and funds making their way back to the region from placements abroad. The bulk of the OBU business is in foreign exchange, but the Arab banks particularly and certainly some of the bigger foreign corporations actively pursue wholesale banking business.

The OBUs are licensed by the Bahrain Monetary Agency which was created in 1973 to direct, supervise and control the banks with extensive central banking powers. The BMA allows a lot of freedom to banks and pursues an open-door policy. It offered certain benefits such as exemption from tax and exchange controls in order to attract the banks which at that time were looking for a Middle East home to replace Beirut. Despite the liquidity shortages due to world recession hitting most of Bahrain's major industries, there is still no indication of the policymakers imposing any controls on the freedom of money or people. The benefits that accrue from the OBUs in terms of employment opportunities, legal fees to Bahraini firms and the social aspect of housing, as well as the mandatory licence fee payable in Bahraini dinars of US$26,500 per unit per year – regarded as a small proportion of the overall advantages – indicate that it is unlikely that any constraints other than the normal monthly accounting demands of the BMA will be placed on the OBUs.

The Agency works through the Bahrain Association of Banks (BAB) so that any problems from either sector can be openly discussed and the BMA's policy of carefully scrutinising applicants for new OBU licences can be followed. As far as the commercial banking sector goes, the BMA stopped issuing additional licences in 1976, to protect the business of the present 18 commercial banks allowed to conduct business in Bahrain. These banks continue to show through their deposits and soaring profits that there is still plenty of money around in the small private investors' accounts. Even in the slowdown year of 1982 deposits increased by US$111.4 million to US$1.88 billion over 1981. And by March 1983 deposits had continued in an upward trend adding a further US$28 million to the banking sector. At the end of 1981, 1,500 Bahrainis were employed in the 1,887 jobs available in the commercial banks. And of the four registered Bahraini banks, one of which is the Bahrain Islamic Bank, three of them account for on average 49.14 per cent of the total profits earned by all the commercial banks.

1984

In addition to the commercial and offshore banking units, Bahrain is determined to extend its activities from a money market to that of a fully fledged financial market. In this cause the BMA offered in 1977 investment banking licences which nine banking firms took advantage of to offer specialised investment and merchant banking business. There are six international money brokers and 44 representative offices of international banks. There are in addition two specialised banks, the Housing Bank and the Bahrain Islamic Bank. In an effort to inject further confidence in Bahrain as an international centre the BMA has actively encouraged the setting up of insurance and reinsurance companies of which there are now 20. The first, Norwich Winterthur Insurance (Gulf) of the UK was set up in 1950 and the latest, the Arabian Insurance Company (ARIC), is the US$3 billion giant that caused such a sensation when it opened its doors in Bahrain in 1980.

By granting permission for the establishment of a new brand of corporate bodies in 1977, the government opened another avenue for further diversification of the economy and created an exempt company status. The business of these companies covers such diverse areas as shipping, cargo, aircraft leasing, management services, oilfield services, financial consulting, investment and trading among others. These companies in 1981 numbered 78. In addition, eight exempt companies have been granted OBU status and seven of them investment banking licences.

So from its first taste of twentieth century technology in the 1930s, when the first oil industry venture in the region came into production and the first telephone exchange was placed in service, Bahrain now boasts the most diversified industrial economy of the region. With ALBA, the Arab Shipbuilding and Drydock Repair Yard, and the new petrochemical and steel pelletisation plants as well as a broad base of manufacturing nest factories and now the international financial centre of OBUs, brokers, investment, insurance and exempt companies and the most comprehensive telecommunications network in the region keyed into computers and satellites, Bahrain is a very significant part of the developing Arab world.

1985

Iran/Iraq War: Escalation But No Panic – A Time-Zone Midway Between Europe and the Far East – Decline of Bahrain's Role as a Service Centre for Saudi Arabia – Exempt Companies – Meagre Oil Resources Dwindling – Iran Relinquishes Longstanding Claims to Bahrain – Viability of Bahrain Depends on Saudi Goodwill – Small Number of Dissenters – The Economy Loses its Buoyancy – Major Activity is in the Gas Field – Search For New Outlets Becomes a Matter of Survival – Aluminium Price Recession – 'No More Heavy Industry, Let Us Digest What We Have'

An international newspaper headline in June 1984 described Bahrain as being 'on the front line of the Iran/Iraq War'. When Iraq hit the first Saudi tanker south of Kharg Island and Iran extended its retaliatory attacks to the rest of the Gulf, newsmen and camera crews converged on the nearest state that would let them in, and for several weeks on-the-spot war stories were date-lined Bahrain. But no reporters were able to climb to the rooftops to see the flames of burning tankers lighting up the night sky. The nearest most of them got to the action was when scarred ships were towed to the anchorage for damage inspection or transfer of cargo.

Ashore, Bahrainis went about their daily business discussing US interest rates, the price of shares on the local stock market or the football results – and hoping the war would go away. Its escalation brought concern, but no panic. For one thing, the island was considered to be a much safer place than Kuwait, whose financial and logistical support for Iraq laid it open to direct punitive attacks, and whose maritime supply lines were more vulnerable. Meanwhile the threat of Iranian-backed political upheaval within Bahrain itself seemed to have receded.

Offshore Banking and Commerce

Wars and rumours of wars have not frightened away any of the regional and international banks which go to make up Bahrain's US$60 billion offshore banking market, even though its development owes a good deal to the eclipse of Beirut. Over the last nine years nearly 80 offshore bank units (OBUs) and 60 representative offices have set up in Bahrain in order to be close to the flow of oil funds; most of the free world's major banks are now there but there is still interest among the Japanese for establishing locally-incorporated subsidiaries.

© KONINKLIJKE BRILL NV, LEIDEN, 2023 | DOI:10.1163/9789004686335_009

As a financial centre, Bahrain has the advantages of a time-zone midway between Europe and the Far East, good telecommunications and air links, a liberal regulatory framework and a tolerant attitude towards expatriates and their customs.

The recycling of surplus petrodollars has not worked as directly as the earlier OBUs expected, since there has been no large-scale switching of governmental deposits to Bahrain and much of the business revolves within the Arab world. The growth of the market has been based on private sector liquidity and inter-bank dealing, although strong locally-based institutions such as the Gulf International Bank (GIB) and the Arab Banking Corporation (ABC) certainly began to attract official deposits as they became well established.

The major concern for the offshore banking community, apart from the Gulf War and the pervasive international debt crisis, has become the decline of Bahrain's role as a service centre for Saudi Arabia. Project lending into the Kingdom has been the mainstay of many OBUs, but with the drop in oil revenues and cuts in government spending such loan opportunities have diminished, and are being further restricted by the policy of the Saudi Arabian Monetary Authority (SAMA) which militates in favour of Saudi banks. The withholding tax on interest paid by Saudi borrowers to foreign lenders has now begun to be enforced, albeit patchily, and banks leading Saudi riyal syndications have to seek the permission of SAMA before inviting foreign lenders in. Meanwhile in February 1984 SAMA began to curb the flow of riyals into the Bahrain market by calling for special 90-day deposits (equivalent to treasury bills) from local commercial banks.

If the Saudi market is closing up, there could still be attractive opportunities for reconstruction and trade in Iran and Iraq once the war is over, although some analysts fear the release of vast quantities of oil on to an already glutted market. Certainly the ending of hostilities would diminish the regional risk factor which has led to intermittent funding problems for a number of banks. The volume of business in the offshore banking market has fluctuated constantly since assets and liabilities reached a peak of US$61.1 billion in August. By the end of the year they stood at US$59 billion and fell to a low of US$55.5 billion in July 1983. The recovery to US$62.7 billion in December 1983 was thought to reflect substantial window-dressing, and sure enough January 1984 saw a plunge to US$57.97 billion – not much above the level of a year earlier.

Business was up again in February and March 1984 (US$59.95 billion and US$63.46 billion), down in April (US$61.6 billion), up in May (US$63.2 billion). A slight fall-off to around US$62.5 billion was expected in June 1984. Clearly the growth rates of the past are unlikely to be repeated, but the market has the maturity to withstand a few shocks, and often the fluctuations mark the activities of just one or two major players. Individually, there is no guide to the performance of branches of foreign banks, but the locally-based institutions have generally consolidated their positions. The Arab Banking Corporation, the Gulf International Bank, Arlabank International, Kuwait Asia Bank and Riyadh-based The Arab Investment Company (TAIC) all showed profit growth in the first half of 1984.

Two years after the launch of the OBU concept at the end of 1975, the Ministry of Commerce introduced regulations to encourage the incorporation of offshore or 'exempt' commercial companies (ECs). The 'exemption' is from provisions of the Commercial Companies Law which require majority Bahraini ownership, or in the case of foreign branches, local sponsorship. Such companies are not permitted to trade in the Bahrain market. By mid-1984 more than 150 ECs had been registered, including 13 public shareholding companies, all of them Gulf-owned. Within the overall total are 15 insurance companies, 24 OBUs and investment banks, a number of investment and management consultants, and companies in the business of oilfield and industrial services, oil trading, contracting, catering, transport and the distribution of goods.

The only 'brass plate' operations are to be found among the Kuwaiti-controlled investment and quasi-investment companies, which suffered badly from their involvement with the Souk al-Manakh (the unofficial Kuwaiti stock market which collapsed in 1982, leaving a US$90 billion legacy of post-dated cheques). The shares of these and other locally-quoted Gulf companies lost more than half their May 1983 value over the following 12 months, and the general loss of confidence spread to Bahraini bank and company shares.

Offshore banking and the (short lived) Concorde flights from London probably did more to put Bahrain on the world map than its historical role as a pearling centre, or the discovery in 1932 of the first oil in the lower Gulf. Well-heeled businessmen can no longer fly supersonic, but Bahrain's international airport is an important staging post for long-haul carriers such as Qantas and British Airways, and is also the home base of the region's national airline, Gulf Air. Its seaport (Mina Salman) is among the most modern in the Gulf, thanks to a recently completed US$36 million expansion of the container terminal and the introduction of computerised control.

As an oil producer, Bahrain is on its way out. Its resources have always been meagre and, short of a major new find, crude production, currently running at under 42,000 barrels per day (bpd), will have dwindled to nothing by the end of the century. Oil is exported only in the form of products, and when running at full capacity the 250,000bpd Bahrain Petroleum Company (BAPCO) refinery (once, but no longer, the biggest in the Middle East) takes 80 per cent of its feedstock by submarine pipeline from Saudi Arabia.

Industrial diversification based on more abundant reserves of natural gas started in 1971 with the commissioning of the Aluminium Bahrain (ALBA) smelter, which led to downstream expansion into aluminium powder (1972), extrusions (1977), cables (1978) and flat products (end-1985). An OAPEC-owned ship repair yard with a drydock designed for VLCCs of up to 500,000dwt was opened in 1977. Further joint venture projects which will be operational in 1985 are an iron pelletising plant and an ammonia and methanol complex.

Pearls ceased to have any economic significance in the early 1930s, when the Japanese cultured pearl industry knocked the bottom out of the market. Fortunately for Bahrain, many of those whose livelihood had depended on the pearling fleet found more regular and better-paid work with BAPCO, then a subsidiary of Caltex. Natural pearls can still be bought at a price, but no boats have worked the pearl banks from Bahrain for more than 10 years.

Repercussions of the Islamic Revolution

Under the Shah, Iran relinquished its longstanding claims to Bahrain before the island became fully independent from Britain in 1971. The renewed threat from the Khomeini regime was ideological rather than territorial. When it was realised for the first time since the Middle Ages, that the Shi'a had their own nation in Iran, a wave of religious excitement swept through the under-privileged Shi'a populations of the Gulf. In Bahrain, the ruling Sunni sect is outnumbered by a combination of indigenous Arab Shi'a (the Bahama) and Iranian immigrants. The Bahama were dispossessed by the conquering al-Khalifa two centuries ago, and their sense of historical injustice is as keenly felt as any present day discrimination. Among these people the appeal of fundamentalist Islam was stronger than elsewhere; the Shi'a matems (meeting houses) swayed to the music of Tehran, and demonstrations which spilled out on to the streets became as much political as religious.

It was a short step from mourning the death of seventh-century martyrs to protesting against the execution in 1980 of a Shi'a Imam, Mohammed Baqr al-Sadr, at the hands of the Iraqi Ba'ath, and to shouting slogans against the al-Khalifa regime in Bahrain. These manifestations found no sympathy among the older Shi'a, nor among the moderates who had joined the establishment and reached positions of affluence and limited authority. They were as shocked as their Sunni compatriots when a group of young fundamentalists was arrested in December 1981, accused of plotting a violent *coup d'état*. A formidable collection of weapons was photographed and shown to the public, and there seems little doubt that personal targets had been identified. The 77 detainees were mostly Bahraini students and working-class youths in their teens and early twenties, with a sprinkling of Saudis, one Omani and one Kuwaiti. All of them were Shi'a, unconnected with the more secular Aden-backed Popular Front for the Liberation of the Arabian Gulf (PFLOAG) or other radical splinter-groups formed by political exiles.

If the psychological wounds are now healing, it is because Iran was made the scapegoat of the affair and no blood was shed on either side. While the conduct of the interrogation and trial could be criticised, retribution was remarkably moderate, with sentences ranging from life imprisonment for three ringleaders to a minimum of five years. Nothing could have been better calculated to provide a contrast with the apparent lack of concern for human life in Iran, and to suggest that what has been happening there is a distortion of Islam. Meanwhile the authorities in Bahrain have tightened their security grip and the discovery early in 1984 of a cache of arms buried near a Shi'a village led to the closure of the already suspect Islamic Enlightenment Society. However, the arms were not thought to have been of recent importation and only two arrests were reported in local newspapers. While it is hard for a foreigner to know what is happening below the surface, local discontent seems at least temporarily to have gone off the boil.

Immigration has always been closely monitored and the bombings in Kuwait at the end of 1983 served to intensify the scrutiny of potentially turbulent Arab nationals from outside the Gulf. Because of this longstanding policy Bahrain has never developed the degree of dependence on the skills of Palestinians, Libyans, Syrians and Iraqis seen in other labour-hungry Gulf states, although Egyptians seem to be regarded as 'safe'.

Political Development

Bahrain has neither a Kuwaiti-style elected parliament nor an advisory council of leading citizens like Qatar and the United Arab Emirates (UAE). The important policy decisions are made in the ruling family council rather than in the cabinet (Council of Ministers), whose function is managerial.

No ministerial initiative gets far without the support of Sheikh Khalifa bin Salman al-Khalifa, the Prime Minister and brother of the Emir. The key cabinet portfolios of foreign affairs, interior and defence are held by the ruling family, together with justice and Islamic affairs, housing and labour. The death of the al-Khalifa education minister more than two years ago led to a redistribution of responsibilities but no new appointment – presumably for want of a sufficiently senior and able member of the family to replace him.

At the time of writing, Minister of Development and Industry Yusuf Ahmed al-Shirawi was looking after cabinet affairs in addition to his own portfolio, and the seven al-Khalifa were outnumbered by nine commoners, of whom five were Shi'a.

The experiment in democracy which followed independence and the drafting of a new constitution was short-lived, and there appears to be no strong popular pressure to revive it – either because the liberals are unwilling to accept a watered-down version with no real power, or because the lid is firmly pressed down on anything that smacks of political opposition. In any case only some form of shura (consultation) which poses no threat to the traditional regime would pass muster with the Saudis – on whose goodwill the viability of Bahrain depends.

The National Assembly, elected in 1973 and dissolved two years later with the arrest of the hard-core radicals, is now described by members of the educated, commercial middle class as 'unrepresentative'; if so, it was because they themselves were too reticent and too busy with their private affairs to shoulder their public responsibilities. Intransigent right-wing (mainly religious) and left-wing factions in the assembly combined to bring about a confrontation with an authoritarian government which was equally unprepared to give ground, while a weak centre party acquired the reputation of 'government yes-men'. No legislation was passed, tempers became frayed and government moved to end a situation which it believed could only lead to civil disorder.

From the 1920s onwards, the response to a succession of reform movements has been much the same, although young hotheads who have once been political prisoners or exiles have been known to reappear in later years as respected members of society.

The Emir's majlis is still a place where citizens may present petitions, but they come as vassals rather than as exponents of a point of view, and the 'pressure group' is a foreign concept to Bahrain. Nevertheless there exist a small number of dissenters, even within the appointed cabinet, who have come to terms with the political system sufficiently to want to improve it from within rather than to destroy it from outside.

Labour Representation

One democratic initiative which rather surprisingly survived both the abortive coup and Saudi distrust was the formation of joint consultative committees between management and labour in eight major companies, and the election in 1983 of the first officially recognised General Committee for Bahraini Workers. The joint committees are empowered to discuss wages and conditions of work, although conditions are mainly governed by a labour law which extends protection to both Bahraini and expatriate employees and which is actively enforced. The labour representatives have so far been cautiously feeling their way and no one uses the term 'trade union'. The degree of autonomy permitted to the General Committee is not great. Every step it takes must be approved by the ministry of labour, and political affiliations are specifically barred. It may be dissolved if it 'makes any resolution or acts in any way contrary to the internal or external security of the state or which may disturb national unity or the interests of the state'.

Foreign Policy

Bahrain is neither big enough nor rich enough to have an independent voice in foreign affairs. It generally follows the Saudi line, or the consensus of the Gulf Co-operation Council (GCC). Politically and economically, Bahrain sees its future in the GCC, although it is also a member of the United Nations, the Arab League, the Islamic Conference Organisation and other regional groupings such as the Organisation of Arab Petroleum Exporting Countries (OAPEC).

The Saudi-Bahrain Causeway

Economic dependence on Saudi Arabia will be further increased by the completion in December 1985 of Ballast Nedam's US$564 million contract to build a 25km bridge and causeway link between the two states. The feeder roads and the twin border posts halfway across are additional to the main contract, and almost the entire cost is being borne by Saudi Arabia.

Bahraini landowners are convinced the island will become a weekend retreat for Saudi families, and are building villas and leisure developments to meet the anticipated demand. One project is a 7-km long 'resort area' on the south-west coast. Hoteliers also see the causeway as the solution to their under-occupancy problems, and few people believe Bahrain will 'go dry', although the availability of alcohol may be more limited. Bahrain's Chamber of Commerce recently concluded from a study among its members that savings in freight costs would be passed on to the consumer. But although prices have always been lower in the Saudi market, it is by no means clear that Bahraini bargain-hunters will be able to do their shopping across the causeway without paying duty, since the GCC 'common market' arrangement covers only goods produced within the community, not imported cars and videos.

As long as Saudi ports continue their ban on trans-shipment trade, Bahrain's well-organised container port could pick up some extra business on the strength of fast onward delivery by road; but this presupposes clarification of the transit and bonding regulations to eliminate the risk of containers being held up and unstuffed midway, at the Saudi border post.

The Economy

Bahrain is weathering the effects of the oil glut better than many of its Gulf neighbours, partly because of the progress towards economic diversification and partly because Saudi Arabia has maintained the level of production at the offshore Abu Safa oilfield, which it owns jointly with Bahrain, in order to protect its small partner's half share of the revenues. These revenues are negligible in Saudi terms, but they account for over 56 per cent of Bahrain's oil income and 38 per cent of the total 1984 budget. While the cash receipts on Abu Safa could be affected by a further drop in official crude prices, Bahrain has nothing to fear from price discounts or a lowering of OPEC production ceilings, provided always that it retains Saudi goodwill.

But, inevitably, the economy has lost its buoyancy; 1983 saw the first deficit on the trade account in four years and the balance of payments position was expected to deteriorate in 1984, leading to a further drain on the country's meagre reserves. These were estimated at US$1.6 billion in 1982 and US$1.5 billion the following year.

As in all the Gulf states, the level of domestic economic activity depends on government spending, which is being held down to avoid a budget deficit. There have been no delays in payments to contractors or cancellation of projects, but the four-year (1982–85) economic social and development plan has been extended over a further two years. The plan calls for investment of some US$4 billion, mainly in infrastructure, housing and education. The US$1 billion new town, Madinat Hamad, continues to be given a high priority.

Efforts to expand the agricultural sector are hampered by the shortage of good quality water, and to some extent by the land tenure system, which gives little incentive to working farmers. But the island is now almost self-sufficient in eggs and, for a few of the cooler months, in fresh vegetables, while local broiler chickens and fresh milk, as well as locally-milled flour, are available in cold stores. There are also moves to revive the fishing industry and experimental fish-farming is just getting under way.

The slower pace of investment in projects has led to fuller utilisation of the budget allocations; in 1982 only 60 per cent of the funds earmarked for public projects were actually spent, but the uptake reached 81 per cent in 1983 and was expected to rise to 90 per cent in 1984. An improvement in administrative efficiency may have helped, although contractors still complain of bureaucratic delays.

Aid and loans, including a BD30 million (US$80 million) issue of government Development Bonds at the end of 1983, are making a significant contribution to the economy – more significant than is apparent from the budget estimates, which do not take into account either the US$1.0 billion GCC defence fund, which benefits Bahrain and Oman, or bilateral assistance from Saudi Arabia (the causeway, water desalination, religious endowments and youth and sport activities), Kuwait (school building) and Abu Dhabi (desalination).

The improved performance of the aluminium industry, which provides Bahrain's only major export other than refined oil products, is unlikely to be matched by the banking and financial sector, and few analysts expect a general upturn before 1986. Much of the optimism appears to be based on hopes of a business boost from the causeway, and from the new joint-venture industries as they come into production, but the prospects for the international oil market are giving rise to acute anxiety.

Oil and Gas Production

The state acquired 100 per cent ownership of oil production resources in 1979 and the state-owned Bahrain National Oil Company (BANOCO) took over full responsibility for management of the onshore producing field in January 1982. Although the value (at official prices) of Bahrain's domestic crude production is not much more than half the revenue it obtains from the offshore Abu Safa oilfield, the regular annual decline of 5–6 per cent was slowed in 1983 because of an intensive well 'workover' programme, and the off-take of just over 15 million barrels from the 252 active wells was very close to that of 1982. The introduction of enhanced recovery methods has been under study during 1984.

The major activity is in the gas field, where a development drilling programme for the deep Khuff zone (2,735 to 3,350 million) will be completed by 1986. The drilling contractor is the Kuwaiti-owned Santa Fe International. This programme will boost gas production by 80 per cent to 670 million standard cubic feet a day (mmscfd), to keep pace with the demands of oilfield reservoir engineers, power stations and desalination plants as well as meeting the feedstock and energy requirements of new industries. There will then be a moratorium until 1989, while BANOCO assesses the performance of the 21 wells.

Exploration

More than US$20 million has been spent over the past three years in a renewed search for untapped hydrocarbon resources on and off shore. At the end of 1983 a 2,672 square km offshore block formerly operated by a US consortium was reassigned to the Kuwait Foreign Petroleum Exploration Company (KUFPEC) under a production-sharing agreement which gives the lessor 80 per cent of any oil found.

Meanwhile a decision was expected late in 1984 on whether to go ahead with exploratory drilling either in the remaining offshore area, on the basis of new seismic data collected by Western Geophysical in 1982, or below the known Bahrain field, where France's Compagnie Générale de Géophysique conducted a deep survey in 1983. A further aerial survey to help in interpreting the onshore and offshore seismic data was carried out in mid-1984. Even a small discovery

1985

would spin out the oil age a little longer, although the record of 11 dry holes over the past 30 years does not encourage high hopes.

Oil Refining

The Bahrain Petroleum Company (BAPCO) was restructured in 1981 as a 40–60 joint-venture between Caltex Petroleum Corporation and the Government of Bahrain, to operate the 250,000bpd refinery and the marine terminal. As it turned out, this was the last of the good years for refiners worldwide, as crude throughput reached a record high of 259,000bpd, compared with 197,000bpd in 1982 and 175,000bpd in 1983.

As the oil glut began to drive product prices down, margins on the refining operation slid into the red, the more rapidly in Bahrain because of the shareholders' dependence on crude purchased at official Saudi prices. Although the government has its 'cushion' of domestic crude, this makes up only a quarter of its throughput entitlement, and neither shareholder has risked Saudi displeasure by buying discounted crude on the world spot market.

To offset its losses, Caltex processed fixed quantities of Bombay High crude on behalf of the Indian government in 1983 and 1984, but a similar fee-earning deal discussed between the Bahrain and Saudi governments had not been put into effect by mid-year. In the first half of 1984 crude runs were at near capacity but began to fall off with the summer slackening of demand. Because product prices remained depressed the volume savings in costs per barrel were still not enough to bring in a profit. Cost-cutting measures include a 25 per cent reduction in manpower over the four years to 1986, with the loss of 1,000 jobs. This is being achieved either by non-renewal of contracts, or in the case of the 800 or so Bahrainis affected, by natural wastage, retirement and redeployment. In 1983, a separate services division was set up to manage employee facilities such as housing, transport, medical and educational services, and to save money by selling any surplus capacity outside BAPCO.

The government's share of refinery output is marketed by BANOCO, which made 40 per cent of its international sales in 1983 to the Gulf region, compared with 28.5 per cent to the Far East. As new Gulf refineries come on stream regional demand for BAPCO's products will fall off, and the search for new outlets will become a matter of survival. Domestic consumption is small (about 6 per cent of the government offtake), although it is rising by 10 per cent a year.

Gas Liquefaction

The Bahrain National Gas Company (BANAGAS) project has proved to be one of Bahrain's best investments, since the associated gas which it uses as raw material had no previous economic value and was vented at the wellheads. Built in

1979 at a cost of US$90 million, the gas-gathering system and liquefaction plant achieved full pay-back in 18 months and averaged a US$60 million profit in each of the next three years. A purchasing agreement with Caltex takes care of any marketing worries.

Because of the minority foreign shareholding (Caltex and APICORP each 12.5 per cent) the government nets back 45 per cent of the profit in income tax, as well as 75 per cent of whatever remains for distribution as dividends. In 1983 BANAGAS sold 80,000 tonnes of propane, 84,000 tonnes of butane and 1.2 million barrels of naphtha. The residue gas was piped to Aluminium Bahrain (ALBA) at the rate of 108mmscfd, so conserving Khuff gas for other consumers.

Manufacturing Industry

The establishment of ALBA was the first and most difficult step towards industrial diversification. At times its protagonists in the government must have been close to despair as the smelter failed to work to its technical specifications, local labour found it hard to adapt to the potroom environment, foreign backers pulled out and metal had either to be stockpiled or sold at below production cost. Even today, when ALBA has become the hub of a thriving local industry, there are conflicting views on whether captive aluminium users should be getting a better deal on prices.

The smelter went into limited production in 1971 but did not operate economically until 1976. During that time the government bought out four of the foreign shareholders (leaving only Kaiser Aluminium with 17 per cent and Breton Investments with 5.1 per cent), and set up a trading company (BALCO) to market its 77.9 per cent share of metal production. In 1979 the Saudi government (through SABIC) became a 20 per cent shareholder in ALBA, after having helped to finance the mountain of unsold metal.

But the policy of stockpiling against a more favourable market had by then paid off, enabling the surviving original shareholders to recoup their losses. Another price recession, described as the worst in the history of the world aluminium industry, took effect in 1981–82, but the prospects for 1984 are the best for three years.

Since it was completed in 1973 at a cost of US$240 million, the 120,000 tonnes-a-year smelter has undergone major modifications. By 1981 a US$120 million investment in new production facilities had boosted capacity to 170,000 tonnes a year, while billet-casting capacity was doubled (to 60,000 tonnes) in 1983.

The four older potrooms of the six now in production are set to be modernised over the next six years in a US$93 million retrofit programme, if trials are successful; and in mid-1984 it had been decided to invest another US$2 million in improving equipment to cast rolling slab for the 40,000 tonnes-a-year Gulf Aluminium Rolling Mill Company (GARMCO), now under construction in Bahrain for completion in November 1985. This US$125 million pan-Gulf project is owned by the governments of Bahrain, Kuwait, Saudi Arabia, Qatar, Oman and Iraq, and was the first of the regional enterprises to be successfully promoted by the Doha-based Gulf Organisation for Industrial Consulting (GOIC).

Bahrain Atomisers International was the first satellite plant to ALBA, set up as long as 12 years ago. But the Bahrain government is only just beginning to take a real interest in it, after reaching a pooling agreement on sales of aluminium powder with its 49 per cent partner, Breton Investments.

BALEXCO, the government-owned extrusion plant, has had a greater impact on the economy, since it supplies more than two dozen local workshops and assembly plants as well as customers throughout the region. The market leader among the local private enterprises is al-Zamil Aluminium Factory, part of a family-owned group with one foot in Bahrain and the other in Saudi Arabia.

Al-Zamil is now investing US$1.5 million in a new factory and paint line, to apply polyester powder paint finishes to aluminium and steel for BALEXCO and other users.

BALEXCO itself has achieved moderate success despite having to contend with uncontrolled foreign dumping in its regional market. In 1983 the plant operated at 80 per cent of its 4,500 tonnes-a-year anodising capacity, with some additional sales of mill-finished extruded section, and 1984 started strongly with full order books. The new paint finishes should further boost sales in 1985. BALEXCO's premium products are architectural systems and curtain walling manufactured under licence from Technal (France) and Alusuisse.

Midal Cables, the only one of the primary aluminium users to be privately-owned, improved its position in the Saudi market when it admitted Saudi Cables Company of Jeddah as a 29 per cent shareholder in 1982, four years after the start of production. This left Olex Cables of Australia, the main supplier of technology, with only 20 per cent, the balance being held by one of Bahrain's leading mercantile families through Zayani Investments. By the end of 1984 MIDAL will have become the first cable-maker in the Gulf to produce its own aluminium alloy, for which it bought a second rod mill earlier in the year. With the addition of new holding and tilting furnaces, rod capacity will be increased to 40,000 tonnes a year and cable-making capacity to 24,000 tonnes. In 1983 MIDAL exported 17,000 tonnes of finished product but there is no local demand as yet.

Manpower planners believe that more than a third of the 40,000 young Bahrainis who will be seeking jobs over the next 10 years can be absorbed by manufacturing industry, even though existing plants are trimming manpower for maximum cost-efficiency and the new projects under construction are not labour-intensive. Given moderate economic expansion and political stability, employment growth in the banking and finance sector is projected at 100 per cent (4,600 new jobs), but in three other sectors it will at best remain static. These are agriculture and fishing (reflecting the scarcity of natural resources), extractive industries (because of dwindling oil reserves) and construction (because a building boom cannot be sustained indefinitely). It is particularly important, therefore, to encourage the development of small-scale industries financed by the private sector, and the incentives being offered include the provision of feasibility studies, concessionary land leases in industrial areas and a 'free zone' for exporters.

Although the government had to work hard to drum up investment support for an US$8 million furniture factory, built with the aid of a soft loan from Abu Dhabi, a US$1 million sulphuric acid project is going ahead quite independently and a number of export-substitution industries, such as paper products, plastics and the assembly of air-conditioning units, are well-established; the output of multi-coloured plastic bags is so prolific as to decorate every tree and fence when a strong wind blows in from the desert. The older Mina Salman industrial area is full and at least three more are being developed, partly with an eye to the downstream possibilities of the aluminium rolling mill.

Ship Repairing

The Arab Shipbuilding and Repair Yard (ASRY) is fortunate in that its backers are seven OAPEC member states who are prepared to see the project through hard times, as part of a strategic plan to get involved in all aspects of the oil industry including the servicing of its own tanker fleets. Although the yard (with its Portuguese partners, Lisnave Shipyards SA) has secured a satisfactory share of the work available worldwide, with an estimated 12 per cent of the VLCC repair market and drydock occupancy of over 80 per cent, prices have reflected the depression in the shipping industry and owners have increasingly deferred repairs. However, in six years of operation ASRY has yet to break even, although average revenues of US$30 million a year in 1981–82 led to forecasts that profitability was just around the corner.

Then came a reversal, with throughput sharply down in 1983 and total revenues (before operating costs) amounting to no more than US$17.5 million; at the beginning of 1984 a US$3.00–4.00 million order for repairs to a jack-up rig struck a more encouraging note.

Whatever the figures say, ASRY has effectively broadened the industrial base, introduced new skills and enhanced Bahrain's reputation as a maritime service centre, already established by two smaller yards.

New Industrial Projects

For many years after the establishment of ALBA and later the ASRY ship repair yard, the theme of development planning was 'no more heavy industry, let us digest what we have'. But the willingness of other Arab states to invest in Bahrain and to stop its economy running out of steam brought about a change of direction, and the first of the new generation projects is the US$300 million Arab Iron and Steel Company (AISCO) pelletising plant, due to go into production in the third quarter of 1984.

The justification for siting the plant in Bahrain is the availability of cheap energy; otherwise there is no significant Bahraini input, no raw material and no local demand for the 4 million tonnes a year of product; it is hoped that the direct reduction steel plants in Qatar and Saudi Arabia will be major customers. Iron ore fines will be shipped in and pellets will be shipped out – although AISCO does have a plan for its own steel plant on the drawing board. The shareholders in the company are the Arab Mining Company (owned by several Arab governments) and Gulf corporate and private investors.

Within sight of AISCO across the main shipping channel is the Gulf Petrochemical Industries Company (GPIC) ammonia and methanol complex, due for commissioning in 1985. GPIC was originally conceived as a joint-venture between Bahrain and Kuwait, but Saudi Arabia came in as an equal partner at a later stage.

Total project costs are put at US$450 million, and output at 1,000 tonnes a day of each product. Kuwait has agreed to handle exports of ammonia for the first five years of production, and the Saudi Basic Industries Company (SABIC) will market the methanol. An even bigger investment – possibly as high as US$2 billion – was envisaged for an 80,000bpd hydrocracking unit. The Heavy Oil Conversion Company (HOCC) has already been formed as a joint-venture between Bahrain (40 per cent) and its GPIC partners, and a detailed techno-economic study was completed by Lummus in March 1983. But the whole project is being re-assessed in the light of a changing oil market, and if it goes ahead at all it will probably be less than half the size.

The Domestic Banking and Financial Markets

The major developments on the local (onshore) banking scene have been the award of the first new licence since the opening of the Islamic Bank in 1979, and the restructuring of the domestic branch of Grindlays Bank with a 60 per cent Bahraini shareholding. The newcomer is the BD40 million (US$106 million) Bahraini Saudi Bank, owned equally by private investors in each state. It plans to be operational by the end of 1984 and to bring Saudi business into Bahrain through its shareholders, who include a son of King Fahd; at a later stage it will also function as an OBU. The limited domestic market is dominated by three local and two old-established British banks, who between them hold over 80 per cent of the aggregate assets and make nearly 90 per cent of the profits, while another 13 branches of foreign banks scramble for what is left. Although 1983 operating profits rose by over 20 per cent to the equivalent of US$77.2 million, almost all of the increase came from the local banks. At the same time, the local banks were deprived of extraordinary earnings on offshore company share issues, which amounted to over US$80 million in 1982; since the stock market crisis erupted in Kuwait no more publicly-quoted ECs have been floated in Bahrain.

Domestic bankers are not enthusiastic over 1984, but they hope that by 1985–86 economic recovery in the industrialised world will have had a favourable impact on the oil market, with a corresponding relaxation of budgetary constraints in the producing countries and an expansion of business. This expansion would be accelerated by an early end to the Gulf War and, to a lesser extent, by a return to normality in Kuwait once the debt problems have finally worked themselves out.

Major new commercial legislation is expected to be enacted in Bahrain either at the end of 1984 or in early 1985, to set up a formal stock exchange and to regulate the insurance sector. Initially the stock exchange is likely to list only the 20-odd Bahraini joint stock companies and the 13 Bahraini-registered Gulf companies (ECs), but other Gulf companies may be included later. There is talk of going international with a fully computerised system, and both Bahrain and the UAE see themselves as a suitable location for an integrated Gulf exchange serving all the GCC states. As it is, a start will be made with a traditional trading floor and a long period of learning and adjustment will be necessary before anything more ambitious is attempted.

The creation in 1980 of the US$3 billion Arab Insurance Group (ARIG) lent considerable importance to Bahrain as an insurance centre, despite the small local market, and the new insurance law aims to ensure that only adequately-capitalised companies can operate there as well as to protect national interests. Scanrisk, a Scandinavian joint-venture specialising in loss prevention and risk management, and BAII Insurance Services, primarily a re-insurance broker, are prominent among the offshore companies, while leading firms of loss adjusters and the major ship classification societies are represented.

Meanwhile ARIG itself has become established in the international re-insurance market and has demonstrated that early fears of political bias were unfounded; nor has it become a 'dustbin' for the poor quality business rejected by others. ARIG is owned by Kuwait, Libya and the UAE and currently 5 per cent (US$150 million) of its capital is paid up.

1986

Shi'a Disaffection – Aluminium Bahrain – Gulf Co-operation Council –
Expatriates – State-run and Quasi State-run Operations – Migration From
Iran – Weekly Majlis – Four-Year Development Plan – Banking Recession –
'Low Risk, Low Reward' Strategy

Bahrain has emerged from the hiatus of 1983–84 (when for a time the regional
order looked threatened by the Iranian revolution and the fall in oil prices)
with strengthened confidence in its ability to deal with most contingencies, but
deeply concerned at the gathering regional recession. The increasing economic
problems of its most important neighbour, Saudi Arabia, on which traditionally it relies for economic and military assistance, is particularly worrying. Furthermore, although the direct threat from Iran may have receded, the deportation from London in June 1985 of six Bahrainis on suspicion of plotting to
overthrow the government indicates that the spectre of Shi'a Muslims disaffection is still alive.

Utilising Resources

Placed strategically off the coast of Saudi Arabia, the island of Bahrain has long
excited the territorial ambitions of its larger neighbours. Iran only relinquished
an ancient claim to the island in 1970, while Saudi Arabia cast covetous eyes
over the prosperous trading post on its doorstep before its own oil boom radi-
cally altered its relationship with the island and the rest of the region. Now
Saudi Arabia is happy to underwrite Bahrain's independence as a buffer against
incursions from the north and supports the state financially through the Gulf
Co-operation Council (GCC) – whose diplomatic positions Bahrain also holds in
its relations with the rest of the world – and with bilateral aid.

Bahrain has had to capitalise on its skills and industries over the past five decades to survive. As the seat of the Residency under British rule, Bahrain came
to be an important military and communications centre. It was also the first
state in the lower Gulf to find oil (in 1932) and to produce it commercially. Although oil has been making a diminishing contribution to revenues since the
early 1970s, the island's economy is inextricably tied in with the industry
through the 250,000 barrels a day (bpd) Sitra Refinery. Built 50 years ago, the
refinery has been the training ground for a technical and management cadre
unique to the Gulf. This cadre, together with the British-trained civil service

© KONINKLIJKE BRILL NV, LEIDEN, 2023 | DOI:10.1163/9789004686335_010

and the trading skills of the merchant community, have dictated the economic development of Bahrain. They determined the decision in the late 1960s and early 1970s to develop heavy industry and offshore banking.

Bahrain was a decade ahead of the rest of the Gulf in utilising its cheap gas as a feedstock for energy-intensive heavy industry. The policy has only been partially successful because of adverse market conditions. There were, for instance, plans for an integrated steel works but these had to be scaled down to an iron ore pelletisation plant. The plant, which is run by the Arab Iron and Steel Company (AISCO), went through trials at the beginning of 1985 and has had a sticky entry into commercial operations. The Arab Shipbuilding and Repair Yard (ASRY), the OAPEC-financed dry dock, has been kept going on subventions since completion in 1977 and looks no nearer breaking even now as it did then.

On the other hand, the Aluminium Bahrain (ALBA) smelter, commissioned in 1971, has been a great success and has been steadily expanding production. It has succeeded in generating a number of downstream industries including aluminium powder (1972), extrusions (1977), cable (1978) and flat products (late 1985). Similar hopes are fostered for the Gulf Petrochemical Industries Company (GPIC), a company jointly owned by the Saudi Basic Industries Corporation, the Kuwait Petroleum Company and the state-owned Bahrain National Oil Company, that it will spawn a downstream petrochemicals industry. It is due to come on-stream commercially in late 1985, producing methanol and ammonia.

Bahrain and the Gulf Co-operation Council (GCC)

In the mid-1970s Bahrain could rely on generous Arab grants and loans to finance its heavy industry development, but now funds are much less readily available.

The creation of the GCC in 1981 and its rapid development from a purely military alliance into the beginnings of a regional common market and an agency for integrating economic activity, was consequently a godsend for Bahrain both in formalising the economic needs of the region and in identifying the specialised contribution Bahrain could make to them. Minister of Development and Industry, Yusuf al-Shirawi, has been a forceful advocate of the GCC and adept at promoting Bahrain's interests within it.

Bahrain has much to gain from the GCC as a communications centre and as the headquarters for Gulf Air. The integration of power and gas supplies will help industry while the elimination of tariffs within the GCC has opened up lucrative markets for those companies geared to take advantage of them. Co-ordinated planning will also help eliminate the kind of costly duplication that has ASRY and ALBA competing with the dry dock and aluminium smelter in Dubai. Bahrain may be the beneficiary of only one GCC-funded industrial project, however (the aluminium rolling mill that comes on-stream in late 1985), although it still hopes to be the site of a GCC-funded regional tyre plant.

Battle to Create Jobs

The biggest single problem facing the Bahrain government is to create jobs for the estimated 60,000 young Bahrainis who will be seeking employment during the next ten years. The 250,000 indigenous population is growing at a phenomenal 10,000 a year. Industry is expected to provide 15,000 new jobs and, given reasonable market conditions, the services sector should provide another 5,000. There is also scope for creating jobs by squeezing out a large part of the 130,000 expatriates currently working in Bahrain.

However, the authorities face a number of conflicting policy aims. The government aims to trim the civil service by 5 per cent a year for the next three years forcing more Bahrainis into the private sector. But Bahrainis generally dislike working for their compatriots. In the private sector they enjoy few of the rights and none of the status of working for the government or for state-run organisations. The private sector is consequently almost entirely manned by expatriates. Conditions have become so bad that Asians have requested shipment home and a Bahrain court recently legalised a strike by foreigners in a company that had failed to pay them.

State-run and quasi state-run operations (like the shipyard, the aluminium smelter and the refinery) have shed up to 50 per cent of their manpower over the past few years in an effort to contain costs and improve competitiveness. Most of the cuts have been in the foreign workforce but further savings will increasingly have to be made at the expense of the unskilled and semi-skilled Bahraini workforce which mostly comes from the Shi'a villages in the centre of the island.

The government, ever sensitive to the political implications of making Shi'as redundant, has told the refinery not to sack Bahrainis. The Sitra Refinery, however, has already instituted a programme to cut the present workforce of 3,700 by another 15 per cent, over the next three years.

The Shi'a and Political Reform

The indigenous Shi'a Muslims have never forgotten that the ruling al-Khalifa family dispossessed them when they took over Bahrain in 1783 and promoted their co-religionists from the mainstream of Sunni Muslims to key positions in government and trade. The Shi'a population, leavened by migrations from Iran, is better represented now in Bahraini society. But the Shah's resurrection of

Iran's ancient claim to Bahrain touched the Sunni establishment on a raw nerve, and the advent of the Iranian revolution disseminating its own brand of Shi'a fundamentalism poses an equally potent threat.

In the post-war era, Bahrain has been the most advanced state in the region, both socially and economically; and as such has had an active political life. A militant labour movement was one of the legacies inherited by the state on independence in 1971, and this movement led the clamour for constitutional reforms. However, the elected National Assembly convened in December 1973 was too contentious. It was prorogued in August 1975, leading radicals were arrested and plans for fully fledged trades unions were shelved – to the evident relief of the House of al-Saud which had viewed with alarm the spread of democracy through the peninsula. There has been no talk of reconvening the National Assembly, only the suggestion of a Majlis al-Shura (consultative assembly) on the lines already mooted by the Saudi government for the past two decades.

The al-Khalifas rule in the traditional paternalistic way. They take the important policy decisions in family council where the views of the Prime Minister, the Emir's brother, Sheikh Khalifa bin Salman al-Khalifa, are particularly influential. The 18-man cabinet, in which the al-Khalifas hold eight portfolios including the key posts of foreign affairs, interior and defence, as well as Premier, is little more than an executive instrument. The system works because Bahrain is small and the Emir sufficiently accessible through his weekly majlis (audience) for grass roots' opinion to reach the decision-makers.

Growing Problems with Security

Nevertheless, the basic problem of the Shi'as, who account for more than 60 per cent of the population (a percentage that is growing, due to their higher birth rate), remains. All 77 detained in December 1981 for their involvement in a well-planned plot to overthrow the government were Shi'a, mostly Bahraini students or young workers, apparently owing allegiance to Tehran. In early 1984 an arms cache was found in a Shi'a village, and in June 1985 six Bahrainis were deported from London on suspicion of plotting to overthrow the government.

Since the December 1983 bombings in Kuwait the security forces have taken a higher profile, keeping a much closer eye on their expatriate Arab communities and tightening up considerably on immigration. New measures have been introduced to combat the alarming spread of drug abuse, and press censorship has been tightened: three foreign journalists have been expelled from Bahrain since the beginning of 1984. Despite the more pronounced police presence and the growth of fundamentalism, Bahrain has not entirely lost its liberal image.

The Causeway

The causeway, which runs from the north-west tip of the island 25 kilometres across the Gulf of Bahrain to the Saudi mainland just south of al-Khobar, will have a profound effect on virtually all aspects of the island's life. Apart from the deep psychological adjustments Bahrainis will have to make to the fact that their country will no longer be an island, there are the disturbing and unsettling effects it will have on business.

The optimists point to the advantages for Bahrain's trade and industry of being opened up to the large Saudi market. The causeway is particularly welcomed by the construction industry which hopes it will give a fillip to sagging real estate prices, and to the tourist and other service industries which have their eyes on the lucrative east coast catchment area. At present east coast visitors have to fly the short hop across from Dhahran to Bahrain – the most expensive flight, kilometre for kilometre, in the world. Although in principle GCC nationals will be able to drive across the causeway (a facility by no means assured Westerners), there are doubts as to how the causeway will work in practice. The problem of drunkenness will be closely monitored. Cynics believe the authorities would not be above causing delays to those crossing the causeway, which, with summer temperatures reaching the lower 40s°C, would temper the ardour of the most determined tipplers.

The trading community has deep anxieties about the causeway – anxieties that soothing official predictions and the periodic meetings of the Dammam and Bahrain Chambers of Commerce do nothing to assuage. Traders hope that the island's principal port, Mina Salman, will become a staging post for the mainland; already there are plans to expand its container facilities. But Mina Salman's fortunes depend on the tariff policies adopted by the GCC in general and Saudi Arabia in particular, for goods imported into a GCC country and shipped on; at present each country has its own tariff regulations.

Bahrain traditionally has imposed high tariffs, having been forced to use import duties as a form of state revenue, and there are fears that the flow of goods across the causeway, especially consumer durables and cars on which mainland mark-ups are much lower because of the higher volume of trade, will be from Saudi Arabia into Bahrain. Indeed, some small traders and industrialists fear they will not be able to survive the tidal wave of dumped goods which has built up in Saudi Arabia during the recession.

The prospects for private investment are mixed. Bahrain cannot offer the cheap loans, free land and utilities provided for Saudi entrepreneurs. On the other hand, established companies like the Bahrain Aluminium Extrusion Company (BALEXCO), which already has established outlets in the Kingdom, welcome the opportunities for expansion which the causeway will bring.

Consumers will also benefit from the increased competition and there is not a little schadenfreude at the discomfiture of the trading community which is about to see its cosy cartels smashed. Inevitably a fair number of small and inefficient businesses will go to the wall, a prospect that the Minister of Development and Industry, Yusuf al-Shirawi, views philosophically.

Balancing the Budget

The government has faced a difficult task in steering the economy to greater self-sufficiency at a time when the tide of recession has been moving so strongly against it. In 1984 the trade deficit doubled to BD140 million (US$368 million). But this was probably overstated as it included purchases for the causeway and the Gulf University for which Bahrain is not paying. In 1986, too, import substitution industries will begin making an impact on the trade balance.

Equally important has been the success the government has had in stabilising revenues and expenditures. In 1983 the budget went into deficit for the first time for many years, principally because of a 17 per cent fall in oil revenues. The refinery also had a particularly bad year but ALBA swung back into profit and in 1984 increased profit by another US$10 million to US$40 million. Although oil prices continue depressed, production from the onshore Dukhan oilfield has been maintained at 42,000bpd, and in 1984 the refinery increased throughput to its barrel per day break even point. Saudi Arabia is believed to have maintained production of the offshore Abu Safah oilfield at 120,000bpd, thereby securing this important source of income.

By also raising commercial fees and duties on luxury imports and holding current expenditure at BD535 million, the government was able to return a small BD10 million surplus on its accounts for 1984.

The government's success in balancing the books has raised the possibility of speeding up the four year Development Plan which had been extended by two years to 1987 because of the island's financial difficulties. Actual capital spending has, in fact, remained fairly constant from 1983 to 1985, disbursement rates improving as capital budgets have come down.

The aim now is to reduce current expenditure by 5 per cent a year for the next three years. For the 1985 financial year (which is the same as the calendar year) that means reducing current expenditures from BD364 million to BD346 million and transferring the savings to the capital budget which is boosted to BD229 million. Over a quarter of capital spending is earmarked for housing which is in chronically short supply in Bahrain. The completion of the US$1 billion new town at Madinat Hamad should ease the housing crisis and there are other major projects in hand.

One of the more intriguing projects awaiting development is for a massive reclamation scheme in the waters between Bahrain and Qatar for housing development. Bahrain is also spending a great deal on power generation. Capacity has doubled to 950MW in the past three years but studies indicate that the island will need a further 800MW over the next 10 years to meet private and industrial demand. Desalination, to combat Bahrain's growing water crisis, will absorb a lot of power. The water shortage is limiting the development of agriculture. Bahrain is already self-sufficient in eggs and poultry.

Industrial Development

Increasingly the government will expect members of the private sector, both Bahraini and other GCC nationals, to take up industrial investment where the government has left off. Already this is happening. The iron ore pelletisation plant recently completed by AISCO was the first major project in Bahrain to be predominantly privately financed. Recently the government has relented a little from its spartan attitude to private investment by building, with the help of a US$32 million Kuwaiti government loan, an industrial estate at North Sitra. Original investors in the Mina Salman industrial zone were given an expanse of shallow water and were left to reclaim the land and install utilities at their own expense. Most of the available sites at North Sitra have been snapped up.

Lack of capital has not proved an obstacle to viable projects in Bahrain but it is generally felt that many entrepreneurs are holding back until the causeway is opened, to gauge its effect.

Local plants are producing paint, syringes, fibre-glass, plastic containers and shoes, and there is now an air conditioner assembly plant in Bahrain. The GCC-financed Gulf Aluminium Rolling Mill Company (GARMCO) is expected to generate a whole new aluminium fabrication industry and create up to 1,000 new jobs, making aluminium the largest industrial employer in the country. GPIC's petrochemical plant should similarly create intermediate industries.

The demands of a more integrated industrial base are also throwing up new industries. Local interests are building a caustic soda plant following the success of the newly established sulphuric acid plant in providing a raw material which was otherwise being imported at great expense.

Maximising the Use of Hydrocarbons

Bahrain's hopes of finding more oil are slim. The Kuwait Foreign Petroleum Exploration Company (KUFPEC), a subsidiary of the Kuwait Petroleum Company, is currently prospecting a 200 square km concession in Bahrain's northern waters with no great hope of making a significant find. The island is therefore dependent on its ageing onshore oilfield at Dukhan, now down to almost half its peak production, and revenue from the offshore Abu Safah oilfield which Saudi ARAMCO operates. It sees no benefit from this crude, as the Kingdom pays Bahrain's half share of production in cash and so it is wholly reliant on Dukhan for domestic feedstock for the refinery. The balance is made up by Saudi Arabian crude bought at OPEC prices – a principal reason for the refinery's difficulties, as its products have to be sold on depressed spot markets. In 1985, this heavy dependence on Saudi Arabian oil has been slightly reduced by small purchases of Indian crude. The long-term viability of the refinery depends on assured, reasonably priced supplies. The commissioning of another 825,000bpd of new refining capacity in the Kingdom is particularly worrying to Bahrain.

The associated gas from the Dukhan oilfield also services a highly profitable gas-gathering plant; the cleaned gas then goes direct to the aluminium smelter. The use of oil and gas as a feedstock for local industry has made it doubly imperative to squeeze the last barrel out of the declining field. Careful husbandry and new recovery techniques have staunched the decline at 42,000bpd and it now seems, with a US$60 million five-year recovery programme recently sanctioned, that the life of the oilfield will be extended considerably beyond the early 1990s deadline given six years ago.

Bahrain is relying on gas from the Khuff zone to meet its future energy needs. The present 400 million standard cubic feet a day (scf/day) draw-down production should be good for another 50 years, but already production capacity is being raised to 600 million scf/day. Some 40 per cent of production is used to maintain pressure in the Dukhan oilfield and is significantly reducing the return of condensates in the associated gas. The remainder is used for power generation, desalination, and industrial and other needs.

Banking

Ten years after international and regional banks first flocked into Bahrain as a service centre for the oil-rich Arab world, the market has lost its momentum. There is still a good basic operation with a solid clientele, and the presence of the Arab Banking Corporation (ABC) and the Gulf International Bank (GIB) is a stabilising factor. But new banks with big capitals are struggling to find profitable outlets for their funds, while others with years of experience in the region face the need to change their strategy or go elsewhere.

The Region

In Saudi Arabia, which has traditionally accounted for 70 per cent of the banks' regional market, oil production hit a 20-year low and government spending patterns changed accordingly. As money flowed less freely to the private sector, management weaknesses emerged in companies that had once been rated as prime borrowers. At the same time lenders into the Kingdom began to realise that Islamic (Shari'a) law affords them little protection against defaulters. Although there were cries of anguish two years ago, when the Saudi Arabian Monetary Agency (SAMA) legislated in favour of home-based banks by restricting the participation of Bahrain OBUs in Saudi riyal syndications, the restriction was a blessing in disguise, some bankers now say. It certainly helped those who were not fully aware of the legal and banking environment in Saudi Arabia to minimise their mistakes.

In Kuwait, the problems of reduced oil revenues have been compounded by the lingering aftermath of the 1982 stock market crash, which has effectively strangled private enterprise, while a series of banking crises has troubled the UAE.

Bahrain banks have never participated to a significant extent in the direct recycling of petrodollars, which continued to be channelled towards the mainstream money centres. But they did find rewarding business opportunities in the financing of contractors for government projects (advance payment bonds, working capital and performance guarantees) and in the deployment of private wealth.

As a result of the regional economic downturn, the quality of their lending portfolios has begun to deteriorate. The individual and corporate borrowings of Kuwaiti merchants and Saudi contractors have become as liable to rescheduling as Third World sovereign debt, and the required provisions against loan losses (plus the build-up of non-performing loans) has had an increasing impact on profitability.

To the economic constraints must be added the political risk factors of Bahrain's proximity to the Gulf war and to revolutionary Iran, plus the tendency of foreign bankers to put into the same package airliner hijackings in Beirut and wars and acts of terrorism throughout the Middle East. Political risk has affected both inter-bank funding, on which the OBUs depend for an average 70 per cent of their resources, and the development of an active capital market.

Comings and Goings

Against this gloomy background, most foreign banks in the market are cutting back on overheads and waiting out the recession, although the departure of Security Pacific in August led others to question the ultimate viability of their Bahrain operation. The Californian bank had been one of the first, back in 1983, to close its OBU dealing room, ostensibly as part of a global reorganisation.

Midland Bank, Barclays Bank and Bank of Oman have subsequently closed their Bahrain dealing rooms, while a few more banks have quietly curtailed their foreign exchange activities. This must jeopardise the profitability of at least two of the six money-brokers, whose aggregate earnings dropped sharply in 1983 and failed to recover in 1984 despite the application of volume discounts to encourage dealers to put more of their transactions through brokers.

There can be few banks in the market which are not economising on manpower. Although targeted cuts were well-publicised at Bank of America, Chase Manhattan Bank and Bankers Trust Company, others simply did not replace employees who left or re-deployed expatriate staff in other offices.

The loss of Security Pacific followed the less surprising departure of Continental Illinois National Bank and Trust Company, in the wake of its US bail-out, and of the Banco do Comércio e Indústria de São Paulo (COMIND) which had sought unsuccessfully to use Bahrain as a source of funds for its Brazilian head office. Spain's Banco de Vizcaya and the Canadian Imperial Bank of Commerce have not maintained an active OBU operation for some time, although both have held on to their licences. Citibank Bahrain, on the other hand, has given up on the development of a regional bond market and has relinquished the investment banking licence (IBL) which it obtained five years ago for its Capital Markets Group. Instead, Citibank has opened a regional representative office for its investment bank, in addition to the well-entrenched OBU which carries a lot of weight in the market.

The OBU of Overseas Trust Bank is still functioning, after a three-day weekend closure when the Hong Kong government launched its lifeboat, while Bank Negara Indonesia has bucked the trend by upgrading its representative office into the sole new OBU of the past year.

Many representative offices are no more than 'toe in the water' operations, and Italy's Banco di Roma was among those which found the water too chilly. Marine Midland Bank, Texas Commerce Bank and First National Bank of Houston were not expected to renew their licences in 1986. By contrast, three Japanese financial institutions (Nomura Securities, Yamaichi Securities and Sumitomo Bank) used their representative offices as stepping stones to locally-incorporated investment banking subsidiaries, which appear to be both busy and profitable. Their success over the last two years has attracted the attention of New York securities broker Smith Barney Harris Upham (which has Middle East shareholders) and the London merchant bank Robert Fleming & Co. These two have recently set up their listening posts on the island, despite the much earlier withdrawals of Lazard Fréres and Kleinwort Benson.

Bankers' Society Proposals

The Bankers' Society of Bahrain has suggested to the Bahrain Monetary Agency (BMA) that it should not issue further licences at this time (although there is hardly a queue of applicants) and that smaller locally-incorporated banks should be encouraged to merge. The most likely candidates are Arab Asian Bank, Kuwait Asia Bank, Bahrain Middle East Bank (BMB), United Gulf Bank (UGB), Bahrain International Bank (BIB) and the Bahraini Kuwaiti Investment Group (BKIG), but no group of shareholders has shown any enthusiasm for a merger except on their own terms, and the BMA is not disposed towards coercion.

The Society has further suggested that the BMA should renew its efforts to convince the Saudis that Bahrain is a financial centre of proven reputation, to which the SAMA might safely commit more of its reserves. That reputation, in the Society's view, would be further enhanced by the creation of a lender of resort for locally-incorporated banks which are the prime responsibility of the BMA. In addition to five dinar-based onshore banks (FCBs) these now number 25 dollar-based OBUs and IBLs whose combined capital reserves far exceed Bahrain's modest foreign reserves.

A statutory reserve requirement provides a readily available cushion for the FCBs, and the BMA is currently discussing with them some form of deposit insurance. There is no such safety net for the offshore banks, although the BMA has been steadily increasing its prudential control, and the law provides for it to take over the administration of a banking firm whose liquidity and solvency are in jeopardy.

Early in 1985, when this appeared to be the case with Arab Asian Bank, the BMA acted as arbitrator between the shareholders and ensured an orderly take-over of the bank and its overseas subsidiaries by a minority shareholder, Middle East Financial Group (MEFG). MEFG is owned by the Bin Mahfouz and al-Kaaki families of Saudi Arabia, which also control the National Commercial Bank. By mid-1985 there had been no official explanation of the disaster at Arab Asian, which had an equity base of over US$70 million but had delayed publication of its 1984 results sheet. Disaster it must have been, since the take-over bid amounted to a nominal US$1. The most worrying aspect of the affair was the secrecy surrounding the arrest and lengthy detention without charge of the bank's Bahraini founder and chief executive Hussain Najadi, who was also denied his legal right to consult privately with his lawyers.

Investment Banking

There was further unsettling news from United Gulf Bank (UGB), which had signalled its intention to switch from commercial to investment banking following a US$5.4 million consolidated loss in 1984. (The loss was mainly due to write-downs at United Gulf Investments (UGI), a wholly-owned subsidiary, plus a 50 per cent drop in operating income at the bank, as a result of poor treasury performance and the build-up of non-performing loans.)

In June 1985, a statement from UGB's directors revealed that the immediate impact of the change in strategy would be the run-down of the loan portfolio, the release of half its staff of nearly 80 – including the general manager recruited only nine months earlier – and withdrawal from the financial futures and foreign exchange options markets. The still unfinished multi-storey headquarters building is likely to be put up for offers, following the successful sale and lease-back of BMB's building earlier in 1985. UGB anticipates cost savings of US$5 million a year, and the gradual deployment of at least US$150 million of its US$250 million capital into investments. Meanwhile it posted a US$2 million profit for the half-year, despite another US$90,000 loss from its subsidiary UGI.

Also placing more emphasis on investment are Kuwait Asia Bank, which opened a full Australian branch in the latter half of 1985, and announced a 60 per cent improvement in interim profits (to US$2.5 million after provisions); BMB which was expected to add a US subsidiary to its acquisition of 41 per cent of a small Swiss Bank; and the BIB, which has moved into longer-term fixed interest securities and is on course to better last year's profit of US$1 million.

Others were geared to investment from the outset. In addition to a number of real estate deals, INVESTCORP acted as financial intermediary in the leveraged buy-out of Tiffany & Co, the New York jeweller, and participated in the acquisition and placement of shares in Whittaker Corporation's luxury power boat divisions. Meanwhile, the more modestly capitalised Trans-Arabian Investment Bank (TAIB) has added a trade finance house in New York (Creditcorp International) to its finance and real estate subsidiaries in Geneva and Florida.

Market Leaders

But all of these banks are small fry compared with the pan-Arab majors, ABC and GIB, which between them represent nearly one third of the total assets of the Offshore Banking Unit market. By the summer of 1985, these assets were still fluctuating around US$60 billion, a level reached at the end of 1982. Future trends will depend on the fortunes of the two market leaders, and of the ability of branches of the big US, European and Japanese banks to adapt to the new business environment in the Gulf. GIB continues with its 'low risk, low reward' strategy and expects to maintain its assets at close to US$7 billion.

For the first half of 1985 the Bank reported a profit of US$33.25 million, up 5 per cent compared with the US$31.7 million profit of the previous June; it does not specify provisions. ABC has achieved more vigorous growth, mainly through aggressive foreign acquisitions such as Spain's Banco Atlántico and Hong Kong's Sun Hung Kai Bank. The 1985 interim profit (consolidated) was up 10 per cent to US$76 million; assets rose 19 per cent over the 12 month period, to US$11.82 billion.

Investment Companies

In an effort to control the growing number of Bahrain registered offshore investment companies, particularly those which are publicly quoted, the BMA decided in 1982 to issue newcomers with investment banking licences (IBLs). However, the decision was taken just before the collapse of the Kuwaiti stock markets and the only licensed investment company, Bahraini Kuwaiti Investment Group (BKIG), has never functioned as a financial institution: all its capital was invested in Gulf listed and unlisted securities. After the necessary provisions and write-offs BKIG posted losses of US$30.7 million in 1983 and US$63.8 million in 1984, while net worth fell from US$192 million to US$98 million.

The unlicensed offshore investment companies present an equally sorry picture. Among them the Bahrain International Investment Centre had 1984 losses of US$27 million, Pearl Investment US$45 million, Gulf Investment US$69 million and Gulf Consolidated Services and Industries US$32 million.

Domestic Banking

The assets of the domestic banking market amount to no more than US$5 billion, shared between 20 banks. The only foreign banks with substantial retail business are Standard & Chartered, which as the Eastern Bank pioneered banking services in both Bahrain and the Gulf in 1920, and the British Bank of the Middle East (BBME), which even in 1944 was still 13 years ahead of the first indigenous bank.

Today, however, the six local banks led by the National Bank of Bahrain and the Bank of Bahrain and Kuwait (BBK) hold 67 per cent of the aggregate assets, and transact 70 per cent of the contra business (largely because they have a monopoly on government bonding and guarantee services). These six banks also made 88 per cent of the 1984 profits, with the Bahrain Islamic Bank showing up particularly well on a return on assets basis. Banque Paribas and the National Bank of Abu Dhabi made losses while the profits of most other foreign banks were minimal.

1987

Conflict With Qatar – Hostages Taken – Peninsula Shield – Oil Production Rises (Slightly) – Spending Slashed – Retrenchment – Housing Provision – Overdue Debts – Shifting Patterns of Employment – Averting Unemployment – Emerging Labour Force

Bahrain has managed to survive for another year relatively unscathed by the raging conflict between Iraq and Iran; but the country, traditionally noted for its stability, has been beset by problems of its own. In April 1986, Bahrain was drawn into an open territorial conflict with Qatar, a fellow member of the Gulf Co-operation Council (GCC), and as a result security on the island has been tightened. In addition, plummeting oil revenues have affected infrastructure projects and public spending. In spite of the introduction of cost-cutting measures, an effort has been made to diversify and expand the economy, and Finance Minister Ibrahim Abdul-Karim, has said that in the near future Bahrain will be seeking short term soft loans and exploring more innovative methods of raising finance. However, Bahrain is caught in a bind. The heavy industry and services sectors, which are the mainstay of Bahrain's diversification programme, are not yet strong enough to provide a sufficient hedge against further recession in the oil market, and it is largely government spending which determines the liveliness of the economy.

Bridging the Gulf

Bahrain technically ceased to be an island in 1986 with the opening on 26 November of the 25km King Fahd Causeway (Sheikh Isa bin Salman al-Khalifa having agreed to the name) costing US$1 billion, which was financed by Saudi Arabia. The new bridge emphasises the country's links with its Arab allies in the six-member GCC, and in particular its links with Saudi Arabia which has been supporting Bahrain politically and financially for decades.

While the Causeway is expected to bring long term economic benefits to Bahrain, it has been built primarily to enhance the country's security vis-a-vis the perceived military threat from Iran in the north. As an adjunct, a US$2 billion military base, financed solely by Bahrain, is being constructed on the island just south of the point where the Causeway comes in.

The Causeway was due to be opened officially in December 1986, once all the approach roads had been completed. The bridge was already used, albeit on a limited scale, much earlier in the year: first by football supporters attending the Gulf Soccer Tournament (held in Bahrain in April), and later by pilgrims on route to the holy city of Mecca in Saudi Arabia. To what extent the causeway will facilitate the freer movement of people and goods between the countries remains unclear, but it is understood that stringent security will operate at border posts. The expatriate dream of living in Bahrain and commuting to jobs in the Eastern Province of Saudi Arabia appears unlikely to materialise in the short term. Initially at least, the unhindered passage of people might benefit only citizens of the GCC.

Bahrain has continued to develop closer ties with the Gulf alliance, but in an unfortunate turn of events, Qatar (a fellow member of the GCC) occupied Fasht Dibal, a tiny reef lying midway between the two countries, in April 1986. The reef is the site of a coastguard station which Bahrain was in the process of building at the time of the occupation.

Twenty-nine expatriate contract workers were taken as hostages (two Britons and a Dutchman were included among the mainly Filipino and Thai workers) and were only released after weeks of negotiations initiated by Saudi Arabia. The conflict, over border delineation, appeared to be under control by late May, with GCC states overseeing a gradual return to normal relations between the two countries.

In an ironic twist of fate, at the time of the occupation the GCC was celebrating five years of industrial and political co-operation as a bloc bounded by common language, history and religion.

Some bold initiatives have been taken by the GCC in the area of defence. Since its creation, in May 1981, GCC states have been developing a unified air defence strategy, and in 1984 the Peninsula Shield rapid development force was set up. Some 5,000 men are now based in Saudi Arabia's Eastern Province, acting as the mainstay of the Shield. Also within the GCC framework, the six states have recently decided to establish a sophisticated air alert network to protect navigation in Gulf waters. This move is in direct response to the intensification of attacks on shipping in local waters by both Iraq and Iran. As an additional measure, a BD10 million food stockpile – enough to keep Bahrain supplied for six months – was set up under GCC auspices in 1985.

Prospects and Problems for an Oil Dependent Economy

While Bahrain was the first Gulf country to strike oil (in June 1932 at Jebel al-Dukhan) its reserves have proved to be much smaller than those of neighbouring Kuwait and Saudi Arabia. At present rates of recovery the country may run out of oil at the end of the century. This is a serious problem as the oil sector still accounts for two thirds of government revenues and around 80 per cent of the country's export earnings. But Bahrain also has reserves of natural gas which are so far under-exploited. Failing a new oil strike natural gas may well replace oil as the country's main source of energy in the next century.

Since 1975, Bahrain's oil output has been steadily declining at a rate of about five per cent a year. In 1985 however, the Bahrain National Oil Company (BANOCO) managed to stem the tide somewhat by reactivating some old wells and by upgrading maintenance services on existing wells. As a result of these measures daily production figures have risen slowly but steadily and now stand at 41,800 barrels per day (bpd).

In an effort to increase output, BANOCO has been drilling offshore exploratory wells under a 35-year production sharing agreement with the Kuwait Foreign Petroleum Exploration Company (KUFPEC). It is thought that positive results are just around the corner, and both KUFPEC and BANOCO have been using advanced survey techniques which were not previously available. The results of the year-long search are not yet known but the empirical evidence for the existence of additional pockets of oil is mixed. The ARAMCO operated Abu Safah oilfield, for instance, which lies 40 miles off Bahrain's north-west coast has a capacity of 100,000bpd, however, in the past 30 years over eleven dry holes have been sunk in Bahrain's offshore waters.

Bahrain's ageing 250,000bpd refinery ran by the Bahrain Petroleum Company (BAPCO) has also undergone rationalisation in 1986. Only two to three years ago output at the refinery was steadily dwindling, and the operation was said to be running at a loss. This was probably due in part to the costs of buying oil from Saudi Arabia (at Organisation of the Petroleum Exporting Countries (OPEC) fixed prices) and then having to sell on the refined products in a depressed market. However, BAPCO's aggressive marketing policies coupled with the firm's strong resolve to cut costs and increase efficiency is beginning to bear fruit, and Saudi crude is now being bought at netback prices (this involves discount deals in which the price of oil is related to the price of refined products). As a result, BAPCO's chairman, Mr Yusuf al-Shirawi, who is also Minister of Development and Industry, has said that the refinery has 'turned the corner'. In this improving climate, Bahrain is now considering a plan to upgrade the refinery in a three-stage scheme costing US$900 million. If it is approved, the plan envisages an upgrading of the plant to enable it to produce gas oil and jet fuel which are expected to be in greater demand in the 1990s than fuel oil and naphta.

BANOCO's development programme, on the other hand, has been designed to keep pace with the growing requirements of the country's power stations and desalination plants, as well as to meet the energy needs of the new heavy industries.

1987   113

Tailoring the Budget

It was with these assets at hand that in mid-1986 Bahrain faced the reality of a dramatic fall in the price of oil. Within a single year the price of oil had dropped from US$26 per barrel down to about US$14. Every US$1 fall has cost the island BD15 million, according to Finance Minister Karim, and he anticipated an additional loss of between US$90–US$120 million in revenues by the end of the year.

Taking the expected fall in the price of oil into account, the government came up with a new budget in January 1986. While the budget envisaged record spending it also introduced some strong cost-cutting measures. At the time, Finance Minister Karim noted that the next two years would be a crucial testing period for the effectiveness of the new budgetary policies.

Projecting a total of BD1,110 million in government spending in 1986/87, the budget set out to define key contingency financing measures, related to a range of US$26 to US$16 per barrel in the price of oil on world markets. As, in fact, the price dipped below US$16 per barrel the government announced that additional emergency measures would have to be taken to combat the shortfall in revenues.

Accordingly a restructured budget saw spending slashed by 15 per cent. The first area to suffer was transport as the government announced that it was to shelve its plans to build and improve secondary roads. Furthermore, plans to construct new government buildings, water and electricity plants, and the completion of the Mina Salman Port Development Scheme (planned to coincide with the opening of the Causeway) could also be delayed as a result of the cutbacks. Increases in selected service charges were introduced; notable amongst these are a BD2 airport departure tax, higher immigration and passport fees, and the introduction of water metering, car registration fees and labour permit charges.

In spite of these measures the government still expected to fall short of covering its revised planned expenditure of BD550 million by about BD80–90 million. Also, the government said that it might have to resort to seeking soft term loans in the near future. As a complementary measure, the cabinet approved an increase in the debt ceiling from US$80 million to US$265 million, and machinery has been set up for the issuing of treasury bills – if and when required. Grants from Saudi Arabia and Kuwait, received in the third quarter of 1986 totalled US$100 million, the government added.

On the positive side, the country is already spending less on imports. Total non-oil imports and exports fell by just under 10 per cent in 1985, with exports falling faster than imports (the peak came in 1983 with a record BD207 million worth of exports, but the figure is now down by 37 per cent). A helpful step was taken by BATELCO, the partly state run telecommunications company, which chipped in with a tremendous sacrifice by cutting its international direct dialling (IDD) call and telex charges by a full 15 per cent on 1 September 1986. This move followed another 15 per cent cut in charges on 1 January. (Last February, Bahrain was the first country in the world to complete technical acceptance tests on the newly available third TV channel of the Intelstat satellite positioned over the Indian Ocean.)

Among the projects which could suffer from the introduction of cost-cutting measures is a planned US$7 million Ministry of Foreign Affairs building. The future of the Fasht al-Adham new town project is also in doubt, although in general housing is one field which so far has engaged serious attention by the authorities and almost 25 per cent of capital expenditure in the country's latest development plan was assigned to the provision of housing. Bahrain's ambitious and highly desirable Zallaq Beach project, designed as a premier tourist attraction, is also slipping in priority. Among the private sector projects now in doubt is the construction of a 23 storey high tower bloc of apartments containing a restaurant, shops, swimming pools, recreation areas and car parks, which was to have been built by a Kuwaiti publisher, Mr Ahmed Jarallah.

On the other hand, a number of vital projects are still expected to get the go-ahead. These include the proposed US$50 million new terminal for the international airport, and a new BD4 million multi-storey car park building. Also the highly successful company Gulf Air, the regional air carrier of Bahrain, Qatar, Oman and Abu Dhabi is set to start building its own 4-storey US$10–15 million headquarters in Bahrain.

Stimulating the Economy: New Laws

New laws aimed at stimulating the economy came into effect on 1 September (1986). According to this package of measures, employers' and workers' contributions to the state pension funds and health services will be reduced to ease the burden on companies. GCC nationals will also be allowed to buy up to 25 per cent of the shares of Bahraini companies, as long as the company retains a 51 per cent majority Bahraini holding. The government also made a commitment to the development of the Bahraini stock market into an international centre.

The decision to set up an international stock exchange came after several postponements – at a time when the 1982 Kuwait Souk al-Manakh crash is still not too distant a memory. The rationale behind this renewed commitment is that while the value of Bahraini company shares was dragged down in the wake of the Kuwaiti debacle, their collapse had more to do with a loss of faith than the actual performance or net worth of the companies concerned. The stock market hopes to open its doors to other Gulf investors while it will also provide price quotes when other markets are closed.

Another law effective from August will allow for the refund of import duties on re-exported goods, effectively giving such goods the same status as transit goods. These changes are deemed as beneficial to the island's traders.

Other measures include allowing companies to buy shares in their own concerns, to protect their value. Meanwhile, banks have also been encouraged to reduce interest rates on Bahraini depositors' long term debt. In addition, approval has been given for the issuance of preference shares – where the holder receives a fixed dividend while taking no part in the running of the company.

In the wake of a succession of bad debts, falling oil revenues and a reduction in opportunities for new businesses, banks operating out of Bahrain are preparing for a period of retrenchment. Assets of the seventy or so offshore banking units (OBUs) have been shrinking steadily, falling by over 12 per cent since January 1984, and reaching a new low of US$54.27 billion in the first quarter of 1986. Some banks have been forced to move their operations out of the country, and in the depressed climate collecting interest on Saudi loans also remains a problem, despite strenuous efforts by regional governments to tighten up and enforce debt legislation. On the positive side, bankers noted that with so many banks either winding down or leaving, those bold enough to stay would be able to share out relatively larger slices of the cake when the upturn in the economy finally came.

The cost of living on the island, often cited in the past as a main obstacle to profitability, has been declining for the past 18 months or so. During 1985 alone, according to the Central Statistical Organisation, it had fallen by more than five per cent for expatriates and three per cent for Bahrainis. Lower housing costs were the main reason for this fall and rents dropped by 22 per cent during this period. No doubt these figures came as a welcome relief to the island's bankers who, in 1984, calculated the annual cost of running an average size OBU as being BD420,000 (according to a *Gulf Banking and Finance* survey).

Banks Get Imaginative

Throughout the island, banks have had to be innovative and forward looking in 1986. Many banks have taken a more aggressive and dynamic approach to their foreign exchange operations. Opportunities have been seized in mergers and acquisitions, and the expansion of advisory services, debt restructuring, trade finance and investment and commercial banking. The formerly 'laid-back' Gulf International Bank (GIB), owned by the seven littoral Gulf states, shed its 'sleeping giant' tag, raising its profile with the opening of a multi-product dealing room and by revamping its public relations image. GIB has also issued uncommitted Eurocommercial paper, a first by a Middle East bank, as well as providing forfaiting services to Saudi exporters in sectors such as petrochemicals.

Arab Banking Corporation (ABC), Bahrain's largest bank, is also being restructured. In the next two years it intends to place more emphasis on investment banking – though commercial banking will still predominate in its activities. Much of ABC's investment banking effort will be channelled through the bank's London merchant subsidiary, ABC International.

No major US or European bank has withdrawn from Bahrain so far, which is in itself a positive sign. There was also no stressful take-over of a bank on the lines of the 1985 buyout of Arab Asian Bank. In spite of these developments, not all banks have such an optimistic prognosis. Bahrain's largest domestic bank, the Bank of Bahrain and Kuwait (BBK) announced in May that it had problems with collecting 'overdue debts'. About 85 per cent of those problem loans originated in Kuwait, say sources in BBK, and the collateral pledged against the bank's loans had in many cases dropped by more than 85 per cent. BBK's mainly Kuwaiti shareholders saved the bank from closure by covering its BD54 million losses. In addition, BBK has now brought in a team of lawyers in a bid to adopt a tougher stance toward awkward debtors.

Other Arab banks based in Bahrain did better than expected; many saw their profits dented but not totally squeezed. Arlabank had a disappointing year but suffered no losses. In addition, two banks which had recorded large losses in the past – Bahrain International Bank (BIB) and United Gulf Bank (UGB) – said that their spruced up investment operations were now bearing fruit.

Banks in Bahrain are consequently experiencing a turbulent period. Some sceptical observers advocate a complete pullout, predicting that the boom years are over for good. More optimistic observers argue that sooner or later Gulf oil will experience a second boom, most likely by the mid-nineties. Furthermore, it is believed that in spite of some obvious corporate problems, Gulf states, and by implication, their royal families are nowhere near bankruptcy.

As if to echo the optimists, the same laws which are aimed at stimulating the economy will also affect the banking sector, directly and indirectly. While the new lower interest rates have threatened to undermine profits, the Bahrain Monetary Agency (BMA) has said it will pay interest on 50 per cent of all reserve funds placed with the agency (to be calculated on a monthly basis, but paid annually). Also, the recommended rates for Bahraini dinar deposits have been reduced for a third time in 1986 so as to offset the effects of cheaper borrowing.

Mergers and the Role of the BMA

Following a recommendation of the BMA, talks were held early in 1986 on the possible mergers of UGB, Kuwait Asia Bank, Bahrain Middle East Bank, BIB, and the Bahrain Kuwait Investment Group (BKIG). All five banks are, in the main, Kuwaiti owned. No definite agreement was reached, but further discussions as

1987 117

to the viability of a merger cannot be ruled out. In the meantime, BKIG announced in the late summer of 1986 its readiness to merge with the Bahrain International Investment Centre, pending the completion of formalities. Both banks, it may be remembered, lost millions in the 1982 Souk al-Manakh debacle in Kuwait. In another recent move the BMA took over the administration of al-Samahji Exchange Company's money changing activities, after the BMA claimed that the company had violated money exchange regulations.

Promoting Heavy Industry

The new Arab Iron and Steel Company (AISCO) pelletising plant, the Gulf Aluminium Rolling Mill Company (GARMCO) works, Gulf Petrochemical Industries Company's (GPIC) twin ammonia and methanol plant and the well established Aluminium Bahrain (ALBA) form the backbone of Bahrain's heavy industrial base.

ALBA has been largely profitable since its establishment in the early 1970s, and this year shareholders were asked to provide extra financing for a projected BD60 million modernisation scheme to increase the plant's production capacity by 25 per cent by 1991.

The aluminium industry in Bahrain saw a welcome downstream development this year with the start-up in February of the GARMCO plant at Sitra Island, the first in the Middle East. Bahrain has a 20 per cent stake in this pan-Gulf venture.

Bahrain's second oldest heavy industry venture was the Arab Shipbuilding and Repair Yard (ASRY). The yard saw high occupancy rates in 1986 but it still failed to turn a profit, some 10 years after its establishment.

Bahrain's newest industrial ventures have yet to be tested. The GPIC plant is jointly owned by Kuwait, Saudi Arabia and Bahrain. It started production in September 1985 but already it has been hit hard by the imposition of a 13 per cent European Economic Community (EEC) customs tariff on imports of methanol from Bahrain. GPIC has now drawn up a comprehensive plan of lowering costs and improving productivity to 'combat the price fall' and it is seeking a rescheduling of its debt repayments.

Future prospects have also been revised for the BD100 million AISCO iron ore pelletiser plant which recently received approval to reschedule its loan repayments. AISCO is a pan-Arab venture in which Bahrain has only a small and indirect stake but the Minister of Development and Industry, Mr Yousef Shirawi, would still like to see it operating on a sound footing, partly as it could provide many jobs for young Bahrainis, as ALBA did 15 years ago. Sources in AISCO say that it has now found markets for its products but that prices are still too low. One alternative available to the government is to set up a downstream steel venture which would consume part of AISCO's output. Such a bold move could emulate the successful expansion of aluminium and related industries in Bahrain.

Changing Employment Patterns

The economic downturn in the Gulf has already shifted the patterns of employment in Bahrain, as it did in other Gulf countries one or two years ago. An estimated 1.0 million expatriate workers were sent home from the Gulf in the period 1984–85, and the exodus is still continuing, though not in the massive proportions that some observers anticipated. Bahrain's own expatriate workforce has declined by about 4,000 workers since January. This was the first recorded drop in foreign manpower in the country. In a single sweep, 700 jobs were axed in March by Rezayat, Brown and Root, the marine oil services company.

Yet even as the outflow continues, and the ranks of Europeans in particular are being depleted, other nationalities are seeing their numbers boosted. This trend seems to be applying to the whole Gulf region, and it reflects a concern by cost-conscious companies to reduce labour costs. Filipinos and Asians in particular have been willing to work for less money. Workers staying on in Bahrain were not infrequently being asked to sign new contracts which reduced their fringe benefits and/or slashed their salaries. Free medical care, education for children and other perks formerly taken for granted, were often reviewed and in many cases scaled down. In the prevailing situation, the government tried its utmost to increase the number of jobs available to Bahrainis. It encouraged restrictions on foreign labour and introduced incentives for hiring local people. At the same time, the government announced a number of 'good-will measures' which guaranteed that foreign companies would have no problems extending the work permits of their expatriate employees.

As applications for new work permits have dropped in any case, the government's target of cutting by two thirds the number of new work permits issued to expatriate workers could probably be met without resorting to any seemingly over-restrictive measures. But a crackdown has been ordered on workers who swap jobs and leave their original sponsors. Jobless workers will now have to simply go home. The Labour Directorate has said that offending companies will be prosecuted and illegal workers will be deported. Wives of expatriate employees have also been shifted from the job scene. At the same time, the Labour Department has been pressing local banks, which had made job cutbacks, to help in finding new jobs for their redundant Bahraini employees.

A government special programme to train 10,000 Bahrainis for the local job market, first launched back in 1981, now boasts more than 1,000 graduates.

Hundreds are still in the programme, learning skills such as management, accounting, data processing, and secretarial work. A massive manpower plan to introduce 1,800 more Bahrainis into the island's hotel industry is about to be launched and the industry's workforce is expected to be 60 per cent Bahraini within the next 5–8 years. The tasks of averting unemployment are truly daunting as Bahrain is said to be heading for a population explosion. Urgent appeals have been made by Bahraini doctors in favour of proper family planning policies.

Unless positive action is taken the country's population could double by the year 2000, and reach 600,000. More than 40 per cent of the country's population is under the age of 15 and the average number of children per family is seven. Bahrain's baby boom is likely to affect adversely the island's plan to become self-sufficient in food production. The Bahrain Family Planning Association has warned however that heavy increases in population will result in valuable agricultural land being utilised for schools, health centres and other basic amenities.

Tourism: A New Option

With its excellent air links, balmy winter climate and well-established de luxe hotels, not to mention its highly commendable 'tolerant' ways of living, Bahrain could prove to be a popular tourist spot in the future. A lot of research still needs to be done however, to examine the viability of tourism as a substantial income earner. Two groups of potential visitors have been identified so far: the Far East-Europe travellers who might appreciate a short two-to-three night break, and Gulf tourists who traditionally preferred destinations outside the region. Already a campaign has been launched to attract more visitors, and travel agents from different parts of the world have toured the island and assessed its facilities. A major new conference for travel agents is being planned for 1987 by the private sector interested in new business opportunities.

Still in its infancy is a project to develop Bahrain's numerous archeological sites for tourism. In the past these sites, such as the famous burial mounds, were poorly presented to the public and photographs were either forbidden or at least discouraged. But all this is about to change, the government says, and in future information centres will be provided at important sites. Visitors will also be allowed to take photographs.

While many of Bahrain's future tourist sites are several thousand years old, a more modern focus of interest will no doubt be provided by the two storey tower restaurants (60 metres high) located on the Bahrain-Saudi causeway. Tourists will be able to visit the restaurants without having to cross passport and customs controls. Erected on each side of the causeway, the restaurants will give sightseers a panoramic view of the historical union between Bahrain and Saudi Arabia.

Bahrain's sustained drive to open up the country for tourism can also be seen in the framework of efforts to stimulate the economy. The Prime Minister, Sheikh Khalifa bin Salman al-Khalifa, revealed recently that both Gulf residents and other foreign visitors to Bahrain will be able to obtain 7-day visas on arrival at the airport. Previously, visitors could obtain only 72-hour visas. A tourist relations superintendent has been appointed and new maps and pamphlets will be printed.

Gulf Air, the national air carrier of Oman, Abu Dhabi, Qatar and Bahrain, faces the uphill task of switching from a reliance on domestic regional markets (formerly 80 per cent; in future about 40 per cent) to a greater emphasis on international markets. This is due to the massive departures of expatriates from the Gulf. Meanwhile, the international airport in Muharraq is to be expanded.

In Conclusion...

Bahrain's future is closely linked to the fortunes of its Gulf neighbours. Since the six states of the Gulf Co-operation Council are collectively expected to lose about US$60 billion in 1986 (according to the Kuwait-based Shal Office for Economic Studies) as a result of the drop in oil prices and the lower value of the dollar, their development plans will be severely affected. In addition to the obvious economic consequences, the political climate is still uncertain as the six-year old Iran-Iraq war still poses a danger of spreading.

In the coming 18 months, the government must weigh the country's assets prudently, if Bahrain is to retain its past role of a financial and service centre for the region. To pull through, the country must draw on all its past experience and reputation as a sound provider of services, labour and excellent communications – at a time when the industrial, oil and banking sectors are going through difficulties. There are signs, however, that the Bahraini government, fully aware of the crisis, has been searching for remedies.

In the short term, Bahrain's most challenging task will be to find training opportunities and work for its burgeoning ranks of school leavers seeking their first jobs. One thing already appears clear: even if the government succeeds in tiding the country over the current recession, the emerging labour force of young Bahrainis will have to substantially lower its sights. Gone are the days when Gulf nationals with proper academic credentials could view proper academic credentials as an automatic passport to high-flying job prospects.

1988

Transformation Under Way – Coup Attempt – Inter-Gulf Trade – Dwindling Oil Reserves – Increased Commercial Sophistication – Over Manned Bureaucracy – Major Projects Held Back – Five-Year Development Plan

When the oil boom was at its height in the late 1970s and early 1980s, surplus finance flooded out of Saudi Arabia in search of investment opportunities. International banks rushed to secure a presence in this rare haven of prosperity, and Bahrain with its British educational and administrative structure was the ideal location. Bahrain rapidly became the offshore service centre for the richer surrounding states. Peel off the veneer of international business in search of oil profits, and Bahrain is revealed to be a relatively prosperous developing country. If that prosperity is to continue, Bahrain has to become the hub of a regional economy, not a transient haven for expatriate business. This vital transformation is under way.

Effect of War

It is all too readily assumed that the fortunes of a small Gulf state like Bahrain must be badly affected by the Iran/Iraq War, now moving into its eighth year. Western attention was at last drawn to the war in 1987 because of US military involvement – a result of Kuwait's decision to seek international protection for its shipping.

Yet, for the people of the Gulf, and especially for the government of Bahrain, the current international phase of the war is arguably less dangerous than in the first months of 1980, when the newly declared Islamic Republic of Iran sought to press home the claim of the former Shah to Persian sovereignty over Bahrain and several smaller islands. Iranian efforts to incite Shi'ite communities in all Arab Gulf states led to an abortive coup attempt in Bahrain which provided a chance for the security forces to flex their muscles and tighten control without ever endangering the state. The Bahraini Shi'ite community never showed much enthusiasm for the revolution across the waters and has maintained a low profile in recent years.

If Bahrain is suffering from the war, it is more because of reductions in marine traffic and hence in servicing requirements. Bahrain had staked considerable investment on the tanker-servicing industries, from ship repair to bunkering. The threat to large vessels and the increased insurance premiums may have reduced sea-borne trade, but it is difficult to assess the extent to which any downturn in shipping business is directly war-related, or a result of the decline in the oil market.

War in the region and fluctuations in oil market conditions may be sufficient to divert foreign business from the Gulf, but such an attitude is short-sighted. It reveals a lack of understanding of the measures introduced in Bahrain and other Gulf states to create an effective regional economy that does not depend entirely on external factors over which the states of the region have no control.

The Causeway: a Bridge to New Markets

The opening of the King Fahd Causeway linking Manama, the main island of the Bahrain archipelago, with the Eastern Province of Saudi Arabia in November 1986 gave rise to the usual speculation: Bahrain's leisure industry would suffer from Saudi prohibitionism, said some; the US$1.0 billion example of advanced engineering was primarily for military purposes, said others. Few listened to Bahraini ministers, who patiently explained to all who would listen that Bahrain suffered from high prices and limited markets because every item had to be imported at high cost by air, or with long delays by sea. Not all Bahrainis by any means could afford to fly to Dhahran to visit close relatives of Saudi nationality living in the Eastern Province. Not everyone could face the rigours of the trip by dhow. The causeway is the realisation of a dream begun when the Emir of Bahrain, Sheikh Isa bin Salman bin Hamad al-Khalifa, visited King Faisal of Saudi Arabia in 1966. The studies were initiated at a time when there was no war in the Gulf, when the price of oil was around US$1 a barrel, and when the Gulf was known only to oilmen, diplomats and a small band of expatriates.

Officially opened in late 1986, the Causeway had been traversed by 58,000 tourists by the end of February 1987. That month marked the end of initial trial procedures and the causeway was opened to traffic on a 24-hour basis. Although juggernauts are banned, trucks are allowed on the causeway at off-peak periods. At present only Gulf Co-operation Council (GCC) traffic is allowed to make the crossing, and plans are in hand to introduce an identity card to speed up processing of vehicles and passengers at passport control posts at either end of the causeway. Although it is too early to assess the impact of the new access to Bahrain for Saudi tourists, there is no doubt that the hotel industry has derived immediate benefit to compensate for a fall in business from international visitors. No extra restrictions have been imposed on Bahraini night-clubs and leisure facilities as a result of the opening of the causeway, but Bahrain's law does not permit driving after consumption of any alcohol, for which severe penalties are imposed.

The development of the tourist trade in both directions is one of the targets of the Causeway authorities in both countries. Gulf citizens do not enjoy the kind of seaside activities favoured by expatriates in the region, but the quiet coasts and oases of east-coast Saudi Arabia, as well as the opportunity to drive to other Gulf destinations, will offer welcome alternatives to Cairo and Europe.

Other aspects of that policy are the boosting of inter-Gulf trade, and regional stabilisation of living costs and economic opportunities. Hardly had the Causeway opened when the first effects of regional parity were felt in Bahrain as the price of meat was lowered in March 1987 by 20 per cent to average US$2.65 per kg – the same price as in Saudi markets. The cost of fresh foodstuffs and many other items will fall as Bahrain begins to benefit from integration with the Saudi Eastern Province markets. Saudi Arabia, with a population of 12 million, can buy at better prices than Bahrain with its resident population of 411,660, of whom 66 per cent are Bahraini nationals. The cost of transporting produce and goods by road from wholesale distribution centres in the industrialising Eastern Province into the small Bahraini market must result in major price reductions for Bahraini consumers.

New Opportunities for Industry

If Bahraini consumers can expect to benefit from the causeway, so too can the growing band of industrialists. Aluminium Bahrain (ALBA) was the first big industrial project in the region, and it was initially set up to allow international aluminium users to benefit from Bahrain's cheap energy resources to smelt raw aluminium. Although the company's fortunes have wavered, it is now basically Gulf-owned, with the Bahrain government holding 57.9 per cent of the equity and the Saudi government 22 per cent. Of the original consortium of international owners Kaiser Aluminium and Breton Investments remain as minority shareholders. ALBA's sales and profits have fluctuated with world markets, but looking to the future, the smelter is the nucleus of the GCC's first integrated industry.

At present ALBA is undergoing a two-phase US$79 million expansion scheme aimed at increasing production to around 200,000 tonnes a year without increasing power consumption – a critical factor in maintaining cost effectiveness.

As well as exporting primary aluminium, ALBA now supplies a range of intermediate industries, including BALEXCO, Midal Cables and, latterly, the GCC joint-venture Gulf Aluminium Rolling Mill Company (GARMCO). Midal Cables was the first Bahraini company to use the causeway for an export shipment and is looking to expand its markets rapidly in Saudi Arabia and beyond. ALBA's primary aluminium-exporting operation, BALCO, has begun freighting primary aluminium to other intermediate users in the kingdom. GARMCO, already producing 40,000 tonnes of rolled aluminium annually (mainly for export), is expected to sign contracts for a US$35 million foil mill early in 1988, while talks are under way between GARMCO and Iraq's state-owned aluminium industry on the possibility of producing discs for use in the manufacture of household utensils, an industry with immense prospects in the Gulf region. Markets which did not exist, or were inaccessible, in 1971 when ALBA began production now provide the opportunity for Bahrain to become the centre of a highly profitable regional aluminium industry.

A second heavy industrial project set up as a joint venture has yet to enjoy similar success because of short-term pressures. The Arab Iron and Steel Company's (AISCO) US$300 million plant was commissioned in 1985 to produce 4.0 million tonnes of iron ore pellets a year. The pellets are used by direct-reduction method steel plants of the type installed in Saudi Arabia, Qatar and Iraq. These plants were expected to take a minimum of 50 per cent of the pelletisation plant's output, while the remainder would go to Egypt and South-east Asia. But steel plants work on long-term supply contracts, and no purchaser would risk ordering from a new producer until the volume and quality of its output was guaranteed. As the company's unsold stocks mounted along with the burden of interest payments on loans of US$200 million, AISCO's creditors called in their loans and refused to accept rescheduling offers. The plant was closed and its future hung in the balance in mid-1987 as British Steel presented a detailed report on its technical and commercial feasibility. British Steel was understood to have produced an optimistic report, and it seemed likely that the plant would survive at the time of writing. If it survives, in ten years' time, or less, AISCO's prospects will no doubt look as bright as ALBA's as the regional steel industry expands and integrates.

Another joint venture involving Bahrain, Saudi Arabia and Kuwait is the Gulf Petrochemical Industries Co marketing difficulties Gulf Petrochemical Industries Company (GPIC), which is also facing marketing difficulties at a time when the oil and petrochemicals markets are glutted. Once again it is the infant survival stage which is vital, for there is no doubt, as Industry and Development Minister Yusuf al-Shirawi has said, the market for Gulf petrochemicals is set to grow substantially in the 1990s as the region's oil industry witnesses another, more modest boom.

Oil Revenues Still Vital
Despite diversification into new industries, Bahrain remains dependent on the oil industry for its foreign currency earnings. Although the oil sector provided only 19.6 per cent of GDP in 1986 compared with 24.5 per cent for the finance

sector, 11.6 per cent for manufacturing industries, and 11.1 per cent for commerce, oil products accounted for 70 per cent of government revenues in 1985. Refined oil-product exports increased in 1986 by 41 per cent to 89 million barrels, valued at US$1,670 million. Oil revenues for the first half of 1987 (January to June) totalled US$307.6 million compared with US$405.7 million for the same period of 1986, and were 30 per cent down on budget estimates, but as oil product prices hardened in mid-1987 a significant improvement was expected for second-half sales.

Most of Bahrain's oil exports are in the form of products refined at the Sitra Refinery, for which a planned US$900 million development scheme is being studied by joint owners the Bahrain Petroleum Company (BAPCO) and Caltex. The purpose of the scheme is to allow the refinery to throughput higher value products than at present. At the same time efforts are being made to enhance recovery of oil from Bahrain's Awali oilfields to feed the refinery, which has been under-supplied since Saudi Arabia cut its oil supply to Sitra Refinery. Awali currently produces 41,900bpd, and reserves, at 140 million barrels, are sufficient to last to the end of the century. The Abu Safah offshore oilfield, owned by Saudi Arabia but granted to Bahrain, was out of action for some time in 1987 for maintenance, but is back to production at 100,000bpd. Unfortunately, explorations in Bahrain's own offshore waters have failed to produce positive results.

Although oil reserves are limited and dwindling, Bahrain enjoys substantial reserves of gas. The Bahrain National Gas Company's US$65 million LPG complex expansion plan was approved in January 1987 and will increase capacity to 340 thousand standard cubic feet (mscf) per day. Gas is the basis of Bahrain's cheap energy on which its industrial development plans are all based, and with more major users of electricity now on stream, such as GPIC and GARMCO, finance has been allocated for increasing capacity from the current level of 930MW. At one time it was suggested that total capacity should be raised by 800MW by 1995, but requirements have been reassessed in the light of plans for a GCC grid-sharing scheme, and because of lower expectations of population growth.

At the height of the oil boom it had been calculated that the population of Bahrain would reach 700,000 by the turn of the century; planners have now settled for 476,000 with fewer than 100,000 expatriates. Water consumption is expected to rise dramatically, however, and meters are being installed in all properties. In an effort to prevent waste of what is an extremely expensive resource in the region, domestic consumers face tariffs which rise from a modest 45 fils per cubic metre for the first 50 metres per month to a heavy 450 fils for units over 150cu metres.

No Budget Alarms

The revised two-year budget for 1986–88 announced in January 1986 allowed for expenditure of BD1,100 million equally divided between the two years, but the poor state of the oil market in 1986 led to expenditure being slashed by 15 per cent. The first half of 1987 produced a budget deficit of US$31 million (BD13 million), but there was no panic in view of the improvement in oil prices as the Organisation of the Petroleum Exporting Countries (OPEC) agreements stabilised the per barrel price of crude at close to the US$18 mark. The deficit was funded by an issue of Treasury bonds on the local finance market, the first time that the Bahrain government had taken such a step since 1983.

In December 1986 the Bahrain Monetary Agency began issuing treasury bills at a weekly rate of BD2 million, following the Saudi example of the Bankers Security Deposit Account, with the aim of mopping up excess liquidity and providing a mechanism for banks to buy and sell as required. Other measures taken in 1987 to further the sophistication of the financial market in Bahrain included the long-awaited establishment of a stock exchange. The law to establish the stock exchange, ratified in March, allows dealing in 30 domestic stocks, bonds and paper issued by public institutions. But the performance of the exchange will be closely monitored to ensure that the stock value of companies is based on performance, and that the kind of speculation which led to the crash of the Souk al-Manakh, the unofficial stock market in Kuwait, cannot occur in Bahrain. A number of Bahraini investors and financial institutions lost money in that crash, and the hard lessons of rash speculation have been learned.

The banking sector itself is looking to develop new forms of business. Offshore banking, which was the vogue of the late 1970s has lost some of its glitter, mainly because Saudi Arabia took steps to prevent the flight of capital to international markets via Bahrain's OBUs. At the end of June 1986 the 73 registered OBUs had assets totalling US$51 billion, down 10.2 per cent on December 1985 and 20 per cent less than in March 1984. But Bahrain's financial sector is no longer dependent on offshore units of foreign banks, set up purely to drain profits out of the Gulf. Bahrain is the home of a number of major Arab-owned banks, including the Gulf International Bank (GIB) and the Arab Banking Corporation (ABC), which are fast becoming leading players in the world banking scene.

Interviewed in the weekly *Middle East Economic Digest* (28 March 1987) ABC President Abdulla al-Saudi said, 'No imagination – no business: you have to create and convince others that business is profitable. The days of receiving deposits and giving loans have no chance in today's markets.'

Both big banks are handling bill issues for local corporations. ABC handled a US$60 million revolving facility for INVESTCORP in April 1987, while GIB managed a US$100 million loan for the Bahrain-based regional airline Gulf Air, which made a US$13.3 million loss in 1986 resulting in 550 job losses in the airline's worldwide staff. Both issues were oversubscribed, but there is simply not enough business within the region to sustain major banks, and so both are hunting for business in international markets and looking for ways to channel the vast financial resources of the Gulf states into profitable investment avenues.

Tightening Commercial Regulations

On the domestic front, 1987 also saw efforts to increase sophistication in the commercial sector with the issuing of a new Commercial Companies Law which took effect on 1 June. The law covers basic rules of company formation, accounting, record keeping and business procedures. Rights and obligations under certain types of commercial contracts are covered, and clear distinctions are made between the role of a distributor and an agent acting on behalf of a foreign company. All aspects of customer banking and commercial instruments are also included in the new regulations. The law updates existing statutes which have been unchanged since 1969. A bankruptcy law was also expected to be promulgated later in the year.

New laws, however, do not create jobs. For some years employment for the well-educated youth of the country has been a primary concern of government planners. With 40 per cent of the population under 21, the issue of job opportunities is going to be critical to the social stability of the country in the next decade. Since the end of the 1970s the government has challenged young people to acquire useful skills through a programme called Train 10,000. The youth responded and now have the right to demand jobs. But Bahrain does not have the financial resources to carry the burden of an over-manned bureaucracy and to siphon graduates from the employment market as occurs in other countries in the region.

Although the big state ventures like ALBA and the Arab Shipbuilding and Repair Yard provide a large number of industrial and administrative jobs, and the banks offer work for the better educated, there are not enough opportunities for young people to earn a living and to acquire practical experience to complement classroom knowledge.

Women account for 55 per cent of the available national workforce in Bahrain. In an effort to provide them with suitable work opportunities, expatriate wives are being forced out of the labour market. Measures to encourage companies to create more jobs include the cutting of social security contributions payable by employer and employee. But the real answer to the problem of youth employment being faced throughout the region is the gradual replacement of foreign labour in all areas of the economy with indigenous labour. This point was stressed by the Prime Minister at a seminar on private sector investment held in March 1987, during which he called on the private sector to use its accumulated wealth to develop the national economy instead of waiting for the government to provide the finance to fuel the economy as in the past. But private sector employers claim that local labour is too expensive and not adequately trained, and indeed the government has been forced to allow the re-issuing of work permits to existing expatriate labour when contracts expire.

Adjusting budgets to the lower revenues of the past three years has meant that a number of major projects have been held back, although 1986 marked the beginning of a five-year BD1,200 million development plan. It seemed likely, as population growth figures were scaled down, that housing project plans for Fasht al-Adham – a massive land reclamation scheme – might remain on the shelf, but tourist projects like the US$5.3 million tourist beach complex at Sanabis and the US$5 million King Faisal sea-front highway were likely to be completed by the end of 1988. A military air base at Suman was originally to be funded by the GCC as part of its aid to improve regional defences, but the GCC funding is not likely to be forthcoming under present economic circumstances and Bahrain will foot the bill itself. The contract for construction of the base went to Taiwanese company Ret-Ser for the low bid of US$89.2 million. Completion is scheduled for early 1990.

In general, construction sector work continued to decline in 1986/87 with a 9 per cent decrease in new building permits. In addition, no new foreign engineering consultancies will be allowed to register in the country, although the 50 or so existing licences will be renewed.

Steady Development Without Booms

As the glitter of the oil boom era fades and normal standards of economic growth are applied to the Gulf states, it becomes apparent that Bahrain is not faring badly for a developing country. Despite a continued dependence on oil revenues it has a better base for diversification than most developing countries, given its well-developed communications, an increasingly sophisticated financial sector, a young industrial base and a well-educated, youthful population. Its prospects will depend to a large extent on the ability of the state and the private sector to make best use of their collective resources to gain a permanent foothold in the wider markets of the Gulf and the Arab world beyond. The Gulf states have the capital and the markets to allow Bahraini industries, services and commerce to flourish, provided that the Bahrainis can offer the required products at the right price. It may be that the 1990s will see Bahrain exporting skilled and professional labour to neighbouring states, manufacturing spare parts for major industries in Jubail, as well as providing much-needed research and development facilities through the newly opened Arab Gulf University. As the Gulf states look forward to the 1990s in the confident hope that demand for oil will force prices up, Bahrain will look to reap the benefits of its current efforts and sacrifices.

1989

Improved Security – US Navy – Royal Navy – Sense of Insecurity – Income Tax Rejected – Debt Provisions – Industry's Mixed Messages – Post-War Business Boom?

For Bahrain, the cease-fire between Iran and Iraq in July 1988 produced the promise of improved security for which all the Gulf Arab states had been craving for so long. In addition, it created the prospect of a quick revival of regional business activity, on which Bahrain's fortunes as a financial services centre had largely been founded, as contractors sought to capitalise on the expected reconstruction boom following the end of hostilities. Even before Iran finally accepted the United Nations Security Council Resolution 598 on the Iran/Iraq War on 18 July, there had been the first faint glimmers of an improvement Bahrain's economy.

Political Tests

Bahrain's small size normally dictates that it adopts a low profile in regional and international affairs, preferring generally to shadow the policies pursued by Saudi Arabia, with which it has a particularly close association. However, in 1987–88, this staunchly pro-Western emirate, as the main support base for the US Navy in the waterway, was in the forefront of Western naval escort operations in the Gulf. The Bahrainis also provided important assistance for the British Royal Navy's Armilla Patrol.

Bahrain has been central to the US Navy's Gulf patrols ever since the United States first established a permanent presence there in 1949. The Americans then took over former Royal Navy installations in Bahrain when Britain withdrew its permanent presence from the Gulf in 1971.

In September 1987, US President Ronald Reagan wrote to the Emir, Sheikh Isa bin Salman al-Khalifa, specifically to thank him for Bahrain's support for the United States. On 29–30 July 1988, the British Prime Minister, Margaret Thatcher, also paid a brief visit to Bahrain, her first since 1981, to thank the government for assisting the Royal Navy. Bahrain also received more tangible dividends for its help.

Whereas neighbouring states like Saudi Arabia and Kuwait have seen significant requests for American arms blocked by the US Congress, Bahrain was given the go-ahead on 18 December 1987 to buy 60–70 of the controversial Stinger

---

© KONINKLIJKE BRILL NV, LEIDEN, 2023 | DOI:10.1163/9789004686335_013

anti-aircraft missiles, worth US$7 million, albeit with stringent conditions attached to the sale, including a pledge to return the weapons to the United States within 18 months.

Bahrain's armed forces are tiny, with only about 2,800 active personnel. However, like the other member states of the Gulf Co-operation Council (GCC), it has been building up its defences, spurred on by the sense of insecurity caused by the Gulf War. As well as the Stingers, Bahrain ordered a US$400 million arms package from the United States in early 1987, including a dozen F-16 fighter jets for its nascent air force, scheduled for delivery from early 1989 onwards. It ordered a further four F-16s in 1988.

The Bahrain Navy has also been building up a force of West German-built helicopter-carrying and missile armed fast patrol boats, while the ground forces took delivery of 60 American-made M-60 tanks in 1987 and 1988. As a further sign of Bahrain's earnestness about maintaining its security, Sheikh Isa announced on 31 March 1988 the appointment of Sheikh Khalifa bin Ahmed al-Khalifa, who had previously been chief of staff of the defence forces, as defence minister in place of the Crown Prince, Sheikh Hamad bin Isa bin Salman al-Khalifa. The new minister now acts as deputy to Sheikh Hamad, who retains his position as commander-in-chief of the defence forces.

On the wider international horizon, Bahrain, like Saudi Arabia, has been slower than its fellow GCC members to establish formal diplomatic relations with the Soviet Union. Nevertheless, on 21 June 1988, Bahrain held its first formal talks with the Union of Soviet Socialist Republics (USSR) when a visiting Soviet envoy had meetings with senior Bahraini officials, as well as discussions with the Emir, and there have been several reports that negotiations on establishing formal ties were close to being concluded.

Budget Reflects Uncertainty

For most of 1988, the economic climate in Bahrain was uncertain. As a result, the government's 1988 budget covered just one year, whereas previous practice had been to issue budgets for two years at a time. The authorities hope to return to a two-year budget for 1989/90. The 1988 budget projected total government spending at BD490 million (US$1,250), compared with the previous budget's projected two-year total of BD1,100 million (US$2,945 million). Given the fall in consumer prices in 1987, this implied little real change in spending levels. The budget anticipated a deficit of BD60 million (US$159 million), and the government announced a threefold increase in the public debt ceiling from BD100 million (US$265 million) to BD300 million (US$796 million) for the three-year period to 1990, and planned to issue new Treasury bills and long-term development bonds as a way of boosting the financial market.

The government anticipated that oil would provide BD252 million (US$670 million) of revenue, or 58 per cent of total public sector income, excluding debt financing. Oil is therefore still the government's main earner, although the proportion of total revenue it provides is down from a high point of 80 per cent in 1982. Oil production in 1987 averaged 117,000 barrels a day (bpd), which included half of the output of the offshore Abu Safah field, which Bahrain shares with Saudi Arabia.

Oil, in the form of refined products, accounts for 70 per cent of export earnings. Bahrain's 250,000bpd Sitra Refinery, operated by Bahrain Petroleum Company (BAPCO), is one of the oldest in the Gulf, and studies were under way during 1988 to modernise the complex, at an estimated cost of US$1,200 million. There were several reports during 1988 that the Bahraini government was negotiating to buy the 40 per cent stake in BAPCO owned by Caltex of the United States, although the authorities would clearly face considerable difficulties in financing such a buy-out.

The authorities raised non-oil revenues in the 1988 budget by increasing duty on tobacco by 20 per cent and on alcohol by 25 per cent. Postal charges were raised on 1 March 1988, but the costs of water, power and petrol were left unchanged. The authorities have also so far rejected the idea of introducing local income tax. However, as part of the budget package, they did announce a drive to improve the efficiency of government departments and public sector organisations.

Finance Picks Up

There was further evidence of uncertainty about Bahrain's economic prospects to be found in the continuing delays over establishing a local stock exchange. A nine-member board was approved in November 1987, and at the beginning of 1988 it was expected that the exchange would start trading in June. However, the timetable was subsequently put back to the fourth quarter of 1988. The plan is that 30 Bahraini companies will be listed initially, but it is hoped eventually to attract other Gulf concerns, and maybe even international stocks.

The banks themselves showed some signs of recovery in 1988 from the slump which had developed from about 1983 onwards. Bahrain's role as a financial centre developed in the 1970s, with the establishment of commercial and investment banks, and particularly offshore banking units (OBUs). These institutions were attracted by the boom in lending to the Gulf Arab states, especially Saudi Arabia, and chose Bahrain as a base because of its good communications and mature and fairly liberal infrastructure. However, the stagnation of regional business, and problems caused by heavy exposure in Latin America, led to a substantial contraction. Among British clearing bank OBUs, the Midland

Bank withdrew in November 1987, following Lloyds Bank's decision to do the same earlier in the year. Barclays Bank retained a representative office for the collection of debts.

As 24-hour financial trading seems to be centring increasingly on Tokyo, New York, and London, the long-term viability of Bahrain as an attractive financial centre must also be in some doubt. However, in 1988 at least, the number of OBUs seemed to stabilise at about 65, having fallen from a high of 74 in 1985. The OBUs' total assets also recovered from a low of US$51.2 billion in 1986 to US$63.5 billion at the end of 1987, and their assets in the first quarter of 1988 were 18 per cent higher than in the same period of 1987. The impact of OBUs on Bahrain's economy is clearly considerable. In January 1988, the Finance and National Economy Minister, Ibrahim Abdul-Karim Mohammed, estimated that the OBUs contributed BD200 million (US$530 million) to the economy each year.

Bahrain-based commercial banks saw their performance affected by the need to make substantial debt provisions in 1987. One of the biggest, the Bank of Bahrain and Kuwait (BBK) reported a net loss of BD23.4 million in 1987, due entirely to the need to make provisions of BD29.2 million, nearly ten times higher than BBK's provisions in 1986. Al-Ahli Commercial Bank reported a net loss for 1987 of BD5.5 million. However, bankers were expecting 1988 to see improved figures, with less need for large provisions, some important opportunities for project lending in Bahrain, and perhaps also the first signs of new business related to the Gulf cease-fire. On 11 August 1988, the Gulf International Bank (GIB), which had had to make provisions of US$220 million in 1986, declared a post-tax profit of US$25.4 million for the first six months of 1988, up 14.3 per cent on the equivalent results for the previous year. GIB is jointly owned by the governments of Bahrain, Saudi Arabia, Kuwait, Iraq, the UAE, Oman, and Qatar.

There has been a noticeable switch to investment banking on the island, in an attempt to attract more private wealth in the Gulf. The October 1987 stock market slump raised doubts about the wisdom of this trend, but a number of new institutions have established themselves in the field recently. During 1988, the number of investment houses reached 19.

One institution which attracted particular attention in 1988 was the INVESTCORP, which during 1988 took a significant stake in the Italian luxury goods house, Guccio Gucci SpA. INVESTCORP, which was established in 1982, made profits of US$28.8 million in 1987, up from US$15.5 million in 1986.

Daiwa Securities Company and Nikko Securities Company, sought leave in 1988 to upgrade their representative offices to full investment banks. In contrast to the trend of Western financial institutions cutting back their operations in Bahrain, Japanese securities houses have been expanding strongly, to capitalise on Gulf demand for yen-based stocks and bonds.

Industry's Up and Downs

The Bahraini government, which always understood that with oil reserves unlikely to last much beyond the mid-1990s, the island's oil revenue would be limited, was quick to set a course for diversification of the economy.

The message from industry in 1988 was mixed. In January, the government introduced legislation which gave local producers a ten per cent price advantage over foreign suppliers on all government contracts. GCC suppliers were to receive five per cent preference, and the private sector was also to be encouraged to give preference to GCC producers. This was in line with legislation being introduced in other GCC states. To avoid abuse of the new practice, such as falsifying the origin of goods, the authorities declared that any violations would be liable to result in a two-year ban on competing for government contracts.

Fears that the causeway link with Saudi Arabia, opened in December 1986, would cause a spate of bankruptcies among Bahraini merchants, overwhelmed by imports of cheaper goods from larger Saudi Arabian competitors, remained unfounded. Indeed, the causeway was giving a healthy stimulus to business.

The services sector appeared buoyant. Hotel occupancy rates were at record levels, and the movement of aircraft and passengers through Bahrain's international airport was up 12 per cent in the first half of 1988 compared with the previous year. Work also began on expansion of the airport's terminal building facilities, at a cost of US$61 million.

The first major industry to be developed on the island was Aluminium Bahrain (ALBA), established in 1968. In 1987, ALBA's smelter produced 180,344 tonnes of aluminium, over 10,000 tonnes above the plant's rated capacity. The plan for 1988 was to produce 180,765 tonnes. In July 1988, ALBA finalised finance worth US$82 million for an expansion plan that would take capacity to 205,000 tonnes. A second-phase expansion is also planned, to increase capacity to 300,000 tonnes, at an estimated additional cost of over US$120 million.

In January 1986, the Gulf Aluminium Rolling Company (GARMCO) began operating at Sitra, producing sheet and coil aluminium from unprocessed slabs supplied by ALBA. In its first full year of operation, GARMCO exceeded its output target by 22 per cent. However, it recorded a net loss of BD4.6 million (US$12.7 million). GARMCO, which is owned 20 per cent each by Bahrain, Saudi Arabia, Kuwait, and Iraq, and ten per cent each by Oman and Qatar, hoped to be in profit in 1988, but plans for a US$35 million, 6,000 tonne foil plant, which was expected to be in operation by the end of 1988, are two to three years behind schedule. Another major project in the offing was the expansion in capacity of the Bahrain National Gas Company's (BANAGAS) gas liquefaction plant from 170,000 tonnes a year to 250,000 tonnes. It was expected that the US$70 million contract would be awarded in the third quarter of 1988.

In 1977, the Arab Shipbuilding and Repair Yard Company (ASRY), financed by the Organisation of Arab Petroleum Exporting Countries (OAPEC), began operations. It has a 450,000 tonne-capacity dry dock. Its activity in recent years has been hit by the general slump in world shipping, and the economic fallout from the tanker war. However, one side-effect of the conflict, the 'tanker war', helped it to its first ever annual profit in 1987, and its turnover in that year of just over US$22 million was nearly double that of 1986, with average occupancy of the dry dock running at close to 90 per cent. About a quarter of the value of all work carried out by ASRY in 1987 was related to damage caused by the tanker war. Whether, with an end to hostilities, the upturn in general shipping business in the Gulf will be enough to compensate for the drop in war-related work remains to be seen, but during 1988 ASRY was planning to purchase a second-hand 80,000 tonne-capacity floating dry dock. In contrast to ASRY's success, the Bahrain Slipway Company announced in January 1988 that it was to cease operating.

The other major industrial casualty on the island was the Arab Iron and Steel Company (AISCO), formed in 1981, which opened an iron pelletising plant in 1984. It was owned by shareholders from Bahrain, Kuwait, Jordan, and the UAE, but was closed in 1986. During 1987–88, negotiations were under way for AISCO's takeover by the Kuwait Petroleum Company, through a subsidiary called the Gulf Industrial Investment Company.

Given the mixed fortunes of the banking sector and heavy industry, it is unsurprising that unemployment is becoming an issue of concern in Bahrain. The authorities may be hoping that the various protection measures they have introduced will also help stimulate local manufacturing and lighter industries and services.

Outlook

Bahrain's political stance during the Iran/Iraq War still puts it firmly in the staunchly pro-Western, Arab camp, even though it has been exploring the possibility of improving relations with the Soviet Union. Like all the Gulf States, Bahrain will be breathing a sigh of relief at the cease-fire. The apparent prospect of a post-war business boom in the Gulf also bodes well for the island, with the possibility of revitalising the financial sector, which was already showing some signs of recovery, and new opportunities for Bahraini industry. Bahrain, and Bahraini businesses, will have to fight hard in what will be a very competitive atmosphere.

1990

Upswing in Gulf Business – Contacts With Iran Increased – Relationship
With Washington – Economic Challenges – Stock – Unemployment –
Negligible Debt – High Reserves

Among Bahrainis, the wave of optimism which initially greeted the Iran/Iraq
War cease-fire in August 1988 was undoubtedly dampened to some extent by
the lengthy stalemate in the UN-sponsored peace talks between Iraq and Iran,
the continued unpredictability of Iranian politics in the post-Ayatollah
Khomeini era (he died in 1989), and the fact that the anticipated post-war reconstruction boom was slow to materialise. There was still a degree of confidence that the fighting between the Iraqis and Iranians had actually come to an
end, that Tehran was embarked on a new course of moderation, and that a
strong upswing in Gulf business activity would eventually come. And Bahrain's
economy, in particular, with its strong banking sector and what, by regional
standards, is a relatively diversified industrial base, still stands to be a major
beneficiary of any such rejuvenation. At the same time, significant economic
challenges lie ahead, not least by the fact that Bahrain faces increasingly stiff
competition in the future, both regionally and internationally, in its traditional
spheres of expertise.

A Changing Political Scene

On the surface, the tiny island of Bahrain – actually two main islands, and over
30 smaller ones – has appeared extraordinarily stable ever since it regained full
independence from Britain in 1971.

Following the 1979 Islamic revolution in Tehran and the start of the
Iran/Iraq War in 1980, Bahrain's staunchly pro-Western, pro-Iraqi policies have
caused some friction between the island and Iran. But, to complicate the picture, there is a particular history of ancient entanglements between the two
countries. In 1783, the Arab rulers of Zubara, ended nearly two centuries of Persian domination of Bahrain. Their descendants still run the island today.

Following the toppling of the Pahlavi regime, the new Islamic Republic of
Iran also revived old claims to sovereignty over Bahrain. Throughout the 1980's
the Bahraini authorities were vigilant in detecting any Iranian inspired challenges to their authority. Yet, in spite of this, at the end of the decade the government was stable. The authorities clearly operate a relatively efficient

© KONINKLIJKE BRILL NV, LEIDEN, 2023 | DOI:10.1163/9789004686335_014

security service. The ruling family, led by the Emir, Sheikh Isa Bin Salman al-Khalifa, also remains popular. The al-Khalifas have adopted relatively benevolent policies towards their inhabitants, and have remained quite close to the community. And Bahrainis still enjoy what, by regional standards, is a markedly liberal society.

But Bahrainis still have more reason than most to view anxiously the evolution of the government of the new Iranian president, Hashemi Rafsanjani. Since the Iran/Iraq War cease-fire, Bahrain has gradually increased its contacts with Iran again. But the process looks likely to be a slow one. Indeed, the Bahrainis themselves hosted the first post-war Gulf Co-Operation Council (GCC) summit in December 1988, at which the member states agreed to take a cautious approach to the issue of relations with Iran. They linked the full normalisation of ties to a lasting settlement in the Iran/Iraq War and a commitment by Tehran not to interfere in their internal affairs.

The Bahraini defence budget increased steadily in the late 1980s. The 1988 figure was BD66.5 million (US$176.4 million) which was actually BD10 million (US$26.5 million) higher than originally planned, and well ahead of the 1987 total of BD51.5 million (US$136.6 million). And the planned defence budgets for 1989 and 1990 were BD69.4 million (US$184 million) and BD72.9 million (US$193.4 million) respectively.

But in modern times Bahrain, because of its small size, has generally relied on outsiders for protection. Between 1861 and 1971 that protection came from Britain, and links between the two countries remain strong. But now, the ultimate guarantor of Bahraini security is the United States.

Indeed, Bahrain probably has a stronger strategic relationship with Washington than any other Gulf state except Saudi Arabia, and possibly Oman. When the British withdrew their permanent presence from the Gulf in 1971, the US Navy took over the former Royal Navy installations in Bahrain as their main facility in the region, and it provided a lynchpin for American tanker escort operations in the War in 1987–88. In 1985, the US Army Corps of Engineers also began work on a large new military air base in the south of the island. It was due to be completed in 1989, at a cost of about US$90 million, and it undoubtedly figures prominently in US contingency plans for reinforcing its presence in the Gulf in an emergency. At least the closeness of the relationship between Manama and Washington gave the Bahrainis access to pieces of advanced US military technology which were denied to some of their neighbours by the pro-Israeli lobby in the US Congress. In particular, Bahrain bought a squadron of F-16 fighter jets in 1988 to bolster its fledgling air force.

At the regional level, Bahrain has close co-operation with Saudi Arabia. Indeed, the causeway between Bahrain and Saudi Arabia's Eastern Province, opened in 1986, was probably intended as much as a political signal to Tehran of this fact as it was meant to facilitate economic links between the island and Saudi Arabia. And, on most aspects of regional and international policy, Manama closely shadows Riyadh.

But one area in which Bahrain's policy was actually ahead of Saudi Arabia's was that of relations with the communist bloc. Like Riyadh, Manama had been increasing its contacts with the Soviet Union. Then in April 1988 it also became the latest Gulf Arab state to establish full diplomatic relations with China. Saudi Arabia was now the only GCC state not to have full formal links with Beijing. In part, this trend was a sign of a maturing foreign policy throughout the Gulf. At the same time, while these closer ties were unlikely to threaten the basic relationships between the GCC states and the West, they were also partly a recognition that major trading opportunities exist in the Soviet Union and China, particularly now that both countries were embarked on economic restructuring programmes.

Slow Growth and Deficits

On the economic front, early forecasts for 1989 predicted annual growth only slightly higher than that achieved in 1988. Moreover, the government's two-year budget for 1989–90, published at the beginning of 1989, appeared to confirm the suspicion that the country's economy still faced a number of medium-term challenges.

First, the authorities predicted an increase in the planned government budget deficit, to BD100 million (US$256 million) in each year. Total government spending for 1989 was projected at BD530 million (US$1,406 million), and for 1989 BD560 million (US$1,432 million).

One problem for the Bahraini authorities has been the continued sluggishness of the oil market. The island's own oil deposits have always been modest: its own oilfield produces only about 42,000 barrels per day (bpd). But Saudi Arabia supplies about 200,000bpd to feed the Sitra Refinery. And oil revenue remains the government's main source of income.

Another difficulty has been that continued high public spending levels will exacerbate Bahrain's mounting trade deficit problem. Of course, ultimately, the hope is that the development spending will allow import substitution by broadening the island's industrial base.

Finance at the Crossroads?

The banking sector has long been a mainstay of the Bahraini economy. But, for most of the 1980s, it was depressed by the contraction of local business and the need to provision for substantial bad debts, particularly in Latin America.

In the mid-1970s, Bahrain established itself as a major centre for offshore banking units (OBUs) attracted by the prospects of business in the then oil-rich Gulf. The OBUs make a substantial contribution to the domestic economy. And, after years of contraction, in the late 1980s they were showing some sustained signs of recovery.

Seven of the top eight OBUs showed profits in 1988, compared to just two in the previous year. Indeed, the largest, the Arab Banking Corporation, showed record net profits of US$142 million. The total assets held by the OBUs were also up for the second successive year, to stand at the end of 1988 at US$68.1 billion.

The results for the local commercial banks, however, remained mixed. The National Bank of Bahrain was among the leaders to record profits substantially higher than in 1987. But the total assets of the commercial banks declined in 1988 by 4.2 per cent, and overall loans and advances were also down.

It seemed that the financial market would be boosted by the government's need to finance its budget deficit, chiefly by issuing treasury bills. The industrial expansion planned by the government should also provide new lending opportunities. And there was still the promise of substantial reconstruction business, and a general revival of Gulf business activity.

Nevertheless, rationalisation of the banking sector seemed inevitable. Certainly, Bahrain will not be able to take its traditional pre-eminence in the financial field forgranted. As the relative attraction of the Gulf has declined with the slump in the oil market, so Bahrain will have to compete more on level terms with other offshore banking centres like Hong Kong. And the post-war era is also likely to be marked by increased regional competition, since Bahrain's neighbours are also developing their own financial systems.

Stock Exchange Opens

Perhaps the most significant development for Bahrain's economy in 1989 was that, after much delay, its stock exchange finally opened in June. Initially, a total of just 29 local and joint venture companies were registered, with a total capitalisation of approximately US$1,600 million.

The Bahrainis clearly have ambitions to host the main regional stock trading centre, dealing in shares of GCC and even other foreign companies. Certainly the reservoir of untapped Gulf investment funds is very great. And Bahrain still has the advantage over potential rivals like Kuwait of its financial track record and a pool of resources at hand among its OBUs. In the light of the opening of the stock exchange, the Bahraini government was also apparently planning a major privatisation programme. That, at least, could provide funds to help alleviate its budget problems, although the authorities are likely to want to retain their stakes in the island's major industrial concerns.

Diversification: a Watchword

Even so, the government made plain its ambitious plans to diversify the economy further, and at the same time attract investors from the main industrialised countries – and especially from the United States, Britain and West Germany – to set up new joint ventures.

Leading this particular drive was the head of the Industrial Development Centre (IDC) of the Ministry of Trade and Development, Sheikh Homoud bin Khalifa al-Khalifa. The next aim, he said, was for Bahrain to replace 30 per cent of its imports in the next five years. And he pointed out that the government itself has allocated US$2.6 billion to industrial projects over the next five years.

IDC officials pointed to a number of incentives for investment in Bahrain. These include a 70 per cent government contribution to the cost of feasibility studies for proposed projects, the possibility of 100 per cent foreign ownership, subsidised energy, the duty-free import of the necessary plant and raw materials, personal and corporate tax exemption, no restrictions on the repatriation of income, and duty-free access to other GCC markets. The priority areas for the government were apparently aluminium and related industries, petrochemicals, engineering, electronics, and healthcare.

A desire to create significant numbers of new jobs was also behind the campaign. Bahrain, like the other Gulf States, faces a mounting threat of unemployment. According to the most recent figures from the country's Central Statistics Bureau, 34 per cent of the population is at present under 14 years of age. Hence, the local labour force is expected to double by the end of the century.

Better Industrial Performance

As it is, Bahrain's industrial base is already very broad for a country of its size. In the hydrocarbons sector, the Sitra refinery continued to operate close to its 250,000bpd capacity. But it is one of the oldest refineries in the Gulf, and the Bahrain Petroleum Company (BAPCO), which operates it, plans a major modernisation programme to increase its efficiency, particularly in the area of high-value refined products. The total cost of the BAPCO programme is expected to be US$640 million.

Meanwhile, in 1989 work had started on the US$74.5 million expansion of the Bahrain National Gas Company's (BANAGAS) gas liquefication plant. The contractor is the Tokyo-based JGC Corporation. It is intended to increase the capacity of the BANAGAS plant from 110 million cu ft/d to 170 million cu ft/d.

Bahrain and the Future

At the start of the new decade, perhaps the biggest danger is that political stability could foster stagnation. The ruling al-Khalifa family are fortunate to be assisted by several able ministers. But the new, harsher competitive atmosphere which is likely to pervade the post-war Gulf will not allow any complacency regarding development plans.

Bahrain is a country with a strikingly rich heritage as testified by its 4,000-year-old Dilmun civilisation, its ancient temples and monuments, its Portuguese and Islamic forts, its longstanding trade relations, its mature and confident people and a continuity and prosperity that are the fruits of many years of stability. The diversity of natural resources and an extended history have provided firm foundations and rich inspiration for a unique cultural heritage.

A visitor to Bahrain will be able to see the world's best natural pearls; the Gulf's oldest mosque; some 170,000 ancient burial mounds extending as far as the eye can see and covering some 30 square kilometres; the site of the Gulf's first oil well; the world's longest causeway, 25 kilometres long; the construction of traditional dhows; the 'Tree of Life' standing on its own amid a stretch of semi-arid desert, a unique collection of illuminated Korans and manuscripts; herds of Arabian oryx; villages where traditional crafts such as pottery, basket weaving, rush matting and embroidery are still flourishing and a great deal more. Bahrain's islands are a main staging post for birds on their spring and autumn north-south migrations. Bahrain's hotels and communications are the best in the Middle East, thus ensuring that visitors will have a very comfortable stay while at the same time they can easily get in touch with anywhere in the world with a telephone or fax machine.

Bahrain's climate is comparatively the most temperate in the Gulf all the year round, making it possible to participate in a wide variety of outdoor activities. The seas off the coast of Bahrain are shallow and warm and are ideal for swimming, fishing, sailing, windsurfing and sub-aqua diving; and facilities for all these and other sports are readily available.

In the past year the development of Sanabis Beach resort has progressed steadily. A complex of hotels, chalets, restaurants and cafes as well as an ultra-modern and spacious exhibition hall are expected to open in the near future. A holiday resort is being developed on al-Dar Island, and a beach hotel will be built at the Bandar Resort.

Several old mansions with distinctive architecture, including the house of Sheikh Isa bin Ali al-Khalifa and the Bayt Siyadi (Siyadi House) on Muharraq Island, have been renovated. Regular trips on well equipped dhows and organised tours of the Wildlife Park and Sanctuary have been introduced, although a plan to build a hotel in the park has been deferred. Bahrain's new US$28 million Bahrain National Museum complex, arguably the best in the Middle East, offers a wealth of artefacts and exhibits that reflect the islands' long and fascinating history.

Gulf Air, which has made a profit in the past year, is expanding its fleet. It plans to buy 12 Airbus A-320s and a further six Boeing 767s, with another 12 A-320s and six 767s on option. Expansion work on the terminal lounge at Bahrain airport is near completion. A new 62,000 square foot Air Cargo Terminal has a mechanical handling system capable of accommodating 57,300 metric tonnes of cargo a month. Handling procedures have also been improved.

Bahrain's licensed restaurants, relaxed atmosphere, luxurious and moderately-priced hotels, excellent communications, sunny weather and warm waters, historic sites, traditional bazaars and modern shops all combine to make the visitor's stay interesting and enjoyable.

Outlook

Bahrain has chosen to diversify its economy to reduce its dependence on oil, and thus maximise the exploitation of its other assets, such as strategic position, relatively skilled labour force, plentiful supplies of natural gas and an advanced telecommunications system.

Several plans to expand Bahrain's major industries were approved in 1989. The economy remained buoyant, and the balance of payments in 1988 was around US$480 million in surplus compared to a deficit in the previous year. The trade deficit fell by BD37.1 million in 1988. Bahrain's oil trade surplus rose in 1988 to BD289.1 million from BD286.8 million in the previous year, while the value of non-petroleum exports in 1988 rose by BD68.2 million. The rate of inflation continued to fall for the fourth successive year. The Bahrain Stock Exchange opened in June 1989. Non-Bahraini Gulf citizens are allowed to trade in the 29 local and joint-venture companies quoted on the exchange.

Container cargo unloaded at Mina (Port) Salman had risen by 50.7 per cent at the end of June 1989, compared with the same period in 1988. A new US$185 million port for container vessels is planned, as the volume of both imports and exports is expected to increase. There is a proposal to link the port with a new industrial zone.

In July 1989 the Government signed a US$73 million agreement for the purchase of Kaiser Aluminium's 17 per cent stake in ALBA. A US$1,440 million project to more than double the production capacity of ALBA's aluminium smelter by 1993 was approved in 1989. Work on a US$74 million project to expand BANAGAS' LPG facilities began in late 1988 and is scheduled to be completed in 1990. BANAGAS has a plan to build a US$365 million–US$500 million polypropylene and methyl tertiary butyl ether plant.

Other projects planned include a US$100 million urea plant at Gulf Petrochemical Industries Company, a second dry dock and diversification at Bahrain Aluminium Extrusion Company. The government approved a US$380 million plan to increase water desalination capacity by 30 million gallons a day and power output by 180MW by 1993. A second causeway linking Manama and Muharraq is being designed.

BAPCO's US$500 million-US$1.00 billion programme to modernise the refinery has been postponed.

By the end of June 1989, the Arab Shipbuilding and Repair Yard Company (ASRY) had doubled its revenue compared with the same period in 1988. Occupancy at the dry dock averaged 95 per cent in 1989, compared with 84 per cent in 1988. The increase in the number of ships repaired at ASRY is expected to continue with Saudi Arabia, Kuwait, Iraq and the UAE playing a basic role in meeting world demand for oil.

In the banking sector, 1989 was a year of moderate revival and reasonable profit. Assets of 58 operating offshore banks at the end of June 1989 totalled US$67 billion, a 2.7 per cent increase on end of March 1989.

Bahrain's international debt is negligible while its reserves are high. Despite the recent recession, the economy has prospered and the diversification programme is proceeding successfully. With the end of the Iran/Iraq War and the increased trade opportunities in the region, Bahrain looks forward to the future from the basis of a reassuringly solid economy.

1991/92

Military Upheaval – Economic Uncertainty – Iranian Threats – Financial Sector Viability – Construction Projects – Water – Transition and Trial

Even before the new Gulf crisis caused by the Iraqi invasion of Kuwait, 1990 presented a mixed picture for Bahrain. The Bahraini government appeared content to maintain the island's traditionally low diplomatic profile in the region, and important steps were taken on the path towards economic diversification and liberalisation. But there was disappointment that the end (in 1988) of hostilities in the Iran/Iraq War still had not produced the expected business recovery, and the long-term future of Bahrain's financial sector remained in doubt. Of course, Iraq's invasion of Kuwait on 2 August 1990 changed the entire equation. Suddenly, Bahrain found itself close to the centre of a major new military upheaval in the Gulf. The crisis plunged the region into a new period of economic uncertainty.

Facing up to the Crisis

Like most of the Arab Gulf states, Bahrain has long been suspicious of Iraq's regional ambitions. That, in part, is why Bahrain took the opportunity of Baghdad's preoccupation with the Iran/Iraq War to found the Gulf Co-operation Council (GCC), which does not include Iraq, in 1981.

Nevertheless, most of the threats to Bahrain's security in recent years seem to have emanated from Iran. Following the 1979 Islamic revolution in Iran, the Tehran government revived historic Persian claims to Bahrain; and there were disturbances on the island in 1979–80. Whereas the ruling al-Khalifa family is Sunni Muslim, the majority of Bahrainis, like the Iranians, are Shi'a.

In December 1981, the Bahraini authorities said that they had uncovered a *coup d'état* attempt, allegedly supported by Iran. Again, in January 1988, the government declared that Iran had been linked to an alleged sabotage plot to blow up the island's Sitra oil refinery.

To counter the potential threat from Iran, Bahrain had been brought increasingly within Saudi Arabia's sphere of influence. To underline this fact, a causeway between Bahrain and Saudi Arabia's Eastern Province was opened in 1986. It provided a strategic as well as an economic link between the two countries. On an international level, Bahrain has also maintained as strong a strategic relationship with the United States of America (US) as any Gulf emirate.

© KONINKLIJKE BRILL NV, LEIDEN, 2023 | DOI:10.1163/9789004686335_015

1991/92   145

Bahrain has provided the major facility for the US Navy's Middle East force in the Gulf, and the US has built a major air base in the south of the island which, it was clearly intended, would be of use to US forces in the event of a regional emergency. These links between Bahrain and the US have meant that the Bahraini armed forces have been given access to certain sensitive US military equipment, the purchase of which has been denied to some of their neighbours.

Despite the various political alarms of the 1980s, the Bahraini government has appeared essentially stable, and contacts with Iran have slowly improved since the Iran/Iraq War cease-fire in 1988. But Bahrain's close ties with both Riyadh and Washington, plus its small size and geographical location near Saudi Arabia's oil-rich Eastern Province – and particularly its proximity to the Dhahran Air Base, the focal point of the US military build-up in the Gulf after Iraq's invasion of Kuwait – all placed it in an especially vulnerable position close to the forefront of the Gulf crisis.

The GCC proved rather ineffective in the face of Iraq's aggression against Kuwait. And Bahrain's own armed forces totalled just 3,350 men, with only 12 combat aircraft and about 50 US-made M60-A3 tanks.

The United States quickly deployed forces to Bahrain, and Britain despatched a squadron of 12 Royal Air Force Tornado GR1 strike aircraft, plus supporting air defence troops, at the end of August, following a visit by the junior defence minister, Alan Clark. British Defence Secretary Tom King also visited Bahrain for talks at the end of August. In September, the British government also announced the deployment of additional Tornados.

Economic Shockwaves

The crisis quickly threw the economy, and particularly the financial sector, into uncertainty. It certainly hit Bahrain's hopes of attracting new foreign investment. In the immediate aftermath of the Iraqi invasion of Kuwait, there were reports of large-scale departures by the expatriate workforces in Bahrain and the other Gulf states. There was also a rush to hard currency, and the government had to take measures to increase foreign currency supplies and protect banks by freezing fixed deposits. Even so, the *Middle East Economic Digest* reported in September that deposits with offshore banking units (OBUs) had slumped by 40 per cent since the beginning of the crisis.

The tension also raised doubts about the long-term viability of Bahrain's financial sector. In the 1970s, Bahrain established itself as a major centre for OBUs. However business was depressed for most of the 1980s because of the contraction of local business – caused both by the Iran/Iraq War and the slump in the oil market – and the need to make provision for substantial bad debt, particularly in Latin America. Activity was already proving slow to recover even before the Iraqi invasion, with a number of foreign banks announcing reductions in their operations in early 1990. Bahrain also faced new challenges to its traditional pre-eminence as a regional financial centre. The OBUs' total assets recovered from a low of US$51.2 billion in 1986 to stand at US$68.1 billion at the end of 1988. But they had fallen again to US$67 billion in 1989.

The government budget deficit in 1989 had been smaller than had been forecast at BD58 million (US$154 million), thanks to higher-than-expected oil revenues. But economic growth remained sluggish. And, despite higher oil export earnings, the trade deficit widened markedly to BD97.2 million (US$258 million) in 1989, an increase of 42 per cent over the previous year. This was due mainly to a large rise in commodity imports.

On 6 July 1990, Bahrain signed an economic trade and technical co-operation agreement with the People's Republic of China. The signing took place during the visit to Beijing of Bahraini Foreign Minister Sheikh Mohammed bin Mubarak al-Khalifa, the first visit to China by a senior Bahraini minister since the two countries established full diplomatic relations in 1989. A Chinese embassy was opened in Bahrain in March 1990.

Another important accord was signed in June 1990, when Bahrain and Britain agreed to co-operate in combating drug trafficking. It is thought that Bahrain, because of its strength in the financial sector, is an important centre for the laundering of drugs money, particularly between the Indian sub-continent and Europe.

The fortunes of Bahrain's local commercial banks were mixed. The largest local bank, the Bank of Bahrain and Kuwait, made profits of BD5.1 million US$13.5 million) in 1989, up from just BD1.00 million (US$2.6 million) in 1988. But the Al-Ahli Commercial Bank announced a loss of BD4.00 million (US$10.6 million) in 1989. The National Bank of Bahrain recorded profits of BD5.4 million (US$14.3 million) for the first half of 1990, up from the BD4.8 million (US$12.7 million) level for the same period in 1989.

Taking Stock

After much delay, the Bahrain Stock Exchange was opened in June 1989. Initially, it listed just 29 companies. And, in early 1990, it was trading a daily average volume of just 331,000 shares, with an average total value of BD82.535 (US$18.925).

The island's strong financial infrastructure may give the Bahrain Stock Exchange an edge over other regional markets in attracting GCC business and investors and plans include the establishment of mutual funds and unit trusts, for which new legislation would be required.

Trading in the initial 29 listings was originally limited to Bahraini and GCC nationals. Subsequently, the Bahraini-based Arab Banking Corporation issued equity open to non-Arab, non-resident investors. But the attraction of non-Gulf investment was not going to be a major short-term feature of the Bahraini market's plans, even before the new crisis, and the exchange's further development in the light of the Gulf War crisis must be in doubt.

The exchange did assist the flotation in May 1990 of the Bahraini government's 42 per cent stake in the Bahrain Hotels Company. Plans were also in hand in 1990 to float at least part of the government's stake in the Bahrain Aluminium Extrusion Company (BALEXCO). These moves were expected to presage a series of state sell-offs, to help liberalise the economy. But privatisation plans are unlikely to include the government's stakes in many of the island's major industrial concerns, so will not produce any substantial funds to help alleviate the government's budget deficit problems to any great extent.

Still Set on Diversification

Some important steps were taken in 1990 in the government's plans to diversify the economy. Bahrain's economy has always been relatively diversified by Gulf standards, as its oil revenues have always been modest.

On 6 March 1990, Aluminium Bahrain (ALBA) inaugurated an initial US$125 million expansion scheme. But ALBA is also responsible for by far the biggest development project on the island, designed virtually to double its smelting capacity to about 450,000 tonnes a year. The estimated cost of the ALBA expansion programme is US$1.440 million. On 17 July 1990, ALBA signed a US$650 million medium-term syndicated loan to finance the first part of the project. It also planned to raise a further US$450 million in export credits for the purchase of plant and equipment.

The international aluminium market was looking strong in 1990. The ALBA expansion is due for completion in 1992. In the short term, the Gulf War crisis raises a question mark over the precise timetable for the project. But Iraqi and Kuwaiti plans to expand their own aluminium industries will certainly have been set back by the affair, and that will surely have a beneficial effect in terms of the expected demand for ALBA's production.

It has been widely assumed that the ALBA project will have a positive spin-off for the other commercial and industrial sectors of the Bahraini economy, quite apart from the potential export boost it should provide once the plant is in commission. But the size of the programme has, at the same time, apparently forced the postponement of the plans of the Bahrain Petroleum Company (BAPCO) to modernise its Sitra Refinery. BAPCO did refine 90.2 million barrels of oil in 1989, slightly up on the 1988 figure, with 81 per cent of the crude coming from Saudi Arabia. But the Sitra Refinery is one of the oldest in the Gulf, and clearly not fully efficient by modern standards. The total cost of the BAPCO modernisation plan had been put at US$640 million.

The Bahrain National Gas Company (BANAGAS) did commission its new gas plant, expanded at a cost of US$74.5 million, during 1990. The main contractor for this project was the Tokyo-based JGC Corporation.

Notwithstanding Iraq's invasion of Kuwait, the Arab Shipbuilding and Repair Yard Company (ASRY) signalled its intention to proceed with its plan to build a second dry dock, to complement its existing 450,000 tonne graving dock. The design consultant for the work is the British Halcrow-Burns company. The new dock will be 300 metres long, 52 metres wide, and have a capacity of up to 180,000 deadweight tonnes. The project, the estimated cost of which has been put at US$55 million, also includes a new 400 metre quay.

The new dock should help ASRY to tackle work on medium-sized and smaller vessels more efficiently than it can at present. Even so, ASRY made a profit of US$10.5 million in 1989, having recorded its first ever small operating profit in 1988. Although the 1989 figure was achieved with a 95 per cent occupancy rate, profits for the first half of 1990 were up 30 per cent compared to the corresponding period of the previous year, with ASRY operating close to full capacity. But, even in the early weeks of the Gulf crisis, fears about the safety of navigation in the Gulf quickly hit ASRY's business. And this may create doubts about ASRY's long-term plans for a third dock.

The Bahraini government continued to make plans during 1990 for the construction of a new container port and free trade zone, at an estimated cost of BD70 million (US$185 million). The inner channel of Mina Salman cannot accommodate the largest of the new generation of container ships. The cabinet chose Hidd, on the second island of Muharraq, as the site for the new facility, in preference to Fisht al-Adham, which was considered to be too exposed, and would have cost twice as much to develop as the Hidd site.

Among other important construction projects, the government delayed the selection of contractors for a new bridge crossing between Manama and Muharraq, which had been expected in August 1990. The estimated cost of the project is BD20 million (US$55 million). Bahrain-based Gulf Air also plans to build a new headquarters on reclaimed land next to Bahrain airport's terminal building, at a cost of BD5 million (US$13 million). Gulf Air itself made a profit in 1989 of BD27.7 million (US$73.6 million), substantially in advance of expectations, helped by the sale of eight old Boeing 737s. The airline – owned jointly by Bahrain, Qatar, Abu Dhabi and Oman – is engaged in a major modernisation of its fleet, with orders and options on up to 36 new aircraft. But its revenues in 1990 and 1991 are sure to be affected by the impact of the Gulf War.

For the future, BANAGAS was reportedly planning further expansion. And the Gulf Petrochemical Industries Company (GPIC) had plans for a new US$110 million plant.

Manpower, Power and Water

To cope with an expanding population, the government continued to emphasise the priority it placed on Bahraini-isation. The goal is for Bahrainis to make up half the private sector workforce by 1994. This could be advanced further if the reported expatriate exodus following the Iraqi invasion of Kuwait proves to be permanent.

In November 1989, the government approved a major new power and water plan. Under the scheme, US$72 million was to have been spent increasing the generating capacity of the main Riffa power station from 700MW to 880MW. But, in September 1990, this idea was abandoned, and it was decided to revert to a previous plan to link the new 800MW power station being built as part of the ALBA expansion to the national grid. The Sitra Island power station is also to be upgraded during 1991. These provisions will certainly be needed, as it has been estimated that peak electricity demand will be approaching the island's current 980MW generating capacity by 1992.

The water resource problem is even more acute, with the island's natural reservoirs being seriously depleted. The government had attempted to impose a daily consumption limit of 60 million gallons, but demand has reached as high as 67 million gallons. As a result, the power and water plan allocated US$305 million for the construction of two new reverse osmosis desalination plants, each with a capacity of 15 million gallons a day. Between them, the two new plants should nearly double Bahrain's production capacity, which currently stands at 35 million gallons a day.

Outlook

The early 1990s were always going to be years of transition and trial for Bahrain, even before the events of August 1990. The optimistic hope that an end to the Iran/Iraq War would bring about a rapid and significant upswing in regional economic activity had largely evaporated, notwithstanding the partial recovery in oil prices.

The Bahraini financial sector faced rationalisation and the need to seek new business beyond the region, as local activity seemed unlikely to sustain it in its existing form, particularly with growing competition from other regional centres. The shock of the new crisis, as well as creating serious short-term difficulties, quickly reawakened fears about the general long-term stability of the region and its reliability as a financial market.

The long-term impact on economic activity of the Iraq invasion of Kuwait remained unclear. The Bahraini government appeared to have a clear vision of the need to broaden the country's industrial base, albeit that its plans were always going to be very expensive. The crisis was inevitably going to knock some of the island's developments off course. But, ultimately, the official judgement in favour of diversification seems correct. It simply remains to be seen whether the viability of each individual project can be maintained.

What does seem clear is that the political map of the Gulf is destined for radical revision. And Bahrain, despite its small size and minimal ambitions, might come under pressure from its Saudi and Western allies to shoulder a significant share of any future security burden, which might include a new security structure and the stationing of significant foreign forces in the region for an extended period. The Bahraini government might decide this is a price worth paying. But it might also create new domestic tensions, particularly among radical elements and those sympathetic with Iran, which took a belligerent stand against suggestions of a large permanent foreign military presence in the Gulf.

1993/94

Border Problems – Budget Problems – Human Resources – Foreign Companies Law – New National Assembly Planned – Open Skies Policy – Plunging Aluminium Prices – Stock Market Expansion

Although Bahrain remains politically stable, it does have a border problem. Its dispute with Qatar over a clutch of islands, reefs and sandbanks which lie close to the Qatari peninsula will be heard in the International Court of Justice in February 1994. The area is potentially rich in both oil and gas and would certainly be an advantage to Bahrain. Budget problems have also cropped up in recent years but tourism and banking are still growth areas. New laws to encourage foreign investment have been enacted.

Budget
Although the budget deficit for 1992 was not as much as earlier estimated, the figure rose to US$190.3 million from US$59.6 million in 1991. The Ministry of Finance predicted a reduced deficit of US$167 million in 1993, due largely to a rise in oil income from a field lying between Bahrain and Saudi Arabia where production will increase from 70,000 barrels per day (bpd) to 100,000 barrels. At present the revenue from a 250,000bpd refinery, supplied mainly by Saudi Arabia, is the mainstay of the economy. Bahrain's trade deficit widened during 1992 as non-oil imports rose without a compensating increase in exports. The trade gap rose to US$724.8 million from US$600 million in 1991, a sharp contrast with the US$48.8 million surplus registered in 1990.

The deficit was partly covered by a net inflow of US$313.5 million in transfers and similar payments to yield a net balance of payments deficit of US$411.3 million. Overall exports declined to US$3.39 billion whilst imports rose to US$4.13 billion. The biggest factor in the jump in imports was a 21.7 per cent increase in imports of machinery and transport equipment, which covers not only construction and development requirements, but also the residents' healthy appetite for new cars.

Offshore banking units in Bahrain appear to have recovered from the doldrums of the 1990–91 Gulf crisis, with assets reaching US$69.8 billion in 1992 – a 30.7 per cent increase over the 1991 figure. The Bahrain Monetary Agency estimated that the aggregate budget for the offshore units in 1991 was US$53.4 billion. The island state of about half a million people has established itself since the oil boom years of the 1970s as an offshore banking centre for the Gulf region. More than 50 offshore units operate in Bahrain at present. Onshore, the island's 19 commercial banks increased their assets by 2.9 per cent in 1992 to US$7.18 billion.

In a sign of growing confidence, the National Bank of Bahrain reported a sharp increase in its net income for the first six months of 1993 compared with the same period in 1992. The new figures for 1993 showed a rise of US$4.7 million, from US$15.7 million to US$20.4 million. Bank officials claimed the increase was a result of strategic expansion plans both in the domestic and international markets. On the local scene, total loans, advances and overdrafts increased from BD153.7 million in June 1992 to BD183.6 million in June 1993, while customer deposits remained stable at BD446 million.

Introduction of its own portfolio management capability, whereby a sizeable proportion of the inter-bank assets are placed in short term floating securities of the highest credit standing, has resulted in the Bank's assets growing from BD653 million in June 1992 to BD758 million in June 1993. Having proved that they can manage their own funds successfully, the Bank's next step will be to offer its services to other clients.

New Foreign Companies Law

In a move to attract new business, the government of Bahrain was reported to have decided to permit foreign companies and individuals to register their offices without the need for their physical presence in the country. It is understood that those wishing to take advantage of the new law will be allowed to obtain their commercial registration certificate without being obliged to be domiciled in Bahrain.

The law will cover a wide spectrum of activities except banks, financial institutions, insurance companies and investment organisations for which the existing procedures, including approvals of the Bahrain Monetary Agency, will continue to apply.

The minimum capital outlay for registration of such companies will be BD2,000 with an annual fee of BD250. The new law will allow organisations to conduct their commercial activities in Bahrain without the need to establish an expensive office as well as incurring other expenses.

The government has made it clear that it is determined to increase the share of nationals in the work force and achieve self-sufficiency in human resources. Ministry officials have said that work permits for the employment of foreign nationals are no longer renewed as a matter of course. Applications are apparently critically scrutinised, and in the event of the availability of nationals with the required qualifications, the company concerned will be asked to appoint the latter. Just how far the measures will help the government achieve their objectives remains to be seen.

Plans to appoint a new consultative National Assembly were announced by Sheikh Isa bin Salman al-Khalifa in December 1992. This move was widely interpreted as a response to the recent international pressure for democracy in the region. However, the specifics of this reform have yet to be made clear. Political parties are illegal in Bahrain.

Tourism Potential

Seeking to widen its area of income, Bahrain is actively promoting tourism to the island. Results so far indicate that there is good potential. A large amount of funding has been set aside by the government to improve the existing beaches and to develop new points of interest. The Riffa Fort, a significant part of Bahrain's history, has undergone a major face-lift and renovation programme. Scuba diving and dhow boating trips are some of the other attractions.

In another move to attract tourists, the island is to have its own 18-hole golf course with a clubhouse and hotel. A new desalination plant will provide water for the greens and fairways as well as the surrounding tree plantations. The project, to be completed by 1996, will be done in three phases. Far Eastern tourists will be a major target of this development.

Bahrain International Airport has been undergoing expansion. Its handling capacity will be increased to ten million passengers a year by March 1994. The new facilities will be the culmination of a US$100 million project which is designed to take the airport into the twenty-first century. As well, in a bid to attract more airlines, the Directorate of Civil Aviation Affairs has implemented a more balanced open skies policy as well as restructuring the airport handling charges. This more aggressive marketing attitude has paid some dividends, with 18 new carriers beginning operations in the 18 months starting from January 1992. A satellite terminal to handle the expected increase in traffic is in the planning stages.

Gulf Air – based in Bahrain and owned by the governments of Oman, Qatar, Abu Dhabi and Bahrain – plans to go public by early 1995. In preparation for such a move the company has been strengthening its capital base, and has made provision to transfer all its profits for the next couple of years to its capital reserves. In line with the decision, US$16 million of the US$21 million profits from 1992 have been transferred to the company's capital reserves, making it a fully paid up company. Gulf Air's board are also seeking to increase the company's authorised capital from US$100 million to US$150 million in 1994.

Gulf Air has been undergoing an ambitious US$2.2 billion modernisation and fleet expansion programme. By the middle of 1993 the airline's fleet comprised

154   1993/94

of 24 Boeings, six Airbuses and eight Lockheed TriStars. A number of new destinations have been added to the airline's network including Jakarta, which
brought the total number of airports served by Gulf Air to 46. However, other
Gulf airlines such as Emirates and Oman Air have been given permission to fly
on the previously exclusive Gulf Air routes, which may cut into its profitability.

Aluminium Production Up

Following the latest US$1.45 billion expansion, Aluminium Bahrain (ALBA) is
now the biggest supplier of aluminium in the Gulf. With its new production
level of 460,000 tonnes per year, the company now boasts the world's biggest
smelter outside the Commonwealth of Independent States (CIS). Since com-
mencing production in 1971, ALBA's capacity has been increased three times
from the initial 120,000 tonnes per year to its present record level. In the first 12
weeks of 1993, total production output was 104,637 tonnes, almost 2,500 tonnes
above target. However, this latest increase in capacity comes at a time of plunging aluminium prices. In three years the price has fallen from around US$2,200 a
tonne to below US$1,100.

ALBA sells its product through the Bahrain Saudi Aluminium Marketing
Company, with around 100,000 tonnes being sold around the Gulf, mostly in
Bahrain, and the rest going to East Asia and Japan. Officials of the company say
that they are more concerned with production costs than demand and in this
area ALBA compares very favourably. Only time will tell whether this policy will
see the company through difficult times in view of the unfavourable pricing
structure. Setting price aside, the company has introduced new environmental
standards. For instance, raw materials can now be recycled back into the process, resulting in no bi-products and no waste.

The Bahrain Aluminium Extrusion Company (BALEXCO), which was set up
by the government to process aluminium billets from ALBA, plans to add a second press, thereby increasing its capacity by 5,000 tonnes. The company has
been producing around 5,000 to 6,000 tonnes a year, and in 1992 it had a record
year with a production total of 7,000 tonnes. At present the company suffers
from stiff competition from other Gulf states as well as from the Far East and
there have been calls to implement some form of import duty.

Stock Market

In June 1993 the Bahrain Stock Exchange celebrated its fourth anniversary with
hopes of absorbing the large liquidity due to a lack of major investment opportunities in the Gulf. The market, which is the second oldest in the Gulf after Kuwait, has witnessed a steady expansion since its launch on 17 June 1989. Officials predict an upturn in business with the opening of new outlets and the

easing of restrictions on shareholding by foreigners. It has been mooted that new laws may well be introduced allowing long term residents of the island to trade shares in Bahraini companies even if they are not citizens. Keen to expand its financial sector, Bahrain has been at the forefront of moves in the Gulf to open its doors to the outside world.

Foreigners from outside the Gulf can now trade shares in two Bahrain based banks, Arab Banking Corporation and Bahrain International Bank, but these institutions were required to win individual government approval. Bahrain set up its stock market to attract investment and reverse an outflow of funds after a decline in oil prices slashed their revenue to US$70 billion in 1992, from more than US$180 billion in 1981.

With Kuwait still trying to re-build its economy, Bahrain's trading floor is now the second busiest in the region after the Saudi Arabia market, where turnover exceeds US$2 billion a year. The turnover in Bahrain, where around 30 banks and companies trade their shares, surged to around US$164 million in 1992 from US$106 million in 1989. The number of shares jumped to 190 million from 61 million. In terms of capitalisation, the Bahraini market is currently the third biggest in the Gulf after Saudi Arabia and the UAE, standing at around US$4.17 billion at the end of 1992.

Fisheries

Infosamak, a project established in 1986 to foster the fisheries sector in the Arab world, received a new lease of life in the middle of 1993 with six countries agreeing to re-orient the project as a new organisation and provide financial and other resources. The new Bahrain-based entity will be called Centre for Marketing Information and Advisory Services for Fishery Products in the Arab World and will foster co-operation between Arab countries with the idea of improving the yield from the fisheries sector. The United Nations Food and Agricultural Organisation (FAO) for the Near East, which is based in Cairo, will play a supervisory and advisory role in the project. The six countries involved are Bahrain, Syria, Tunisia, Morocco, Mauritania, Yemen and Oman.

1995

Exports and Imports Gap – Hawar Islands Dispute – Oil Exploration Prevented – The Importance of ALBA – GCC Export Success – Banking Centre of the Gulf – Tourism a Billion Dollar Industry – Regional Headquarter Choice

As Bahrain's oil runs out, and oil income falls, the country is boosting its push for the diversification of the economy, and increasing its incentives for foreign investors. Bahrain's renaissance in the post-Gulf War (Kuwait) period may well prove to have received its biggest boost with new regulations allowing 100 per cent foreign ownership, a more favourable option for many international companies than, say, setting up in Dubai's Jebel Ali Free Zone.

Economy

The long-term trend for Bahrain is a widening gap between exports and imports, putting further pressure on the island to diversify its revenue sources. Bahrain's gross domestic product (GDP) reached US$4.2 billion in 1993, having seen growth of 4 per cent that year, and forecast to be sustained at 4 per cent in 1994. Annual inflation remained under 2 per cent.

Bahrain's government budget for 1994 is BD675 million, up from 1993's figure of BD463 million. The budget deficit is likely to rise to BD75 million during 1994 even though incomes are up and expenditure is being tightly controlled. Bahrain saw budget deficits through the 1980s, which were temporarily reversed in 1990 due to the anomalous effects of the Gulf War when a surplus of BD26 million was recorded.

Oil

Bahrain's oil reserves are estimated at between 70 million and 200 million barrels, and this is expected to be exhausted early in the next century. The government is continuing its oil exploration, although recent work offshore around the North Islands in 1992 was unsuccessful, while exploration of the more promising area near the Hawar Islands is prevented by its dispute with Qatar over the sovereignty of the islands.

Government income rose slightly as a result of increased oil output – up from 70,000 to 100,000 barrels per day (bpd) in 1993 – from the Abu Safah oilfield which is shared with Saudi Arabia – although not all the oil from this field comes to Bahrain. The Bahrain government is reported to be seeking to increase production from this field to 200,000bpd of heavy crude. Despite increased production, oil income was hit by low oil prices in 1993 and during 1994; the effect is significant as oil and gas revenues make up 63 per cent of government income (BD314 million out of BD498 million in 1992). Since 1975 oil's contribution to GDP has dropped from 36 per cent to 17 per cent, while banking and insurance has increased its contribution from 3 per cent to 12 per cent.

Bahrain is not a member of the Organisation of the Petroleum Exporting Countries (OPEC) and so is not faced with quotas, but it is a member of the Organisation of Arab Petroleum Exporting Countries (OAPEC). Also it is equally vulnerable to the lowering of world oil prices when OPEC members over-produce – and looks with trepidation to the re-introduction of Iraq's quotas on to the oil market.

Bahrain's one on-shore field, operated by the Bahrain National Oil Company, produces some 42,000bpd. It is combined with 220,000bpd of Arab Light crude bought from Saudi Arabia at preferential rates, and imported via a sub-sea pipe-line to be refined by the Bahrain Petroleum Company (BAPCO). Refined products comprise: gasoline 8.0 per cent, naphtha 14.00 per cent, kerosene 18 per cent, jet fuel 1.0 per cent, heavy distillates 3.0 per cent and LPG 0.3 per cent. Gasoline production is now increasing as a percentage. Modernisation of the BAPCO refinery is being carried out in a three year two-phase programme covering the building of a single modern primarily crude processing unit and the addition of a small methyl tertiary butyl ether (MBTE) plant; phase one is costing US$200 million and phase two will cost US$350 million.

Gas

Bahrain has some 7.0 trillion cu ft of natural gas, of which 6.1 trillion is non-associated natural gas located in the Khuff formation of the Arab Zones, and the remainder is in natural gas liquids below the Mauddud Formation. This is considered sufficient to last 20–25 years at current rates of extraction, but increased utilisation by industrial projects could up consumption by 50 per cent by the end of the decade. Some 256 billion cu ft of natural gas was produced in 1992, all of which was used domestically.

Natural gas is used in power generation (31 per cent), maintaining oilfield pressure (34 per cent) at the ALBA aluminium smelter (5 per cent), and for an LPG plant. Wet gas is processed by BANAGAS which has an intake capacity of 265 million cu ft per day. In 1992 its six compressor stations and two processing units produced 4.7 million barrels of LNG, 117,000 tonnes of propane, 109,000 tonnes of butane and 196,000 tonnes of naphtha with a value of BD24.4 million (US$64.7 million).

158   1995

Despite its dwindling reserves, Bahrain is expected to continue developing its downstream industries – with the option of buying in Saudi feedstock later if necessary – as its population growth demands continual industrial expansion. The US$450 million Gulf Petrochemical Industries Company (GPIC) plant processes Khuff gas into ammonia and methanol. GPIC plans to build a new US$140 million urea plant at the existing site during 1995 to produce some 1,750 tonnes per day of fertilisers.

Industry

Taking advantage of low energy costs on the island, the energy-intensive aluminium smelting industry performs well locally as an international player. Bahrain's biggest non-oil industry is its aluminium smelter, ALBA, which completed a major US$1.2 billion expansion in late 1993, that has also boosted downstream industry. The expansion included an 800MW combined cycle power plant increasing generating capacity to 1,340MW to bring aluminium production up 465,000 tonnes. As consumption averages 900MW, the plant provides excess power to the state power grid. The workforce, estimated at about 1,800 by mid-1980, is 85 per cent Bahraini. Downstream industries using the aluminium feedstock include the GARMCO aluminium rolling mill, Midal cable plant, BALEXCO extrusion plant, a small automotive wheel plant, and a fly mesh plant. ALBA plans a US$12 million 6,000 cubic metres per day reverse osmosis desalination plant, with surplus for sale to local industries,

As the government seeks to boost revenue and encourage the private sector, it has proposed two privately financed utilities, and sell offs have included Trafco (a general trading and food processing company) and a fisheries project, a dairy project and date project. Plans are for the government to reduce its shareholding in the National Bank of Bahrain; in 1993 that bank saw a net profit of BD16.3 million, an increase of 41 per cent over the previous year. Part privatisation of Bahrain Aluminium Extrusion Company (BALEXCO) is also on the cards. BALEXCO is to see its paid up capital rise by 50 per cent during 1994 to BD12 million, with more than half its shares privately held, and its extrusion capacity doubling by the end of 1994 with the introduction of a 5,000 tonne per year extrusion line. Within three years the State of Bahrain could liquidate its holding, and the introduction of a third line would triple early 1994 capacity. Additional activities to be introduced include scrap recycling, die making and broadening its product range.

The government-run Bahrain National Cold Storage and Warehousing Company (BANZ) has been privatised in a BD500,000 deal which included five trawlers, ice plant, maintenance workshop and deep freeze storage. Annual production is 6,000 tonnes which meets 35 per cent of domestic needs; the new

Bahrain Fishing Company aims to treble or quadruple its production for export, which may be aided with a BD500,000 government injection.

Other current industrial projects include a new US$13 million sulphur derivatives plant set up by the National Chemical Industries Corporation (NACIC) to produce 10,800 tonnes of sodium sulphate and 7,200 tonnes of sodium metabisulphite per year – due on stream by the end of 1994/early 1995. Future plans include the production of sodium bicarbonate and sodium thiosulphate. The 55 per cent shareholder United Gulf Industries Co (UGIC) plans to set up another four projects in 1994/95; two more speciality chemicals projects and two metals projects. In addition, the government has discussed privatising existing electricity transmission and generating capacity.

This could prove controversial as low rates are currently charged, and summer shortages of power and associated desalinated water supplies are common. Bahrain's water consumption is the world's highest per head, at some 60–70 million gallons per day. Of which 35–40 million gallons comes from non-replenishable ground water. The water table is dropping given the growing population and industrial usage, including construction. There are three desalination plants, but more are needed.

Agriculture

Urban development has reduced the limited agricultural land, and agriculture now contributes just one per cent to GDP, although the island is self-sufficient in eggs, poultry and fish, and exports dates. Traditional agriculture is also an inefficient use of groundwater, with unlimited extraction from bore-holes run along channels during the heat of the day – rather than night sprinkler systems to minimise evaporation.

Foreign Trade

Bahrain remains a trading island, even though its tariffs tend to be higher than most of its neighbours. And trade with Saudi Arabia has continued to boom since the completion of the King Fahd Causeway across to the Kingdom in the mid-1980s. According to the Central Statistics Organisation, in 1993 Bahrain saw the value of its non-oil exports rise 47 per cent to BD450.7 million, which helped reduce the trade deficit to BD494.9 million, from BD684.2 million in 1992. Imports dropped by 4.4 per cent in 1993, to BD954.3 million, of which imports from the Gulf Co-operation Council (GCC) countries dropped 3.3 per cent to BD90.6 million. Exports to the GCC countries, however, rose 36 per cent over 1992, with Saudi Arabia accounting for BD72 million, the United Arab Emirates (UAE) BD26 million, Kuwait BD16 million, Qatar BD9 million and Oman BD4.5 million.

Banking and Finance

Bahrain established itself as the banking centre of the Gulf in 1975 when it allowed the establishment of Offshore Banking Units (OBU's) and introduced a range of inducements which attracted six major international money broking firms. There are now almost 90 OBU's on the island with assets of some US$70 billion, as well as 50 representative offices and foreign exchange and money brokers. In addition, there are nearly 60 local and foreign exempt companies using Bahrain as a base for their activities and over 60 insurance companies.

The Bahrain Monetary Agency oversees the banking and financial sector, which still enjoys no taxes , requiring just a BD10,000 annual operation fee. The banking sector remains an important source of foreign revenues and a major employer on the island and Bahrain's financial sector has an average daily foreign exchange turnover of US$3 billion. There were 29 companies traded on the Bahrain Stock Exchange in 1993, with a total market capitalisation of BD2 million. This comprises five commercial banks, six investment banks, five insurance companies, seven service companies, three industrial companies and three hotel groups.

Probably the biggest recent boost in Bahrain's drive to attract foreign investment was the move in early 1994 when Bahrain introduced commercial legislation to allow registration of companies with 100 per cent foreign ownership – allowing them to operate within the domestic market and offshore, whilst at liberty to hold extra general meetings (EGMs) and annual general meetings (AGMs) outside Bahrain – unusual in the Gulf. A Marketing and Promotions Board has been set up to encourage inward investment, particularly for export-oriented industrial and service companies, citing other incentives such as no tax, subsidies for Bahraini staff, power, land, customs exemptions, export credits and tariff protection as well as duty-free facilities for transit and re-export goods.

Tourism

Tourism is now reported to be becoming the biggest single industry on the island, both in terms of profitability and of turnover according to Tariq Almoayed, Bahrain's Minister of Information. Yearly revenues from tourism have been put at more than US$1 billion. Some 500,000 visitors stayed in Bahrain's hotels during 1993, of which 75 per cent were Gulf nationals. More than 300,000 visitors a month cross the King Fahd Causeway from Saudi Arabia. Short stay local visitors form the majority of tourists, but business people, conference delegates and a few international travellers as well as stop-over visitors swell the numbers further. Long haul tourism is now being promoted. Visitor numbers are forecast to rise by some 8 per cent a year, and the average stay is expected to rise from 1.4 nights to 2.9 nights by 1996. The number of hotel rooms in classified hotels is due to increase from a current total of 5,600 rooms to 8,000 rooms by 1996. Current totals comprise 37 classified hotels and eight non-classified, with seven five-star hotels, three four stars, ten two star and four one star.

Transport

Bahrain International Airport handles some 19,000 flights a year, of which about 16 per cent are cargo flights, the remainder passengers – totalling around 3.5 million passengers. The airport saw an US$80 million renovation completed in 1991, boosting capacity to five million a year. In 1994 the second phase of the BD37.8 million expansion will be completed increasing the capacity to 10 million passengers. A new cargo terminal comprises 6,000 sq metres of covered warehousing, has extensive refrigeration and cold room facilities.

Regional carrier Gulf Air is headquartered in Bahrain, resulting in many benefits for the island. Gulf Air made BD million in 1993 and has far more local flights than any other airline in the region – serving 51 destinations and adding direct services to China, Moscow and New York in 1994. Consequently Bahrain has been selected by leading courier companies such as DHL, Worldwide Express and UPS as their regional base. DHL is building a US$9 million distribution centre at the airport.

Since the opening of the causeway to Saudi Arabia, some shippers unload in Mina Salman for trucking of goods to Saudi Arabia; the causeway has, however, killed dhow traffic from the island. Work on a new US$200 million super-port was scheduled to start in 1994, to cover a 640 hectare site south of Hidd, requiring extensive land reclamation. The integrated development will include the new port, duty free zone and industrial area.

Demand for ship repair operations at the Arab Shipbuilding and Repair Yard Company (ASRY) is forecast to rise in 1994. International and regional competition in this market remains fierce but the yard is flexible and able to take vessels up to 500,000dwt.

Outlook

Bahrain's oil wealth looks set to dwindle unless the Hawar islands dispute is settled with Qatar and new discoveries are made. This would totally transform Bahrain by allowing it to capitalise on its other advantages – a liberal, stable and educated society, excellent communications and transport infrastructure, proximity to Saudi Arabia, and pro-business government. Without oil Bahrain must continue to rapidly diversify its economy, increasing industrialisation and development of service industries, including high tech industries. To do this, the government is expected to continue providing generous incentives to foreign investors – and with 100 per cent ownership now allowed, Bahrain has tipped the balance in its favour as a site for regional headquarters.

While there are potential tensions with a minority in the Shi'a population, they have little support and the security services are able to contain the situation with ease. But if the economic situation were allowed to deteriorate, they could form the nucleus for dissent. For this reason, Saudi Arabia is likely to bail out Bahrain if it ever faces serious economic difficulties, as it has its own Shi'a minority and does not want trouble on its border. The success of Bahrain as a service centre for the Gulf appears to have alleviated this particular problem, and the future of Bahrain looks to be that of a middle income country trying to balance its imports and exports.

1996

Shi'a Protests – Sunni-Dominated Régime – GCC Support – Zubara – Development Schemes Delayed and Cancelled – Aluminium Production Cut – Stock Market Integration – Oil Reserves – Developing Downstream Industries

Sporadic anti-government protests and related violence which erupted in late-1994 and continued into the first part of 1995 has underscored the potential seriousness of Bahrain's recent economic difficulties. The problems posed by falling income from oil, a growing budget deficit and the resultant cuts in government grants and subsidies have meant that the authorities are less able to quell dissent through hand-outs as they have done in the past.

Dissent
Until recently, protest by some members of the local Shi'a community towards the ruling family was never allowed to get out of hand and had been dealt with efficiently by Bahrain's strict security services. The ruling al-Khalifa family are from the Sunni branch of Islam and the Shi'a community (which are in a majority in Bahrain) often complain that they are the victims of discrimination by the Sunni-dominated régime. This situation is epitomised by the higher unemployment rate suffered by Shi'as and by the fact that they are able to join the civil service but not the police or armed forces.

The current disturbances originated in November 1994 when joggers from a charity marathon were stoned by Shi'a villagers as the event wound its way through the outskirts of the capital. The police stepped in and made a number of arrests which sparked wider demonstrations. Many traditionalists dislike jogging's Western connotations – especially the fact that brief clothing is worn and that females participate in the sport.

Sheikh Ali Salman, a charismatic Shi'a cleric with Iranian contacts, not only objected to the arrests which followed the disturbances but combined his protest with calls for a return of Bahrain's parliament – this got him arrested in the first week of December 1993. (The authorities had dissolved parliament, which had a Shi'a majority, in 1975 after less than two years of existence.)

Salman's outspokenness further fanned the flames of dissent and resulted in his deportation, along with three other clerics. The demonstrations and arrests are giving dissenters what they lacked in the past – a forum to broadcast their

164   1996

convictions, a rallying point for their cause, and a reason to riot. Unrest continued in varying degrees in the first quarter of 1995 and was mainly centred around the capital. The death toll was up to 13 by mid-April – three police and ten civilians. Militants set fire to a petrol station, two power transformers and the offices of the Bahrain International Exhibition; six anti-government suspects allegedly admitted to carrying out these acts. In late March 1995 an Islamic bank situated in a Shi'a suburb was burned by protesters who reiterated the call for the release of prisoners. Amnesty International reported that over 700 arrests were made between December 1994 and April 1995. The Gulf Co-operation Council (GCC), of which Bahrain is a member, issued a statement on 19 April 1995 saying that it was fully in support of measures taken by Bahrain to quell dissent and restore order. Business activities, for the most part, have not suffered much as a result of the protests.

The government blames 'an external party organisation that is backed by an external power' for the recent unrest – a veiled reference to the exiled Islamic Front for the Liberation of Bahrain and to Iran. If the dissent becomes so fractious that it starts looking like Bahrain's rulers could be overthrown, the al-Khalifa family know that they can call on Saudi Arabia for economic and other assistance. Saudi Arabia has its own Shi'a minority concentrated in the east and does not want to encourage regional Shi'a-led destabilisation.

Hawar Dispute

Bahrain is in dispute with Qatar over the Hawar Islands and their reefs off the south coast of Bahrain. The region could have considerable oil deposits but the fact that the sovereignty question remains unresolved has prevented exploration of this area. Observers say that if this dispute is settled in Bahrain's favour it could revitalise the country's flagging oil industry.

Qatar has taken the Hawar dispute to the International Court of Justice (ICJ) in The Hague, an action which Bahrain disapproves of and has chosen to boycott. The Bahraini position is that the ICJ has no jurisdiction to hear a case brought unilaterally by Qatar. On 15 February 1995 the court ruled that it did indeed have jurisdiction to hear the dispute but Bahrain continued to assert that it would not accept any ICJ judgement. To add a new wrinkle to the dispute, Bahrain has now counter-claimed that Zubara, which is located on Qatar's west coast 105 kilometres north of Doha is rightfully Bahrain's. Zubara, the traditional home of Bahrain's ruling family, was lost to Qatar about a century ago.

Economy and Industry

The government has predicted that it will run-up budget deficits in 1995 as well as 1996, of US$324 million and US$302 million respectively, to be financed by treasury bills and government bonds. Oil revenues are expected to be some US$250 million less than in 1993/94. Non-oil revenues should reach US$578 million in 1995 according to the government; this would be an increase of 8 per cent over the previous year. Expenditure is to be cut by almost US$90 million in 1995 to US$1.7 billion where it will remain for the following year. Saudi Arabia and Kuwait contribute money to Bahrain through grants but this important source of government revenue has decreased substantially in the past two years because of financial restraints being experienced in the donor countries.

Bahrain's less-than-rosy financial picture has forced the government to delay and cancel some of its development schemes. However, in January 1995 it announced that a series of modest projects will be undertaken in the healthcare, textile, food and engineering sectors. The largest of these is the carbon black factory which will require an investment of between US$60 and US$70 million. The second largest, with a proposed capital investment of between US$7 and US$8 million, is a chocolate and speciality confectionery production line. Bahrain now has access to the European Union's (EU) equity investment funds for small and medium-sized industrial joint ventures and this will likely be utilised for a number of these new projects. The EU can fund up to 20 per cent of the equity for projects alongside local and European partners.

In March 1995 the government announced that it planned to build 20 new hotels to help meet expected future demand as tourism grows. At present Bahrain hosts some 1.7 million tourists each year but the government is keen to boost these figures to four million before the turn of the century. The new hotels will cost between US$6 million and US$30 million each.

Gulf Petrochemical Industries Company, whose profits came to BD126.4 million in 1994, plans to construct a 1,700 tonne per day urea plant; the contract to build the plant is expected to be signed in mid-1995 and will cost US$200 million. It is estimated to take just under two years to build.

Aluminium became very profitable for Bahrain in the past year as world prices rose substantially – this industry is now the country's biggest export earner. Aluminium Bahrain (ALBA) intends to increase the capacity of its third reduction line by 36,500 tonnes – bringing the company's total capacity to 496,500 tonnes.

The output for 1995 will be 460,000 tonnes, which it had sold by the end of the first quarter of 1993. Production in 1994 was cut by 10,000 tonnes to 450,000 tonnes in accordance with an understanding among international aluminium producers to trim back their output to shore up prices.

Bahrain Aluminium Extrusion Company (BALEXCO) has announced that it will have a third aluminium extrusion line built which would increase production to 21,000 tonnes of extruded products by 1996. The company's net profits were up 8 per cent in 1994, reaching BD2.17 million. Total sales were 7,661 tonnes in 1994, an increase of 8 per cent, which brought in BD10.7 million.

BATELCO, the Bahrain Telecommunications Company, saw its net profits rise to BD24.2 million in 1994 – 15 per cent more than in the previous year due to a good performance from its international telephone division.

Finance

The stock exchanges of Bahrain and Oman are being linked under an agreement reached on 15 March 1995 – the first arrangement of its kind in the Middle East. In April 1995 the initial step was taken towards integration when the shares of a Bahraini bank and an Omani company were listed on the bourses of both countries. Together the two exchanges have US$8.1 billion worth of capital.

Bahrain has 21 specialised and commercial banks. The country's largest commercial bank, National Bank of Bahrain, saw its profits fall by 24 per cent in 1994, to BD12.27 million. It blamed this performance on interest rate rises that increased the cost of funding its investment portfolio and on the failure of the bond market to recover after the February 1995 crash. The Bank of Bahrain and Kuwait also saw its profits fall in 1994 – to BD7.5 million from BD10 million in the previous year. The bank blames low oil and aluminium prices in the first quarter of 1994 and unfavourable interest rates for the poor showing. The Al-Ahli Commercial Bank had a solid growth year in 1994 when its profits rose by 30 per cent to BD4.73 million. And the Bahraini Saudi Bank posted a 6 per cent rise in profits, to BD2.8 million.

Energy and Transport

The government is continuing its oil exploration with its eye steadily on the clock. Bahrain's oil reserves will be exhausted early in the new millennium; they are estimated at anywhere between 70 million to 200 million barrels, with local consumption running at a quarter of output each year. Since 1975, oil's contribution to gross domestic product (GDP) has dropped from 36 per cent to 17 per cent, while banking and insurance has increased its contribution from 3 per cent to 12 per cent. Bahrain is not a member of the Organisation of the Petroleum Exporting Countries (OPEC) and so is not faced with quotas, but it is a member of the Organisation of Arab Petroleum Exporting Countries (OAPEC). It made a considerable fortune when oil prices soared in the 1970s but is equally vulnerable to the lowering of world oil prices when OPEC members over-produce as they have in the past few years.

Bahrain's one on-shore oil field, operated by the Bahrain National Oil Company, produces some 42,000 barrels per day (bpd). It is combined with

220,000bpd of Arab Light crude bought from Saudi Arabia at preferential rates, and imported via a sub-sea pipeline to be refined by the Bahrain Petroleum Company (BAPCO). Refined products comprise gasoline, naphtha, kerosene, diesel, fuel oil, jet fuel, asphalt, heavy distillates and liquid petroleum gas (LPG). BAPCO is planning to modernise its ageing refineries with a US$300 million expansion. This will involve upgrading petrol production by installing a single new crude unit; at present production is done through four units. Further modernisation is expected to go ahead once phase one is completed.

According to reliable estimates Bahrain had some 5.3 trillion cu ft of natural gas in reserve in 1994. This could last two decades at current rates of extraction, but increased utilisation by industrial projects could send consumption up 50 per cent by the turn of the century. The gas is used exclusively domestically, in power generation, maintaining oil field pressure, at the ALBA aluminium smelter, and for an LPG plant. Despite its dwindling reserves, Bahrain is expected to continue gas production and may have to resort to using Saudi feedstock.

Gulf Air made a profit of BD8 million in 1994 according to preliminary figures; this was a drop of 35 per cent from the previous year. The airline cancelled its order for six long-haul Boeing 777 aircraft originally ordered in November 1993 after taking a hard look at its future needs. The jets were to be delivered between 1998 and 2000 and would have cost up to US$1.7 billion. Increased competition in the region and a re-grouping after a period of rapid expansion were the main reasons behind the cancellation.

The country's Bahrain International Airport handled 3.3 million passengers in 1994, an increase of 9.7 per cent. Arrivals totalled almost 1.4 million passengers. There were 38,400 passenger flights which is an increase of 9.6 per cent from 1993's figure. The growing economic recovery in Europe, the increasing numbers of long-haul charters and the growth experienced by Gulf Air are all behind the increase in numbers.

1997

Unrest – Organised Protest – Executions – Urban Terrorism – Hawar Dispute – Development Loans – Islamic Banking – Development Projects – Gas Reserves

Bahrain continues to experience difficulties both in economic and political terms. The unrest which broke out in late 1994 is still continuing and although it is so far unlikely to act as more than a minor irritant to the economy, international political concern is mounting.

Politics

None the less, of late the unrest has been mounting in Bahrain. In the past, this situation was largely ascribed to economic schisms within the population. However, the character of the opposition movement is now changing, and taking on a religious nature. It is this fact which continues to worry foreign governments and businesses.

Bahrain was, until 1971, a British colony, and on independence adopted some of the characteristics of a Western democratic state. In 1975, however, the constitution was suspended and monarchical rule instigated by the ruling al-Khalifa family, who are members of the minority Sunni Muslim group in Bahrain rather than the majority Shi'a community. It is this aspect which now gives the unrest new force. The Shi'a Muslim community has for some time, experienced both considerable political and economic discrimination; they live predominantly in rural areas, suffer higher rates of unemployment and are barred from employment in the police or security services.

The unrest originally commenced when villagers stoned a group of joggers who were making their way through the village (jogging has certain Western associations), the police responded by arresting a number of people, and this sparked wider demonstrations.

Organised protest was initiated by several groups – certain sections of the middle class (some of whom are, rather embarrassingly, Sunni), rural Shi'a citizens and increasingly, women. Most prominent within the original protest movement was one woman, a professor of University of Bahrain and a member of a wealthy Sunni family. She had been joined by a number of prominent Shi'a and Sunni doctors, academics, lawyers and civil servants; many of these have now had to resign from their jobs. Increasingly it seems that women have been in the front line; using screaming tactics at the university (making lectures impossible), boycotting schools and stone throwing at members of the predominantly Pakistani security forces.

Some anti-government activities have gone further and there have been many reports of arson and some bombings, although the sporadic nature of such events suggests undirected anger, rather than a campaign. The response of the government has been repressive, featuring detentions, beatings and – according to Amnesty International – show trials. One such trial ended in March 1996 with the first execution in Bahrain for over 20 years.

Three other men were likewise sentenced to death in July for burning down a restaurant, and killing several migrant workers in the process. Due to international pressure the case was referred to the Appeal Court, which has however ruled that it has no jurisdiction over the State Security Court which issued the original sentences. The fate of the three men is now to be decided by the Emir personally. It looked likely, however, that he would not repeal the Security Court's decision. To do otherwise would put at considerable risk the international support the country requires to overcome its current financial and employment problems.

Although at one stage the government maintained that the unrest was organised by a previously unknown group called Hezbollah-Bahrain who received financial and military backing from Iran, this is no longer the case. Largely due to mediation by the Syrian foreign minister, Farouk al-Shara, both countries have now ceased their war of words, although relations are still tense. This has not, however, solved the problem of what is rapidly becoming urban terrorism. Nor is there an end in sight to the dispute with Qatar over the Hawar islands near Zubara.

Dispute with Qatar

Relations with Qatar have worsened over the last year with regard to the disputed Hawar Islands, controlled by Qatar since the 1930s. The Qatari government has apparently not abided by a 1990 agreement whereby no building work would be carried out on the islands, which are just off Bahrain's coast. Qatar has refused to accept either direct or mediated negotiation and referred the case to the International Court of Justice (ICJ) in The Hague.

The ICJ was expected to rule on the case by the end of 1996, but at the time of writing had not done so. In any case Bahrain has stated that it will refuse to accept the Court's judgement as it considers it has no jurisdiction in the matter. The government has stated that it would not be attending the December summit of the Gulf Co-operation Council (GCC) due to the fact that it is being held in Qatar.

Unemployment

One matter which the unrest has highlighted is the country's relatively high unemployment. Bahrainis are the most literate and highly educated citizens in the Gulf – if anything they are over-educated – and thus a considerable number of manual jobs are taken by guest workers. Officially unemployment is currently at 1.4 per cent, yet other estimates suggest that the true figure is between 15 and 30 per cent. The Labour and Social Affairs Minister, Abdel-Nabi al-Shoala, has recently accepted that there is a link between unemployment and the unrest, and has announced a series of measures to reduce unemployment.

One of the main problems is that a sizeable proportion of the workforce is comprised of foreign nationals, who have few rights and enjoy lower pay than their Bahraini counterparts. Within the public sector the number of Bahraini nationals accounts for 90 per cent, yet in the private sector by contrast they only constitute some 30 per cent. The latest economic development plan envisages raising the number of Bahraini nationals within the private sector by 5 per cent a year. It hopes to achieve this by making it more expensive to employ non-Bahrainis and establishing training facilities for nationals.

These measures are expensive; the Bahraini economy is not in a suitable state to bear this new burden. The government has thus obtained a number of development loans which it is hoped will see Bahrain through the political crisis. These loans have been sourced from the Islamic Development Bank (IDB), Saudi Arabia, Kuwait and the United Arab Emirates (UAE). In total the loans amount to US$83 million.

Economics and Banking

Bahrain's economy is one of the more diversified in the Gulf and the country places little reliance on oil as a means of generating foreign currency. It is, however, the least self-reliant of the five Gulf States and depends on cash support from Kuwait and Saudi Arabia, in addition to free imports of crude oil for its refinery at Sitra.

Prior to the discovery of oil in the region it was one of the richest emirates owing to the abundance of pearls, along with its rich agricultural heritage and geographical trade position. When oil was discovered in 1932 Bahrain was the first Gulf state to exploit the limited reserves that it possesses. Since then, of necessity, the economy has diversified and oil's significance has declined to the situation today where it contributes a mere 12 or 13 per cent of GDP. However some 60 per cent of government revenue is derived from oil production, and public consumption as a proportion of GDP is almost as high as private consumption.

Islamic economics is also an increasing force in the Bahraini equation, mirrored by the growth in banking facilities. Several conventional Western orientated banks have opened specific facilities to offer Islamic banking products in the region; Bahrain is the natural choice for such ventures. The US-based Citibank has opened the Citi Islamic Investment Bank as an offshore facility and others will undoubtedly follow. The Arab Banking Corporation and ABN-Amro have also announced their intention to establish similar subsidiaries.

Industry

Aluminium exports are now one of Bahrain's biggest earners as a result of increasing world prices. The whole manufacturing sector is dominated by Aluminium Bahrain (ALBA) which smelts alumina imported from Australia and is one of the largest smelters in the world with a current capacity of 460,000 tons per year. ALBA is reportedly planning further increases of 25,000 tons per year by 1997. One of the secondary industries based on the smelter, Gulf Aluminium Rolling Mill Company (GARMCO) has recently completed an expansion of capacity at its existing rolling mill to produce 120,000 tons per year of aluminium foil and is now building a new plant at Sitra which, when complete, should produce another 20,000 tons per year. GARMCO is a joint venture between the Gulf states and Iraq, although Bahrain is the largest shareholder with 25.5 per cent.

Iron and steel production is also to rise with Indian involvement in a third project. The Bahrain Ispat Company will operate, under control of the Indian Ispat Group, a new US$290 million plant which will have a capacity of 1.2 million tons per year of iron briquettes produced from iron pellets. The iron pelleting plant built by Arab Iron and Steel Company (AISCO) was rescued by Gulf Industrial Investment Company (GIIC) and production restarted in 1988. Recent demand from Iran, the biggest customer, has increased, and facilities have been modernised to cope with the extra production required. With the establishment of the briquette plant and its requirement for a substantial capacity of pellets, further expansion will be necessary.

Two other projects with Indian participation, are under way with Nippon Denro Ispat raising equity for a US$250 million project and Prakesh Industries building a new steel rolling mill. The latter is to be operated by a wholly-owned subsidiary, the Bahrain Iron and Steel Company, and is expected to have an initial capacity of 200,000 tons per year at a cost of US$25 million.

Energy Developments

One seemingly insuperable problem is the rapidly rising demand for electricity. At present Bahrain has a generating capacity of 1,652MW, but this includes the peak capacity available from ALBA and BAPCO which are not part of the national grid under the control of the Ministry of Electricity and Water. Domestic demand is forecast to continue rising from the current average of 1,000MW to 1,100MW in 1998 and 1,600MW in 2005. The government has been pursuing a number of development projects, the most recent involving British Gas. That project, a combined water and electricity project to generate some 500MW, appears to have been dropped. The government has now given up hope of private sector financing for generating and desalination facilities, and has now obtained development loans to part-finance a new project at Hidd, near the capital, Manama. This project will cost some US$360 million for the first phase and is expected to generate 260MW electricity and produce some 135 million litres per day of water.

The rest of the capital is provided for by the recent increase in oil prices and the extra barrels per day that Bahrain receives from the Abu Safah oilfield and which Bahrain used to share with Saudi Arabia. The field, although straddling the Saudi Arabia-Bahrain border, is operated by Saudi ARAMCO and Bahrain is hoping that its share will be increased again in future years, especially as domestic oil sources are expected to run dry early in the next century. Exploration has been continuing but so far with little success. It is in this context that the country has been steadily developing its gas reserves, as have of course, neighbouring states. Reserves are estimated at 263 billion cubic metres which should allow production to continue for between 40 and 60 years.

1998

Demand for Greater Representation – Consultative Council – Political Violence – Execution of Dissidents – Relations with Iran Improve, but not with Qatar – Stock Market Opens – Important Regional Centre for Islamic Banking – Surplus Trade Balance –Employment Opportunities

Improved economic performance in 1997 has lowered the intensity of political conflict in the tiny Gulf state of Bahrain. Sheikh Isa bin Sulman al-Khalifa's monarchist regime has refused to reinstate the National Assembly which was dissolved 1975. Since 1994, the government has been under pressure to come up with a solution as political violence has dented Bahrain's international image. Offers to expand the mandate of the current Consultative Council by including debate on social, cultural and health matters and increasing its membership from 30 to 40 have been dismissed by opponents for falling far short of their demands.

This demand for greater representation is fuelled by two factors. First, the disillusion of the unemployed (estimated to be at least 15 per cent, although official figures are 1.36 per cent) and second, by religious tendencies within the political structure, whereby the ruling family comprises minority Sunni Muslims while the majority of Bahraini nationals are Shi'a Muslims. The Shi'as feel excluded from power and exploited by the Sunnis. This situation has been compounded by alleged foreign support from Shi'a dominant Iran.

The conflict has manifested itself in a number of ways. Over the last three years there have been incendiary attacks on financial and tourist targets in the capital, Manama, and rioting in the villages on a weekly basis. The opposition has also organised miniature strikes and boycotts of companies linked with the ruling family. However, the intensity and frequency of these events had tailed off by the end of 1997 as strong oil revenues and government expenditure created more economic opportunities for the local population.

The government continues to maintain its authority through the judiciary. Suspects linked with the opposition movement are tried in the State Security Court, with no right of appeal. Various governments and international organisations have expressed concern over the court's procedures which include the use of written confessions extracted under interrogation.

Over 140 people have been tried by the court since the violence escalated at the start of 1996 and the Red Cross estimates that there are over 1,400 political prisoners in Bahrain. Public outrage at the public execution of dissidents which took place in 1996 has been compounded by the death through ill health in jail of the opposition leader Abdel-Amir al-Jamri in July 1997. The judiciary now favours the use of long sentences in preference to capital punishment. In August 1997, eight activists were tried in absentia and sentenced to between five and 15 years' imprisonment.

According to anecdotal evidence, on most issues the government is traditionally divided between Sheikh Isa's brother, the prime minister, Sheikh Khalifa bin Salman al-Khalifa, and his son, the Crown Prince Hamed bin Isa bin Salman al-Khalifa. The latter is known for adopting a more hawkish approach to problem solving. Even so, on the question of containing the unrest, there is a high degree of uniformity between the two camps, suggesting that there is little opportunity for negotiations with the opposition. According to many Bahrainis the Emir himself remains aloof from the unrest.

Foreign Relations

Bahrain has received a mixed reaction to its troubles from fellow Gulf Co-operation Council (GCC) members. Faced with its own internal unrest, Saudi Arabia has become increasingly concerned that any concessions by the Bahrain government will encourage the Shi'a inhabitants of Saudi Arabia's oil-rich Eastern Province to rebel. Consequently, Saudi Arabia continues to encourage the crackdown, going as far as to allow its own National Guard to play a major role in quelling the disturbances.

However, relations with Qatar have soured further as a result of the unrest. Relations between the two states have been strained since 1991 when a dispute erupted between the two countries over ownership of the Hawar Islands off the west coast of Qatar. Both have since bowed to Saudi pressure to resolve the issue. But relations again deteriorated over Bahrain's support for the deposed Emir of Qatar, Sheikh Khalifa bin Hamad al-Thani. In retaliation, Qatar broadcast an interview with Bahrain's opposition leaders that could be heard in Bahrain. With the new Emir of Qatar determined to carve his own path in domestic politics by opening up the local political system, relations between the two countries are likely to remain tense.

Bahrain's relationship with Iran improved significantly in November 1997 when Manama and Tehran agreed to exchange ambassadors. Considering the diplomatic small-fire between the two countries over Iran's alleged support of terrorists, this is a significant step and should be seen as part of a closer rapprochement of Arab states in the latter half of 1997. In June 1996, Bahrain had accused Iran of plotting with the military wing of Hezbollah-Bahrain, the terrorist group, to forcibly oust their government. This rapprochement is likely to continue in 1998 as Bahrain's foreign policy remains set firm on establishing tighter unity between GCC members, as a counter to emerging trade blocs like the European Union (EU) and the North American Free Trade Area (NAFTA).

The Economy

After sluggish performance in 1996, the government attempted to kick-start the economy and dampen current unrest by spending more in 1997. Increased revenue enabled the government to boost expenditure on wages and allowances, which had been frozen for several years, and allow for increased employment opportunities in the public sector. Capital expenditure – which had borne the brunt of the government's cuts in previous years – was expected to rise even more sharply.

The government announced plans in 1997 to invest US$2.8 billion in public sector projects over the next three years – specifically in industry and infrastructure, including the long-awaited power and water desalination plant at Hidd. The government has also indicated that it plans to go ahead with a port and industrial free zone at Hidd which could include a new causeway linking the port to the mainland.

Increased government spending comes on the back of boosted revenues arising from higher than expected oil revenues and Saudi Arabia's decision in 1996 to concede its share of the output from the Abu Safah oilfield, which the two countries used to share. The government received additional loans from a number of Gulf States, including Saudi Arabia, Kuwait and Abu Dhabi, provided on favourable terms to reflect political support for the Gulf State. An Emiri decree has also extended the state's borrowing limit by BD300 million to BD600 million.

Bahrain is attempting to broaden its financial sector by developing international capital markets, Islamic banking and fund management. As a result, the government has introduced a number of measures such as the opening of the stock market to attract greater activity. In this, they have been helped by the Bahrain Monetary Agency's impressive track record in ensuring a well-regulated banking sector.

The sector has been described by the American credit ratings agency, Moody's, as 'having the capacity to remain among the most forward-looking central banks in the Gulf'. As a result, Bahrain has developed into an important regional centre for Islamic banking, with Citibank opening its Islamic subsidiary in Manama, and the Bahrain Islamic Bank experiencing a positive response to a private equity placement, aimed at increasing paid in capital from US$15 million to US$50 million. Despite this, it faces a stiff challenge from Dubai as the regional financial centre.

176   1998

Political uncertainty continues to hang over the sector, and other problems persist such as the high level of non-performing loans. Assets in offshore banking units have also continued their steady slide downwards, begun in 1996.

Industry and Tourism

Aluminium Bahrain BSC (ALBA) completed its expansion plans in 1997 to become the world's largest smelter as well as one of the lowest-cost producers. Aluminium currently accounts for approximately 14 per cent of Bahrain exports. The expansion has increased production to 500,000 tonnes per year.

The government plans to develop tourism, again as a means of achieving a diversified economy and creating employment opportunities. However, the sector has been badly affected by political uncertainty, with hotels reporting sharply reduced occupancy rates. While joint public and private tourism projects will go ahead in the short-term, the industry will be sensitive to the possibility of further political unrest, especially if opposition groups resume targeting luxury hotels in the capital, Manama.

Trade

For the second year running Bahrain produced a surplus trade balance which increased from US$442.1 million in 1995 to US$569.7 million in 1996 due to stronger oil exports. According to official figures, non-oil export revenues fell by 13 per cent (BD543 million compared to BD624 million in 1995) while oil export revenues rose 22 per cent to BD1,187 million compared to BD923 million in 1995 due to higher prices and the transfer of Saudi output from the Abu Safah oilfield to Bahrain. Non-oil import revenues fell by 3 per cent to BD868 million (BD897 million in 1995) while oil imports grew by 25 per cent to BD671 million from BD500 million in 1995. The increase in oil imports was to supply Bahrain's refineries. Official figures for the first three quarters of 1997 suggest that oil revenues were significantly lower than in 1996. By the end of the third quarter of 1997, oil export revenues totalled BD757.9 million as compared to BD851.5 million for the same period in 1996. Although oil prices have remained high (averaging US$19.60 per barrel) in 1997, prices have declined slightly from the US$20.60 average in 1996 (prices reached a high of US$22.00 per barrel). As Bahrain's main export markets are Japan, South Korea and Taiwan, exports are likely to be affected in 1998 as these nations struggle to recover from the financial crisis they endured at the end of 1997.

Employment

Bahrain's political situation has made the provision of employment opportunities a prime concern for the government over the last two years.

Unemployment continues to be highest among young Shi'a Bahrainis, based outside the capital where most of the demonstrations have taken place. Public spending increases, which began in 1996 and continued in 1997, are providing employment opportunities, particularly in the construction industry.

The government has followed a policy of 'Bahraini-isation' to dissuade the private sector from employing expatriate labour. The Ministry of Labour and Social Affairs has increased the cost of issuing and renewing work permits and set up an amnesty, which ended in November 1997, allowing illegal immigrants to formally register or leave. The government has also restricted or barred entry for certain job categories to foreigners. Parastatals are giving preference for contracts to companies employing the highest number of Bahrainis. As a way of deflecting criticisms that Bahrainis do not have sufficient training, a job centre has been established and training programmes set up.

Privatisation

Privatisation has been limited because of fears that restructuring would involve job losses and provoke further political unrest. This has scuppered government plans to solicit large amounts of private sector and foreign investment through the divestment of public companies. However, foreign investment rules have been liberalised, opening Bahrain to fully foreign-owned companies for the first time and including the listing of foreign companies and corporate bonds, as well as the introduction of a new auditing law.

Outlook

Bahrain's political and economic stability is primarily due to the rise in oil prices in 1997. Expectations that prices will remain above US$18.50 per barrel for 1998 are unrealistic as economic and financial turmoil in Asia reduces global demand for oil. As Bahrain's main export markets are Asian, export levels are likely to fall further in 1998. The government may be able to engineer growth in the short-term through its expenditure plans, but falling oil prices will have a significant impact on its ability to stimulate economic growth through investment.

1999

Shi'a Demands – Human Rights Abuses – Unemployment – Hard Line Policy
– Utilities Problems – Local Loans to Government – Offshore Exploration

With only limited oil reserves, Bahrain has long been regarded as the poor relation of the Gulf states. Ironically, this has saved the tiny emirate from the dramatic collapse in revenue experienced by its neighbours in 1998. Nonetheless,
Bahrain has not completely escaped the financial constraints imposed on the
region by falling oil prices.

Reduced Tension

The collapse in the price of crude could not have come at a worse time for the
Emir, Sheikh Isa bin Salman bin Hamad al-Khalifa who, since 1997, has been determined to spend his way out of Bahrain's political unrest. Demands, largely
by the Shi'a majority, for the reinstatement of the National Assembly dissolved
in 1975, have continued, with the government's opponents unwilling to accept
the government appointed Consultative Council.

Even so, throughout 1998, opposition to the government shifted into a lower
gear. While the Emir abandoned earlier attempts to reach a compromise with
his opponents, his government did respond to concerns expressed by numerous international organisations over widespread human rights abuses. As a result, 1998 saw a significant reduction in the number of political detainees dying
in Bahrain's prisons. The lack of Shi'a martyrs meant fewer opportunities for
the mass rallies and rioting in the villages which so characterised the unrest in
1997. Instead, violence is now largely limited to attacks on the Asian community, whom many Shi'a hold responsible for their own unemployment. The government is sensitive to such accusations and is attempting to cutback on the
hiring of foreigners, who are regarded by local employers as better trained and
less expensive than locals.

The combination of a young population facing a slack labour market (unemployment is estimated to be as high as 25 per cent among the Shi'a) and limited
oil revenues to bankroll public sector jobs means that tackling unemployment
continues to be a prime concern for the government. As in previous years, the
bulk of government revenue in 1998 was given over to spending on wages and
allowances. The government continued its training programmes and launched
a campaign aimed at persuading older public servants to take early retirement.

However, a psychological blow was dealt to the Shi'a opposition movement by the Emir's success in improving relations with its Shi'a neighbour, Iran. Prior to 1998, Bahrain had accused Iran of sponsoring a number of alleged coup attempts by the opposition. Although Iran provided little practical support to the opposition, the restoration of diplomatic relations with Bahrain deprived the opposition of a significant source of moral support. Throughout 1998, Bahrain's relations with fellow members of the Gulf Co-operation Council (GCC) also remained warm. Saudi Arabia in particular continued to encourage the hard line policy followed by the Emir towards the Shi'a, determined to prevent any spill over from Bahrain's troubles to its own Shi'a population in the oil-rich Eastern Province. But practical support by the other Gulf states in the form of soft loans and direct aid was limited by their own loss of revenues. The one problem in relations with other GCC members was with Qatar, which remained locked in a bitter dispute with Bahrain over ownership of the disputed Hawar Islands off the west coast of Qatar. Their relationship worsened in 1998 due to Bahrain's plans to build a causeway from the Hawar Islands to the main Bahrain Island.

Financing Gap

With over 50 per cent of government income derived from oil, the fall in oil prices has hit government revenue hard. In November 1997, Brent crude slipped from over US$19 per barrel before plummeting to US$12 per barrel over the course of 1998. As a result, the government announced that the 1998 budget deficit would reach BD100 million (US$266 million), an increase of 35 per cent on the 1997 deficit. However, political sensitivities continued to prevent the government from introducing revenue raising measures such as boosting domestic levels of taxation or services charges. In 1998, both taxation and services charges accounted for a paltry 15 per cent respectively of total revenue.

As a result, despite massive shortages in utilities such as power, the government remained loathe to raise prices to reflect costs. Instead the government tried to ring-fence charges in order to limit them to the expatriate workforce. For example, while rising health costs forced the government to consider measures such as mandatory health insurance, this was to apply to foreign workers only. In addition, fear that privatisation would prompt restructuring and job losses, so provoking further political unrest, meant that only modest sales of state-owned assets took place during 1998.

Instead, the government looked once again to Arab countries to provide grants and direct aid to help plug the fiscal gap. But borrowing from Gulf neighbours has been limited due to their own financial constraints, leaving the budget to be primarily funded through an increase in domestic borrowing. Local commercial bank loans to the government rose dramatically throughout 1998 and, for the first time, bonds were issued to the public. But however pain-free in the short-term, resorting to government borrowing will put a burden on future expenditure and on future generations of Bahrainis. For the meantime, interest payments on government debt remain comparatively low, a relief for the government in view of its limited revenues for current expenditure.

As usual, the lion's share of expenditure – almost 80 per cent – was allocated to current expenditure. Political considerations precluded a reduction in spending, although financial constraints limited the increase to BD572 million from BD554 million in 1997. On capital expenditure, the government's ability to cut costs was hampered by plans to invest BD900 million (US$2.4 billion) in public sector projects over the 1998–2002 period. This got off to a modest start with BD157.500 allocated under the 1998 budget. Nonetheless, the government warned that non-essential projects would not be undertaken, and there were signs that the much-vaunted plans to build a port and industrial free zone at Hidd, as well as a causeway linking the port to the mainland, would also be delayed.

Economy

As the major source of government revenue, oil continues to be the driving force of the economy. The fall in oil prices meant that the non-oil industry, primarily manufacturing, trade, the financial sector and the leisure industry which had recorded steady growth in 1997, all contracted in 1997. Consumer confidence was further undermined by high consumer interest rates of around 12 per cent. On the plus side, price inflation was curtailed by the weak economy and high interest rates. The government's increased domestic borrowing also served to reduce money supply and relieve inflationary pressures.

There was an increase in private sector activity in 1988, although much of this was in the oil sector. US major Chevron carried out offshore explorations, the first of its kind for over a decade, while Jeddah-based refining and marketing company Petroma and Hutchinson of the US also announced plans to build a US$5 billion oil refinery. This is due to come on stream in 2000, and will produce middle distillates to meet an expected European shortage of jet fuel.

There were further signs in 1998 that Bahrain is starting to realise its full potential as a financial centre, despite the strong regional competition from Dubai. Market capitalisation of the local stock exchange increased by over 60 per cent throughout the course of the year. Market sentiment was also bullish with the 37-index ending the year on a high, second only to the United Arab Emirates (UAE).

Confidence in the local banking sector has also been boosted by Bahrain's well-regulated environment. However, US credit rating agency Moody's warned that banking profits in 1998 are likely to have been undermined by the fall in oil revenues. Despite the premium rates local banks charge for personal loans, these traditionally account for the largest proportion of banking activity. But the downturn in consumer confidence recorded in 1998 is expected to have undermined the asset quality of loans. In the past, defaults have hit banks' operating profits, with local banks traditionally having less success in recovering their loans than their Western counterparts.

Despite such activity in the private sector, the perennial complaint that Bahrain – along with most other Gulf States – has failed to create a self-sustaining private sector still holds true. Only two locally owned companies made it into the 1998 top 50 Middle East companies by market capitalisation, the Arab Banking Corporation (ABC) and investment bank INVESTCORP. However the ABC is an offshore bank, and INVESTCORP holds all of its assets outside of Bahrain. And despite the government's rhetorical commitment to diversifying the economy away from the oil and banking sectors, there are no Bahrain-owned manufacturing companies in the top 50. In fact, the state continues to dominate the manufacturing sector, largely through its ownership of the Aluminium Bahrain smelter.

The fall in oil values was also felt in the external accounts. For the first time in four years, the trade balance was pushed into the red, despite a fall in Bahrain's traditionally high import bill. In the first quarter of 1998, the trade deficit was BD3.9 million reversing a surplus of BD44.2 million recorded in the previous quarter. By mid-1998 the trade balance levelled at BD4 million. Although low oil values will continue to undermine the trade balance, Bahrain is not as dependent on Asian countries for export markets as many Gulf states and so has not been as hard hit by the financial crisis there.

The Future

These are difficult times for Bahrain. On the one hand, the unrest has quietened down and, because of its limited oil revenues, it has not been hit as hard as other Gulf states by the fall in the price of oil. However the economy will continue to slow, hindered by low oil prices – Standard & Poor's predict oil prices remaining in the vicinity of US$13–15 per barrel.

In an environment of low oil prices, Bahrain needs successfully to pursue a policy of increased private sector activity if it is to remain one of the region's upper-middle-income countries. Although the government has traditionally been wary of ending subsidies and increasing prices, funding constraints could force it to consider seriously running utilities on a commercial basis. With much Asian investment being abandoned due to that region's financial crisis, the amount available worldwide for direct foreign investment has shrunk. The government can consequently ill afford the continuation of even low-level tension. Nor can it afford to maintain its own ambivalence towards private sector investment in state assets or services. There is no doubt that many in the government hope that oil prices will soon return to their pre-1998 highs, allowing Bahrain immediately to forgo all necessary reforms. But it seems that in the short- to medium-term at least, their dreams are likely to be disappointed.

2000

Improved Prospects – Political Reform Falters – Policy Changes – Worsening Living Standards – Ruling Family Divisions – Oil Revenues Climb – Tight Monetary Policies – Political Unrest Vulnerability

With oil prices buoyant it was almost inevitable that the small island state of Bahrain would see a return to growth in 1998. An improved political atmosphere is the result of the improved prospects for political reform, with the young Emir, Sheikh Hamad bin Isa al-Khalifa, eager to play a more active role in the political process, despite opposition from his influential uncle, the current prime minister, Sheikh Khalifa bin Salman al-Khalifa.

Superficial Reform

However, the pace of political reform has faltered despite the early promise shown by the new Emir, Sheikh Hamad. This development has disappointed many but surprised few, given the country's seemingly engrained legacy of political and social unrest. The major source of instability stems from the long-standing tension between the poorer Shi'a Muslim community (estimated at 55 per cent of the population) and the ruling, but minority, Sunnis. On succeeding his late father, Sheikh Isa bin Salman bin Hamad al-Khalifa, who died in March 1999, Sheikh Hamad sought to establish himself as a reformer. Key to this was bringing an end to the country's political troubles.

An important first step was the release of 300 members of the Shi'a community who had been detained during the political unrest of 1996–97. The Emir released Sheikh Abdul-Amir al-Jamri, a prominent Shi'a cleric, who had been sentenced to 10 years in jail and ordered to pay a fine of US$15 million after a conviction for spying and provoking unrest. In a major policy change, the government also announced its intention to recruit more Shi'a nationals into the defence force. In the past, the government has filled senior posts with Pakistani and Indian nationals, suspicious of links between the Shi'a community and the state of Iran.

In the view of many local observers, however striking these moves may be, they are largely superficial. The Emir has done little to tackle the chronic unemployment and worsening living standards that are particularly felt by the Shi'a community. Although a visible easing in social tensions has been apparent, without improved employment prospects further unrest is inevitable. With

© KONINKLIJKE BRILL NV, LEIDEN, 2023 | DOI:10.1163/9789004686335_022

power concentrated in the hands of leading Sunni families, the Shi'a majority have few alternative avenues of protest.

None the less, more ambitious reforms are unlikely, as the Emir seeks to strengthen his political power base and to gain leverage over the influential prime minister, Sheikh Khalifa bin Salman al-Khalifa, who is considered a hawk on questions of reform. The death of the late Emir triggered a considerable degree of speculation that Prime Minister Khalifa would go so far as to contest the succession. In the end this did not happen, but his influence over government policy remains considerable. This was made patently clear following the announcement of a 'new' cabinet, three months after Sheikh Hamad's succession; it included no more than three new faces.

The reform process is expected to suffer as the Emir and the Prime Minister jockey for political influence. The Emir has proposed an expanded role and higher profile for the country's sole consultative body, the Majlis al-Shura. Hedging his bets, he also stated that the proposed change would need to be 'appropriate' for Bahrain, and it is thus likely to fall well short of representing any serious degree of democratic reform. Crucially, it is unlikely to give a true voice to the opposition movements active both inside and outside the Kingdom. In this respect, a cautious proposal mooting the promise of local elections along the lines of the Qatari municipal elections that took place in 1999 holds greater promise, although when these elections might take place remains unclear.

Economic Reform

Divisions within the ruling family have not prevented the Emir from making substantive changes to economic policy in a bid to attract foreign investment and remove barriers to business. Notably, a decision was made to allow Gulf Co-operation Council (GCC) nationals to enjoy 100 per cent ownership of companies listed on the Bahrain Stock Exchange (BSE). Perhaps more significant, however, was the ground-breaking provision made for non-GCC nationals to own up to 49 per cent of such companies.

In the past, Bahrain has fiercely resisted anything resembling what it perceived to be foreign intervention in the domestic economy. The irony here is that Bahrain remains heavily dependent on foreign companies for the efficient operation of its oil exploration, production and refining activities. In this respect, it differs little from its neighbours. So it is that moves to invite greater foreign participation in the country's highly protected oil sector were bolstered by an agreement reached with the US company Texaco (Chevron) in August 1999. This is intended to boost oil exploration in Bahrain.

It is only the second decision of its type to be reached since an agreement with Chevron in February 1998. Chevron (formerly called Texaco) was one of the Seven Sister oil companies which dominated the global petroleum industry from the mid-1940s until as recently as the mid-1970s.

Fiscal Adjustment

The government's financial position is prone to changes in its oil fortunes. The protracted slump in oil prices in 1998 led the government to calculate its 1999 budget on a conservative price of US$12 per barrel. However, oil prices surged following the decision of the Organisation of the Petroleum Exporting Countries (OPEC) agreement to cap production in March 1999. Higher oil income contributed to a narrowing of Bahrain's fiscal deficit from initial estimates of BD160 million to some BD80 million, equivalent to 4.2 per cent of GDP.

The improved revenue outlook is certainly welcome, given that the government has managed to maintain expenditure throughout the oil price slump. This policy led to a dramatic widening in the fiscal deficit and a sharp rise in the public sector borrowing requirement. Indeed, in itself the composition of Bahrain's government spending remains a source of concern. The political imperative to maintain recurrent expenditure even during a time of low oil income inevitably means that capital expenditure must be cut. In turn, this has negative repercussions for sustainable growth.

Nevertheless, fiscal consolidation appears not to be a priority for the government. There were no significant announcements in 1999 that were aimed at either broadening the revenue base or cutting back on expenditures. Indeed, in announcing a reduction in tariffs on consumer goods and foodstuffs in late December 1999, the government failed to explain where the lost revenue would be made up. Moreover, there is little scope for introducing new taxes or service charges, given the enduring potential for social unrest.

A Change in Oil Fortunes

As is the case with most Gulf States, the price of oil is the main determinant of economic growth in Bahrain. Despite efforts at diversification, the contribution of the commodity to gross domestic product (GDP) remains significant, at 15 per cent. Although this is well below that of other GCC states, oil accounts for some 70 per cent of government revenues. In Bahrain, the level of government spending plays a crucial role in determining growth. One way or another, the private sector is largely reliant on contracting or supplying to state-owned enterprises. A rise in oil revenues, therefore, is transmitted through to the private sector via an expansion in government spending.

The benefit of the steep climb in oil revenues was not expected to be felt until early 2000. Despite this, weak private consumption trends were marginally reversed as a result of improved confidence in growth prospects. In addition, the decision to reduce tariffs on most consumer goods and foodstuffs in late 1999 is expected to provide a temporary stimulus to consumption. In the absence of an income or sales tax, disposable income in Bahrain is relatively high, a situation which further underpins positive consumption trends.

Elsewhere, a combination of weak consumer demand, price controls, and numerous state subsidies served to suppress inflationary pressures throughout 1999. The effect of higher oil prices on inflation is not expected to feed through to the real economy until mid-2000. The threat of imported inflation is low, with the dinar fixed to the US dollar. Moreover, the new governor of the Bahrain Monetary Agency is expected to continue to pursue a tight monetary policy, further curbing inflationary pressures. Defence of the pegged rate of BD0.376 per US$ against downward speculatory pressure, in conjunction with the public sector's heavy financing requirements, ensured that interest rates remained high throughout 1999. These contributed to the slowdown in private sector investment during the year.

External Balance

The economic structure of the Kingdom's trade profile remains heavily biased towards oil exports and therefore subject to fluctuations in world oil prices. The trade surplus in 1999 was estimated at some 5.1 per cent of GDP, well below surpluses of around 25 per cent of GDP recorded between 1995 and 1997.

Imports continue to undermine the trade balance, being equivalent to 68 per cent of GDP – Bahrain imports significant quantities of oil from Saudi Arabia for its refineries. Moreover, the country is compelled to import the majority of its consumer goods due to the small size of the domestic manufacturing sector. Over the course of 1999, weak consumer demand resulted in a smaller import bill. However, this did not offset the negative effect of low oil export revenues earlier in the year.

Largely the result of transfers, in the form of remittances from expatriates working in Bahrain, the current account deficit stood at an estimated 7.2 per cent of GDP in 1999. This was a significant improvement on the 16.8 per cent deficit in 1998.

Financing the current account deficit presents few problems, as long as Saudi Arabia and Kuwait are willing to provide loans on concessional terms. Moreover, a steep rise in oil prices typically narrows the deficit.

Although the fall in oil prices was rumoured to have resulted in speculatory pressure on the dinar, the pressure to devalue can be held in check so long as the bulk of exports are denominated in US dollars – devaluation would not add to export price competitiveness. Moreover, the IMF's revision of Bahrain's balance of payments merely highlighted the importance of capital flows to the overall external balance. Maintaining market confidence in the pegged rate was crucial to resisting speculatory outflows of capital over the course of 1999.

Oil Initiatives

At the end of the year, in December 1999, the Bahrain Government formed the Bahrain Petroleum Company, (BAPCO), by merging the Bahrain National Oil Company, which was the national oil exploration and production company, and the Bahrain Petroleum Company (formed by Standard Oil Company of California in 1929 and confusingly also often known as BAPCO). The 'new' BAPCO is wholly owned by the Government, and the company is continuing with the upgrade of its 250,000bpd capacity refinery at Sitra. One other project was the reduction of the sulphur content of the diesel fuel produced from a range of 0.75 per cent to 1 per cent, down to 0.05 per cent. The refinery modernisation project also included an in-line blending project, an unleaded gasoline project, a new kerosene plant, and instrumentation rehabilitation. Chevron (United States) continues to evaluate offshore blocks 1, 2, and 3. Texaco, also of the United States (and now owned by Chevron) reinitiated petroleum exploration activities in late 1999. Crude oil reserves are officially reported to be 210 million barrels, and natural gas reserves are estimated to be 122 billion cubic metres.

Outlook

GDP growth in 2000 is forecast at 2.8 per cent, following a 1.0 per cent contraction in 1999. As the Emir pursues more ambitious economic reforms, a marginal rise in foreign capital inflows should boost investment in the non-oil sectors, fostering private sector activity. At the same time, as the region benefits from rising oil income, growth in the financial and tourism sectors should accelerate. On the downside, Bahrain will remain vulnerable to political unrest – the Emir has not yet addressed the root causes of social tension: chronic unemployment and falling living standards. Moreover, substantive reform will be deferred so long as the new Emir finds it necessary to compete for political influence with the current Prime Minister.

Risk assessment

Economic	Improving
Political	Improving
Regional Stability	Satisfactory
Stock Market	Poor

2001–02

New Emir – Political System Liberalisation – National Assembly – Respect for Human Rights – Hawar Resolution in Sight – Rising Unemployment – Financial Services – Stock Exchange – Tele-Density

With the new millennium came a change in Bahrain's fortunes. Long criticised for its harsh treatment of Shi'a dissidents, moves by the government to open up the political system have at last guaranteed stability on the Island. The government was also praised for its efforts to liberalise the economy, while oil price rises provided a welcome boost to government finances. For Bahrain's still new King (from 14 February 2002), Sheikh Hamad bin Isa bin Salman al-Khalifa, the upturn in fortunes has come as a great relief.

Domestic Political Reforms

The year 2000 saw liberalisation of the political system move tentatively forward. The al-Khalifa family continue to dominate the government, holding all key cabinet positions. The prime minister, Sheikh Khalifa bin Salman al-Khalifa, nominates all 40-members of the Majlis al-Shura (Consultative Council) which comments on bills but has no legislative authority. However, in October 2000 Crown Prince, Sheikh Salman bin Hamad bin Isa al-Khalifa, announced a new National Action Charter, which will see the Majlis al-Shura replaced by a National Assembly elected by universal suffrage. Elections are scheduled for 2004. It is not yet clear if political parties will be allowed, or whether the new assembly, like the Majlis al-Shura, will be limited to a purely advisory role. Local elections are also expected to take place for the first time next year.

Liberalisation has come on the back of two factors. The first is the ascendancy of Sheikh Hamad bin Isa al-Khalifa, who became Emir following the death of his father, Sheikh Isa bin Salman al-Khalifa, on 6 March 1999, shortly after a meeting with United States defence secretary, William Cohen. Both Sheikh Hamad and his son Sheikh Salman are keen to end the sectarian politics of the Sheikh Isa era, and have frequently adopted a conciliatory approach towards the Shi'ite-led opposition movement which led mass demonstrations that rocked the island in the mid-1990s. The restoration of a National Assembly had been a major plank in the opposition movement's manifesto. Sheikh Isa had been more susceptible to the influence of Prime Minister Sheikh Khalifa, who was believed to be behind the harsh treatment meted out to Shi'ite dissidents.

Then, on 14 February 2002, Emir Hamad bin Isa al-Khalifa, declared Bahrain a kingdom, and proclaimed himself the first king – King Hamad. As King he is Supreme Commander of the Defence Forces and chairs the Higher Judicial Council. His powers include appointing the prime minister and members of the upper house of the National Assembly.

The second impetus to liberalisation comes from the increasingly warm relations enjoyed with Iran since President Mohammad Khatami came to office in May 1997. Khatami, a moderate, is determined to improve relations with his Gulf neighbours. Diplomatic relations were restored with Bahrain at the end of 1998 and a number of economic co-operation agreements have been signed. Prior to President Khatami's election, the Bahrain authorities had accused the Islamic Republic of Iran of fomenting trouble among the island's Shi'ite majority, who share a common ethnic and religious background with the Iranians.

However, reconciliation has not yet been fully achieved. Few Shi'ites have forgotten the draconian methods used by the government to crack down on their own people, including long term periods of detention without trial, and torture documented by UK-based Amnesty International. There remain at least a few hundred political prisoners, including some imprisoned under local law permitting three-year detention without trial. If Sheikh Hamad is to succeed in winning over the community, then he will have to continue with the promised political reforms, in particular the National Action Charter's commitment to establishing 'respect for human rights'. Economic prospects for the community will also have to improve. Shi'ites have traditionally been discriminated against in the labour market, with unemployment estimated to be as high as 30 per cent, well above the officially estimated 6 per cent national average. High population growth among the community will also increase the need for government funded low-cost housing.

Foreign Policy

The long standing dispute with Qatar over the Hawar Islands, situated at the norhern end of Qatar's Dukhan oilfield, also inched closer to a resolution in 2000 when the case came under arbitration at the International Court of Justice (ICJ) at The Hague. Bahrain's national pride would be dealt a serious blow by the loss of the Islands, which make up 30 per cent of its sovereign territory. There is also speculation that the Islands may contain oil deposits, so a judgment in favour of Qatar could represent a significant financial loss to Bahrain as well. Over the past few years the government has determinedly stepped up the amount of building carried out on the Islands, as a means of boosting its claim.

Economy

Cutbacks in government spending dampened growth in 2000. However, the rebound in oil prices helped push growth upwards to 2.6 per cent according to government estimates. With Bahrain's oil reserves limited to the Awali field at Jebel Dukhan, which is declining at one per cent per annum, and the offshore oil field, Abu Safah, the government has continued to look to the service sector to provide growth and employment. According to the World Trade Organisation (WTO), services are the largest sector in Bahrain, contributing around 50 per cent of employment.

In its October 2000 Trade Policy Review report on the Bahraini economy, the WTO stresses the importance of speeding up economic reforms if any significant economic growth is to be achieved. The reality is that although lower economic growth and declining public revenue, (mainly derived from taxes on petroleum and natural gas), have prompted Bahrain to implement economic reforms aimed at further diversifying the economy and raising economic growth to accommodate a growing population, the results have been indifferent.

The liberalisation programme may have gone some way towards addressing the rising unemployment among Bahrainis (particularly in predominantly Shi'a areas) and towards raising private investment. But foreign investment, particularly in key sectors of the economy has been sluggish, suggesting that accelerated reform would better meet Bahrain's targets of economic diversification and growth.

Bahrain's Most Favoured Nation (MFN) tariff on imports is relatively low, averaging 7.7 per cent in 2000, with tariffs on alcohol and tobacco products considerably higher than for other products. The WTO notes that escalation in the tariff provides greater protection for finished products although in some sectors there is a de-escalation in the tariff, providing greater protection to primary products and intermediate goods. The report also notes that Bahrain's tariff average at 35.6 per cent is significantly higher than the simple average tariff, introducing an element of uncertainty for traders and investors by providing Bahrain with scope to raise applied tariffs at will. There also appears to be some discrepancy between trade-related legislation and practice, potentially reducing transparency and predictability in Bahrain's trade regime.

The report also notes that Bahrain has few non-tariff barriers and recent tariff reductions have taken place in the context of the Gulf Co-operation Council's (GCC) Unified Economic Agreement which is to be completed by 2005. Bahrain's trade and investment relations are particularly strong with other members of the GCC to which it grants preferential treatment on tariffs, investment and government procurement.

In addition to trade reform, the WTO notes that Bahrain has also attempted to open up the economy to private investment and to reduce the size of the public sector which dominates key economic activities and is an important source of employment for Bahraini nationals. Efforts include full or partial privatisation of several companies, especially in services, and contracting out of some government services to private sector providers. Given that private investment, while allowed in several activities, has not taken place in sectors with a major public sector presence. However, the report stresses the need for a more systematic and stepped up privatisation programme to increase private investors' confidence in the economy and to attract foreign investment.

It goes without saying that Bahrain has a well-developed financial services sector and liberalisation has been pursued to try and strengthen the sector further. Banking, especially offshore banking, has grown rapidly and policies regulating offshore banking, are liberal. Foreign investment restrictions in onshore banking are up to 49 per cent for non-GCC nationals and up to 100 per cent for GCC nationals. Bahrain is also trying to develop its Stock Exchange which began operating in 1989. Financial services was also the only sector in which Bahrain made commitments under the General Agreement on Trade in Services (GATS). Liberalisation has also been proceeding in other services, notably telecommunications, and transport, although more slowly than in financial services.

The petroleum and manufacturing sectors tend to be dominated by the public sector. As part of its diversification strategy, Bahrain has targeted investment in downstream activities related to Bahrain's existing energy intensive industries and is providing supporting infrastructure to attract investment in these activities. A number of investment incentives, including reduced infrastructure costs such as free rental for a two year period and reductions in electricity tariffs are already provided to encourage investment in manufacturing.

The report concludes that despite these efforts, important sectors such as petroleum and telecommunications appear to be essentially closed to private investment, whereas reform in services, other than financial services, has been piecemeal. An acceleration and deepening of economic reform will therefore not only be important for economic growth, but would also send a positive signal to potential investors. In the view of the WTO, the predictability and transparency of the trade and investment regime would be enhanced were Bahrain to more actively notify details of any new legislation to the WTO.

Budget

The 1999–2000 budget was drawn up with revenues based on an oil price of US$12 per barrel. However, budgetary calculations were invalidated by oil's rapid price recovery averaging US$18 in 1999 and over US$25 in 2000. The budget forecasts a deficit of BD160 million (US$421 million) for 2000, although due to oil price rises, the final figure will be far below this.

As usual, current expenditure took up the lion's share of the budget, accounting for 82 per cent in both 1999 and 2000. This was an increase on 1998, when 78 per cent was given over to current expenditure, although its final percentage is estimated to have been above this. The greatest item of current expenditure was public sector salaries, which accounted for 60 per cent of total expenditure. By contrast, absolute sums allocated to capital spending fell. In 1998, BD158 million (US$415.8 million) was earmarked for capital expenditure compared to BD130 million (US$342 million) for each of 1999 and 2000.

The budget's low capital expenditure reflects the government's cautious attitude towards expenditure. This is a result of the government's determination to eliminate the budget deficit by 2006. Fiscal reform is a response to budgetary deficits caused by low petroleum revenue; an oil price collapse in 1997–98 left benchmark Brent crude at below US$10 per barrel, its lowest real price since 1972. However some much-needed manufacturing projects aimed at boosting economic growth were finally given the go-ahead in 2000. The majority government owned Aluminium Bahrain (ALBA) announced that a US$1.4 billion expansion will take place. This will boost Bahrain's aluminium output by up to 50 per cent over the next two years raising production to 750,000 tonnes a year of primary aluminium. A financial advisor on the project is to be appointed by the end of 2000. The Bahrain Petroleum Company (BAPCO) will also spend US$800 million to upgrade and modernise its ageing Sitra oil refinery. And with Bahrain's electricity power consumption growing at 5 per cent per annum and manufacturing projects cancelled due to limited power and water services, the government has finally conceded to pressure to upgrade utilities. The Ministry of Electricity and Water is funding a US$1 billion expansion at the Hidd power and desalination complex. The ALBA expansion will also include the provision of an extra 250MW power output.

World Trade Organisation

With full membership of the WTO due by 2003, Bahrain's transitional adjustment period will soon end. In October, a WTO report praised Bahrain for the rapid liberalisation of its financial services. This has boosted the sector's contribution to GDP to around 23 per cent and helped Bahrain develop into the region's leading banking centre. Up to 49 per cent of the total equity of a local bank or insurance company may be held by foreign nationals, and up to 100 per cent is permitted for Gulf Co-operation Council nationals. There are no foreign ownership restrictions for offshore banks. At the start of 2000 there were 176 financial institutions including 19 full commercial banks (FCBs), 48 offshore banking units (OBUs) and 33 investment banks (IBs). Additional reforms include the raising of foreign equity ownership limits in firms listed on the Bahrain Stock Exchange (BSE) from 24 per cent to 49 per cent and from 49 per cent to 100 per cent for GCC nationals. At the end of 2000, the government was studying the possibility of opening the BSE still further to foreign participation, through 100 per cent ownership of listed companies.

In early 2000, Bahrain was also praised by the Canada-based Fraser Institute for its economic openness. The report's conclusions were similar to that of the US-based Heritage Foundation published at end 1999, which rated Bahrain fourth in its list of most open economies. The government was commended for its liberal economic polices, particularly low corporate and personal taxes, and its commitment to free trade. In January 2000, Bahrain reduced its Most Favoured Nation tariff on imports to average 7.7 per cent. The reports also praised Bahrain for the institutional support underpinning foreign investment, in particular, a strong legal system and reductions in bureaucracy. Early in 2000, the government announced the establishment of a Higher Council for Economic Development; its mandate includes reducing the waiting time for approving foreign direct investment (FDI). Other reforms passed in 2000 included allowing GCC citizens to own real estate. Foreign-owned companies conducting business through a local agent were also given the right to change agents.

However, according to the WTO, as noted above, reforms to sectors other than financial services have been piecemeal. Up to 100 per cent foreign ownership is allowed in new industrial companies but local agents are still required in some sectors. Further reform is required, such as the speeding up of the privatisation process, and the encouragement of foreign investment in key sectors of the economy such as transport and manufacturing. Despite the government promises that privatisation of transport would take place in 2000, this failed to materialise. The WTO also pointed out that despite reductions in MFN tariffs, the bound tariff average at 35.6 per cent is significantly higher than the simple average tariff, providing Bahrain with scope to raise applied tariffs within their bindings.

Telecommunications

Although Bahrain is bound by the WTO's General Agreement on Trade In Services (GATS), to negotiate the opening of all internationally traded services, the telecommunications market is not yet liberalised. Bahrain's failure to sign the February 1997 WTO agreement providing international market access commitments, means the national incumbent Bahrain Telecommunications Company (BATELCO), retains exclusive rights to provide telecommunications services in domestic, regional and international fixed line, cellular and data services. As a result, Bahrain has not benefited from new market entrants instituting roll-out programmes, leading to low 'tele-density', particularly in non-urban areas. However, BATELCO has been privatised, with 39 per cent owned by the government and 20 per cent by the UK's Cable and Wireless. The remaining 41 per cent is traded on the exchange, where it is Bahrain's second largest listed company.

Outlook

The major challenge for the government will continue to be creating employment opportunities. Bahrain has a very young population with 38.9 per cent under 15 years of age. Unemployment has been exacerbated by the rise in the number of expatriates who, the Central Statistics Organisation (CSO) estimates, now make up more than 40 per cent of the population. According to the WTO report, the liberalisation programme has gone some way towards creating employment through raising private investment. In contrast to some Gulf countries, as many as 35 per cent of the local workforce is employed in the private sector. The WTO has recommended that the government step up the privatisation programme in 2001 to attract further levels of private investment and so create greater employment opportunities.

Risk Assessment

Economic	Satisfactory/good
Political	Improving/satisfactory
Regional Stability	Good
Stock Market	Improving

2003/04

Municipal and National Elections – Political Liberalisation – 2002 Constitution – Social Issues – Terrorist Threats – Protests – Overt and Covert Support for Washington – Entrenched Economic Elite – Bahraini-isation – Telecommunications Liberalisation

King Hamed bin Isa al-Khalifa's promise to introduce democracy to the tiny island was boosted by the holding of municipal and national elections during 2002. The democratisation process is a necessary factor in keeping in check tensions between the ruling Sunnis and the majority Shi'a.

The King has instituted a process of political liberalisation since his accession to the throne in 1999, including establishing a bicameral parliament with an elected lower house and an appointed upper house, instituting a nominally independent judiciary, dismantling the security laws and security courts, encouraging exiled opposition figures to return and allowing trades unions. However, the process has been tightly controlled to ensure that the ruling family and its close associates maintain control of both political and economic power.

Elections

The first municipal elections were successfully held in April and May 2002. A disappointingly low turnout of just over 50 per cent of the electorate voted in the two rounds of the elections, which returned conservative Islamists to all 50 seats. Although the Shi'a comprise around 66 per cent of the population they gained control of only 23 seats, because of a distorted allocation of electoral districts.

The same process was applied to the national elections, which were held in October (two years earlier than originally promised), with constituencies ranging from as low as 500 voters in Sunni areas to 12,000 in Shi'a wards. As a result, the national elections were boycotted by a number of political societies (political parties remain banned), including the al-Wefaq National Islamic Society (the main Shi'a political group), the National Democratic Action Society (leftist), the Nationalist Democratic Rally (pan-Arab) and the Islamic Action Association (also pro-Shi'a). The societies were also protesting against the 2002 Constitution which gives the appointed upper house greater powers than the elected lower house. The previous Constitution of 1972, although never adhered to, gave the former less power. In addition, the four societies organised a

© KONINKLIJKE BRILL NV, LEIDEN, 2023 | DOI:10.1163/9789004686335_024

protest, which was attended by 10,000–20,000 people, the day before the first round of the elections.

Despite the protests the turnout was 53.2 per cent of registered voters, slightly up from the 51.28 per cent turnout in the municipal elections. However, the figure disguises considerable differences between the constituencies, with estimates as low as 20 per cent in some of the Shi'a areas. In addition, voters had their passports stamped, sparking fears that failure to vote could lead to problems in the future when dealing with the state bureaucracy. Although the outcome is not clear cut because of the lack of political parties, the lower house is dominated by Islamists and conservatives. However, if a split does occur it will be between Sunni and Shi'a, particularly over social issues. The dominance of conservative Islamists will result in the new legislature becoming a blocking agent to further political and economic changes implemented from above, as happens in Kuwait. In mid-February 2003 it voted against approving the issue of a US$500 million Eurobond on the grounds that it was un-Islamic because the loan pays interest. In addition, the funds were to be used to fund ventures at which alcohol would be available.

Although the full extent of the reforms will take several years to become apparent, they will make a major contribution in reducing tension in the country and undermining the violent opposition to the government, which dominated the political environment from the mid-1990s to the end of the decade. This is an important consideration given that the situation in Iraq and Israel tends to spill over into domestic politics, as has been seen by the regular demonstrations concerning these issues since September 2000. In addition, the societies that boycotted the election have agreed not to resort to violence to achieve their ends, but to work with the government through a process of dialogue.

Although tensions have been held in check, two incidences have occurred since the beginning of 2003, which indicate that the political reform process is not being implemented to the satisfaction of all members of the community. At the New Year, youths, mainly from the Shi'a community, went on the rampage in Manama, destroying cars and property. This unusual incident was followed in mid-February by the arrest of five Sunni Bahrainis on suspicion of planning a terrorist attack against American targets. A number of guns and ammunition, along with powdered chemicals, were also discovered according to official sources.

In the international sphere, the King has maintained a fine balance in relation to the US, which bases its Fifth Fleet on the island and provides a regional security umbrella for Bahrain and the GCC states. The government has supported Washington's war-on-terrorism, and covertly backed the war on Iraq in 2003, whilst openly criticising US policy in the region, particularly in relation to

Israel. However, anti-US sentiment on the street will increase unless a satisfactory political solution in Iraq is found, which includes US withdrawal.

It's Still Oil

Unlike the other GCC states Bahrain has limited hydrocarbon reserves, its output is only 35,000 barrels per day (bpd) but it receives in excess of 200,000bpd of crude oil via a pipeline from Saudi Arabia. Although oil production's contribution to gross domestic production (GDP) has declined from around 32 per cent in the 1970s to less than 15 per cent, the per barrel oil price continues to be a significant determinant of Bahrain's economic health. Oil still accounts for over 60 per cent per cent of the value of exports and for around 50 per cent of government revenues. Revenues from oil accrue to the government, which then recycles them into the economy through its expenditure programmes. In addition, there is a significant degree of state-ownership in Bahrain; as such, the state is the largest employer and key economic investor. The dominance of the government in the economy has resulted in its expenditure policies dictating real growth rates.

Despite the seemingly entrenched dominant position of the government, the Bahraini economy appears to be in good shape. GDP growth in 2001 was recorded at 4.1 per cent. Encouraging indicators included low levels of debt (under 5 per cent of GDP), increasing foreign reserves (US$1.63 billion at the end of 2002), a positive trade balance, low inflation (consistently under one per cent), and low interest rates. The rate of GDP growth had eased since the year 2000, when the annual growth rate was 7 per cent compared to the previous year. This rate was in turn one per cent higher than the figure of 6 per cent recorded in 1999. In 2000 GDP was put at US$9,063 million. The absolute value of Bahrain's GDP in 2000 rose by US$1,481 million with respect to the 1999 figure. The GDP per capita of Bahrain in 2000 was US$14,215, an impressive US$2,005 higher than in 1999, when it was US$12,210.

However, the King is committed to economic liberalisation and diversification from oil dependency. The government's economic policy is based on attracting investment in six sectors: hydrocarbons, financial services and tourism (which are already well developed), information technology and communications, healthcare and education. Although Bahrain faces increasing competition from Dubai in the financial services sector, which accounts for over 20 per cent of GDP, it has the advantage of history and a well-regulated environment. In addition the authorities are responding by promoting the fast growing Islamic financial sector. However, much of the diversification relies on oil revenues; the funds that pass through the banking system are largely oil-derived, while tourism is aimed at the Gulf Arab market.

Privatisation has been limited, primarily due to the entrenched interests of the economic élite, which appears unwilling to relinquish its role in the economy. However, when the government issued Decree No 41 in October 2002 the process was boosted, permiting gradual privatisation in the tourist and communications sector, transport, electricity and water, the ports and airport service, the oil and gas sector and the postal service. The government has already initiated the process for liberalising the telecommunications sector, with the licence for the second mobile telephone network due to be awarded in April 2003.

After a number of years of relative austerity, the government boosted its spending during 2002 and this trend was continued with the announcement of the budget for 2003 and 2004 (the government sets its budget every two years), which was approved in October 2002. Based on an oil price of US$18 per barrel, the main provisions are budgeted revenues of US$2.14 billion in both 2003 and 2004, compared with a budget of US$1.79 billion for 2002. The budget projects a 6.5 per cent increase in expenditure in 2003 (to US$2.96 billion) and a further increase of 2.0 per cent in 2004 (to US$3.02 billion). The projected deficits will be less than anticipated as oil prices are forecast to remain higher than the planned US$18 per barrel.

The reason behind the end of the austerity measures is to promote socio-economic development, in particular addressing the problems of unemployment and of alienation of the Shi'a Muslim community. The socio-economic priorities include the reduction of unemployment through the programme of Bahraini-isation and by developing human resources, the provision of new low-cost housing; and the decentralisation of power.

The policy of Bahraini-isation aims to discriminate in favour of locals in the job market. The government is addressing the policy by: 1) a ban on the employment of foreigners in some occupations; 2) pressure on illegal foreign workers to legalise their positions or leave; and 3) a US$66.3 million fund to help the unemployed. In early 2003, the government also announced its intention to stop issuing visas to expatriates after 2005, except in certain unspecified sectors. However, the Bahraini-isation programme has not yet met with any significant success, thus ensuring that unemployment remains a contentious issue.

The high levels of unemployment, officially around 4 per cent but acknowledged to be 15 per cent by Crown Prince Salman bin Hamad al-Khalifa in January 2003, continue to threaten stability. The problem is exacerbated by the presence of migrant workers, who comprise around 60 per cent of the workforce.

Unemployment cuts across all levels of the population, including graduates, many of whom have been educated in the West. These graduates have been at the forefront of a series of peaceful demonstrations held throughout 2002 and 2003. While these protests do not immediately threaten political stability, they place greater pressure on the government not only to speed up the Bahraini-isation but also to implement further economic liberalisation. Furthermore, among the young (who make up the majority of the labour force), the figure is estimated to be as high as 25 per cent.

Political tensions remain latent but a breakdown of the political liberalisation process could see a return to the violence of the 1990s. These tensions will continue to be affected by the uncertain regional situation. The long-term success of the economy will depend on the ability of the government to overcome entrenched interests and adopt an economic programme of liberalisation and diversification.

Risk Assessment

Economic	Good, Improving
Political	Good, Stable
Regional Stability	Poor
Stock Market	Under-developed

2005/06

Bi-Cameral Parliament – Dominance of Conservative Islamists – Monetary Union – Key Structural Areas – Inter-Generational Equity – Customs Union – Cosmopolitan Living Environment

Since his accession as Emir in 1999 (and later as King in 2002), Hamad bin Isa bin Salman al-Khalifa has instituted a process of political liberalisation, including establishing a bicameral parliament with an elected lower house and an appointed upper house. He has also instituted a nominally independent judiciary, dismantled the State Security Law and Security Courts, encouraged exiled opposition figures to return and permitted the formation of trades unions. However, the process has been tightly controlled to ensure that the ruling family and its close associates maintain control of both political and economic power. Bahrain is likely to remain vulnerable to political unrest – the King has not yet addressed the root causes of social tension: chronic unemployment and falling living standards. Tensions in Bahrain will continue to be affected by the uncertain regional situation, such as the aftermath of the 2003 Iraq War and relations with an increasingly unstable Saudi Arabia and also Iran, which for decades laid claim to Bahrain.

Elections

The first municipal elections had been successfully held in the first half of 2002. Just over 50 per cent of the electorate voted in the two rounds of the elections, which returned conservative Islamists to all the seats up for election. Although Shi'a Muslims account for around 70 per cent of the Muslim population, they gained control of less than half the seats, because of a distorted allocation of electoral districts.

The same process had been applied to the national elections, which were held in October 2002, with constituencies ranging from a low 500 voters in Sunni areas to 12,000 in Shi'a wards. As a result, the national elections were boycotted by a number of political societies (political parties remain banned), including the main Shi'a political group, the Islamic National Wefaq (Accord) Society, the leftist National Democratic Action Society and the pan-Arab Nationalist Democratic Rally. The societies were also protesting against the 2002 constitution which gives the appointed upper house greater powers than the elected lower house.

Turnout in the national elections was 53.2 per cent of registered voters, slightly up from the 51.3 per cent turnout in the municipal elections. However, the figure disguised considerable differences between the constituencies, with estimates as low as 20 per cent in some of the Shi'a areas. In addition, voters had their passports stamped, sparking fears that failure to vote could lead to problems in the future when dealing with the state bureaucracy. Although the outcome of the elections is not clear-cut because of the lack of political parties, the lower house is dominated by Islamists and conservatives. However, if a split does occur it will be between Sunni and Shi'a, particularly over social issues. The dominance of conservative Islamists could result in the new legislature obstructing further political and economic changes, as happens in Kuwait. In mid-February 2003, the chamber voted against approving the issue of a US$500 million eurobond on the grounds that it was un-Islamic because the loan pays interest. In addition, the funds were to be used to fund ventures involving alcohol.

Tensions

Although reforms will need several years to take effect, they should make a major contribution in reducing tension in the country and undermining the opposition to the government, which has dominated the political environment from the mid-1990s to the end of the decade. The tensions generated in Iraq and Israel tend to spill over into domestic politics, fomenting regular demonstrations over these issues since September 2000. The societies which originally boycotted the election have, however, agreed not to resort to violence to achieve their ends, but to work with the government through a process of dialogue. Although tensions have been held in check, there were some incidents in the first half of 2003 which indicate that the political reform process still has some way to go.

The Economy

The kingdom has also stepped up promotion of its status as the key financial centre in the Gulf region. From 1995–2005, the number of banks, insurance companies, investment houses and other financial organisations establishing themselves in Bahrain has more than tripled, to 300. In its 2004 Overview of the Bahraini Economy the Washington-based International Monetary Fund (IMF) went as far as commending the Bahraini authorities for their prudent management of the economy, which has resulted in consistently high GDP growth, low inflation, what was described as a 'manageable' debt situation, and positive social and development indicators. The IMF endorsed the Bahraini authorities' strategy to improve the country's competitiveness and growth prospects through continued openness, diversification away from oil and gas production and institution building. In the view of the IMF, Bahrain's most notable success has been in the financial sector where, through the deployment of appropriate regulations and innovations in both conventional and Islamic finance, Bahrain has become recognised as a regional hub.

The IMF considered that the main challenge over the medium term will be to build on Bahrain's earlier successes by sustaining non-oil growth and creating employment opportunities for the growing Bahraini labour force. However, this will require further progress in a large number of key structural areas, in particular reducing the role and size of the public sector while encouraging Bahrain's private sector development and investment, eliminating rigidities, particularly in the labour market, as well as continued adherence to (or the development of) principles of good governance in public sector institutions and the corporate sector.

In particular the IMF commended the Bahrain government for its commitment to maintaining a prudent fiscal policy. It noted that in the 2004 budget, increases in capital expenditure for infrastructure modernisation and utilities will be more than offset by increased revenues from oil receipts, and that a small fiscal surplus is to be achieved. For the medium term, the IMF considered that the authorities' plan to scale back capital expenditure to contain any emerging macroeconomic imbalances should be complemented by fiscal reforms aimed at 'further strengthening fiscal institutions and enhancing the non-oil revenue base, thereby reinforcing growth and diversification efforts.' The IMF welcomed the intention to establish an oil stabilisation fund by the end of the year, in order to preserve hydrocarbon wealth for future generations. Some IMF directors expressed the view that to safeguard what was termed 'inter-generational equity', expanding the economy's productive base and developing its human resources will be as important as accumulating financial assets.

The IMF also agreed that adopting a broad-based consumption tax – preferably, a value added tax – should ideally be carried out in the context of a future co-ordinated tax regime under the Gulf Co-operation Council (GCC). Nevertheless, they encouraged the authorities to start laying the foundations for such a tax, and to adjust various fees and charges to reflect costs more closely. As regards expenditure, the IMF cautioned that the public sector wage bill has risen sharply in recent years, while welcoming steps taken by the authorities to contain it in order to promote medium-term fiscal sustainability and strengthen the budget's capacity to withstand oil price shocks.

The current peg of the dinar to the US dollar is considered satisfactory by the IMF and that it continues to serve the economy well. The IMF also welcomed the increased monetary co-operation and harmonisation developing in the context of the GCC, with the declared objective of achieving monetary union by 2010. Efforts to improve further prudential practices in the financial sector through the consolidation of supervision under the authority of the Bahrain Monetary Authority were also welcomed. The IMF also welcomed the authorities' intention to undertake a Financial Sector Assessment Programme (FSAP).

The IMF considered the Bahraini authorities' focus on liberalisation and structural reforms aimed at promoting private sector-led growth and creating job opportunities to be adequate. It welcomed the privatisation of public utilities and encouraged the authorities to press ahead with their structural reform agenda to promote wider private sector participation, including through further privatisation in the infrastructure and utilities sectors. The emphasis placed in the Bahraini authorities' programme to reduce unemployment among Bahraini nationals on vocational training and initiatives to unify benefits in the public and private sectors and to make private sector employment more attractive was encouraged. The IMF felt that a minimum wage, if set at too high a level, could impede efforts to reduce unemployment and affect competitiveness. Instead the Bahraini authorities were encouraged to use price and market-based interventions to encourage the employment of Bahraini nationals. They advised that if unemployment insurance is introduced, it should be designed so as to minimise its impact on the budget and on work incentives.

External Relations

By 2010, Bahrain will see its economy aligned more closely with the other GCC member countries of Kuwait, Oman, Qatar, Saudi Arabia and the United Arab Emirates (UAE). A customs union between the GCC countries was introduced in 2003, with duties on goods imported into GCC countries fixed at a harmonised rate of 5 per cent. No duties are applied to imports from other GCC states. A single currency pegged to the US dollar is to be introduced within the GCC countries in 2010. There are also plans to introduce EU-style economic convergence criteria in the run-up to the single currency.

In the international sphere, the King has maintained a fine balance in relation to the US, which bases its Fifth Fleet on the island and provides a regional security umbrella for Bahrain and the other GCC states. Bahrain has been awarded the informal status of 'major non-NATO ally' of the US, placing Bahrain among a very small group of nations which enjoy this status, including Jordan and Egypt. This award is testament to Bahrain's long-standing political, military, economic and cultural relationship with the US. The government has openly supported the US's war on terrorism, assisting the US in the 2003 Iraq War, while openly criticising US policy in the region, particularly in relation to

Israel. However, anti-US sentiment on the street will increase unless a political solution in Iraq, which includes a complete US withdrawal, is found to satisfy ordinary Bahrainis.

Abuse of Guest Workers

Bahrain generated news in 2005 over its treatment of guest workers, who make up about one third of Bahrain's population. In September, Alem Teklu, an Ethiopian citizen, went public with her story of having fallen victim to people traffickers and enduring virtual slavery in Bahrain. With the assistance of the International Organisation of Migration (IMO), Ms Alem drew attention to the plight of thousands of young Ethiopians who are trafficked to the Middle East, often suffering corporeal punishment, imprisonment, forced marriages and sexual abuse on arrival.

Oil Still Counts

Bahrain's 125 million barrels of proven oil reserves are located in the onshore Awali field, the first oilfield to be developed in the Gulf. Discovered in 1932, Awali's crude oil production peaked at more than 75,000bpd in the 1970s, but has declined since then. Bahrain also has potential oil reserves offshore in the Gulf of Bahrain. These areas became available for exploration and potential exploitation following the International Court of Justice's March 2001 resolution of a territorial dispute between Bahrain and Qatar over the Hawar Islands located between the two countries. The court awarded sovereignty over the islands to Bahrain, allowing Qatar to retain the neighbouring islands of Zubarah and Jinan. Bahrain has since awarded two blocks off the country's south-eastern coast to Petronas of Malaysia and another block to ChevronTexaco. Both companies have since begun to explore their concessions. The Calgary-based EnCana Corporation has also become involved in offshore exploration.

Bahrain also receives oil via submarine pipeline from Saudi Arabia. Some of this oil comes from the Abu Safah offshore oilfield, which lies in Saudi Arabian waters. All the field's 140,000bpd of production is donated to Bahrain. The Saudi petroleum company ARAMCO has undertaken development work aimed at increasing Abu Safah's production capacity to as much as 300,000bpd by 2004. The remainder of the oil that Bahrain receives from Saudi Arabia comes from the oilfields around Dammam. Unlike the Safah oil which it receives as a gift, Bahrain purchases the Dammam oil, albeit at a discounted rate.

Unlike other Gulf States, Bahrain exports refined petroleum products rather than crude. The country's only refinery, Sitra, is located south of Manama and has a current capacity of 248,900bpd. Bahrain exports most of the Sitra refinery's products to India and the Far East. The Sitra Refinery was built in 1936 and has been modernised several times. At present, the Bahrain Petroleum Company (BAPCO) is carrying out a US$600–US$900 million modernisation programme, which will increase overall capacity. It will also introduce hydrocracking facilities to allow production of 40,000bpd of low sulphur diesel. This project was due to be completed during 2004. In 2002, the government authorised BAPCO to initiate a study of the feasibility of building a US$1.5 billion petrochemical complex at Sitra.

Consolidation of Bahrain's state-owned petroleum sector began in 2000, when the upstream Bahrain National Oil Company (BANOCO) began merging into BAPCO. The merger was completed in 2002. The new entity, the Bahrain Petroleum Company BSC, is charged with the exploration, production, refining, marketing and distribution of Bahraini oil for domestic use and the international market.

Economy

Due in large measure to its liberal environment, Bahrain has evolved into a regional financial centre. The business centre of Manama, the capital city of Bahrain, is home to leading international financial and commercial institutions, including Salomon Smith Barney, HSBC, Coca-Cola, IBM, UPS and Ericsson, Citicorp, American Express, Nomura Investment Banking, Arab Banking Corporation, Gulf International Bank, DHL and INVESTCORP. The presence of such corporations in Bahrain is testament to its liberal and transparent economy and cosmopolitan living environment.

Bahrain was a founder member of the World Trade Organisation (WTO) and has been consistently ranked amongst the top most economically free countries in the world over the past eight years, by the Heritage Foundation and the *Wall Street Journal*. Bahrain has also been rated as the freest economy in the Middle East and the Arab world.

Economic performance in 2003 was steady, with real gross domestic production (GDP) growth of 4.9 per cent up on the 4.1 per cent recorded in 2002. Some observers forecast GDP growth of 5.4 in 2004, increased foreign reserves of US$1.76 billion at the end of 2003, a positive trade balance of US$1.38 billion and inflation of only 0.4 per cent. Short-term interest rates were 1.1 per cent. The government's economic policy is based on attracting investment in six sectors: hydrocarbons, financial services and tourism (which are already well developed), information technology and communications, healthcare and education.

Although Bahrain faces increasing competition from Dubai in the financial services sector, which accounts for over 20 per cent of GDP, it has the advantage of history and a well-regulated environment.

In addition, the authorities are responding by promoting the fast growing Islamic finance sector. Much of the diversification relies on oil revenues; most of the funds passing through the banking system are oil-derived.

Privatisation has been limited, primarily due to the entrenched interests of an economic elite unwilling to relinquish its role in the economy. However, the process was boosted in 2002, when the government issued a decree, which permits gradual privatisation in the tourist and communications sector, transport, electricity and water, the ports and airport services, the oil and gas sector and the postal service. The government has already initiated the process for liberalising the telecommunications sector.

Bahrain has adopted an overall strategy of creating an open economy. Inward investment plays an important role in this strategy, bringing in new expertise, knowledge and funding. Bahrain was the first country in the Gulf to exploit its oil commercially in the early 1930s. It was also the first to develop non-oil industries. In the twenty-first century, Bahrain now has a number of well-established, non-oil dependent industries, as well as the infrastructure needed to sustain them.

The selection of Bahrain as the regional base for so many major international companies underlines the attractive investment climate that Bahrain has created. As well as duty-free access to the larger GCC market.

Bahrain's inward investment regulatory and promotional activities are undertaken by its Economic Development Board (EDB). The EDB is responsible for formulating and overseeing Bahrain's economic development strategy. The EDB's principal objective is to attract foreign direct investment (FDI) to Bahrain and has identified six, previously mentioned, main economic sectors which capitalise on Bahrain's competitive advantages and present significant investment opportunities going forward.

Outlook

Bahrain has taken constructive steps to minimise the fallout of declining hydrocarbon exports, which currently generate around 70 per cent of Bahrain's total foreign trade earnings. The high price of oil in 2005, and the likelihood that prices will remain high, especially if sanctions are imposed on Iran in 2006, has also delivered extra income for further diversification. Bahrain's reputation as the region's financial hub remains intact, although Bahrain will have to continue to monitor developments in Dubai, where efforts are being stepped up to establish a rival financial centre. Unemployment cuts across all levels of the population, including university graduates, many of whom have been educated in the West. These graduates have been at the forefront of a series of peaceful demonstrations held throughout 2002 and 2003. While these protests do not immediately threaten political stability, they place greater pressure on the government not only to speed up 'Bahraini-isation' but also to implement further economic liberalisation. Furthermore, among the young (who make up the majority of the labour force), the unemployment rate is estimated to be as high as 25 per cent.

Political tensions remain latent but a breakdown of the political liberalisation process could see a return to the violence of the 1990s. These tensions will continue to be affected by the uncertain regional situation. The long-term success of the economy will depend on the ability of the government to overcome entrenched interests and adopt an economic programme of liberalisation and diversification.

Risk assessment

Economic	Good, improving
Political	Good, stable
Regional stability	Poor
Stock market	Underdeveloped

2007

Offshore Banking – Awali Production Declines – Financial Sector Triples – Draft Labour Law – Monetary Agency – Democratic Credentials – Election Boycott

The Kingdom of Bahrain has worked hard to emphasise its strengths and minimise its weaknesses since becoming an independent state in 1971. Faced with declining oil and gas reserves, the government has invested heavily in the aluminium production and financial services sectors. Even prior to the Iraqi elections of December 2005, when several women and ethnic minorities were elected to parliament, Bahrain had set the pace in developing Arab democracy.

Long a regional financial services centre specialising in offshore banking, Bahrain has for some time been intent on further diversifying its generally liberalised economy. For the time being, however, the country remains heavily dependent on the oil sector. Petroleum revenues make up about two-thirds of government revenue and export earnings. Hydrocarbons also provide the foundation for what have become Bahrain's two major industries: refining and an aluminium smelter. Accordingly, oil prices dramatically affect Bahrain's economy. The relatively high oil prices of recent years have helped Bahrain's real gross domestic product (GDP) to grow at 5.4 per cent in 2004 and at 6.9 per cent in 2005. Growth for 2006 was estimated to be 7.1 per cent. These relatively strong growth rates, however, have not kept unemployment from becoming a growing economic and political problem. Inflation, on the other hand, is well under control – 2.6 per cent for 2006, the same rate as 2005.

Oil and Gas

All of Bahrain's 125 million barrels of onshore proven oil reserves are located in the Awali oilfield, the first oilfield to be developed in the Arabian Gulf. Discovered in 1932, Awali's crude oil production peaked at more than 75,000 barrels per day (bpd) in the 1970s, but has declined since then. As of early 2006 Awali was producing around 35,000bpd of crude oil.

In addition to Awali, Bahrain might have undiscovered oil reserves offshore in the Gulf of Bahrain. These areas became available for exploration and potential exploitation following the International Court of Justice's (ICJ) March 2001 resolution of a territorial dispute between Bahrain and Qatar over islands located between the two countries. The court awarded sovereignty over the

© KONINKLIJKE BRILL NV, LEIDEN, 2023 | DOI:10.1163/9789004686335_026

Hawar Islands to Bahrain. Bahrain has since offered concessions to foreign investors. Bahrain also has natural gas reserves of about 3.25 trillion cubic feet (Tcf), much of it associated gas from the Awali oilfield.

In addition to what is produced in its territory, Bahrain purchases Arab Light crude oil via a submarine pipeline from Saudi Arabia, which it refines for export at its Sitra Refinery. To support the Bahraini economy, Saudi Arabia gives Bahrain the right to market and sell 150,000bpd of Arab medium crude oil from the Abu Safah offshore field. This oil is exported through the Saudi terminal at Ras Tanurah, but sales are handled by the Bahrain Petroleum Company (BAPCO), and Bahrain receives the revenue.

Unlike other Gulf States, Bahrain exports refined petroleum products rather than crude oil. The country's only refinery, at Sitra, is located south of Manama and has a current capacity of 248,900bpd. Bahrain exports most of the Sitra refinery's products to India. The Sitra Refinery was built in 1936, and has been modernised several times, including the recently completed US$900 million modernisation project, which increased overall capacity, and kept its product up-to-date with current Indian fuel standards. It also introduced hydrocracking facilities to allow production of 40,000bpd of low sulphur diesel.

With no new significant oil or gas finds in recent years, Bahrain has not only had to maximise production efficiency in its existing fields, at Awali and Abu Safah, but also invest heavily in aluminium production. The state-owned Aluminium Bahrain (ALBA) already contributes 8.00 per cent of Bahrain's GDP and this share is expected to increase to around 12 per cent once the new smelter line becomes fully operational.

The Kingdom has also stepped up promotion of its status as the key financial centre in the Gulf region. From 1995–2005, the number of banks, insurance companies, investment houses and other financial organisations establishing themselves in Bahrain more than tripled, to 300. In December 2005, Bahrain was named the winner of the internationally prestigious Financial Centre of the Future award, in the Middle East and Africa category. This was welcome news in Bahrain, as it now faces competition for its status as the region's financial centre from the Dubai International Financial Centre (DIFC).

International Monetary Fund
In June 2004, the International Monetary Fund (IMF) published its assessment of the Bahrain economy. The IMF notes that although endowed with smaller oil resources than its neighbours, Bahrain has established a refreshing policy of openness and diversification. In the view of the IMF Bahrain has become one of the most advanced economies in the region with liberal exchange rate, trade,

and investment regimes. The IMF considers that Bahrain's macroeconomic performance has fared well relative to the other countries of the Gulf Co-operation Council (GCC). Bahrain's diversification efforts have resulted in the development of non-oil activity in manufacturing (in particular, aluminium) and various non-financial services, including tourism. In addition, efforts to establish Bahrain as a regional banking and financial services hub have, in the opinion of the IMF, been successful.

Despite all these diversification efforts, however, Bahrain's economy remains heavily dependent on oil and gas. Rapid population growth, combined with labour market rigidities and a shortage of marketable skills have resulted in high levels of unemployment among Bahraini nationals. Public sector wages and benefits are among the highest in the region.

Bahrain's macroeconomic performance has been strong in recent years, with GDP growth exceeding 5.5 per cent in 2003, up from 5 per cent in 2002. Non-oil growth performance rose from about 6 per cent in 2002 to 6.5 per cent in 2003, underpinned by strong growth in manufacturing (mainly aluminium) and financial services. Prices increased only slightly (by about one per cent). The IMF reported that there existed a growing confidence in the economy. In part due to higher oil prices and low interest rates, the Bahrain stock market produced sizeable returns, growing by 28 per cent in 2003.

Bahrain's consolidated fiscal position improved and registered an overall deficit of 1.8 per cent of GDP in 2003, largely on account of higher oil prices. While the share of total expenditure relative to GDP has varied significantly in recent years, capital spending has increased in 2002/03. Notwithstanding higher oil prices, the external current account position was estimated to have registered a deficit in 2003. The increase in crude oil imports was more than offset by higher exports of refined products. Non-oil exports were relatively flat while imports rose by 17 per cent. Service receipts were strong, mostly on account of additional tourism revenues.

There has also been progress in the area of structural reforms. The government has completed the privatisation of the country's public bus network, liberalised the telecommunications industry, and also established a regulatory authority in 2003. Legislation to improve the transparency of privatisation transactions was also passed in 2003. Progress in privatisation of public utilities has been slow, however, due to concerns of increasing unemployment, although plans are under way to involve the private sector in the operation of the newly built Hidd power generating project.

In its report, the IMF registered concern at the high levels of unemployment. The authorities have adopted active labour market policies of matching job seekers with potential private sector employers and promoting the acquisition of marketable skills through training. A draft Labour Law is being discussed with the trades unions and the private sector, emphasising vocational training and stipulating equal levels of remuneration for public and private sector employees. The introduction of a minimum wage is being considered.

Concluding the report's summary, the IMF praised Bahrain's success in developing a financial sector, which it describes as 'one of the main engines of growth for Bahrain's economy and one of the most vibrant in the region.' The Bahrain Monetary Agency (BMA) has consolidated the supervision and regulation of the financial sector (including banks, insurance, and capital markets) under one umbrella; and Bahrain is at the forefront in developing Islamic financial services.

In a separate study focusing entirely on Bahrain's financial sector, published in March 2006, the IMF notes that it is enjoying good results and steady growth in a favourable environment. The IMF refers to what it labels 'soundness indicators' as suggesting that the system is robust. The banking sector is well-capitalised. Asset quality has been improving and provisioning is high. The sector's profitability surged in 2004–05, but in recent years the return on equity has been moderate for many institutions. The insurance sector is also well-capitalised. Those indicators available for the non-financial sectors show that household debt relative to disposable income is low but rising, and that the corporate sector is on average not highly leveraged.

These favourable liquidity conditions have caused regional equity and real estate markets to surge. Consumer lending has grown rapidly, although it slowed in 2005 following a tightening of loan-to-income limits. Possible regional geo-political disturbances constitute another risk factor, although Bahraini financial institutions have withstood such shocks in the past. Results from a comprehensive stress testing exercise, where due allowance was made for the risk-sharing features of Islamic institutions, suggests that banks as a whole could withstand even a severe shock. Nonetheless, individual banks may be vulnerable to a 'boom and bust' in credit, or adverse movements in interest rates or equity prices. Hence, the authorities need to closely monitor rising exposures, and eventually a pre-emptive tightening of prudential requirements may be warranted.

The BMA, which has had supervisory authority over the entire financial system since 2002, has modernised prudential requirements and is enhancing its supervisory capacity. The regulatory framework, which is designed to accommodate both conventional and Islamic institutions, is largely in conformity with the relevant regulatory standards. The payments and securities settlements systems are reliable and efficient, and are in the process of being upgraded. Prudential supervision and notably that of banks is generally effective, while that covering the smaller insurance sector is developing rapidly. A significant challenge is to ensure that the BMA has the staff and skills to keep up with expansion of the financial sector and innovations in its products. The positive reputation of the BMA contributed to Bahrain's attractiveness as a financial centre.

In the view of the IMF, the BMA also endeavours to be both transparent and consultative. Under current legislation, it is not formally fully independent, and some of its powers are not comprehensively specified in law. However, several of these and other shortcomings relative to international standards should be largely remedied once the proposed Central Bank of Bahrain and Financial Institutions Law 2006 (CBBFIL) is passed and the new licensing framework introduced. A number of issues deserve attention. These include proper implementation by both the BMA and financial institutions. This implies improved staff quality, which in turn will need to be bolstered both by competitive remuneration and on-going training. At the same time, the effectiveness of supervision could certainly be improved by better management techniques. The adequate provision of supervisory resources is an especially important question now, at a time when a large number of applications are being received for bank licences. New ventures are generally likely to be riskier than established ones. In the view of the IMF, the BMA should begin to require collateral for all lending to banks.

The BMA, according to the IMF, has broadly adequate powers of enforcement and bank resolution, which it has used effectively, but more contingency planning would be valuable. When conditions eventually become less benign, the authorities may have to cope with a wave of mergers in the banking and insurance sectors, where many institutions are small. Many financial institutions appear to face a shortage of appropriate local investment vehicles, which limits the development of the sector. Trading in securities markets remains thin, in large part because most Bahraini investors follow a 'buy and hold' strategy. Also, efforts could be pursued to make Bahrain a more attractive location for the issue of private tradable securities. Finally, the IMF suggests that legislation needs to be drawn up to make terrorist financing an offence.

A Democracy, as it Were

Although political power is overwhelmingly dominated by the al-Khalifa family – its members include the King, crown prince, prime minister, deputy prime minister, defence minister, foreign minister and finance minister – Bahrain has made much of its democratic credentials in recent years, 2005 being no exception. Bahrain caused a stir in the pan-Arab and local media when, in April, Alees Samaan became the first woman and non-Muslim anywhere in the Arab world to chair a house of parliament. Ms Samaan, a Christian, stood in as speaker of Bahrain's upper house, the Majlis al-Shura (Consultative Assembly), by default, as she was the most senior parliamentarian available in the absence of the elected speaker and his deputies. That the event was permitted to occur at all was unprecedented in a region dominated by patriarchal societies. In November 2005, Bahrain hosted the Forum for the Future, which brought together leaders from the Middle East and the Group of 8 (G8) countries to discuss political and economic reform in the region.

Elections

It had been hoped that the elections scheduled for September 2006 would turn out to be a more inclusive affair than those held in 2002. The majority Shi'a community largely boycotted these and not a single woman candidate won a seat. King Hamad subsequently appointed six women to the Majlis al-Shura. A poll conducted in January 2006 revealed that the electorate was much more favourable to voting for female candidates and some Shi'a community leaders indicated a greater willingness to participate.

In the event, Bahrain held its second set of parliamentary (national) and municipal elections in November and December 2006. All registered political societies participated in the elections and a Shi'a society, al-Wefaq National Islamic Society, now represents the largest single bloc inside the Council of Representatives. Thirty-two of the Council's 40 members represent Sunni and Shi'a Islamist societies. One woman, Lateefah al-Qauod, ran uncontested and became the first woman elected to parliament in Bahrain.

Outlook

Bahrain has taken constructive steps to minimise the fallout of declining hydrocarbon exports, which currently generate around 70 per cent of Bahrain's total foreign trade earnings. The high price of oil in 2005, and the likelihood that prices will remain high, especially if sanctions are imposed on Iran in 2006, has also delivered extra income for further diversification. Bahrain's reputation as the region's financial hub remains intact, although Bahrain will have to monitor developments in Dubai, where efforts are being stepped up to establish a rival financial centre.

Risk Assessment

Politics	Fair
Economy	Good
Regional stability	Fair

2008

Moves to Modernise – Left at the Post – Corruption – Threat of Instability – Enhanced Due Diligence – Unemployment Benefits – Robust Economic Performance – Shi'a Unemployment – New Offshore Licensing Round

February 2008 saw further developments in Bahrain's gentle reform process, started some twenty years earlier by the island state's Crown Prince, Sheikh Salman bin Hamad al-Khalifa. The changes have sought to increase efficiency and end corruption, while creating a functioning national parliament.

Continued Reforms

The moves to modernise, spearheaded by the Crown Prince, have not always been welcomed by the more conservative rearguard of Bahrain's extensive Ruling Family, a well-entrenched bureaucracy and even elements of the island's business community. The mix is further complicated by the fact that Bahrain's Ruling Family and the higher echelons of society are Sunni, while 65 per cent of the population are Shi'a. What has all the makings of a potentially explosive mix has in fact worked well, as an enlightened Royal Family has exercised a measured and well thought-out balance in its rule.

As Gulf rulers go – and he has in time become recognised as Bahrain's *de-facto* ruler – the Cambridge educated Crown Prince is, at 39, still a young man. He has grouped much of Bahrain's decision making machinery within the Economic Development Board (EDB), headed up Sheikh Mohammed bin Essa al-Khalifa. In theory, the EDB's steadily increasing powers represent the erosion of parliament's already limited powers. But the gradual strengthening of the EDB appears to have been welcomed, rather than opposed, by parliament.

Bahrain's National Assembly (parliament) was reactivated in 1999, and there have since been two elections to the lower house. What protests there have been over parliament's lack of power have come from disaffected, rather than specifically motivated, Shi'a. Sunni-Shi'a community tensions in Iraq have not helped, but the particular complaints of the more marginalised elements of the Shi'a population focus on exclusion from senior government jobs and other more petty forms of discrimination.

The apparent loser in a January 2008 government re-shuffle was Bahrain's Prime Minister Sheikh Khalifa bin Salman al-Khalifa, who was on holiday at the time.

Economic Diversification

In a number of respects, Bahrain has been left at the post in the Gulf's economic development stakes. In the 1970s, along with Kuwait, it boasted the area's most developed infrastructure, enjoying a close relationship with the southerly emirate of Abu Dhabi (with which it shared its currency for a period) and the UK. The only thing that Bahrain really lacked was oil; its meagre resources were totally out-gunned, not only by the vastness of Saudi Arabia's oilfields, but also by those of Kuwait, Abu Dhabi and even Oman. Before too long, it would also be overtaken by Qatar's natural gas reserves. The refining capacity that had enabled Bahrain to keep up with its neighbours was also quickly overtaken.

In response, Bahrain sought to diversify into less certain areas of economic activity, not always successfully. Its drydock project was soon eclipsed by that of Dubai and its partially owned (along with Abu Dhabi and Oman) flag carrier airline, Gulf Air – once the Gulf region's major carrier – succumbed to years of inadequate management, with the result that Bahrain ceased to be the regional hub it had once been. The state holding company Muntakalat pulled off a high profile coup in persuading the Formula One organisers to choose Bahrain for the region's Grand Prix. Muntakalat also has a 30 per cent shareholding in the McClaren Formula One operation. Bahrain has the Middle East's largest aluminium smelter, which has been a commercial success. It is operated by Aluminium Bahrain (ALBA). ALBA has increased its capacity to 750,000 tons per year (tpa) to meet growing demand. Bahrain's stock exchange claims to be among the most important in the region, although only some 50 companies are listed. Bahrain also has a well-established banking sector covering investment services, offshore and Islamic banking.

Corruption Allegations...

In early 2008 ALBA brought a legal action against the US company Alcoa, one of its major suppliers for many years. The *Wall Street Journal* observed that the allegations represented an 'unusually sweeping assertion' by a foreign government of improper behaviour by a US corporation. According to ALBA, Alcoa had steered payments to a group of small companies abroad in order to pay kickbacks to a Bahraini 'senior government official' following overcharging to ALBA. Under a contract signed in 2007, the US investigation company Kroll Associates Bahrain has uncovered a number of cases of corruption in state-owned companies. As a result, officials have been arrested. In ALBA's case Alcoa had assigned supply contracts to a series of companies incorporated by a Canadian businessman of Jordanian origin, Victor Dahdaleh. The legal action claimed that 'these assignments served no legitimate purpose and were used as a means to secretly pay bribes and unlawful commissions as part of a scheme to defraud ALBA. ALBA alleged that in 2005 a supply contract was inflated by some US$65 million. Since 1990 ALBA had made some 80 payments to the offshore companies, most of which were for amounts in excess of US$15 million.

... and Banking Ripples

In March 2008 a ripple of concern went through Manama's banking circles when the US Treasury imposed sanctions on Bahrain's Future Bank, a subsidiary of Bank Melli Iran. Bank Melli was accused by Washington of playing a central role in financing Tehran's nuclear and ballistic missile programmes. The action froze any assets Future Bank held in the USA. This shot across Bahrain's bows followed the visit to Bahrain of US Treasury Secretary Stuart Levey in February 2008. Mr Levey had urged Bahrain's monetary officials to exercise 'enhanced due diligence' in guarding against money laundering and nuclear proliferation activities.

Foreign nationals are permitted to have 100 per cent ownership of Bahrain based businesses without needing a local sponsor. The attractiveness of setting up shop in Bahrain has generated strong flows of foreign direct investment (FDI), making Bahrain the Gulf leader in this respect. Nevertheless, Bahrain's economy has to come to terms with three long term problems. First comes the depletion of its oil reserves. Second, the unacceptably high levels of youth unemployment. Bahrain is one of the first Gulf States to introduce unemployment benefits. Third, like its neighbours, Bahrain cannot afford to ignore the threat of instability, which risks having lasting effects on Bahrain's economic prospects. Average forecasts for the period 2008–11 which suggest an annual GDP growth rate of around 4.8 per cent are based on continued macroeconomic stability. Understated government forecasts for oil prices may enable fiscal equilibrium to be maintained.

In the medium term, it looks as though the high oil prices will continue to boost Bahrain's economy. This manifests itself principally in increased government expenditure, but any increased activity will inevitably boost the financial sector. Government efforts to address unemployment and housing shortages should also show through positively.

Crisis, What Crisis?

According to the International Monetary Fund (IMF) in its March 2007 overview of Bahrain's economy, the Kingdom's macroeconomic performance during 2005/06 was strong. Real GDP grew by an annual 7.75 per cent, reflecting strong expansion in the non-oil sectors of financial services, construction and manufacturing. This was supported by prudent macroeconomic policies, further improvements in the investment environment, and favourable economic conditions in Bahrain's neighbouring countries. While non-oil GDP grew by 10 per cent a year, oil GDP actually declined by 5 per cent. As a result, Bahrain remains the lowest oil-dependent economy in the Gulf Co-operation Council (GCC) member states with the share of the hydrocarbon sector in total GDP declining to 15 per cent in 2006. Inflation remained subdued at below 3 per cent during in 2005/06, and – according to the IMF, Bahrain's unemployment rate declined from 15 per cent in 2005 to 4 per cent in mid-2007. Financial stability has not been affected by the correction in the GCC equity markets or the recent global sub-prime credit turmoil. It is to be noted that Bahrain's overall fiscal position registered only moderate surpluses in 2005/06, as the increases in oil revenues were largely offset by lower non-oil receipts and higher capital spending. Capital expenditure increased by over 2.5 per cent of GDP, but restrained current spending helped maintain an average overall fiscal surplus of about 3 per cent of GDP. As a result, public debt declined by 5 percentage points, to 23 per cent of GDP by the end of 2006.

Internationally high oil prices have helped to strengthen the external position, with high current account surpluses. Despite strong import growth, the current account surplus averaged 12 per cent of GDP in 2005/06, driven mainly by growth in exports of hydrocarbon products and aluminium. At the same time, the Central Bank of Bahrain's gross official reserves increased to about US$3 billion by the end of September 2007, equivalent to 2.9 months of imports of goods and services. Bahrain's real effective exchange rate depreciated by 2.8 per cent in 2005 and by an additional 2.9 per cent in 2006, reflecting the weakening of the US dollar.

In 2007 Bahrain's financial sector performance and the legal framework continued to improve. The IMF noted that solvency, profitability and asset quality indicators all strengthened in 2006 and the first nine months of 2007. At the same time, the equity market remained remarkably stable during the GCC equity market turmoil of 2005/06 and strengthened subsequently, with the price index rising to a historical high after a 15 per cent gain.

The passage of a new Central Bank of Bahrain (CBB) law in September 2006 established the CBB as a single regulator of the country's financial services industry, covering banking, insurance, and the capital markets. The authorities have also made good progress in implementing the 2005 Financial Sector Assessment Programme (FSAP) recommendations, including those pertaining to the Anti-Money Laundering/Countering Financing of Terrorism (AML/CFT) rulings.

The IMF also noted that the Bahraini authorities have embarked upon comprehensive reforms to reduce further the costs of doing business by streamlining regulations and creating the necessary infrastructure in partnership with the private sector. They have initiated a public services outsourcing and dereg-ulation programme, and have also embarked on a four-pillar labour reform process to enhance productivity and employment. A comprehensive overhaul of the education system is also under way.

Unsurprisingly, the outlook for 2007/08 remains favourable. With the strong expansion of the non-oil sector, real GDP growth is projected to average 6.5 per cent a year in 2007/08. Inflation is expected to reach 3.5 per cent in 2007, but is likely to decline gradually thereafter as world non-fuel commodity prices de-cline, and domestic supply bottlenecks subside. The IMF expects the overall fis-cal surplus to average 2.75 per cent of GDP in 2007/08, mainly due to higher oil revenues, while the external current account is expected to register re-cord-high surpluses, in the order of 15 per cent of GDP.

The IMF commended the Bahraini authorities' prudent macroeconomic pol-icies and the progress with structural reforms, which, together with the sharp increase in oil prices, have resulted in Bahrain's robust macroeconomic perfor-mance. A key medium-term challenge for the Bahraini authorities will be to boost long-term economic growth while maintaining macroeconomic stability and reducing the economy's dependence on oil and vulnerability to oil price swings.

Social Tensions

As is the case with most Gulf States, despite high levels of unemployment among the Shi'a, Bahrain has long been dependent on imported labour. Most of this comes from the Indian sub-continent. This over-dependence sits uncom-fortably alongside the absence of many human and political rights for the im-migrant community.

In a January 2008 interview with the pan-Arab newspaper Asharq al-Aswat, Bahrain's labour minister Majid al-Alawi touched a raw nerve when he claimed that the Gulf was facing an Asian 'Tsunami' because Gulf nationals are 'lazy' and 'spoilt'. The Minister went further in his interview, expressing what many considered to be the alarmist view that the estimated 17 million foreign nation-als working in the Gulf represented 'a danger worse than the atomic bomb or an Israeli attack'. His remarks were endorsed and expanded upon by Mansour al-Jamri, the newspaper's Bahraini editor, who stated that foreign labour should not be classified as temporary, since for the most part they had become virtually permanent members of the community. Mr al-Jamri further expanded on his theme, suggesting that the political influence of a renascent India could well end up making the Gulf States part of a 'Commonwealth of India' as its for-mer citizens assume greater confidence and responsibility in both private and public sectors.

The Oil Still Counts

Bahrain is the Gulf's smallest oil producer. None the less, oil still accounts for about 75 per cent of total government revenues. Bahrain's total energy consumption is mostly provided by natural gas. According to the *Oil and Gas Journal* (OGJ) and as reported by the US Energy Information Administration (EIA), Bahrain's oil reserves in January 2007 were a modest 125 million barrels, located entirely in the Awali Oilfield. Bahrain shares with Saudi Arabia on a 50/50 basis the 300,000 barrels per day (bpd) of the offshore Abu Safah oilfield. The state-owned Bahrain Petroleum Company (BAPCO) is responsible for all exploration and production for both domestic and international markets. As part of wider government reorganisation, the National Oil and Gas Authority (NOGA) replaced the oil ministry in 2005 to become the national regulatory authority.

Although Bahrain is one of the Gulf's oldest oil-producing states, its estimated oil production in 2007 of 35,000bpd was less than half the production levels of the 1970s. Between 2007 and 2015 BAPCO expects to drill a further 700 new wells in the Awali oilfield, in the expectation of producing an additional 12,000bpd. This is forecast to offset any further declines in production. The NOGA has also opened a new licensing round for offshore exploration and production projects. Bahrain's notional refining capacity of 250,000bpd at BAPCO's Sitra refinery was surpassed in 2006, when the refinery ran at an annual rate of 263,000bpd. The OGJ reports that in January 2007 Bahrain's natural gas reserves were 3.25 trillion cubic feet (Tcf). The last recorded figures (for 2004) suggest that domestic natural gas consumption and production, at an annual rate of 344 Bcf, were in equilibrium.

Risk Assessment

Economy	Good
Politics	Fair
Regional stability	Fair

2009

Backwater – National Action Charter – Gentle Reform Process –
Hydrocarbons Decline – Safe Haven Investment Location – From Emir to
King – Potential New Oil Reserves

In the twenty-first century, the Gulf States had certainly arrived on the international stage. Not a week would go by without the names of Dubai or Abu Dhabi hitting the headlines. However, the same could hardly be said of Bahrain which, to those who had followed the Gulf's development over thirty years or so, seemed to have missed a number of boats. Once the regional hub, whose airport was the natural first stop for international airlines, as well as being the home of the first regional airline, Gulf Air, Bahrain by 2009 seemed to be something of a backwater.

Towards Constitutional Maturity

In November 2000, Bahrain's ruler, Sheikh Hamad al-Khalifa had established a committee to see through the transformation of Bahrain from a hereditary emirate to a constitutional monarchy within two years. The resulting National Action Charter was later presented to the public in a referendum in February 2001. In what was the first public vote in Bahrain since the 1970s, 94.8 per cent of the voters overwhelmingly endorsed the charter. That same month, Sheikh Hamad pardoned all political prisoners and detainees, including those who had been imprisoned, exiled or detained on security charges. He also abolished the State Security Law and the State Security Court, which had permitted the government to detain individuals without trial for up to three years.

One year later, in February 2002, Sheikh Hamad pronounced Bahrain a constitutional monarchy and changed his status from Emir to King. He also announced that the first municipal elections since 1957 would be held in May 2002, and that a bi-cameral parliament, with a representative lower house, would be reconstituted with parliamentary elections in October 2002. As part of these constitutional reforms, the government created an independent financial watchdog empowered to investigate cases of embezzlement and violations of state expenditure in July 2002.

Turnout for the May 2002 municipal elections was 51 per cent, with female voters making up 52 per cent of voters. Turnout for the parliamentary elections of 2002 – the first in almost three decades – was 53 per cent in the first round

© KONINKLIJKE BRILL NV, LEIDEN, 2023 | DOI:10.1163/9789004686335_028

and 43 per cent in the second round, despite the fact that four political societies, including the largest Shi'a society, organised a boycott to protest constitutional provisions enacted by the King that gave the appointed upper chamber of parliament voting rights equal to the elected lower chamber. The new parliament held its first joint sitting in December 2002.

The Reforms Continue

There were further developments in Bahrain's gentle reform process (started some twenty years earlier) in 2008, by the island state's Crown Prince, Sheikh Salman bin Hamad bin Isa al-Khalifa. The changes have sought to increase efficiency and end corruption, while creating a functioning national parliament. The moves to modernise, spearheaded by the Crown Prince, have not always been welcomed by the more conservative rearguard of Bahrain's extensive ruling family, a well-entrenched bureaucracy and even elements of the island's business community. The mix is further complicated by the fact that Bahrain's ruling family and the higher echelons of society are Sunni Arabs, while 65 per cent of the population are Shi'a. What has all the makings of a potentially explosive mix has in fact worked well, as an enlightened royal family has exercised a measured and well thought-out balance in its rule.

As Gulf rulers go – and he has in time become recognised as Bahrain's *de-facto* ruler – the Cambridge educated Crown Prince is, at 39, still a young man. He has grouped much of Bahrain's decision making machinery within the Economic Development Board (EDB), headed up Sheikh Mohammed bin Essa al-Khalifa. In theory, the EDB's steadily increasing powers represent the erosion of parliament's already limited powers. But the gradual strengthening of the EDB appears to have been welcomed, rather than opposed, by parliament.

Bahrain's parliament was reactivated in 1999, and there have since been two elections to the lower house. What protests there have been over parliament's lack of power have come from disaffected, rather than specifically motivated, Sh'ia. Sunni-Shi'a community tensions in Iraq have not helped, but the particular complaints of the more marginalised elements of the Shi'a population focus on exclusion from senior government jobs and other more petty forms of discrimination. The apparent loser in a January 2008 further government re-shuffle was Bahrain's Prime Minister, Sheikh Khalifa bin Salman al-Khalifa, who was on holiday at the time.

Economic Diversification

In a number of respects, Bahrain has indeed been left at the post in the Gulf's economic development stakes. In the 1970s, along with Kuwait, it boasted the area's most developed infrastructure, enjoying a close relationship with the southerly emirate of Abu Dhabi (with which it shared its currency for a period) and the UK. The only thing that Bahrain really lacked was oil; its meagre resources were totally out-gunned, not only by the vastness of Saudi Arabia's oilfields, but also by those of Kuwait, Abu Dhabi and Oman. Before too long, it would also be overtaken by Qatar's natural gas reserves. The refining capacity that had once enabled Bahrain to keep up with its neighbours was also quickly overtaken.

In response, Bahrain sought to diversify into less certain areas of economic activity, not always successfully. Its drydock project was soon eclipsed by that of Dubai and its partially owned (along with Abu Dhabi and Oman) flag carrier airline, Gulf Air, succumbed to years of inadequate management, with the result that Bahrain ceased to be the regional hub it had once been. The state holding company Muntakalat pulled off a high profile coup in persuading the Formula One organisers to choose Bahrain for the region's Grand Prix. Muntakalat also has a 30 per cent shareholding in the McClaren Formula One operation.

Bahrain has the Middle East's largest aluminium smelter, which has been a commercial success. It is operated by Aluminium Bahrain (ALBA). ALBA has increased its capacity to 750,000 tons per year (TPA) to meet growing demand. Bahrain's stock exchange claims to be among the most important in the region, although only some 50 companies are listed. Bahrain also has a well established banking sector covering investment services, offshore and Islamic banking.

Global Crisis, Impact on Bahrain Modest

The global financial crisis that saw many countries teetering on the verge of bankruptcy obviously had adverse consequences for global economic prospects. During 2008, world output grew by 3.4 per cent, down from a growth of 5.2 per cent in 2007. Growth projections for 2009 indicated a low of 0.5 per cent growth, with an improvement to 3.0 per cent expected for 2010. Before developing into a global crisis, the initial effects of the turmoil had limited direct impact on the economic performance of the GCC economies. In September 2008, the financial crisis entered a more serious phase and with oil prices declining substantially, sustaining high levels of growth became a big challenge for all GCC countries.

Although the initial impact of the crisis on the Bahraini financial system was relatively modest, according to Bahrain's Central Bank economic effects were more immediate as real gross domestic production (GDP) growth fell to 6.3 per cent in 2008, down from 8.4 per cent the previous year. This was largely due to a shrinkage in non-oil output, especially financial services. The inflation rate remained low at 3.5 per cent during 2008.

Despite the inevitable effects of the crisis, Bahrain's sovereign credit ratings remained favourable. The credit ratings agency Fitch's rating for Bahrain's long term foreign currency debt remained at A (with a stable outlook) in 2008. Local currency debt ratings remained A+ (stable). Another major credit rating agency, Standard and Poor's ratings for foreign and local currency debt also remained unchanged at A (stable) in 2008. Notwithstanding the turmoil, the Bahraini government continued to introduce various policies aimed at strengthening the domestic economy. It continued the implementation of labour market reforms, advanced the government initiative and continued the upgrade of general infrastructure. It also entered into several trade agreements. The private sector is expected to benefit from these reforms, thereby strengthening further the foundations for economic diversification.

Bahrain's money supply continued to grow during 2008, mainly through a growth in savings deposits. Broad money (M2) grew by 18.4 per cent, due principally to increases in domestic and foreign currency private sector deposits. With US monetary policy changing to combat the financial and economic turmoil, interest rates in Bahrain showed mixed trends. Given the dinar's peg to the US dollar, exchange rates have been influenced by economic developments in the United States. For most of 2008, the real effective exchange rate decreased against other major world currencies and bilateral rates of the dinar against other currencies also showed some depreciation. The financial sector continues to be the largest contributor to Bahrain's economy, accounting for 26.6 per cent of real GDP in . The total assets of retail banks (including foreign assets) stood at BD23.9 billion as at the end of the year, an increase of BD5.3 billion or 28.3 per cent over 2007. This growth is attributed mainly to growth in domestic assets, which increased from BD8.0 billion at end-2007 to BD11.1 billion at end-2008 (a 38.6 per cent growth rate). Total outstanding credit facilities extended by retail banks to the different sectors of the domestic economy amounted to BD5,887.6 million as at end of 2008. The consolidated balance sheet for wholesale banks decreased in 2008. Total wholesale bank assets fell by 3.8 per cent to reach US$188.9 billion at year-end, down from US$196.3 billion in 2007. External sector indicators for 2008 reflected the global economic disturbances with Bahrain's current account surplus narrowing to BD848.6 million, compared to BD1,092.9 million in 2007. The capital and financial account registered a net outflow of BD837.2 million, while the direct investment account shows a noticeable increase in net inflow of BD65.2 million (up from BD32.7 million in 2007). The net international investment position rose to BD5,774.9 million by the end of the year (from BD4,949.4 in 2007). With the global financial crisis affecting financial markets around the world, the Bahrain All Share Index closed 34.5 per cent down at the end of the year with virtually all sectors showing year-on-year declines. The only exception was the hotel and tourism sector with a 23.0 per cent year-on-year increase.

Economy: IMF *Approval*

According to the International Monetary Fund (IMF) Bahrain's macroeconomic performance during 2005/06, was strong. Real gross domestic product (GDP) grew by a healthy 7.75 per cent a year, reflecting a strong expansion in financial services, construction, and manufacturing. In the view of the IMF, this performance was supported by prudent macroeconomic policies, further improvements in the investment environment, and favourable economic conditions in neighbouring countries. Although non-oil GDP grew by an annual 10 per cent, oil GDP declined by 5 per cent over the same period. As a result, Bahrain remains the lowest oil-dependent economy in the Gulf Co-operation Council (GCC), with the share of the hydrocarbon sector in total GDP declining to 15 per cent in 2006. Inflation remained subdued at below 3 per cent during 2005–06, and (rather surprisingly) the unemployment rate declined from 15 per cent in 2005 to 4 per cent in mid-2007. Financial stability has not been affected by the correction seen in the GCC equity markets or the recent global sub-prime credit turmoil. Bahrain's overall fiscal position registered moderate surpluses in 2005/06, as increases in oil revenues were largely offset by lower non-oil receipts and higher capital spending. Capital expenditures increased by over 2.5 per cent of GDP, but restraint in current spending helped maintain an average overall fiscal surplus of about 3 per cent of GDP. As a result, public debt declined by 5 percentage points, to 23 per cent of GDP by end-2006.

High oil prices have certainly helped to strengthen Bahrain's external position, as indicated by the high current account surpluses registered. Despite strong import growth, the current account surplus averaged 12 per cent of GDP in 2005–06, driven mainly by the growth seen in exports of hydrocarbon products and aluminium. At the same time, the Central Bank's gross official reserves increased to about US$3 billion by the end of September 2007, equivalent to 2.9 months' expenditure of imports of goods and services. Bahrain's real effective exchange rate depreciated by 2.8 per cent in 2005 and by an additional 2.9 per cent in 2006, reflecting (inter-alia) the weakening of the US dollar.

Money growth accelerated in response to a large foreign assets accumulation and also to strong private sector credit growth. Broad money grew by 15 per cent in 2006, and at an annualised rate of 31 per cent in the first nine months of 2007, with credit to the private sector growing at a strong pace. Following the cut in the US Federal Reserve 'Fed funds' rate in September 2007, in November 2007 the Central Bank lowered its key policy interest rate to ease upward pressure on the dinar.

The Economy Matures

Bahrain's reputation as a relatively 'safe haven' investment location seemed justified as not only the financial sector performance, but also the legal framework, continued to improve. Solvency, profitability and asset quality indicators all strengthened in 2006 and the first nine months of 2007. At the same time, Bahrain's equity market remained remarkably stable during the Gulf Co-operation Council (GCC) equity market turmoil of 2005/06 and strengthened subsequently, with the price index rising to a historical high after a 15 per cent gain. The passage of a new Central Bank of Bahrain (CBB) law in September 2006 established the CBB as a single regulator of the country's financial services industry, covering banking, insurance, and the capital markets. The IMF noted that the Bahrain authorities have also made good progress in implementing the 2005 Financial Sector Assessment Programme (FSAP) recommendations, including those pertaining to Anti-Money Laundering/Countering Financing of Terrorism (AML/CFT).

The authorities have also embarked upon comprehensive reforms to reduce further the costs of doing business by streamlining regulations and creating the necessary infrastructure in partnership with the private sector. Bahrain has initiated a public services outsourcing and deregulation programme, and has embarked on a four-pillar labour reform process to enhance productivity and employment opportunities and on a comprehensive overhaul of the education system.

The outlook for 2007/08 remains favourable. Reflecting a strong expansion in the non-oil sector, real GDP growth is projected to average 6.5 per cent a year in 2007/08. Inflation is expected to reach 3.5 per cent in 2007, but would decline gradually thereafter as world non-fuel commodity prices decline, and domestic supply bottlenecks subside. The overall fiscal surplus is projected to average 2.75 per cent of GDP in 2007/08, owing mainly to higher oil revenue, while the external current account is expected to register record-high surpluses, in the order of 15 per cent of GDP.

Oil Industry Expansion

Between 2007 and 2015 BAPCO expects to drill a further 700 new wells in the Awali Field, in the expectation of producing an additional 12,000bpd. This is forecast to offset any further declines in production. NOGA has also opened a new licensing round for offshore exploration and production projects. More important than crude oil production, however, is Bahrain's refining industry. The country's only refinery is located south of Manama and has a capacity of 248,900bpd. The Sitra Refinery was built in 1936, and has since undergone several modernisations. BAPCO has announced a US$900 million modernisation programme that entails the addition of supplemental hydrocracking facilities, which will allow Sitra to produce a wider range of petroleum products including low sulphur diesel and gasoline.

Bahrain also has untapped potential oil reserves offshore in the Gulf of Bahrain. In March 2001, the International Court of Justice resolved a territorial dispute between Bahrain and Qatar over islands located between the two countries. Sovereignty over the Hawar Islands was awarded to Bahrain, while Qatar retained the neighbouring islands of Zubarah and Jinan. Resolution of the territorial dispute allowed Bahrain to offer concessions located off the country's south-eastern coast to foreign investors. Bahrain has natural gas reserves of about 3.2 trillion cubic feet (Tcf), most of which is associated gas from the Awali Oilfield. Gas production and processing are the responsibility of the majority state-owned Bahrain National Gas Company (BANAGAS).

Risk Assessment

Regional Stability	Good
Economy	Fair
Politics	Fair

2010

Rankings – Foreign Influences – Dense Population – Religious Balance Tilts – Societies – Islamic Finance Centre – Iranian Suspicions – Regenerating Oil Production

Bahrain's energetic ruler, King Hamad bin Isa al-Khalifa, inherited the throne in 1999, since when he, and his eldest son Crown Prince Sheikh Salman bin Hamad bin Isa al-Khalifa have set about introducing reforms which, it is claimed, will bring Bahrain into the twenty-first century. In the immediate post-Second World War period, Bahrain was for a long while the most developed state in the Gulf, the hub of the region's business and communications. Airlines slipped their crews in Bahrain, banks and Lebanese advertising agencies chose Bahrain for their first presence in the booming Gulf. The Gulf's first English language newspapers were also based in Bahrain.

Remarkably, Bahrain has the highest rating of any Middle East country on the conservative-leaning, Washington based Heritage Foundation's *Index of Economic Freedom* world rankings, placed 13 in 2009, followed by Qatar in 39th place. Bahrain has moved up from 19 in 2008, and now finds itself ahead of most European countries, only Denmark, Ireland, Switzerland and the United Kingdom coming ahead. The United Arab Emirates (UAE) was placed 46, Jordan 52.

Progress

The neo-colonial atmosphere that had characterised much of the Gulf in the period following the First World War saw Bahrain become the seat of the so-called British Political Agent (a form of lesser viceroy), at the centre of the network of Trucial States and tribal fiefdoms. A combination of close political ties with Britain, and the fact that Bahrain's oil revenues could never rival those of its neighbours, meant that the island state retained a greater openness to foreign influences. Another almost unspoken influence was the fact that although most of the population are Shi'a, the ruling al-Khalifa family are Sunni, producing something resembling a political impasse. The post Second World War development of the small island rapidly led to the appearance of a modern, liberal state. Membership of the World Trade Organisation (of which it was a founder member in 1995) and other international agencies later conferred upon Bahrain a status that other Gulf States could at the time only aspire to. Appearances can deceive however. Despite this patina of modernity, in 2010 *de facto* Bahrain is still ruled by a single family; democracy may have a toehold, but little more. The majority Shi'a population, accounting for between 60 and 70 per cent of the population, harbour the inevitable resentments of any marginalised group, religious or otherwise.

Tensions

Surprisingly, Bahrain is also one of the most densely populated countries in the world; about 89 per cent of the population live in the two urban centres of Manama and al-Muharraq. Approximately 66 per cent of the indigenous population is originally from the Arabian Peninsula and Iran. Bahrain also has a large foreign labour force – roughly half the population – with many immigrant workers coming from the Indian sub-continent. Citizens of the Co-operation Council for the Arab States of the Gulf – more commonly known as the Gulf Co-operation Council (GCC) – countries are able to assume Bahraini nationality, an innovation that has raised concerns among Bahrain's vociferous, and essentially Shi'a, opposition groups that the religious balance may be tilted in favour of the Sunni population. Official estimates are that some 40,000 foreign citizens have been naturalised since the 1960s.

In Bahrain's first attempt at anything like universal suffrage since the 1970s, a referendum was held in 2001 on proposals to transform Bahrain from a hereditary emirate to a constitutional monarchy within two years; almost 95 per cent of those polled endorsed the charter. Approval meant that Sheikh Hamad could change his title from Emir to the rather grander 'King'. In only the second round of national (parliamentary) and municipal elections, held in late 2006, the al-Wafaq society, representing the Shi'a population, became the largest single group in the Council of Deputies. Thirty-two of the Council's 40 members represent Sunni and Shi'a Islamist 'societies', the *noms de guerre* for Bahrain's political parties.

Economy Quietly Doing Well

The global financial crisis inevitably affected Bahrain's economy from 2008. According to the International Monetary Fund (IMF) gross domestic product (GDP) growth dropped to 2.9 per cent in 2009, from 6.1 per cent in 2008, owing to lower levels of non-oil activity, largely attributed to a drop in financial services activity. Bahrain's inflation has remained low compared to the levels seen in some other GCC countries, partly reflecting government subsidies and infrastructure development projects that helped to limit housing bottlenecks.

The IMF also noted that financial developments elsewhere also inevitably had an effect on Bahrain's external position. The appreciation of the US dollar in 2008–09 generated a reversal of speculative capital inflows. Some locally-incorporated banks incurred losses on their international portfolios and saw a sharp decline in deposits, but parent banks or shareholders injected capital and increased deposits or credit lines as necessary. Overall, these steps worked, containing the balance of payments deficit. None-the-less, international reserves declined from 7.5 months' worth of imports in 2007 to 5.5 months in 2008.

Buoyant hydrocarbon revenues financed a strong increase in public spending in 2008. The fiscal stimulus continued, with the non-oil primary deficit increasing to 33 per cent of non-oil GDP, from 27.5 per cent in 2007. The rise in spending reflected higher current outlays; capital spending declined. The 2009 budget foresaw an increase in the non-oil primary budget deficit of 1.5 percentage points of non-oil GDP; higher current spending was expected to offset any further decline in capital expenditure.

Net foreign assets had increased during the first half of 2008, owing to high oil prices and speculative capital inflows. Despite the introduction of higher capital charges on property investments in 2007 and an increase in reserve requirements from 5 to 7 per cent in January 2008, Bahrain's banks continued to channel significant resources to domestic lending, further fuelling credit growth to the private sector. Despite these strains, the financial sector appeared to be surviving the global financial turbulence. Unlike elsewhere in the region, the Central Bank of Bahrain (CBB) did not have to shore up retail banks, mainly because parent banks and/or shareholders provided support to maintain solvency and liquidity. Consequently, liquidity has been maintained in the system and core retail banks have been able to preserve their balance sheets.

At the start of the financial crisis over 370 offshore banking units and representative offices were located in Bahrain, as well as 65 American firms. Bahrain has made a particular effort to establish itself as the leading Islamic finance centre in the Arab world. There are 32 Islamic commercial, investment and leasing banks as well as Islamic insurance (takaful) companies, reportedly the largest concentration of Islamic financial institutions in the Middle East.

Friendly Relations

As a matter of informed common sense, in addition to maintaining friendly relations with its largest financial backers, Saudi Arabia, Kuwait and the UAE, Bahrain has worked to improve its relations with Qatar and has proper, but hardly cordial, relations with Shi'a Iran. The withdrawal of the British from the Gulf under the East of Suez policy in the 1970s meant that for the remainder of the twentieth century, Iran was the Gulf's only military superpower. The simple fact, and the knowledge that Iran has long harboured strategic designs on Bahrain, meant that relations were inevitably strained. The discovery in 1981 of an Iran-sponsored coup plot in Bahrain did not improve matters, and they have not improved much since. Bahraini suspicions of the Iranian role in local political unrest in the mid-1990s persisted.

Maritime Settlement

In March 2001 the International Court of Justice (ICJ) announced its judgment on a long-standing maritime delimitation and territorial dispute between Bahrain and Qatar. The judgment awarded sovereignty over the Hawar Islands and Qit'at Jaradah to Bahrain and sovereignty over Zubarah (part of the Qatar Peninsula), Jinan Island and Fasht ad Dibal to Qatar. The peaceful settlement of this dispute has allowed for renewed co-operation, including plans to construct a causeway between the two countries. Since the 1991 Gulf War, the US has replaced the UK as the principal supplier of military hardware and assistance. Military exercises are conducted on a regular basis to increase the Bahrain Defence Forces's (BDF's) readiness.

Oil: Modest, but Enough for the Moment

All of Bahrain's 125 million barrels of onshore oil reserves are located in the Awali oilfield, the first oilfield to be developed in the Gulf. Discovered in 1932, Awali's crude oil production peaked at more than 75,000 barrels per day (bpd) in the 1970s, but has declined since then. However modest, Bahrain's oil sector accounts for around two-thirds of total government revenue. Although the first state on the Arabian Peninsula to produce crude oil, in comparison to its neighbours in the Gulf it has always had a modest, though vital output. The Kingdom has however been very successful in extending oil production even after some analysts predicted reserves would be depleted by 1997. In 2009 it still produced some 35,000bpd from the Awali field. The main source of petroleum now comes from its shared production with Saudi Arabia in the Abu Safah oilfield providing Bahrain with a further 150,000bpd. Despite this Bahrain urgently needs to acquire additional energy resources to sustain its industrial expansion since current domestic oil reserves are now put at little more than 125 million barrels and 92 billion cubic metres of gas. The ICJ's 2001 ruling ending the territorial dispute with Qatar meant that the offshore oil reserves in the Gulf of Bahrain became available for exploration and potential exploitation. Bahrain has since offered concessions to foreign investors. In November 2001, Bahrain had also awarded two blocks off the country's south-eastern coast to Petronas (Malaysia) and another similarly located block to ChevronTexaco of the USA.

The consolidation of Bahrain's state-owned petroleum sector began in January 2000, when the upstream Bahrain National Oil Company (BANOCO) began merging into BAPCO. The merger was completed on 1 June 2002. The new entity, the Bahrain Petroleum Company BSC, was charged with the exploration, production, refining, marketing and distribution of Bahraini oil for domestic use and the international market. In 2005, the Bahrain government issued a Royal decree establishing the National Oil and Gas Authority (noga), which replaced the Ministry of Oil. Noga has regulatory and oversight authority, as well as policy-making functions over the oil sector. Unlike other Gulf States, Bahrain exports refined petroleum products rather than crude oil, with most exports going to India and other Asian markets. According to the 2010 BP Statistical Review of World Energy, Bahrain had modest natural gas reserves of 0.09 trillion cubic metres in 2009, and production of 12.8 billion cubic metres.

The twenty-first century saw real expectations that the decline in production could be reversed with the help of foreign investment. It was hoped that output from the Awali oilfield would double with new technology able to exploit hitherto non-viable reserves.

Buoyant crude prices also stimulated investor interest, with bids to regenerate Bahrain's oil production. The offshore blocks under development completely lap Bahrain's entire 7,400 square kilometres area. Wider exploration is also under way in co-operation with both Qatar and Iran.

Risk Assessment

Economy	Good
Politics	Fair
Regional Stability	Fair

2011/12

Gulf Staging Post – Iranian Interference – Rumblings of Dissent – Violent Periods – Saudi Troop Reinforcements – Royal Family Wrong-Footed – An Uprising, Not a Revolution – A Deepening Human Rights Crisis – Decency and Tolerance? – The World's Newest Pariah State

Bahrain is a small island (less than 50km long, and only 15km across), with a population of one million, (roughly half of whom are not Bahrainis), little oil and, at least in comparison to its wealthy near neighbours, lacking a mouth-watering sovereign wealth fund. During the Second World War Bahrain served as a base for military aircraft and ships from both the US and the UK. In the period immediately after the war, it was the Gulf's staging post, where the aircraft of the British Overseas Airways Corporation (BOAC) and Australia's Qantas (Queensland and Northern Territories Air Services) refuelled on their flights half way round the world. In what at the time was the seminal work on the region, *The Arabian Peninsula* published in 1954, Richard Sanger wrote that 'although its size and limited resources prevent Bahrain from becoming an important business and trading centre, wise expenditure and the investment of its oil revenues and wages have already brought the highest standard of living.' Mr Sanger also noted that the oil revenues had been 'quite fairly and usefully administered. Approximately one third has gone to the King to be spent by him and his family for their personal needs and charities. One third is invested so that Bahrain will have wealth to fall back on when oil production ends. And one-third is used for the operation and modernisation of the islands.' In 1953, it seemed, all was sweetness and light in the island state where a Sunni majority ruled over a Shi'a minority.

February – the Cruellest Month?
In the early twenty-first century, Bahrain continued as a relatively calm island, where thirsty Saudi Arabians could breach the island's fastness and drive over the 26km King Fahd Causeway, completed in 1986, linking the island to Saudi Arabia. But times change; immigration and birth rate differentials had seen to it that in the second half of the twentieth century, Bahrain's Sunni Muslim rulers held increasingly uncertain sway over the Shi'a Muslim majority. In the first ten years of the century, an estimated 65,000–100,000 Sunnis were added to the electoral roll, concentrated in large-scale government housing projects.

Nevertheless, since the 2003 end of Saddam Hussein's rule in Iraq, Bahrain has found itself isolated as the only Shi'a majority country ruled by a Sunni élite. Many observers concur that Shi'a Iran has long sought to exacerbate tensions between the two communities. A desire to interfere in the internal affairs of Bahrain has long featured, albeit discreetly, in Iranian foreign policy. Iran has from time to time claimed Bahrain as its fourteenth Iranian province; the basis of this claim dates back to the eighteenth century when for a short period Bahrain recognised Iranian sovereignty. The periodic resurgence of the claim flies in the face of history; if anything it has probably lead to a modest level of Arab nationalism, evident in the rival nomenclature 'Persian' and Arabian Gulf. Understandably, Bahrain's rulers are nervous of any Iranian interest in their country's affairs.

In the run up to Bahrain's elections in October 2010 rumblings of dissent surfaced, anticipating similar undercurrents in Egypt, Libya, Syria, Tunisia and Yemen. As many as 150 protesters were detained in the October protests, principally involving Shi'a political and human-rights leaders, but including some who had done no more than join in the protests. Bahraini opposition leaders accused the US of ignoring these protests. The US Ambassador J Adam Ereli was reported as saying that 'Bahrain is important to the United States for security issues. But that doesn't mean we don't raise human rights issues as well.' The US State Department, like many others, failed to appreciate the seriousness of the situation.

In late February 2011 matters came to a head, as Bahrainis lived through one of the most violent periods in the small island's history. What had become something of a peaceful backwater saw something of a bloodbath when nervous Sunni troops, unable to control crowds of protesters in Manama's Pearl (Lulu) Square (in fact a roundabout) opened fire, killing seven Shi'a protesters and wounding scores, possibly hundreds, more. Interestingly, although most of the protesters were Shi'a, a number came from the Sunni Muslim community, equally incensed about the lack of true democracy, the prevalence of corruption and fundamental inequalities. Some degree of reason eventually prevailed on the part of the government when the Crown Prince, the government's *de facto* spokesman, ordered the troops back to their barracks.

The Bahraini protesters had seen from events in Egypt just how effective a well-organised street protest could be. Pearl Square took on some of the aspects of Cairo's Tahrir Square, with tents accommodating thousands of demonstrators, a Bahraini 'Speakers Corner' and numerous, for the most part free of charge, food stands.

If things had looked grim for the government in February 2011, by March they had taken a turn for the worse. Invoking the collective defence clauses of the Gulf Co-operation Council (GCC) on 14 March 2,000 troops from Saudi Arabia and the United Arab Emirates (UAE) moved in to shore up the beleaguered al-Khalifa régime. The troop reinforcements lost no time in propping up their Bahraini counterparts, clearing public areas of protesters and dismantling the Pearl Square encampments. Unconfirmed reports suggested that the 'invasion' had resulted in the deaths of a further seven demonstrators. The operation provided the Iranian government with something of a public relations coup, a result that irritated many of the younger demonstrators who, again following the Egyptian example, seemed for the most part anxious to maintain the non-sectarian nature of their protest.

Getting it Wrong

Bahrain's bigger, and wealthier, neighbours to the south and east were understandably nervous, not only about the possible outcome of the Bahrain Uprising, but also about any possible Iranian intervention. It later emerged that Bahrain (as well as Oman) had been promised an annual aid stipend (from the US) of US$1 billion for the next ten years.

Nervous? Us?

Bahrain is the base for the US Navy's Fifth Fleet; no small matter in the overall picture. The fleet comprises around 30 warships and 30,000 officers, sailors and staff. Immediately after the arrival of GCC troops in Bahrain US Secretary of State Hillary Clinton telephoned the Saudi foreign minister Prince Saud al-Faisal to express her concern. Mrs Clinton was quoted as saying: 'the security challenges cannot be a substitute for a political resolution.' While in Tunisia she had earlier said of the invasion that 'We have said not only to the Bahrainis but to our Gulf partners that we do not think the security is the answer to what is going on.' The US was, predictably if improbably, joined by Iran in complaining about the Saudi presence in Bahrain. Iran sees Sunni Saudi Arabia as its sparring partner in the region.

Bahrain's royal family certainly appeared to have been wrong-footed by the Pearl Square demonstrations. After the shooting incident, King (the constitution promulgated in 2002 established Bahrain as a constitutional hereditary monarchy whose head of state is the King) Hamad announced the release of 23 political prisoners. This gesture was not so much made willingly, but reluctantly in response to its imposition by Manama's protesters as a pre-condition to talks. Following the Saudi example, King Hamad also announced a one-off payment of 1,000 dinars to every Bahraini family. As has been the case in Egypt and in Libya, as well as in Yemen, events in Bahrain added up to an uprising rather than a revolution, lacking as it did an obvious leader.

The common perception of the Bahraini régime prior to the uprising was one of mild decency and tolerance. But the official response to the Pearl Square demonstrations was certainly not one of dialogue and discussion, nor of any degree of give and take. It was one of intolerance, harsh repression and summary punishment. The regime which, either by actually inviting or at least agreeing to the incursion of troops from Saudi Arabia and the UAE, had already shot itself in the foot, made matters even worse by detaining over 500 people. Human rights groups reported on the deaths of four Bahrainis in detention; there were also reports of torture. The arrival of foreign troops in Bahrain was certainly a public relations disaster for the government. But there was worse: in April a military court sentenced four young Bahrainis to death for their alleged role in the death of two policemen. Three others received life sentences for their alleged role in the deaths. Amnesty International's Middle East director went on record as saying that 'Bahrain is in the grip of a deepening human rights crisis and the severity of the sentences... will do nothing to reverse that.' Significantly, a number of Bahraini politicians joined local human rights activists in acknowledging that the damage done to the country's reputation was beyond repair.

In mid-June 2011, a Bahraini military court tried 23 doctors and 24 nurses who had treated injured protesters. This was seen by virtually all neutral observers as a sad detachment of the regime from principled behaviour. The doctors and nurses' lawyers complained they had been tortured in custody. This was certainly not the behaviour expected of a once respected constitutional monarchy. The London daily *The Times* went so far as to describe Bahrain as 'the world's newest pariah state'. The charges ranged from stealing medicine to stockpiling weapons to taking over a hospital. The defendants' lawyers challenged the military court's jurisdiction, also requesting that their clients receive independent medical examination.

Knowing it was on the ropes of international politics the Bahraini regime forlornly seized on the prospect of reinstating the Formula One Grand Prix that had been cancelled in March 2011 because of the protests. Crown Prince Salman had pounded Europe's political pavements in May 2011, meeting with the UK's David Cameron and other leaders, optimistically endeavouring to restore his government's tattered image. It was reported that he had also been in touch with the Formula One President Bernie Ecclestone. Local press reports alleged that in April a quarter of the staff employed at the Bahrain International Circuit (where the Grand Prix was to have been held) had been sacked. Those who lost their jobs were, reportedly, all Sh'ia. The government's decision to end on 1 June 2011 the state of emergency that had been in place since 15 March was thought to have more to do with reinstating the Grand Prix than any humanitarian concerns. The deadline for re-scheduling the Grand Prix was 3 June. At first it seemed as though the event would go-ahead. By mid-June, however, the decision to hold the Grand Prix seemed to have been reversed, not out of any moral or even political concerns, but because the risks to drivers and track officials were too high.

Oil Gone

Bahrain is the oldest oil-producing state in the Gulf. The first strike was in 1932 and commercial production began in 1934 by the Standard Oil subsidiary, Bahrain Petroleum Company (BAPCO), from the Awali oilfield. Petroleum production and refining account for more than 60 per cent of Bahrain's export receipts, and 70 per cent of government revenues. Most of Bahrain's total energy consumption comes from natural gas, with the remainder supplied by oil. Hydrocarbons also provide the foundation for Bahrain's two major industries: petroleum refining and aluminium smelting. Bahrain's proven oil reserves stood at 125 million barrels in January 2011, according to the US-based *Oil & Gas Journal* (OGJ), all of which are located in the Awali field. In addition to the 46,000 barrels per day (bpd) produced in its territory, Bahrain and Saudi Arabia share the 300,000bpd of oil production from the offshore Abu Safah field. This figure is actually counted in Saudi oil production figures, but half of the output is allocated to Bahrain.

Unlike other Gulf States, Bahrain exports refined petroleum products rather than crude oil. Bahrain's domestic oil pipeline network is rather limited, focused primarily on delivering crude oil from the Awali field to the refinery at Sitra. Because domestic production is much lower than the country's refining capacity, Bahrain imports about 210,000bpd of Arabian Light crude oil from Saudi Arabia via a sub-sea pipeline linking the two countries. BAPCO (owned 60 per cent by the government and 40 per cent by Caltex since 1981) refines this crude oil and exports much of it via tanker. Most of Bahrain's exports go to India and other Asian markets.

Bahrain's production remained relatively stable over the first decade of the twenty-first century. As domestic consumption has surged since 2005, exports have decreased proportionately. Perhaps surprisingly, the self-contained nature and presence of Bahrain's hydrocarbons production has meant that it has been to a degree cocooned from the effects of the uprising seen in the first few months of 2011. Exports were originally expected to continue to decrease in 2011, having already fallen from 27,000bpd in 2005 to 3,000bpd in 2009. However, any diminished levels of domestic demand resulting from the uprising may well make more production available for exports.

2013

Military Tribunal Convictions – Vindictiveness – Reform Agenda –
Continuing Unrest – Job Creation – Key Challenge – Fiscal Unsustainability –
Decline in Bank Assets

In 2012 Bahrain continued to face international criticism as the island state's appeal court decided to uphold the convictions and sentences of 13 men convicted by military tribunals for anti-government protests during the Arab Spring of 2011. The appellants had originally been sentenced in mid-2011 to between two years and life in prison on charges that included espionage, subversion and terrorism. The Bahrain government, whose international promotion relies heavily on the tag-line 'Business friendly' insisted that the men had a fair trial. The island's Information Affairs Authority was quoted in *The Guardian* (UK) as claiming that 'The court provided all assurances of a fair trial through a team of 17 defence attorneys selected by the defendants'. Amnesty International, which attended the first trial, called the appeal court's ruling 'outrageous', adding its view that: 'Today's court decision is another blow to justice. It shows once more that the Bahraini authorities are not on the path of reform but seem rather driven by vindictiveness.'

This small Arabian Gulf state where the Shi'a majority is ruled by the Sunni al-Khalifa dynasty, was shaken in February 2011 by protests which became known locally as the Pearl Revolution. Seen as a Gulf manifestation (virtually the only Gulf manifestation) of the Arab Spring, the more confrontational aspects of the Pearl Revolution ended when Saudi Arabian led Gulf Co-operation Council (GCC) forces intervened. The government has pledged reforms but both the US and Britain have repeatedly criticised it for moving too slowly. Bahrain is home to the US Navy's Fifth Fleet and is a key strategic asset – and potential liability – in any confrontation with Iran. At the end of 2011 Bahrain appeared to be simultaneously paying lip-service to a reform agenda while endeavouring to crack down on continuing unrest. King Hamad bin Isa al-Khalifa had announced constitutional reforms intended to bring about greater accountability. The King had also ordered the rebuilding of mosques knocked down by the government and had appointed two distinguished British lawyers to begin an overhaul of the judicial system. The government claimed that it was reinstating those people – for the most part Shi'a – who had lost their jobs following their support of the protests. Bahrain's trades union representatives disputed the government's claims that this was the case. The measures were intended as much as anything to reassure Bahrain's Western allies, notably the US. Bahrain not only provides strategic Gulf port facilities for the US Fifth Fleet, but is also home to the British naval presence in the Gulf. And to a lesser extent, the proposed reforms were aimed at placating a restive Bahraini population.

King Hamad's government had also appointed a Bahrain Independent Commission of Inquiry (BICI), chaired by the Egyptian lawyer Professor Cherif Bassiouni. The Bahraini government could hardly have expected to be congratulated on its handling of affairs. Whether it had expected such a critical assessment, however, was unlikely. The report highlighted human rights abuses and the torture of detainees by the police and other security forces as they had confronted protests in February and March 2011.

Clutching at Straws

It was not altogether surprising that Bahrain's royal family and the hard-pressed government on which it was super-imposed should take whatever opportunity it could to demonstrate that, contrary to the bulk of international news coverage, all was well in downtown Manama. Thus, claims that Bahrain is 'the most economically free nation in the Middle East and North Africa region (MENA) and 'the seventh freest economy in the world' made by the Canadian based Fraser Institute, a right-wing lobby group seeking (ironically enough in the case of Bahrain) 'a free and prosperous world through choice, markets and responsibility' were unsurprisingly seized upon by the government. The Fraser Institute index measured the degree to which the policies and institutions of countries are supportive of economic freedom. Bahrain achieved an overall score of 7.94 out of 10, marking it ahead of the United States and Japan. The other top 10 nations are Hong Kong, 8.90; Singapore, 8.69; New Zealand, 8.36; Switzerland, 8.24; Australia, 7.97; Canada, 7.97; Mauritius, 7.90; Finland, 7.88; and Chile, 7.84. Bahrain led the rankings in the GCC, followed by the United Arab Emirates (UAE), 7.83; Qatar, 7.70; Kuwait, 7.66; Oman, 7.64; and Saudi Arabia, 7.06. Economic freedom was measured in five different areas: size of government, legal structure and security of property rights, access to sound money, freedom to trade internationally and regulation of credit, labour and business. No reference is made to other freedoms (normally available in Canada) such as the right to demonstrate, to a free press, to strike, to vote in free elections for an elected government. The Bahrain government welcomed other reports highlighting Bahrain's economic strengths. In early 2012 Bahrain was ranked no less than first in the Middle East and twelveth place worldwide in the 2012 *Wall Street Journal*/Heritage Foundation Index of Economic Freedom.

The Stuttering Economy

Bahrain's Economic Development Board (EDB) expected 4–5 per cent gross domestic product (GDP) growth in 2012, driven primarily by increases in crude oil production, manufacturing and government spending. While a fall in private sector demand and a surplus of commercial properties has slowed construction, government spending was projected to compensate and fuel construction for infrastructure, social housing and other social spending projects such as schools and hospitals.

A budgeted US$10 billion ten year GCC fund is likely to be dedicated to projects such as these, in addition to expenditure already budgeted. The increase in Bahraini oil output and higher oil prices were also expected to produce large current account surpluses. The EDB notes that while the political situation was difficult to predict, it was likely to affect hotels, restaurants and trade more than oil output and manufacturing, as the former sectors depend highly on tourism which has been seriously affected by the continued unrest. Manufacturing, on the other hand, is geographically isolated in industrial areas, is focussed on exports and employs a majority of non-Bahrainis, all attributing to less risk of disruption by protests.

Despite relatively strong growth, fiscal deficits remain a looming issue for Bahrain as high oil prices are expected to diminish in the coming years. Employment is also seen as a decisive issue, as the EDB estimates about 7,000 jobs will need to be created for Bahrainis annually to 2020 to keep unemployment levels from rising. These two issues are seen as the key challenges faced by the government in the short to medium term. It should be noted that both the Institute for International Finance (IIF) and the International Monetary Fund (IMF) have projected less optimistic growth outcomes for Bahrain, 3.7 per cent and 2.0 per cent respectively for 2012.

Annual real output growth in Bahrain was 2.2 per cent in 2011 as the economy recovered faster than expected in the second half of the year. After a sharp fall in output in the first quarter of 2011 due to the unrest, output returned to previous levels in the third quarter and grew by 3.2 per cent in the first quarter of 2012 compared to the same period a year earlier.

According to the National Bank of Kuwait's (NBK) GCC Economic Outlook Bahrain's 2.2 per cent rate of growth in 2011 was its lowest rate since 1994. The NBK expected GDP growth to pick up to 3.5 per cent in 2012, supported by continued moderate growth in oil GDP and a recovery in the non-oil sectors that were affected last year. 2013 is likely to see growth accelerate further, to 4 per cent, as confidence and stability improve and economic activity gradually returns to 'pre-turmoil' norms. The sectors disrupted in 2011 – including tourism, retail trade, business services and construction – are all expected to see a steady recovery. As for the sectors that had performed well despite the unrest – manufacturing, government services and local financial institutions – these should continue to see improved growth. The NBK expected non-oil GDP to pick-up to 3.5 per cent in 2012 and to 4 per cent in 2013. This is still much weaker than the 8 per cent average witnessed in the period prior to the unrest.

After remaining flat for the first two months of 2012, the NBK noted that consumer price inflation jumped in March to almost 5 per cent – the highest rate in three years. The rise was driven by a sharp easing in the rate of deflation in housing rents, reflecting a base effect as last year's plunge in rents fell out of the annual comparison. But lower food price inflation helped push the headline rate of inflation back down. The NBK expected inflation to average around 3 per cent in 2012 and in 2013 underpinned by a recovery in domestic demand.

No official figures have been released for 2011, but the budget deficit was expected to have narrowed significantly to 1–2 per cent of GDP helped by record oil revenues. 2012 was forecast to see a similar deficit, but in 2013 the NBK expected lower oil prices to push the budget deficit higher to around 3 per cent of GDP. Moreover, the deficit could turn out larger in the case of a sharp fall in oil prices. Bahrain's budget break-even oil price for 2012 is the highest in the Gulf at an estimated US$115 per barrel.

In 2011 Bahrain's current account surplus expanded strongly on the back of higher oil prices which more than offset the deterioration in the services, income and transfers balances. Higher oil production and an improvement in services inflows from tourism receipts are likely to keep the current account surplus high in 2012 and 2013, at around 13 per cent and 10 per cent of GDP respectively.

When oil prices collapsed in late 2008, persisting throughout 2009, Bahrain's government budget was exposed. The Kingdom swiftly moved to its first large deficit in the decade, which was BD446 million (US$1,183 million) representing 6 per cent of nominal GDP for the year. By the end of 2009, government debt had risen to 25 per cent of GDP and in 2010 it exceeded 35 per cent. However, Bahrain's government debt to GDP is well below the ratios now apparent in Japan, the US, the UK and many European nations. Given the Kingdom's recent two-notch credit rating downgrade by several agencies (which cited not only political instability but concerns about fiscal unsustainability), interest rates on debt were expected to rise, putting pressure on the exchange rate. The issue of fiscal sustainability for Bahrain was identified as a serious concern by several international organisations, including the International Monetary Fund.

The prospects for Bahrain's banking sector are mixed. Retail banks – little affected by the unrest – will continue to perform robustly as domestic demand improves. For wholesale banks, whose assets saw significant declines, the outlook is less clear. Encouragingly, the annual decline in assets of wholesale banks has receded. Nevertheless, a significant recovery is contingent on political stability and wholesale banks' ability to attract foreign funding. On a more global level, the recovery is also subject to a potential break-up of the euro-zone that could have spill-over effects on Bahrain's all-important financial sector, as was the case with the global financial crisis.

A positive sign is the sharp improvement in credit growth. Annual growth in private sector bank claims increased from a mere 2 per cent in April of last year to more than 17 per cent by the end of the first quarter of 2012 – the fastest rate recorded since May 2009. Personal loans in particular jumped in the second half of 2011 and have continued growing at a rapid pace – by more than 20 per cent year on year in the earlier part of 2012. Business loans, although growing at a slower pace, have also seen a significant pick-up, growing by an annual 14 per cent at the end of the first quarter of 2012. This compared to negative growth at the same time last year.

In March 2012, the annual decline in total bank assets came to a halt for the first time in a year. The loan books of retail banks have continued to grow well reaching a record high of US$69 billion. The bigger banking segment, wholesale (or offshore) banks, saw the year-on-year drop in assets recede significantly in March, though this is largely due to a base effect. Wholesale bank assets stood at US$130 billion at the end of the first quarter 2012, well below the plus US$200 billion in assets held during 2008. Uncertainties regarding Bahrain's stability could continue to undermine the wholesale banks' ability to attract foreign funding.

In the first half of 2012 the Central Bank of Bahrain (CBB)'s key policy rate – the one week deposit rate – remained unchanged at 0.5 per cent. Monetary policy has been based upon the exchange rate peg against the US dollar since 1980. Meanwhile, the dinar stood at just under BD0.5 per euro at the end of May 2012, almost 11 per cent stronger than a year earlier. The CBB's official reserves fell by more than US$0.7 billion in the first quarter of 2011 after some capital flight, but had regained US$0.3 billion of this by the third quarter of 2011. After falling for most of 2011, the Bahrain Dow Jones stock index held relatively steady at just below 100 points in the first four months of 2012, before slipping slightly near the end of the first half. Nevertheless, the index was still down by some 16 per cent year on year by mid-2012 reflecting the unrest-related declines of 2011.

Energy

After remaining almost unchanged since 2005, total oil production picked-up in 2011, following a ramping-up of production at Bahrain's ageing Awali oilfield. Production there jumped by more than 10,000 barrels per day (bpd) to 42,500bpd and is expected to reach 100,000bpd within a couple of years. Total oil GDP – which includes output from the Abu Safah oilfield which is shared with Saudi Arabia – was up 3.4 per cent in 2011 and was expected to continue to grow at around 4 per cent in 2012 and 2013. Bahrain is the oldest oil producer in the Arabian Gulf, exporting much of its oil in the form of refined petroleum products rather than crude oil. However, Bahrain has a small hydrocarbons production capacity, much of which is derived from the joint Abu Safah oilfield with Saudi Arabia. Despite its relatively low volumes of oil production, Bahrain's oil sector accounts for about 70 per cent of total government revenues. Bahrain has modest natural gas reserves and it consumes all the natural gas that it produces. Bahrain was integrated into the GCC power grid in 2009, ensuring adequate electricity supply even in emergencies. Overall, crude oil production, grew by 6.5 per cent in the fourth quarter of 2011. This growth is part of the planned expansion of the Bahrain field through the Tatweer Petroleum deal, which aims to increase Bahrain oilfield production to more than 100,000bpd in the coming years (from an initial production of around 30,000bpd prior to 2009).

Bahrain's government plays a majority role in the energy sector, both in electricity generation and regulation. State-owned companies dominate the market, with the national electricity regulator, Electricity and Water Authority (EWA), being chaired by the Minister of Electricity and Water. The Ministry of Electricity and Water is responsible for generation, transmission and distribution of electricity and remains the sole transmitter and distributor in the country.

In January 2010, in an effort to improve energy security, Bahrain awarded an oilfield contract to Occidental to more than double production from the Bahrain oilfield. the National Oil and Gas Authority (NOGA) estimates that domestic demand for oil will increase by at least 3 per cent a year over the coming year, reaching 45,000bpd by 2011. The country is also on course to establish connections with the electricity grid of the UAE and in the long-term, with Oman. However, plans to implement nuclear power in the country have faced problems due to a lack of local experience and the high demand for nuclear expertise in the area.

Risk Assessment

Politics   Poor

Economy   Fair
Regional Stability   Fair

2014

Imprisoned Human Rights Defenders – 'Honest and Open Discussions' – HRW Criticism – No Willingness to Change – *Annus Horribilis* – Bond Issue – Fiscal Improvement

In June 2013 a number of human rights organisations asked the European Union (EU), ahead of its ministerial meeting later in the month with the Gulf Co-operation Council (GCC), to call for the release of those 'currently detained and imprisoned for peacefully exercising their rights'. The organisations' statement highlighted the continued crackdown by the authorities in Bahrain on human rights defenders and peaceful opposition activists. It also deplored the failure of the EU to make what it termed 'explicit calls for the immediate and unconditional release of human rights defenders, Twitter activists and bloggers and leaders of peaceful protests.' Specific reference was made to the cases of imprisoned human rights defenders Naji Fateel, Abdulhadi al-Khawaja, Nabeel Rajab and human rights defender Zainab al-Khawaja who, only days before the GCC/EU meeting was sentenced to two additional months in jail in relation to charges of assault against two policewomen inside prison.

Interfere, Restrict, Control

Following the meeting, the EU delegation issued a cautious statement, lamely noting that 'We do have honest and open discussions on issues, for instance on human rights. We may have different perspectives at times, but we're able to have that honest dialogue.' The acting president of the independent Bahrain Centre for Human Rights, Maryam al-Khawaja (whose father, Abdulhadi al-Khawaja was sentenced to life imprisonment for his part in the 2011 democracy demonstrations and whose sister Zainab is imprisoned) said she was 'very disappointed' by the comments, made by the EU's Catherine Ashton, not generally known for her familiarity with Middle Eastern affairs. Ms al-Khawaja said that 'The regime barely received a slap on the wrist' from the EU.

The US based non-governmental organisation (NGO) Human Rights Watch (HRW) was altogether more forthright in its criticism of the Bahraini government. In its June 2013 report, entitled *Interfere, Restrict and Control*, HRW noted that 'Since independence from Britain in 1971, social, cultural and sports clubs, as well as civil and professional organisations, have been pivotal in shaping po-

© KONINKLIJKE BRILL NV, LEIDEN, 2023 | DOI:10.1163/9789004686335_032

litical debate. With political groups of any sort prohibited until 2001 NGOs had often served as forums for discussing social, economic and political issues.'

However, government actions and legislation have often undermined the ability of such groups to function. Despite a limited flowering of civil society since 2001, civic, political, and labour organisations have functioned with difficulty, with the authorities harassing, arresting and prosecuting their leaders and members. This has intensified in the wake of the widespread pro-democracy demonstrations that took place throughout much of the country in February and March 2011. In particular, the Ministry of Social Development has far exceeded international standards in its restrictive scope and 'routinely exploited its oversight role to stymie the activities of NGOs and other civil society organisations', said HRW.

Today, freedom of association is under even greater threat due in part to draft legislation that is even more restrictive than the current Law of Associations (No 21/1989), which authorities use – in the words of one Bahraini activist – 'to interfere, restrict and attempt to control the activities of civic organisations.'

Adding to the international criticism of the régime, in 2013 the Paris-based European Union Institute for Security Studies was quoted by Judy Dempsey in the *International Herald Tribune* (IHT) as saying that Bahrain's Prime Minister, Sheikh Khalifa bin Salman al-Khalifa – who has been in power since 1971 – showed no willingness to change. According to the Institute's report 'Bahrain is caught between reforms it is not willing to undertake and an uprising it is unable to suppress.' Feeling itself to be on the back foot, it also emerged that the Bahraini government had cancelled an official visit scheduled to be made by the United Nations' special rapporteur on torture and other abuses, Juan E Méndez. On the Transparency International Corruption Perceptions Index Bahrain ranked 53 in 2012, well down on the 36th position achieved in 2006 when it was ranked 4th among Middle East countries, behind only the United Arab Emirates (UAE), Qatar and Israel.

Conflicting Loyalties

In 2013 Bahrain was still feeling the effects of 2011 – Bahrain's annus horrabilis – when this small Arabian Gulf state had been shaken in the February of that year by protests which became known locally as the Pearl Revolution. Seen as a Gulf manifestation of the Arab Spring, the more confrontational aspects of the Pearl Revolution had ended when Saudi Arabian led GCC forces had intervened. The Sunni government (of a Shi'a majority) had pledged reforms but both the US and Britain have repeatedly criticised it for moving too slowly. Bahrain is home to the US navy's Fifth Fleet and is a key strategic asset in any confrontation with

Iran. By 2012 Bahrain appeared to be simultaneously paying lip-service to a reform agenda while endeavouring to crack down on continuing unrest, even though King Hamad bin Isa al-Khalifa had announced constitutional reforms intended to bring about greater accountability. The King had also ordered the rebuilding of mosques knocked down by the government and appointed two distinguished British lawyers to begin an overhaul of the judicial system. The government claimed that it was reinstating those people – for the most part Shi'a – who had lost their jobs following their support of the protests. Bahrain's trades union representatives disputed the government's claims that this was the case. The measures had been intended as much as anything to reassure Bahrain's Western allies, notably the US. To a lesser extent, the proposed reforms were aimed at placating a restive Bahraini population.

King Hamad's government had also appointed a Bahrain Independent Commission of Inquiry (BICI), chaired by the Egyptian lawyer Professor Cherif Bassiouni. The Bahraini government could hardly have expected to be congratulated on its handling of affairs, but whether it had expected such a critical assessment, however, was unlikely. The report highlighted human rights abuses and the torture of detainees by the police and other security forces as they confronted the 2011 protests.

The Economy

According to Reuters, Bahrain's underlying economic strategy is – or at least was – based on becoming a regional financial hub, a decision it had been obliged to take as it lacks much of the petrodollar wealth of its Arab and Iranian neighbours. However, the political unrest that manifested itself in 2011, in which the government confronted mainly Shi'ite-led pro-democracy protests, hit Bahrain's economy hard and, *inter alia* raised pressure on the government to boost spending. As outlined in the 'Energy' section below, output in the hydrocarbons sector, which accounts for a quarter of Bahrain's US\$30 billion economy, grew by 1.3 per cent in the January–March 2013 period compared to the meagre 0.4 per cent rise seen in the final three months of 2012. Hydrocarbon output jumped 8.0 per cent on an annual basis in the first quarter after falling by the same amount in October–December. Last year (2013), Bahrain reported a drop in crude oil output from its key Abu Safah field, which it shares with Saudi Arabia and which contributes nearly 67 per cent of budget revenue.

Growth in Bahrain's financial sector, which accounts for roughly 16 per cent of gross domestic product (GDP), slowed to 0.3 per cent quarter-on-quarter in January-March 2013 from 1.4 per cent in the previous three months. In the hospitality sector, which had nose-dived during the 2011 turmoil, output crept up by 0.5 per cent in January–March, after a 0.1 per cent rise in the fourth quarter of 2012. In the view of the analysts polled by Reuters in April 2013, Bahrain's GDP growth was expected to ease slightly to 3.3 per cent in 2013 from the 3.8 per cent registered in 2012.

In its May 2013 assessment of the Bahraini economy, the International Monetary Fund (IMF), noted that the economic situation had improved in 2012 following the downturn in non-oil GDP seen in 2011, due largely to the continuing crisis in the euro-zone and the persistent domestic political unrest. As oil production for the year contracted, (for the most part because of a disruption in the Abu Safah oilfield that was rectified by the end of 2012), non-oil economic activity rebounded, supported by government spending. According to the IMF, activity in manufacturing, hotels and restaurants and insurance picked up significantly, accompanied by a moderate recovery in construction and retail banking. Inflation was again in positive territory after the 2011 deflation, supported by the improvement in housing rents.

In the view of the IMF, Bahrain's external position also seemed to improve in 2012 due to a decline in capital outflows and to the strength of the current account position, which remained strong with an estimated surplus of 18.2 per cent of GDP. Official reserves increased from US$4.2 billion at end-2011 to about US$4.9 billion in 2012 (18 per cent of GDP and close to 10 months of import cover, excluding imports of crude oil).

Financial market developments reflected the rebound in the wider economy. Private-sector credit and deposit growth were solid at 6 per cent and 5 per cent, respectively. In addition, there were tentative signs that investor confidence had improved. The deleveraging in the wholesale segment of the banking sector appeared to have stabilised and several market-based indicators had moved into more positive territory. The government's bond issue of US$1.5 billion was four times over-subscribed at a coupon of 5.8 per cent; both bond yields and CDS spreads were back to pre-2011 levels. In January 2013, Standard & Poor's revised Bahrain's outlook to stable from negative. Nevertheless, the stock market index declined by 7 per cent in 2012.

The fiscal outcome in 2012 was estimated to have been better than expected. The overall fiscal deficit for 2012 (excluding extra-budgetary operations) was estimated at 1.0 per cent of GDP, reflecting high oil prices, a consolidation in capital spending and a reduction in subsidies and transfers that resulted from scaling back gas subsidies for industrial users. Including extra-budgetary operations, the overall deficit was estimated at 2.6 per cent of GDP.

Energy

Bahrain is, along with Oman, one of only two countries bordering the Arabian Gulf that is not a member of the Organisation of the Petroleum Exporting

Countries (OPEC). Bahrain produced 48,000 barrels per day (bpd) of total petroleum liquids in 2012, the least of any country in the Gulf. It has set a goal of increasing total petroleum production to 100,000bpd by the end of the decade. Bahrain's refinery capacity far exceeds domestic crude oil production capacity. Bahrain has a 254,000bpd export refinery at Sitra. Most of the feedstock is imported from Saudi Arabia, so that net exports for Bahrain are only about 5,000bpd. Plans are under way to expand the refinery's capacity by 100,000bpd by 2017.

Saudi Arabia and Bahrain share production of the 300,000bpd Abu Safah offshore oilfield in Saudi Arabia, which is connected to Bahrain's Sitra refinery via pipeline. Bahrain intends to replace the ageing pipeline system from Saudi Arabia with the planned new Arabia pipeline, a 71 mile, 350,000bpd pipeline running between the Abqaiq complex in Saudi Arabia and Bahrain's refinery at Sitra.

As with oil, Bahrain is a small producer of natural gas and produced 14.2 billion cubic metres of natural gas in 2012, an increase of 6.9 per cent on 2011. In order to meet future natural gas needs, Bahrain plans to import gas from a number of sources, either via pipeline from Qatar or via imports of liquefied natural gas (LNG) following the awarding of a contract to construct a new LNG terminal. Bahrain has over 3 gigawatts of electricity generating capacity, almost all of which is conventional thermal fired. The Kingdom has recently begun to develop solar and other renewable power. It is also taking part in the GCC's plan to integrate the electric power grids of all GCC countries.

Risk Assessment

Regional Stability	Poor
Economy	Fair
Politics	Poor

2015

Government's Maladroit Actions – Reconciliation Talks – Bahrain Independent Commission of Inquiry (BICI) – 'Foreign Interference' – Moderate Economic Growth – New Crown Prince Out Manoeuvered? – First to Produce Oil, First to Cease Oil Production?

Once described as an 'unlikely candidate for Utopia', since the heady days of the 1970s, Bahrain's international standing had by 2013 diminished to the point of near extinction. In 'pre-oil' times, Bahrain had already grown rich on agriculture, pearl-diving, shipbuilding and regional trade. In the twentieth century it had seen the end of its pearl diving prosperity, fortuitously replaced by petroleum. In the 1970s another crop loomed – cash. Bahrain quickly established itself as a regional banking centre, only to be later eclipsed by Dubai in the United Arab Emirates. None the less, with prosperity came free education, free medical care and full employment. There was no income tax.

In the latter part of 2013, and the earlier months of 2014 Bahrain continued to discover that it was being judged by its actions rather than its words. Government reassurances that political and economic reforms are under way are flatly contradicted, not only by opposition spokesmen and women, but more worryingly by the government's often maladroit actions.

In 2013 opposition activists in Bahrain found themselves sharing the frustrations of their counterparts in Tunisia and Morocco as the Arab Spring turned in to something of a forgotten revolution. In Bahrain, the street protests continued, facing a government that preferred to opt for tear gas rather than dialogue. Quoted by Christina Lamb in the London *Sunday Times*, Falah Rabeea of the human rights group Bahrain Salam for Democracy and Human Rights claimed that 'A country that orders more canisters of tear gas than it has people does not seem committed to reform.'

Opposition
In July 2014 Bahrain's Ministry of Justice sought court approval to suspend the activities of the al-Wefaq National Islamic Society, the principle Shi'ite Muslim opposition group, in a move that looked certain to derail efforts to restart reconciliation talks between the government and opposition groups. The closure spoke volumes to Bahrain's Shi'a majority. The purported reason for the three month closure was to enable the group to 'correct its legal status'.

© KONINKLIJKE BRILL NV, LEIDEN, 2023 | DOI:10.1163/9789004686335_033

The ministry claimed that the group had lost its legal status after four of its general conferences were annulled due to a lack of delegates and a failure to comply with requirements for transparency in convening these conferences.

The suspension followed charges against al-Wefaq's leader Sheikh Ali Salman, and his assistant, Khalil al-Marzouq. Both had been charged with holding an illegal meeting with Tom Malinowski, US Assistant Secretary of State for Democracy, Human Rights and Labour (see below). Mr al-Marzouq was cleared of terrorism charges in June 2014, raising hopes that the talks between the government and the opposition could be reinstated. al-Wefaq, which says it advocates non-violent activism, had boycotted talks with the government after Marzouq's arrest in September 2013.

Friendly Relations: The US?

Bahrain's relations with the US are at best 'sensitive'. The US Fifth Fleet is stationed in Bahrain, which gives the US the perfect base to monitor – and intervene as necessary – events in Iran, Syria and Iraq. The presence of the base makes any Iranian initiatives in the region unlikely. The Sunni Bahraini royal family considers Shi'a Iran to be its principle threat. The sensitivity of the US relationship was raised several notches in July 2014 when Bahrain chose to order Tom Malinowski to leave the Kingdom immediately, because he had 'intervened flagrantly' in Bahrain's internal affairs. Mr Malinowski was declared *persona non grata* after he allegedly 'held meetings with one particular opposition grouping (presumably al-Wefaq – see above), apparently to the detriment of others, thereby contravening diplomatic norms and flouting normal interstate relations'.

The US State Department said that the United States was 'deeply concerned' about Bahrain's demand that Malinowski leave immediately, stating that the visit had been co-ordinated with Bahrain in advance and that the Bahraini government was 'well aware' that visiting US officials would often hold meetings with opposition groups. The State Department also riposted that Bahrain had imposed requirements on Mr Malinowski's visit that violated diplomatic protocol, advising that 'The government insisted – without advance warning and after his visit had already commenced – that a Foreign Ministry representative be present at all of Assistant Secretary Malinowski's private meetings with individuals and groups representing a broad spectrum of Bahraini society, including those held at the US embassy.'

It is not the first time that US actions in Bahrain have created political controversy. Last year, Bahraini lawmakers urged the government to stop the US ambassador in Bahrain from interfering in domestic affairs and meeting government opponents.

Following the events of 2011, the Bahraini government invited an independent inquiry to report on its handling of the trouble in 2011. The Bahrain Independent Commission of Inquiry (BICI) said that the authorities had used widespread and excessive force, including torture to extract confessions. On the back foot, the Bahraini government announced that it had taken steps to address the problems by dismissing those responsible and introducing cameras at police stations. This response was generally considered inadequate by human rights groups. In 2013, Bahrain ranked 57 out of the 177 countries surveyed in the Transparency International Corruption Perceptions Index.

Friendly Relations: The European Union (EU)

In mid-2014 King Hamad directed ministries and government departments to investigate claims that what was termed 'foreign interference' in Bahrain's affairs continued. The *Gulf Daily News* reported that an enquiry was under way to see whether individuals and institutions received foreign aid to carry out activities which violated the law. Under its expanded scope, even scholarships, training programmes and competence-building initiatives provided by foreign think-tanks, research institutes, centres or foundations for government and non-governmental establishments would be scrutinised. In what appeared to many as an exercise in paranoia, the government announced that regulations would be enforced to ensure that such schemes were not exploited as a cover to interfere in Bahrain's internal affairs.

Meanwhile, Gulf Co-operation Council (GCC) representatives had threatened to boycott a top-level meeting between GCC foreign ministers and their EU counterparts under the auspices of the United Nations Human Rights Council (UNHCR) allegedly due to a controversial UN statement on the human rights situation in Bahrain. Endorsed by 46 countries, a UN statement to be read out at the meeting praised some of what it described as 'positive steps' that had been taken in Bahrain, but at the same time expressed concerns over reported cases of violence, harassment and ill-treatment and criticised the fact that the BICI's recommendations had allegedly not been implemented in full. The Bahrain delegation dismissed these claims, countering that the statement 'failed to take into account the tangible improvements officially documented' and was undermining 'the unrelenting and sincere efforts undertaken by Bahrain to carry out its human rights obligations.' EU sources confirmed that the meeting had been postponed.

The Economy – The IMF View

In May 2014 the International Monetary Fund (IMF) published its assessment of the Bahraini economy, noting that gross domestic product (GDP) had grown by

5.3 per cent in 2013, supported by a rebound in the hydrocarbons sector, while Bahrain's non-oil activity growth slowed to 3 per cent, largely reflecting weak investment sentiment and the delay in the 2013/14 budget approval. However, within the non-oil activity, transport and tourism continued to expand, reflecting buoyant activity in the service sector, particularly hotels and restaurants and social and personal services. Unemployment remained low, at 4.2 per cent at the end of February 2014. Inflation picked up in late 2013 (to 4 per cent year on year at end 2013) reflecting price increases in housing, but had fallen in March 2014 to 2.3 per cent year on year. Private sector credit growth remained moderate at about 6.6 per cent at the end of 2013 (6.2 per cent in 2012), while deposits grew by 9 per cent for the same period (4.6 per cent in 2012).

The IMF reported that the fiscal deficit had continued on a rising trend in 2013, although by less than budgeted. The better fiscal turnout was largely related to the under-spending of the capital budget. The overall deficit (including extra-budgetary operations) was estimated at 4.3 per cent of GDP, up from 3.2 per cent of GDP in 2012 – the fiscal breakeven oil price increased to US$125 per barrel in 2013 from US$119 per barrel in 2012. Government debt increased by eight percentage points of GDP in 2013, to 44 per cent of GDP. Although the government had increased its reliance on external financing, government external debt as a share of GDP remained low, at 20 per cent of GDP. Bond yields and Credit Default Swap spreads were now back to their pre-2011 levels, but were still higher than the levels experienced in late 2012 and early 2013. The current account remained strong with an estimated surplus of 7.8 per cent of GDP in 2013. Official reserves coverage fell marginally from about 10 months of imports in 2012 to nine months in 2013.

According to the IMF, Bahrain's banking sector was in good health, and the performance of the challenged Islamic retail banks has improved marginally. The capitalisation of the banking system was high on average and the ratio of non-performing loans (NPLs) to gross loans had continued on a downward trajectory. The Islamic retail banking segment had been tackling high NPLs due to concentrated exposures to local and regional real estate; while capital buffers for this sector declined slightly in 2013, the capital adequacy ratio remained high. After several years of posting losses, the banking sector's profitability had moved into positive territory, with the Islamic banking segment undergoing some consolidation in 2013. Bahrain had not been affected by recent market volatility. Its stock market index increased by 17 per cent in 2013 and by about 7 per cent from the start of 2014 to the end of March 2014.

In the view of the IMF, Bahrain's economic outlook was characterised by moderate growth and higher public debt, with average annual inflation projected to be subdued in 2014 and over the medium term. The most immediate policy challenges were to correct the fiscal imbalances and stabilise government debt. Over the longer term, the challenge was to reduce Bahrain's fiscal dependence on oil revenues and resume robust economic growth.

The Economy – the View from the Street

When beleaguered Bahrain announced plans in December 2013 to cut fuel subsidies, it looked like a possible step towards economic reform in a region where welfare systems prevailed. Bahrain's National Oil and Gas Authority announced that it would gradually increase the pump price for diesel fuel, aiming to double it by 2017. But, almost inevitably, the plan soon got bogged down in domestic politics. Some members of Bahrain's largely ineffectual parliament simply objected to the price rises, others boycotted their weekly meeting in protest. The Prime Minister announced in parliament that the proposed initiative might need to be reviewed. Six months later it remained unclear if the subsidy cuts would be implemented.

Although the IMF reported healthier growth figures, the growth in its financial industry was considered to be half-hearted. Sporadic, often violent political and street unrest did little for the government's attempts to promote itself as a regional hub. In an ideal world, the government would like to break away from its traditional economic model, deploying greater funds to investment and the development of the economy. But reducing welfare payments is perceived to target precisely those – largely Shi'a – Bahrainis who already consider themselves marginalised and under-privileged.

Although the IMF figures suggested that Bahrain's economy had recovered since the protests of early 2011, civil unrest – often violent – was a daily occurrence in villages throughout the island. Thus Bahraini society had become increasingly divided. Its medical and teaching professionals opposed to their treatment, its commercial and financial executives filling Manama's restaurants alongside the (Sunni) Saudi Arabians who flock over the causeway to Manama at the weekend.

The appointment in March 2013 of Cambridge educated Crown Prince Salman bin Hamad bin Isa al-Khalifa as First Deputy Prime Minister raised the hopes not only of Bahrain's business sector, but also of many human rights activists. Initially both were probably disappointed, as the Crown Prince found himself outmanoeuvred by the more entrenched members of the royal family.

The Immediate Future

Bahrain looks set to avoid any economic crisis indefinitely because of support from neighbouring Saudi Arabia, whose Sunni rulers have a geopolitical interest in supporting the country. Following the 2011 uprising, Saudi Arabia, the

United Arab Emirates (UAE) and Kuwait pledged US$10 billion aid to Manama. This gesture helped Gulf companies and individuals to continue viewing Bahrain as a safe, convenient business centre. However, mere survival as an economic satellite of Saudi Arabia is not quite what was hoped for.

As long as the talks between the government and opposition on ending the unrest remain deadlocked, it is doubtful that Bahrain will feel secure enough to reform its tax and subsidy systems. Political crises of the sort still faced by Bahrain make root and branch changes of the sort needed in Manama virtually impossible.

Hydrocarbons and Energy

In 1932 prospectors first obtained oil in Bahrain. Well Number 1, as it was to be called, continued to flow for decades, operated by the Bahrain Petroleum Company. At the site of the well is a plaque commemorating a discovery which changed the world's geo-political structure. Bahrain, along with Oman, is one of only two countries bordering the Arabian Gulf that is not a member of the Organisation of the Petroleum Exporting Countries (OPEC). Bahrain produced 48,000 barrels per day (bpd) of total petroleum liquids in 2012, the least of any country in the Gulf. It has set a goal of increasing total petroleum production to 100,000bpd by the end of the decade although the longer term likelihood is that Bahrain, the first Gulf state to produce oil, will also be the first to cease production.

Any analysis of the sources of Bahrain's growth shows a worrying picture. Most growth comes from the oil industry, which is vulnerable to swings in global prices. And Bahrain has less ample oil reserves than its rich neighbours – its proven reserves could run out in a decade or so at current rates of production, according to US government estimates.

The resources sector, which consists almost entirely of oil and provides over a fifth of GDP, led growth in the fourth quarter of 2013, expanding 14.6 per cent from a year earlier. Bahrain's refinery capacity far exceeds domestic crude oil production capacity. Bahrain has a 254,000bpd export refinery at Sitra. Most of the feedstock is imported from Saudi Arabia, so that net exports for Bahrain are only about 5,000bpd. Plans are underway to expand the refinery's capacity by 100,000bpd by 2017.

Saudi Arabia and Bahrain also share production of the 300,000bpd Abu Safah offshore oilfield in Saudi Arabia, which is connected to Bahrain's Sitra refinery via pipeline. Bahrain intends to replace the ageing pipeline system from Saudi Arabia with the planned New Arabia pipeline, a 71-mile, 350,000bpd pipeline running between the Abqaiq complex in Saudi Arabia and Bahrain's refinery at Sitra.

As with oil, Bahrain is a low level producer of natural gas – 446 billion cubic feet of dry natural gas in 2011. In order to meet future natural gas needs, Bahrain plans to import gas from a number of sources, either via pipeline from Qatar or via imports of liquefied natural gas (LNG) following the awarding of a contract to construct a new LNG terminal.

People to watch: Cambridge educated Crown Prince Salman bin Hamad al-Khalifa.

Risk Assessment

Politics	Poor
Economy	Fair
Regional Stability	Fair

2016

Heavy-Handed Response to Street Protests – al-Wefaq Election Boycott – iPhones for Voters – Bahrain Joins the Yemen Coalition – GDP Growth, Low Unemployment – Vision 2030: Competitiveness, Integrity and Sustainability – New Pipeline Planned – Prison Riots – Torture Allegations

Bahrain's November 2014 elections saw a turnout of 52.6 per cent of the electorate, a figure reportedly welcomed by the authorities as 'satisfactory'. Many Bahrainis chose not to vote in what they saw as a less than democratic exercise. This was the first legislative election since the uprisings – initially considered to be related to the Arab Spring – of early 2011. The main issue surrounding the elections was the stance of the principle opposition (Shi'a) al-Wefaq grouping whose 18 parliamentarians had resigned from the 40-seat lower house (the Assembly) in the early days of the uprising in protest at the Bahraini's heavy-handed response to the street protests.

What, No Opposition?
Their demands ignored, the al-Wefaq deputies chose to continue their boycott. This was in the face of intense government and even international pressure. al-Wefaq were not the only abstainees – three smaller opposition groupings joined them. The opposition's absence called into question the legitimacy of the election, explaining the government's relief at the turnout, although the official figure was itself challenged. The controversy inevitably meant that the actual results seemed of secondary importance. Given the dilution of the assembly's political importance it came as no surprise that no more than four candidates from the political groupings were actually elected, the other 36 were so called independents thought to be aligned to the government. Bahrain's Sunni parties, including the al-Manbar al-Islami and al-Asalah groupings, which represent Islamists affiliated with the Muslim Brotherhood and Salafism. Not one of the 10 al-Fatih Coalition (Sunni) candidates was elected despite their apparent pro-government popularity during and following the anti-government street protests. The apparent collapse of support for these often populist pro-government groupings came as something of a surprise.

The constitutional basis of Bahrain's elections dates back to the 2002 Constitution which established a two-chamber parliament: the appointed upper chamber – effectively by the King – and an elected lower chamber. Despite this apparently democratic system, it is the King, not parliament, who appoints the prime minister. Legislation needs to be approved by both houses, giving the King a blocking right on any new legislation. The King may at any time declare marshal law.

By Appointment...

According to the Bahrain Watch (BW) website, the Directorate of Election and Referendum is responsible for conducting Bahrain's elections. It is headed by the Minister of Justice, who is also appointed by the King. In the November 2014 elections, requests by the Bahrain Transparency Society (BTS) to allow international monitors were rejected, although domestic monitors were permitted. BW noted that the absence of robust observation of the electoral process compounded concerns about the official results.

Also according to BW, the government had proposed to condition eligibility for government jobs and services on electoral participation, and issued a statement that was interpreted as a threat to remove the right to vote for anyone who had failed to vote in this election.

Those who did vote in the elections were entered into a raffle, where they could win one of twenty i-phones. According to the Bahrain Centre for Human Rights, the government repressed protests and arrested over 60 people in the run-up to the elections.

Criticism?

According to Human Rights Watch (HRW), the government of Bahrain remained hyper-sensitive to any form of criticism. In early 2015 Bahrainis were given a further reminder that the Bahrain government brooked no criticism. In a statement, the Bahraini Ministry of Interior cautioned against criticism of the government's decision to send eight fighter jets to take part in air-strikes in Yemen as part of the Saudi-led, US-backed coalition against Houthi forces. It warned against 'any attempt to exploit the situation through division or sedition, or issuance of statements against the approach Bahrain has taken.' The Ministry 'would take appropriate steps against individuals that put the safety and security of the country at risk,' it added. This tough talk came after Bahrain's al-Wahdawi political society had condemned the Gulf coalition's air strikes as a 'flagrant aggression that violated international law.' Bahrain's police promptly arrested the society's secretary; Fadhel Abbas and another unnamed individual were blamed for 'exploiting the situation in Yemen to disrupt the peace and endanger security and civil order', according to the Interior Ministry. The Justice Ministry also announced that it would file a lawsuit demanding the dissolution of al-Wahdawi.

The action against al-Wahdawi was, according to HRW, merely the latest example of Bahrain's intolerance of speech critical of the government. During 2014 and early 2015, human rights activists and members of the political opposition have been arrested and prosecuted, often for peaceful criticism of the authorities, and the government invested itself with further powers to arbitrarily strip critics of their citizenship and the rights that attach to it.

The Economy

According to the International Monetary Fund (IMF), in its May 2014 assessment of the Bahraini economy, Bahrain's gross domestic production (GDP) grew by 5.3 per cent in 2013, supported by a rebound in the hydrocarbons sector, while non-oil activity slowed to 3 per cent, largely reflecting weak investment sentiment and the delay in the 2013/14 budget approval. Within non-oil activity, transport and tourism continued to expand, reflecting buoyant activity in the service sector, particularly hotels and restaurants and social and personal services. Unemployment remained low, at 4.2 per cent at end-February 2014. Inflation picked up in late 2013 (4 per cent year on year at the end of 2013) reflecting price increases in housing, but had fallen in March to 2.3 per cent year on year. Private sector credit growth remained moderate at about 6.6 per cent at end-2013 (6.2 per cent in 2012), while deposits grew by 9 per cent for the same period (4.6 per cent in 2012).

The IMF noted that Bahrain's fiscal deficit continued on a rising trend in 2013, although by less than had been budgeted. The improved fiscal result was largely related to under-spending on the capital budget. The overall deficit (including extra-budgetary operations) was estimated at 4.3 per cent of GDP, up from 3.2 per cent of GDP in 2012–the fiscal breakeven oil price increased to US$125 per barrel in 2013 from US$119 per barrel in 2012 (NB although by the end of 2014 the price per barrel had fallen to between US$50 and US$60 per barrel). Government debt increased by eight percentage points of GDP in 2013, to 44 per cent of GDP. While the government had increased its reliance on external financing, government external debt as a share of GDP remained low, at 20 per cent of GDP. The current account remained strong with an estimated surplus of 7.8 per cent of GDP in 2013. Official reserves coverage fell marginally from about 10 months of imports in 2012 to nine in 2013.

According to the IMF, Bahrain's banking sector was in good health, and the performance of the 'challenged' Islamic retail banks had improved marginally. The capitalisation of the banking system was high on average and the non-performing loans (NPLs) to gross loans ratio had continued on a downward trajectory. The Islamic retail banking segment had been tackling high NPLs due to concentrated exposures to local and regional real estate; while capital buffers for this sector declined slightly in 2013, the capital adequacy ratio remained high. After several years of posting losses, the sector's profitability has moved into positive territory, with the Islamic banking segment undergoing some consolidation in 2013. The stock market index increased 17 per cent in 2013 and about 7 per cent since the start of 2014 (up to the end of March 2014).

The IMF considered that Bahrain's economic outlook was characterised by moderate growth and higher public debt, with average annual inflation estimated to be subdued in 2014 and over the medium term. The most immediate policy challenges were to correct the fiscal imbalances and stabilise government debt, while balancing growth and debt sustainability considerations. Over the longer term, the challenge is to reduce fiscal dependence on oil revenues and resume robust economic growth.

The Economic Vision 2030 – Derailed?

The Economic Vision 2030, launched by His Majesty King Hamad Bin Isa al-Khalifa in the inauspicious month of October 2008, embodied a comprehensive vision for the Kingdom of Bahrain that aimed at 'creating a clear approach to develop the kingdom's economy while focusing on the main objective which was to improve the standard of living of all Bahraini citizens.' The Vision had been launched after four years of discussions with a group of decision makers in the public and private sectors, including government institutions and related entities in addition to a number of think-tanks and international institutions. The Economic Vision 2030 rather optimistically focuses on crystallising an integrated socio-economic government vision and focuses on three basic principles which are competitiveness, integrity and sustainability. The events of 2011 have clouded the government's vision somewhat.

After the launch of the Economic Vision 2030, the Kingdom of Bahrain had begun an institutional economic reform programme that at the time was in line with the objective of the Economic Vision 2030. This led to the preparation of a national economic strategy that represented a roadmap to achieve the vision. *Force majeure* after the events of 2011, the strategy has needed continuous revision to adapt to the international changes and the government's work programme.

Energy

As one of the smaller oil exporters Bahrain, alongside Oman, looked likely to face rapidly rising debt levels and negative credit ratings following the 2014 slump in oil prices. The Kingdom is, also in the company of Oman, one of only two countries bordering the Arabian Gulf that is not a member of the Organisation of the Petroleum Exporting Countries (OPEC). The Bahrain Petroleum

Company (BAPCO) and the National Gas Company (BANAGAS) dominate Bahrain's hydrocarbon industry.

According to the US government Energy Information Administration (EIA), Bahrain produced 48,000 barrels per day (bpd) of crude oil and lease condensate in 2013, the smallest amount of any country in the Arabian Gulf. Total petroleum production capacity at the Bahrain Oilfield was expected to rise to 100,000bpd by 2018.

Saudi Arabia and Bahrain share production of the 300,000bpd Abu Safah offshore oilfield in Saudi Arabia, which is connected to Bahrain's Sitra refinery via pipeline. The two countries intend to replace the ageing pipeline system from Saudi Arabia with a new 71 mile pipeline by 2016. The planned pipeline will transport 350,000bpd of crude oil from Saudi Arabia's Abqaiq plant to Bahrain's Sitra Refinery. Bahrain's refinery capacity far exceeds domestic crude oil production capacity. Bahrain has a 267,000bpd export refinery at Sitra and plans are underway to expand the refinery's capacity to 360,000bpd by 2017.

As with oil, Bahrain is a small producer of natural gas. According to the BP Statistical Review of World Energy 2014, Bahrain produced 558 billion cubic feet (Bcf) of natural gas in 2013, up from about 480Bcf in 2012. In order to meet growing domestic needs, Bahrain plans to increase its imports of natural gas. The government plans to complete construction of a 400 million cubic feet per day (MMcf/d) LNG import facility in the beginning of 2017. Potential pipeline projects involving Iran and Qatar have been put on hold.

Bahrain had about 4 gigawatts of electricity generation capacity in 2012, almost all of which was fossil fuel fired. A 5-megawatt solar project came online at the start of 2014 and a 25-megawatt waste to energy plant will come online by 2015. Bahrain is also taking part in the Gulf Co-operation Council's (GCC) plan to integrate the electric power grids of all GCC countries.

Jaw, but no Law

A March 2015 riot at Bahrain's notorious Jaw Prison ended up with a fierce response from the authorities, and allegations of police torture. Reportedly, prisoners were subjected to tear gas, beaten up and left in a courtyard, where they were stripped to their underwear for a few hours and were left in the courtyard for three days until tents were put up. As reported by the *International Business Times* journalist Gianluca Mezzofiore, inmates were summoned one by one and apparently tortured. The reports of alleged torture and human rights violations came just after Amnesty International published a report accusing the Bahrain government of human rights abuses – with documented episodes of torture and mistreatment of detainees, continued jailing of activists and bans on protests in the capital.

The jail disturbances had started in March 2015 due to poor conditions and overcrowding in the prison. One of the prison buildings alone had a capacity of 456 but was containing 1,020 prisoners. A government newspaper reported that the unrest was the result of violence by prisoners after a confrontation between prison guards and three visitors. Local human rights groups claimed that the security forces had used excessive force against prisoners. The reaction of the Bahraini government was to call in riot police, mostly formed by Pakistani and Jordanian guards, who surrounded the main buildings of the prison and then broke inside.

Sayed Ahmed Alwadaei, the director of Advocacy at the Bahrain Institute for Rights and Democracy reported to Mr Mezzofiore that: 'they used tear gas and gunshots. One guy was shot at a very close range. Everyone was beaten and asked to stand down.' Bahrain's police media centre at the Ministry of Interior denied the torture allegations. The testimonies of the alleged violations were submitted to the UN for breaches of international human rights.

Amnesty Report

After the crackdown on the Bahrain pro-democracy uprising in 2011, led by Saudi forces, Bahrain has plunged deeper into sectarian conflict between the wealthy ruling Sunni (al-Khalifa) minority and the Shi'a majority. King Sheikh Hamad bin Isa al-Khalifa had pledged to implement the recommendations of an independent commission of inquiry but the reforms were progressing slowly and reconciliation talks had stalled.

There have for some years been allegations of torture and abuse in the Jaw prison. Well over its 1,200 prisoner capacity, it houses upwards of 2,000 prisoners by the Bahrain Centre for Human Rights' estimates, many of them protesters and activists imprisoned for doing no more exercising their free assembly, expression and association rights. One such prisoner had been in solitary confinement since his detention in 2012. Tortured and abused, Ali al-Taweel (aka Altaweel) was on death row for the alleged murder of a policeman, for which he was coerced into confessing. After a reported two attempts, and barred from contact with the outside world, in early 2015 he had handed his lawyer a suicide note.

Rather than hold its errant torturers to account, Bahrain was thought to be covering up its abuses. And instead of trying to improve the situation, the government allowed its deterioration, which by 2015 was if anything worse than during martial law in 2011. No one has been held accountable, and there is no sign that anyone will be. The introduction of an Ombudsman, and a National Institute for Human Rights, were modest 'reforms' which the Bahrain government claimed as a success story.

2017

Iran's Territorial Ambitions – List of 68 Terrorist Groups – Lebanese Residents Deported – Economic Vulnerabilities Rise – Fiscal Deficit Remains High – GCC Funding – Economic Malaise and Uncertainty.

Since 2011 Bahrain has not been a happy country. That unhappiness re-emerged violently in July 2015 when Reuters reported that a bomb had killed two policemen and wounded six in the deadliest such attack in Bahrain for some time. Rather precipitously, state media stated that the explosives resembled those that had been seized a few days earlier, which had apparently been smuggled from Iran.

The Iranian Dimension

Sunni-ruled Bahrain had long accused Iran of stirring up unrest among its majority Shi'ite population. Tensions between the two countries had risen in early 2016, eventually resulting in Bahrain recalling its ambassador from Tehran. Neighbouring Gulf States also recalled their ambassadors to Iran in protest at the attack on the Saudi Arabian embassy in Tehran following the execution of the Shi'a cleric Sheikh Nimr al-Nimr and 46 other suspected opponents of the Saudi Arabian government. While its response to the situation appeared to be a gesture of neighbourly support, the Iran-inspired problems that faced the Bahraini government were unique. In no other Gulf State did a Sunni minority rule over a Shi'a majority. Furthermore, Bahrain was the only area of the Gulf to which Iran had long held territorial ambitions.

Quite apart from the Iran inspired problems faced by the Bahraini authorities, the withdrawal of Bahrain's ambassador was also a timely gesture of solidarity with neighbouring Saudi Arabia. The ruling Sunni al-Khalifa family knew that it might well need Saudi support in coping with the widespread discontent among Bahrain's Shi'a Muslims population. There was a recent precedent: in 2011, 1,200 Saudi Arabian, and 800 United Arab Emirates troops had calmly driven over the causeway into Bahrain as part of a force operating under the aegis of the Gulf Co-operation Council (GCC). The six-nation regional coalition of Sunni rulers was understandably concerned over the increasing threat to Bahrain's rulers. Matters were not improved by the nuclear agreement reached between Tehran and a grouping of global powers. This had also created increased nervousness in Bahrain and its Gulf Arab neighbours, who felt that the

© KONINKLIJKE BRILL NV, LEIDEN, 2023 | DOI:10.1163/9789004686335_035

nuclear agreement meant less foreign pressure on Iran to contain its aspirations of regional expansion and intrigue.

Terrorism, and Paranoia?

In April 2016 the Bahraini authorities published a list of 68 Islamist militant groups it classified as 'terrorist'. Perhaps predictably, Lebanon's Shi'a Hezbollah movement, already branded as 'terrorist' by the GCC and the Arab League, came top of the list. Other organisations included on the list were al-Qaeda and its branches in Yemen and North Africa, as well as the al-Nusra Front in Syria and the Islamic State group (ISIS). Nigeria's Boko Haram, Egypt's Islamic Jihad and al-Murabitoun in Mali were also listed. Less well-known names such as the al-Ashtar Brigades and Resistance Brigades, as well as the clandestine February 14 Coalition were all believed to be Shi'ite groups in Bahrain. Other GCC members that had published similar lists were Saudi Arabia and the UAE.

In March 2016 the GCC had formally branded Hezbollah as a terrorist organisation, reflecting the deterioration of relations between Iran, Hezbollah's Shi'ite backer and puppetmaster, and the Sunni monarchies, notably Saudi Arabia. The Gulf monarchies had already sanctioned Hezbollah in 2013 in reprisal for its armed intervention in Syria in support of its embattled President Bashar Assad. The move by the GCC followed an announcement by Saudi Arabia that it was cutting U$4 billion in aid to Lebanese security forces. Saudi Arabia and other Gulf States also urged its citizens to leave Lebanon. After the GCC decision Bahrain deported several Lebanese residents for links to Hezbollah.

The 2015 bombing outside a girls' school in the Shi'ite village of Sitra had been the first in Bahrain for several months, and the worst since March 2014, when a blast killed three policemen. Iranian officials had failed to comment on the bombing. Tehran doggedly denied any interference in Bahrain, but openly supported opposition groups seeking greater rights for the Shi'a majority. Sporadic violence aimed at Bahraini security forces had become the norm since widespread, Shi'ite-led, pro-democracy protests were put down by the government in 2011. In addition to the police fatalities, the bomb also wounded another six policemen, two of them critically and two who were stable but in intensive care.

Bahrain Watch

In February 2016 following the arrest and deportation of four American journalists from Bahrain, the Bahrain Watch blog estimated the total number of journalists, suspected activists, aid workers and NGO observers that have been denied access to the country at over 250. The February deportees – Anna

Therese Day and three members of her camera crew – were in Bahrain with valid visas to report on the demonstrations surrounding the anniversary of the pro-democracy movement. It appears the authorities were displeased that the journalists had not reported to the Information Affairs Authority who stated that 'security authorities detained four US nationals during the incident as a result of their involvement in the criminal acts.' This restriction on mobility as well as the way journalists are hunted down, prosecuted and then deported, amounted, in the view of Bahrain Watch, to an official policy of treating journalists as criminals. Worryingly, even government sponsored events such as the Manama Dialogue in December 2015 saw accredited participants arrive in Bahrain, only to be taken from their hotel rooms and deported.

The Bahraini government's rather cack-handed policy of either rejecting visa applications by journalists, or refusing entry at the airport and even deporting journalists who had already been allowed entry was perceived as part of a systematic policy to make it difficult for international media to report directly on protests and repression in Bahrain. This unsubtle censorship was arguably succeeding in reducing interest, and certainly increasing the cost and the risks of reporting from inside Bahrain. Bahrain Watch also pointed out that its report did not include Bahraini journalists or observers working inside the country, many of whom had been jailed with sentences of up to 15 years imprisonment.

In February 2016, the distinguished Emirati academic, Abdulkhaleq Abdullah, was denied entry into Bahrain to attend the Gulf Development Forum on Water Security, with no reason being given. Gulf citizens are allowed to travel to other GCC states without a visa but joint security agreements meant that border agencies retained lists of *personae non grata*.

Among the Gulf States, it is not only its religious make-up that sets Bahrain apart from its neighbours. Alongside Dubai, it is unique in not solely depending on oil revenues for its prosperity. However, an assessment of the Bahraini economy prepared in January 2016 by the International Monetary Fund (IMF) concluded that the large decline in oil prices had substantially lowered export and fiscal revenues. Given that the oil price decline was expected to persist over the medium term, Bahrain's external and fiscal vulnerabilities had intensified and at the same time consumer and investor sentiment had also weakened.

The IMF noted that Bahrain's economic growth had slowed during 2015, estimated to have reached 3.2 per cent, which was lower than the 4.5 per cent achieved in 2014. The overall fiscal deficit and government debt in 2015 had been projected to be 15 per cent and 63 per cent of gross domestic product (GDP), respectively. The external current account deficit was estimated at 3.8 per cent of GDP.

In early 2016, the Bahraini authorities had announced significant fiscal measures to strengthen revenues, including increases in the retail prices of fuel products, electricity, and water. As a result of weakening market confidence, and reflecting the dampening effect of the necessary fiscal measures on aggregate demand, GDP growth was expected to slow further in 2016, down to 2.25 per cent, and inflation was expected to rise to around 3 per cent.

Despite the implementation of the measures referred to above, the lower projected oil prices in 2016 implied that the overall fiscal deficit would remain high, at over 15 per cent of GDP, and narrow only gradually over the medium term. A substantial increase in debt was projected and a sizeable fiscal adjustment was urgently needed to restore fiscal sustainability, reduce vulnerabilities, and boost investor and consumer confidence.

In the view of the IMF, fiscal measures in the near term might include the implementation of a value added tax (VAT), which had been agreed at the Gulf Co-operation Council (GCC) level. Rationalising spending on social transfers, which were large, was expected to create substantial savings. Significant progress in reducing the wage bill, which was higher in Bahrain (as a share of spending) than in all other GCC countries, could be made in the near term by freezing wages. Over the medium term, sizeable further consolidation could be achieved in the context of a civil service review and would help support the goal of boosting private sector employment of Bahrain nationals. Other measures were also needed to raise non-oil revenue and help finance the provision of government services. Reforms to strengthen the fiscal framework would support the process of fiscal consolidation.

The IMF also considered that the Bahraini banks' strong capitalisation and liquidity would help them weather the slowing pace of economic growth. The Central Bank of Bahrain continued to strengthen its regulations and the supervision of the financial sector, which would support the continued development and stability of the financial system. The exchange rate peg to the US dollar continued to serve Bahrain well, and would be supported by fiscal consolidation.

...and from Kuwait

In its early 2016 Economic Outlook the National Bank of Kuwait (NBK) noted that the Bahraini economy was expected to recover in 2016 and 2017, as gains in the non-oil sector began to offset some of the weakness in the oil sector. The NBK took a slightly more positive view than the IMF, projecting annual growth of three per cent in 2016. The NBK expected non-oil growth to be around 3–4 per cent in 2016 and 2017, largely due to strong fiscal expenditure and Gulf Co-operation Council (GCC) funds targeted at housing and infrastructure. The GCC had begun to play a significant role in Bahrain's economic development, scheduled to deliver funding of around US$1 billion annually over a ten year period up to 2025. At the same time, according to Bahrain's Economic Development Board (EDB) some US$20 billion was to be invested in industrial and infrastructure projects.

Despite these impressive investment plans, the NBK remarked that Bahrain's non-oil GDP remained susceptible to the internal political problems and divisions that had beset Bahrain since the days of the Arab Spring. While many of these concerns and some of the unrest had quietened down, business optimism was still fragile and acting as a brake on the all-important financial sector (the biggest contributor to the economy after the oil sector) as well as the construction and tourism sectors.

However uncertain the economy, at least overall inflation – 1.6 per cent up to the end of September 2015 – appeared to be manageable. Food (3.2 per cent) and rent (3.1 per cent) inflation were higher, but the NBK expected headline inflation to be around the 2.5 per cent mark in 2016. Despite this good news, Bahrain was expected to turn in one of the highest budget deficits in the GCC member countries. Bahrain's official figures had originally been based on an oil price of US$120 per barrel. The NBK expected the budget deficit to remain between 14 and 16 per cent of GDP in 2016 and 2017.

In the prevailing atmosphere of political tension, the NBK considered any significant reduction in public spending to be unlikely. However, credit growth, and especially personal lending had remained surprisingly strong in 2015. The reclassification of financial institutions made in 2015 meant that an accurate assessment of credit growth was difficult. The reclassification had a greater effect on business credit; business loan growth was estimated at 2.5 per cent in 2015, much less than the figure for personal credit which was estimated at 13.8 per cent.

The continuing backdrop to Bahrain's economic malaise was the drain on government finances, eroded not only by government spending but also by low oil prices. The negative climate also extended to the banking sector; commercial bank assets dropped by 2.1 per cent in the year to June 2015. Losses in the wholesale sector also affected the sector. Asset growth in the more domestically oriented banks slowed from an annual rate of 2.9 per cent in May 2015 to 0.5 per cent in May 2015. Economic uncertainty has also constrained Bahrain's stock market trading where investor sentiment reflected the general malaise into 2016.

Energy

Bahrain is, along with Oman, one of only two Gulf states that is not a member of the Organisation of the Petroleum Exporting Countries (OPEC). Bahrain can hardly be considered a major oil producer, producing – according the US government Energy Information Administration (EIA) – 48,000 barrels per day (bpd) of crude oil and lease condensate in 2013, the smallest level of any Arabian Gulf state. Total petroleum production capacity at the Bahrain Field (does this mean the Awali oilfield or the Abu Safah) was, however, expected to rise to 100,000bpd by 2018

Saudi Arabia and Bahrain share production of the 300,000bpd Abu Safah offshore field in Saudi Arabia, connected to Bahrain's Sitra refinery via pipeline. According to the EIA, Bahrain intended to replace the ageing pipeline system from Saudi Arabia with a new 71 mile pipeline in 2016. The planned pipeline will transport 350,000bpd of crude oil from Saudi Arabia's Abqaiq plant to the Sitra refinery. Refinery capacity far exceeds domestic crude oil production capacity. Bahrain has a 267,000 bpd export refinery at Sitra. Plans were underway to expand the refinery's capacity to 360,000bpd by 2017.

As with oil, Bahrain is a small producer of natural gas. According to the BP Statistical Review 2014, Bahrain produced 558 billion cubic feet (Bcf) of natural gas in 2013, up from about 480Bcf in 2012. In order to meet growing needs, Bahrain plans to increase imports of natural gas. The government plans to complete construction of a 400 million cubic feet per day (MMcf/d) LNG import facility in early 2017. Potential pipeline projects from Iran and Qatar have been put on hold.

The Bahrain Petroleum Company (BAPCO) and Bahrain National Gas Company (BANAGAS) dominate Bahrain's hydrocarbon industry. Bahrain had about 4.0 gigawatts of electricity generating capacity in 2012, almost all of which was fossil fuel fired. A 5.0 megawatt solar project came online at the start of 2014 and a 25 megawatt waste to energy plant will come online by 2015. Bahrain is also taking part in the GCC's plan to integrate the electric power grids of all GCC countries.

Risk Assessment

Politics	Poor
Economy	Fair
Regional Stability	Fair

2018

Early Social Development – Pearling Prosperity – Confused and Sullen
Aquiesence – Bahraini Doctors and Lawyers – One-sided Stalemate – First
Executions for Twenty Years – Shared Grievances – Khalij al-Bahrain –
Political and Social Uncertainties – Hesitant Investment Climate

It is difficult to believe that until the 1970s Bahrain could rest on its reputation
as a major trading (and once pearling) centre. This was at a time when both Qatar and the Trucial States (also known as the Trucial Coast and later to become
the United Arab Emirates (UAE)) were little more than small coastal settlements. In his excellent book *The Merchants* (John Murray, 1984) the author Michael Field noted that although Bahrain had seen the first discovery of oil in the
Arabian Peninsula, '... it proved to be very small by Arabian standards and to be
the only one ever found on the island.' But the discovery of oil did enable Bahrain (and Kuwait, its more affluent neighbour to the north) to embark on serious economic and social development long before the lower Gulf States were
able to do so.

Development

Bahrain opened its first school in 1919, and began girls' education ten years
later. These social developments placed the island kingdom way ahead of all its
neighbours. Bahrain in the 1920s was by far the most important and cosmopolitan centre on the Gulf coast. Mr Field notes that 'It was richer than the other
towns. It had prosperous communities of Indian and Persian merchants.' It was
the main pearl market and home to the Gulf's largest pearl fishing fleet – some
300 vessels. Qatar and the Trucial Coast each sent out some 200 craft, Kuwait
100 and Saudi Arabia only 50. For centuries Bahrain was the recognised centre
of the Middle East pearl industry, with a population thought by many observers
to enjoy the highest per capita income in the world.

Bahrain was also the anchorage where the steamship lines called most regularly, the port through which most of the imports of the mainland were
trans-shipped. The British Political Agent – who answered to Bombay – was
based in Bahrain (until 1946 he was based in Bushire in Iran) and oversaw British interests throughout the lower Gulf. Bahrain's development policies were
strengthened and given focus by the arrival, in 1926, of Charles Belgrave as advisor to the Sheikh. From 1934 onwards, Mr Belgrave's task (as a *de facto* minister)

© KONINKLIJKE BRILL NV, LEIDEN, 2023 | DOI:10.1163/9789004686335_036

became easier as the oil revenues began to flow. By the mid-1920s six schools had been opened.

Mr Belgrave arrived in Bahrain having answered an advertisement in the Personal Column of the London daily *The Times* seeking 'a young gentleman' of public school education 'for service in an Eastern State'. Seen by many of his contemporaries and later historians as an anachronism, his description in David Holden's *Farewell to Arabia* (1966) as 'a living symbol in the Gulf', rang true. Mr Holden continued 'Perhaps it was the island nature of Bahrain that enabled the Raj to stamp its image more clearly here than in other parts of the Gulf'. The relative emancipation of educated Bahrainis was very much a product of what was seen as Bahrain's Welfare State – not only were schools and hospitals established, there was also created what Mr Holden described as 'a demand for more benevolence and less paternalism' on the part of the Island's rulers'. The British government, confronted from 1952 onwards with growing Nasserism and nationalism, came up with proposals for democratic institutions in Bahrain.

This was rejected by the ruling family and Bahrain's 'under-employed, educated youngsters were demanding a trades union, a modern code of law and the removal of Charles Belgrave. Bahrain seemed to simmer and occasionally to seethe in unison with the rest of the Arab world.'

Mr Holden summed up the island's post-Suez situation thus: 'Characteristically vague but heated aspirations fire them. Socialism, democracy, independence and Arab unity are their idols. Nasserism and Ba'athism, the two conflicting theologies of the Arab revolution, are their principal ways of worship... With Ba'athists and Nasserists divided; Baghdad, Cairo and Damascus dancing a three-cornered jig, Saudi Arabia and Egypt carrying their enmity to the brink of open war; Iran continuing to claim her ancient rights in Bahrain; and Iraq setting an alarming example by her attempt to annex Kuwait, there has been no agreed, or agreeable, future for the young Bahrainis to anticipate and no coherent theory for them to espouse, save to wait and see. They have subsided, in consequence, into confused and sullen acquiescence.' All that is missing from this perceptive analysis of Bahrain's internal problems is mention of the tensions that exists between the minority Sunnis and the majority Shi'a.

By the 1970s Bahrain saw itself as a service centre, connected to the region by the first regional airline, Bahrain-based Gulf Air, hosting the region's first offshore financial centre and the location of the Gulf's first drydock. With less austere religious customs than the Wahhabi strictness of neighbouring Saudi Arabia, with the advent in 1986 of the King Fahd Causeway, it became something of a leisure centre for both Saudis and expatriates. Oil accounted for around 70 per cent of Bahrain's GDP.

But Bahrain's limited oil income meant that its government could not provide more than a minimal welfare state. Hence, as Mr Field pointed out, its citizens had to be prepared to do genuinely productive jobs. The government faced the need – unheard of in other Gulf States – of building up industries with the objective of providing jobs for the island's inhabitants. In the 1970s Bahrainis accounted for three quarters of the Aluminium Bahrain (ALBA) workforce. In 1984 Mr Field noted that 'Bahrain is the one place in Arabia, outside the Aramco headquarters at Dhahran (Saudi Arabia), where a large part of the indigenous population has forsaken the dishdasha (the long white 'thobe' traditionally worn in the Gulf) for western dress. During the working day it has been found that western dress is more practical. Again in contrast to neighbouring states, by the 1970s there were Bahraini doctors and lawyers and in other professions which was not the case elsewhere in the Gulf.'

In terms of its government structure, Bahrain did not differ much from its neighbours. Its ruling family came from the Anaizah tribe in the north-west of the Nejd (as did the Kuwaiti ruling family) and settled on the Gulf coast in the early 1700s. Strangely, in Bahrain the Shi'a population made up almost all the original settlers. However, the ruling al-Khalifa family are Sunni; the Shi'a population regards itself as an oppressed grouping. Tensions between the religious groups flared alarmingly in 2012–13 following the Arab Spring to such a point that a Gulf Co-operation Council (GCC) force largely made up of troops and equipment from Saudi Arabia and the UAE was despatched across the causeway to maintain peace. Shi'a Iran has long harboured claims on Bahrain.

Things Aren't What They Used To Be – and How

Its population cowed with the assistance of intervention from its larger Gulf neighbours, Bahrain sadly exemplifies how the Gulf's Sunni rulers have sought to cope with demands for greater representation. In Bahrain, six years of protest and oppression have brought about something approaching a one-sided stalemate. The Shi'a opposition may still be seen as an enemy of the ruling Sunni, but by 2017 the heart had gone out of that opposition.

According to a report in the London *Economist*, in Bahrain at the beginning of 2017 there were over 2,500 political prisoners. Hundreds of Bahrainis have sought exile, a large number have been banned from travel, and some 300 stripped of their nationality. In January 2017 three Bahrainis – the first in twenty years – were executed.

It would, in many respects, have made sense for Bahrain's disaffected Shi'a and Sunni to set aside their differences; after all, the grudges most of them held against the al-Khalifa ruling family were largely shared. At the top of the list was the presence of a ruling family that seemed indifferent to their aspirations. The days in which Bahrain's Shi'a and Sunni subjects could share their grievances still prevailed, just. Both communities resent a ruling family that hoards ministerial posts. The King's uncle, Khalifa bin Salman, is the world's longest serving prime minister, having been in place for 46 years. The King himself has ruled since the death of his father in 1999. Although the al-Khalifas monopolise power, they seek to spread the pain of austerity. In line with Economic Vision 2030, the economic programme devised for Bahrain by the US consultants McKinsey & Company, subsidies on such basics as meat have been cut. But some of the proposed measures appear to be in the 're-arranging of deckchairs' category. On the macro-economic level the current oil price would have to double to permit the budget to be balanced. In 2017 the ratings agency Standard and Poor's judged Bahrain's debt to be down to the junk level.

Despite the shared grievances, the government's fiscal measures have fallen most harshly on the Shi'a community. Fellow Gulf States have given billions in aid to prop up the Kingdom, but much has been channelled into building housing for Sunnis and for foreigners. New mansions, compounds and high-rise blocks screen rundown Shi'a villages. Undulating parks along the Corniche beautify Sunni districts. The authorities have also chipped away at the demographic majority of the Shi'a, who once made up 60 per cent of the population. A rash of new Hindu temples, Christian churches and Sunni Muslim mosques testifies to an influx of non-Shia foreigners. Unusually for a Gulf State, Bahrain has opened its doors to Syrian Sunnis from Jordan's refugee camps. An acrid xenophobia often characterises Shi'a discourse: a common Shi'a observation is that even the ruling al-Khalifa, who arrived in Bahrain from the Arabian hinterland in 1783, are in fact 'foreigners'.

Communal tension is less apparent in the few places where Sunnis and Shi'a live together. But sects that once shared the same streets in new towns built in the 1980s now seem to be moving apart. The Hamad Town district is a case in point, where the flags of Shi'a saints are displayed in the homes on one side of the main thoroughfare; Bahraini flags of loyalist Sunnis fly on the other. Reportedly, intermarriage is also less common. Alone among the Gulf states, Bahrain still marks Ashura, the holiest day in the Shi'a calendar, as a public holiday, but divisions are widening. In a telling vignette, *The Economist* noted that although some Sunni grandmothers still bake pomegranate cakes that are a traditional Ashoura delicacy, their husbands who 'once joined the chest-beating Shi'a Muslim rites, now furtively watch from afar'. For many Sunnis, 'Shi'a villages are no-go areas.'

Matters were not eased when in late 2018 the so-called 'Islamic State' (IS) put out an hour-long video of a Bahraini ideologue from the same tribe as the Royal Family appealing for Sunni suicide bombers to attack the island's Shi'a. And on

New Year's Day militant Shi'a broke into a high-security jail, freeing ten dissidents and prompting the official opposition to consider whether it might not be more effective as an underground movement.

Oil – Pennies in Heaven?

A different kind of underground development appeared imminent in 2018 when news broke that a new oilfield had been discovered off the coast of Bahrain. The government announced the discovery of the Khalij al-Bahrain oilfield, its largest oil and gas find since 1932, situated off Bahrain's west coast and estimated to contain at least 80 billion barrels of shale oil, roughly the same amount as Russia. Additionally, it is thought that the associated gas field holds some 10–20 billion cubic feet of natural gas.

No announcements on the possible timing for further exploration and production have yet been made. But the discovery could be, quite literally, a godsend. In spite of efforts toward economic diversification, Bahrain's modest oil and gas sector still remains an overwhelmingly important contributor to Bahrain's economy. This importance is increased by the fact that the Kingdom's two other major industries, aluminium smelting and petrochemicals, are both highly oil-intensive. Some of the required crude oil for export and internal consumption comes from an onshore oilfield, Awali, which is managed by the Tatweer Petroleum Company – a subsidiary of Bahrain's National Oil and Gas Authority (NOGA). Awali's production amounted to 50,000 barrels per day in 2015.

A much larger offshore oilfield, however, is jointly owned with Saudi Arabia. Following the signing of an agreement in 1958, the two countries evenly split the Abu Safah oilfield's production of some 300,000 barrels of crude per day. Although the Saudi Arabian giant Saudi Aramco operates the field, Bahrain takes care of the refining and marketing of its own half of the output. The country's share is pumped into a pipeline taking it to the Sitra refinery on the mainland.

However, the elation of the new discovery needed to be tempered by the fact that 'tight' (shale) oil is often contained in deep rock formations, requiring advanced technological solutions, and increasing the cost of production. Bahrain Petroleum Company (BAPCO), a subsidiary of NOGA, is reportedly in talks with international oil companies that have some expertise in the extraction of shale oil.

The process involved, hydraulic fracturing or fracking is used for the extraction of oil pockets trapped in porous shale rocks. The complex procedure often entails the pumping of high pressure water into deep horizontal wells to fracture the rocks and release the trapped oil content. The US is a market leader in fracking, producing about 6.5 million barrels of tight oil per day in 2018, according to the US Energy Information Administration (EIA). The new discovery did not preclude other exploration activities. It was reported that the Italian oil company Eni was about to sign a memorandum of understanding with Bahrain's Ministry for Offshore Exploration activities.

The timing of the new discovery, however, was less than perfect. In Europe, the US and Asia huge sums were being invested by car and truck manufacturers to develop electric engines. The short term arithmetic for Bahrain's new discoveries may well hold up, but the longer term is less promising in a world where demand for petroleum products looks like diminishing. Additionally, Bahrain's production costs, compared to, say, those of Saudi Arabia, will be high. And with additional shale and conventional crude production, Bahrain will need more refining capacity.

A new refinery is expected to be commissioned sometime in 2022/23, according to BAPCO. The expansion programme will eventually boost the Sitra refinery's capacity of 260,000 barrels per day to over 360,000. Bahrain is not a member of the Organisation of the Petroleum Exporting Countries (OPEC), which gives it a degree of freedom. For the most part Bahrain feels it appropriate to reflect OPEC trends, but if it chooses, it can go its own way.

The Economy

In its 2018 overview of the Bahraini economy, the International Monetary Fund (IMF) noted that the decline in oil prices since 2014 and the absence of 'buffers' had led to a rise in Bahrain's fiscal and external vulnerabilities. Public debt increased to 89 per cent of gross domestic product (GDP), with large fiscal and external current deficits persisting. Reserves remained low, covering only 1.5 months of prospective non-oil imports at the end of 2017.

Overall output, according to the IMF, grew by 3.8 per cent in 2017, underpinned by the resilience of the non-hydrocarbon sector, and combined with a robust implementation of Gulf Co-operation Council (GCC) funded projects as well as strong activity in the financial, hospitality, and education sectors. Fortunately, Bahrain's well developed banking system remains stable with large capital buffers.

However, in the view of the IMF, less good news was that growth was projected to decelerate over the medium term. And in spite of any planned fiscal consolidation measures, both fiscal and external deficits looked likely to continue over the medium term, due to Bahrain's large and growing interest bill. The IMF warned that any delays in implementing a credible fiscal plan and seeing changes in market sentiment as global financing conditions tighten, are likely to present the risks of a downturn.

The IMF welcomed the resilience of growth in Bahrain as noted above, while also noting downside risks to the outlook 'stemming from the rise in fiscal and external vulnerabilities, tighter global financing conditions, delays in fiscal adjustment, and lower energy prices.' Against what was a potentially negative background, the IMF called (not for the first time) for additional sustained efforts to improve Bahrain's fiscal and external positions, preserve financial sector resilience, and support diversified, inclusive growth.

Bahrain's continued fiscal reform efforts were welcomed by the IMF, but the Organisation also noted that public debt is expected to increase further over the medium term and that Bahrain's reserves are projected to remain low. This, in the optimistic view of the IMF, might be overcome by a comprehensive package of reforms, aimed at reducing fiscal deficits over the medium term. The Bahrain authorities' commitment to continue subsidy reforms, to cut non-productive spending and to raise non-oil revenues by introducing a value-added tax (VAT) by 2019 was welcomed by the IMF. But it also considered that additional steps are needed to put Bahrain's public finances on a sustainable trajectory, 'striking the right balance between revenue and expenditure measures while protecting the most vulnerable.' The need to introduce taxation, including a corporate income tax, while containing the public wage bill and targeting subsidies to the poorest was considered important by the IMF, which looked forward to the influence of the newly established debt management office in developing a contingent financing strategy to mitigate financing risks and costs. In broader terms, the IMF also encouraged the Bahraini authorities to strengthen their macro-fiscal framework and increase fiscal transparency and accountability, securing public support and awareness, and enhancing market confidence. No small order given the socio-religious constraints that confronted the Bahrain government.

Looking at the external economy, the IMF accepted that the exchange rate peg remains appropriate for the economy, delivering as it did a clear and credible policy anchor, and at the same time keeping inflation low and stable. The IMF emphasised the importance of fiscal adjustment in supporting the peg and in rebuilding international reserves and altogether ensuring external sustainability. But the IMF did recommend a gradual unwinding of the Central Bank of Bahrain's (CBB) lending to the government.

The IMF also welcomed the CBB's continued efforts to implement the 2017 IMF Financial Sector Assessment Programme (FSAP) recommendations to strengthen further the regulation and supervision of the financial sector. It emphasised the need for Bahrain to develop a well-defined emergency liquidity assistance framework, deepen the interbank market, and enhance and improve the supervision of Islamic banks and insurance companies. Something else flagged by the IMF was the need for close monitoring of the build-up of household debt. The IMF was impressed by the Bahraini authorities' initiatives to streamline business regulations, with a view to promoting private sector development, diversification, and job creation. It also approved of the recent developments in enhancing small and medium sized enterprises' (SMEs) access to finance, as well as recent labour market reforms both to increase flexibility and to promote employment in the private sector. This required further structural reforms to boost productivity and competitiveness through more privatisation plans and public-private partnerships, and measures to strengthen the education system and support greater female labour force participation.

Outlook

As noted above, the political and religious oppression meted out by the government, especially since 2011, has had a doubly negative effect, not only on the Bahraini government which has been unable to enter into any serious discussion with domestic opposition groups. The harsh treatment of political opponents has also resulted in imprisonment, exile and – for the first time in 30 years – the death penalty being carried out.

The welcome given to the new oil discoveries has also been reserved. The government and Bahrain's business community are well aware that the shale gas discoveries need foreign investment if they are to be developed. But they also know that faced with political and social instability and uncertainty, foreign investment will be harder to secure, and will carry a higher price tag. In a context of lower oil prices, and already high production costs, this makes the ultimate return less attractive.

2019

Attempts to Redress the Religious Imbalance – Frustrated Demands – Perceived Instability – Astride Three Middle East Fault Lines – Friends in the West – ALBA Expansion

In many respects, despite the country's tribulations following the events that ensued from the 2011 Arab Spring, Bahrain can probably still (just) be described as the most mature of the Gulf States. Bahrain's oilfield was not only the first to be discovered in the Gulf, it was in commercial production nearly fifteen years before that was the case in Kuwait. Writing in 1966 David Holden (*Farewell to Arabia*) noted that Bahrain's government had an annual income of 'less than US\$9 million from all sources. Spread among the whole population of nearly 150,000, this is not much more than one twentieth of Kuwait's per capita income. Where Kuwait spends US\$750 a year on the education of each child of school age, Bahrain makes do with a modest US\$50.00 and must scale down her other services in proportion.'

Bahrain's maturity is largely down to the fact that its institutions – schools, courts, and the civil service – date back to the years before full independence in 1971 and are not subject to the Wahhabi strictures to be found in Kuwait and Saudi Arabia, or to the lesser puritanism encountered in Qatar. The British influence over Bahraini affairs was probably a mixed blessing, as was Bahrain's ability to adopt modern trends and while allowing disproportionate riches to exist alongside them. The country's development was also conditioned by the fact that, probably due to its island status, Bahrain's links with the Arabian Peninsula were less important than those with India and even Britain. The Persian (Iranian) influence has also been significant; although the last Persian 'occupation' was almost 300 years ago, it explains the fact that despite the al-Khalifa (Sunni) government's efforts to redress the religious balance, the Shi'a majority still exists.

A central irony of Bahrain's political development has been the resistance of the Ruling Family to the suggestions, almost even the demands, of the departing 'colonial power', that more democratic institutions be introduced. The tentative response in 1954 of the Ruler, Sheikh Isa al-Khalifa, to popular demands for the establishment of a trades unions was so hesitant and guarded that the frustrated demands inevitably went a stage further, requesting (in 1955) the establishment of an elected legislature. The political climate in Bahrain became

© KONINKLIJKE BRILL NV, LEIDEN, 2023 | DOI:10.1163/9789004686335_037

one of mounting discontent. This coincided with, and was accelerated by, events in the wider Arab World – President Nasser's arms agreement with the Soviet Union and the dismissal of the Baghdad Pact.

The invasion by Britain and its allies of the region around the Suez Canal in the autumn of 1956 brought matters in Bahrain to an unpleasant head. British troops were called on to restore order. The advent of 26 year old Sheikh Isa bin Salman bin Hamad al-Khalifa as Ruler (Hakim) in 1961 five years after the 1956 riots saw a 'phoney', paternal, calm take over. Not that the causes of discontent had disappeared. Sheikh Isa and his advisers simply took the decision not to permit any further concessions to Bahrain's political activists.

Nevertheless, the perceived instability of Bahrain, combined with the modernising trends apparent in Bahrain's Gulf neighbours – by 1964 wealthier Kuwait had a national assembly and a functioning civil service that no longer depended on royal patronage – meant that the emerging Gulf States were more likely to look to Kuwait than Bahrain as the model to follow.

Arab Spring, Sprung

It has been argued that the advent of the Arab Spring movement in November 2011 did not necessarily assist the improvement of Bahrain's political aspirations. Unlike its neighbours, Bahrain sat right on three major Middle Eastern fault lines: first, the sectarian division, wherein a majority of its citizens were Shi'a, living in a country where the Ruling Family and most of society's upper echelons were Sunni. Second: Bahrain also sat abreast of the relationship between its often vociferous Arab allies and its 'friends in the West' who not only provided cash and resources, but also saw Bahrain as the regional hub for land, air and sea military forces. Finally Bahrain was seen by many neutral observers as merely paying lip service to the development of social, political and educational advancement. The ill-treatment of alleged political opponents was well documented by the BICI/Bassiouni Commission reports.

In mid-July 2019 protests broke out following the execution of two Shi'a activists on purported terrorism-related charges. The tension that grew over the weekend in the Sunni-led kingdom, needed to be seen against the confused backdrop of a notional Western ally that had been cracking down harshly on dissent since a failed 2011 uprising. Thus it was that the Bahrain Police Force fired tear gas to disperse hundreds of demonstrators in the Bilad al-Qadeem suburb where one protester allegedly died from gas inhalation in the protests.

However, a government spokesperson said in a statement sent to Reuters that the man had died from natural causes.

People also took to the streets in several Shi'ite villages and neighbourhoods on the outskirts of the capital Manama in late July in response to the execution by firing squad of Ali al-Arab, Ahmed al-Malali and a third man in the Jaw Prison, south of Manama. Amnesty International reported that in May 2019, the Bahraini Court of Cassation had upheld Ali al-Arab and Ahmed al-Malali's convictions and death sentences. The two men were convicted of offences which include 'forming and joining a 'terrorist' group', following a doubtful mass trial. Security officers had allegedly tortured and ill-treated them both. The third man was convicted of murder in another case. Videos and pictures posted on social media showed demonstrators clashing with security forces, burning tires and building roadblocks.

The protests were seen as the most significant unrest in more than two years in the island state, which is the headquarters of the US Navy's Fifth Fleet, since authorities in 2017 executed three Shi'ite men convicted of killing three policemen in a bomb attack. Bahrain, with its Shi'a Muslim majority, is precariously ruled by a Sunni royal family. It is the only one of the Gulf monarchies to have faced serious unrest during the Arab Spring protests that swept the Middle East and North Africa in 2011.

Asked about the demonstrations, the government spokesperson told Reuters that Bahrain upholds constitutional rights for freedom of expression and peaceful assembly, but 'any acts of disorder that disrupt public safety require legal actions to be taken' in accordance with internationally recognised standards.

Keeping a Lid on Dissent

The ruling al-Khalifa family has kept a lid on dissent since the mostly Shi'ite opposition staged a failed uprising in 2011. Saudi Arabia sent in troops to help crush that unrest in a mark of concern that any major unrest or power-sharing concession by Bahrain could inspire its own Shi'ite minority. Activists abroad have called for further protests over the executions referred to above, which were criticised by international rights groups claiming that the men's confessions were obtained through torture, which Manama denies. 'There are calls and there will be more protests in the coming days, but the repression is very violent and authorities are retaliating with collective punishments,' said Ali Alaswad, a senior member of the dissolved opposition group al-Wefaq, who has lived in exile in London since 2011.'The regime uses executions as a vengeance tool,' said al-Wefaq's Alaswad. The Bahraini authorities have denied targeting the opposition and say they are protecting national security.

But the leading opposition group, al-Wefaq, is banned and its leader, Ali Salman, is now in prison on doubtful charges of spying for Qatar. A secular leftist group, Wa'ad, was also dissolved. Former members of al-Wefaq and Wa'ad are not permitted to stand for election.

Sunni Islamist parties are still free to operate, but they hold few seats in parliament. International election monitors are banned.

As political freedom shrinks, inequality has been exacerbated by an economic crisis. Although the non-oil sector generates 80 per cent of gross domestic product (GDP), oil provides 70 per cent of government revenue. When prices crashed earlier this decade Bahrain's fiscal deficit soared, hitting 18.4 per cent of GDP in 2015. The government has since cut spending. Electricity and water subsidies were reduced for expatriates and wealthy Bahrainis. An early-retirement scheme, launched last month, aims to trim the public payroll. More than 9,000 workers have applied for it.

These measures have helped, although this year's deficit is still projected to be 8.9 per cent of GDP. A new 5 per cent value added tax, due to be introduced in January, will raise more revenue. But it will also strain families already struggling to pay their bills. Wages are almost flat and the median monthly private-sector income, BD416 (US$1,106), is 41 per cent below its public-sector counterpart. The higher-paying government jobs tend to go to Sunnis. Shi'as are mostly excluded from the security forces.

The Shi'a, who often live in poorer areas, also bear the brunt of Bahrain's housing shortage. One minister has proposed importing cheap prefabricated homes. But there is little money for that. Public debt has soared to 88 per cent of GDP and foreign reserves, at US$2.3 billion, are barely enough to cover a month of imports. In October 2018 Saudi Arabia, Kuwait and the United Arab Emirates (UAE) had to step in with US$10 billion in aid.

Bahrain has thrived as a banking hub and, since the opening of the Causeway, an alcohol- serving tourist trap for Saudis. Both Qatar and Saudi Arabia are now trying to build up their own financial centres (and Dubai, in the UAE, already has a very successful finance sector). The Saudi Crown Prince, Mohammed bin Salman, has allowed cinemas, concerts and other diversions in a bid to keep Saudi tourists (and their money) at home. Bahrain's banks still employ 14,000 people, most of them nationals. And despite the advent of Saudi Arabia's new 'nightlife', it certainly cannot compete with that of Manama, where bars serve alcohol and the sexes mingle freely. But firms established in Bahrain are certainly nervous. Bahrain has long relied on its wealthier neighbours for business and charity. Now they are also competition. One thing is certain. The people of Bahrain will have little say over how it deals with these economic challenges.

In May 2019 the workers at ALBA, Bahrain's aluminium smelter, were about to finish a US$3 billion expansion. Bahrain would soon produce 1.5 million tonnes of aluminium a year, more than 2.0 per cent of global output. Following the expansion, ALBA's payroll would increase by 500, to 3,700. Almost 90 per cent of ALBA's staff are Bahraini citizens, meaning that firm will end up employing 2.0 per cent of the national workforce, accounting for some 15 per cent of GDP. All six members of the Gulf Co-operation Council (GCC) have (often grandiose) plans to wean their economies off oil. Bahrain is in many ways a forerunner of this effort. It built a financial sector back in the 1980s. More recently it passed a bankruptcy law, allowed 100 per cent foreign ownership of firms and introduced flexible visas that allow some migrants to undertake freelance work.

Compared with other Gulf States, the job market in Bahrain looks vibrant. Two-thirds of citizens work in the private sector, compared with 55 per cent in Saudi Arabia and 10 per cent in Kuwait. Unemployment is 4 per cent. In Saudi Arabia, where joblessness is three times higher, the government is raising work permit fees to drive out migrants. In Bahrain such fees are low. Most migrants toil in low-wage jobs that locals spurn. Bahrainis do not want to lay bricks.

Bahrain ploughs 80 per cent of the take from work permit fees back into the domestic economy through Tamkeen, which offers subsidised loans and grants to help businesses buy equipment and training. Though it has a few national champions, Bahrain has tried harder than other GCC states to cultivate small firms. Businessmen praise its simpler bureaucracy. A local restaurateur says he needs nine licences to operate a fast-food joint in his native Kuwait. Meanwhile, Bahrain has consolidated its permits into one.

Yet the fiscal picture is bleak. Oil provides about 70 per cent of government revenue – and there is not enough of it. Last year's deficit was a yawning 12 per cent of GDP. Wealthier Gulf countries had to offer a US$10 billion bail-out. Bahrain trimmed subsidies for power and water consumption in 2016. But more reforms planned for the following years were simply postponed for fear they would trigger unrest.

Cutting subsidies is only part of the equation. But even though Bahrain introduced a 5 per cent value added tax in January 2019, a corporate or income tax seems politically impossible. Without new taxes the Gulf States will struggle to balance their budgets. State jobs still pay 70 per cent more than those in the private sector, a figure that has grown over the past decade as the monarchy doled out increases and stipends to buy political calm. The gap fuels unrest in a country where the Shi'a majority is often frozen out of state jobs. Flexible work permits might slowly drive up wages in migrant-heavy sectors – but it seems that disaffected employers are trying to sabotage the programme.

Oil still accounts for more than half of Bahrain's exports. Sameer Abdulla Nass, the head of the Chamber of Commerce, complains that 100 per cent foreign ownership has brought only 'retail and restaurants', not industry. Bankers talk giddily about fintech as a growth industry, though in a venture capital firm overlooking the Gulf, investors complain that universities do not produce enough entrepreneurs. Nor do they provide the sort of training that might help graduates land well-paid technical jobs.

Bahrain has done well at convincing its citizens to try the private sector instead of counting on cushy state sinecures. But it has not upended the social contract, whereby oil pays the bills and foreigners do the manual labour. 'Some day, it will have to,' according to Mr Nass, 'We have no choice.'

Oil to the Rescue?

A new, massive oil discovery in Bahrain could help the island kingdom dramatically improve its economic and fiscal strength, according to analysts at Moody's credit ratings agency.

In early April 2018, Bahrain's Oil Minister, Sheikh Mohammed bin Khalifa al-Khalifa announced its biggest discovery of hydrocarbon deposits in decades, estimated to be at least 80 billion barrels of tight oil and between 10 and 20 trillion cubic feet of deep natural gas.

These newly identified deposits have been found off Bahrain's west coast. Although they still need to be verified by an international oil consortium as being technically and economically recoverable it could be a boon for the Bahraini economy. Bahrain's budget deficit was as high as 17.8 per cent of gross domestic product (GDP) in 2016 and the International Monetary Fund (IMF) predicted there would be a deficit of 11.9 per cent of GDP in 2018. But, while improving, Bahrain's debt factor continues to be a concern for both ratings agencies and the IMF.

As such, a new oil discovery could be just the thing Bahrain needs to boost its recovery. 'The find... could stimulate private investment in the country's energy sector in the near-term, and in the medium-term could increase government oil and gas related revenue, and reduce the country's fiscal and current account deficit,' considered Moody's analysts. Like other Gulf nations, Bahrain is keen to diversify its economy away from oil, but revenues from oil exports still make up the bulk of government income. Hydrocarbon-related revenue accounted for 75 per cent of government revenue in 2017, down from 87 per cent in 2013. Although Bahrain is one of the smallest oil exporters in the region, it is the Gulf Co-operation Council's (GCC) oldest oil producer, while remaining its littlest, having started production in the 1930s. Bahrain's hydrocarbon endowment is relatively small, Moody's noted, with an output of around 198,000 barrels per day (bpd) of which around 150,000bpd comes from an offshore field that it shares with Saudi Arabia. By contrast Saudi Arabia produces 12.3 million bpd.

Bahrain's onshore oil reserves are estimated to be around 125 million barrels which, at the current rate of production, would last less than seven years, the analysts noted, making the new discovery of as much as 80 billion barrels very important. 'A significant oil and gas discovery could improve Bahrain's economic and fiscal strength by allowing the kingdom to boost its rate of hydrocarbon production (and hence GDP) and/or to extend its current rate of production for a number of additional years,' according to Moody's.

Welcome Boost

If the latest discovery of oil proves viable and leads to a large increase in Bahrain's oil production, and associated fiscal revenue, it could therefore materially reduce the Kingdom's budget deficit and improve its balance of trade. Moody's downgraded Bahrain's credit rating last year to B1 with a negative outlook. It said the downgrade was driven by its view that the credit profile of the Bahraini government would 'continue to weaken materially in the coming years, predominantly because, despite some fiscal reform efforts, there is a lack of a clear and comprehensive consolidation strategy.'

The agency also expected Bahrain's government debt burden and debt affordability to deteriorate significantly over the coming two to three years. There is hope that a recent recovery in oil prices will also help the economy, with Reuters reporting the Central Bank of Bahrain (CBB) governor as saying in February that he hoped growth would be spurred by this – although he warned about the budget deficit. Brent crude is currently trading around US$73.00 and West Texas Intermediate crude around US$67, a big improvement from 2014 when prices dipped below US$30 a barrel causing the Bahrain economy to struggle more than its richer neighbours.

Bahrain reportedly asked a number of its Gulf allies for financial aid last year. The aid was said to have been required to avert a currency devaluation as the CBB struggled to keep the currency, the Bahraini dinar, pegged to the dollar. The CBB said in December that it was committed to the peg, which means it has to maintain a fixed exchange rate to the dollar by buying or selling its currency. The IMF warned in August that Bahrain 'urgently needed' to take more steps to stabilise state finances and support the dinar's peg to the dollar, Reuters reported. Moody's analysts said that pressure on the peg now was higher than ever, explaining the current state of Bahrain's finances.

'Oil exports accounted for 55 per cent of total goods exports in 2017. When oil prices declined after mid-2014, the dollar value of Bahrain's oil exports dropped significantly and the country's current account swung from surpluses averaging 8 per cent of GDP in 2012–13, to deficits averaging 3.7 per cent of GDP in 2015–17,' the analysts said. 'The reserves have since recovered on the back of large sovereign external bond issuances, including US$3 billion in international bonds in September 2017 and US$1 billion in international sukuk (Islamic bonds) in April 2018. But with foreign reserves of US$2.8 billion at the end of November covering only 1.4 months of imports of goods and services and less than 10 per cent of Bahrain's short-term external debt, pressure on Bahrain's pegged exchange rate regime is now at its highest since the formal peg of the Saudi rial to the dollar was introduced in 2001.'

Moody's Blues

In its August 2019 report, Moody's took the view that the credit profile of Bahrain (B2 stable) reflects a sharp and persistent deterioration in the government's balance sheet, which has intensified since the oil price decline in 2014, Moody's observed that 'Bahrain's public finances are highly sensitive to oil price fluctuations because of a very high share of oil-related revenues in government revenue and a very high fiscal breakeven oil price,' according to a Moody's senior analyst, adding that 'The sovereign debt is also highly susceptible to government liquidity and external vulnerability risks.'

However, Moody's noted that Bahrain does have some credit strengths, notably a very high per capita income, a diversified economy (when compared with fellow Gulf Co-operation Council states) and a positive net international investment position. Together, in the view of Moody's, these factors provide some 'shock-absorption capacity'. Critically, Bahrain's credit profile is also bolstered by the financial support package committed in 2018 by neighbouring GCC governments, equivalent to more than 25 per cent of GDP. Moody's also considered that a rapid fiscal consolidation that stabilised and eventually decreased the government's debt burden would be positive for the sovereign credit profile. As would a sustained rebuilding of the Central Bank's foreign-currency buffers, that materially decreased external vulnerability. Conversely, however, any slower than expected fiscal consolidation might endanger potential GCC disbursements or undermine an already fragile investor confidence.

2020

Human Rights – Banking Reforms – FinTech: High Hopes – Oil Price Plunges – Diversification Again – New Discoveries – New Pipeline – Asset Rich, Cash Poor

Whatever hopes that were held by the Bahraini government that its international image might begin to improve by 2019 were largely dashed by the annual report of the US based Human Rights Watch (HRW) in which it observed that the Bahraini authorities had continued the repression of dissidents as well as attacking freedom of expression and assembly. HRW confirmed that the Bahraini government had continued to crack down on peaceful dissent during 2018, virtually eliminating all opposition. No independent media were allowed to operate in Bahrain in 2018, and ahead of the parliamentary elections due to be held in November 2018, parliament banned members of the (already dissolved) opposition parties from being able to run.

The Bahraini authorities certainly took no chances. Peaceful dissidents were arrested, prosecuted, ill-treated, and stripped of citizenship. The HRW director for the Middle East, Lama Fakih, did not mince her words: 'the Bahraini authorities have demonstrated a zero tolerance policy when it comes to free media, independent political thought, and peaceful dissent,' said Ms Fakih. 'Despite the stream of arrests and convictions of dissidents, Bahrain's allies have failed to use their influence to improve Bahrain's rights record at home or abroad.'

The government detained a former member of parliament, Ali Rashed al-Asheeri, after he tweeted about boycotting the elections. He was released on bail three days after the election. On 4 November the Bahrain High Court of Appeals overturned the previous acquittal of a prominent opposition member, Sheikh Ali Salman, sentencing him to life in prison on espionage charges. Salman is the leader of Bahrain's opposition group, al-Wefaq, which was outlawed in 2016. The report also brought the case of upholding the 5-year jail term against Nabeel Rajab and sentencing Duaa al-Wadaei to prison *in absentia* as well as attacking female human rights defenders, held in the Isa Town Prison, Hajer Mansoor Hasan, Najah Yusuf, and Medina Ali by the prison officials.

HRW stressed that the oversight bodies did not investigate credible allegations of prison abuse or hold officials who participated in and ordered widespread torture during interrogations since 2011 accountable. 'According to one human rights group, in 2018, the courts stripped 305 people of their citizenship, bringing the total since 2012 to 810', said the report, adding that 'Bahraini prisons held 14 people on death row.' The organisation added that 'despite significant human rights concerns in Bahrain and its participation in the Saudi Arabian-led coalition in Yemen, which is committing serious violations of international humanitarian law, the United States State Department approved five major weapons sales to Bahrain between January and November.'

FinTech Future?

Once a regional pioneer in the world of international finance and banking, as the twenty-first century wore on it had become clear that Bahrain had, in effect, fallen well behind its closest rival, Dubai. To widespread surprise in 2019 and in early 2020 Bahrain's banking regulators and administrators seemed to be set on introducing an ambitious series of reforms and initiatives, aimed at encouraging the banking community to embrace innovation and entrepreneurship in the age of fintech. Although the Bahraini authorities saw the future of fintech as one of the main drivers of the island's growth, a 2017 article in the London *Sunday Times* observed that 'Too often, fintech seems like little more than a trendy re-branding exercise.' Nevertheless, there were a number of self-styled experts who were convinced that 'the fintech revolution is coming'.

A public-private partnership, Bahrain FinTech Bay (BFB) claims to be the largest fintech hub in the Middle East, with partners that include governmental bodies, financial institutions, corporates, consultancy firms, universities, associations, media agencies, venture capital and fintech start-ups. The stated objective is to bring together the full spectrum of financial market participants and stakeholders. To this end, the Central Bank of Bahrain (CBB) has created a fintech innovation unit of its own, with – it also claims – the relevant regulatory backup. It has released new regulations for crowd-funding and draft rules for crypto-assets. It intends to roll out this so-called 'open' banking before the end of 2020. The CBB has also announced that the first phase of a national on-line 'know your-customer' system is imminent.

The chief executive officer of the BFB, Khalid Saad announced that during the previous two years 'Things have been happening'. The goal, he stated, is 'to future-proof the financial sector and 'reposition the country as an innovator'. It was also claimed that the BFB is part of a broader effort to diversify Bahrain's economy and reduce its vulnerability to fluctuating oil prices. Cynics couldn't help wondering how many times they had heard that this objective was considered an important part of the government's economic policy.

'Regulatory changes are encouraging the embrace of fintech,' Rasheed al-Maraj', Governor of the Central Bank of Bahrain, said in a paper prepared for the 2020 Gateway Gulf Investor Forum in Manama (the event was postponed due to the Covid pandemic). But ultimately, he concluded, 'what matters is the value new technology brings to improve the quality of people's lives. Beyond economic diversification and growth, broader goals include job creation and financial inclusion.'

Something of a buzzword, fintech (an abbreviation of 'financial technology') is used to describe a range of new technologies that seek to improve and automate the delivery and use of financial services. Essentially, fintech is used to help companies, business owners and consumers better manage their financial operations, processes, and lives with specialised software and algorithms that are used on computers and, increasingly, smart phones. The term was initially applied to the technology employed at the back-end systems of established financial institutions. Since then, however, there has been a shift to more consumer-oriented services and therefore a more consumer-oriented definition. Fintech now includes different sectors and industries such as education, retail banking, fundraising and investment management.

Not specifically relevant to Bahrain, fintech also includes the development and use of crypto-currencies such as bitcoin (and others). While that segment of fintech may make the most headlines, the generally accepted view is that the major opportunities still lie in the traditional global banking industry. However, Bahrain's innovations did at least suggest that the government is at pains to establish a fintech niche for itself. Early indications indicate progress. The BFB reportedly has over 50 established partners, including big names such as American Express, Cisco and Microsoft. Of its 28 associated start-ups, two have graduated beyond simple optimism – one in open banking, the other a crypto-asset exchange. While numbers are not broken out for fintech specifically, Bahrain's Economic Development Board (EDB) reports that direct investment in Bahrain experienced a year-on-year growth of 138 per cent during the first nine months of 2018. Mr Saad of the BTB observed that 'One of the biggest successes has been a 'mindset shift' in the last year.'

Following a visit of an International Monetary Fund (IMF) mission in February 2020, the organisation offered praise, while encouraging vigilance. The IMF head of mission, Bikas Joshi, noted that 'efforts at supervisory and regulatory vigilance, and to further enhance the Anti-Money Laundering/Countering Financing of Terrorism framework, are welcome. Bahrain has been a leader in fintech, promoting opportunities while revising regulations and collaborating with other regulators.

Economy
Bahrain recorded 1.8 per cent year-on-year growth in 2019 and 2.4 per cent in nominal terms, according to the latest figures published by the Information

and Government Authority. This compared to an annual growth rate of 1.8 per cent in 2018 in real terms and 6.1 per cent in nominal terms. The oil sector rebounded in 2019, growing at an annual rate of 2.2 per cent, having contracted by 1.3 per cent in 2018 due to planned maintenance in the first quarter of 2018. The non-oil sector continued its positive growth, albeit at a slower pace, expanding at a rate of 1.7 per cent (3.6 per cent in nominal terms). The growth of the non-oil sectors is a testament to the successful economic diversification and development initiatives pursued under the guiding principles of the Economic Vision 2030.

Non-oil growth in 2019 received a boost from the manufacturing, hotels and restaurants sectors. Having recorded an annual growth rate of 4.7 per cent in the third quarter of 2019, the manufacturing sector continued to grow by 5.2 per cent in the fourth quarter of 2019, spurred on by the completion of ALBA's sixth production line.

Moreover, the hotels and restaurants sector recorded the highest non-oil sector annual growth at 6.8 per cent. Preliminary results point to a decline in growth in the fourth quarter of 2019. Despite negative growth of 0.4 per cent in real terms and 0.3 per cent in nominal terms during the final quarter of the year, the non-oil private sectors grew by 2.7 per cent in real terms in the fourth quarter of 2019 or by 3.4 per cent in nominal terms.

The government services sector growth decelerated during the quarter after the government's implementation of fiscal measures to lower expenditure and improve the budget deficit. After a bout of lower risks, the Covid-19 pandemic has emerged as a major disruption to the near-term economic outlook.

Despite the initial optimistic expectations for economic growth in 2020, a global recession is now all but certain. Policymakers around the world – led by the US Federal Reserve – have returned to aggressive stimulus measures. For Bahrain, this has entailed a monetary stimulus as interest rates have been reduced and the government has adopted a BD4.3 billion stimulus package to counter the effects of the crisis. Furthermore, oil prices have plunged significantly since their highs at the end of December 2019, adding to the pressure on the global economy.

With a Little Help From My Friends

A relatively oil-rich island nation (at least following the more recent discoveries) of 1.6 million people set in the Arabian Gulf between Saudi Arabia and Qatar, Bahrain has been forced to seek the support of its neighbours to calm the debt and currency markets when low petroleum prices helped push its public finances into disarray. Economic growth dropped to under 2.0 per cent in the final quarter of 2018, according to the IMF, but at the end of 2018 Bahrain could at least consider itself to be asset rich. Although for at least the next five years, discounting any significant rise in the price of oil, the island Kingdom looked likely to be cash-poor.

This has prompted Bahraini officials to reinforce their diversification efforts. As noted above, fintech counts among the priority sectors targeted, along with manufacturing, logistics, information and communication technologies, tourism, health care and education. Bahrain's financial services account for nearly 17 per cent of GDP, ranking only just behind oil and gas, at 19 per cent to 20 per cent respectively. The Central Bank of Bahrain counts close to 400 institutions under its regulatory wing, including an impressive list of prestigious international banks such as Standard Chartered and JP Morgan.

Once a regional hub for financial services, Bahrain has lost ground to Dubai; but the sector's backbone remains strong. Bahrain has been a financial hub in the region going back five decades, with a long tradition in financial services. It is hoped that Bahrain could recover its place vis-à-vis Dubai by using fintech that is forward looking as a launching pad. Fintech has also helped in appealing to a new generation of Bahraini wealth, young entrepreneurs, innovators and creators who are not satisfied with the products currently offered. Opportunities exist for the financial sector's entrepreneurs, venture capitalists and their customers. Islamic finance also offers a significant opportunity for Bahrain's banking community. In a report released in 2019, the EDB claimed that the country is the leading Islamic finance hub in the Middle East and North Africa region and the number two worldwide. A recent example of progress on this front is the interesting partnership between the Islamic Bank and PayPal to expand the bank's digital offerings and offer additional services. In 2018, the BFB announced the launch of the Global Islamic and Sustainable Fintech Center with over a dozen international partners.

An important opportunity for Bahrain's financial sector is the development of fintech solutions through Sharia-compliant procedures. One example is technology, which can be used to enable Islamic financial institutions to improve transaction transparency. 'Smart' contracts can also be implemented for Islamic contracts, which are based on the Shariah, enabling, in principle, the seamless execution of extensive contractual obligations.

In April 2019, King Hamad bin Isa al-Khalifa paid a visit to Paris, leading a delegation of Bahraini fintech entrepreneurs. An opportunistic French government, it appeared, was not bothered by Bahrain's unsatisfactory human rights record. The accompanying delegation met with tech entrepreneurs at Station F, the world's largest start-up campus; at the coding school Ecole 42; and at the fintech incubator Le Swave. Agreements were discussed, contracts were signed.

Diversification – Again?

Once the regional banking hub, Bahrain lost pride of place to Dubai in the 2000s. Today, the Gulf Co-operation Council's (GCC) smallest state aspires to leverage fintech innovation to reclaim its leading position. In 2019, Bahrain signed agreements with companies and institutions in France, the US, Turkey, India and China, which anticipated the launch of a venture capital fund based in Manama.

Bahrain has long sought to diversify its economy. Unlike its oil-rich neighbours, it started looking for alternative sources of revenue in the 1970s. A strong banking system quickly became the focal point of this strategy. As a result, while oil currently accounts for less than 20 per cent of GDP, the financial services are not far behind, making up 16.5 per cent. Today, Bahrain is home to some 400 financial institutions, including more than 114 licensed banks. Total banking assets reached US$201 billion in April 2019, according to CEIC, and are growing steadily.

A major selling point for Bahrain has always been its strategic location as a gateway to the Gulf region and its position as an entry point to the GCC's largest market, Saudi Arabia. A regional financial services base in Bahrain will put any business at the centre of one of the most potent concentrations of wealth on the planet. However, a strong banking infrastructure won't automatically make Bahrain a financial services leader since virtually all its close neighbours – the other five GCC states – are in the same race. In order to differentiate itself from its competitive neighbours, Bahrain is betting on its low cost of doing business, advanced regulation and efficient administration. A 2018 report by the global accountancy firm KPMG indicated that Bahrain enjoys a cost advantage of 35 per cent when it comes to the annual operating costs for a financial services firm when compared to those of the Dubai International Financial Centre or the Abu Dhabi Global Market. To attract foreign money and talent, Bahrain allows 100 per cent foreign ownership of companies and imposes zero corporate or income taxes; a relatively new bankruptcy law makes it easier for entrepreneurs to take risks, fail and start again. Bahrain is also home to the region's first fund of funds. One year after inception, the US$100 million al-Waha Fund of Funds had allocated half of its resources to five regional venture funds that will set up a presence in Manama. Underpinning these initiatives is Bahrain's reputation for administrative efficiency – a selling point with many foreign entrepreneurs, for whom time means money. Thanks to diversification, non-oil sectors account for 80 per cent of the economy and grew by a healthy 4.3 per cent in 2018. But oil still contributes the bulk of government revenues (75 per cent), making the kingdom vulnerable. After a couple of years of low oil prices, government debt, which was 30 per cent of GDP in 2010, now stands at an all-time high of 93.4 per cent and is expected to reach 100 per cent in the next three years. The 2.4 per cent economic growth forecast for 2019 depends upon a US$10 billion aid package from GCC neighbours. The Kingdom introduced a 5 per cent value added tax (VAT) in January; but unpopular measures, such as cutting subsidies or levying taxes, seem unlikely for fear of social unrest.

Bahrain's government debt burden will continue to rise, due to political and social considerations, Moody's concluded in December 2018 as it upgraded Bahrain's banking outlook from negative to stable. Moody's considered the credit challenges to be set against Bahrain's key credit strength – its relatively diversified and dynamic economy. Fintech, Manama hopes, will be one successful way to leverage those advantages.

IMF Relaxation

Overall economic activity was subdued in 2018. The IMF notes that oil output is expected to have declined by 1.2 per cent, while non-oil output growth decelerated to 2.5 per cent, driven by slowdowns in the retail, hospitality, and financial services sectors. The continued implementation of GCC-funded projects has supported growth in the construction sector. Overall growth in 2018 is estimated at 1.8 per cent, with inflation edging up to 2.1 per cent, mainly driven by higher food and transport prices. With higher oil prices, the reduction in utility subsidies, and the new excise taxes, the overall deficit in 2018 fell to 11.7 per cent of gross domestic product (GDP), down from the 14.2 per cent seen in 2017. Public debt in 2018 increased to 93 per cent of GDP. The current account deficit widened to 5.8 per cent, while reserves remained low, covering only about one month of prospective non-oil imports by the end of 2018.

According to the IMF, economic growth was anticipated to remain around 1.8 per cent in 2019. The Bahrain authorities' Fiscal Balance Programme (FBP), underpinned by the 2019/20 budget, has provided a commendable framework to arrest the decline in fiscal and external buffers since 2014. The introduction of VAT in January 2019 was a particularly significant step. The various measures envisaged under the FBP are expected to further reduce the fiscal deficit over the medium term, but the IMF considered that Bahrain's public debt would nevertheless continue to increase.

As a consequence, the government's additional reform efforts, anchored in a more transparent medium-term agenda, will be needed to ensure fiscal sustainability and support the currency peg, which continues to provide a clear and credible monetary anchor. Further revenue measures, including a direct taxation system such as corporate income tax, could be considered and spending reforms should be designed to protect the most vulnerable. The implementation of the Voluntary Retirement Scheme (VRS), said the IMF, is expected to reduce the public wage bill over the medium term. The ultimate impact on public service delivery and public finances should be carefully assessed based on public sector restructuring plans and contingent liabilities of the VRS.

In the view of the IMF, the banking system remains stable. Continuing efforts at supervisory and regulatory vigilance, and to further enhance the AML/CFT framework, are welcome. Bahrain has been a regional leader in fintech, promoting opportunities while revising regulations and collaborating with other regulators.

Sustained structural reforms were expected to help support inclusive growth and further economic diversification. This requires developing a dynamic private sector, while transforming the role of the government without sacrificing necessary public services. Targeted education and labour market reforms would help promote opportunities and improve productivity. Efforts to place greater emphasis on vocational education and retraining are welcome, particularly as technology is rapidly changing the nature of work. Reforms to streamline regulations should further improve efficiency and catalyse private investment. Improving access to financing for small and medium enterprises, said the IMF, would invigorate further the private sector's contribution to the overall economy. Bahrain certainly sees a particularly ripe opportunity to be a leader in information and communication technologies (ICT). In December 2018, the CBB issued rules to enable open banking by the end of June. The new legal set-up borrows from the EU's second Payment Services Directive. The new regulatory framework seems to be attracting multinationals. The Chinese tech group Wonder News has invested US$50 million in a new regional office; the French insurance group AXA is building a six-story MENA headquarters; and in Bahrain's biggest coup to date, Amazon Web Services (AWS) is setting up its first data centre for the region in Manama.

Fintech is far from being the only star to which Bahrain is hitching its economy. Direct investment reached a record US$830 million in 2018, a 13.2 per cent year-on-year increase, according to the EDB. Financial services and ICT accounted for 13 per cent of that amount; while tourism, real estate, education, health care, manufacturing, transport and logistics made up 87 per cent. Like its neighbours, Bahrain has a general road map for the future, Vision 2030, which drives a US$32 billion infrastructure plan across a variety of sectors – including oil.

Energy

The discovery of a giant offshore reserve at Khalij al-Bahrain has certainly enlivened Bahrain's energy prospects. When Bahrain discovered the massive hydrocarbon resources in its waters in early 2018, the find was hailed as having the potential to transform its energy future. Without question, the new oil discovery could help Bahrain return to a more balanced economic keel. The credit agency Moody's saw the discovery as 'dramatically' improving the Kingdom's economic and fiscal strength. Oil Minister Sheikh Mohammed bin Khalifa al-Khalifa had announced that the west coast discovery was simply the biggest discovery of hydrocarbon deposits in decades, estimated to be at least 80 billion barrels of tight oil and between 10 and 20 trillion cubic feet of deep natural gas. The next step was to have the discovery verified by an international oil consortium as being technically and economically recoverable.

Like other Gulf States, Bahrain has been keen to diversify its economy away from oil, but revenues from oil exports still make up the bulk of government income.

Hydrocarbon-related revenue accounted for 75 per cent of government revenue in 2017, down from 87 per cent in 2013. Although Bahrain is one of the smallest oil exporters in the region, it is the GCC's oldest oil producer. Bahrain started commercial production in the 1930s. Its hydrocarbon reserves are relatively small, Moody's noted, with an output of around 198,000 barrels per day (bpd) of which no less than some 150,000bpd comes from an offshore field that it shares with Saudi Arabia.

Bahrain's onshore oil reserves had been estimated to be around 125 million barrels which, at the current rate of production, would last less than a meagre seven years. Thus the new discovery can be seen to be vitally important. Moody's noted that Bahrain could either boost its rate of hydrocarbon production or extend its current rate of production for a number of additional years.

Moody Moody's
If the latest discovery of oil proves viable and leads to a large increase in Bahrain's oil production, and associated fiscal revenue, it could materially reduce the Kingdom's budget deficit and improve its balance of trade. In 2018 Moody's downgraded the government of Bahrain's long-term debt ratings to B2 from B1 and maintained a negative outlook. The key driver for the rating downgrade is the rise in Bahrain's external and government liquidity risks to particularly elevated levels, constraining access to market financing to a greater extent than Moody's previously envisaged.

Despite the higher oil prices seen over the past year, the government's gross borrowing needs remain very high and its foreign exchange reserves are very low. Meanwhile, heightened external and government liquidity pressures have failed to accelerate the implementation of the much vaunted fiscal reforms, which Moody's expects to remain very slow. Also, the B2 rating assumes that Bahrain's GCC neighbours will provide some financial support, following a broad statement made in June 2018, without which Bahrain's creditworthiness would be significantly weaker.

Moody's negative outlook reflects the risk that the promised financial support from the GCC countries is neither timely or comprehensive enough to maintain Bahrain's credit profile at B2 through the series of debt repayments.

There is some hope that the recent recovery in oil prices will also help the economy to recover. Brent crude is currently trading around US$73 and WTI around US$67, a big improvement from 2014 when prices dipped below US$30 a barrel. Bahrain has reportedly asked a number of its Gulf allies for financial aid. The aid was reportedly required to avert a currency devaluation as the Central Bank of Bahrain struggled to keep the Bahraini dinar pegged to the dollar. The IMF warned in August 2018 that Bahrain 'urgently needed' to take more steps to stabilise state finances and support the dinar's peg to the dollar. Moody's noted that the pressure on the peg was higher than ever.

Oil exports accounted for 55 per cent of total goods exports in 2017. When oil prices declined in the second half of 2014, the dollar value of Bahrain's oil exports dropped significantly and the country's current account swung from surpluses averaging 8 per cent of GDP in 2012–13, to deficits averaging 3.7 per cent of GDP in 2015–17. The reserves have since recovered following large sovereign external bond issuances, including US$3 billion in international bonds in September 2017 and US$1 billion in international sukuk (Islamic bonds) in April 2018. But with foreign reserves of US$2.8 billion at the end of November covering only 1.4 months of imports of goods and services and less than 10 per cent of Bahrain's short-term external debt, pressure on Bahrain's pegged exchange rate regime is now at its highest since the formal peg of the Saudi rial to the dollar was introduced in 2001.

nogaholding

Nearly one year after the new oil and gas discoveries were first announced, Bahrain has taken its first steps to explore the reserves held in the Khalij al-Bahrain offshore field. The oil is estimated to be more than 80 billion barrels of tight oil and the gas between 10–20 trillion cubic feet, according to nogaholding, Bahrain's state oil and gas company. However, the full economic picture of the reserves remains unknown, as estimates are based on P50 estimates, which assume that only 50 per cent of the hydrocarbons represents a commercially feasible value proposition for extraction. The consultancy firm Wood Mackenzie has cautioned that the newly discovered energy reserves are 'technically challenging and potentially high-cost to develop'. The US oil field services corporations Schlumberger and Halliburton have assisted Bahrain in realising the pre-Khuff discovery, and have carried out exploratory drilling and appraisal work on the Khalij al-Bahrain resource on behalf of nogaholding and the Bahrain Petroleum Company (BAPCO).

Since the original oil discoveries in 1932, investment in Bahrain's oil and gas sector has not yielded much by way of profit for foreign exploration and production companies. So the proposals for prospective partners based on the 2018 discoveries not only need to be well thought out and soundly based, they need to be attractive to foreign investors. Previous oil contracts had less than attractive terms by accepted international standards and as a result, the international oil company partners made meagre returns. New fiscal terms will be needed to attract suitable partners.

Outlook

For a country that produces as little as 41,000bpd, despite being located in an oil-rich region, and has to grapple with declining output from its few fields, a discovery the size of Khalij al-Bahrain offers the prospect of eventually transforming not only its energy sector, but also improving the wider aspects of its economy. Meanwhile, hopes are pinned on the development of its financial sector, with particular emphasis on fintech applications, helping it turn a corner in its economic fortunes.

The target date for the commercial production from the new oil discoveries is only five years away. In October 2018, Bahrain commissioned the new pipeline it has been building since 2014. This will allow the Sitra refinery to receive increased volumes of crude production from neighbouring Saudi Arabia. Built at an estimated cost of US$400 million, it originates from Saudi Aramco's Abqaiq plants and will enable BAPCO's Sitra Refinery to receive its full requirement of crude.

The Islamic Calendar

With the advent of the twenty-first century, the general use, and importance of the Islamic (Hijri) calendar had diminished throughout the Gulf States, largely replaced in official circles by the internationally used Gregorian calendar. However, the traditionally important dates and festivals of Islam were still determined according to the Islamic calendar.

The Islamic calendar is based on the date the Prophet Mohammed left Mecca for Medina. In the Christian calendar, this corresponds to 16 July 622. The departure from Mecca became known as the Hijrah (a word meaning 'withdrawal of affection' rather than 'flight' as it is usually translated) and the years of the new era are therefore known in non–Muslim countries by the term Anno Hegirae (AH), by analogy with Anno Domini.

The Hijri era is based on pre-Islamic tradition, with necessary revisions. The year is a lunar one and consists of twelve months, each lasting for one lunation, the period it takes for the moon to revolve around the earth, or rather between two new moons.

The moon's revolution takes roughly 29 1/3 days, but the effect of the Earth's own movement means that the observed elapsed time, which is what the Islamic Calendar is concerned with, is slightly longer, 29 1/2 to be precise. Twelve such months amount to 354 days, which is about 11 days shorter than the solar year of 365 days. To correlate two such astronomical events in terms of a third (the revolution of the Earth on its own axis, which is the basic unit, the day, of all systems of chronology, including both the Christian and the Islamic calendars) obviously poses problems. Because 12 lunar months are shorter than one solar year, the Islamic calendar does not keep time with the seasons and 'advances' by about 10, 11 or 12 days each year in relation to the solar year. Thus 12 lunar months, measured from the cyclic appearance of 12 crescent new moons, define a year that averages just over 354 days. Indeed, the Prophet himself proscribed such practice in the Khutbah at his Farewell Pilgrimage: 'a year is twelve months, as at the time of Creation', a formula that is echoed in the Koran (Sura IX, 36).

This somewhat confusing difference between lunar and solar calendars was the bane of priests, administrators, historians, emperors and rulers for centuries. Ancient Egypt had recourse to no less than five different calendars during the period from 3000 BC to AD 500, while the Babylonian ruler Hammurabi some 500 years ago was compelled to make calendrical pronouncements concerning the intercalation of an extra month when astronomical movements did not seem to be harmonious with seasonal events or with calculated dates: 'Since the year has a deficiency, let the month which is beginning be known as the second Ululu. But the taxes which are due in Babylon on the 25th day of the month Tashritu should be paid on the 25th day of the second Ululu.'

Intercalation, the practice of adding an extra day or month into the calendar in order to keep it astronomically aligned, has through the centuries, been carried out in different ways according to different religious and civil requirements.

In lunar calendars, that is, those that use months of 29 days or 29 or 30 days, a whole month is generally added every third year or so on order to correct the 11.5 day difference between the lunar and solar years. This was the method used in the ancient Mesopotamian and pre-Islamic Middle Eastern calendars and was long used in Israel and China.

With solar calendars, intercalation tended in the past to be either more sporadic, or peculiar to a certain civilisation until Julius Caesar's time. In one of Ancient Egypt's calendars, for example, the twelve thirty day months were supplemented by five 'epagomenal' days at the end of each year, when the five principal deities were deemed to have been born, but this system naturally got the year out of phase with the natural year of 365.22 days. As a result this Egyptian Civil – or 'wandering' – year gradually moved, 'wandered', through the seasons by one day every four years returning to the same place after 1,460 days or so! After this cycle had occurred at least twice during Egypt's long history, it was proposed in around 230 BC that a sixth epagomenal day was added every fourth year in order to check the wandering; but the idea was ignored even though this had been the main purpose of the Canopus Decree put out by Ptolemy First. It was Julius Caesar, some 200 years or so later, who picked up this idea originally proposed by Ptolemy's Greek-Egyptian astronomers in Alexandria, and it was from his Julian calendar that the Civil calendar originated.

In the Islamic calendar there is no attempt to keep the New Year at a specific time in the seasonal year, that is, in accordance with the sun's movements. The year comprises 12 cycles of the moon and intercalation only occurs to keep this pattern in check. Each lunar 'synodic' cycle (ie from new moon to new moon) averages 29.53 days, so a year made up of months alternating between 29 and 30 days is not accurate enough after a few months have elapsed.

In order to correct this, the twelfth month, Dhu al-Hijjah, therefore in some years has 29 days, and 30 days in others according to a thirty-year cycle. This lunar year – 354 days in some years, 355 days in others – then moves through the seasonal year in such a way that in 32.5 years it passes through all the seasons, somewhat like the old Egyptian Wandering Calendar but in only a fraction of the time!

THE ISLAMIC CALENDAR

Before proceeding to look at the Islamic calendar it is worth considering how the Western, or Gregorian calendar evolved. One of the many tasks that Julius Caesar set himself on becoming emperor was that of sorting out the Roman Republican calendar. This had fallen into chaos and was three months behind the seasons, thanks very largely to a combination of meddlesome priests and political manoeuvrings in the latter days of the Republic – certain none too scrupulous leaders extended or reduced their terms of office according to their wishes by the simple means of declaring that the calendar was wrong! Julius Caesar sought the advice of the Alexandrian Sosigenes, who in turn looked to the earlier Ptolomaic astronomers; they had first defined a sixth epagomenal day every fourth year, and Sosigenes followed suit by proposing that the year 46 BC should have 445 days in order to make up the three month deficiency, and that thereafter the year should consist of 365 days for three years and 366 every fourth.

Julius Caesar accepted the suggestion and decreed that the extra day in the leap year should be placed after 23 February and before 24 February, that is on the sixth day before the calends of March. Hence the old term bissextile for such a year with two sixth days before the calends (the word is still used in France).

The day after 23 February was formerly when the extra month was intercalated into the old 355 day Republican lunar calendar. The new year would begin on 1 March, as some of the present month names remind us. September, for example, is the seventh month (septem being the Latin for seven) and December the tenth (from decem meaning the tenth). The fifth month, formerly Quintilis, was renamed after Julius, and the sixth, Sixtilis, after Julius' successor, Augustus. Because Augustus' admirers thought him equal to – if not greater than – the great Julius, a day was taken from the already depleted February and added to August, which until then had only 30 days, thus making it equal in length to Julius' month.

Julius' calendar served the empire and the kingdoms that emerged after the Romans had departed for over 1,500 years, But its 365 1/4 day year was not, alas, accurate enough. It was eleven minutes and 14 seconds too long. Over a few decades such an error would not be easily noticed. But over 130 years it accumulates to one day. The Venerable Bede noted in AD730 that the Spring Equinox was about three days late, and Roger Bacon noted the error which by the thirteenth century had grown to seven days.

But it was not until Pope Gregory's time in the sixteenth century that anyone did anything about correcting the matter, so after carrying out the necessary research, Pope Gregory decreed in March 1582 that the day following 5 October in that year should be designated 15 October. And it was so. In Protestant England, however, where anything that issued from a pope was naturally disregarded on principle, it was not until 1752 when the calendar error had accumulated to eleven days, that corrections were made. In that year, the day after 2 September was called 14 September.

Unfortunately – understandably – the mass of the population wondered what on earth was going on especially as many of them had lost eleven days pay, and inevitably rioting followed. At the same time the beginning of the year was moved from 1 March to 1 January, a fact that causes some problems to present-day historians trying to piece together the timing of past events. In order to avoid the 11 minutes per year accumulating in the future, Gregory decreed that the century's years should not be leap years unless they were divisible by 400. For instance, the years 1700, 1800 and 1900 were not leap years, whereas 2000 was.

Easter is now fixed in the modern Gregorian calendar by a complicated formula which contrives to place it on the Sunday after the first full moon after the day that follows the Spring Equinox; it is usually 21 March but is sometimes the 22 March. Other Christian movable feasts – such as Lent and Pentecost – are geared to Easter.

In the Islamic calendar certain dates are now given according to the Gregorian calendar, particularly in connection with business or official functions. It is not unknown for mistakes to be made, so for many years it was advisable for visitors to the Gulf States to double check both dates in both calendars. The most common source of errors was the fact that the Islamic day begins at sunset, and in rare cases dates would be given for that – evening-beginning-day; since most business is carried out during daylight hours, however, the date given was usually correct.

In Hijri leap years, the month Dhu al-Hijjah at the end of the year will have 30 days instead of the normal 29. The all-important month of Ramadan ends with the great holiday of Eid al-Fitr. Other important festivals that 'move' according to the Gregorian calendar are:

Eid al-Adha – 10 Dhu al-Hijjah

al-Hijjah – New Year 1 Muharram

Ashura – 10 Muharram

The Prophet's Birthday – 12 Rabi al-Awal (Mawlid al-Nabi))

Lailat al-Miraj – 27 Rajab

Lailat al-Qadr – 27 Ramadan (The Night of Power or of the Decree)

Ramadan, the important ninth month in the Islamic year commemorates the gift of the Koran to teach and guide the people. The last ten days of the month are particularly sacred and the 27th day is Lailat al-Qadr when tradition holds that the revelation of the Koran was actually made.

THE ISLAMIC CALENDAR

The tradition of fasting during the daylight hours of Ramadan is one of the Five Pillars of the Islamic faith and is generally taken very seriously throughout the Islamic world; it includes not only refraining from eating but abstinence from drinking and sexual intercourse. The rules apply each day of the month and last from dawn when 'a white thread may be distinguished from a black' until nightfall when the two threads become indistinguishable again. As with the Islamic months the beginning and end of Ramadan may not occur on the actual calendar date but when a reliable witness (or Qadi) has actually sighted the new moon. This procedure has been somewhat modernised with the advent of satellite imagery. No longer can it be delayed by heavy skies or clouds. The first three days of the month after Ramadan, Shawaal, naturally have an air of festivity about them following the abstinences of the previous 30 days; this is the time of the Feast of Eid al-Fitr, the 'Breaking of the Fast', one of the two great feasts or Bairam of the Islamic Year. At this time people go visiting their families and friends, give presents to each other and visit the graves of relatives. The other great Bairam of al-Adha lasts three days from the tenth day of the month Dhu al-Hijjah. It celebrates Ishmael's ransom of a ram, which people often commemorate by the sacrifice of an animal and distributing the meat to the poor.

Arabic Naming Practice

Traditional Arabic names consist of five parts: the *ism*, *kunya*, *nasab*, *laqab* and *nisba*.

The *ism* is the given name, that is to say the names given to children at birth

The *kunya* is an informal name used within family circles. Almost a family 'nickname' and does not constitute a part of a person's 'official' or formal name and would not normally be seen in print. It is however an important identity component.

The *nasab* is the patronymic and starts with bin or ibn, which means 'son of', or 'bint', which means 'daughter of'. It acknowledges the father of the child. Matronymics are not used in Arabic. The nasab generally follows the ism, so that you have, for example, Mohammed ibn Faysal Ahmed, which means Mohammed, son of Faysal Ahmed. A daughter would be Miriam bint Abdul Aziz. In principle, the names of grandfathers and grandmothers can be added. There are variations within this formula.

In Iraq, for example, the nasab is normally omitted. The use of bin, ibn or bint is not, however, essential. Mohammed bin Abdullah means exactly the same as Mohammed Abdullah. However, bin, ibn or bint can be put in front of a distinguished ancestor.

The *laqab,* when used, would normally follow the ism. It generally assumes a religious or favourably descriptive dimension. Thus 'Abdullah al-Rashid ibn Faysal Darwish' is Abdullah the rightly guided son of Faysal Darwish.

The *nisba* corresponds to the 'Western' surname. Significant territorial exceptions are Egypt and Lebanon where the nisba is not used; the laqab includes its meaning. Elsewhere, the nisba is often used as the last name and usually represents an occupation, a geographic location, or a tribe or family.

One divergence from Western practice is that Arabic women do not take their husband's names when they marry. They retain the names they were given at birth. Children, however, take their father's name.

The use of 'al' is delightfully vague. If it is included in front of a family name it translates as 'the family'. Unfortunately this practice has been adopted by the region's social climbers anxious to improve their own status. Similarly, although 'sheikh' is a respectful term applied to tribal and religious leaders it is occasionally used by junior civil servants and employees to address their line managers and employers.

This is akin to the use of academic titles ('doctor' and 'licenciado') in Latin American countries.

We are indebted to Beth Notzon and Gayle Nesom of the University of Texas for their paper on the often complicated subject of Arabic nomenclature. Thanks also, to Michael Field (who for some years edited the *Middle East Review*) for his helpful Appendix *Note on Arab Names* in: *The Merchants: the Big Business Families of Arabia*, originally published in 1985 by the Overlook Press, Woodstock, N.Y.

Notes

AB-4 Pipeline: Commissioned in 2018, a 71-mile, 350,000 barrels per day (bpd) pipeline running between the Abqaiq complex in Saudi Arabia and Bahrain's refinery at Sitra.

Abadan: the British-owned Anglo-Persian Oil Company built its first pipeline terminus oil refinery on the offshore Iranian island of Abadan, starting in 1909 and completing it in 1912, with oil flowing by August 1912. The refinery's production rose from an annual 33,000 tons in 1912–13 to 4,338,000 tons in 1931. By 1938, it was the largest in the world. During the First World War, Abadan saw combat between Iranian forces and British and Indian troops. Abadan was a significant logistics centre. In 1951, Iran nationalised its oil industry and Abadan's refining operations came to a stop. Rioting broke out and it was not until 1954 that a settlement was reached, permitting a consortium of international oil companies to manage production and refining. After the total nationalisation, Iran's focus switched to domestic requirements and a pipeline from Abadan to Tehran was built.

Abbas, Mahmoud (also known as Abu Mazen): (b. 1935) President of the Palestinian Authority since January 2005. Abbas was a founder member of the Palestinian political wing, Harakat al-Tahir al-Watani al-Falistin (Fatah) (Movement for the National Liberation of Palestine). Mr Abbas worked his way up the Palestine Liberation Organisation (PLO) hierarchy but remained opposed to force. He played an important role in obtaining international agreement on the 1993 Oslo Peace Accords between Israel and the PLO. Mr Abbas' position was weakened by the division within the Palestinians produced by the 2005 elections in Gaza, which were won by the hard-line Hamas grouping, opposed to negotiating with Israel. Under Abbas, the Fatah group retained control of Palestine and the West Bank. Mr Abbas could take credit for the improved security situation under Fatah, and the strong support he had orchestrated from the international community, best symbolised by the rapprochement with the United Nations (UN). Before becoming the Fatah leader, Mr Abbas had fallen out with his predecessor Yasser Arafat, opposed to PLO violence and the Hamas leaders in Gaza. However, his failure to secure an independent Palestine had lost him popularity within the Palestinian community, to the extent that a majority of Palestinians wanted him to resign. By 2017 his potential successors were already jockeying for position.

Abu Dhabi: (literally translates as 'Father of the Gazelle') the richest

NOTES

member state and the seat of government of the United Arab Emirates (UAE) (population est. 2.7 million 2020). In 2020 Abu Dhabi city's estimated population was 1.5 million. A British protectorate from 1892, Abu Dhabi is the westernmost and the largest of the UAE's six emirates, reaching from the Khor al-Odaid on the frontier with Qatar to the border of Dubai near the Jebel Ali. Its area is 67,000sq km, representing almost 90 per cent of total UAE territory and significantly larger than Bahrain's 785sq km. Until the late 1970s Abu Dhabi consisted mostly of desert.

Abu Mazen: see Mahmoud Abbas above.

Abu Safah (aka Abu Safaah or Abu Saafa) oilfield: in the early 1980s increased output from the offshore Abu Safah oilfield, some 70 kilometres off Bahrain's north-west coast, compensated for lower production from other Bahraini fields. At the time, Bahrain shared the production from Abu Safah with Saudi Arabia. However, in 1996 Saudi Arabia agreed to concede to Bahrain its share of the output from the oilfield. But the empirical evidence for the existence of additional pockets of oil in the Abu Safah field was mixed. The field's capacity was 100,000bpd, a figure that showed no signs of increasing. In a 30 year period, over eleven dry holes were sunk in Bahrain's offshore waters.

Aden: a port city that in the days of the British Empire was one of the busiest in the world. In 1968 the British government under Prime Minister Harold Wilson decided to leave Aden as part of its East of Suez colonial restructuring policy. Under colonial rule, Aden had been seen as offering protection for the Gulf, particularly Kuwait and its oil. At the time, the maintenance and protection of oil supplies was inextricably linked to maintaining sterling's role as an international reserve currency. Once this policy was abandoned, the UK government hoped sterling would continue to be a major trading currency.

Afghanistan (Soviet invasion): the deployment of Soviet (USSR) troops in Afghanistan began in August 1978. The withdrawal of Soviet troops started in May 1988, and ended in February 1989. Bahrain had been slower than other Gulf Co-operation Council (GCC) members to establish formal diplomatic relations with the Soviet Union. Nevertheless, on 21 June 1988, Bahrain held its first formal talks with the USSR when a visiting Soviet envoy had meetings with senior Bahraini officials, as well as discussions with the Emir; there were several reports that negotiations on establishing formal ties were close to being concluded.

Ahli United Bank (AUB): the AUB was formed in May 2000 following a merger between The United Bank of Kuwait and al-Ahli Commercial Bank. In 2018 the AUB had a net income of US$940 million, nearly 4,000 employees and 150 branches, making it Bahrain's largest bank and with a market capitalisation of US$5.34 billion, and Bahrain's leading private company.

Al-Ahlia Saudi Insurance: began operations in 1982 in Bahrain with a total capital of US$15 million. The company, which is a joint venture between Saudi Arabian, Bahraini and Hong Kong interests, intended to open branch offices in Jeddah, Riyadh and Dammam.

Airborne Warning and Control System (AWACS): the 1982 agreement of the United States to provide Saudi Arabia with advanced AWACS radar equipped aircraft and the extension of their cover to Bahrain in 1982 helped to alleviate fears at the time that the effectively defenceless country would have no warning of imminent danger.

Ajam: a Shi'a community in Bahrain of Persian origin, that was once considered supportive of the al-Khalifa government. The term originally meant 'mute' in Arabic, but in Bahrain the word was applied to those unable to speak Arabic properly. Ajam eventually came to be used specifically to refer to Persians, as they were one of the first major civilizations Arabs encountered as they spread across the globe. For the most part, Persians never fully adopted Arabic as their home language.

Persian migration into Bahrain goes back to the days of the Sassanids and the Achaemenid empire. Esti-mates vary, but the Ajam are thought to number some 100,000, or around 14 per cent of Bahrain's population.

al-Ajmi, Sheikha bint Hassan al-Khrayyesh: born in Kuwait and the second wife of the (current, 2022) King of Bahrain, Hamad bin Isa bin Salman al-Khalifa.

Alaswad, Ali: a senior member of the dissolved opposition group al-Wefaq, living in exile in London since 2011.

al-Alawi, Majid: a former Minister of Labour Affairs and Minister of Housing. Al-Alawi was the architect of a number of labour reforms. However, his reforms were not without controversy, and, as Minister, al-Alawi often faced opposition. Following the 2011 government crackdown on protests in Bahrain, al-Alawi appeared to have resigned. He was for a time one of the exiled leaders of the London-based opposition movement, the Bahrain Freedom Movement. He returned to Bahrain in the early 2000s to participate in the re-formed political process after King Hamad appeared to have begun a process of reconciliation and democ-ratisation.

al-Alawi, Sayed Mahmoud: (b. 1902, d. 1994. Head of the Finance Directorate and Bahrain's first post-independence Minister of Finance.

ALBA: see Aluminium Bahrain.

ALBA-Alcoa lawsuit: under a 2007 contract, the US investigation company Kroll Associates Bahrain uncov-ered a number of cases of corruption

NOTES

in state-owned companies. In ALBA's case, Alcoa appeared to have assigned supply contracts to a series of companies incorporated by a Canadian businessman of Jordanian origin, Victor Dahdaleh. The legal action claimed that 'these assignments served no legitimate purpose and were used as a means to secretly pay bribes and unlawful commissions as part of a scheme to defraud ALBA.' ALBA alleged that in 2005 a supply contract was inflated by some US$65 million. Since 1990 ALBA had allegedly made some 80 payments to the offshore companies, most of which were for amounts in excess of US$15 million.

Alcoa: Alcoa and the Saudi Arabian Mining Company (Ma'aden) formed a joint venture in 2009 that created the world's largest, lowest cost fully integrated aluminium facility. The project included a bauxite mine situated in central Saudi Arabia, which is connected by rail to an integrated facility consisting of an alumina refinery, smelter, and casthouse on the Arabian Gulf coast. The plant began operations in December 2012, and in 2015 the smelter reached full capacity, producing 740,000mtpy of aluminium. The Saudi Arabian plant represented serious competition for ALBA.

Allah: The sole deity of Islam.

alumina: (aluminium oxide) a chemical compound of aluminium and oxygen. It is the most commonly occurring of several aluminium ox-

ides. An almost colourless crystalline substance, it is generally used as a starting material for the smelting of aluminium metal.

aluminium: the Gulf Co-operation Council (GCC) region produced 5.3 million mt/year of aluminium in 2018, up from 5.15 million mt/year in 2017, according to *World aluminium.* Total global production in 2018 was 64.34 million mt/year. A number of Gulf aluminium producers were upgrading or expanding their production to meet both local and international demand.

Aluminium Bahrain (ALBA): founded in 1968, ALBA is one of the world's largest aluminium producers and a major industrial company in the Middle East. By January 1976 the Bahrain government had increased its shareholding in the smelter to 77.9 per cent. The other two remaining shareholders are Kaiser Aluminium (US) 17 per cent and Breton Investments (Netherlands) with 5.1 per cent. This change in ownership persuaded the Bahrain government to start marketing its own share of the metal rather than allowing it to be sold by Amalgamated Metal Corporation as its agents.

The smelter was completed in 1972. Output in 1980 totalled 125,954 tonnes, even though the plant's official capacity at the time totalled only 120,000 tonnes a year. Production rose to around 170,000 tonnes by the end of 1982 as a result of the installation of a new potline. On 6 March

1990, ALBA inaugurated an initial US$125 million expansion scheme. This was by far the biggest development project on the island, designed to virtually double ALBA's smelting capacity to about 450,000 tonnes a year. The cost of the expansion programme was estimated at US$1.440 million. In July 1990, ALBA signed a US$650 million medium-term syndicated loan to finance the first part of the project. It also planned to raise a further US$450 million in export credits for the purchase of plant and equipment. The increased capacity was expected to boost production by 540,000 tonnes to 1.5 million tonnes per year. Products included extrusion billet, foundry alloys, rolling slabs, standard ingots and liquid metal.

In 2018, ALBA's revenue stood at US$2.4 billion – putting it at second place in Bahrain's top ten companies. In 2018 the majority – 83 per cent – of its 3,186 employees were Bahraini nationals. ALBA's principal competitor is the smelter based in Dubai (UAE) which began production in 1979.

Aluminium billets: the billet is one of the most widely used aluminium product forms globally. Billets are created directly through continuous casting or extrusion or indirectly through hot rolling ingots.

Americans for Democracy and Human Rights in Bahrain (ADHRB): a lobby group based in Washington, USA. The ADHRB was initially formed in 2002 following a number of conferences that brought together the Bahraini-American community in the United States. It was formally incorporated as a non-profit organisation in 2008. In that time it has built relationships with many pro-democracy and human rights NGOs, including Amnesty International, Freedom House, Human Rights Watch, Human Rights First, the Project on Middle East Democracy (POMED), and others. It has also developed relationships with US congressional offices and executive branch agencies. The ADHRB has also been influential in securing several congressional briefings and hearings on human rights abuses in Bahrain. The 2016 ADHRB paper on the human rights issues confronting Bahrain is a comprehensive statement of government plans, actions and failures.

Amir: (more commonly spelt Emir) a title used by Gulf rulers and other dignitaries. The original sense was 'army commander'.

Amnesty International: a global human rights NGO based in London that is active in supporting Bahraini human rights activists both in Bahrain and in the UK. Amnesty International went as far as accusing the UK of 'lending cover' to Bahrain during the crackdown on human rights activists. Following the Pearl Roundabout events, the Middle East director of Amnesty International went on record as saying that 'Bahrain is in the grip of a deepening human rights crisis and the severity of

NOTES

the sentences... will do nothing to reverse that.' When, in 2012 Bahrain's appeal court decided to uphold the convictions and sentences of 13 men convicted by military tribunals for anti-government protests during the Arab Spring of 2011, *The Guardian* newspaper of London called the appeal court's ruling 'outrageous', adding its view that: 'Today's court decision is another blow to justice. It shows once more that the Bahraini authorities are not on the path of reform but seem rather driven by vindictiveness.'

In 2017, Amnesty International published a report entitled *No one can protect you: Bahrain's year of crushing dissent*, which reported that in the year from June 2016 to June 2017, more than 150 critics of the régime, and in some cases their relatives, were arrested, tortured, threatened or banned from travel by the Bahrain authorities.

Anglo-Persian Oil Company: later to become British Petroleum (BP). After the First World War (1914–18) geologists of Anglo-Persian began to seek oil deposits in what was still known as Trucial Oman. In 1935 the Iraq Petroleum Company (IPC), a subsidiary of Anglo-Persian, secured concessionary rights through agreements with 'the Rulers and governments of the entire Arabian peninsula excluding the newly proclaimed Kingdom of Saudi Arabia'.

Appeal Court: Bahrain has a dual court system, which comprises both civil and Sharia courts. The Sharia courts mostly deal with domestic (family) matters (marriage, divorce, and inheritance). While Sharia courts of first instance are located in most communities, a single Sharia Court of Appeal sits in Manama. Appeals considered to be beyond the jurisdiction of the Sharia Court of Appeal are taken to the Supreme Court of Appeal, which is part of the civil (non-Sharia) system.

The civil court system consists of summary courts and a supreme court. Summary courts of first instance are located in all communities and include separate domestic, civil, and criminal sections. The Supreme Court hears appeals from the summary courts.

al-Aqsa Mosque: located in the Old City of Jerusalem, the al-Aqsa Mosque is the third holiest site in Islam (after Mecca and Medina). The mosque was built on top of the Temple Mount, known as Haram esh-Sharif in Islam. Muslims believe that Mohammed was transported from the Sacred Mosque in Mecca to al-Aqsa Mosque during the Night Journey. Originally constructed some 20 years after the nearby Dome of the Rock Islamic shrine (Qubbat al-Sakhrah in Arabic), the al-Aqsa is Jerusalem's biggest mosque, enabling some 4,000 worshippers to pray at the same time.

al-Arab, Ali: executed by firing squad in July 2019 after being convicted of terrorism.

Arab/African Summit Conference (March 1977): the goal of this first conference of its kind was to bring about a balance of interests between Arab oil states that – thanks to the Organisation of the Petroleum Exporting Countries' (OPEC) petroleum revolution of the early 1970s – had acquired substantial foreign currency revenues. With financial help from the newly wealthy Arab states, both the economic development of capital-poor, but resource- and water-rich African states had been helped. Thus it was planned that the supply of food (the so-called 'breadbasket strategy') and raw materials from Africa to the Arab states would be achieved. One of the summit's concluding declarations stated that: 'The African and Arab Heads of State and Government reaffirm the need to strengthen their peoples' united front in their struggle for national liberation and condemn imperialism, colonialism, neo-colonialism, Zionism, apartheid, and all other forms of discrimination and racial and religious segregation, especially under the forms in which they appear in southern Africa, Palestine and the other occupied Arab and African territories.'

Arab and Allied Military Forces: a generic term used to describe the coalition forces that united to evict occupying Iraqi forces from Kuwait in February 1991.

Arab Bank: headquartered in Amman, Jordan, the Arab Bank is one of the Gulf's older banking establishments, having been founded in Palestine in 1930. When the League of Nations created British Mandate for Palestine withdrew from Palestine in 1948 and customers had to leave the country, the bank's ability to redeem all claims in full stood it in good stead. Today the bank operates extensively throughout the Gulf and is a major player in Bahrain's financial sector.

Arab Bank for Economic Development in Africa (Banque Arabe pour le Développement Economique en Afrique) (BADEA): founded in 1974, BADEA is headquartered in Khartoum (Sudan). The Bank, owned by eighteen Arab countries, including – since 1971 – Bahrain, began operations in March 1975.

Arab Banking Corporation (ABC): often known as Bank ABC, an international bank headquartered in Manama, with an international network in the Middle East, North Africa, Europe, the Americas and Asia. Bank ABC was founded in 1980, and is listed on the Bahrain Bourse. The major shareholders are the Central Bank of Libya and the Kuwait Investment Authority. By market capitalisation at US$1.23 billion (source: Reuters Eikon, Markaz Research 2018), it is one of Bahrain's top ten companies.

Arab Boycott: see League of Arab States.

Arab Co-operation Council (ACC): a regional grouping that was inaugurated in Baghdad in February 1989 by the heads of state of Egypt, Jordan, Iraq and North Yemen. The

NOTES

creation of the Gulf Co-operation Council (GCC) prompted the formation of the ACC. However, following the Iraqi invasion of Kuwait, the ACC became defunct.

Arab Free Trade Area (AFTA) (aka the Greater Arab Free Trade Area (GAFTA)): a pan-Arab free trade zone founded in 1997 by 14 countries: Bahrain, Egypt, Iraq, Kuwait, Lebanon, Libya, Morocco, Oman, Qatar, Saudi Arabia, Sudan, Syria, Tunisia and the United Arab Emirates. Jordan joined in 2004,the West Bank and Yemen in 2005, and Algeria in 2009. GAFTA is supervised and run by the Arab League's Economic and Social Council (ESC). The members participate in 96 per cent of the total internal Arab trade, and 95 per cent with the rest of the world by applying wide-ranging conditions.

Arab Fund for Economic and Social Development (AFESD): the Kuwait-based AFESD is an autonomous regional Pan-Arab development finance organisation. Its membership consists of all the member states of the Arab League which includes Bahrain. The Fund commenced operations in early 1974.

Arab Gulf states: a loose generic term used in referring to the Arab states located on the western shore of the Arabian (Persian) Gulf. These are Bahrain, Kuwait, Oman, Qatar, Saudi Arabia and the United Arab Emirates (UAE).

Arab Gulf University: the idea of the university came about after the fourth meeting of the General Convention of Arab Education for the Gulf, in 1979. The university was established by the six GCC Countries (Bahrain, Kuwait, Oman, Qatar, Saudi Arabia, UAE) and Iraq in 1980. In 2018, the university awarded the first of several tenders for the construction in Bahrain of a new multi-phase US$1 billion medical city that is to house the university's new campus. The King Abdullah bin Abdulaziz (of Saudi Arabia) Medical City was to be built in the Southern Governate of Bahrain on land donated by King Hamad bin Isa al-Khalifa.

Arab Insurance Group (ARIG): a joint-venture of the governments of Kuwait, Libya and the United Arab Emirates, established in 1981 with a total capital of US$3 billion, a figure which – in theory – makes it almost a rival of the huge London syndicate, Lloyds. The Group was started in response to Lloyds' decision to declare the Gulf a war-risk area, a move that was taken even before the outbreak of the Iran/Iraq War in September 1980.

Arab Investment Banking Corporation (Investcorp): established in 1982.

Arab Iron and Steel Company (AISCO): owned by shareholders from Bahrain, Kuwait, Jordan and the UAE. In late 1981 AISCO was chosen as prime participant to operate a new pelletising plant to be located east of the drydock, with its own 100MW power plant and a 3,000 cubic metres-a-day desalination complex as well as a separate deep-water jetty offshore. Production was expected to total some four million tonnes of pellets a year. However, the turnover predictions for the plant were not realised and it was closed in 1986. During 1987–88, negotiations were under way for AISCO's takeover by the Kuwait Petroleum Company, through a subsidiary called the Gulf Industrial Investment Company.

Arab/Israeli war (October 1973): this war, known to Arabs as the October 1973 War and to the Israelis as the Yom Kippur War, laid the foundations for a new understanding of their region's realities in the Arab countries. The war was seen by many Arabs as legitimate revenge.

Earlier, in June 1967, Israel had mounted attacks on Egypt, Jordan and Syria that lead to the Israeli occupation of remaining Palestine as well as the Egyptian Sinai desert, and Syria's Golan Heights. In the space of some six days, the Israeli army virtually neutralised the forces of three Arab countries and occupied territory that was some three and a half times its size. Generally known as the Six Day War.

Arab League: See League of Arab States.

Arab (Arabian) Light crude: type of crude oil used as a price marker. Normally a blend of light crudes from various fields, high in sulphur.

Arab Maritime Petroleum Transport Co: a maritime tanker company established in 1973 by the member countries of the Organisation of Arab Petroleum Exporting Countries (OAPEC) to provide maritime transport of hydrocarbon substances for the benefit of its member states.

Arab Monetary Fund (AMF): a regional Arab organisation, founded in 1976, which started operations in 1977. The AMF has 22 member countries (Jordan, United Arab Emirates, Bahrain, Tunisia, Algeria, Djibouti, Saudi Arabia, Sudan, Syria, Somalia, Iraq, Oman, Palestine, Qatar, Kuwait, Lebanon, Libya, Egypt, Morocco, Mauritania, Yemen, and Comoros.)

The AMF objectives include:

- correcting disequilibria in the balance of payments of member States
- striving for the removal of restrictions on payments between member States
- establishing policies and modes of Arab monetary co-operation
- providing advice on policies related to the investment of the financial resources of member States in foreign markets
- promoting the development of Arab financial markets
- paving the way towards the creation of a unified Arab currency.
- promote trade among member states.

Arab Nationalist Movement: (also known as the Movement of Arab Nationalists) was a pan-Arab nationalist organisation influential in much of the Arab world, particularly

NOTES

within the Palestinian movement. It was established in 1951 by George Habash. Internal disagreements led to its disintigration by 1970.

Arab News: established in 1975, the Saudi-based *Arab News* is the largest circulation English language daily newspaper in Saudi Arabia.

Arab Petroleum Investment Corporation (APICORP): created by the Organisation of Arab Petroleum Exporting Countries (OAPEC) in 1975, Apicorp is a commercially-focused financial institution charged with providing financing options to the Arab energy industry. Over four decades, Apicorp has worked to raise capital access and enhance the financial stability and performance of the Arab energy industry.

Arab Shipbuilding and Repair Yard Company (ASRY): (aka Arab Company for Shipbuilding and Repair), it employs 1,500 people and is located at al-Hidd. The company was founded in 1977 by seven OAPEC member countries: Bahrain, Kuwait, United Arab Emirates, Iraq, Qatar, Saudi Arabia and Libya.

The company offers a wide range of shipbuilding and vessel repair services as well as the construction of tugs, work and crew boats, and offshore service vessels.

Arab Spring: a popular movement the origins of which were in Tunisia and which in 2011 brought about political reform (in Tunisia), political change (in Egypt), regime change (in Tunisia and Yemen) and political chaos (in Libya). The movement's common denominator was discontent over economic hardship, and opposition to *de facto* dictatorships and autocratic rule. The Arab Spring triggered protests in Bahrain, but elsewhere its effects did not appear to reach the Arabian Gulf. However, the Doha (Qatar) based al-Jazeera media group broadcast a documentary entitled *Shouting in the Dark* in which Bahrain was described as 'abandoned by the Arabs, forsaken by the West and forgotten by the world.' The authors of *Bahrain's Uprising* Ala'a Shehabi and Marc Owen Jones considered that 'the narrative of most reporting was around Shi'a protestors struggling against a Sunni ruling family. Beyond this 'ahistoricism', the myriad grievances, including unemployment, land usurpation, corruption and the politics of exclusion, were concealed. Yet these were critical factors that united Bahrainis at the start, until state repression temporarily crushed the momentum of the movement.'

Arabian Gulf: (aka Persian Gulf by Iran) since the 1960s the term 'Arabian Gulf' has become more widely used. The Gulf was known historically and internationally as the Persian Gulf as Persia (Iran) was the region's only recognised body politic. Iran insists that this is the only correct term. The Turkish Ottoman authorities used the term Gulf of Basra.

Arabian Light crude: see Arab Light crude above.

Arabian Peninsula: a geographical term that includes Kuwait, Oman, Qatar, Saudi Arabia, the United Arab Emirates (UAE) and Yemen. It also includes the southern areas of Iraq and Jordan. The largest body politic on the Peninsula is Saudi Arabia. The Peninsula, plus Bahrain and the Socotra Islands constitute the geo-political concept of 'Arabia.'

Arabian Sea: a term used to refer to a region within the northern Indian Ocean bounded on the north by Iran and Pakistan, on the west by the Gulf of Aden and the Arabian Peninsula and on the east by India.

Arafat, Yasser: (b. 1929, d. 2004) Chairman of the Palestinian Liberation Organisation (PLO) from 1969 until his death.

ARAMCO: state-owned Saudi Arabian oil company. In late December 2019, a share offering of ARAMCO shares took place. The shares were offered at 32 Saudi riyals, (US$8.53 a share), valuing the company at US$1.7 trillion. The IPO was expected to raise US$25.6 billion.

Argus Sour Crude Index (ASCI): a weighted system used to determine pricing for crude oil.

Army: see Royal Bahraini Army.

al-Asalah: a Sunni political grouping which represented Islamists affiliated with Salafism in Bahrain's March 2014 Assembly elections. Not one of the 10 al-Fatih Coalition (Sunni) candidates was elected despite their apparent pro-government popularity during and following the anti-govern-

ment street protests. The apparent collapse of support for these often populist pro-government groupings came as something of a surprise.

Asharq al-Aswat: in a January 2008 interview with the pan-Arab newspaper Bahrain's labour minister, Majid al-Alawi, touched a raw nerve when he claimed that the Gulf was facing an Asian tsunami because Gulf nationals are 'lazy' and 'spoilt'. The minister went further in his interview, expressing what many considered to be the alarmist view that the estimated 17 million foreign nationals working in the Gulf represented 'a danger worse than the atomic bomb or an Israeli attack'. His remarks were endorsed and expanded upon by Mansour al-Jamri, the newspaper's Bahraini editor, who stated that foreign workers should not be classified as temporary, since for the most part they had become virtually permanent members of the community.

Ashburton, John: (b. 1928, d. 2020) (Baron Ashburton) A member of the British Baring merchant-banking family. He was a director of British Petroleum (1982–92) and its Chairman from 1992 to 1995.

al-Ashtar Brigades: (see also Saraya al-Ashtar) a Shi'a opposition group based in Bahrain that featured on the Bahraini government's 2016 list of 68 terrorist groupings.

Ashura (aka Ashoura): The 10th day of the month of Muharram (the first month of the Islamic calendar). Ashura is celebrated by Muslims as a

NOTES

whole. It is a day of fasting to commemorate the day Noah left the Ark, and the day that Moses was saved from the Egyptians by God. For Shi'a Muslims, Ashura is a solemn day of mourning the martyrdom of Hussein, grandson of the Prophet Mohammed, in 680AD at Karbala (now a city of 700,000 in Iraq). It is marked with mourning rituals and passion plays re-enacting the martyrdom. Shi'a men and women dressed in black also parade through the streets slapping their chests and chanting. The great schism between Sunnis and Shi'as occurred when Imam Ali did not succeed as leader of the Islamic community at the death of the Prophet. Ali was murdered in 661AD and his chief opponent Muawiya became caliph. Caliph Muawiya was later succeeded by his son Yazid, but Ali's son Hussein refused to accept his legitimacy and fighting between the two resulted. Hussein and his followers were later massacred in the battle at Karbala. The deaths of Ali and Hussein gave rise to the Shi'a cult of martyrdom and to a sense of betrayal and struggle against injustice, oppression and tyranny.

associated gas (APG): natural gas that comes from oil wells is typically termed 'associated gas'. This gas may exist separately from oil as 'free gas' or it can be dissolved in the crude oil. Once separated from crude oil it often exists in mixtures with other hydrocarbons such as ethane, propane, butane and pentanes. APG can be con-

verted to power at high efficiency utilising Jenbacher gas engines. The power generated can be used for the provision of electricity and heating on-site whilst eliminating the cost of diesel deliveries to remote areas. The utilisation of APG as a fuel for a generator is one way of reducing carbon dioxide emissions that might otherwise result from diesel fuel consumption.

Atlantic Richfield (ARCO): US oil company headquartered in Los Angeles and purchased by British Petroleum (BP) in 2000.

AWACS: see Airborne Warning and Control System above

Awali Oilfield: the first oilfield to be developed in the Gulf. Discovered in 1932, Awali's crude oil production peaked at more than 75,000bpd in the 1970s, but subsequently declined. (Renamed Bahrain Oilfield, see below.)

Ba'ath (Hizb al-Ba'ath al-Arabi al-Ishtiraki): (aka Ba'ath, Ba'th and Baath) The Ba'ath political philosophy traces its origins to a Damascus discussion group of the 1940s. Fundamental tenets of Ba'athism are: 'unity' of all Arabs; 'freedom' from outside domination and 'socialism' of a particularly Arab type. The first Ba'ath communiqué was issued in July 1943. It stated: 'We represent the spirit of Arabism against materialistic Communism. We represent living Arab history against dead reaction and contrived progressivism. We represent complete Arab nationalism against the empty nationalism which does not go beyond lip-service and which all ethics refute. We represent the gospel of Arabism against professional politics. We represent the new Arab generation.' (*The Ba'ath and the Creation of Modern Syria*, (translation by David Roberts), New York, St Martin's Press, 1987.) Outside Syria, the only country where the Ba'ath political philosophy gained political popularity was in Iraq under the Saddam Hussain dictatorship.

Ba'athists: followers of the Ba'ath movement, members of the Ba'ath Party, (both of which are generally referred to as 'the Ba'ath').

Baghdad: the capital city of Iraq. Population (2016) approximately 8,765,000. It is the largest city in Iraq and the second largest city in the Arab world, after Cairo.

Baghdad Pact: a defensive co-operation organisation created to promote shared political, military and economic goals. It was founded in 1955 by Turkey, Iraq, Great Britain, Pakistan and Iran. Based on the structure and values of the the North Atlantic Treaty Organisation (NATO), the main purpose of the Baghdad Pact was to prevent communist incursions and foster peace in the Middle East. It was renamed the Central Treaty Organisation, or CENTO, in 1959 after Iraq pulled out of the Pact.

Bahrain Agricultural Foods Storage and Security (BAFCO): a shareholding company formed in 2015, BAFCO is a processor, importer and exporter of agricultural products and foodstuffs.

Bahrain Aluminium Extrusion Company (BALEXCO): the oldest non-hydrocarbon industry in the Gulf, commenced operations in 1970. BALEXCO was established in 1977 as the region's first aluminium extrusion plant. In its field BALEXCO rapidly established itself in the production of high quality extrusions and systems, used mainly as aluminium doors, window frames and other products that are required in the construction industry. Since its establishment, BALEXCO has left a marked influence on the extrusion industry, increasing its capacity more than three times and expanding into markets in the GCC countries, the Middle East and West Asia.

Bahrain Association of Banks (BAB): established in 1979 by a ministerial decree, BAB unites all banking institutions in Bahrain to promote the country as the Middle East's financial hub. It is licensed by the Central Bank of Bahrain and, including indigenous banks, there are nearly 50 members including other banks from within the Middle East and major global banks.

Bahrain Aviation Fuel Company (also known as BAFCO but not to be confused with the entry above): incorporated in 1985 in which the Bahrain National Oil Company (BANOCO) (see notes below) has 60 per cent shares, Chevron Asia Pacific Holding 27 per cent and BP 13 per cent. BAFCO

NOTES

provides aircraft fuelling services and is based at Bahrain International Airport.

Bahrain, background to independence: the Bahrain archipelago was ruled in the sixteenth century by Portugal and intermittently from 1602 until 1783 by Persia (Iran). The Persians were expelled by an Arabian family (precisely by whom and exactly when is still disputed) that established the current ruling dynasty. In 1861 Bahrain became a British protectorate. In 1971, after Britain (as part of the East of Suez withdrawal) withdrew from the Gulf, Bahrain became fully independent. Oil was found in Bahrain in 1932, but until the 2018 Khaleej al-Bahrain field discovery (which was estimated to contain around 80 billion barrels of shale oil) Bahrain was expected to be the first Gulf state to run out of oil. With 40 per cent of the population of the nine Lower Gulf states in the early 1970s and a more advanced economy, Bahrain had originally insisted on a proportionate say in the running of the proposed federation of Gulf states. When this proved unacceptable to the others, Bahrain opted for full independence.

Bahrain Bourse: established in 1987 as the Bahrain Stock Exchange, it became known as the Bahrain Bourse in 2010. Trading globally, it is a member of the Union of Arab Stock Exchanges, World Federation of Exchanges (WFE), Africa & Middle East Depositories Association

(AMEDA) and Association of National Numbering Agencies (ANNA). Self-regulating, in 2019 the Bourse had a market capitalisation of US$23 billion.

Bahrain Centre for Human Rights (BCHR): founded in 2002 by Abdulhadi al-Khawaja and Nabeel Rajab. The centre has been the most prominent human rights group since the March 2011 crackdown on protests (led by Saudi Arabian troops, with a UAE contingent in support, both acting in the name of the Gulf Co-operation Council (GCC)). The BCHR was one of the more vocal protest groups alongside the Bahrain Human Rights Society (BHRS). Between February 2011 and May 2014 the BCHR reported that 'up to 98 people were killed directly by the government's use of force.'

Bahrain Defence Force: consists of the Royal Bahraini Air Force, Royal Bahraini Army, Royal Bahrain Navy and the Royal Guard. The current Commander-in-Chief (2022) is Field Marshal Khalifa bin Ahmed al-Khalifa. The 2020 budget was US$1.4 billion (4.1 per cent of GDP).

Bahrain Development Bank (BDB): aims its services at self-employed professionals and small and medium enterprises by providing conventional and Islamic investment banking services.

It proactively encourages entrepreneurs through its BDB Rowad Platform to develop ideas and grow new enterprises.

Bahrain dinar (BD): In June 1966, India devalued the rupee, which, even in its lesser role as the Gulf rupee, had long been the *de-facto* currency of the Gulf States, including Bahrain. To avoid following this devaluation, several of the states using the rupee decided to adopt their own currencies. Qatar and most of the Trucial States adopted the Qatar and Dubai riyal, while Abu Dhabi initially adopted the Bahrain dinar, but changed to the dirham in 1973.

The Bahrain dinar became the country's official currency after the Bahrain Currency Board was established in 1964 and the first issue of new currency notes and coins was issued on 7 October 1965, when it replaced the Gulf rupee as legal tender. The Bahrain Monetary Agency came into being in 1973 and the second set of notes and coins was issued in 1978/79.

The trading code for the dinar is BHD. Since 1980 the currency has been pegged to the US dollar at a rate of BD0.376 = US$1.0.

Bahrain dissidents (espionage allegations): in late 2017, Bahrain's public prosecutor charged two leaders of the country's banned main opposition party (the al-Wefaq National Islamic Society) of spying for Qatar. This followed the severing of ties with Qatar amid a regional diplomatic dispute. According to the Bahrain News Agency (BNA) Bahraini Sheikh Ali Salman, Secretary General of the al-Wefaq party (Bahrain's largest political party until the resignation of its MPs in 2011), and Sheikh Hassan Sultan also of Bahrain were accused of colluding with Qatar to carry out 'hostile acts' in Bahrain and damage its national interests and prestige. The two men allegedly met Qatari officials as well as affiliated agents inside the Lebanese Shi'te militia Hezbollah. They were accused of revealing defence secrets to, and receiving financial support from, Qatar. The prosecutor ordered that both men be taken into custody. Mr Salman was already serving a four-year prison sentence for inciting hatred and insulting the Interior Ministry, after he was arrested in 2015.

Bahrain Field: see Bahrain Oilfield below.

Bahrain FinTech Bay: claims to be the largest FinTech hub in the Middle East. Located in Manama, the Bahrain FinTech Bay is a dedicated FinTech co-working space designed to position Bahrain as a regional FinTech hub. Its partners include governmental bodies, financial institutions, commercial corporates, consultancy firms, universities etc.

Bahrain Fishing Company (BFC): (40 per cent UK Ross group, 60 per cent Bahraini) although overshadowed by the oil industry, for some time fishing remained an important economic sector in Bahrain, both for exports and domestic consumption. The BFC caught and froze prawns for export. However, the company was closed in 1979.

Bahrain Forum for Human Rights, aka Bahrain Human Rights Forum (BFHR): founded in Beirut in 2011, an independent gathering on human rights with specific reference to violations in Bahrain. Following the Arab Spring events in early 2011, Bahrain saw popular protests demanding humanitarian improvements. However, the absence of fair policies meant that the Bahrain authorities over-reacted, enforcing systematic violations on dissident civilians, institutions and NGOs. The BFHR seeks to improve human rights by publishing human rights documents and recording violations. It also seeks to expose violations and highlight the importance of prosecution by national courts and in international courts to prosecute those involved in established violations.

Bahrain Freedom Movement (BFM): a London-based Shi'a Islamist opposition group formed in the 1990s. It was originally led by Mansur al-Jamri, the son of the high profile Shi'a cleric, Abdul Amir al-Jamri. In 2007 BFM members lead street protests in Manama over the detention of a Shi'a cleric who was returning from Iran. The protests turned violent and a number of the demonstrators were arrested. In 2010 further protests occurred involving BFM members. In 2013 the BFM leader Said bin Shehabi agreed to the formation of a tri-partite coalition with the Haq and WAFA opposition groups. The coalition was named the Coalition for the Republic. In the ensuing elections no BFM members were elected.

Bahrain Human Rights Monitor aka *The Monitor*: established in London to join a group of local, regional and international human rights organisations concerned with monitoring and developing human rights in Bahrain, and promoting Bahraini citizens' rights. *The Monitor* aims to strengthen relations between civil society, official bodies and international human rights organisations to better defend citizens' rights. It also provides ideas, analyses and news items, advising human rights organisations, issuing reports and publications and contributes to conferences, and workshops to strengthen civil society.

The Monitor aims to track both negative and positive human rights developments in Bahrain, trying to provide an overview of the human rights situation. Thus, *The Monitor* claims its activities go beyond research and press coverage, extending to daily developments in human rights.

Bahrain Human Rights Observatory (BHRO): established in 2011 as one of at least eight independent human rights NGOs.

Bahrain Human Rights Society (BHRS): established at the same time as the BHRO, after the March 2011 crackdown (led by Saudi Arabian troops, with a UAE contingent in support, both acting in the name of the Gulf Co-operation Council). The BHRS was one of the more vocal protest groups, alongside the BFHR.

Bahrain Independent Commission of Inquiry (BICI): (aka the Bassiouni Commission as it was chaired by the Egyptian lawyer Professor Cherif Bassiouni). Between February and March 2014 the BICI reported that as many as ninety-eight people were killed directly by the government's excessive use of force.

The government established the BICI in July 2011, following the repression of the pro-democracy movement in February of that year. The commission consisted of a panel of international human rights experts who set out to assess the authorities' violations during the 2011 pro-democracy movement. The BICI later made recommendations to the government on how to prevent similar events from happening again. In November 2011, the BICI presented its report to King Hamad. The report made 26 recommendations, aiming to trigger reforms that would end the Kingdom's apparent abuses.

A number of the recommendations addressed the lack of accountability of government authorities accused of ill-treatment and torture. The commission sought to address the Bahraini courts' apparent dismissal of due judicial process and the arbitrary detention of peaceful political activists. The commission also addressed the problem of a sectarianised public security force that it claimed lacked training in 'the human rights dimensions of detention and interrogation.' The recommendations also sought the reinstating of Bahraini workers and students dismissed from businesses and schools for their participation in the pro-democracy protests.

King Hamad publicly accepted the BICI and openly called for the full implementation of all 26 recommendations to address the continued human rights violations. In March 2012, just four months after the presentation of the BICI to King Hamad, the government declared 'most' of the recommendations had been implemented, with the rest soon to follow.

In September 2015, the government claimed that 19 of the 26 recommendations had been fully implemented.

In May 2016 the government announced the full implementation of all 26 BICI recommendations. In commemoration, King Hamad presented the BICI commission chairman, Professor Bassiouni, with the Bahrain First Class Medal. Official media quoted Professor Bassiouni as commending the government for implementing all of the BICI recommendations. However, Professor Bassiouni later stated that he was wrongfully quoted, and said that the government had only implemented ten of the 26 recommendations.

A 2013 US State Department report found that the government of Bahrain had only implemented five of the

26 BICI recommendations, noting that 'much work remains' for Bahrain to realise its promise of fulfilling all BICI recommendations. In a Congressional report released in June 2016, some five months late, the State Department released its second analysis of the BICI recommendations. The timing was less than fortunate; the second report coincided with a number of clumsy acts of repression.

In the three weeks leading up to the release of the report, the government exiled the political activist Zainab al-Khawaja, implemented travel bans against members of a delegation of human rights advocates due to participate in the 32nd Session of the Human Rights Council (HRC), arrested the prominent human rights defender Nabeel Rajab, shut down Bahrain's largest opposition political party, al-Wefaq, and revoked the citizenship of Sheikh Isa Qassim. The State Department ignored all these acts of repression in their overdue report, and strangely failed to include any implementation assessments.

Meanwhile, the ADHRB, the BCHR, and BIRD all concluded that the government had actually only fully implemented two of the 26 BICI recommendations.

These were recommendation No 1718, which urges the National Security Agency (NSA) to give up law enforcement and arrest powers, and recommendation 1722 (i), which called on courts to commute the death sentences of those defendants charged for murder during February and March 2011.

In fact a large number of the BICI recommendations had yet to be implemented. Recommendation 1722 (b) – to establish an independent oversight body to investigate allegations of torture – was often cited as implemented and given as an indication of progress made by the government. It was certainly true that the government had established an Ombudsman's office and a National Institute of Human Rights. However, neither of these institutions were independent nor impartial. The staff employed by these 'oversight' bodies were often former government employees; and both entities were subordinate to the Special Investigations Unit (SIU), which had a history of ignoring allegations or enacting reprisals against victims who complained of torture.

The BICI recommendation 1722 (h) which called on the government to drop charges and commute sentences of all persons convicted of crimes related to peaceful dissent was ignored in practice. The Bahraini authorities continued to detain individuals for exercising their right to free speech. Nabeel Rajab remained in government detention on charges related to his posts on social media. Abdulhadi al-Khawaja, Zainab al-Khawaja and Maryam al-Khawaja had all been sentenced following charges relating to speeches they had made. Abdulhadi was in the Jau

Prison on a life sentence and both Maryam and Zainab were effectively exiled. Bahraini courts had sentenced to prison sentences two prominent political leaders, Sheikhs Ali Salman and Sharif, for peaceful speeches that they gave criticising Bahraini government abuses. Sharif was released after serving his one-year sentence. By November 2016, five years after the report's publication, according to the ADHRB, the government still had to implement 24 of the BICI recommendations. More gravely, between February and March 2014 the BICI itself reported that as many as ninety-eight people were killed directly by the government's excessive use of force.

Bahrain Institute for Political Development (BIPD): a government sponsored body founded in 2001, the BIPD stresses the importance of co-operation, communication and partnership with official and civil bodies to enhance the state of political development, including the dissemination of the culture of democracy, the development of political awareness with the participation of all groups in political life in its various forms, and the stimulation of institutions. The BIPD also seeks to activate the citizen's role in the change process, by providing training and research programmes and organising conferences and meetings that are appropriate and open to different groups of people.

Bahrain Institute for Rights and Democracy (BIRD): a London based lobby group, a non-profit organisation focusing on advocacy, education and awareness for the calls of democracy and human rights in Bahrain. The BIRD works by engaging with victims of human rights abuse in Bahrain to provide them recourse to aid and justice. The BIRD also engages with key international actors and governments to advocate for policies that support human rights in Bahrain. The BIRD also works alongside NGO coalitions, international bodies, members of the British-Bahraini community, Bahraini activists, and the UK public to raise awareness of the human rights situation in Bahrain.

Bahrain International Airport (BAH): Located in Muharraq, just 7km from Manama, the international airport is the hub for the national carrier Gulf Air and there are some 37 additional airlines operating from the airport providing flights to neighbouring countries and to major international destinations.

Bahrain International Bank (BIB): in mid-2004 the Bahrain authorities formally launched the liquidation of the BIB after nearly three years of post-9/11 creditworthiness problems. While poor management and strategy caused the failure, in the view of the banking community the Bahrain Monetary Agency (BMA) could have acted sooner and more decisively. While the BIB was at the time the only bank to collapse in Bahrain, it was one of three banks that were troubled during the previous year. Together, these banks' problems had tarnished Bahrain's image as a well-regulated banking centre.

Bahrain Islamic Bank: a commercial bank, founded in 1979 and based in Manama. It was one of the six foreign owned banks operating in Bahrain in 1985. It was also the first Islamic bank in Bahrain.

Bahrain Ispat Company: established in 1996, the company was to operate under the control of the Indian Ispat Group. The new US$290 million plant was to have a capacity of 1.2 million tons per year of iron briquettes produced from iron pellets.

Bahrain Justice and Development Movement: in August 2011 the Bahraini authorities blocked access to the website of the Bahrain Justice and Development Movement, a London-based group that had only been founded one month earlier. Consisting mainly of Bahraini exiles, it sought both to denounce human rights violations in Bahrain and to advocate democratic reforms. The website had been about to post an article in which Ali al-Aswad, a former parliamentarian now living in exile, said he feared a civil war could break out in Bahrain. Without elaborating, the authorities accused the site of 'breaking Bahrain's laws'.

Bahrain Maritime and Mercantile International (BMMI): in 1980 Gray MacKenzie (see below) formerly owned by the Inchcape Group, formed a joint venture with local shareholders to form the Bahrain Maritime and Mercantile International group. When Inchcape divested its shareholding in 1999, BMMI became a wholly Bahraini owned public shareholding company.

Bahrain Middle East Bank: is a wholesale, publicly listed bank formed in 1982. It provides corporate finance and investment advice on mergers and acquisitions as well as underwriting and asset management services. It also advises on private equity investments in a number of sectors.

Bahrain Monetary Agency (BMA): replaced the Currency Board (established in 1964) in 1977 to regulate the domestic banking market. The first chairman of ALBA, Alan Moore, was given the job of setting up the Agency. In 2006 the BMA was replaced by the Central Bank of Bahrain.

Bahrain National Gas Company (BANAGAS): was set up in April 1979 as a joint venture between the Bahrain National Oil Company (BANOCO) (75 per cent), Caltex (12.5 per cent) and the Arab Petroleum Investments Corporation (12.5 per cent). In 1989 work started on the US$74.5 million expansion of the BANAGAS gas liquefication plant.

The contractor was the Tokyo-based Japan Gas Corporation. The expansion was intended to increase the capacity of the BANAGAS plant from 110 million cu ft/d to 170 million cu ft/d.

Bahrain National Oil Company (BANOCO): established in 1976 to enable the Bahrain government to gain a foothold in its country's petroleum business with a 60 per cent joint venture share in BAPCO (see notes below). By 1981, the state owned company had assumed full responsibility for the production of oil and gas from the Bahrain Field.

Bahrain Oilfield: discovered in 1932, the Bahrain Oilfield measures approximately 15 kilometres (nine miles) long and five kilometres (three miles) wide, an area of some 400sq km. Originally known as the Awali Oilfield, it is a geologically complex field and consists of 16 oil reservoirs and four Khuff gas reservoirs in addition to deep pre-Khuff reservoirs. The oil reservoirs lie between 380 metres (m) and 2,000m and gas is found as deep as nearly 4,000m. Situated below Jebel Dukhan, Well No 1 was the first ever oil well in the southern part of the Arabian Gulf. The well, which was operated by the Bahrain Petroleum Company (BAPCO), produced its first oil in October 1932 at an initial rate of 9,500bpd. In 1970 the oilfield peaked at 79,000bpd, and after that it started to decline.

The Bahrain oilfield uses the large Khuff gas reservoir as fuel and feedstock for power and industry such as electricity generation, aluminium smelting, petrochemicals, water desalination, refining and others. Some of the Khuff gas is re-injected into the oil reservoirs to maintain reservoir pressure and stimulate production whereas some is used to lift oil from wells artificially. In 2009, seeking to revive the mature Bahrain Field, the government of Bahrain formed a new joint venture company, Tatweer Petroleum, through a Development and Production Sharing Agreement (DPSA) with three strategic partners: the Bahrain-based National Oil and Gas Holding Co (nogaholding), US-based Occidental Petroleum and Abu Dhabi-based Mubadala Petroleum. In December 2009, Tatweer Petroleum took over operation of the Bahrain Field.

Bahrain Petroleum Company (BAPCO): the Bahrain Petroleum Company's inception marked the start of a radical transformation the impact of which was felt in Bahrain and across the region. From a country known for its pearl trade, Bahrain became a pioneer in the oil and gas sector and led the change towards an industrial economy.

In January 1929 BAPCO was formed by the Standard Oil Company of California (SOCAL) in the era of the late Sheikh Isa bin Ali al-Khalifa. History was made in 1932 when oil was discovered at Well Number One in Jebel al-Dukhan – marking the first such discovery in the Arabian Gulf. In June 1934, the first ever shipment of Bahrain crude oil was exported, to Japan, from the Sitra terminal on board *El Segundo*, the Standard Oil Company's tanker.

NOTES

The Bahrain Refinery (also known as the Sitra Refinery), was opened in 1936 with a capacity of 10,000 barrels per day (bpd) and by 2021 was producing 270,000–280,000bpd.

Increased activities at the refinery meant the need for more trained and qualified oil workers to move to Bahrain with their families. From temporary housing near the first oil well in 1933, the foundation for a dedicated township was laid and was named Awali by the then Ruler of Bahrain, Sheikh Hamad bin Isa al-Khalifa. Awali grew with modern facilities and amenities, and was the first in Bahrain to have central air-conditioning plants.

BAPCO was reconstituted in 1981 as a joint venture company owned 60 per cent by the Bahrain government and 40 per cent by Caltex. Today (2023), it is wholly-owned by the government, with the 267,000 barrels per day (bpd) Bahrain Refinery (see below). Exports account for 95 per cent of production with crude oil and refined products going to the Middle East, India, the Far East, South-east Asia and Africa. A US$4.2 billion project to expand and upgrade the refinery will increase output to 380,000bpd with improvements in energy-efficiency and cleaner products.

Bahrain Refinery: (often referred to as the Sitra Refinery), opened in 1936 with a capacity of 10,000bpd and by 2019 was producing 260,000bpd of crude oil and 40,000bpd of low sul-

phur diesel. In November 2021 Bahrain was planning to upgrade and expand the Sitra Refinery so that by 2024 its sole processing facility would be to handle new crudes, including heavier grades, according to S&P Global Platts. The expansion was to increase Sitra's processing capacity to about 370,000–380,000bpd from 270,000– 280,000bpd. The refinery is owned and managed by BAPCO.

Bahrain Salam for Democracy and Human Rights (SALAM DHR): an NGO founded in August 2015 that endeavours to preserve universal principles of dignity and respect by shielding democracy and human rights.

Bahrain Ship Repairing and Engineering Company (BASREC): Since its establishment in 1963, BASREC has conducted a wide range of repairs and maintenance on vessels working in and around the Arabian Gulf. The company's facilities include a 120 metre x 18.5 metre floating dock with a lifting capacity of up to 6,000 tons deadweight, two 80-metre long slipways, both having a capacity of up to 1,000 tons, and two repair quaysides, both consisting of a 6 metre minimum water depth; it can accommodate vessels of up to 170 metres in length. Additional facilities include small craft, barges, and a 20-metre light float.

Bahrain Slipway Company: operated by Gray Mackenzie and owned by private Bahraini investors, the company announced in January 1988 that it was to cease operating. It had specialised in work on small craft such as tugs and supply vessels. It blamed a weak market for its decision to close.

Bahrain Steel: a wholly owned subsidiary of the Foulath group, established in Bahrain in 1984. Located on the Foulath Complex in the Hidd Industrial Area, Bahrain Steel operates two iron ore pelletising plants with a total production capacity of 11.0 million tons per year. Over time, Bahrain Steel has established its reputation as a market leader and is one of only three merchant pelletizing plants in the world and the only such operator in the Middle East region.

Bahrain Stock Exchange: see Bahrain Bourse above.

Bahrain Telecommunications Company (BATELCO): the principal telecommunications company in Bahrain operating and managing the GSM mobile telecommunication and fixed line networks. BATELCO also provides internet and web hosting services, as well as telecommunications systems and accessories retail outlets. By market capitalisation at US$1.10 billion in 2018 Batelco was one of Bahrain's top ten companies.

Bahrain Transparency Society (BTS): founded in 2001 by the Minister of Labour and Social Development, the BTS was Bahrain's first and only NGO specialised in promoting transparency and anti-corruption. It is an active member of Transparency International and a member of several Arab networks. BTS's objective is to promote a culture of transparency, anti-corruption and good governance within the government, private sector, media and civil society.

Bahrain University: see University of Bahrain below.

Bahrain Uprising: in the introduction to their book *Bahrain's Uprising* the authors Al'a Shehabi and Marc Owen Jones summarise the events of 2–11 February 2011 thus:'Bahrain experienced near-revolution. Its opposition trend was massive in size, cross sectarian (at least at the outset), and existentially threatening to the regime. At the height of the unrest in February 2011, well over a hundred thousand Bahrainis marched in protest, an astonishing number given the tiny island country's citizen population of less than 1.3 million. If Charles Kurzman's estimate that modern revolutions seldom involve more than one per cent of the population, then what transpired was correct.

Bahrain Watch: in 2014 a 'Stop the Shipment' campaign by the anti-corruption group Bahrain Watch forced the South Korean government to stop a shipment of tear gas bound for Bahrain.

Bahraini Saudi Bank: offers retail and commercial banking services and claims to have a niche market by providing specialised services to Bahrain's commercial sector.

Bahraini Women's Day: an annual celebration highlighting the role

NOTES

women play in public life and in the progress of Bahrain, promoting the contribution women make to legislative and municipal affairs. Patron of the event is Princess Sabeeka bint Ibrahim al-Khalifa, wife of King Hamad bin Isa al-Khalifa, the King and President of the Supreme Council for Women (SCW).

Bahraini-isation: in 1991 the goal was for Bahrainis to make up half the private sector workforce by 1994. This target was to be advanced further if the reported expatriate exodus following the Iraqi invasion of Kuwait proved to be permanent. In 1997 the government continued its policy of Bahraini-isation to dissuade the private sector from employing expatriate labour. The Ministry of Labour and Social Affairs increased the cost of issuing and renewing work permits and set up an amnesty system, which ended in November 1997, allowing illegal immigrants to formally register or leave. The Bahraini government also restricted or barred entry for certain job categories to foreigners. Parastatals were giving preference for contracts to companies employing the highest number of Bahrainis. The Bahraini-isation policy continued into the twenty-first century, albeit less stringently applied.

Ballast Nedam: the construction contract for the Saudi-Bahrain causeway (completed 1986) was awarded to the Amsterveen (Netherlands) firm Ballast Nedam. The budgeted cost of the venture was US$564 mil-

lion – which at roughly US$30,000 a metre made the causeway the most expensive civil engineering project of its type in the world. Saudi Arabia had agreed to bear the total cost.

Bank of Bahrain and Kuwait (BBK): a 50/50 joint venture between Bahraini and Kuwaiti interests. The bank made profits of BD5.1 million (US$13.5 million) in 1989, up from just BD1 million (US$2.6 million) in 1988. BBK is a commercial bank offering deposits, loans and credit cards since 1971. By market capitalisation at US$1.26 billion (2018), it is one of Bahrain's top ten companies.

Bank Melli Iran: the Tehran based Bank Melli was accused by Washington of playing a central role in financing Tehran's nuclear and ballistic missile programmes.

Banoco Arab Medium: the name given to the crude oil produced in Bahrain. Varieties, or grades, are valued based on their crude qualities. According to McKinsey's Energy Insight, BANOCO has an API (gravity) rating of 31.8 and a sulphur content of 2.45.

Banque Arabe Internationale d'Investissement (BAII): a consortium bank based on Arab and international capital. It was 50 per cent owned by major international banks, notably the BNP (France), Bank of America, UBS (Switzerland) and ABN (Netherlands). The other 50 per cent was owned by major banks from the Arab League countries. It described itself as the 'most Arab of French banks, and the most French of the banks from the Arab League countries'. After losses amounting to some 300 million French francs in 1990, the bank's position worsened in 1991, to the extent that after injecting a further 600 million francs in 1992, the BNP – by then the 98.3 per cent shareholder – decided that the bank would withdraw from all banking activities except for the management of private wealth funds.

Banque Franco-Arabe d'Investissements Internationaux (FRAB): was established in Paris in 1969 by the Kuwait Investment Company in partnership with the French Société Générale and the Société de Banque Suisse.

Banque Paribas: in 1985 one of six foreign-owned banks operating in Bahrain. Banque Paribas is one of the few international banks to have its Middle East Headquarters in Bahrain. This was a decision taken in the 1990s reflecting the perceived quality of Bahrain's supervisory authorities.

Basel III: a set of international banking regulations developed by the Bank for International Settlements (BIS) to promote stability in the international financial system. The Basel III regulations are designed to reduce damage to an economy by banks that take on excess risk.

Basra: (aka Basrah) an Iraqi city (population: 2.15 million in 2017) on the Shatt al-Arab, the eastern shore of the upper Arabian Gulf. The Persian occupation of Basra from 1775 to 1779 resulted in the diversion of maritime trade between India, Arabia and Europe to Kuwait. Basra is Iraq's main port, although it does not have deep water access. Vessels unable to enter Basra are unloaded at the port of Umm Qasr. In July 1982 Iranian troops sought to encircle Basra. Bahrain's government viewed this as a sign that Tehran might seek to export its brand of militant Islam throughout the Gulf. With a Shi'a majority, Bahrain's Sunni rulers saw this as a worrying possibility.

Bayt Siyadi (Siyadi House): built in 1931 on Muharraq Island by the pearl merchant Abdullah bin Isa Syadi and still (2020) a private residence. Within the same complex a mosque had been built in 1910. A majlis or meeting hall was also built on the site in 1850 and extended in 1921. A number of buildings on the so-called Pearling Path have been refurbished to form a UNESCO World Heritage site.

Begin, Menachem: (b. 1913, d. 1992) an Israeli politician, founder of the right-wing Likud Party and the sixth Prime Minister of Israel. Before the creation of the State of Israel he was the leader of the Zionist militant group Irgun. As head of the Irgun, he first targeted the British military in Palestine, later attacking the Arabs in what became known as the 1947–48 Palestine Civil War.

The British government considered Begin to to be the leader of 'a terrorist organisation'. Elected to the

NOTES

first Knesset (parliament), as head of the Herut party that he had founded; after years in opposition he eventually won the 1977 election.

His most important achievement as Prime Minister was to sign a peace treaty with Egypt in 1979, for which he and the Egyptian President Anwar Sadat shared the Nobel Peace Prize. However, the Begin government began to promote the construction of Israeli settlements in the West Bank and the Gaza Strip. As if this was not bad enough, Begin authorised the the invasion of Lebanon in 1982 allegedly to attack the PLO military presence there. As the Israeli military involvement in Lebanon deepened, the Sabra and the Shatila massacres shocked world public opinion and Begin found himself increasingly isolated internationally.

Belgrave, Charles: (*nota*: even though Charles Belgrave's period in Bahrain precedes the years covered in these pages, his presence in Bahrain probably accounted for many of the Kingdom's administrative, social and educational advances). In 1925 Charles Belgrave answered an advertisement in the London *Times* for a young administrator to work in an 'Eastern State'. Belgrave was eventually offered the position of Adviser to Sheikh Hamad bin Isa bin Ali al-Khalifa, beginning his new role in April 1926 at a tense time for Bahrain. Sheikh Hamad had been installed as deputy ruler by the British three years earlier when his father Sheikh Isa bin

Ali al-Khalifa was forced to step down. Tensions remained between the new ruler and factions within Bahrain that still supported his father and refused to recognise his abdication; Hamad was regarded as Deputy Ruler until his father's death in 1932. Although Bahrain was nominally independent, Britain had long dictated its foreign policy.

In 1900, British regional power was strengthened by the creation of the post of British Political Agent in Bahrain.

Belgrave, *en principe*, no more than an employee of the Sheikh, was in reality closely tied to British colonial aims in the region. He soon became a powerful figure in Bahrain, known simply as 'The Adviser'. In short, he ran Bahrain's government, was the head of its police force and – in the absence of an organised legal code – personally operated its courts. He also oversaw a programme of modernisation that included the creation of an education system, a police force, a health service and an extensive series of public works. During this transitional period, power became centralised, leading to a further consolidation of the British and al-Khalifa family's positions.

A review by the British Library of contemporary documents makes it clear that Belgrave's role encompassed a wide range of matters. However, by the 1950s, many Bahrainis took exception to the amount of power he held. By then, Belgrave had come to represent British imperialism in the Middle East at a time of lively Arab nationalism. After the Suez Crisis, Britain's standing in the region had plummeted, and The Adviser was viewed by many Bahrainis as a serious impediment to the transition to democracy. Eventually, in April 1957, Charles Belgrave was forced to leave and was never to set foot in Bahrain again.

blockade: in mid-2017 an air, land and sea blockade was unexpectedly imposed on Qatar when four countries – Saudi Arabia, the United Arab Emirates (UAE), Bahrain and Egypt (the so-called 'quartet') – severed diplomatic and trade ties with Doha.

On 5 June, the Ministries of Foreign Affairs in Bahrain, Saudi Arabia, the UAE and Egypt had all issued statements announcing the severing of diplomatic relations with Qatar. Subsequently, the quartet closed its land borders, and imposed a land, sea and air embargo on Qatar. It was claimed that Qatar sought to support 'terrorism', had 'maintained intimate relations with Iran' and meddled in the internal affairs of their countries. Qatar responded by saying that the decision was a 'violation of its sovereignty'. The tension between Qatar and its neighbours was not completely new. Differences had been expressed in 2014, to the extent that Saudi Arabia, the UAE and Bahrain had withdrawn their diplomats. At the heart of the dispute was Qatar's controversial support for political

Islamist movements, including the Muslim Brotherhood, as well as complaints about the reporting of the Doha-based *al-Jazeera* news channel.

In late 2019 there were press reports that the dispute and the blockade had been ended. Although the Gulf leaders signed a statement ending the blockade, Bahrain however, seemed rather hesitant, still sending mixed signals. The uncertainty over resuming travel between Qatar and Bahrain was perhaps the most telling of these. There appeared to be a lack of clarity over the degree of 'resumption'. The Bahraini foreign minister, Abdullatif al-Zayani, announced that the Kingdom's relations with Qatar would go back to the *status quo* that prevailed before June 2017 when travel between the GCC countries was visa-free for citizens. But Mr al-Zayani later accused Qatar of 'not taking any 'initiative' to solve its problems with his country'. It was also reported that Qataris were being denied entry to Bahrain via the King Fahd Causeway, the only land access between the countries.

A Bahrain foreign ministry statement accused Qatar of 'not making any gesture to resolve the outstanding issues with Bahrain'. It referred to 'pending files' and 'the damage' the Kingdom had suffered for decades as a result of Qatari policies, but did not specify what the 'issues' might be. The consensus was that Bahrain and Qatar have had territorial disputes in the past, notably the issue of the Hawar

NOTES

Islands, which had been resolved in 2001, but which the Bahraini government had revived during the period of the blockade.

It was not until 5 January 2021 at a meeting of representatives of all six GCC countries held in al-Ula (Saudi Arabia) that the Quartet agreed to lift the three and a half year blockade and resume diplomatic relations with Qatar.

BP Statistical Review of World Energy: over 60 years old, the publication is the longest running compilation of global energy statistics available. Collected down the years, it has become widely recognised as a key source of data on energy markets, useful to business, policy, academia, journalists and the public alike, underpinning with facts discussions about energy or the environment. Since its creation, the *Review* has expanded from six typewritten pages plus one page for graphical illustrations to an internet database that can be used for very detailed analysis. Behind the published data are about 300,000 single data entries – at the last count – and growing every day.

Yet, in a world ever more concerned with the commercial value of data, it is freely available to all who wish to use it, without wishful thinking, politics or spin. It is no more than a portrait in numbers of global energy production, consumption, trade, reserves and prices. These numbers contain the story of energy in the last

half of the 20th century and the beginning of the 21st.

Bramco Group: the Bahraini company, together with the Swiss company, IMF AG, formed a joint-venture and won the US\$7.8 million contract to supply 450,000 tons of aggregate from two quarries in the UAE for the 584 concrete piles required to support the bridging structures of the Bahrain/Saudi Arabia causeway.

Breton Investments: in 1977 the Dutch company held a 5.1 per cent shareholding in Aluminium Bahrain (ALBA). It ceased to be a shareholder in 2010.

British Bank of the Middle East (BBME): A British owned bank that operated in many Middle East countries, originally known as the Imperial Bank of Persia.

After the Second World War, in 1949, the bank's concession expired and the name was changed, this time to The British Bank of Iran and the Middle East. Following political upheaval in Iran in the 1950s, the Bank was no longer allowed to operate in Iran, once again changing its name – to the BBME.

In January 1960 the Hongkong and Shanghai Banking Corporation (HSBC) acquired 99.5 per cent of the Bank's shares. In 2016, the Bank confirmed that it had transferred its place of incorporation and head office from Jersey (UK) to the Dubai International Financial Centre. As a result of the transfer, the Bank, now known as the

Hongkong Bank of the Middle East (HBME), became regulated by the Dubai Financial Services Authority.

British Broadcasting Corporation (BBC): the BBC closed its Arabic television service in 1996 but continued with its Arabic (and Persian) language broadcast radio programmes.

British Foreign Office: the British political presence in the Gulf was properly established in the late eighteenth century as the 'factories' (more accurately trading posts) of the East India Company were replaced by British 'Residencies' and 'Agencies'. Britain's principal concern was the protection of the route to India, and secondly preventing other European states from establishing a presence; which meant that mini-states, like Kuwait, were of collateral importance. Between the mid-eighteenth century and mid-twentieth centuries, posts were established in Bushir (Iran), Muscat (Oman), Basra (Iraq), Bahrain, Kuwait and Sharjah (later to become part of the United Arab Emirates (UAE)).

Following the signature in 1820 of the General Treaty of Peace between Britain and the rulers of the Arabian Gulf coast, the Gulf States were no longer permitted to build large ships or coastal fortifications. Reference was also made in the treaty to the ending of the slave trade. Britain was granted the right to police the waters of the Gulf. The British presence also began to concern itself with matters political as well as the commercial role inherited from the East India Company.

British Petroleum (BP): originally formed as the Anglo-Persian Oil Company a subsidiary of the Burmah Oil Company, exploiting deposits originally found in Persia in 1908. The company's early history was not easy – following a cash crisis, and prompted by Winston Churchill who could see oil replacing coal as the Royal Navy's principal fuel, the UK government became a major shareholder in the company.

Ironically, the British Petroleum brand had originally been created by a German company as a way of marketing its products in Britain. During the First World War, the British government seized the company's assets, and the Public Trustee subsequently sold them to Anglo-Persian in 1917. After the First World War (1914–18) geologists of Anglo-Persian began to seek oil deposits in what was still known as Trucial Oman. In 1935 the Iraq Petroleum Company (IPC), a subsidiary of Anglo-Persian, secured concessionary rights through agreements with 'the Rulers and governments of the entire Arabian Peninsula'.

British – role in Bahrain: given its strategic island location in the Arabian Gulf, dominated to the west by Saudi Arabia and to a lesser extent by Qatar to the east, and also by Persia's historical claims to Bahrain, Britain provided overt protection to both Bahrain's government and its ruling family, from the mid-1800s until the

NOTES

country's independence in 1971. During most of that period Bahrain was the seat of the British Political Residency (from 1863 until 1947). Less overt protection has continued since. Then, in 2018, with the aim of boosting its presence in the Middle East, Britain opened a £40 million naval base at Mina Salman staffed by 500 soldiers, sailors and airmen. Strong ties between Britain and Bahrain's royal families have existed for many years for the sake of diplomacy and trade. The opening of the UK's new Bahrain naval base by HRH Prince Andrew was no exception, with a large entourage of the al-Khalifa dynasty in attendance. Generating worldwide media coverage, these events – particularly that of King Hamad bin Isa al-Khalifa's attendance with Queen Elizabeth II at the 2018 Windsor Horse Show – have attracted considerable protests from human rights activists, who claim that Britain is nurturing Bahrain's dictatorship atrocities against their citizens.

Brown and Root Marine: one of the world's largest marine engineering companies operating in the Far East, Middle East and Gulf of Mexico, and a fabrication yard in Bahrain.

Cable and Wireless: a British company, that traced its history back to the 1860s. In the 1970s it was one of the main telecommunications providers in the Gulf. Bahrain's failure to sign the February 1997 World Trade Organisation (WTO) agreement opening up greater international market access meant the national incumbent Bahrain Telecommunications Company (BATELCO), retained exclusive rights across the board to provide telecommunications services. As a result, Bahrain failed to benefit from the new market entrants instituting rollout programmes, leading to low 'tele-density'. However, by 2000 BATELCO had been privatised, with 39 per cent owned by the government and 20 per cent by Cable and Wireless. The remaining 41 per cent was traded on the Stock Exchange.

Cairo: Egypt's capital city. Population 19.5 million (2018).

Caltex: the petroleum brand name of America's Chevron Corporation. It was founded in 1936 and was instrumental in the development of the Bahrain Petroleum Company (BAPCO). In 1981 Caltex became a 40 per cent shareholder alongside the Bahrain government's 60 per cent.

Camp David Accords: the 1978 Egyptian-Israeli peace accords signed under the aegis of US President Jimmy Carter. The agreement defined the future of the Sinai region (taken by Israel in the 1967 Arab-Israeli war) and the establishment of an autonomous regime in the West Bank and Gaza.

Causeway: See King Fahd Causeway below.

CEIC Data: founded in 1992 by a team of expert economists and analysts, CEIC Data is now part of the Emerging Markets group of companies. It provides data insights into more than 213 economies. Its customers are economists, analysts, investors, corporations, and universities around the world.

Census: the census of April 1971 revealed that the total population of the Bahrain islands had reached 216,000, with an estimated growth rate of 3.3 per cent per annum. The April 2020 census showed a population of 1,501,636.

Central Bank of Bahrain (CBB): following Bahrain's independence, the CBB's forerunner, the Bahrain Monetary Agency, was established in 1973, replacing the Currency Board that had been established in 1964. It was re-launched as the Central Bank of Bahrain in 2006 to implement monetary policy, regulate Bahrain's banking sector, act as the government's fiscal agent, promote Bahrain as a major international centre of finance and manage foreign currency, cash and gold reserves.

Central Boycott Office (CBO): See League of Arab States.

Central Statistics Organisation (aka Statistical Bureau): first established 1 October 1967 under the supervision of the Ministry of Finance and National Economy. Its original name was the Statistics Office and its objective was to provide statistical information on Bahrain.

On full independence the government embarked on a process of improvement and development of the Statistics Office to provide information and data.

Central Treaty Organisation: see Baghdad Pact above.

Chevron: Chevron made one of the Middle East region's first major oil discoveries in Bahrain in 1932. Some ninety years later, in April 2019, the Bahrain-based Oil and Gas Holding Company, known as nogaholding, announced that it had signed a letter of intent with Chevron, covering a joint evaluation study of the Khalij al-Bahrain basin and potential liquefied natural gas (LNG) procurement opportunities. The letter of intent was signed in Manama by Sheikh Mohammed bin Khalifa al-Khalifa, Bahrain's Minister of Oil, and Jay Pryor, vice president of Corporate Business Development, Chevron Corporation. Under the agreement, Tatweer Petroleum, a nogaholding subsidiary, was to work with representatives from Chevron to study the offshore potential of the basin, a recent discovery that spans 2,000 square kilometres in shallow waters off Bahrain's western coast.

Jay Pryor noted that Chevron had been present in Bahrain since 1929 and were 'excited to build on our relationship with Bahrain as the country enters a new phase of energy progression and to provide support in two areas that are a significant strength in Chevron's portfolio – tight oil and LNG.'

China, Peoples Republic of: in July 1990, Bahrain signed an economic, trade and technical co-operation agreement with the People's

NOTES

Republic of China. The signing took place during the visit to Beijing of the Bahraini foreign minister, Sheikh Mohammed bin Mubarak al-Khalifa, the first visit to China by a senior Bahraini minister since the two countries established full diplomatic relations in 1989. A Chinese embassy was opened in Bahrain in March 1990.

Citibank Bahrain: for over half a century, Citibank Bahrain has played an active role in the financial sector of Bahrain as well as the Middle East. Citibank Bahrain is a leading player in corporate and investment banking, consumer banking and Islamic banking. The company's clients include global multinationals operating in Bahrain, Bahraini corporates and financial institutions, public sector corporates and individuals.

The consumer banking arm of Citibank that was launched in 1989, is considered a leader in the local credit card market and is a major provider of personal loans and wealth management products.

In 2015, Citibank Bahrain launched its call centre which provided services to more than 200,000 customers in Bahrain and across the region.

Citi Islamic Investment Bank (CIIB): the CIIB was incorporated in Bahrain in 1996 as a fully owned subsidiary of Citicorp Banking Corporation. The CIIB is licensed by the Central Bank of Bahrain as an Islamic wholesale bank and was the first Islamic bank established by a major international financial Institution. Citi

had been active in the Islamic finance industry since 1981, when it opened its first Islamic 'window' in London. The CIIB has been able to leverage Citibank's global network and products to provide innovative Islamic banking products and solutions.

Clinton, Hillary: (b. 1947) First Lady of the United States (1993–2001) and was US Secretary of State in the first term of the Obama administration from 2009 to 2013. Mrs Clinton once reportedly telephoned the Saudi foreign minister, Prince Saud al-Faisal, to express her concern about events in Saud Arabia. Mrs Clinton was quoted as saying: 'security challenges cannot be a substitute for a political resolution.'

Cohen, William: (b. 1940) a Republican politician from the US state of Maine. He served as Secretary of Defence under the (Democratic) President Bill Clinton from 1997 to 2001.

Commercial Companies Law (June 1987): the revised law covered the basic rules of company formation, accounting, record keeping and business procedures. Rights and obligations under certain types of commercial contracts were covered, and clear distinctions made between the role of a distributor and an agent acting on behalf of a foreign company.

All aspects of customer banking and commercial instruments were also included in the new regulations. The law updated existing statutes, most of which had remained unchanged since 1969.

common currency: the term to be used for the GCC's proposed currency was thought to be 'khaleeji', Arabic for 'of the Gulf', and traditionally associated with the Gulf States. This name was turned down in late 2009 and no official name was agreed prior to the withdrawal of the agreement for a GCC common currency. The name 'dinar' had been suggested as it was already used by two Gulf states (Bahrain and Abu Dhabi). The term 'dinar' is mentioned in the Quran (Koran), it being the currency used during the prophet Mohammed's lifetime.

GCC sources had suggested that the currency might be linked to the US dollar or would tie-up with a basket of currencies in which the US dollar would have the lion's share. The currencies of Saudi Arabia, the UAE, Qatar, Oman, and Bahrain are pegged to the US dollar. The exception is Kuwait's dinar, which is pegged to a basket of currencies including the US dollar and the euro.

It had been provisionally agreed in May 2009, at the GCC consultative summit held in Riyadh, that Saudi Arabia would host the new currency's Gulf Central Bank. The UAE differed, noting that a number of GCC institutions were already headquartered in Saudi Arabia. The UAE then backed off the idea of a GCC common currency. The technical reason given was the lack of a precursor unit of account. The currency, had it been adopted, would have been the sole legal tender in the remaining GCC countries. Oman and the UAE confirmed that they would not adopt the new currency until further notice. The terms of what would be called the GCC Monetary Agreement were later published. The new currency was originally to be introduced in 2010. It soon appeared that this deadline would not be met on time due to the global financial crisis and a lack of sufficient co-operation between the GCC member states. In 2010, it was still thought in some quarters that a GCC common currency between the four states of Saudi Arabia, Kuwait, Bahrain and Qatar might proceed. However, that was before the 2017 dispute with Qatar. By mid-2019, no significant developments had been announced.

Common Market: a GCC 'common market' was launched in January 2008 with plans to create a fully integrated single market. This initially eased the movement of goods and services. However, implementation lagged behind after the 2009 financial crisis. The creation of a customs union began in 2003 and was completed and fully operational by January 2015 when the common market was also further integrated, allowing full equality among GCC citizens to work in the government and private sectors, social insurance and retirement coverage, real estate ownership, capital movement, access to education,

NOTES

health and other social services. Some barriers remained in the free movement of goods and services. The co-ordination of taxation systems, accounting standards and civil legislation was also in progress. The homogeneity of professional qualifications, insurance certificates and identity documents was underway.

Commonwealth of Independent States (CIS): created in 1991 following the collapse of the Soviet Union. Very much Russia's answer to the perceived progress of the European Union (EU). Its founding member states were: Armenia, Azerbaijan, Belarus, Georgia (ended its membership in 2008), Kazakhstan, Kyrgyzstan, Moldova, Russia, Tajikistan, Turkmenistan and Ukraine.

Constituencies: there are eight of these – Manama, the capital, accounts for roughly half the population, followed by Muharraq, the second largest island, with an estimated population of 50,000.

Constituent Assembly: See Consultative Assembly below.

Constitution 1973: Bahrain's first constitution was declared in 1973, just two years after Bahrain became an independent country. Bahrain became a constitutional monarchy on 14 February 2002 when Sheikh Hamad bin Isa al-Khalifa declared himself King. Bahrain's regime became a hereditary constitutional monarchy.

Constitution 2002: In 2001 Emir Hamad put forward the National Action Charter which was intended to

return Bahrain to constitutional rule. However the opposition objected to a proposed amendment to the 1973 Constitution which would change the legislature from unicameral to bi-cameral.

The Charter stated that 'the legislature will consist of two chambers, namely one that is constituted through free, direct elections and whose mandate will be to enact laws, and a second one that will have members with experience and expertise who will be able to give advice as necessary. The opposition saw this statement as too ambiguous, and remained opposed to the Charter.

Emir Hamad responded by meeting the spiritual leaders of the Shi'a Islamist opposition. He subsequently signed a document clarifying that only the elected lower house of the parliament would have legislative power, while the appointed upper house would have a strictly advisory role. Upon this assurance, the main opposition groups accepted the Charter and called for a 'Yes' vote in the national referendum. The Charter was accepted in the 2001 referendum with 98.4 per cent approval.

However, in 2002 Emir (now King) Hamad promulgated the 2002 Constitution, without any public consultation, in which both the elected and the royally-appointed chambers of parliament were given equal legislative powers, thereby going back on his 2001 promise. As a result, the elections due to be held later in the year were boycotted by all the (largely Shi'a) opposition.

Constitutional Courts: Bahrain's first court was established in 1922 and today (2022) there are two main law courts – one covering civil law, the other for Sharia law. A supreme court of appeal was set up in 1989, known as the Court of Cassation and a National Safety Court, ruled by the military, was created in 2011 – at the time of the Bahrain Uprising – to try activists, protesters and opposition leaders.

Consultative Assembly (Majlis al-Shura aka Constituent Assembly and Consultative Council): elections for the Assembly were first held in December 1972. All candidates ran as independents. A total of 15,385 votes were cast (although not all constituencies were contested), giving a turnout of 88.5 per cent. However, only some 12.5 per cent of the population were registered voters in 1972. The Constituent Assembly had been charged with drafting and ratifying a constitution, following Bahrain's independence from Britain in 1971.

Voters had to be male and aged over 20.

The assembly consisted of twenty-two elected members and eight delegates appointed by the Emir, (later King), and the twelve members of the Council of Ministers. The Constitution drafted by the Assembly was adopted and known as the 1973 Constitution. The Assembly's upper house now (2022) has 40 royally-appointed members.

Council of State (aka Council of Representatives (Majlis al-Nuwab)): Elections for the Council, the lower house of the National Assembly, were expected to be held by November 2022. The Council was created by the 2002 Constitution and consists of forty members elected by universal suffrage. Members are elected for four-year terms using a 'two round' system, with a second round being held of the top two candidates if no candidate receives 50 per cent in the first round. The forty seats of the Council of Representatives together with the forty royally-appointed seats of the Consultative Council form the National Assembly. Elections were last held in November 2018.

coup d'état (attempted 1981): Political unrest had simmered in Bahrain since the country's full independence from the UK was declared in 1971. One of the most dramatic manifestations of the unrest was the failed *coup d'état* by a militants grouping in 1981. The Bahraini regime alleged they were operating under the auspices of the Islamic Front for the Liberation of Bahrain.

COVID-19: in the two year period from the Pandemic's inception in late 2019 to the end of 2021 Bahrain registered 311,000 cases of infection and just under 1,300 deaths.

crowd-funding: a term used to describe the raising of capital from a large number of individual investors to fund a new business. The Crowd-funding concept lends itself to the use of social media; it has also led to the development of designated crowd-funding websites aimed at alerting small investors to potential opportunities. The overall objective is to widen the pool of investors.

crypto-asset (aka crypto-currency): there are a number of types of crypto-asset in the market, more commonly known as crypto-currencies. Crypto-assets require a number of cryptographic techniques to access the related digital assets. In essence they are a medium of exchange for financial transactions. As the name suggests, a crypto-currency is 'hidden' or 'secret,' reflecting the secure technology employed to record who owns what, and for making payments between users. In short a crypto-currency is no more than a type of electronic cash. Although they can only exist electronically, crypto-currencies use a transactional peer-to-peer system. There is no central bank or government department to manage the system or step in if something goes wrong. This means there are what the Bank of England describes as 'significant risks'. There are no banks or central authorities on hand to protect the users. If funds are stolen, no third party is responsible for recovering them.

Currency Board: in 1964, the Bahrain Currency Board was established and issued a new Bahrain dinar banknotes and coins on 7 October 1965.

Daawa: see Islamic Daawa Party.

Dahdaleh, Victor: allegedly the architect of a corruption scheme affecting ALBA and the American giant Alcoa which had assigned supply contracts to a series of companies incorporated by Mr Dahdaleh, a Canadian businessman of Jordanian origin.

The ALBA legal action claimed that 'these assignments served no legitimate purpose and were used as a means to secretly pay bribes and unlawful commissions as part of a scheme to defraud ALBA'. ALBA alleged that in 2005 a supply contract was inflated by some US\$65 million. Since 1990 ALBA had made some 80 payments to the offshore companies, most of which were for amounts in excess of US\$15 million.

Daiwa Securities Company: in 1988 applied to upgrade its representative office to one of a full investment bank. In contrast to the trend of Western financial institutions cutting back their operations in Bahrain, Japanese securities houses were expanding to capitalise on Gulf demand for yen-based stocks and bonds.

Damascus: (aka Dimashq) the Syrian capital city and the largest city of Syria. Damascus claims to be the oldest continuously inhabited city in the world. Population 4 million (est), or 6.5 million including greater Damascus.

al-Dar Island: is a group of resort islands near Sitra, They lie 12km (7.5 miles) south-east of the capital city Manama on the Bahrain archipelago.

death sentence: in July 2021 the Qatar-based broadcaster al-Jazeera reported that the use of the death penalty in Bahrain had dramatically escalated over the previous decade, specifically since the 2011 Arab Spring uprising. Reports by the Bahrain Institute for Rights and Democracy (BIRD) and the human rights group, Reprieve, claimed that death sentences had risen by more than 600 per cent, with at least 51 people sentenced to be executed since anti-government protests erupted in 2011.

Defence Budget: Bahrain's Defence Budget increased steadily in the late 1980s. The 1988 figure was BD66.5 million (US$176.4 million) which was actually BD10 million (US$26.5 million) higher than originally planned, and well ahead of the 1987 total of BD51.5 million (US$136.6 million). The planned defence budgets for 1989 and 1990 were BD69.4 million (US$184 million) and BD72.9 million (US$193.4 million) respectively.

desalination plants: the 1991 power and water plan allocated US$305 million for the construction of two new reverse osmosis desalination plants, each with a capacity of 15 million gallons a day. Between them, the two new plants were expected to nearly double Bahrain's production capacity, which stood at 35 million gallons a day.

development bonds: Bahrain's first development bonds were launched in the autumn of 1977. This was the first time any Gulf government had borrowed domestically. There were a number of reasons for the creation of the bonds: first the need to test out additional sources of finance for the government, second to mop up excess liquidity in the banking system, and third to provide a secure domestic investment for Bahrain's growing pension and other institutional funds. The first US$25 million of bonds were well received by local institutions and at the time the Bahrain government was considering widening the market for the second tranche, due in the autumn of 1978. It was also considering development bonds as a means of financing revenue generating projects.

Development Plan (Four Year): the government plan for the period 2019–22 set out three strategic priorities:

- Upholding the values of the State and Society
- Financial sustainability and Economic Development
- Supporting an Enabling Environment for Sustainable Development

Dhahran: a major administrative centre for the oil industry, located in the Eastern Province of Saudi Arabia. Together with the nearby cities of Dammam and al-Khobar, Dhahran forms part of the area commonly known as greater Dammam. Dhahran was a key marshalling and deployment centre for US troops during the Gulf War (1990–93). In 1996 a terrorist attack on a Dhahran US troop barracks killed over a dozen soldiers.

NOTES

Dilmun: an ancient Sumerian kingdom (circa 2,000BC) centred on Bahrain and a shipping point between Sumer (Mesopotamia) and the Indus Valley (Pakistan).

dinar: see Bahrain dinar above

Directorate of Election and Referendum: the government department responsible for conducting Bahrain's elections. It is headed by the Minister of Justice, who is appointed by the King.

Dow Jones: the Bahrain Stock Exchange index is operated by the Bahrain branch of the US financial information company.

Dubai: the name is thought to be derived from the Arabic word for a young locust and possibly refers to a stretch of sand or desert where locusts lay their eggs.

Dubai's area is approximately 15,000sq miles (38,900sq km), with a population at the end of 2020 according to the Dubai Statistics Centre of approximately 3.38 million (in 1969 the population was estimated at 60,000). Dubai's early history is ill-documented, but it appears to have been a dependency of Abu Dhabi until 1833 when, after prolonged disputes, some 800 members of the Bani Yas tribe, lead by Maktoum bin-Butti, left Abu Dhabi and settled in Dubai. By the twenty-first century Dubai was established as the commercial hub of the United Arab Emirates (UAE). The city of Dubai is the largest conurbation in the UAE.

Dukhan: exploration for oil in Qatar's Dukhan fields began in 1935. The first oil strike at Dukhan was made in October 1939 by a company then known as Petroleum Development Qatar, and the first well was drilled in 1940. In 1948 and 1949 the Qatar Petroleum Company (QPC) was bringing on stream Qatar's first, and only, on-shore field at Dukhan. The first shipment of crude oil was exported from Qatar on 31 December 1949. The production capacity of the Dukhan field in 2021 was around 335,000bpd.

Dulsais: Iranian aluminium smelter competing internationally with Bahrain's ALBA.

East India Company: Founded in 1600 by merchants in London, the Company's mission was essentially mercantile. The name was a misnomer – its first activities were focused on Persia, where it was well received and granted (1617) a monopoly on all silk leaving Persian ports. In 1619 an English 'factory' (trading post) was established at Jashk. The Company's representatives later established a representation at Bandar Abbas which for some 50 years became a centre of commercial activity. It also began to take an interest in the opportunities offered by India. Such had been the Company's initial success that it was soon emulated, and surpassed, by the Dutch East India Company. Dutch trade and influence prevailed in the Gulf until 1765, when the Dutch presence ceased. Until the end of the seventeenth century the Company continued as an essentially commercial operation. That changed when in 1688 it took over the government of Bombay from the Portuguese. It was allowed to raise a small military force but its presence in Bandar Abbas had become precarious and was relocated to Bushire.

By the beginning of the nineteenth century, pirate fleets in the Gulf had begun to pose a chronic threat to the company's cargoes – of gold and silver outwards to India, and of silks and spices in the opposite direction.

Finally, the Company sent a significant flotilla to the Gulf and attacked Ras al-Khaimah, the pirates' stronghold, reducing the town and the pirate fleet to ashes. The Gulf rulers signed a peace treaty agreeing to the cessation of plunder. Another treaty was signed in 1835, followed by the Treaty of Maritime Peace in Perpetuity in 1853. Until 1858 all Gulf contacts of a diplomatic or administrative nature were conducted through the Company. Thereafter, the responsibility moved to the government of India in Bombay.

East of Suez: a rather vague geographical term used by the British Foreign Office to include the Arabian Gulf, the Indian sub-continent and South-east Asia. Its most prominent use was to describe the British strategic withdrawal from the areas in question. In 1968, the United Kingdom's Labour government, led by Harold Wilson, was obliged to come

to terms with its diminished international position. A combination of financial constraints, a developing reluctance to be involved in imperial adventures and after the withdrawals from Aden and Cyprus, an awareness of anti-colonial hostility, lead to the East of Suez withdrawal. In 2013 there were press reports that the UK government was considering a partial reversal of the East of Suez decision. This represented a strategic reorientation of defence and security requirements towards the Gulf region. The new British presence was to be focused in the United Arab Emirates (UAE), where the Royal Air Force (RAF) would use the al-Minhad base. The Royal Navy had always kept three minesweepers and at least one frigate or destroyer in the Gulf, supported by a small permanent staff in Bahrain.

Eastern Province, Saudi Arabia (aka Ash Sharqiyah and the Eastern Region): the eastern-most of the 13 provinces of Saudi Arabia. It is the largest province by area and the third most populous after the Riyadh Province and the Makkah Province. In 2017, the population was 4,900,325. Of these, 3,140,362 were Saudi citizens and 1,759,963 foreign nationals The province accounts for some 15.00 per cent of the entire population of Saudi Arabia. More than a third of the population is concentrated in the Dammam metropolitan area. The Province is the home of most of Saudi Arabia's Shi'a population.

NOTES

Economic Development Board (EDB): set up in 2003 to be responsible for formulating and overseeing Bahrain's economic development strategy. The EDB's principal objective is to attract foreign direct investment (FDI) to Bahrain.

By 2004 it had identified six main economic sectors able to take advantage of Bahrain's competitive edge. These included: information technology and telecommunications, education and training services, tourism, healthcare services, downstream activities and financial services. The driving force behind the positioning of much of Bahrain's decision making machinery was the EDB, which in 2022 was headed up by Prince Salman bin Hamad al-Khalifa. In theory, the EDB's steadily increasing powers represented an erosion of parliament's already limited powers. But the gradual strengthening of the EDB appeared, rather perversely, to have been welcomed, rather than opposed, by parliament.

Economic Development Plan (2006): this envisaged raising the number of Bahraini nationals within the private sector by 5 per cent a year. It was hoped to achieve this by making it more expensive to employ non-Bahrainis and establishing training facilities for nationals. However, these measures were expensive and the Bahraini economy was not in a suitable state to bear this new burden. The government decided to seek a number of development loans which it was hoped would see Bahrain through the political crisis. These loans were sourced from the Islamic Development Bank (IDB) (Saudi Arabia), Kuwait and the UAE, a total of US$83 million.

Economic Vision 2030: launched by King Hamad Bin Isa al-Khalifa in October 2008, the concept embodied a comprehensive vision for the Kingdom of Bahrain that aimed at 'creating a clear approach to develop the Kingdom's economy while focusing on the main objective which was to improve the standard of living of all Bahraini citizens.'

The Vision had been launched after four years of discussions with a group of decision makers in the public and private sectors, including government institutions and related entities in addition to a number of think-tanks and international institutions. The Economic Vision 2030 rather optimistically focussed on 'crystallising an integrated socio-economic government vision' with three basic principles: 'competitiveness, integrity and sustainability'.

Electricity and Water Authority (EWA): Bahrain's national electricity regulator, chaired by the Minister of Electricity and Water.

Emir (Amir): a title used by Gulf rulers and other dignatories. The original sense was 'army commander'.

Emirates: the Dubai based Emirates airline formed in October 1985 with US$10 million provided by the government of Dubai via the Investment Corporation of Dubai. The airline remains government owned and has been self-financing since the initial investment. By late 2016 Emirates ranked among the top ten airlines in the world in terms of passengers flown, and had become the largest airline in the Middle East in terms of revenue, fleet size, and passengers carried.

Despite its name, the airline does not fly to the UAE's capital city Abu Dhabi.

EnCana Corporation: Canadian oil company, headquartered in Calgary.

Energy Information Administration (EIA): This US government department is the statistical and analytical agency within the US Department of Energy. The EIA collects, analyses, and disseminates energy information to assist in policymaking, understanding markets, and improving public understanding of energy and its role in the economy and the environment. The EIA is the US' principal source of energy information.

Ereli, J Adam: the United States Ambassador in Bahrain in 2010–11. When Bahraini opposition leaders accused the US of ignoring the growing level of street protests, Mr Ereli was reported as saying that 'Bahrain is important to the US for security issues. But that doesn't mean that we don't raise human rights issues as well.' None the less, it appeared that the United States, with many others, failed to appreciate the seriousness of the situation.

Etihad Airways: the second flag carrier airline of the United Arab Emirates. Based in Khalifa City, near Abu Dhabi International Airport.

Eurodollar: US dollar-denominated deposits at foreign banks or held at the overseas branches of American banks. Because they are held outside the United States, eurodollars are not subject to regulation by the Federal Reserve Board, including reserve requirements. Dollar-denominated deposits not subject to US banking regulations were originally held almost exclusively in Europe, hence the name 'eurodollar'. They are also widely held in bank branches in the Bahamas and Cayman Islands.

Europe-Arab Bank: part of Arab Bank group (see above).

European Bahrain Organisation for Human Rights (EBOHR): a human rights group aiming to improve standards of human rights in Bahrain through active lobbying, including holding the Bahraini government accountable in its commitment to international human rights law along with promoting a human rights culture through media including, but not limited to, media-related awareness campaigns.

European Central Bank (ECB): established in 1998, with its headquarters in Frankfurt, Germany, the ECB is the central bank for the European currency, the euro, and administers monetary policy within the

Eurozone, the name given to the then 19 countries of the European Union using the euro. It is one of the largest monetary areas in the world.

European Community (EC): forerunner of the European Union (EU). Originally there were three international European organisations governed by the same set of institutions, the European Coal and Steel Community (ECSC), the European Atomic Energy Community (EAEC or Euratom) and the European Economic Community (EEC).

The latter was renamed the European Community (EC) in 1993 by the Maastricht Treaty, which also formed the European Union. The European Coal and Steel Community ceased to exist in 2002 when its founding treaty expired. The European Community was subsumed into the EU by the Treaty of Lisbon in 2009. Euratom remained an entity distinct from the EU, but governed by the same institutions.

European Currency Unit (ecu): forerunner of the euro.

European Economic Community (EEC): forerunner of the European Union (EU).

European Union (EU): an economic and political union of 27 (2021) European member states. With almost 500 million citizens, the EU is the world's largest single market. In 1988 Bahrain, as a member of the Gulf Co-operation Council, signed a co-operation agreement with the EEC (later to become the EU) for trade and investment. On-going co-operation continues and also includes energy and climate change. According to the European Commission (2020), EU exports to the GCC amounted to €67.5 billion. EU imports from the GCC accounted for only €29.6 billion.

European Union Institute for Security Studies: in 2012 the Paris-based Institute was quoted in the *International Herald Tribune* (IHT) as saying that Bahrain's Prime Minister Sheikh Khalifa bin Salman al-Khalifa – in power since 1971 – showed no willingness to change. According to the Institute's report 'Bahrain is caught between reforms it is not willing to undertake and an uprising it is unable to suppress.'

Exempt Company: a joint stock company that has been exempted from some or all of the requirements of the Law of Commercial Companies by the Minster of Commerce and Agriculture. An exempt company must register and situate its main office in Bahrain, but is set up to conduct its activities outside Bahrain.

F-5 fighter jets: in 1982 Bahrain ordered a number of F-5 military aircraft from the US, as well as 60 air-to-air missiles as part of a major programme to improve its air force.

F-16 fighter jets: in 1987 Bahrain ordered a US$400 million arms package from the US, the most notable feature of which were a dozen F-16 fighters for Bahrain's nascent air force, scheduled for delivery from early 1989 onwards. Bahrain ordered a further four F-16s in 1988.

Fasht al-Adham: island off the east coast of Bahrain, famous for its diving reef.

Fasht Dibal: a small reef lying midway between Bahrain and Qatar. It was occupied by Qatar in April 1986. The reef is the site of a coastguard station which Bahrain was in the process of building at the time of the occupation. Twenty-nine expatriate contract workers were taken as hostages (two Britons and a Dutchman were included among the mainly Filipino and Thai workers) and were only released after weeks of negotiations initiated by Saudi Arabia. The conflict, over border delineation, appeared to be under control by late May, with states overseeing a gradual return to normal relations between the two countries. In an ironic twist of fate, at the time of the occupation the GCC was celebrating five years of industrial and political co-operation as a group of countries sharing a common language, history and religion.

Fatah: see Harakat al-Tahir al-Watani al-Falistin below.

Fateel, Naji Bahraini: human rights activist and a board member of the Bahrain Youth Society for Human Rights (BYSHR). Since 2007 and during the 2011 Bahrain Uprising he was imprisoned and reportedly tortured. In August 2020, Mr Fateel began a hunger strike to protest about conditions in Bahrain's jails and the denial of their rights to practice their religions. In May 2014 the Appeals Court of Bahrain upheld a 15 year sentence against Mr Fateel. Five years later, in September 2019 he was transferred to solitary confinement and was prohibited from receiving visits and telephone calls from his family and legal representatives.

February 14 Coalition: a clandestine Shi'ite opposition group that featured on the Bahraini government's 2016 list of 68 terrorist groupings.

Fifth Fleet: the Fifth Fleet of the United States Navy is responsible for US naval forces in the Arabian Gulf, Red Sea, Arabian Sea, and the coast of East Africa as far south as Kenya. It shares a commander and headquarters with US Naval Forces Central Command (NAVCENT).

Finance Ministry: In 1975, Emiri Decree No (13) was issued, in accordance with which the Ministry of Finance was formed. In the same year, economic affairs were separated from Finance, and Emiri Decree No (15) of 1975 renamed the Ministry of Commerce and Industry as the Ministry of Commerce, Agriculture and Economy. In June 1976, Emiri Decree No (5) was issued, whereby the Ministry of Finance and the Ministry of Commerce, Agriculture and Economy were renamed. The Ministry of Finance was renamed as the Ministry of Finance and the National Economy.

financial sector: Bahrain's financial sector is well-developed and diversified, consisting of a wide range of conventional and Islamic financial institutions and markets. There is also a stock exchange, listing and trading both conventional and Islamic financial instruments. The sector is therefore well-positioned to offer a wide range of financial products and services, making it the leading financial centre in the Gulf region. The sector is the largest single employer in Bahrain, with Bahrainis representing over 80 per cent of the work-force in the sector.

Overall, in 2006, the banking sector contributed 27 per cent of Bahrain's gross domestic product (GDP), making it one of the key drivers of growth in the country. In December 2006, the banking sector's assets stood at over US$180 billion, more than twelve times the country's annual GDP. Despite these successes, the Bahraini banking industry faces a strong threat from its regional rivals. For example Dubai is aggressively marketing the Dubai International Financial Centre (DFIC), an initiative which has the potential to undermine Bahrain's role as the regional financial hub. Qatar and Saudi Arabia are also striving to become leading financial centres in the region. In addition, there is an increasing number of foreign banks establishing themselves in Bahrain

Financial Sector Assessment Programme (FSAP): the global financial crisis showed that the health and functioning of a country's financial sector has implications for its own

and other economies. The International Monetary Fund's (IMF) FSAP is a comprehensive analysis of a country's financial sector. It is tied in to the IMF's Article IV consultations.

FinTech: regarded by many as something of a buzzword, FinTech (an abbreviation of 'financial technology') is used to describe a range of new technologies that seek to improve and automate the delivery and use of financial services. Essentially, it is used to help companies, business owners and consumers better manage their financial operations, processes, and lives with specialised software and algorithms that are used on computers and, increasingly, smartphones.

The term was initially applied to the technology employed at the back-end systems of established financial institutions. Since then, however, there has been a shift to more consumer-oriented services and therefore a more consumer-oriented definition. By 2020 FinTech had come to include different sectors and industries such as education, retail banking, fundraising and investment management.

Although not specifically relevant to Bahrain, FinTech also includes the development and use of crypto-currencies such as bitcoin (and others). While that segment of FinTech may make the most headlines, the generally accepted view is that the major opportunities still lie in the traditional global banking industry.

However, Bahrain's innovations did at least suggest that the government is at pains to establish a FinTech *niche* for itself.

FinTech Bay: see Bahrain FinTech Bay above.

Fiscal Balance Programme (FBP): In September 2021 the credit ratings agency Fitch recommended a reboot of Bahrain's Fiscal Balance Programme (FBP), including a rise in the VAT rate, which could improve the trajectory of the country's public finances. Fitch considered that progress with other fiscal measures would be necessary, in addition to the VAT increase, to bring the budget deficit to balance, based on current oil price assumptions. Bahrain's government planned to raise the VAT rate to 10 per cent from 5 per cent, from January 2022, alongside other measures. Fitch estimated that such a VAT rise could raise an additional 1.5–2.00 per cent of GDP in revenue. Fitch's forecasts, which did not assume any VAT increase, forecast the budget deficit falling to 7.9 per cent of GDP in 2021, from 16.8 per cent in 2020. Bahrain launched its FBP at the end of 2018, targeting a balanced budget in 2022, a target Fitch expected to be reached later than government forecasts. However, the Covid-19 pandemic blew the FBP off course, disrupting activity and pushing down oil prices.

food stockpile: as a strategic defensive measure against the perceived Iranian threat, a BD10 million food stockpile – enough to keep Bahrain supplied for six months – was set up in 1985. Bahrain imports over 80 per cent of its food requirements.

Foreign Companies Law: in a move to attract new business, in 1992 the government of Bahrain was reported to have decided to permit foreign companies and individuals to register their offices without the need for their physical presence in the country.

Those wishing to take advantage of the new law were to be allowed to obtain their commercial registration certificate without being obliged to be domiciled in Bahrain. The new law was to cover a wide spectrum of activities, except banks, financial institutions, insurance companies and investment organisations, for which the existing procedures, including approvals of the Bahrain Monetary Agency, would continue to apply.

The minimum capital outlay for registration of such companies was to be BD2,000 with an annual fee of BD250. The new law would allow organisations to conduct their commercial activities in Bahrain without the need to establish an expensive office as well as incurring other expenses

FRAB-Bank: see Banque Franco-Arabe d'Investissements Internationaux.

Fraser Institute: a Canadian based right wing lobby group that in 2012 claimed that Bahrain is 'the most economically free nation in the Middle East and North Africa' (MENA) region' and 'the seventh freest economy in the world'. The Institute's overall objective was the creation of 'a free and prosperous world through choice, markets and responsibility', which was unsurprisingly endorsed by the Bahraini government. The Institute's international index measures the degree to which the policies and institutions of countries are supportive of economic freedom. In 2012 Bahrain achieved an overall score of 7.94 out of 10, marking it ahead of the United States and Japan. The other top 10 nations were: Hong Kong, 8.90; Singapore, 8.69; New Zealand, 8.36; Switzerland, 8.24; Australia, 7.97; Canada, 7.97; Mauritius, 7.90; Finland, 7.88; and Chile, 7.84. Bahrain led the rankings in the GCC, followed by the United Arab Emirates (UAE), 7.83; Qatar, 7.70; Kuwait, 7.66; Oman, 7.64; and Saudi Arabia, 7.06. Economic freedom was measured in five different areas: size of government, legal structure and security of property rights, access to sound money, freedom to trade internationally and regulation of credit, labour and business. No reference is made in the index to other freedoms such as the right to demonstrate, to a free press, to strike or to vote in free elections for an elected government.

Future Bank: In March 2008 the US Treasury imposed sanctions on Bahrain's Future Bank, a subsidiary of Bank Melli Iran. Bank Melli was accused by Washington of playing a central role in financing Tehran's nuclear and ballistic missile programmes. The action froze any assets Future Bank held in the USA. This shot across Bahrain's bows followed the visit to Bahrain of US Treasury Secretary Stuart Levey in February 2008. Mr Levey had urged Bahrain's monetary officials to exercise 'enhanced due diligence' in guarding against money laundering and nuclear proliferation activities.

G-8 (Group of 8): the world's largest economies: Canada, France, Germany, Italy, Japan, Russia, UK and USA. Originally the Group of 7 (G-7) until Russia joined in 1997. It reverted to G-7 when Russia withdrew in 2014.

gas-gathering: a gas gathering system is a system of gathering lines, flowline networks, and processing facilities. Together the system works to move natural gas (a similar system can be used for oil installations) from the wells to the main storage site/facility, or processing plant. There are two types of gathering systems: the radial and the trunk line. A radial gathering system employs a central header pipeline, while a trunk-line gathering system has several header pipes. A gathering system is also known as a collecting system or gathering facility.

Gaza Strip (Gaza): 40km long and 10km wide, the Gaza Strip is the narrow piece of land along the Mediterranean coast between Israel and Egypt. Gaza is home to more than 2.05 million Palestinians (2020). The Gaza Strip's shape was defined by the

Armistice Line, following the creation of Israel in 1948, and the subsequent war between the Israeli and Arab armies. Egypt administered the Strip for the next 19 years, but Israel captured it during the 1967 Arab-Israeli war.

In 2005, Israel pulled out its troops, and the thousands of Jews who had settled in the territory had to leave Gaza.

However, Israel still exercised control over most of Gaza's land borders, as well as its territorial waters and airspace. Egypt controlled Gaza's southern border. Following its election victory, in June 2007 Hamas assumed control of Gaza, ousting the forces of Fatah led by Palestinian Authority President Mahmoud Abbas and effectively splitting Gaza from the West Bank (see below) in terms of its administration.

General Agreement on Trade in Services (GATS): a treaty of the World Trade Organisation (WTO) that entered into force in 1995. All members of the WTO are parties to the GATS. The fundamental principles of the GATS apply, in principle, to all service sectors.

General Committee for Bahrain Workers: a body appointed in the early 2000s with responsibility for the supervision of employees' rights, enshrined by a draft law granting workers internationally recognised rights.

General Tenders Law: introduced to secure transparency in the award of government tenders.

General Treaty of Peace: signed in 1920 between Britain and the rulers of the Arabian Gulf coast. See British Foreign Office above.

Global Islamic and Sustainable FinTech Center (GISFC): the launch at Bahrain FinTech Bay (BFB) of the GISFC built on the success of the BFB's diverse network of partnerships locally, regionally and internationally. It aims to help accelerate the use of FinTech to drive the next phase of growth in Islamic finance, whilst also focusing on sustainable, social and responsible innovation. The launch of the GISFC reaffirms Bahrain's position as a global leader in Islamic finance and banking. (See FinTech above.)

Gray MacKenzie: see Bahrain Maritime and Mercantile International above.

green coke: Pitch from a coal tar filtration plant is fed into a coker unit at high temperature and pressure. The light products produced in the cracking process in the coker drums are then routed back to refining units. The remainder in the coker is a solid black substance known as green coke or raw coke and contains around 90 per cent fixed carbon.

gross domestic product (GDP), gross national product (GNP): GDP refers to and measures the purely domestic levels of production, whereas the GNP of a given country measures the production levels of any citizen or nationally owned entity, regardless of where in the world the actual production process is taking place. GNP also measures the compensation and investment income received by nationals working or investing abroad. GNP is less commonly referred to than GDP, but is considered by many economists to be a better measure of national output. GNP can be either higher or lower than GDP, depending on the ratio of domestic to foreign manufacturers in a given country. In broad terms, in 2016 China's GDP was US$300 billion greater than its GNP, according to some estimates, due to the large number of foreign companies manufacturing in the country. Conversely, the GNP of the USA was US$250 billion greater than its GDP, because of the amount of US owned production taking place outside the country.

Although both calculations attempt to measure the same thing, generally speaking, GDP is the more commonly used method of measuring a country's economic activity.

The Guardian: British daily newspaper (originally founded and based in Manchester as the *Manchester Guardian*) known for its liberal views and general focus on human rights affairs.

Gulf: Term generally used to refer to the Arabian Gulf (al-Khalij al-Arabi). Iran calls it the Persian Gulf. The term 'Arabian Gulf' is used adjectivally to describe the coastal states of the Arabian Peninsula. The United Nations and other international bodies have traditionally used the Persian Gulf (Khalij-e Fars) as the accepted term. That had also been the official position of the US and many other countries, a state of affairs that appeared to be changing in the twenty-first century.

Gulf Air: Bahrain based airline and national carrier of the Kingdom of Bahrain. Gulf Aviation (later Gulf Air), commenced operations in 1950, becoming one of the first commercial airlines established in the Middle East. In its heyday in the late 1980s – when Bahrain still considered itself to be the Gulf's commercial and transport hub – the airline planned to buy 12 Airbus A-320s and a further six Boeing 767s, with another 12 A-320s and six 767s on option.

The government of Bahrain was originally a shareholder alongside Abu Dhabi, Bahrain, Oman and Qatar. In 2002 Qatar sold its shareholding in Gulf Air coinciding with the launch of its own airline Qatar Airways. Similarly Abu Dhabi sold its shareholding in 2010 and Oman in 2007, as each launched its own national carrier. In 2018 Gulf Air still served 47 cities in 26 countries in three continents.

Gulf Aluminium Rolling Mill Company (GARMCO): in 1981 there were plans to set up an aluminium rolling mill in North Sitra. A US firm was awarded a contract to survey the site in early 1982. Saudi Arabia, Iraq, Kuwait and Bahrain each had a 20 per cent share in GARMCO, while Oman and Qatar were to have 10 per cent each. In 1983 an agreement was signed between Kobe Steel (Japan) and Gulf state shareholders of GARMCO to build the 40,000 ton capacity rolling mill. ALBA was to provide much of GARMCO's feedstock and the region was expected to absorb 80 per cent of its production. With Gulf demand for aluminium rolled products forecast in the region of 240,000 tons per annum over the following decade, the US$106 million plant was anticipated to be a cost-effective exercise.

Gulf Aviation: see Gulf Air above.

Gulf of Bahrain: an inlet of the Arabian Gulf on the east coast of Saudi Arabia, separated from the main body of water by the peninsula of Qatar. The King Fahd Causeway crosses the western section of the Gulf of Bahrain.

Gulf Common Market: one of the unfulfilled objectives of the Gulf Co-operation Council.

Gulf Co-operation Council (GCC): A regional co-operation body established in 1981 and headquartered in Saudi Arabia (Riyadh) with the objectives of improving the co-ordination, integration and inter-connection between the member states (Bahrain, Kuwait, Oman, Qatar (membership temporarily suspended from 2017 to 2021), Saudi Arabia and the UAE) in order to achieve greater unity.

The emphasis is on economic and financial affairs, commerce, customs and communications and education and culture.

Gulf crisis: somewhat vague term used to refer to the events surrounding and following the Iraqi invasion of Kuwait in 1990.

Gulf Development Forum on Water Security: in February 2016 the Forum attracted publicity for all the wrong reasons when the distinguished Emirati academic Abdulkhaleq Abdullah was denied entry into Bahrain to attend the Forum with no reason being given.

Gulf Finance House (GFH): a Bahrain based financial investment group. It is listed on three regional stock markets including the Bahrain Bourse and is considered – by market capitalisation at US$1.42 billion (source: Reuters Eikon, Markaz Research 2018) – to be one of Bahrain's top ten companies.

Gulf Industrial Investment Company (GIIC): a Kuwait Petroleum Company subsidiary.

Gulf International Bank (GIB): a Bahraini bank established in 1976 as a conventional wholesale bank jointly owned by Saudi Arabia, Kuwait, the United Arab Emirates, Qatar, Oman, Iraq and Bahrain. It is licensed by the Central Bank of Bahrain, headquartered in Manama and has a number of overseas branches. As an offshore bank headquartered in Bahrain, the GIB was not supposed to deal with commercial institutions trading in the island; however, it appeared that, *force majeure*, the Bahraini government has been prepared to make specific exceptions.

Gulf Investment Corporation (GIC): in January 1982 the GCC member states agreed to set up a joint investment corporation as part of the GCC's efforts to establish a Gulf common market. The GIC, equally owned by the six Gulf Co-operation Council states (GCC), is headquartered in Bahrain.

Gulf Organisation for Industrial Consulting (GOIC): founded in 1976 by the Gulf Co-operation Council (GCC) member states (UAE, Bahrain, Saudi Arabia, Oman, Qatar and Kuwait, and – in 2009 – Yemen). A regional organisation created to achieve industrial co-operation and co-ordination between GCC member states.

Gulf Petrochemical Industries Company (GPIC): incorporated in 1979, owned equally (33.3 per cent each) by the Oil and Gas Holding Company, Bahrain; SABIC Agri-Nutrients Investment Company, Saudi Arabia; Petrochemical Industries Company (PIC), Kuwait.

Gulf-Riyad Bank: In 1997, after some years of uncertainty, the Bahrain-based Gulf Riyad Bank was closed because its shareholders, Crédit Lyonnais of France and Riyad Bank of Saudi Arabia, no longer saw it as a useful investment. The bank stopped taking new business in 1993. The bank was founded in the late 1970s, when Western banks began to set up in the Gulf to capture petrodollar flows and Arab banks teamed up with them in order to get access to international markets. Since then, Arab banks have gained in expertise and prefer direct representation in the West.

Gulf states: a term generally understood to include, Bahrain, Kuwait, Qatar and the UAE. It can sometimes also include Oman, but not generally Saudi Arabia, although both these countries are members of the Gulf Co-operation Council (GCC).

Gulf University: established in 2001, the Gulf University is a private establishment.

Gulf War: a term used when referring to the Coalition offensive that followed the Iraqi invasion of Kuwait in 1990/93. It was originally used to describe the 1980–88 war between Iran and Iraq which came to be referred to as the Iran/Iraq War.

The Hague: capital city of the Netherlands and location of the International Court of Justice (ICJ).

Haig, Alexander: (b. 1924, d. 2010). US Secretary of State 1981–82.

Hakim: one of the names of God in Islam, meaning 'The All-Wise'.

Hamad Town: (aka Madinat Hamad) (est. 2022 population 52,718). Set up as a 'housing town' with council houses for those unable to afford the high private sector prices elsewhere in Bahain. In 1990 the government had welcomed to Bahrain those Kuwaitis suffering from the effects of the Iraq invasion, providing free houses and school facilities. In 1991 the Kuwaitis returned home and the

Bahraini government gave the houses to the people of Hamad Town free of charge.

Since 1991 it has formed part of the Northern Governate. It is culturally diverse, with a proportionally mixed Shi'a-Sunni population of varying socio-economic backgrounds.

Hamas: see Harakat al-Muqawama al-Islamia below.

Haq Movement for Liberty and Democracy: an opposition political organisation, founded in November 2005 with Hasan Mushaima as its secretary. In September 2021 Mr Hasan, who is serving a life sentence, refused a conditional release on grounds it would be 'humiliating' and reiterating his right to freedom without restriction.

Harakat al-Muqawama al-Islamia (Hamas) (Islamic Resistance Movement)): the largest and probably the most influential Palestinian militant movement.

Hamas evolved from the Muslim Brotherhood, the religious and political organisation founded in Egypt by the organisation's spiritual leader, Sheikh Ahmed Yassin. Yassin founded Hamas as the Muslim Brotherhood's local political arm in December 1987, following the eruption of the first intifada, a Palestinian uprising against Israeli control of the West Bank and Gaza. In its early years Hamas divided its strategy into social programmes – schools, hospitals etc – and a militant offensive carried out by its Iss al-Din Qassam Brigades.

In the reign of Jordan's King Hussein (1952–99), Hamas was headquartered in Jordan, but his successor, King Abdullah II, had the movement's headquarters closed, causing the leadership to move to Qatar.

In January 2006, Hamas won the Palestinian Authority's (PA) general legislative elections, defeating Harakat al-Tahir al Watani al-Falistin (Fatah), the party of the PA's president, Mahmoud Abbas. Following the Gaza elections, Ismail Haniyeh, the Hamas prime minister and senior figure in Gaza, often appeared at odds with Khaled Meshal, Hamas's overall leader, who lives in Syria. Hamas has refused to recognise Israel, instead carrying out suicide bombings and attacks using mortars and short-range rockets. Hamas has launched attacks both in the Palestinian territories of the West Bank and Gaza Strip. In Arabic, the word 'hamas' means 'zeal'.

Harakat al-Tahir al-Watani al-Falistin (Fatah) (Movement for the National Liberation of Palestine): the Palestinian political party elected in the West Bank.

Hawar Islands: (aka Huwar) a group of 16 islands just off Bahrain's coast that had traditionally formed part of Bahraini territory. All but one of the islands are administered by Bahrain. The small, uninhabited island of Jinan is administered by Qatar. Bahrain's relations with Qatar had worsened during 1996 due to the disputed islands, which had been

NOTES 353

controlled by Qatar since the 1930s. The Qatari government appeared to ignore a 1990 agreement whereby no building work would be carried out on the islands, which are just off Bahrain's coast. Qatar also refused to accept either direct or mediated negotiation and referred the case to the International Court of Justice (ICJ) in The Hague.

The ICJ was expected to rule on the case by the end of 1996, but its verdict was later delayed. Bahrain had stated that it would refuse to accept the Court's judgement as it considers it has no jurisdiction in the matter. The Bahrain government also announced that it would not be attending the December 1996 summit of the Gulf Co-operation Council (GCC), due to the fact that it was being held in Qatar. In 2001 the ICJ awarded sovereignty over the Hawar islands and of the smaller Qit'at Jaradah to Bahrain, allowing Qatar to retain the neighbouring islands of Zubarah and Jinan. Bahrain promptly awarded two exploration blocks off the country's south-eastern coast, one to Petronas of Malaysia and the other to ChevronTexaco.

Heritage Foundation: the US based publishers of the *Index of Economic Freedom* world ranking, on which Bahrain ranked 13 in 2009. However, on the 2021 Index, Bahrain had slumped to 40, and had been overtaken by both the UAE (14)and Qatar (21). See *Wall Street Journal* below.

Hezbollah (aka Hizbollah): a militant Shi'a religious grouping founded in 1982 and originally headquartered in Damascus, but mostly operational in Lebanon, where it is a significant political force. Hezbollah is a major provider of social services, operating schools, hospitals and agricultural services for thousands of Lebanese Shi'ites. Hezbollah's political standing was bolstered after a wave of violence in May 2008 prompted Lebanon's lawmakers to compromise with the militant group. In August 2008, the country's parliament approved a national unity cabinet, giving Hezbollah and its allies veto power with eleven of thirty cabinet seats.

Hezbollah also operates the al-Manar satellite television channel and broadcast station. It also groups members of the 1980s coalition of groups known as Islamic Jihad and has close links to Iran and Syria. Syria had continued to permit the Iranian resupply, via Damascus, of Hezbollah in Lebanon.

Hezbollah-Bahrain: in 1996 was already thought to be receiving financial and military backing from Iran.

al-Hidd (aka Hidd): one of Bahrain's smaller towns with a 13,000 largely Sunni population. Located on Muharraq Island, it has a port and is well known for its sea crab industry. It is also well known for its Bahraini premier league football team. Hidd is the location of the Arab Shipbuilding and Repair Yard Company (ASRY).

Higher Council for Economic Development: early in 2000, the Bahrain government announced the establishment of this body with a mandate that included reducing the waiting time for approving foreign direct investment (FDI).

Hongkong Bank of the Middle East (HBME): see British Bank of the Middle East above.

Houthi: (aka al-Houthi, or Ansar Allah – 'Supporters of God') a Shi'a (Zaidi sect) rebel Islamist grouping in northern Yemen, generally known as 'the Houthis'. The name 'Houthi' comes from the leadership of Hussein Badreddin al-Houthi. The Houthis were originally a grouping opposed to the rule of former Yemeni President, Ali Abdullah Saleh, whom they accused of corruption and of being an American 'lackey'. Mr Hussein was killed by the Yemeni army in a 2004 Houthi insurgency, led by Mr Hussein's brother Abdul-Malik. The Houthi's war-cry is simple enough 'God is great, death to the US, death to Israel, curse the Jews, and victory for Islam'.

The Houthis participated in the 2011 Yemeni Revolution and in the GCC sponsored National Dialogue Conference. However they rejected the outcome, opting for an alliance with former President Saleh. With the support of Iran, the Houthis soon controlled Sana'a and much of North Yemen. Since 2015 Houthi forces have been resisting the Saudi-led coalition, of which Bahrain is a member.

Human Rights Watch (HRW): a US based NGO. In its June 2013 report on Bahrain, entitled *Interfere, Restrict and Control*, HRW noted that 'Since independence from Britain in 1971, social, cultural and sports clubs, as well as civil and professional organisations, have been pivotal in shaping political debate. With political groups of any sort prohibited until 2001 NGOs have often served as forums for discussing social, economic and political issues.'

Hussein, Saddam: (b. 1937, d. 2006, by hanging). Born in Tikrit, Iraq, Saddam Hussein was a secularist whose political ascendancy was assisted by his affiliation to Iraq's Ba'ath party until he eventually assumed the presidency. Under his rule, segments of the populace enjoyed the benefits of oil wealth, while those in opposition faced torture and execution. In 1990 he was responsible for the short-lived Iraqi invasion of Kuwait. Believing Iraq to possess nuclear weapons, the USA, aided and abetted by the government of Tony Blair in the UK, chose to invade Iraq and depose Saddam Hussein. After the military conflict with USA-led armed forces, Hussein was captured in 2003. He was tried for treason and executed in 30 December 2006.

Huwar: see Hawar above.

hydrofracking: Hydraulic fracturing, informally referred to as 'fracking,' is an oil and gas well development process that typically involves injecting water, sand and chemicals under high pressure into a bedrock formation via the well. This process is intended to create new fractures in the rock as well as increase the size, extent, and connectivity of existing fractures. Hydraulic fracturing is a well-stimulation technique used commonly in low-permeability rocks like tight sandstone, shale, and some coal beds to increase oil and/or gas flow to a well from petroleum-bearing rock formations.

Imperial Bank of Persia: see British Bank of the Middle East above.

Industrial Development Centre (IDC): a division of the Ministry of Trade and Development. In 1989 Bahrain aimed to replace 30 per cent of its imports over a five year period. The Bahrain government itself had allocated US$2.6 billion to the development of industrial projects.

Information and eGovernment Authority (iGA): the government entity in charge of supervising the digital agenda of the Kingdom of Bahrain. It plays a key role in modernising government services and supporting the digital infrastructure needed to execute the digitalisation strategies spelt out under the directions of the Supreme Council for Information and Communication Technology (SCICT). In line with Bahrain's Economic Vision 2030, the iGA aims to deliver better government eServices to the public through the single platform of the National Portal, bahrain.bh.

International Court of Justice (ICJ): in March 2001 the ICJ passed judgement in the territorial dispute between Bahrain and Qatar over the Hawar Islands. The ruling was broadly in favour of Bahrain. (see Hawar Islands above).

International Herald Tribune: a Paris-based English language daily newspaper jointly owned by the *New York Times* and the *Washington Post*. In 2013 the *Washington Post* sold its shareholding to the *New York Times*, since when the name changed to the *International New York Times*.

International Labour Organisation (ILO): an agency within the United Nations which brings together government, employer and worker representative to promote decent work standards in different parts of the world. Bahrain has been a member since 1977 since when it has ratified 10 ILO conventions.

International Monetary Fund (IMF): The IMF is an organisation of 190 countries (in 2022), 'working to foster global monetary co-operation, secure financial stability, facilitate international trade, promote high employment and sustainable economic growth, and reduce poverty around the world.' The IMF came into existence in 1944 to meet the challenge of rebuilding national economies after the end of the Second World War.

As the post-war reconstruction phase came to an end, the IMF became charged with overseeing the international monetary system to ensure exchange rate stability and encouraging members to eliminate exchange restrictions that hinder trade.

Investcorp Bank: one of Bahrain's top ten companies by market capitalisation at US$750 million (source: Reuters Eikon, Markaz Research 2018). Founded in the US in 1982, the company manages global investments and has a significant presence in the Gulf with offices in Bahrain, Abu Dhabi, Riyadh and Doha as well as New York, London, Mumbai and Singapore. It claims to have a unique fundraising capability in the Gulf by offering a 'high level of personal service to an investor base of high-net-worth individuals and institutions.'

investment banking licence (IBL): a financial tool devised by the Bahrain Monetary Agency (BMA) for merchant banking activities.

Iran: (population 80.6 million in 2017, World Bank estimate) in the 1960s Shah Mohammad Reza Pahlavi (aka Mohammad Reza Shah) set about the modernisation and westernisation of Iran with the 'White Revolution', a programme of land reform and social and economic modernisation. However, the lack of representative democracy in Iran lost the Shah his authority and legitimacy, making him dependent on Iran's secret police (SAVAK) in confronting those opposition movements critical of his reforms. By 1978 the Shah's policies appeared to have also alienated the clergy; his increasingly authoritarian rule lead to social disorder and eventually to strikes and mass demonstrations.

Martial law was imposed in September 1978 but before long the Shah and his family were forced into exile. In February 1979 the iconic Islamic fundamentalist, Ayatollah Ruhollah Khomaini returned to Iran after 14 years of exile in Iraq and France and in April 1979 the Islamic Republic of Iran was proclaimed following a referendum.

Formerly Persia, Iran has been a constant threat to Bahrain, often claiming ownership of the island. Indeed from the seventeenth century, Persia had controlled Bahrain through Sunni tribes until the mid-1800s when Bahrain became a British protectorate. In the run up to independence in 1971, Sir William Luce, Britain's special envoy to the Gulf, successfully negotiated the Shah of Iran's agreement in 1971 to drop Iran's longstanding claim to Bahrain.

Iran was known to have been developing and utilising clandestine organisations embedded within the Shi'a communities of the Arab Gulf states to conduct acts of sabotage and terrorism, and to generally stoke sectarian violence. Nowhere was this clearer than in the case of Bahrain: Iran's hardliners claimed Bahrain as their fourteenth province. Bahrain had faced a variety of terrorist groups that were trained and deployed un-

NOTES

der the command of the Quds Force of the Islamic Revolutionary Guard Corps (IRGC). The most formidable challenges had been: (1) the Islamic Front for the Liberation of Bahrain (IFLB), (2) the Military Wing of Hezbollah Bahrain (MWHB), and (3) Sacred Defence Bahrain (SDB). While the IFLB was subdued and dismantled following the Shi'a intifada in the 1990s, many of its proponents evaded arrest and joined the other active groups. The MWHB and the SDB survived into the 2000s and have been joined – in a post-2011 security environment – by several others, including the Youth of 14 February and the Saraya al Ashtar (SaA).

Iran/Iraq War: a term used to describe the hostilities between Iran and Iraq which lasted from 1980 to 1988. The cease-fire, in August 1988, provided Bahrain with a new sense of security.

Iranian pressures: Bahrain has long been of strategic interest to Iran which notionally regards it as its Fourteenth Province and a stepping stone towards a wider confrontation with Saudi Arabia. Bahrain has confronted numerous Iran-backed terrorist groups over the years. While Bahraini security operations were able to contain most Iranian terrorist groups, the 2011 upheaval in much of the Arab world provided the Shi'a opposition and Iranian backed groups with new opportunities to destabilise Bahrain. Invoking the collective defence clauses of the Gulf Co-opera-

tion Council (GCC) on 14 March 2000 troops from Saudi Arabia and the UAE moved in to shore up the beleaguered al-Khalifa régime.

The troop reinforcements propped up their Bahraini counterparts, clearing public areas of protesters and dismantling the Pearl Square encampments. Unconfirmed reports suggested that the intervention had resulted in the deaths of a further seven demonstrators. The operation provided the Iranian government with something of a public relations coup.

Iranian threat: Iran has long sought to develop and deploy clandestine organisations imbedded within the Shi'a communities of the Arabian Gulf states to conduct acts of sabotage and terrorism, and to generally stoke sectarian violence. Nowhere is this clearer than in the case of Bahrain where Iran's hardliners claim the island as their fourteenth province. Bahrain has faced a variety of terrorist groups that were trained and deployed under the command of the Quds Force of the Islamic Revolutionary Guard Corps (IRGC).

The deployment of troops from Saudi Arabia and the United Arab Emirates (UAE) to protect vital infrastructure in 2011 prevented the IRGC from playing a more direct role.

The show of force under Operation Peninsular Shield deterred Iranian intervention. In addition, the stationing of the US Fifth Fleet and the UK's new naval station have enhanced

Bahrain's ability to restrict Iran's direct role. However, since both the United States and United Kingdom respond to different threat perceptions, Bahrain's security relies on its alliance to Saudi Arabia and the UAE more so than others.

Iraq: (population 38.27 million in 2018, World Bank estimate) Kuwait's 'noisy neighbour' to the north had long laid claim to Kuwait. The claim's roots lay in a tenuous historical interpretation of the legacy of the Ottoman Empire, during most of which Kuwait was a district within the Iraqi province of Basra. Kuwait, with some justification, could point out that in the latter stages of Ottoman rule, in 1899 it had passed under British protection.

In the late nineteenth century, Britain had signed treaties with the states of the lower Gulf – with Muscat (Oman) in 1891, with the sheikhs of the so-called Trucial coast, and with Bahrain in 1892. For some time Britain had been nervous about the implications of its relations with Ottoman Turkey. However, intelligence reports suggesting that Germany was contemplating building a railway from Baghdad to the Gulf, and that Russia was considering opening a coaling station in Kuwait gave Britain cause for concern. During this period Britain exercised control over Bahrain's foreign relations and was responsible for security. When British protection ended in 1961 Bahrain had in effect become a sovereign nation, recognised as such by many countries – including Iraq. The regional political climate had, however, changed in Iraq when in 1958 Iraq's pro-Western monarchy was deposed by a violent military *coup d'état* led by one Abd al-Karim Qasim.

Islamic Action Association: (pro-Shi'a aka The Association of Islamic Labour) is a political Islamic organisation concerned about the affairs of the country and citizens. It defends the human rights in Bahrain in order to provide a free and decent life where citizens could have honor, dignity and security. The Association works on developing and flourishing the society in accordance with a comprehensive Islamic view. The Association was founded by 410 members in Bahrain where it was registered in the record of the associations and social clubs of the Ministry of Labour and Social Affairs in Bahrain on the first of Ramadan, 1422AH (6 November 2002).

Islamic Daawa Party (aka the Islamic Call Party): See Daawa

Islamic Development Bank: an international financial institution established in Saudi Arabia, in 1973. The purpose of the Bank is to foster the economic development and social progress of member countries and Muslim communities individually as well as jointly in accordance with the principles of Sharia (Islamic law).

Islamic Economics: the knowledge and application of injunctions

NOTES

and rules of the Sharia that prevent injustice in the acquisition and disposal of material resources in order to provide satisfaction to human beings and enable them to perform their obligations to Allah and society.

Islamic financing: The banking sector is the most developed part of the Islamic financial service industry. Other segments of the industry include investment companies, investment funds, insurance (Takaful), and reinsurance (ReTakaful) companies. The sukuk market has remained small and has been dominated by the overseas corporate sector. Islamic banks' market share had increased rapidly between 2005 and 2010 and has since then stabilised at around 38 per cent. As of December 2015, Kuwait had the fifth-largest share of Islamic banking assets and the sixth-largest share of Islamic funds globally.

Islamic Front for the Liberation of Bahrain (IFLB): came to prominence as the front organisation for an attempted coup in Bahrain in 1981 that sought to install an Iraqi Ayatollah based in Iran, Ayatollah Hadi al-Modaressi, as head of a theocratic revolution in Bahrain. In the 1990s the Front became more noted for bomb attacks targeting civilians such as the 1996 bomb attack on a Manama hotel.

The specific aim of the Front was an 'uprising' of all Bahraini Muslims under Imam Khomeini with forces trained and financed by Iran.

al-Modaressi served as Khomeini's 'personal representative' in Bahrain and his brother, Ayatollah Mohammed Taqi al-Modaressi, was thought to be Khomeini's chief operative for exporting the Iranian revolution abroad. One of the Front's commanders, the Iranian Ayatollah Sadeq al-Rouhani, had called for Bahrain to be annexed by Iran.

Islamic Heritage Revival Society: a body devoted to the strict letter of the Koran and opposed to secular rule. However, in the late 1980s the Society won representation in the National Assembly.

Islamic Law: see Sharia below

Islamic National Wefaq Society: see al-Wefaq below

Islamic State (IS): (aka Islamic State of Iraq and the Levant (ISIL) and Islamic State in Iraq and Syria (ISIS)), an extremist Islamic movement that from 2013 onwards described itself as the Islamic State (IS) reflecting its ambition to establish a 'caliphate' based on military might and Sharia rule. The caliphate was to extend from northern Syria (bordering Turkey) to southern Iraq. The dictum at the heart of the IS political and and theological philosophy stated that 'The foundation of the religion is a book (the Quran (Koran) that guides and a sword that supports.'

The debate over whether IS considered itself to be representing the Sunni community hinged on whether it saw itself as enforcing the rule of Allah according to the Quran under the guidance of the movement's Sharia Council, for some time seen as the group's most vital body.

The council's responsibilities included overseeing the speeches of the (self-declared) Caliph Ibrahim (Abu Bakr al-Baghdadi) and those under him, dictating punishments, preaching, mediating, monitoring the group's media, ideologically training new recruits and advising the caliph on how to deal with hostages when it was decided to execute them.

The extent to which IS military or economic strategies and policies were decided without the Sharia Council's approval was not totally clear.

Underneath the main Sharia Council in each district there was a smaller council that made decisions about issues related to the area. There were also two main muftis (a Muslim legal expert authorised to rule on religious matters) under the head of the council – the Mufti of Iraq and the Mufti al-Sham in Syria.

By the end of 2017, ISIL military forces had been routed by the forces of the US-led coalition and the advent of the Russian air force supporting the still beleaguered al-Assad government. At the beginning of 2019 US President Trump announced that US forces were to be withdrawn from Syria since ISIS 'had been defeated'. However, the Pentagon and the CIA both stated that while the ISIS movement had lost most of its territory, as a terrorist organisation it could still count on a large membership dispersed throughout the Middle East.

Islamic Summit Conference (Third) Riyadh, 1981: plans for the creation of the Gulf Co-operation Council (GCC) were finalised at the conference.

Israel (Gaza conflict 2008–14): Israel has twice been in a state of armed conflict with Gaza. In December 2008 Israel launched Operation Cast Lead aimed at curtailing Hamas rocket attacks on southern Israel and in January 2009 it launched a ground invasion.

Then in July 2014 the Israeli Defence Forces (IDF) launched Operation Protective Edge which saw IDF troops enter the Gaza Strip. According to the United Nations (UN) over 2,000 Palestinians (mostly civilians) were killed. The Israeli casualties were some 70, mostly soldiers. A ceasefire was agreed upon on 26 August 2014.

Israel (Lebanon Conflict 2006): also called the 2006 Israel-Hezbollah War and known in Lebanon as the July War and in Israel as the Second Lebanon War.

Iss al-Din Qassam Brigades: the military wing of the Palestinian organisation Hamas; operating in the Gaza Strip.

Istanbul: (population: 15.07 million in 2018) Turkey's largest city, straddling the Bosphorus Strait. Until the construction of the first suspension bridge in 1973, all surface transport between Asia and Europe had to be ferried across the Bosphorus. The Fatih Sultan Mehmet Bridge (Second Bosphorus Bridge) was opened in 1988. The third Bosphorus Bridge was opened in 2016.

Jakarta: (population 10.5 million 2020) the capital city of Indonesia. By population 273.5 million (2020), the world's largest Muslim country.

al-Jamri, Abdel-Amir: the popular outrage at the public execution in Bahrain of dissidents which took place in 1996 was compounded by the death, through ill health, in jail of the opposition leader Abdel-Amir al-Jamri in July 1997.

al-Jamri, Mansour: the Bahraini editor of the pan-Arab newspaper *Al-Wasat* which he founded in 2002. The newspaper was respected internationally for its editorial independence and integrity. Mr al-Jamri controversially stated that foreign labour should not be classified as temporary, since for the most part they had become virtually permanent members of the community. Mr al-Jamri further expanded on his theme, suggesting that the political influence of a renascent India could well end up making the Gulf States part of a Commonwealth of India as its former citizens assume greater confidence and responsibility in both private and public sectors. Following the Bahrain Uprising in 2011 *al-Wasat* was closed down by the Bahrain government which accused Mr al-Jamri of publishing false news. Following

his resignation as editor, the newspaper was allowed to continue publishing. He was subsequently charged and convicted. However, later in 2011 the newspaper's board of directors reinstated him. Eventually, in 2017, the Information Affairs Ministry indefinitely suspended the newspaper, forcing its closure. There was widespread condemnation of the move; Amnesty International of the UK described it as an 'all-out campaign to end independent reporting.'

Japan Gas Corporation (JGC): in 2016 the JGC announced that it was to build new gas processing facilities in Bahrain. These were located in the Bahrain oilfield area south of Awali, near Jebel al-Dukhan, and were to be operated by the Bahrain National Gas Expansion Company (BSC). The project was scheduled for completion in September 2018. It was expected that, by exporting recovered petroleum constituents as commercial products, the plant would contribute to the development of the oil and gas industries in Bahrain.

Jaw Prison (aka Jau Prison): in March 2015 a riot at Bahrain's notorious Jaw Prison ended with a fierce response from the authorities, and allegations of police torture. A very sophisticated Jaw Prison breakout later occured in January 2017 – with the subsequent attempted smuggling of escapees to Iran.

Jebel al-Dukhan (aka Jebel Dukhan): Bahrain was the first Gulf country to strike oil – on 1 June 1932 at

Jebel al-Dukhan. However, until 2018 its known reserves were much smaller than those of neighbouring Abu Dhabi, Kuwait and Saudi Arabia. At mid-1980s rates of recovery Bahrain had been expected to run out of oil by the end of the twentieth century.

This was a serious problem as at the time the oil sector still accounted for two thirds of government revenues and around 80 per cent of the country's export earnings. But there was scope for a degree of optimism – Bahrain appeared to have sizeable reserves of natural gas which were largely under-exploited. Failing a new oil strike (see Khalij al-Bahrain, below) until 2018 it was thought that natural gas might well replace oil as Bahrain's main source of energy and exports in the next century.

Jeddah: (population 4.0 million in 2017). Saudi Arabian port city on the Red Sea. It is the second largest city in Saudi Arabia after the capital city, Riyadh, and is the country's commercial capital. Jeddah is also the principal gateway to Mecca and Medina, two of the holiest cities in Islam.

Jerusalem: (population 936,000). A Holy city located in Palestine but under Israeli control. The (largely) unrecognised capital of the modern nation of Israel, Jerusalem is of great importance to the three Western religious traditions of Judaism, Christianity and Islam.

Most Arab nations could not countenance any proposed 'settlement' of the status of the Israel-Palestine issue that did not include a return to Arab hands of East Jerusalem, without in any way weakening Jerusalem's legitimacy as the keeper of Islam's Holy Places.

However the fact that Israel regards Jerusalem as its 'eternal and undivided' capital, sits uncomfortably with Palestine which claims that East Jerusalem – occupied by Israel in the 1967 war – is the capital of a future Palestinian state. In recognising Jerusalem as Israel's capital in 2017, the US became the first country to do so since the foundation of Israel in 1948. Australia followed the US in 2018, but in October 2022 the decision was reversed by the Labor Party.

Jinan: an offshore island awarded to Qatar in the March 2001 settlement by the International Court of Justice (ICJ). Sovereignty over the Hawar Islands was awarded to Bahrain, while Qatar retained Jinan and the neighbouring island of Zubarah.

Jubail: (population 684,531 in 2021.) a major industrial centre in eastern Saudi Arabia, on the Gulf.

Kaiser Aluminium: in 1977 Kaiser Aluminium of the US (Kaisertech Ltd) held a 17 per cent shareholding in Aluminium Bahrain (ALBA). In 1989 the Bahrain government signed a preliminary agreement with Kaiser Aluminium to purchase its equity interest in ALBA for a sum reportedly between US$70 million and US$75 million. Before the sale, ALBA's capital

NOTES

had been owned 57.9 per cent by the Bahrain government, 20 per cent by the Saudi Basic Industries Corporation (SABIC), 17 per cent by Kaiser Aluminium, and 5.1 per cent by Breton Investments of West Germany. Following the purchase, the Bahrain government would be Alba's majority shareholder.

Kanoo Group: one of the largest and oldest independent, family owned groups of companies in the Arabian Gulf states. Established in Bahrain in 1890 by Yusuf bin Ahmed Kanoo, it began as a classical trading and shipping business to become a major regional commercial business group.

Kanoo Terminal Services: a freight handling company for the Dammam-Riyadh railway line in Saudi Arabia; a joint venture of the Kanoo brothers (Bahrain) organisation and Nedlloyd of Rotterdam.

Kanoo, Yusuf bin Ahmed: b. 1874, d. 1945. At the age of twenty a precocious Yusuf Kanoo began travelling to India from Bahrain to trade. In 1898 he also began to undertake part-time work for the first British representative in Bahrain. His local importance as a source of information for the British and his perceived influence with the British by most Bahrainis gave him a level of notoriety. In 1913 a formal British Political Agency was established on Bahrain and perhaps not by coincidence also in 1913 Yusuf Kanoo obtained his first commercial agency, for the recently created An-

glo-Persian Oil Company. Alongside what was a *de-facto* banking operation, Yusuf Kanoo quickly built up a commercial operation, but his dependence on British patronage meant that this success was short-lived. In the 1920s his wealth and influence faded with the decline of the pearl industry. In the 1930s the process accelerated and although Yusuf Kanoo managed to repay almost all his debts, he never regained his earlier prestige and influnce, neither with the Bahrainis nor with the British. He eventually handed over the running of his business to his nephews, Jassim and Ali, sons of his brother, Mohamed.

Keffiyeh: A square of chequered print material – often red and white or black and white – worn by Arab men as a headdress.

Khaleej al-Bahrain: see Khalij al-Bahrain below.

al-Khalifa, Abdullah bin Ahmed: (b. 1769, d. 1849) ruled as Hakim from 1796–1843, as Co-Regent with Salman bin Ahmed al-Khalifa (1796–1825) and Khalifa bin Salman al-Khalifa (1825–34). Abdullah and his elder brother, Salman bin Ahmed al-Khalifa, began to rule the country together in 1796 when their father, Ahmed, died.

The brothers' reign was, however, less than straightforward. In 1802 Bahrain was invaded and captured by the ruler of Muscat. This state of affairs was short-lived. The ruler of the (then important) Saudi city of

Diriyah, Abdul Aziz bin Mohammed, captured Bahrain and appointed Abdullah bin Ufaysan, as Governor. The brothers Abdullah and Salman al-Khalifa were imprisoned in Diriyah. A series of Ottoman attacks weakened Abdul Aziz bin Mohammed's position as ruler, allowing the al-Khalifa brothers to re-establish their rule.

The exceptional joint rulership of Abdullah and Salman lasted until 1825 when Salman died. His son Khalifa succeeded his father as co-ruler in 1825, but it was accepted that Abdullah was the more important, principal, ruler.

In 1834 Khalifa bin Salman died, and Abdullah became the sole ruler. In 1839 Abdullah signed a treaty with Egypt which obliged him to recognise the supremacy of the Egyptians. Another condition required by the treaty was that a Turkish Agent was to reside in Bahrain to implement Ottoman orders.

Abdullah's rule was challenged by his great-nephew Mohammed bin Khalifa, son of Salman. Following his defeat Mohammed was granted asylum. Although he had defeated Mohammed, in 1843 Abdullah lost the fort of Damman and was removed as Ruler of Bahrain by the British.

al-Khalifa, Ahmed bin Mohammed: (b. 1725, d. 1795) became Bahrain's first ruler (Hakim) 1783–1796 when he assumed sovereignty over Bahrain and its islands in 1783. He was the progenitor of the ruling al-Khalifa family of Bahrain and the first monarch or hakim of Bahrain. All of the al-Khalifa monarchs of Bahrain are his descendants.

al-Khalifa, Ali bin Khalifa: Ruler of Bahrain (Hakim) 1868–1869.

al-Khalifa, Hamad bin Isa bin Ali: (b. 1872, d. 1942) ruled 1932–1942. Although officially recognised as ruler (Hakim) when his father died in 1932, Hakim Hamad was, in effect, a *de facto* ruler before this because his father, Sheikh Isa bin Ali al-Khalifa, was coerced to abdicate by British authorities.

He made an official visit to Britain in 1936 where he met with King Edward VIII. Suffering from diabetes, he resorted to insulin in large quantities and died of a stroke in 1942.

al-Khalifa, Hamad bin Isa bin Salman: (b. January 1950) the current (2022) King of Bahrain. He is the son of Isa bin Salman al-Khalifa and ruled as Emir from 1999, then – following a successful vote for constitutional democracy – declared himself the first King of Bahrain from 2002. He has four wives and 12 children – seven sons and five daughters.

Following early education in Bahrain, he went to Britain where he attended Applegarth College in Surrey and the Leys School in Cambridge. He undertook military training in both the UK and the USA and is a trained helicopter pilot.

He is head of the Royal Bahraini Army and supreme commander of the Bahrain Defence Force. He ap-

NOTES

points the country's prime minister and other ministers – many of whom are members of the royal al-Khalifa family – and he chairs the Higher Judicial Council. From the beginning of his reign, Hamad made efforts to stabilise Bahrain's mood by releasing political prisoners and allowing those in exile to return. He dissolved the State Security Court. Also, he ensured that living standards were improved and was instrumental in promoting Bahrain as a financial hub.

But with many Sunnis in positions of power – the royal family being of the Sunni faith but with Sunnis only accounting for about a third of the Bahraini population – the Shi'ite community were not to be quelled with accusations of government corruption and discrimination. By 2011, mounting tensions resulted in an uprising and the government responded with a brutal crackdown attracting negative reactions from human rights activists around the world. Hamad aimed to appease the nation by ordering that BD1,000 be given to each family to celebrate the tenth anniversary of the National Action Charter referendum. He also apologised publicly for the deaths of two demonstrators.

Further deaths occurred and in June 2011, Hamad commissioned an independent enquiry by the respected US human rights lawyer, Mahmoud Cherif Bassiouni. While applauded by international rulers, activists saw the enquiry as only scratching the surface of the atrocities. Hamad declined the invitation to attend the London wedding of Prince William in 2011 for fear of protests by human rights activists. Even seven years later, when he attended the 2018 Windsor Horse Show, activists were there to show disapproval of his regime.

al-Khalifa, Isa bin Ali: (b. 1848, d. 1932) ruler (Hakim) of Bahrain from 1869 until his death in 1932. His reign lasted 63 years, making him one of the Gulf's longest reigning monarchs. Although he was forced by the British Political Advisor to abdicate in 1923, his abdication was never recognised by most Bahrainis who considered his successor Hamad al-Khalifa only to be vice-ruler until Isa's death in 1932.

al-Khalifa, Isa bin Salman bin Hamad: (b. 1931, d. 1999) ruled as Hakim from 1961–1971, and as Bahrain's first Emir from 1971 to 1999. He was the father of the current (2022) King of Bahrain – Hamad bin Isa al-Khalifa.

One of the highlights during his leadership, was for his country to gain independence from Britain in 1971. At the time, serious consideration was given to joining the proposed United Arab Emirates but the union's constitution was not to Bahrain's liking. Having promoted a moderately democratic parliament, the Emir dissolved it when a security law was refused in 1974 and he took over sole power. He facilitated economic growth during his 38 year reign and the international political world recognised him as an engineer of stability and peace within the Middle East.

al-Khalifa, Khalifa bin Ahmed: (b. 1946) is (2022) the Commander-in-Chief of the Bahrain Defence Force (BDF). In January 1974, Emir Isa bin Salman al-Khalifa appointed him Chief of Staff of the BDF. This was followed in March 1988, by being made Deputy Commander-in-Chief and Minister of Defence. On 29 January 2001, Emir and soon-to-be King of Bahrain, Hamad bin Isa promoted Khalifa bin Ahmed to Lieutenant-General, followed by the titles of BDF Commander-in-Chief on 6 January 2008, and to the rank of Field Marshal in February 2011.

al-Khalifa, Khalifa bin Salman: (b. 1935, d. 2020) a member of the Royal Family and politician who served as prime minister from January 1970 until his death in 2020. He was thought to be the longest-serving prime minister in the world. He took office over a year before Bahrain's independence in August 1971. Under the 2002 Constitution he lost some of his powers. He was also the uncle of the reigning King Hamad bin Isa al-Khalifa and great-uncle of Crown Prince Salman.

al-Khalifa, Mohammed bin Essa: was appointed as Political and Economic Advisor to the Crown Prince's Court in 2012. He was also Chief Executive of the Economic Development Board of Bahrain from 2005 until 2012, and was responsible for ensuring the continued growth and stimulation of the Bahraini economy. He also chairs the Tamkeen (Bahrain Labour Fund) and is a Board member of the Crown Prince's International Scholarship Programme, the Economic Development Board of Bahrain and of Gulf Air. He has also chaired The Young Arab Leaders' Bahrain chapter and Bahrain Polytechnic. He holds a Bachelor's degree in Economic Theory from the American University in Washington DC and a Post Graduate Diploma in Business Studies from the London School of Economics.

al-Khalifa, Mohammed bin Khalifa bin Salman: Hakim (Ruler) from 1834–1842, 1849–1868 and in 1869 (one year only). Mohammed served as governor of Manama.

When his father, Khalifa bin Salman, died in 1834, Mohammed succeeded him as the co-ruler. In 1842 Mohammed challenged the reign of his grand uncle Abdullah bin Ahmed al-Khalifa and declared himself Ruler of both Bahrain and Qatar. Shortly afterwards in 1842 Mohammed was defeated in the battle of al-Nasfah against Abdullah and sought refuge in what was known as the Emirate of Najd.

In early 1843 Mohammed returned to Qatar and then to Bahrain, where in April 1843 he defeated Abdullah and once again became Ruler in 1849.

There followed a period where Mohammed paid an annual tribute to the Emir of Najd. However, in 1850 he

NOTES

failed to pay the amount. Failing to obtain Persian support, Mohammed and his brother Ali were forced by the British Resident to sign a convention which, in 1861 saw Bahrain integrated into the framework of the Trucial System. In 1868 Mohammed was forced to abdicate by the British after an alleged violation of the 1861 convention which prevented him from carrying out maritime piracy. In 1867 he and the sheikhs of Abu Dhabi had together attacked the coast of Qatar. Mohammed was succeeded by his brother, Ali bin Khalifa al-Khalifa, who himself was killed by the forces of Mohammed bin Abdullah al-Khalifa in 1869.

al-Khalifa, Mohammed bin Mubarak: (born 1935) an experienced Bahraini politician and a member of the Royal Family. He served as foreign minister from 1970 to 2005, and has been deputy prime minister since 2005.

al-Khalifa, Sabrika bint Ibrahim: (b. 1948) wife and queen consort of Hamad bin Isa bin Salman al-Khalifa, the current (2022) King of Bahrain and mother of Crown Prince Salman bin Hamad bin Isa al-Khalifa. As head of the Supreme Council for Women, she campaigns for women's political rights in Bahrain and their role in business. She has also addressed the United Nations in her capacity as chief patron of the Society for Women and Children in Bahrain.

al-Khalifa, Salman bin Hamad bin Isa: (b. 1894, d. 1961) ruled as Hakim

of Bahrain from 1942–1961. He was Knight Commander of the British Order of the Indian Empire and of the British Order of St Michael and St George.

al-Khalifa, Salman bin Hamad bin Isa: (b. 1969), appointed Crown Prince in March 2013 and in November 2020 was appointed as Prime Minister after the death of his great uncle, Prime Minister Prince Khalifa bin Salman who had held the position for nearly fifty years. He is also the deputy supreme commander of the Bahrain Defence Force.

Khalij (aka Khaleej): Arab word for 'Gulf' as in Khalij al-Arabi (or Khalij al-Farsi mean Persian Gulf).

Khalij al-Bahrain oilfield: in mid-2018 Bahrain announced its biggest ever discovery of oil and gas reserves, amounting to at least 80 billion barrels of tight (shale) oil and estimated gas reserves of between 10–20 trillion cubic feet (roughly the same amount as Russia), according to the National Communication Centre. Bahrain's National Oil and Gas Authority (nogaholding) confirmed that the oil reserves are located in the Khalij al-Bahrain (Gulf of Bahrain) basin, off Bahrain's western coast. The separate discovery of significant gas reserves in two accumulations below Bahrain's main gas reservoir was also confirmed.

This was the largest discovery of oil in the Kingdom since 1932, when extraction started within the Bahrain oilfield.

Khatami, Mohammed: (b. 1943) an Iranian politician who served as president of Iran from August 1997 to August 2005. He had previously also served as Iran's minister of culture from 1982 to 1992.

At the time of his election in 1997 he was considered to be a moderate, determined to improve relations with his Gulf neighbours. Diplomatic relations were restored with Bahrain at the end of 1998 and a number of economic co-operation agreements were signed. Prior to the Presidential election, the Bahrain authorities had accused the Islamic Republic of fomenting trouble among the island's Shi'ite majority. Later, he was critical of the government of President Mahmoud Ahmadinejad (2005–13).

al-Khawaja, Abdulhadi: a prominent human rights defender and the former president of the Bahrain Centre for Human Rights. He has been in prison for over 10 years (2022), serving a life sentence for 'organising and managing a terrorist organisation', among other charges.

al-Khawaja, Maryam: in 2011 Maryam, the acting president of the independent Bahrain Centre for Human Rights, said she was 'very disappointed' by comments, made by the EU's Catherine Ashton. Ms al-Khawaja said that 'the regime barely received a slap on the wrist' from the EU.

al-Khawaja, Zainab: a Bahraini human rights activist and democracy activist. She came to prominence during Bahrain's pro-democracy uprising that commenced in February 2011. In May 2016 Bahrain's judicial authorities ordered the suspension of her sentence on 'humanitarian grounds'.

She had been detained in the Isa Town Women's Prison with her one year old son, for over three months. The charges brought against her included 'destroying public property' after she had destroyed (twice) a picture of the King of Bahrain.

al-Khobar: the Saudi terminal of the King Fahd Causeway, which provides the only land link between Bahrain and Saudi Arabia.

Khomeini, Sayyid Ruhollah Musavi (Ayatollah): (b. 1902, d. 1989) leader of the 1979 Iranian Revolution. Ayatollah Khomeini was a religious scholar and in the 1920s became an ayatollah, a term for leading Shi'a scholars. In 1962 Khomeini was arrested for his opposition to the pro-Western regime of Mohammed Reza Shah Pahlavi. In 1964 he was exiled, living in Turkey, Iraq and finally France, from where he urged his supporters to overthrow the Shah. By the late 1970s, the Shah had become deeply unpopular and there were riots, strikes and mass demonstrations across the country.

In January 1979 the Shah's government collapsed and in February 1979 Khomeini returned to Iran. In a national referendum Khomeini won a landslide victory. He declared an Islamic republic and was appointed

NOTES

Iran's political and religious leader for life.

King Fahd Causeway: in the years preceding its completion in 1986, the link between Bahrain and Saudi Arabia was expected to be of vital importance in rationalising marketing costs. The 25 kilometre, two-lane dual-carriageway was also expected to take a projected 31,000 vehicles a day. Link roads on both sides of the Gulf were constructed in preparation for the target opening in January 1986.

From the Eastern Province on the Saudi side, Western Europe would be only 5,000 kilometres away. The construction of the venture was awarded to the Amsterveen (Netherlands)-based firm Ballast Nedam for US$564 million – which at US$30,000 a metre makes the Saudi-Bahrain causeway the most expensive civil engineering project of its type in the world (reported costs varied up to US$1.2 billion).

The causeway contract featured severe penalty clauses if extended over the 1986 target date. It was named the King Fahd Causeway and opened on 12 November 1986. The venture was funded by Saudi Arabia and the operator is the King Fahd Causeway Authority (KFCA).

King Faisal Corniche, (the Corniche): in the heart of Manama the Corniche overlooks the sea on the one hand and on the other rubs shoulders with the towers and skyscrapers of Manama.

KIPCO: see Kuwait Projects Company below.

Kobe Steel: of Japan was named at the end of 1981 as prime contractor for the construction of a new pelletising plant in Bahrain to be run by the Arab Iron and Steel Company (AISCO). The plant, which was to be located east of the drydock, will also have its own 100MW power plant and a 3,000 cubic metres per day desalination complex as well as a separate deep-water jetty offshore. Production was expected to total some four million tonnes of pellets a year.

Kuwait, Iraqi invasion of: on the night of 1 August 1990 an Iraqi force crossed into Kuwait without warning. Unprepared, Kuwait's defence forces were rapidly either overwhelmed or destroyed. Some Kuwaiti military retreated to Saudi Arabia, as did the Emir of Kuwait with his family and other government leaders. In less than a day Kuwait City was captured and the Iraqis had established a provincial government. Once its troops and officials were installed, it was soon referred to as Iraq's Southern Governorate. The United Nations Security Council denounced the invasion and demanded Iraq's immediate withdrawal from Kuwait. On 6 August, the Security Council imposed a worldwide ban on trade with Iraq. A military coalition (code name Operation Desert Shield) was formed to eject the Iraqis. The US led coalition was made up of a total of 35 countries, including the USA, Saudi Arabia, the

UK and France (after some hesitation).

The occupying Iraqi army in Kuwait rapidly rose to about 300,000 troops. On 29 November 1990 the UN Security Council passed a resolution authorising the use of force against Iraq if it failed to withdraw by 15 January 1991. Saddam Hussein refused to withdraw his forces from Kuwait, and some 700,000 allied troops, primarily American, prepared in January 1991 for Operation Desert Storm to recover Kuwait. After less than four days, Kuwait was liberated, and most of Iraq's armed forces had either surrendered, retreated to Iraq, or been destroyed. The cost of the war to the United States was estimated by the US Congress to be US$61.1 billion. About US$52 billion of that amount was paid by other countries, of which US$36 billion by Kuwait, Saudi Arabia and other Gulf states.

Kuwait Airways (KAC): Kuwait was the first Gulf state to have its own airline, which in the early 1970s not only flew to Tehran, Bahrain, Dubai and other regional airports, but also to Bombay, London and New York.

Kuwait Foreign Petroleum Exploration Company (KUFPEC): which the Bahrain National Oil Company had a 35-year production sharing agreement. There were times when the two companies thought that positive exploration results were just around the corner.

Kuwait Fund for Arab Economic Development (KFAED): founded in 1961 as the State of Kuwait's agency for the provision and administration of financial and technical assistance to developing countries. The KFAED also administered grants provided by Kuwait's government worth US$1.5 billion, under the framework of the GCC Development Programme.

In December 2019 the KFAED signed a US$100 million loan agreement with Bahrain to help finance the development of a 400-kilovolt (kV) transmission network in Bahrain.

The agreement was part of the financial balance programme signed by Kuwait, Saudi Arabia and the UAE in 2018 with Bahrain. The context of the agreement was the already close Bahrain-Kuwait co-operation, aimed at achieving the Kingdom's long-term plans to secure the electricity and water resources as set out in the Bahrain Economic Vision 2030.

The Minister of Electricity and Water Affairs (EWA) also went on to explain that the project would be instrumental in boosting the capacity and efficiency of power transmission besides tackling the electricity shortage issue and ensuring the safe operation of equipment. The project will also contribute to facilitating the exchange of electric power with the GCC networks.

Kuwait Investment Company (KIC): established in 1961 as the first investment company in Kuwait and the region; its creation coincided with the independence of Kuwait in

NOTES

the same year. The company was something of a role model for the emerging investment industry in Kuwait at the time. The KIC adopted a new strategic plan in 2013, focusing on 'enhancing profitability indicators and shareholders' equity and risk reduction.' During the Iraqi occupation the company announced plans to relocate to Bahrain.

Kuwait Projects Company (KIPCO): an investment holding company in the Middle East and North Africa region. In 2017 KIPCO announced changes to the structure of its Bahrain-based subsidiary, the United Gulf Bank (UGB). These resulted in the establishment of two distinct entities: UGB Holding (which will fully own the existing UGB) and the UGB as a conventional bank governed by the Central Bank of Bahrain (CBB). UGB Holding was to be listed on the Bahrain Bourse, while the UGB was to be de-listed.

labour movements: Bahrain differs from most of its neighbours in that since the discovery of oil in the 1930s organised labour movements have existed in one form or another. Occasional work stoppages and organised strikes were an early response to the inadequate work and accommodation conditions initially introduced by the oil industry.

The first industrial strike in Bahrain was that of Bahrain Petroleum Company (BAPCO) workers in December 1943. At the time BAPCO was a sub-

sidiary of the US Standard Oil Company. In an ironic role inversion, the 1943 strike was successful in large part due to pressure on the company by the Bahraini-British presence. The British government was concerned that the strike might adversely affect the war effort in the Gulf region as a whole.

Later political developments in the 1950s triggered some changes in the Bahraini labour movement. The formation of the General Trade Union (GTU) suggested that the size and influence of the GTU was in fact, a recreation of the wider political leadership, constituted by the National Union Committee (NUC). If the NUC was the overt opposition, the covert opposition was made up of a number of underground groupings of political activists, including a small number of communist activists.

The NUC was formed in 1954 following a series of inter-community disturbances which claimed casualties from both the Sunni and Shi'a communities. The community clashes did little to advance the perceived legitimacy of the opposition both to the British presence and to al-Khalifa rule. Prompted by the popularity of the GTU, the NUC held a series of meetings which adopted a common, 'national unity' platform and presented it to the government and to the British Political Resident. The platform demanded a constitution, an elected legislative assembly, a modern penal code, a constitutional court and the legalisation of labour unions. Some reports suggested that the Bahraini labour union was able to recruit 14,000 Bahraini workers in [its first] three months. The workers' representatives elected to the tripartite commission were entrusted to draw up the first labour code. The NUC/GTU candidates clearly won the election, while their opponents received only some 600 votes out of the 18,000 votes cast.

However, following mass demonstrations in support of Egyptian President Nasser during the 1956 Suez War, the British saw fit to supress both the NUC and the GTU, imprisoning or deporting its leaders and eventually banning all its activities. An inevitable result was the growth of underground movements, suggesting significant disaffection.

The experience of the Iraqi and Iranian militants who had taken refuge in Bahrain in the 1950s stood the nascent Bahraini movements in good stead. This coincided with the growth of the National Liberation Front (NLF), also known as the Communist Party of Bahrain, and the Bahraini section of the Arab Nationalist Movement (later forming part of the Popular Front for the Liberation of Oman and the Arabian Gulf (PFLOAG) as well as the more broadly named Popular Front). Communists and Arab nationalists were prominent in the labour movement following the suppression of the NUC at the end of 1956.

This ban on political activity was not really challenged until March 1965, when the dismissal of scores of BAPCO workers prompted an uprising which demonstrated not only surprising sophistication and militancy, but also serious levels of support for the banned organisations and the key role of the labour movements in the opposition to British rule and the quest for a more equitable social order.

The 'Bahrain Uprising' as it then became known, lasted some three months. A government report stated that: 'Towards the end of March 1965, certain subversive elements took advantage of a strike by the oil company workers over redundancies, to carry out acts such as the attempted blowing up of the oil pipeline to the refinery, the burning of oil company buses, the stoning of European cars, and the destruction by fire of a European warehouse. The strike was settled and with the capture and arrest of the ringleaders of the subversive elements everything was back to normal by mid-April.' The events of 1965 did demonstrate that the bulk of the population, both Shi'a and Sunni, were not on the same page as the Ruling Family and the British officialdom. Although the uprising had ended, widespread labour unrest, in the form of strikes, continued until 1968 when the announcement of an imminent British withdrawal from the Gulf calmed things down. It enabled the hitherto clandestine political organisations to claim Bahrain's declaration of independence in 1971 as their achievement. Expectations of political and social reforms were supported by proposals made by contemporary Bahraini representatives to various Arabian Gulf states' gatherings.

Law of Associations (1989): this stated that all organisations must register with authorities prior to undertaking activities. Used – in the words of one Bahraini activist – 'to interfere, restrict and attempt to control the activities of civic organisations'.

League of Arab States (Arab League): the Arab League was founded in Cairo (where it was headquartered) in 1945 by Egypt, Iraq, Lebanon, Saudi Arabia, Syria, Jordan (Transjordan up to 1950) and Yemen. Member states have to have Arabic as their main language and to consider themselves to be Arabs.

The following countries joined later on the dates shown: Algeria (1962), Bahrain (1971), Comoros (1993), Djibouti (1977), Kuwait (1961), Libya (1953), Mauritania (1973), Morocco (1958), Oman (1971), Qatar (1971), Somalia (1974), South Yemen (1967), Sudan (1956), Tunisia (1958) and the United Arab Emirates (1971). The Palestine Liberation Organisation (PLO) was admitted to membership in 1976. Following its signature of a peace treaty with Israel, Egypt's membership was suspended in 1979 and the League's headquarters was moved from Cairo to Tunis. In 1987

Arab leaders decided to renew diplomatic ties with Egypt. Egypt was readmitted to the League in 1989 and the League's headquarters was moved back to Cairo. The Arab League's boycott of Israel (the Arab Boycott) is a somewhat ineffectual economic measure on the part of Arab League member states in support of Palestine, designed to isolate Israel.

The boycott applies to products and services that originate in Israel, businesses that operate in Israel and businesses that have relationships with other businesses trading in Israel.

The Central Boycott office, originally headquartered in Damascus, has become obsolete and very few states (Syria, Lebanon and Iran) continue to enforce the boycott in any way.

Levey, Stuart: US under secretary of the treasury for terrorism and financial intelligence (2004–11). In February 2008, while visiting Bahrain, Mr Levey reportedly urged Bahrain's monetary officials to exercise 'enhanced due diligence' in guarding against money laundering and nuclear proliferation activities.

low sulphur fuel oil: from 1 January 2020, new regulations on international shipping emissions came into force, reducing the maximum sulphur content of marine fuel oil down to 0.5 per cent, except in the SECA (European) zone where the maximum level is 0.1 per cent.

Luce, (Sir) William GBE KCMG: (b. 1907, d. 1977) worked for the British Government to manage the withdrawal of British troops from the Gulf by the end of 1971. He mediated between Iran and the Gulf states over various disputes and was involved in the formation of the United Arab Emirates and the independence of Bahrain and Qatar.

M-60 Tanks: Bahrain's ground forces took delivery of 60 of the American-made M-60 tanks in 1987 and 1988.

Majlis al-Shura: see Consultative Assembly.

al-Malali, Ahmed: and his fellow detainee Ali al-Arab, were executed on 27 July 2019 despite regional and international protests. The families of the two men were called for exceptional and unscheduled visits on 26 July while the rest of the prison was placed under complete lockdown. Other prisoners were banned from making scheduled calls to their families, in an apparent attempt to restrict the flow of information. These procedures are similar to those followed in January 2017 when three other prisoners were executed, after a seven-year break in the use of the death penalty.

Malinowski, Tom: US Assistant Secretary of State for Democracy, Human Rights and Labour. In August 2014 Mr Malinowski was expelled from Bahrain. The government's decision was endorsed by the Secretary General of the Gulf Co-operation Council (GCC), Abdullatif bin Rashid al-Zayani (a Bahraini) who was reported as saying that Mr Malinowski's actions 'did not reflect the historic bilateral relations between his country and the US'. Mr Malinowski had arrived in Bahrain for a three-day visit. While there, the diplomat had meetings scheduled with al-Wefaq, government officials, and a leading human rights activist, Nabeel Rajab. According to government officials, in meeting al-Wefaq, Mr Malinowski's actions ran 'counter to conventional diplomatic norms'. A later foreign ministry press release endeavoured to smooth over the expulsion by stating that 'The government of Bahrain asserts that this should not in any way affect the two countries' relationship of mutual interests.'

Manama: the capital city of Bahrain which lies on the north-eastern tip of the island and accounts for roughly half the population – 147,074 in the 1973 census, although some estimates put the figure lower, rising to some 650,000 by 2021.

Manama Dialogue: an annual international security and regional diplomatic summit held in Bahrain that brings together high level representation from governments and individuals from across the Middle East and beyond. The 2021 event covered 'key regional security developments ranging from questions about the US security commitment to the region, the growing relationship between the

NOTES

Gulf and Asia, the cautious optimism around de-escalation efforts, the potential role of 'minilateral' diplomacy in the region, and a renewed focus on the Red Sea as a geopolitical arena with its own unique dynamics.'

al-Manbar al-Islami: a Sunni political grouping which in the March 2014 elections represented Islamists affiliated with the Muslim Brotherhood. Not one of its candidates (standing under the aegis of the al-Fatih Coalition) were elected despite their apparent pro-government popularity during and following the anti-government street protests. The apparent collapse of support for these often populist pro-government groupings came as something of a surprise.

Mecca (Makkah): a Saudi Arabian city where the Kaaba (also Ka'ba, and Kabah) the sacred house of Islam, is located at the centre of Masjid al-Haraam (the Holy or Grand Mosque). Followers of Islam make a pilgrimage (Haj) to Mecca. The city is located in and is the capital of Makkah Province, in Hejaz region.

Midal Cables: a joint venture between Olex Cables Company of Australia and the Bahraini merchant family A A Zayani. The company was the first operation to produce stranded aluminium power transmission and distribution cables for the Gulf markets.

Middle East (aka Near East): the region between Egypt in the west and Iran in the east, Turkey in the north

and Oman/Yemen and South Sudan in the south. Saudi Arabia is the largest middle-eastern nation and Bahrain the smallest in area.

Egypt is the largest by population (2021 estimate 101.48 million) followed by Iran (2021 population estimate 85.17 million). Bahrain has the smallest population (2020 census 1,501,636 million).

Middle East (Annual) Review: first published in 1974, an annual title of the UK reference publisher World of Information, in which much of the information published in this volume first appeared.

Middle East Economic Digest (MEED): magazine and business information publisher founded in London by Elizabeth Collard in 1957 as a weekly magazine. Owned for some years by the EMAP conglomerate, in December 2017, MEED was purchased by GlobalData of the UK. The magazine is now headquartered in Dubai.

Middle East Engineering Ltd: the Bahrain-based regional company of General Electric (USA).

Middle East and North Africa (MENA): group of countries usually said to include Algeria, Bahrain, Djibouti, Egypt, Iran, Iraq, Israel, Jordan, Kuwait, Lebanon, Libya, Malta, Morocco, Oman, Qatar, Saudi Arabia, Syria, Tunisia, United Arab Emirates, Palestine, and Yemen.

Mina Salman/Mina Sulman: one of Bahrain's major cargo ports and custom points with 15 container berths within an 80 hectare site. In

2018, Britain opened a US$60 million naval base at the port.

Mina Salman Port Development Scheme: this was originally planned to coincide with the opening of the King Fahd Causeway to Saudi Arabia. However the 1986 slump in government revenues caused by the fall in oil prices forced the Bahraini government to review its budget expenditure levels.

Ministry of Information Affairs (MIA): was created under the Royal Decree No 83 in 2014. It is responsible for setting Bahrain's media policies and regulating the media and communication sector.

In 2011, the MIA's predecessor, the Information Affairs Authority (IAA), was heavily criticised for its response to what, in the wider context of the Arab Spring, became known as the Bahrain Uprising.

The report issued in November 2011 by the Bahrain Independent Commission of Inquiry stated that having reviewed a selection of material from national television, radio and print media relating to the events of February/March 2011, the Commission noted that much of this material contained derogatory language and inflammatory coverage of events, and some may have been defamatory.' However, the Commission did not find evidence of media coverage that constituted hate speech. The Commission also identified numerous examples of defamation, harassment and, in some cases, incitement through social media websites. Both pro- and anti-government journalists were targeted through social media. The Commission also noted that six of the seven daily newspapers are pro-government and the broadcasting service is state-controlled. There was also sufficient evidence to suggest that the [Government of Bahrain] exercised censorship over local media outlets.

The lack of adequate access to mainstream media creates frustration within opposition groups and results in these groups resorting to other media outlets such as social media.

This can have a destabilising effect, because social media outlets are both untraceable and unaccountable, even in extreme cases where they promulgate hate speech and incitement to violence.

Ministry of Labour and Social Affairs: established to provide distinct labour and social services for the beneficiaries through government initiatives and partnerships by local professional experts 'to ensure sustainability, fairness and competitiveness' in the context of Bahrain's Vision 2030.

Ministry of Social Development: according to Human Rights Watch (HRW) (see above) the Ministry 'has far exceeded international standards in its restrictive scope' and 'routinely exploited its oversight role to stymie the activities of NGOs and other civil society organisations'.

NOTES

Monarchy: Bahrain became a hereditary constitutional monarchy on 14 February 2002 when Sheikh Hamad bin Isa al-Khalifa declared himself King.

Moody's: an American business and financial services company. It is the holding company for Moody's Investors Service, an American credit rating agency,

Moore, Alan: the first chairman of ALBA and later director general of the Bahrain Monetary Agency 1975–80.

Morland, Lewis: a well-known cartoonist and artist commissioned to design a set of 12 stamps for the Bahrain government when the postal service became independent in 1966. Mr Morland also produced the first book of cartoons to be published in the GCC, in addition to painting the first formal portrait of Sheikh Salman bin Hamad al-Khalifa, the late ruler (1894–1961). A book of Morland's cartoons – *Bahrain Laughs* – was published in 1978. The 54 cartoons had first appeared in the *Gulf Weekly Mirror*, the first local English language newspaper to be published in the Gulf.

Most Favoured Nation: a most favoured nation (MFN) clause requires a country to provide any concessions, privileges, or immunities granted to one nation in a trade agreement to all other World Trade Organisation (WTO) member countries.

al-Moumen, Qassim Abdullah Ali: allegedly the principal coordinator for the foreign military training within the Saraya al-Ashtar (SaA) who studied at Hawza al-Imam Zain al-'abidin in Bani Jamrah in Bahrain. He is the uncle of Ali Ahmed Abdullah al-Moumen who was among the first to be killed during the 2011 uprising. Nephew Ali became a 'martyr' for the uprising in Bahrain and his death created a following within the Bahraini community.

Mubarak, Hosni: Egyptian president and military leader 1981–2011, following the assassination of his predecessor and political mentor Anwar Sadat. Mubarak followed many of Sadat's policies notably that of rapprochement with Israel. Internally, Mubarak's principal challenge was that of militant Islamists, although under his presidency the Muslim Brotherhood was granted increased freedoms.

Muharram: the first month of the Islamic calendar and one of the four sacred months when warfare is forbidden. It is held to be the second holiest month after Ramadan. The tenth day of Muharram is known as Ashura.

Al-Muharraq city: Bahrain's third largest city, located on Muharraq Island just north-east of Bahrain's capital city Manama. Situated on the waterfront, it has many fine buildings including Sheikh Isa bin Ali House, the Siyadi Mosque and the fifteenth century Arad Fort. The city is home to the National Museum and to the country's leading football club.

Muntakalat: Bahrain's state holding company which in 2007 pulled off a high profile coup in persuading the Formula One car race organisers to choose Bahrain for the region's Grand Prix. Muntakalat also has a 30 per cent shareholding in the McClaren Formula One operation, which helped secure this development.

Muslim: a follower of Islam. The older term Mohammedan should be avoided.

Muslim Brotherhood (Ikhwan al-Muslimin): an Islamic revivalist movement founded in 1928 by Hasan al-Banna, following the collapse of the Ottoman Empire. The Brotherhood grew as a popular movement over the next 20 years, encompassing not only religion and education, but also politics. It later began to carry out terrorist acts inside Egypt, which led to a ban on the movement by the Egyptian government. A member of the group assassinated the prime minister of Egypt, Mahmud Fahmi Nokrashi, in December 1948.

The Egyptian government legalised the Brotherhood in 1948, but only as a religious organisation; it was banned again in 1954 following its insistence that Egypt be governed under Sharia (Islamic law). In 1964, President Gamal Abdel Nasser granted an amnesty to the Brotherhood, however the leaders of the Brotherhood were executed in 1966, and many others were imprisoned. Nasser's successor, Anwar Sadat, promised the Brothers that Sharia would be implemented as the Egyptian law and released all of the Broth-

erhood prisoners; however, the Brothers lost their trust in Sadat when he signed the peace agreement with Israel in 1979; four Brothers assassinated Sadat in September 1981.

The 2011 Arab Spring gave the Brotherhood a degree of respectability and even political power at first, but by 2013 it had suffered severe setbacks. In 2012 the Egyptian Muslim Brotherhood won several elections, including the presidential election when its candidate Mohamed Morsi became Egypt's president. One year later, he was overthrown by the military. The group was then banned in Egypt and declared a terrorist organisation. By 2015 the principal state backers of the Muslim Brotherhood were Qatar and Turkey. In 2015 it was considered a terrorist organisation by the government of Bahrain, as well as those of Egypt, Russia, Syria, Saudi Arabia and the United Arab Emirates.

Najadi, Hussain: founder and chief executive of the Arab Asian Bank which in 1985 appeared to be in trouble. Mr Najadi was jailed and the bank was sold for US$1.00 to the Saudi-owned Middle East Financial Group (MEFG).

Najd (aka Nejd): the geographical central region of Saudi Arabia and location of the country's capital city, Riyadh. The Najd accounts for almost a third of Saudi Arabia's population.

Nasser, Gamal Abdul: (b. 1918, d. 1970) Egyptian prime minister 1954–56, president 1956–70. On be-

NOTES

coming president, Nasser embarked on a programme of confiscation of farm land from Egypt's rich landowners, as well as nationalising banks and industries and the Suez Canal. After the abortive attempt by Britain and France to retain control of the canal (the 1956 Suez Crisis), Nasser ended the British presence in Egypt, following peace negotiations.

National Action Charter: in October 2000 the Crown Prince, Sheikh Salman bin Hamad bin Isa al-Khalifa, announced the introduction of a new National Charter, which would see the Majlis al-Shura replaced by a national assembly elected by universal suffrage. Elections were scheduled for 2004. At the time it was not clear if political parties would be allowed, or whether the new assembly, like the Majlis al-Shura, was to be limited to a purely advisory role. One controversial aspect of the Charter was its stated 'respect for human rights'. Intended to end the popular protests seen in the 1990s and return the country to constitutional rule, it was approved in a national referendum in 2001, in which 98.4 per cent of the voters voted in favour of the document.

National Assembly (Parliament): The first ever National Assembly in Bahrain was elected in 1973 under the statutes of the first constitution which was promulgated in the same year. In 1975 the Assembly was dissolved by the then Emir Sheikh Isa bin Salman al-Khalifa because it re-

fused to pass the government sponsored State Security Law of 1975. The Emir subsequently did not allow the Assembly to meet again or hold elections during his lifetime. After his death in 1999, his son Sheikh Hamad bin Isa al-Khalifa, the new ruler of Bahrain, promulgated the Constitution of 2002. That same year elections were held for the Council of Representatives and Sheikh Hamad appointed the members for the Consultative Council, forming the first National Assembly since 1975.

National Bank of Bahrain: founded in 1957 as Bahrain's first locally owned bank (owned jointly by the government and the private sector) and playing a key role in the local and Gulf economies with branches in Abu Dhabi and Riyadh. Publicly listed on the Bahrain Bourse, 44 per cent of the bank is government owned, nearly 45 per cent owned by shareholders and the remainder by the Social Insurance Organisation. It is ranked number three in Bahrain – by market capitalisation of US$2.21 billion (2018).

National Democratic (Labour) Action Society (NDLAS) (Wa'ad): emerged from the Popular Front for the Liberation of Bahrain In 2002, a clandestine opposition movement of socialist and Arab nationalist orientation. Under the reform movement begun by King Hamad, the exiled leaders of the Popular Front returned in 2002 to participate in the political process through the NDLAS, which was the first legitimate political group in the Arabian Gulf. However the NDLAS boycotted the 2002 parliamentary elections, but took part in the 2006 parliamentary election. In 2017, the party was banned on terrorism charges. The ban was criticised by Amnesty International and the Bahrain Institute for Rights and Democracy.

National Liberation Front (NLF): founded in February 1955, also known as the Communist Party.

National Museum: the Bahrain National Museum was officially opened in December 1988. At the time it was considered one of the finest museums of its kind in the Gulf region. It has long been one of the island's main cultural landmarks. Designed by the architects Krohn and Hartvig Rasmussen of Denmark, the outstanding building is characterised by its white travertine marble facade and is centrally located on an artificial peninsula overlooking the island of Muharraq. The museum complex is composed of two connected buildings with approximately 20,000 square metres of floor space. The main building houses the permanent exhibition area, temporary exhibition halls, an art gallery, a lecture hall, gift shop and café. The Museum is the repository of 6,000 years of Bahrain's history.

National Oil and Gas Authority (NOGA): established in 2005 to assume responsibility for all matters related to oil and gas in the Kingdom. The role of NOGA is to preserve Bahrain's natural resources of oil and gas, to find alternatives and to utilise such resources to achieve a maximum return. It mainly focuses on the regulation of the petroleum and associated industries in Bahrain and on the development of related industries.

National Union Committee: formed in the early 1950s, its membership was drawn from both the Sunni and Shi'a communities. Quoted in *Bahrain's Uprising*, the British Political Agent at the time, Charles Belgrave, wrote that 'the NUC declared that there were no longer any divisions between Sunnis and Shi'a, and that all people in Bahrain were merged in the popular movement.'

The NUC was surprisingly successful in a number of ways. It established Bahrain's first labour union, with 14,000 members signed up during the first three months of existence. It called upon the government to introduce an elected parliament, to allow labour to organise into unions, a codified legal system and the removal of Charles Belgrave and the British influence from the Island. In 1956 members of the Committee, lead by Abd al-Rahman al-Bakir, were put on trial for an alleged attempt to assassinate the Ruler.

Nationalist Democratic Rally: a political group founded in 1991 with close links to the Iraqi-based Ba'ath Party in Bahrain. The organisation is part of a four party opposition alliance opposing the government, which comprises two Shi'a Islamist parties, Al-Wefaq and the Islamic Action Society and the former Maoist National Democratic Action.

natural gas liquids (NGL): a term for those hydrocarbons in the same family of molecules as natural gas and crude oil, composed exclusively of carbon and hydrogen. Ethane, propane, butane, isobutane, and pentane are all NGLs. There are many uses for NGLs, spanning nearly all sectors of the economy.

Near East (aka Middle East): (aka Near East) the region between Egypt in the west and Iran in the east, Turkey in the north and Oman/Yemen and South Sudan in the south. Saudi Arabia is the largest middle-eastern nation and Bahrain the smallest in area. Egypt is the largest by population (2021 estimate 101.48 million) followed by Iran (2021 population estimate 85.17 million). Bahrain has the smallest population (2020 census 1,501,636 million).

Nejd: (aka Najd, see above).

Nikko Securities Company: applied in 1988 to upgrade its representative office to one of a full investment bank. In contrast to the trend of Western financial institutions cutting back their operations in Bahrain, Japanese securities houses were expanding strongly, to capitalise on the Gulf demand for yen-based stocks and bonds.

Nimr al-Nimr: a Saudi Arabian Shi'a cleric executed in early 2016 to-

gether with 46 alleged opponents of the Saudi Arabian government. This followed an attack on the Saudi Arabian embassy in Tehran.

nogaholding: the Kingdom's hydrocarbon and energy investment and development arm. It plays a key role in the implementation of the government's investment strategies.

non-associated gas: natural gas that is produced from a natural gas well, rather than an oil well.

North American Free Trade Area (NAFTA): in September 2018, the United States, Mexico, and Canada reached an agreement to replace NAFTA with the United States-Mexico-Canada Agreement (USMCA), and all three countries had ratified it by March 2020. NAFTA remained in force until the USMCA was implemented on 1 July 2020.

North Atlantic Treaty Organisation (NATO): an intergovernmental military alliance created between 29 North American and European countries in 1949 after the Second World War. In 2004 Bahrain was given the informal status of 'major non-Nato ally' of the United States, placing Bahrain among a very small group of nations which enjoy this status, including Jordan and Egypt.

al-Nusra Front: a Syrian Islamist grouping that featured on the Bahraini government's list of 68 terrorist movements.

OAPEC dry dock: a Bahrain facility planned in 1973 and established in

1977, to be operated by a consortium of Portugese (Lisnave) and Japanese ship-repairers.

offshore banking units (OBU): in January 1988, the Finance and National Economy Minister, Ibrahim Abdul-Karim Muhammad, estimated that the OBUs contributed BD200 million (US$530 million) to the economy each year.

Oil & Gas Journal (OGJ): a petroleum industry weekly publication with a worldwide coverage and readership. It is headquartered in Tulsa, Oklahoma (USA) with offices in Houston, Texas (USA).

Oman (Sultanate of): Oman's area is 82,000sq miles and in 2021 the Sultanate had an estimated population of 5.16 million. Oman also shares borders with Saudi Arabia to the west, and Yemen to the south-west, the United Arab Emirates to the north-west as well as marine borders with Iran and Pakistan.

Haitham bin Tariq al-Said became Sultan on 11 January 2020, following the death of his cousin Qaboos bin Said bin Taimur on 10 January. Qaboos had been ruler since 1970.

Oman Air: the flagship company of the Sultanate of Oman's Civil Aviation sector, commenced operations in 1993.

Starting off as a regional player, Oman Air has witnessed rapid growth, making Muscat a major traffic hub in the Middle East providing a fillip to commercial, industrial and tourism activities.

Organisation of Arab Petroleum Exporting Countries (OAPEC): Kuwait, Libya and Saudi Arabia signed an agreement in January 1968 in Beirut establishing OAPEC. By 1982 the membership of the Organisation had risen to eleven (Algeria, Bahrain, Egypt, Iraq, Kuwait, Libya, Qatar, Saudi Arabia, Syria, Tunisia and the UAE).

Members are Arab countries which rely on the export of petroleum. OAPEC is head-quartered in Kuwait, and is concerned with the development of the petroleum industry by fostering co-operation among its members. The Organisation's mission statement states that it 'is guided by the belief in the importance of building an integrated petroleum industry as a cornerstone for future economic integration among Arab countries'.

Organisation of the Petroleum Exporting Countries: (OPEC) head-quartered in Vienna, Austria. OPEC's members in 2022 were: Algeria, Angola, Congo, Equatorial Guinea, Gabon (suspended membership in 1994 and re-joined in 2016), Iran, Iraq, Kuwait, Libya, Nigeria, Saudi Arabia, UAE and Venezuela (Indonesia had suspended its membership in January 2009; Qatar terminated its membership on 1 January 2019). Described by its critics as a cartel, OPEC's best-known activity is the determination of members' production levels in the light of world supply and demand conditions. In early 2009 OPEC controlled some 76 per cent of world reserves and produced nearly 28 million barrels per day (33 per cent of world consumption). Members of OPEC have their production constrained by the organisation's production targets, in theory. The OPEC+ alliance consists of the 13 OPEC members plus 10 of the world's major non-OPEC oil-exporting nations. It aims to regulate the supply of oil in order to set the price on the world market.

Oryx: There are four species of oryx living in Africa and the Middle East. They are large antelopes with long, spear-like horns. The gemsbok (oryx gazella) is the largest of the oryx species. They are a true desert animal, with a thick, horse-like neck, a short mane, and a compact, muscular body. A defined pattern of black markings that contrast with their white face and fawn-coloured body are prominently displayed during dominance rituals to emphasise the length of their horns and the strength of their shoulders. In addition to the mainland Arabian Peninsula Arabian oryxes, they have also been reintroduced on to Bahrain's Hawar Island. In 2019 the total reintroduced population was estimated to be around 1,000.

Pahlavi Régime (Dynasty) (Iran): the Pahlavi dynasty was the last Iranian royal dynasty, ruling for 54 years between 1925 and 1979. It was founded by a non-aristocratic soldier (Reza Khan) who adopted the name of the Pahlavi language once spoken in the pre-Islamic Sasanian Empire in order to burnish his nationalist credentials.

The Pahlavi dynasty eventually replaced the Qajars in the early 1920s, when the 41-year-old Reza Khan, was promoted by the British General Ironside to lead the British-run Persian Cossack Brigade. Shortly after, under British direction, Reza Khan's 3,000–4,000 strong detachment of the Cossack Brigade reached Tehran in what became known as the 1921 *coup d'état*.

The rest of the country was taken by 1923, and by October 1925 the Majlis (Iranian parliament) decided to depose and exile the ruling Ahmed Shah Qajar. The Majlis named Reza Pahlavi as the new Shah of Iran on 12 December 1925, according to the Persian Constitution of 1906. Reza Pahlavi had originally planned to declare the country a republic, but abandoned the idea in the face of British and clerical opposition. Under pressure from the British, in 1941 Reza Shah abdicated and was despatched into exile, first in Mauritius, then in South Africa. He was replaced by his son Mohammad Reza Pahlavi who was overthrown in 1979.

Palestine: a highly politicised area of the eastern Mediterranean region consisting of the territories making up the modern state of Palestine, including the Gaza Strip and the West Bank (the West of the Jordan River),

Israel and to some people parts of Jordan itself. Parts of the region are known as the Holy Land and are of religious importance to the Christian, Muslim and Jewish faiths. However, since the First World War, religious claims on all or parts of the region have lead to conflicts, massacres and wars.

Palestine Liberation Organisation (PLO): mediation by the PLO in the autumn of 1979 seemed at first to have improved the strained relations between Bahrain and Iran. By the end of the year, however, the resignation of the civilian government in Tehran, the taking of the American hostages at the embassy, and the increasing power of the clergy again led to a revival of Iranian claims to the islands.

Pearl diving: for centuries Bahrain was the recognised centre of the Middle East's pearling industry. Once a major source of income for Bahrain's population, pearl diving was killed off, as elsewhere in the Gulf, by Japan's cultivated pearls and, more importantly, by the advent of oil, which was discovered in Bahrain in 1932. According to Parker T Hart, who in the mid-twentieth century served as US Consul General in Dhahran (Saudi Arabia), pre-petroleum, Bahrain was in some years thought to have the highest per-capita income in the world.

Pearl Roundabout (aka Pearl Square) (Dowar al-Lulu): in February 2011 the Bahrain Online website urged Bahrainis to participate in a 'Day of Rage' on 14 February to demand a 'new constitution written by the people'.

This triggered a fearful government to announce a 1,000 dinar payment to every Bahraini family, a gesture that angered rather than mollified a disaffected population. The Pearl Roundabout was chosen as the venue because of its accessibility, and its proximity to downtown Manama and to the capital's neighbouring villages. Thousands of protestors made their way to the roundabout. After three days of protest, on 17 February government forces attacked the protestors without warning. Somehow, the order to open fire was given, and four demonstrators were killed. Thus, the Pearl Roundabout became a national symbol – occupied for some days by government tanks. In the face of international protest, the government withdrew its tanks from the roundabout. The return of the civilian protestors transformed the Pearl monument into a symbol.

Peninsula Shield: since the establishment of the Gulf Co-operation Council (GCC), in May 1981, the member states have been developing a unified air defence strategy, and in 1984 the Peninsula Shield rapid development force was set up. Some 5,000 men were deployed in Saudi Arabia's strategically important Eastern Province, acting as the mainstay of the Shield.

Persian sovereignty (over Bahrain): Bahrain came into the Persian

NOTES

sphere of influence for the first time in the Sasanian period (224–651). After the Portuguese occupation (1521–1602), it again fell under Persian domination for almost two centuries, despite several Omani invasions, in 1718 and 1738, which caused major devastation and the abandonment of villages, as mentioned by the German explorer Carsten Niebuhr, in the 1760s.

In 1753 the island was re-occupied by the Persians, who remained in charge until 1783, when it was conquered by the Arab dynasty of al-Khalifa, of mainland Bedouin stock descended from the Qajaris.

Iranian claims to the island were renewed several times subsequently, notably at the time of the 1861 and 1871 treaties which established the British protectorate in Bahrain and marked the Turkish conquest of the Hasa in 1871. They were finally abandoned only after a mission of mediation by the United Nations (UN) in 1971, when the emirate achieved its independence.

The urban population, concentrated around the al-Khalifa dynasty in the two cities of Manama and Muharraq, is Sunni. The rural population is Shi'a and is generally estimated at about half or more of the indigenous population. This predominance has given rise to the widely held view that most Shi'a are of Iranian origin and to speak Persian among themselves. But Shi'ism is, in fact, very old on the north-eastern

coast of Arabia and Bahrain. During the Persian domination in the seventeenth and eighteenth centuries, religious influence seems to have flowed mainly from Bahrain to Iran, rather than the reverse.

petrodollars: US dollars paid to an oil-exporting country for the sale of oil, or simply, an exchange of oil for US dollars.

Political Agent: The establishment by the British of the Bahrain Political Agency in 1900 strengthened British interest in the Persian Gulf, establishing a template for increased economic and political involvement in the 20th century. Reporting to Britain's senior official in the Persian Gulf at Bushire, the Bahrain Political Agent helped formulate policies that affected not only Bahrain, but the wider Gulf.

Housed in a structure built at the turn of the century in Manama, the Bahrain Political Agency was altered and enlarged until 1955 when it was replaced by a more modern structure.

Popular Front for the Liberation of Bahrain (PFLB): underground political party created from the split of the Popular Front for the Liberation of Oman and the Arabian Gulf into Popular Front for the Liberation of Oman and the PFLB. It had its origins in the Arab Nationalist Movement.

potline: An inter-connected row of electrolytic reduction pots used in the smelting of aluminium.

Pro-Israeli Lobby: the closeness of the relationship between Manama and Washington in the 1980s provided Bahrain with access to pieces of advanced US military technology which were denied to some of their neighbours by the pro-Israeli lobby in the US Congress. In particular, Bahrain bought a squadron of F-16 fighters in 1988 to bolster its fledgling air force.

al-Qaeda: an Islamist terrorist movement based in Afghanistan and responsible for the 2001 Twin Tower attack in New York. Al-Qaeda and its branches in Yemen and North Africa were prominent on the list of 68 terrorist groupings featured on a list prepared by the Bahraini government.

Qatar: (population 2,788,677, World Bank 2018) 10,500sq km in area Qatar is a peninsula some 160km long, 90km wide. It has land frontiers with both the UAE and Saudi Arabia, and a maritime border with Bahrain. As was the case with most of the Trucial States, in the nineteenth century Qatar suffered from the decline of the pearling industry. Oil was discovered in Qatar some 15 years earlier than in the UAE.

It was almost the last Gulf sheikhdom (Fujairah's recognition was later), to be recognised as an independent state. In terms of social development, Qatar had also been seen as one of the least advanced of the Gulf States. As the pace of development picked up, Qatar's natural inclination was to model itself on Kuwait, its fellow Sunni state to the north, although the Qataris had traditionally been close to Saudi Arabia.

In mid-2017 Qatar found itself accused by GCC member countries Saudi Arabia and the UAE of an allegedly close relationship with (Shi'a) Iran and of supporting the Islamist Muslim Brotherhood. In June 2017 a blockade was imposed by Saudi Arabia, Bahrain, UAE and Egypt (the Quartet) stopping flights between Qatar and the other GCC countries. Sea-routes were also closed and Qatari nationals living in the other GCC countries were threatened with repatriation.

The Quartet alleged that Qatar was supporting terrorist organisations; Qatar denied this. The blockade threatened to cause Qatar severe economic problems.

The blockade was lifted after agreement was reached at a GCC summit meeting in al-Ula (Saudi Arabia) in January 2021. Diplomatic relations were restored.

In 2012 (FIFA) announced that Qatar would be the first country in the Middle East to hold the FIFA World cup final, in 2022. Despite opposition to holding the event in the extreme heat in a small, but rich, country, seven new stadia and surrounding infrastructure were constructed, mostly using immigrant labour. Numerous complaints were made against the contractors for the mis-treatment and under-payment of the workers, a number of whom died during the construction period.

NOTES

al-Qauod, Lateefah: the first woman elected (in 2006) to parliament in Bahrain.

Qit'at Jaradah: an extremely small island situated within the 12-mile limit of both Bahrain and Qatar. According to a report commissioned by Bahrain, at high tide its length and breadth are about 12 by 4 metres, whereas at low tide they can reach 600 by 75 metres. At high tide, its 'altitude' is approximately 0.4 metres. Bahrain claimed that Qit'at Jaradah is under Bahraini sovereignty, since it has displayed its authority over it in various ways, and that this was recognised by the British government in 1947. In this respect it has referred to a number of activities, including the erection of a beacon, the ordering of the drilling of an artesian well, the granting of an oil concession, and the licensing of fish traps.

On the other hand, Qatar contended that Qit'at Jaradah, being a low-tide elevation, cannot be appropriated, and that, since it is situated in the part of the territorial sea which belongs to Qatar, Qatar has sovereign rights over it.

In the judgement of the International Court of Justice (ICJ) certain types of activities invoked by Bahrain such as the drilling of artesian wells would, taken by themselves, be considered controversial as acts performed *à titre de souverain*. The construction of navigational aids, on the other hand, can be legally relevant in the case of very small islands. In the present case, taking into account the size of Qit'at Jaradah, the activities carried out by Bahrain on that island must be considered sufficient to support Bahrain's claim that it has sovereignty over it.

Rabeea, Falah: a leading light of the human rights group Bahrain Salam who claimed in 2013 that 'A country that orders more canisters of tear gas than it has people does not seem committed to reform.'

Rajab, Nabeel: with Abdulhadi al-Khawaja in 2002 Rajab formed the Bahrain Centre for Human Rights.

Rapid Deployment Force (RDF) aka the Rapid Deployment Joint Task Force (RDJTF): an American inspired Gulf wide project drawn up in 1980 (but later de-activated in 1983), the aim of which was the deterrence, essentially against any possible Soviet or proxy invasion in the Gulf thereby 'maintaining regional stability and the Gulf oil-flow westward'. Its area of responsibility included Egypt, Sudan, Djibouti, Ethiopia, Kenya and Somalia as well as Afghanistan, Bahrain, Iran, Iraq, Kuwait, Oman, Pakistan, the People's Republic of Yemen, Qatar, Saudi Arabia, United Arab Emirates and the Yemen Arab Republic. The RDF was later re-organised as the United States Central Command (USCENTCOM).

Ras Tanura: population 153,933 (2018). A Saudi Arabian refinery and port city in Saudi Arabia's Eastern

Province and connected to Abqaiq by pipeline. Ras Tanura was developed by Saudi Aramco (known at the time as the Arabian American Oil Company) after the discovery of nearby oil deposits in the 1930s. It is the principal Gulf pipeline terminal and is capable of accommodating very large tankers.

Ras Tanura is also the location of a major refinery and storage tanks as well as hydro-formers, producing high-octane gasoline.

Reagan, Ronald: (b. 1911, d. 2004) United States President 1981–89. In September 1987, President Reagan wrote to the Emir, Sheikh Isa bin Sulman al-Khalifa, specifically to thank him for Bahrain's support for the US military presence in the Gulf.

REDEC: see Saudi Research and Development Corporation.

refining: the history of refining in Bahrain dates back to 1937 with the opening in Sitra by Sheikh Hamad bin Isa al-Khalifa of the first Bahrain Refinery, with a capacity of 10,000 barrels per day. In 1968 the Bahrain Refinery expansion programme was completed, increasing the plant's capacity to 250,000 barrels per day. In 1987 Bahrain considered a plan to upgrade the Bahrain Petroleum Company (BAPCO) refinery in a three-stage scheme costing US$900 million. The plan envisaged enabling the plant to produce gas oil and jet fuel which were expected to be in greater demand in the 1990s than fuel oil and naphta. In 1997 the Bahrain govern-

ment assumed 100 per cent ownership of the Bahrain Refinery. Later modernisation plans were commissioned in 2001, 2004, 2005, 2007, 2008 and 2013.

In 2019 the base oil refinery plant was one of the largest of its kind in the world. Expansion plans have been delayed until 2024 as a result of the Covid-19 pandemic.

Rejectionist Front (States): The Rejectionist Front (aka Front of the Palestinian Forces Rejecting Solutions of Surrender) a political coalition formed in 1974 by radical Palestinian factions who rejected the Ten Point Programme adopted by the Palestine Liberation Organisation (PLO) in its Twelfth Palestinian National Congress (PNC).

residue gases: a mixture of gases derived as by-product from the distillation of crude oil and the processing of oil products in refineries and the chemical industry. The mixture consists mainly of hydrogen, methane, ethane and carbon dioxide.

Resistance Brigades: a less well known opposition grouping that featured on the Bahraini government's 2016 list of 68 'terrorist' groups.

Reuters: (merged in 2008 with the Canadian Thomson Corporation) a Canadian based news agency long respected for its reporting on the Middle East and its Arab language services.

Thomson Reuters has several hundred editorial staff in the Middle East and Africa region. In 2000 the company launched the Reuters Arabic Online Report, a comprehensive multimedia news publication for Arabic language publishers around the world. The service consists of six distinct channels: Top Middle-East News, Top World News, Business, Sport, Entertainment and Technology News. The stories, written in Arabic, are delivered as multimedia news packages created for the needs and interests of Middle East audiences.

Riffa: Bahrain's second largest city; the population has grown from 79,550 in the 2001 census to an estimated 195,606 in 2018. It is a popular tourist destination and is divided into East Riffa and West Riffa. East Riffa is renowned for its shops and souqs, Riffa Fort, the Royal Golf Club, the Bahrain National Stadium and Royal Women's University.

West Riffa includes Bahrain's top residential area being home to members of the royal family, government officials and business investors. The roundabout landmark Riffa Clock Tower is also in West Riffa.

Riyadh: capital city of Saudi Arabia. Population (2018) 7.68 million.

Rohani, Sadiq (Ayatollah): (aka Grand Ayatollah Sayyid Muhammad-Sadiq Husayni Rohani) (b. 1926) an Iranian Shi'a marja'.

He was one of the first senior clerics to be placed under house arrest under direct order from Grand Ayatollah Ruhollah Khomeini after the 1979 Iranian revolution.

Rohani is a critic of the Iranian government today.

Rowad Platform: see Bahrain Development Bank above.

Royal Bahrain Naval Force: a unit of the Bahrain Defence Force (BDF). Based at Mina Salman Naval Base, consists of seven combat vessels, 31 patrol craft, 10 landing ships, two helicopters and over 700 personnel.

Royal Bahraini Air Force: a unit of the Bahrain Defence Force (BDF). Following independence from the UK in 1971, the Royal Bahraini Air Force (RBAF) was formed in 1977. Combat operations have included the 1991/93 Gulf War and more recently the 2015 military intervention in Yemen. By 1992 it had 650 active personnel and this grew to 1,500 personnel by 2009. Latest figures (2018) show a fleet of 129 aircraft with three fighter squadrons, four helicopter quadrons and two training squadrons. The inventory, mostly supplied by the United States, is topped by Bell attack and utility helicopters and F-16 Fighting Falcon combat aircraft. There is an on-going programme to update the fleet.

In October 2017, Bahrain signed a deal to upgrade its F-16 fleet. The forces's four bases are at Muharraq, Riffa, Sakhir and Isa.

Royal Bahraini Army: a unit of the Bahrain Defence Force (BDF). Following almost two centuries of British protection, Bahrain opted for complete independence with the establishment of the BDF in 1971. The

Royal Bahraini Army, headed by Lieutenant General Khalifa bin Abdullah al-Khalifa, is the BDF's ground force element with 18,000 personnel. These ground troops took part in the Saudi Arabian-led intervention in Yemen, the Yemeni Civil War and the Gulf War (1991/93).

Royal Guard: a unit of the Bahrain Defence Force (BDF). Royal security duties.

SaA: see Saraya al-Ashtar below.

Sadat, Anwar: b. 1918, d. 1981. President of Egypt 1970–81. In signing the disengagement agreement with Israel in 1975, Sadat showed that interests prevailed over alliances. The 1978 Camp David Accords, of which Sadat was the architect, certainly left Egypt isolated among the Arab states. With the exception of Sudan's President Nimeiri, no Arab heads of state attended Sadat's funeral. Only two other Arab countries (Somalia and Oman) were represented.

al-Salam Bank-Bahrain (ASBB): founded in 2006, the ASBB is one of the pioneering Sharia-compliant Banks in Bahrain.

It is licensed and regulated by the Central Bank of Bahrain as an Islamic Retail Bank. ASBB was established with paid-up capital of BD120 million (US$318 million) and was the largest IPO in the Kingdom's history with subscriptions reaching over BD2.7 billion (US$7 billion).

Samaan, Alees: the first woman and non-Muslim anywhere in the Arab world to chair a house of parliament. In 2005, Ms Samaan, a Christian, stood in as speaker of Bahrain's upper house, the Majlis al-Shura (Consultative Assembly), by default, as she was the most senior parliamentarian available in the absence of the elected speaker and his deputies.

Salman, Ali: the leader of al-Wefaq, Sheikh Salman and his assistant, Khalil al-Marzouq were charged with holding an illegal meeting in 2014 with Tom Malinowski, the US Assistant Secretary of State for Democracy, Human Rights and Labour. Mr al-Marzouq was eventually cleared of terrorism charges in June 2014, raising hopes that the talks between the government and the opposition could be reinstated. Al-Wefaq, which claimed to advocate non-violent activism, had boycotted talks with the government after Marzouq's arrest in September 2013.

Sanger, Richard: author of *The Arabian Peninsula* (Yale 1954).

Saraya al-Ashtar (SaA) (al-Ashtar Brigades): operations organised and executed by members of this Iranian-backed militia can be traced to 2007.

At that time, acts of violence had been greatly reduced as the result of co-ordinated police actions and high-profile prosecutions. However, a regrouping and incorporation of members of the (dissolved since 2002) Islamic Front for the Liberation of Bahrain (IFLB) was in process.

Although operating without the SaA brand until 2012, the organisation existed as a clandestine unit that took advantage of the mounting troubles in early 2011 to form a new, radicalised terrorist group in Bahrain. As part of their training exercises, young men in the SaA (all from the Shi'a sect) from some of Bahrain's villages (including Sanabis, Sitra, Diraz, Daih, and Bani Jamra) began the process of militarising demonstrations by using political dissent as a means of triggering strategic riots aimed at attacking Bahrain's security forces. The process followed a pattern: first, groups of young men and women would stage a march or protest in one of the Shi'a villages. The police would be present but would not engage with the protesters. From behind the main part of the protest lines, young SaA members would pelt security personnel with stones. The police would then attempt to arrest those engaging in stone throwing, which posed a danger to public safety. In response, the SaA trainees would scatter and regroup behind prearranged street barricades. Tires would be set ablaze and small arsenals of Molotov cocktails would be hurled at security force vehicles and riot police.

The stated objective was the 'overthrow of al-Khalifa rule'. This objective was reiterated in their public discourse and their online platforms, and also was chanted during the pitched battles that they filmed, edited, and released for propaganda

purposes. Even as its capabilities were enhanced, the SaA did not see its numbers swell and, according to Bahrain's Ministry of the Interior, it retained only three attack cells and a similar number of bomb-making workshops at any given time.

Saudi Arabia: (population 35 million in 2021, UN estimate) a significant neighbour of Bahrain and the biggest country in the Middle East covering 2.24 million sq kilometres. Saudi Arabia is home to Islam's holiest shrines in Mecca and Medina. Also, it is the world's largest oil producer. In 1986, the construction – paid for by Saudi Arabia – of the King Fahd Causeway, linking Saudi Arabia with Bahrain, was completed via a series of five bridges.

Saudi Arabia, aid from: in 1996 Saudi Arabia allocated to Bahrain all the resources of the formerly shared (140,000 barrels per day) Abu Safah oilfield. The objective was to steady Bahrain's finances and shore up political stability.

Saudi Arabian Basic Industries Corporation (SABIC): founded in 1976, a Saudi multinational chemical manufacturing company which is a subsidiary of Saudi Aramco. It is active in petrochemicals, chemicals, industrial polymers, fertilisers, and metals. Ranked among the world's largest petrochemicals manufacturers, SABIC is a public company based in Riyadh. 70 per cent of the Company's shares are owned by Saudi Aramco, with the remaining 30 per cent publicly traded on the Saudi stock exchange.

Saudi Bank: founded in 2011 it subsequently bought BMI Bank in 2014. By market capitalisation at US$580 million in 2018 it was one of Bahrain's top ten companies. It owns the real estate company Manara Developments Company.

Saudi Development Fund (SDF): (aka The Saudi Fund for Development (SFD)) a Saudi Arabian government agency that provides development assistance to developing countries by financing social and infrastructure projects with the aim of improving lives and communities. In 2017 the SFD funded a US$10 million school in Hamad Town (Bahrain), with a capacity of 900 students.

Saudi-Kuwaiti Mediation Mission: in the run up to independence in 1971, Bahrain had pursued the concept of a Federation of Arab Emirates (aka Union of Arab Emirates), a planned amalgamation of Bahrain, Qatar and the six Gulf Emirates (Abu Dhabi, Ajman, Dubai, Fujairah, Ras al-Khaimah, Sharjah), all of which were still under the British protectorate in 1971, and Umm al-Qawain.

The draft 1968 federation would have encompassed some 100,000sq km with an estimated population of 375,000. The capital would have been Sharjah and the first head of the Federation would have been the Emir of Bahrain, (at the time Isa bin Salman al-Khalifa). The ruling emirs would have formed a supreme council, the chairmanship of which would have changed annually.

In February 1968 an Agreement of the Federation had been signed in Dubai. However, when it came to agreeing the details of the Federation's constitution, agreement between the signatory states could not be achieved.

In May 1970 a meeting of the UN Security Council confirmed the wish of the Bahraini people to belong to an independent state with full sovereignty and with the ability freely to establish relations with other countries.

The government also decided to terminate all Bahrain's political and military Treaties and Agreements regulating the special treaty relations between the governments of Bahrain and Britain.

In early 1971 the Saudi-Kuwaiti Mediation Mission submitted further amended proposals for a draft constitution. In a bid to overcome the remaining points at issue, the government of Bahrain agreed to an amended version which represented a watered down version from its earlier conditions. A stalemate was reached leaving Bahrain no option but to look for alternatives.

Saudi Research and Development Corporation: (REDEC), the majority of which is owned by Ghaith Pharaon, had surprised the banking world in December 1985 when it suspended payments on its debt to over 40 major international banks. A consortium of

NOTES

International banks met in Bahrain in June 1987 in a bid to recover more than US$330 million in loans to one of Saudi Arabia's most prominent private-sector companies. The creditors of REDEC were to be presented with a plan to reschedule the company's debt. The creditors included Citibank, the Bank of Boston and Manufacturers Hanover Trust.

schadenfreude: a German expression meaning 'to take pleasure from the discomfort of others'.

Schlumberger: in April 2021 the US global energy firm, Schlumberger, was awarded a contract for a Future Production Enhancement Scheme by Tatweer Petroleum. The value of the contract was US$223.4 million. The project is a performance-based extension contract for the Integrated Performance Management of 15 wells following the success of a pilot project in the Awali Field. In December 2020 Tatweer Petroleum had awarded a contract to the project for provision of oil and gas services to the Cementing and Remedial Cementing Stimulation Services. The value of this contract was US$24.9 million.

Schultz, George: (b. 1920, d. 2021). US Secretary of State 1982–89, considered to be on good terms with a number of Gulf rulers and prime ministers.

Seven Sisters: a term coined after the Second World War to describe the world's then seven largest oil companies: Exxon, Gulf, Texaco, Mobil, Socal (all from the USA), BP

(UK), and Shell (Anglo-Dutch). Following the merger of Exxon and Mobil, and the acquisition by Chevron of both Texaco and the production assets of Gulf Oil, the 'seven' eventually became 'four'.

Shah: (see Pahlavi Régime).

al-Shamil Bank: a Bahraini investment bank established in 1998 covering investment, e-commerce, real estate, financial services and insurance. It has branches in Qatar, Dubai, Kuwait, Sudan and Egypt.

al-Shara, Farouk: a prominent official in the Syrian government who served as foreign minister of Syria from 1984 until 2006. Largely due to Mr al-Shara's mediation, tensions between Bahrain and Iran were eased in 1996. However, although the war of words ceased, relations remained tense.

Sharia: Islam's legal system, derived largely from the Koran, and from fatwas, the rulings of Islamic scholars. The term translates as 'the clear, well-trodden path to water'. In effect, Sharia acts as a code for daily life that all Muslims should adhere to, including prayers, fasting and donations to the poor. In principle it aims to help Muslims understand how they should lead every aspect of their lives according to God's wishes. The legal system of Saudi Arabia is based on Sharia.

Sharjah: the most easterly of the UAE's seven sheikhdoms; the name is probably derived from an Arabic term meaning 'east'. The sheikhdom of Ras al-Khaimah originally formed part of Sharjah but separated in 1866 when the domains of the former ruler of Sharjah were divided among his four sons.

Fujairah also asserted its independence from Sharjah, in 1901. Until the late 1960s, Sharjah, with Bahrain, was one of the two focal points of the British presence in the Gulf. It was the home of the Trucial Scouts and the principal airport of the southern Gulf states.

Sheikh: (also Shaikh, or sometimes Shaykh) a title of respect originally given to a tribal chief, but without precise meaning.

Shell Fisheries: founded in Saudi Arabia as a frozen food storage and distribution business in the 1970s; a new venture was established in Bahrain in 2001 where a state-of-the-art seafood processing factory was built in Salmabad.

Shi'a Muslims: a major branch of Islam whose adherents believe in a system of hereditary Imams the first of whom was Ali, the son-in-law of the prophet Mohammed. Most Shi'ites are Twelvers who believe that there have been twelve Imams, the last of whom is the Imam of the Age, whose revelation will mark the day of Judgement.

Shirawi, Yusuf (aka al-Shirawi): (b. 1927, d. 2004) one of the Middle East's outstanding public servants and intellectuals. He was born in Muharraq, the son of a noted Arabic scholar. During his early lifetime,

Bahrain was considered to be ahead of the region's other states in laying down the beginnings of a modern infrastructure. He graduated from high school in Beirut in 1945 and in 1950 received a degree in chemistry from the American University of Beirut (AUB). After serving as a secondary school teacher in Bahrain, he undertook graduate studies in the UK and in 1955 received a Master's degree in chemistry from the University of Glasgow.

Upon his return to Bahrain he entered public service, holding a number of administrative positions before being appointed Bahrain's Minister of Development and Industry in 1970. In 1977, he approached his counterparts in Kuwait and proposed the establishment in Bahrain of a Kuwait-Bahrain chemical joint venture, which resulted in the formation in 1979 of the Kuwait-Bahrain Chemical Company, a 50/50 partnership between Kuwait's Petrochemical Industries Company (PIC) and the Bahrain National Oil Company (BANOCO). In 1980, SABIC of Saudi Arabia entered the joint venture. After SABIC entered the joint venture, the enterprise was renamed the Gulf Petrochemical Industries Company (GPIC). GPIC had the distinction of being the first and only three-state joint venture in the Arabian Gulf region. Although SABIC, PIC, and the government of Bahrain had equal shares in GPIC, al-Shirawi sought to keep leadership of the company in Bahraini hands. It was agreed that the chair-

NOTES

man of the company would always be a Bahraini. The first and all subsequent CEOs of the company were also Bahraini nationals.

al-Shoala, Abdel-Nabi: (b. 1948) while Labour and Social Affairs Minister in 1996 Mr al-Shoala publically accepted that there was a link between unemployment and social unrest, announcing a series of measures to reduce unemployment.

Sinai Accord: an agreement signed by Egypt and Israel in September 1975. The agreement stated that the conflicts between the countries 'shall not be resolved by military force but by peaceful means'. It also called for 'a further withdrawal in the Sinai and a new UN buffer zone'.

al-Sindi, Murtada Majid Ramadan Alawi: Bahraini-born and currently (2021) residing in Iran, Mr al-Sindi, was designated as a terrorist by the United States for his involvement with the SaA. He was arrested by the Bahraini government five times between 1997 and 2011, has called for armed struggle against the Bahraini government, believing that the phase of peaceful revolution has ended.

Sitra Island: in 1974 the oil port on Sitra Island was expanded to take tankers up to 100,000dwt.

Sitra Refinery: see Bahrain Refinery.

Souk al-Manakh, aka Souq-al-Manakh: in 1980 Kuwait was still the financial centre of the Arabian Gulf. At that time, other centres such as Saudi Arabia, with its broker-based stock market, and Bahrain (which was effectively a satellite market of Kuwait's) were not the sophisticated trading centres that Kuwait had become. However, alongside the formal banking sector and stock exchange there existed a less regulated market, the Souk al-Manakh, where new and innovative stocks, which were not traded on the main stock market (Boursa), could be traded in an air-conditioned car park that had been built over the old camel trading market. The Souq al-Manakh crashed spectacularly in 1982 leaving debts estimated to be as high as US$94 billion. One Jassim al-Mutawa, a former immigration clerk owed US$10.5 billion for personal cheques he had issued to buy stock traded on the exchange. The cheques were not honoured. Nine investors, known as the Magnificent Nine were thought to account for two thirds of the US$94 billion in post-dated checks that proved worthless when the market collapsed.

Soviet Union: see USSR below.

Spot Metal (aka Spot Price): generally refers to the price at which a metal commodity can be sold or purchased immediately, in contrast to futures or forward contracts. The spot price of gold refers to the price of one ounce of gold and the spot price of silver to the price of one ounce of silver.

Standard Oil Co: a US (Ohio) based oil company, established in 1870. Standard's history as one of the world's first and largest multinational corporations came to an end in 1911, when the US Supreme Court ruled that it was an illegal monopoly. However, the income of the subsidiary companies turned out to be larger than the former single enterprise. One of its successors, ExxonMobil, was one of the Seven Sisters (see above). Following the first oil strike in the Arabian (Persian) Gulf in Bahrain in 1932, commercial production began in 1934 by the Standard Oil subsidiary, Bahrain Petroleum Company (BAPCO), from the Awali field.

Standard & Poor's (S&P): a US credit rating agency. S&P is the largest of the Big Three agencies, alongside Moody's and Fitch Ratings.

State Council: anticipating independence in the early 1970s, the administrative apparatus was regulated by Decree No (1) of 1970 establishing the State Council, which was then the cabinet. The State Council carried out all the tasks and responsibilities relating to the administration and organisation of Bahrain's executive affairs, including finance – the preparation of the state budget and the state plan for the development of the national economy.

That Decree was subsequently followed by the issuance of many decrees and resolutions that regulate the government .

State Department: the United States foreign ministry, based in Washington, DC.

State Security Court: abolished in 2001, Bahrain's State Security Law had allowed for the imprisonment of political dissidents for up to three years without trial.

Stinger anti-aircraft missiles: in December 1987 Bahrain was given the go-ahead to acquire 60–70 of the controversial anti-aircraft missiles, worth US$7 million. The purchase came with stringent conditions attached. The most notable was a pledge by Bahrain to return the weapons to the United States within 18 months.

Suez Canal: an artificial sea-level waterway running north to south across the Isthmus of Suez (in Egypt) to connect the Mediterranean Sea and the Red Sea. The canal separates the African continent from Asia, providing the shortest maritime route between Europe, the Indian sub-continent and Asia. The canal extends 193km (120 miles) between Port Said in the north and Suez in the south,

Sukuk (aka Islamic bonds): unlike conventional bonds which are based on a contractual obligation to pay interest to bond-holders, the sukuk holder's income is linked to the performance of the underlying asset which is usually measured in a fixed period of time.

This also exposes the bond-holder's investment to the risk that the asset may lose value. Since 2000, sukuk have become important Islamic financial instruments in raising funds to finance long-term projects. Malaysia issued the first sukuk in 2000. Bahrain followed in 2001.

Sunni Muslims: the Sunni branch of Islam – its largest – reflects the be-

NOTES

lief that on the death of the Prophet Mohammed (in 632AD) no successor to lead the Muslim community had been appointed. Abu Bakr, a close friend of the Prophet (and his father-in-law) was elected by a group of elders as the first Caliph. (This brought the Sunnis into conflict with those Muslims that had adopted the Shi'a interpretation – see above). Some thirty years after the death of the prophet, the power struggle between the two interpretations – essentially two branches of the same family – spilled over into civil war (Fitna) which ended with the rise to power of Syria's Umayyad dynasty which took control of the Caliphate and ruled until AD750. This marked the beginning of Sunni predominance. Sunnis hold that the religion's hierarchical succession should be governed by a consensus of the faithful. After the one-day Battle of Karbala in AD680 between supporters of the prophet's grandson Hussein and the forces of Yazid the First, the Ummayad Caliph, Yazid's forces defeated Hussein's supporters. The cause of the battle was Yazid's insistence that Hussein accept him as undisputed ruler. This division became a permanent split in Islam with all the attendant consequences.

Sects and sub-sects that emerged after the Fitna were dismissed as illegitimate by Sunnis. Islamic Law (Sharia) evolved over the religion's first four centuries, dividing into four different interpretations (madhab)

each reflecting the beliefs and understandings of their founders and the scholars that advised them. By the twenty-first century more extremist Sunni factions such as the Muslim Brotherhood and Hamas had attempted to impose such an interpretation, dividing the Sunni community in their attempts at destroying other religious and secular communities.

Supreme Council for Oil: established in 1980 and chaired by Bahraini Prime Minister Khalifa bin Salman al-Khalifa.

Taif (aka Ta'if): population 688,700 (2020), Saudi Arabia's principal summer resort. It is the site of the tomb of 'Abd Allah ibn Abbas, a cousin of the Prophet Mohammed, and for the graves of two infant sons of the Prophet. It is the site of the signing of the Taif Treaty of 30 June 1934 which demarcated a portion of the Saudi Arabia/Yemen boundary after the brief Saudi Arabia/Yemen war. The city is also noted for its production of fruit and woven coats. It is also the site of a military hospital and the Akramah irrigation dam which was completed in 1956.

Tamkeen: a Bahraini semi-autonomous government agency, founded in 2006 by the National Communication Centre. Its objective is to provide assistance and training to the private sector and to promote the development of the private sector.

Tanker War: during the Iran/Iraq War (1980–88) the anti-shipping campaigns conducted by both sides in the Arabian (Persian) Gulf were known as the Tanker War. In May 1981, Iraq declared that all ships going to or from Iranian ports in the northern zone of the Gulf were subject to attack. The aim was to weaken Iran's ability to fight, initially by attacking ships carrying military supplies to ground war locations but later by attacking ships allegedly carrying Iran's exports.

Iran retaliated by attacking ships belonging to Iraq's trading partners and to countries that were thought to have loaned Iraq money to support its war effort. In 1984 Iraq escalated its effort, opening the second phase of the Tanker War. Iraq deployed its French Super-Etendard combat aircraft. Iran finally retaliated by using more creative tactics when targeting ships.

Tatweer Petroleum: assumed responsibility for the redevelopment of the Bahrain oilfield in 2009. Its main objective is to increase the production of oil and the availability of gas to meet Bahrain's future energy demands.

It is wholly owned by nogaholding, the business and investment arm of the National Oil and Gas Authority of Bahrain.

Tehran (aka Teheran): capital city of Iran. Population (2022 estimate) 9.3 million, 15 million when including greater Tehran.

Texaco: the company began life as the Texas Company, founded in 1902. It adopted the name Texaco in 1959. Texaco was a pioneer in the development of oilfields in the Middle East. In the 1920s, it invested in the nascent oilfields of Bahrain, and in 1936, it became a 50 per cent partner (with Chevron) in developing Saudi Arabia's gigantic oilfields.

Thatcher, Margaret: b. 1925, d. 2013. As British Prime Minister, (1979–90) Mrs Thatcher made an official visit to Bahrain in September 1981. In July 1988, Mrs Thatcher, again paid a brief visit to Bahrain, to thank the Bahraini government for assisting the Royal Navy.

tight oil: aka shale oil, tight oil is processed into conventional oil but given the more complex geological structure of the deposits, is extracted using what is known as fracking, more correctly hydraulic fracturing.

Tornado GR.1: the Tornado is a twin-engine combat aircraft with a variable-sweep wing. Although during its lifetime it was used for several purposes (ground attack, electronic combat/reconnaissance, interceptor), its main role has always been to perform low-altitude penetrating strike missions. The Tornado's baptism of fire took place in 1991 during the Gulf War. The British Royal Air Force Tornado Gr.1s, deployed on Bahrain and Saudi Arabia air bases, were crucial during what became known as Operation Granby during the 1991 Gulf War.

Train 10,000: from the end of the 1970s the government had challenged

NOTES

young people to acquire useful skills through the Train 10,000 programme.

Transparency International: a non-government organisation (NGO). Its Corruption Perceptions Index is widely respected.

In 2012 Bahrain ranked 53, well down on the 36 ranking registered in 2006 when it was ranked four among Middle East countries, behind only the United Arab Emirates (UAE), Qatar and Israel. By 2021 Bahrain ranked 78, (behind Kuwait (73), Oman (56), Saudi Arabia (52), Qatar (34) and the UAE (24).

Trucial States: the seven Trucial States (Abu Dhabi, Ajman, Dubai, Fujairah, Sharjah, Ras al-Khaimah and Umm al-Quwain), occupied the area of eastern Arabia once known geographically as Trucial Oman, a definition attributed to the British Political Agent in Bahrain, Captain F B Prideux. In Arabic the area was known as Sahel Oman (the coast of Oman).

Ultra large crude carriers: (ULCCs) are the very largest ships, with a length of up to 415 metres (1,350 feet) and a capacity of 320,000dwt to more than 550,000dwt. They carry from two million to more than three million barrels of crude.

Union des Banques Arabes et Françaises (UBAF): a financial institution created in 1970, headquartered in Paris and governed by French law. Shareholders come from some 25 countries of the Arab world; it is associated with the Crédit Agricole Corporate and Investment Bank of Paris.

Union of Soviet Socialist Republics (USSR) aka Soviet Union (Soyuz Sovetskikh Sotsialisticheskikh Respublik): until the collapse of the Soviet Union in 1991, Kuwait was the only Gulf state to have diplomatic links with the USSR.

Officially a federal union in which all the states were equal, the USSR which endured from 1940 to 1991 was dominated by Russia and the constituent states had little influence in domestic or foreign policy. The 15 member states were Armenia, Azerbaijan, Belorussia (Belarus), Estonia, Georgia, Kazakhstan, Kirghizia (Kyrgyzstan), Latvia, Lithuania, Moldova, Russia, Tadzhikistan (Tajikistan), Turkmenistan, Ukraine and Uzbekistan.

United Arab Emirates (UAE): formed in 1972 upon the independence of the Trucial States – Abu Dhabi, Ajman, Dubai, Fujairah, Sharjah and Umm al-Quwain; Ras al-Khaimah joined the union a short time after the other six. Abu Dhabi became the capital of the UAE, reflecting its greater oil wealth.

United Arab Shipping Company (UASC): a global shipping company based in the Middle East. Founded in 1976, UASC with more than 185 offices around the world. The company is the largest container shipping line in the Middle East region and adjacent markets, covering over 275 ports and destinations worldwide.

In 2016 the UASC company merged with Hapag Lloyd. The merged company (named Hapag Lloyd (the United Arab Shipping Company was no more) became the world's fifth largest container line, with 230 vessels and a total capacity of 1.6 million tonnes. Under the terms of the deal, the two companies merged their offices across the world, synchronised their IT systems and brought together their fleets, which saw Hapag Lloyd significantly increase its presence in the Middle East. A fifth Hapag-Lloyd regional centre was established in the UAE.

United Gulf Bank: a merchant bank operating within the Kuwait Projects Holding Company (KIPCO) group – one of the biggest holding companies in the Middle East and North Africa (MENA) (see above).

United Gulf Holding Company (UGHC): a merchant bank through its wholly-owned subsidiary United Gulf Bank (see above) and therefore also a subsidiary of KIPCO. By market capitalisation at US$1.23 billion, it is one of Bahrain's top ten companies.

United Nations: an inter-governmental organisation with 193 member states. Formed in 1945 after the Second World War, its founding mission is to maintain international peace and security. Its four additional missions are to protect human rights, deliver humanitarian aid, promote sustainable development and uphold

international law. It has eight specific agencies in Bahrain – the International Civil Aviation Organisation (ICAO), the United Nations Development Programme (UNDP), the United Nations Environment Programme (UNEP), the United Nations Educational, Scientific and Cultural Organisation (UNESCO), the United Nations Information Centre (UNIC), the United Nations Children's Fund (UNICEF), the United Nations Industrial Development Organisation (UNIDO), and the World Meteorological Organisation (WMO).

United Nations Food and Agriculture Organisation: Bahrain has very little agriculture, except in the north where fresh water springs are found.

United Nations Human Rights Council (UNHCR): the Office of the High Commissioner for Human Rights (UN Human Rights) is the leading UN entity on human rights. The UN General Assembly established the Office of the High Commissioner for Human Rights in December 1993 through its resolution 48/141 which also details its mandate. This was just a few months after the World Conference on Human Rights adopted the so-called Vienna Declaration and Plan of Action.

Adopted by 171 States, the Vienna Declaration renewed the world's commitment to human rights. It also called for strengthening and harmonising the monitoring capacity of the United Nations system with regards to human rights.

United Nations Security Council (UNSC): the UN Security Council has primary responsibility for the maintenance of international peace and security. It has 15 members, and each member has one vote. Under the Charter of the United Nations, all member states are obligated to comply with Council decisions.

The Security Council takes the lead in determining the existence of a threat to the peace or act of aggression. It calls upon the parties to a dispute to settle it by peaceful means and recommends methods of adjustment or terms of settlement. In some cases, the Security Council can resort to imposing sanctions or even authorise the use of force to maintain or restore international peace and security.

However, the five permanent members of the Security Council (US, UK, France, China and Russia) have the power to veto any substantive resolution. An abstention from voting does not prevent any draft resolution from being adopted.

United Nations Security Council Resolution 598 (20 July 1987): called on Iran and Iraq to observe an immediate ceasefire, discontinue all military actions and withdraw all forces to the internationally recognised boundaries. It requested the UN Secretary General to dispatch a team of United Nations observers to verify, confirm and supervise the ceasefire and withdrawal of troops. It also urged that prisoners of war be re-leased and repatriated without delay after the cessation of active hostilities.

On 17 July 1988, Iran notified the Secretary General of its formal acceptance of resolution 598, expressing the need to save life and to establish justice and regional and international peace and security. The following day, Iraq also reaffirmed its agreement with the principles embodied in the resolution.

United Nations Special Commission (UNSCOM): formed by the United Nations after the Gulf War (1991–93) to ensure Iraq's compliance with policies concerning Iraqi production and use of weapons of mass destruction.

United Nations Special Rapporteur: in 2013 it emerged that the Bahraini government had cancelled an official visit scheduled to be made to Bahrain by the United Nations' Special Rapporteur on torture and other abuses, Juan E Méndez.

University of Bahrain: established in 1986 as a result of the merger of two public colleges, the Gulf Polytechnic (founded in 1968) and the University College of Arts, Science and Education (1979). In 2020 the university had more than 20,000 registered students and some 2,000 staff.

US Army Corps of Engineers: in 1985, the Corps of Engineers began work on a large new military air base in the south of the main island, Manama, it cost about US$90 million. It was considered to be a main part of

US contingency plans for reinforcing its presence in the Gulf in an emergency.

US Energy Information Administration (EIA): This US government department is the statistical and analytical agency within the US Department of Energy. The EIA collects, analyses, and disseminates energy information to assist in policymaking, understanding markets, and improving public understanding of energy and its role in the economy and the environment. The EIA is the US' principal source of energy information.

United States-Mexico-Canada Agreement (USMCA): in September 2018, the United States, Mexico, and Canada reached an agreement to replace the North American Free Trade Area (NAFTA) with the USMCA and all three countries had ratified it by March 2020. NAFTA remained in force until the USMCA was implemented on 1 July 2020. The new Agreement involved only small changes.

Utub: a clan of the Anaiza tribe of nomads from the Najd branch of the Utub – the al-Khalifa – established themselves as the rulers of Bahrain in the eighteenth century. Another clan of the Anaiza tribe were thought to be the earlier founders of Kuwait.

value added tax (VAT): in 2017 the Bahraini government announced that VAT would be introduced in 2019. The objective was to raise non-oil generated revenue. VAT was implemented in Bahrain on 1 January 2019.

The general VAT rate was 5 per cent from 1 January 2019 until 31 December 2021. From 1 January 2022, the rate was increased to 10 per cent, but transitional provisions apply in certain circumstances under which the 5 per cent rate could still apply on certain supplies made after 1 January 2022 until 31 December 2022. The standard rate applies to most goods and services, with a number of exceptions where certain goods and services may be subject to a zero per cent rate or be exempted from VAT altogether. The mandatory registration threshold is BD37,500 for businesses resident in Bahrain.

very large crude carriers (VLCC): ships with a length of some 330 metres (1,100 feet), and a deadweight (dwt) capacity of 200,000–320,000dwt. They carry in the region of two million barrels. The largest ships that can transit the Suez Canal are known as Suezmax, and are some 275 metres (900 feet) long and have a capacity of 120,000–200,000dwt. They carry about 800,000–1,000,000 barrels.

Voluntary Retirement Scheme (VRS): in October 2019 Bahraini MPs reiterated their support for the government's Voluntary Retirement Scheme, which aimed to reduce the public sector payroll. By then more than 8,000 civil servants were reported to have taken advantage of the programme. The scheme granted a large number of unemployed citizens, especially university graduates,

NOTES

opportunities to fill vacancies in a number of government jobs. The renewed implementation of the scheme was expected to create more than 1,000 jobs for citizens who were on the waiting lists of the Civil Service Bureau, and was expected to contribute to lowering the unemployment rate and increasing the rate of Bahraini-isation in government employment.

al-Wafa: the political umbrella of the Saraya al-Ashtar (SaA) (see above) that is the al-Wafa Islamic movement.

al-Wafa is a Khomeinist movement established in 2009 by Ayatollah Abduljalil al-Miqdad. From its inception, the group rejected the political process that existed in Bahrain, describing it as a charade. It wanted to reform the political system and end what it perceived as systematic discrimination against the Bahraini community. Its political leaders reside in Iran, from where they release their publications. al-Wafa opposes the monarchic system in Bahrain and, since 2011, has called for the downfall of the regime. The group's strategic vision document calls for the establishment of a republic in Bahrain. al-Wafa is inherently anti-Semitic and has threatened to attack anyone holding an Israeli passport whether they are dual citizens of the US or any European state or not, calling it an act of 'resistance'. It seeks a constitution in which Islam plays the central role in legislations. al-Wafa leaders who reside in Iran celebrated the successful operation of smuggling terrorist detainees out of Bahrain into Iran, an operation known as Swords of Vengeance.

al-Waha (aka the Fund of Funds): is a US$100 million venture capital fund which aims to provide funding access to Bahrain's start-up industry.

The fund is focussed on investing in technology, fintech and smart cities with the objective of bringing Bahrain and the MENA region to the forefront of global technological advances, as a hub for venture capital, start-ups and technology companies. The fund is managed by the Bahrain Development Bank.

al-Wahdawi: a Bahraini political society (aka political party) which had condemned the Gulf coalition's (of which Bahrain was a member) air strikes on Yemen which had begun in 2015 as a 'flagrant aggression that violated international law'. Bahrain's police promptly arrested the society's secretary, Fadhel Abbas, and another unnamed individual, each blamed for 'exploiting the situation in Yemen to disrupt the peace and endanger security and civil order'.

Wahhabi (Wahabiyya): followers of Mohammed ibn 'Abd al-Wahhab (1703–92), whose teachings focussed on the Singularity of God (tawhid) and who sought to reverse what they saw as impure innovations within Islam.

Wall Street Journal: in early 2012 Bahrain was ranked first in the Middle East and twelfth place worldwide on the 2012 *Wall Street Journal*/Heritage Foundation Index of Economic freedom.

al-Wefaq National Islamic Society: the principle Shi'ite Muslim opposition group, which, as part of Shi'a society in Bahrain, follows two simple goals: opposition to the current government in Bahrain and change in the structure of society to be based on the rule of the people. Established in 2001, it was founded by more than 100 Shi'a scholars, such as Ali Salman, Saeid Shahabi, Abdul Amir al-Jamri and Sheikh Isa Ahmed Qassim, the leader of al-Wefaq.

In July 2014 Bahrain's Justice Ministry sought court approval to suspend the activities of the al-Wefaq in a move that looked certain to derail efforts to restart reconciliation talks between the government and opposition groups. The closure spoke volumes to Bahrain's Shi'a majority. The purported reason for the three month closure was to enable the group to 'correct its legal status' after four of its general conferences were annulled due to a lack of delegates and a failure to comply with requirements for transparency in convening these conferences.

The suspension followed charges against al-Wefaq's leader Sheikh Ali Salman, and his assistant, Khalil al-Marzouq. Both had been charged with holding an illegal meeting with Tom Malinowski, US Assistant Secretary of State for Democracy, Human Rights and Labour.

Well Number One: in 1932 prospectors first discovered oil in Bahrain. Well Number One, as it was to be called, continued to produce oil for decades, operated by the Bahrain Petroleum Company. At the site of the well is a plaque commemorating a discovery which changed the world's geo-political structure.

West Bank: that part of Palestine on the West Bank of the River Jordan. Following the First World War (1914–18), which marked the end of the Ottoman Empire, the area formed part of the British Mandate of Palestine. After the 1948 Arab-Israeli war, which followed the Second World War (1939–45) the West Bank was annexed by Jordan, which ruled the it until its 1967 capture by Israel in the Arab-Israeli war, which also enabled Israel to annex East Jerusalem. Palestinians have had to accept Israeli occupation since then. The rest of the West Bank, although under *de facto* Israeli rule, was never formally annexed by Israel.

In 2009 the West Bank was under a Fatah government, in contrast to the Gaza Strip, which had been returned to the Palestinians in 2005 and where in 2016 an elected Hamas government held power.

Wood MacKenzie: founded as a small, Edinburgh-based stockbroker. By the 1970s, it had become one of the top three stockbrokers in the UK, re-

NOTES

nowned for the quality of its equity research. In 1973, Wood MacKenzie published its first oil report, having cultivated deep expertise in upstream oil and gas. After periods of ownership by Hill Samuel (Merchant Bank) (UK) and Deutsche Bank (Germany) Wood MacKenzie is now (2021) owned by the Verisk Group (US).

World Trade Organisation (WTO): established in 1995; Bahrain was a founder member. The Organisation provides a forum for negotiating agreements aimed at reducing obstacles to international trade and ensuring a level playing field for all, thus contributing to economic growth and development. The WTO also provides a legal and institutional framework for the implementation and monitoring of these agreements, as well as for settling disputes arising from their interpretation and application.

The current body of trade agreements comprising the WTO consists of 16 different multilateral agreements (to which all WTO members are parties) and two different plurilateral agreements (to which only some WTO members are parties).

Over the past 75 years, the WTO and its predecessor organisation the General Agreement on Tariffs and Trade (GATT) (established in 1947), have helped to create a strong and prosperous international trading system, thereby contributing to unprecedented global economic growth.

The WTO currently has 164 members, of which 117 are developing countries or separate customs territories.

Yemen: the differences between North Yemen and its Marxist neighbour to the South, the Peoples' Democratic Republic of the Yemen (PDRY – consisting of the Hadramaut and Aden) were settled – with mediation by the USSR – in 1990.

However, Yemen's post-independence history is one of political feuds and upheavals.

In March 2015 a Saudi-led coalition, Operation Decisive Storm which included the UAE as well as other Gulf Co-operation Council (GCC) members Bahrain, Kuwait and Qatar, plus Egypt, Jordan, Morocco, and Sudan, launched a military operation in Yemen against Iran backed-Houthi rebels, nominally at the request of Yemen's President Abd-Rabbu Mansour Hadi.

The involvement of so many disparate countries underlined the fact that Yemen had become the epicentre of a proxy war between Saudi Arabia and Iran.

Zakat (zakaat, zakah): almsgiving, one of the five pillars of Islam.

al-Zayani, Abdullatif bin Rashid: b. 1954. Bahraini Foreign Minister (2021) trained as an engineer and started his career as an army officer rising to Lieutentant General. From 2011 to 2020 al-Zayani was the Secretary General of the Gulf Co-operation

Council (GCC), before being appointed Bahrain's Foreign Minister.

Zubara: (aka Zubarah) an offshore island awarded to Qatar (along with the neighbouring island of Jinan) in the March 2001 settlement by the International Court of Justice. Sovereignty over the Hawar Islands was awarded to Bahrain.

Timeline

1816	Bahrain's first treaty with Britain was signed.
1861	The second treaty made it a British protectorate.
1869	Sheikh Isa bin Ali al-Khalifa was named ruler.
1913	A treaty between Britain and Turkey recognised Bahrain as an independent state, but the country remained under British administration.
1923	After more than half a century of peace and stability, Sheikh Isa bin Ali al-Khalifa abdicated in favour of his son, Sheikh Hamad bin Isa al-Khalifa.
1928	Iran claimed ownership of Bahrain; the dispute was not resolved until 1970 when Iran accepted a UN report stating that the vast majority of Bahrainis wanted their complete independence.
1932	Bahrain became the first country in the Gulf to strike oil.
1942–61	Sheikh Hamad died in 1942 and his son, Sheikh Sulman bin Hamad al-Khalifa became ruler.
1961	Sheikh Sulman bin Hamad al-Khalifa died and was succeeded by Sheikh Isa bin Sulman al-Khalifa.
1968	As part of its East of Suez departure programme Britain announced its intention to withdraw from the Gulf by 1971.
1971	Bahrain and Qatar became independent states. Sheikh Khalifa bin Salman al-Khalifa became Prime Minister of Bahrain.
1973–74	Bahrain's constitution was promulgated; it limited the Ruler's powers and established an elected 30-member National Assembly.
1975	The National Assembly refused to ratify a bill to arrest and detain people for up to three years without trial, and as a result was dissolved by the Ruler, Sheikh Isa. The government subsequently ruled by decree.
1981	A political and economic union, the Co-operation Council for the Arab States of the Gulf (CCASG) (generally known as the Gulf Co-operation Council (GCC)) was formed by Bahrain, Kuwait, Oman, Qatar, Saudi Arabia and the United Arab Emirates (UAE).
1986	The opening of the 25km King Fahd Causeway between Bahrain and Saudi Arabia not only gave a boost to business and tourism but was seen as strengthening regional security.
1990	Iraq invaded Kuwait on 2 August.

1991	Bahrain actively supported the allied forces against Iraq in the Gulf military conflict following Iraq's invasion of Kuwait.
1994	The majority Shi'ites staged demonstrations demanding better living conditions and the return of an elected parliament. The Sunnis, once the majority but by the twentieth century in a minority, are dominant in both politics and business.
1999	Sheikh Isa bin Sulman al-Khalifa, who had ruled since 1961, died and was succeeded by his son, Sheikh Hamad bin Isa al-Khalifa. Sheikh Khalifa bin Salman al-Khalifa continued as Prime Minister.
2000	For the first time, non-Muslims and women were appointed to the 40 member Majlis al-Shura (Consultative Council).
2001	A referendum on political reform was approved, under which Bahrain would become a constitutional monarchy with an elected lower chamber of parliament and an independent judiciary.
2002	The state became a constitutional monarchy and Hamad bin Isa al-Khalifa was declared King. As part of the reform process, legislation was approved to allow women to vote in elections and run for national office. In legislative elections (the first since 1973), parliament became a mix of secular and Islamic candidates. The Shi'ite opposition boycotted the election.
2004	The first woman to be appointed head of a government ministry, Nada Haffadh, was made health minister. A free trade agreement was signed with the US.
2005	King Hamad called for increased global co-operation to combat international terrorism. Thousands protested in favour of a fully elected parliament.
2006	Legislative elections were held in which Sunni representatives won 22 seats (out of 40) and Shi'ites won 18.
2007	There were several days of rioting in majority Shi'a areas with protesters demanding compensation for human rights violations between 1980–90.
2008	A common market was created between Bahrain, Kuwait, Oman, Qatar, Saudi Arabia and the UAE, the six wealthiest Gulf States. Citizens of these countries are allowed to travel between and live in any of the six states, where they may find employment, buy properties and businesses and use the educational and health facilities freely.
2009	Iraqi Airways began flights to Bahrain, after a gap of 20 years. The National Bank of Kuwait Bahrain (NBK Bahrain), posted record profits of US$88.9 million for the first two quarters of the year (an increase of 55 per cent over the same period in 2008).

TIMELINE 409

2010 The authorities suspended the news network al-Jazeera's operations in Bahrain and barred its workers from entry following the broadcast of documentaries on the treatment of Asian labourers and poverty in Bahrain. In parliamentary elections, the Shi'a al-Wifaq National Islamic Society (al-Wifaq) won 18 seats (out of 40), the combined Sunni block won 22 seats, including 17 independent delegates.

2011 In March, protesters marched on the Council of Ministers. The Bahraini authorities 'asked' Saudi Arabia to supply 1,500 troops to help their own forces restore order. A day later, security forces used tanks to oust protestors from Pearl Square, ending its two-week occupation. Ambulances were blocked from entering the square to provide aid. Later security militia carried out a sweep of hospitals, arresting any trauma patients being treated. The UN criticised Bahraini officials for commandeering all hospitals and the arrest by various security forces of protestors receiving medical treatment. In April, the Turkish foreign minister, Ahmet Davutoglu, held talks with both the opposition group al-Wifaq and King Hamad. In May, Moody's downgraded Bahrain's sovereign credit rating to 'negative'. In June, the King decreed that the state of emergency that had been imposed in March was to be lifted. Legal trials began before the Court of National Safety of 47 medical personnel arrested for treating demonstrators during the civil unrest; 20 were charged with possessing unlicensed weapons, inciting others to overthrow the monarchy, unauthorised occupation of the hospital and stealing medical equipment; 28 others were accused of spreading false news and lying about the medical condition of some patients (one accused was tried *in absentia*). In July, in a BBC interview, a doctor claimed that he had been subjected to torture and coerced into making a false confession while under arrest; the families of other doctors made similar claims. National reconciliation talks began between the Sunni-led government and Shi'a opposition, al-Wifaq, in which the King said that the dialogue process would be inclusive. However, later al-Wifaq withdrew from the talks, saying the national dialogue 'was not serious' and that they had been allocated too few seats. In September 20 medical staff from the Salmaniya Medical Complex, who had treated injured persons during the February and March demonstrations, were found guilty by the National Safety Court. The security court gave long jail sentences to some 80 protesters. Elections to replace 18 al-Wifaq (Shi'ite) members of

410   TIMELINE

parliament, who had resigned in February, were held on 24 September. The opposition boycotted the elections and voter turnout was very low with fewer than one in five voters casting ballots; four candidates were re-elected due to the lack of any opposition candidate. There were skirmishes between the security forces and opposition youths attempting to reach the Pearl roundabout. In October, after international condemnation on the harshness of the sentences by international medical associations and human rights campaigners, the attorney general announced that after studying the court's judgement the 20 medical staff would be retried by the country's highest civilian court. In November, the government acknowledged that 'excessive force' had been used on pro-democracy demonstrators by security forces and 20 members of these forces were charged with abuse. An official inquiry established that there had been 'instances of excessive force and mistreatment of detainees'.

2012   A demonstration called for 14 February, the first anniversary of pro-democracy protests at the now demolished Pearl Roundabout in Manama, was thwarted by a heavy security presence. Police fired tear gas and rubber bullets at rock-throwing youths. Up to 70 people were arrested, including foreign activists. In April the government endorsed a decision to retry 21 activists, convicted by a military court in June 2011, of plotting against the state. On 14 June, an appeals court convicted nine medics that took part in the 2011 pro-democracy protests for up to five years in prison; nine other medics were acquitted. The most serious charges against all the medics were dropped. The government established Bahrain Independent Commission of Inquiry (BICI) found that the medics had been tortured while in custody. On 1 October, the sentences of nine convicted medics were upheld by the Court of Cassation (the highest appeal court). A new visa system (similar to the European Schengen agreement) allowing multiply entry for foreigners to the six Gulf Co-operation Council (GCC) countries was introduced in November.

2013   The 2013 Bahrain Grand Prix took place on 21 April after being cancelled in 2011 due to the political unrest. On 24 June parliament finally approved the 2013/14 budget. It had been delayed by several months over demands for extra spending to raise public sector salaries by 15 per cent. The measure had been opposed by the cabinet and in the end parliament passed the plan without the pay rise, but with rises in pension payments for both public and private sector

TIMELINE

411

retirees, and higher subsidies for food and other items. The 23rd session of the Joint Council and Ministerial Meeting of the GCC and the EU was held in Manama on 30 June. Some 50 Shi'a Muslims were sentenced on 30 September for up to 15 years for forming a clandestine movement, the 14 February Coalition.

2014 Three policeman were killed in a bombing in March. It occurred on the third anniversary of the start of the 2011 uprising that had seen people take to the streets to demand more democracy and an end to what they perceived as discrimination against the Shi'a community by the Sunni royal family.

2015 The worst attack since March 2014 occurred in July when a bombing took place outside a girls' school in the predominantly Shi'a village of Sitra. It killed two policemen and wounded six other people. Iran has since been accused of causing the continued unrest because it has deliberately stirred up tension between the Sunni population of Bahrain and the majority Shi'a population in Iran. Bahrain recalled its ambassador from Tehran.

2016 A UN appointed panel was tasked with the duty of investigating state harassment of Bahrain's Shi's population and found that there was indeed a systematic structure of harassment against them. The main Shi'ite Muslim opposition group, al-Wefaq, was banned in July.

2017 The main opposition group, the National Democratic Action Society (Waad), was disbanded in June; it had already been banned. In early December Bahrain appeared on the EU's first 'blacklist' of 17 tax haven countries it said failed to match up to international standards. The EU said the move was an attempt to clamp down on the estimated US$650 billion lost to 'aggressive avoidance' every year. A further 47 countries were placed on a 'grey list' and warned to complete their tax reforms. Countries on the blacklist will no longer be eligible for EU funds except where it is to aid development.

2018 In April Bahrain announced the discovery of a large oil and gas field, the first new field since 1932.

2020 On 11 September US President Donald Trump announced on Twitter that Bahrain and Israel had agreed to establish full diplomatic relations, the second Gulf state to do so in two months. The UAE and Bahrain signed agreements (the Abraham Accords) with Israel in Washington on 15 September with President Trump looking on. The deal will formalise relations between Israel and the two Gulf states; the Israeli-Palestinian conflict, which had long been the obstacle to diplomatic progress, was not mentioned. Neither was the suspension of Israel's plans to annex the West Bank, which the UAE had sought before agreeing to the deal. The UAE agreement was substantially more detailed than the Bahrain agreement. The signatories were foreign ministers Abdullatif bin Rashid al-Zayani and Sheikh Abdullah bin Zayed al-Nahyan of Bahrain and the UAE respectively, and President Netanyahu of Israel. Crown Prince Salman bin Hamad al-Khalifa became Prime Minister on 11 November.

2021 To widespread surprise in 2019 and in early 2020 Bahrain's banking regulators and administrators seemed to be set on introducing an ambitious series of reforms and initiatives, aimed at encouraging the banking community to embrace innovation and entrepreneurship in the age of fintech. Although the Bahraini authorities saw the future of fintech as one of the main drivers of the island's growth, a 2017 article in the London *Sunday Times* observed that 'Too often, fintech seems like little more than a trendy re-branding.' Following a visit of an International Monetary Fund (IMF) mission in February 2020, the organisation offered praise, whilst encouraging vigilance. The IMF head of mission, Bikas Joshi, noted that 'efforts at supervisory and regulatory vigilance, and moves to further enhance the Anti-Money Laundering/Countering Financing of Terrorism (AML/CFT) framework, are welcome.' Bahrain has been a leader in fintech, promoting opportunities while revising regulations and collaborating with other regulators.

The Bahrain authorities' Fiscal Balance Programme (FBP), underpinned by the 2019/20 budget, has provided a commendable framework to arrest the decline in fiscal and external buffers since 2014. The introduction of a value added tax (VAT) in January 2019 was a particularly significant step. The various measures envisaged under the FBP are expected to further reduce the fiscal deficit over the medium term, but the IMF considered that Bahrain's public debt would nevertheless continue to increase.

As a consequence, the government's additional reform efforts, anchored in a more transparent medium-term agenda, will be needed to ensure fiscal sustainability and support the currency peg, which continues to provide a clear and credible monetary anchor. Further revenue measures, including a direct taxation system such as corporate income tax, could be considered and spending reforms should be designed to protect the most vulnerable. The implementation of the Voluntary Retirement Scheme (VRS), said the IMF, is expected to reduce the public wage bill over the medium term. The ultimate impact on public service delivery and public finances should be carefully assessed based on public sector restructuring plans and contingent liabilities of the VRS.

Bibliography

al-Baharna, H. (1968). *Legal Status of the Arabian Gulf States: A Study of their Treaty Relations and their International Problems.* Manchester, UK: Manchester University Press.

Barratt, Robin. (2012) *My Beautiful Bahrain.* London: Apex Publishing.

Belgrave, Charles. 1960. *Personal Column.* Hutchinson, London.

Burdett, A. (2006). *Records of Bahrain.* Cambridge, UK: Cambridge University Press.

Ehteshami, A. and Wright, S. (2011). *Reform in the Middle East Oil Monarchies.* Reading, UK: Ithaca Press.

Field, Michael. (1984). *Merchants: the Big Business Families of Arabia.* London: John Murray.

Faroughy, Abbas. 1951. *The Bahrein Islands.* New York: Verry, Fisher.

Fucaro, N. (2009). *Histories of City and State in the Persian Gulf.* Cambridge, UK: Cambridge University Press.

Gardner, Andrew. (2010). *City of Strangers: Gulf Migration and the Indian Community in Bahrain.* Ithaca, NY, US: ILR Press, Cornell University.

Gengler, J. (2015). *Group Conflict and Political Mobilization in Bahrain and the Arab Gulf: Rethinking the Rentier State.* Terre Haute, US: Indiana State University.

Hamid, Mahzer. (1980). *Arabia Imperilled: the Security Imperatives of the Arab Gulf States.* Washington DC, US: Middle East Assessments Group.

Halliday, Fred. (1974). *Arabia Without Sultans.* London: Penguin-Pelican.

Holden, David. (1966). *Farewell to Arabia.* London: Faber and Faber.

Jones, Marc Owen. (2020). *Political Repression in Bahrain.* Cambridge, UK: Cambridge Middle East Studies.

Khalaf, A., al-Shehabi, O., and Hanieh A. (eds.). (2014). *Transit States: Labour, Migration and Citizenship in the Gulf.* London: Pluto Press.

Khuri, F. (1981). *Tribe and State in Bahrain: The Transition of Social and Political Authority in an Arab State.* Chicago, US: Chicago University Press.

Khuzaie, Ahmed, Meredith Sullivan, Zenaty Nour. (2020). *Kingdom of Bahrain: Political Review.* Washington DC, US: Khuzaie Associates LLC.

Gengler, J. (2015) *Group Conflict and Political Mobilization in Bahrain and the Arab Gulf: Rethinking the Rentier State.* Middle East Studies.

Matthiesen, Toby. (2013). *Sectarian Gulf: Bahrain, Saudi Arabia and the Arab Spring That Wasn't.* Stanford California, US: Stanford Briefs.

Nakleh, E. (2011). *Bahrain: Political Development in a Modernizing Society.* New York, US: Lexington Books.

BIBLIOGRAPHY

Sanger, Robert. (1954). *The Arabian Peninsula.* New Haven, Connecticut, US: Yale University Press.

al-Shehabi, Omar. (2019). *Contested Modernity: Sectarianism, Nationalism, and Colonialism in Bahrain.* London, UK: Oneworld Academic.

al-Shehabi, Ala'a & Owen Jones, Marc. (2015). *Bahrain's Uprising.* London, UK: Zed Books.

Smith, Simon C. (2013). *Britain's Revival and Fall in the Gulf: Kuwait, Bahrain, Qatar, and the Trucial States 1950–71.* London, UK: Routledge.

Al-Tajir, M.A. (1987). *Bahrain 1920–1945: Britain, the Shaikh, and the Administration.* London: Routledge.

Tuson, P., Burdett, A., & Quick E. (eds.). *Records of Bahrain 1820–1960.* Slough, UK: Archive Editions.

Wehrey, F. (2014). *Sectarian Politics in the Gulf: From the Iraq War to the Arab Uprisings.* New York, US: Columbia University Press.

Wilson, Arnold. (1928). *The Persian Gulf.* Oxford: Oxford University Press.

Winkler, David F. (2013). *Amirs, Admirals & Desert Sailors: Bahrain, the US Navy, and the Arabian Gulf.* Annapolis, Maryland, US: Naval Institute Press.

Country Profile

Political structure

Constitution

The 1973 constitution was suspended in 1975 and reinstated by royal decree, with significant amendments, in February 2002. By a charter, agreed by referendum, Bahrain was declared a constitutional monarchy in 2002, with a bicameral parliament and independent judiciary. Women were given suffrage and although political parties remained illegal, eleven new political societies were licensed in 2001. The King is the symbol of the country and is inviolate.

Independence date

15 August 1971

Form of state

Constitutional monarchy

The executive

Executive power rests with the King, who is Head of State, he appoints a prime minister and members of the Consultative Council, which is an advisory body that, since 2002, is empowered to make laws. The King may dissolve or extend the term of the Consultative Council. The King has the right to initiate, ratify and promulgate laws. The King is the head of the armed forces and head of the Judiciary.

National legislature

A bicameral National Assembly consists of the Majlis an Nuwab (Chamber of Deputies (sometimes translated as Representatives)) (lower house) which has 40 popularly elected members, and the Majlis al-Shura (Consultative Council) with 40 members appointed by the King. Membership of both houses is for four years. The King may renew membership of the Council and dissolve the Chamber of Deputies by decree. Terms of both houses may be extended by the King for up to two extra years. The King and prime minister present bills to the Chamber of Deputies for consideration before they are passed to the Consultative Council.

Legal system

The judiciary is a constitutionally independent body, whose function and organisation is regulated by law. It is a mixture, based on English common law and Sunni and Shi'a Sharia (Islamic law) traditions, where Sharia is the principal source of law.

The Supreme Court is the final court of appeal for all civil, commercial and criminal matters.

Last elections

The November 2022 parliamentary elections saw relatively high levels of voter turnout. Six candidates won their seats outright in the first round. The other 34 seats were decided in the second round. More than 330 candidates, including 73 women, stood in the original contest. The first round turnout was 73 per cent with around 350,000 registered voters.

A record eight female MPs were successfully elected in the 2022 election, two more than the number in the previous

COUNTRY PROFILE

parliament. Seven incumbent Members of Parliament were re-elected and five members of earlier parliaments were returned to Parliament. Given the restrictions placed on the activities of the so-called political societies, their weak performance was hardly surprising. Of the four Progressive Tribune candidates three won seats, and the National Unity Assembly (NUA) one. All the Salafist Asalah candidates were defeated, although three independent Islamists were successful.

The London-based Bahrain Institute for Rights and Democracy described the vote as a 'sham', saying that other legislation linking voter inclusion to records of previous election participation, appeared to be targeting individuals who had boycotted earlier polls.

Next elections

2026 (parliamentary)

Political parties

Political parties in Bahrain are formally banned; MPs are members of political 'societies'.

Ruling party

There is no ruling party.

Population

1,501,636 million (2020)

Bahrain is the smallest country in the Gulf region and the only island state; it has the smallest population in the region.

Last census

27 April 2010: 1,234,571

Population density

2,120 inhabitants per square km, one of the highest in the world (World Bank 2020).

Annual growth rate

-5.08 per cent annual change (2020) (World Bank/OECD).

Ethnic make-up

Bahrain's inhabitants are mostly Arab, with a sizeable minority of Iranian descent.

Approximately 38 per cent of the population are foreign residents, mostly from South Asia and other Arab countries.

Religions

According to the constitution, Islam is the state religion. Approximately 98 per cent of the indigenous population are Muslim – two-thirds Shi'as and the remainder belonging to the Sunni branch of Islam. There is no exact figure for the number of each; the Sunnis were in the majority up until the mid-1950s but are now in a minority, although remaining in power. The government have attempted to adjust the difference by a programme of naturalising Arab and non-Arab Sunnis for work in the police and military. The remaining 2 per cent are Jewish and Christian.

About half of the foreign population are non-Muslim, including Christians, Jews, Hindus, Baha'is, Buddhists and Sikhs.

Education

Primary schooling lasts for six years between the ages of six and 12. Secondary education lasts for three years and offers students a choice of three main branches: the general, the technical or the commercial.

The government is seeking to establish Bahrain as a regional centre for human resource development. In addition to several universities, there are a number of training centres, such as the Bahrain Training Institute (BTI) and the Bahrain Institute of Training and Finance (BITF) that are designed to prepare local graduates for the modern, technology driven workforce.

There are both government-owned and private schools.

Literacy rate

91 per cent for total adult population (World Bank 2010).

Compulsory years

6 to 15

Enrolment rate

105 per cent boys, 106 per cent girls total primary school enrolment of the relevant age group (including repetition rates) (World Bank).

Health

Health services in Bahrain are of a high quality and all Bahrainis receive free health care from the state. There are a mixture of government and private hospitals, with additional government health centres and maternity hospitals.

Life expectancy

77.42 years (2020 World Data Atlas)

Fertility rate/Maternal mortality rate

The fertility rate for Bahrain in 2021 was 1.934 births per woman, a 1.07 per cent decline from 2020. The maternal mortality rate was 14 per 100,000 live births. (Unicef 2021)

Child (under 5 years) mortality rate

6.8 per 1,000 live births (Unicef 2020).

Welfare

The government provides direct financial assistance to those considered needy in addition to assistance provided by religious organisations and local charitable societies. There are a number of social centres operated by the ministry of labour and social affairs (MoLSA) that provide training and assistance, especially to needy women. Public and private facilities for the elderly, handicapped and orphaned provide first class care, using the latest professional methods, approaches, and equipment. The number of needy families on government assistance lists has been growing for the past decade at double the rate of the population growth.

Family support

Starting from January 2022, it was agreed that levels of financial support for low-income families be increased. The amount of financial support for the three categories of eligibility is as follows: BD110 for the first category in which the income of the head of the Bahraini family is less than BD300, and BD77 for the second category, in which the income of the head of the Bahraini family ranges between BD301–700, and BD55 for the third category in which the income of the head of the family ranges between BD701–1,000.

Main cities

Manama (capital) (estimated population 664,000 in 2021), Muharraq (263,000 in 2020), Ah Rifa (79,550), Madinat Hamad (52,718), Isa (38,090), Jid Hafs (31,375). All figures estimated.

Languages spoken

English is widely spoken. Persian (Farsi), Hindi and Urdu are also frequently used.

Official language/s

Arabic

Media

While press laws guarantee the independence of journalists, criminal penalties may be imposed for infringements, such as insulting the King; self-censorship is widespread.

Bahrain is striving to achieve a status as the primary media centre for the Middle East in competition with Dubai in the United Arab Emirates.

Press

Dailies

In Arabic, *Akhbar al Khaleej* (www.akhbar-alkhaleej.com) also in English, *al Ayam* (www.alayam.com) also in English, *al Meethaq* (www.almeethaq. net) and *al Waqt* (www.alwaqt.com).

In English the *Bahrain Tribune* (www.bahraintribune.com) and *Gulf Daily News* (www.gulf-daily-news.com); also in Arabic *Akhbar al Khaleej* (www.akhbaralkhaleej.com), *Al-Alayam* (www.alayam.com).

Weeklies

In Arabic, *Layalina* (www.layalina mag.com) also available in English and *Sada al-Usbu'*. In English, *Gulf Weekly* (www.gulfweekly.com), has general news and information.

Business

In Arabic, *Akhbar al Khaleej* (www.akhbar-alkhaleej.com) has a business section (also available in English). In English, the online website *Trade Arabia* (www.tradearabia.com), has a comprehensive range of business information topics and a hard copy *Gulf Industry* in English and Arabic, concerning the petroleum industry.

Periodicals

In Arabic, *Huna al Bahrain*, published by the Ministry of Information. In English, *Bahrain This Month* (www. bahrainthismonth.com).

Broadcasting

The state-owned Bahrain Radio and Television Corporation (BRTC) (www. bahraintv.com) operates the national public broadcasting networks.

Radio

BRTC also operates Radio Bahrain (www.radiobahrain.fm) over three wave lengths, in the English language, offering news and current affairs, popular music and classical music. The Radio Bahrain Second Programme broadcasts general and cultural programmes including sports events and the Qur'an in Arabic. There are other private radio stations including Voice FM (www.voicefmbahrain. com), and, via satellite, Radio Sawa Gulf (www.radiosawa.com) and Monte Carlo Doualiya (www.rmc-mo.com) broadcasting in Arabic and French.

Television

BRTC operates five TV channels. The private and independent Orbit Satellite Television and Radio Network (www.orbit.net) operates 48 channels in Arabic and English by subscription. Residents also have access to hundreds of regional channels broadcasting via foreign satellite or cable TV companies.

National news agency
  Bahrain News Agency

Economy

Following the visit of an International Monetary Fund (IMF) mission in February 2020, the organisation offered praise for the Bahrain economy, whilst encouraging vigilance. The IMF Head of Mission, Bikas Joshi, noted that 'efforts at supervisory and regulatory vigilance, and to further enhance the Anti-Money Laundering/Countering Financing of Terrorism (AML/CFT) framework, are welcome.' Bahrain has been a leader in fintech, promoting opportunities while revising regulations and collaborating with other regulators.

According to the Moody's rating agency, Bahrain recorded 1.8 per cent year-on-year growth in 2019 and 2.4 per cent in nominal terms, according to the latest figures published by the Information and Government Authority. This compared to an annual growth rate of 1.8 per cent in 2018 in real terms and 6.1 per cent in nominal terms. Real annual growth was supported by growth in the oil and non-oil sectors. The oil sector rebounded in 2019, growing at an annual rate of 2.2 per cent, having contracted by 1.3 per cent in 2018 due to planned maintenance in the first quarter of 2018. The non-oil sector continued its positive growth, albeit at a slower pace, expand-

ing at a rate of 1.7 per cent (3.6 per cent in nominal terms). The growth of the non-oil sectors is a testament to the successful economic diversification and development initiatives pursued under the guiding principles of the Economic Vision 2030. Non-oil growth in 2019 received a boost from the manufacturing, hotels and restaurants sectors. Having recorded an annual growth rate of 4.7 per cent in the third quarter of 2019, the manufacturing sector continued to grow by 5.2 per cent in the fourth quarter of 2019, spurred on by the completion of ALBA's sixth production line. The hotels and restaurants sector recorded the highest non-oil sector annual growth at 6.8 per cent. Preliminary results point to a decline in growth in the fourth quarter of 2019. Despite negative growth of 0.4 per cent in real terms and 0.3 per cent in nominal terms during the final quarter of the year, the non-oil private sectors grew by 2.7 per cent in real terms in the fourth quarter of 2019 or by 3.4 per cent in nominal terms. The government services sector growth decelerated during the quarter after the government's implementation of fiscal measures to lower expenditure and improve the budget deficit. After a bout of lower risks, the COVID-19 pandemic has emerged as a major disruption to the near-term economic outlook. Despite the initial optimistic expectations for economic growth in 2020, a global recession is now all but certain. Policymakers around the world – led by the US Federal Reserve – have returned to aggressive stimulus measures. For Bahrain, this has entailed a monetary stimu-

COUNTRY PROFILE   421

lus as interest rates have been reduced
and the government has adopted a BD4.3
billion stimulus package to counter the
effects of the crisis. Furthermore, oil
prices have plunged since their highs at
the end of December 2019, adding to the
pressure on the global economy.

External trade

Bahrain is one of six members of the
Gulf Co-operation Council (GCC) free
trade agreement (FTA), a common market between Bahrain and the other five
members of the GCC, which was launched
in 2008. Citizens of these countries are
now allowed to travel between and live in
any of the six states, where they may find
employment, buy properties and businesses and use the educational and
health facilities freely. Bahrain is also a
member of the Greater Arab Free Trade
Area (GAFTA), which co-ordinates shared
standards and specification of Arab products, inter-custom fees and provides a
platform for communication between
members. The export of goods and services accounts for around 70 per cent of
GDP. In the face of falling oil reserves the
government has invested in processed
aluminium, which has become a major
export commodity and supports many
domestic downstream industries

Imports

Main imports are crude oil, machinery, raw materials, chemicals and foodstuffs.

Main sources

China (13.8 per cent of total in 2020),
Saudi Arabia (7.4 per cent), Australia (6.9
per cent), UAE (6.5 per cent).

Exports

Main exports are petroleum and related goods, aluminium, vehicles and au-
tomotive parts, and textiles.

Main destinations

Saudi Arabia (23.9 per cent of total in
2020), United Arab Emirates (12.5 per
cent), US (8.6 per cent), Oman (5.9 per
cent), Netherlands (5.1 per cent).

Agriculture

The agricultural sector typically accounts for 0.3 per cent of GDP and employs around 1 per cent of the workforce.

Apart from being a small island, development of agriculture is limited by labour
shortages, lack of water and salinity of the
soil. The major crop is alfalfa for animal
fodder, although farmers produce modest amounts of crops including dates, wa-
termelons, pomegranates, bananas, pota-
toes, eggplants and tomatoes for the local
market.

Government agricultural plans
emphasise drainage to reduce salinity,
improvement of the soil and new irrigation and cultivation techniques; there
have also been experiments with hydro-
ponics.

The land tenure system, under which
over 60 per cent of cultivable land is held
on three-year leases, discourages the stability needed for development.

The lack of grazing inhibits livestock
production. One large dairy has annual

milk production of 500,000 litres. Small dairy farmers, responsible for 15 per cent of production, have established a co-operative and constructed a milk pasteurising plant.

Fishing

The waters surrounding Bahrain have traditionally been rich fishing grounds, with more than 200 varieties of fish, many of which constitute a staple of the local diet.

The discovery of oil in 1932 led to a steady decline in the fishing industry, which has been unable to meet domestic demand, noticeably since the 1970s. Moreover, pollution in the Gulf, since the 1980s, has increasingly threatened fish production and the shrimp industry.

Fish catches have dropped amid claims of illegal fishing, habitat destruction from land reclamation and environmental pollution that threatens overall fish stocks.

Pearl diving was once a major industry with 40 per cent of Gulf pearl exports coming from Bahrain. Diving has declined sharply since the 1930s, but Bahrain has been a leading pearl testing centre since 1990, and a new pearl and gem-testing laboratory was opened in 2008.

Industry and manufacturing

The industrial sector contributes around 40 per cent of GDP, with manufacturing accounting for some 15 per cent. The sector typically employs an estimated 35 per cent of the labour force. Bahrain's most prominent non-oil indus-

try is the Aluminium Bahrain (ALBA) plant, which supplies various downstream manufacturing plants as well as the Gulf Aluminium Rolling Mill Company (GARMCO). Aluminium is Bahrain's second biggest export after oil. ALBA, one of the world's largest smelters, has expanded production, through its Line 6 Expansion Project (adding an extra 540,000 metric tonnes per annum, in 2020, to the previous one million mtpa). Bahrain also continues to seek new natural gas supplies as feedstock to support its petrochemical and aluminium industries.

In response to fiscal pressures from the effect of low oil prices, the government is gradually lifting the price of gas supplies to industry.

Facing declining oil reserves, Bahrain has invested strongly in communications and transport infrastructure, and worked to attract multinational businesses. It has achieved some diversification, but oil revenue remains 85 per cent of government revenue and 10 per cent of GDP. Low oil prices, most recently during COVID-19, place pressure on the national budget.

More than 50 per cent of the aluminium produced at ALBA is sold on the local and regional market, while the remainder goes mainly to the Far East. Export-oriented small- and medium-sized industries have been attracted to free industrial zones established at Mina Salman, Ma'amir, Abu Gazal and North Sitra, which enjoy tax and duty incentives. Industries located in these areas include plastics, paper, steel-wool and wire-mesh producers, marine service industries, aluminium, asphalt, cable manufacturing, prefabricated building and furniture. Iron and steel production is increasing. The Bahrain Ispat Company, under the control of the Indian Ispat Group (London), operates a plant with a capacity of 1.2 million tpy of iron briquettes produced from iron pellets.

Tourism

Bahrain as a regional destination is a key strategy for its tourist industry. However, the COVID pandemic in 2020 and 2021 and the associated restrictions on international travel have severely hindered plans for the development of the tourist industry.

Government national plans had included marketing Bahrain as a 'high-quality leisure and business tourism destination' for visitors primarily from the Middle East, but also Europe and Asia.

The most significant tourist development in the late 20th century was the opening of the causeway to Saudi Arabia. Many visitors cross the causeway from Saudi Arabia for day-trips. The Bahraini government is concerned that its traditional and historic towns are an asset that could easily be damaged by unfettered development. In July 2012, the coastal and island sites on Muharraq Island, which were the traditional home of the pearling industry, were added to UNESCO's World Heritage List.

Hydrocarbons
Gas
Reserves (end 2020): 2.3tn cu feet

Production: 16.4bn cum

Bahrain's largest oil and gas discovery since the 1930s was announced by the government in 2018. As a result total reserves of natural gas at end 2020 were estimated at 2.3 trillion cubic feet. Natural gas production in 2020 was 16.4 billion cubic metres.
Oil
Bahrain's oil reserves are declining rapidly. However in April 2018, the discovery of a large field of shale oil was announced, with estimated oil reserves of 80 billion barrels, the second largest deposit of shale oil in the world.

Oil accounts for around 87 per cent of government revenue, more than 75 per cent of exports, and around 20 per cent of GDP, but the government has been diversifying the economy especially in the wake of the drop in oil prices. Bahrain's annual refinery output in 2020 was 222,000 barrels per day (bpd), rather less than the 265,000bpd recorded in 2010. Total refining capacity in 2020 was 260,000bpd (BP). The Bahrain Petroleum Company has responsibility for all aspects of the hydrocarbon industry including exploration, production, refining and distribution in both domestic and international markets.
Coal
Bahrain does not produce or import coal.

Energy

Bahrain has 3.9GW of electricity generating capacity, almost all of which is produced from conventional thermal plants. However the Kingdom has recently begun to develop solar and other renewable power. It is also taking part in the GCC's plan to integrate the electric power grids of all GCC countries.

Construction of Bahrain's largest power plant, to provide around 30 per cent of Bahrain's total output, located at al-Dour, was completed in 2012. At a total cost of US$1 billion, it provides an additional 1,250MW of electricity and 181,680 kilolitres of desalinated water. The US electrical engineers GE Energy were contracted to provide five gas turbines, equipped with advanced emission control technologies. Further plans to increase production in other existing plants were to increase generation up to a projected requirement of 3,500MW by 2020.

A Gulf Co-operation Council (GCC) project to link the six member states (Saudi Arabia, Qatar, Bahrain, Kuwait, Oman and the UAE) to an integrated power-grid began in 2005. The first phase of the GCC power grid was completed in July 2009 at a cost of US$1,095 million, linking Saudi Arabia, Bahrain, Kuwait and Qatar through 800km of transmission lines. Kuwait and Saudi Arabia each received an extra 1,200MW of power capacity and the UAE 900MW, Qatar 750MW, Bahrain 600MW and Oman 400MW. In the first phase, a 400kV overhead line linked Kuwait's al-Zour power station with Doha, and a 400kV submarine line to Saudi Arabia with Bahrain. The second phase will link the UAE with Oman. The resulting two mega-grids will be joined in the final phase.

Financial markets

Bahrain has a solid reputation as an international financial hub. Although lagging behind Dubai (UAE), and having lost the political stability it once enjoyed, it remains attractive as a result of a combination of factors: an open and tax-free business climate, central geographical position, low costs, excellent communications and an accommodating government. The financial sector is one of the most diverse in the region and has the largest volume of transactions in the Middle East. The International Islamic Financial Market (IIFM) has attracted a number of major financial institutions to deal specifically in Sharia compliant deals.

At the end of 2021, according to the Central Bank, there were 403 financial institutions in Bahrain. This figure included 103 commercial, and investment banks, of which 79 could be called 'conventional' and 24 'Islamic'. Fifty-one of these financial institutions were also members of the Bahrain Association of Banks (BAB).

Bahrain Islamic International Rating Agency (IIRA) is the sole credit ratings agency set up (in 2005) to provide a ratings system of capital instruments and Islamic financial products in predominantly Islamic countries. IIRA is sponsored by several multilateral development institutions, major banks, financial institutions and ratings agencies. It operates in 11 countries in which it also has shareholders as the Sharia complaint board of directors maintain an independence service

COUNTRY PROFILE

Stock exchange

The Bahrain Bourse (BHB) (Bahrain Stock Exchange (BSE)) is the only licensed stock exchange of the Kingdom of Bahrain with a market capitalisation of US$24 billion offering various types of securities that include: shares, mutual funds, bonds and sukuk and treasury bills. The BHB also offers a comprehensive suite of exchange-related facilities including offering listing, trading, settlement, and depositary services for various financial instruments. Trading is carried out through 12 licensed members and day-to-day trading takes place through an Automated Trading System.

The Investor Online Account Service available on bahrain.bh is provided by Bahrain Bourse and allows investors to access their portfolio to view the details of ownership of owned shares and view all types of securities transactions' details.

Banking and insurance

In 2008 there were some 370 offshore banking units and representative offices in Bahrain, as well as 32 Islamic commercial, investment and leasing banks. Bahrain reportedly has the largest concentration of Islamic financial institutions, including *takaful* (insurance) companies, in the Middle East.

The Central Bank of Bahrain (CBB) has full regulations for its Islamic banking community. An agreement was reached between Saudi Arabia, Kuwait, Bahrain and Qatar to establish a Gulf Monetary Council (GMC) in 2010, but it never got off the ground.

Central bank

The Central Bank of Bahrain (CBB) replaced the Bahrain Monetary Agency on 7 September 2006. It is responsible for maintaining monetary and financial stability. The CBB has full regulations for the Islamic banking community.

Main financial centre

Manama

Time

GMT+3.

Geography

Bahrain is an archipelago of 33 islands. Only three of the islands are inhabited. The main island of Bahrain contains most of the population and is linked by a causeway to the island of Muharraq. Another causeway links Bahrain to Saudi Arabia.

Hemisphere

Northern

Climate

Summer temperatures are hot and humid, reaching 49 degrees Celsius ($^\circ$) in the shade, while January, the coldest winter month, has temperatures ranging from 3° to 28°. Humidity, particularly on the coast, can be extreme. Between December and the end of March the climate is temperate, with temperatures ranging between 19°–25°.

Dress codes

A lightweight suit or lightweight jacket and trousers are advised. A long-sleeved shirt with an optional tie should be worn at business and official meetings but a jacket need not be worn. Women should dress modestly. However, bikinis may be worn on certain beaches and at international hotel swimming pools. The dress code for women is less severe than in Saudi Arabia or some other Islamic countries.

Entry requirements

All visitors must carry photographic ID. It is an offence not to produce ID when requested by a member of the Bahraini authorities and you could be subject to a fine of BD300.

Women arriving in Bahrain alone and without a visa could be refused entry. Lone female travellers are advised to obtain a visa before departure.

Passports

Passports are required by all and should be valid for a minimum period of six months from the date of entry into Bahrain.

Visa

Visas are required by all, except nationals of Kuwait, Oman, Qatar, Saudi Arabia and the United Arab Emirates (UAE). Visas in advance of travel and visas on arrival are available for citizens of eligible nationalities. To determine eligibility and to obtain an e-visa prior to departure to Bahrain, visit the website www.evisa.gov.bh. For details of requirements for business and tourist visas visit: www.bahrainembassy.org/visareq.html. Tourist visas can be obtained on arrival at Bahrain airport, business visas must be applied for in advance. Journalists must make prior arrangements with the Ministry of Information Affairs.

Prohibited entry

Israeli nationals or anyone holding a passport with an Israeli visa/stamp may be denied entry.

Currency advice/regulations

Any currency, including Bahraini, may be freely imported and exported.

Customs

Personal effects are duty free. The duty free allowance is 400 cigarettes or 50 cigars and two bottles of alcoholic beverages, for non-Muslim passengers only, and 227ml of perfume for personal use.

Jewellery, drugs, firearms and ammunition are subject to import permits.

Prohibited imports

Pornographic and obscene literature and pictures, cultured or undrilled pearls.

Health (for visitors)

Medical services in Bahrain are of high quality with a good general hospital in Manama and modern health centres in smaller communities. Medical insurance is advised.

Mandatory precautions

Yellow fever certificate, for visitors arriving from infected areas.

COUNTRY PROFILE

Advisable precautions

Recommended immunisations are hepatitis A and B, polio, tetanus and typhoid. There is also a risk of rabies.

Hotels

There are plenty of first class hotels. A 12 per cent service charge is usual. Major hotels and most restaurants are licensed.

Public holidays (national)

Fixed dates

1 Jan (New Year's Day), 16–17 Dec (National Day).

Variable dates

Eid al Adha (three days), Eid al Fitr (three days), Islamic New Year, Ashura, Prophet's Birthday.

Islamic year

1444: 1 Muharram (approx 1 Jul 2022) – end Dhu al-Hijjah (approx 18 Jul 2023).

The Islamic year has 354 or 355 days, with the result that Muslim feasts advance by 10–12 days against the Gregorian calendar each year. Dates of the Muslim feasts vary according to sightings of the new moon, so cannot be forecast exactly.

Working hours

Thursday and Friday are weekly holidays. Regular hours are subject to change during the month of Ramadan. Some banks and businesses close on Saturday.

Banking

Sat–Wed: 0730–1200; Thu: 0730–1100; some branches are open three days weekly in the afternoon; some offshore banking units close on Sunday; 1000–1330 during Ramadan.

Business

Sat–Thu: 0800–1530 or 0800–1300, 1500–1730.

Government

Sat–Tue: 0700–1415; Wed: 0700–1400. During Ramadan government offices open 0930–1430.

Shops

Sat–Thu: 0830–1230, 1530–1830; large superstores are open Sat–Thu: 0800–1900; late opening Wed and Thu: 0800–1200, 1530–2130; some are open for a few hours on Friday in the Souk.

Mobile/cell phones

GSM 900/1800 services are available throughout the country.

Electricity supply

230V 50 cycles AC everywhere except Awali, which has 120V 60 cycles; various types of plug fitting, normally three-pin flat.

Weights and measures

Metric system (local measures are also used).

Social customs/useful tips

Traditionally much time is spent in exchanging small talk at business meetings; embarking on business matters before the atmosphere is favourable may cause offence. Decisions are often taken by consensus, according to the Arabian tradition, rather than exclusively on the advantages and disadvantages of the case submitted. In business, it is essential to create a mood of trust and to be persistent even when the case is apparently lost. Always shake hands on meeting and leaving. You may find the handshake lasts longer than in the West, but this is a sign of friendship. If you have made a good impression, the handshake on departure may be longer than that on arrival.

Muslims pray five times a day although shops and offices do not close during prayer. Although alcohol is not forbidden by law, like pork, it is forbidden by Islam and should be consumed with discretion. It is polite to avoid eating, drinking or smoking in the presence of Muslims during daylight hours in the month of Ramadan (it is illegal to do so in public).

Unless addressing members of the royal family normal Western forms of address and greeting are usual.

Everyone, including the visitor, is subject to *sharia* (Islamic law) although it is less rigorously applied than in some other Islamic countries.

Security

Visitors to Bahrain should keep in touch with developments in the Middle East as any increase in regional tension might affect travel advice.

Local security precautions, religious and social sensitivities should be observed and respected.

Getting there
Air
National airline

Gulf Air (100 per cent owned by Bahrain since May 2007).
International airport/s

Bahrain International, Muharraq (BAH), 6.5km north-east of city, with bar, restaurant, buffet, bank, shops, hotel reservations.
Airport tax

International departures BD7; not applicable for transit passengers.

Surface
Road

The King Fahd Causeway links Bahrain, Saudi Arabia and Qatar. The toll charges for using the causeway are set in Saudi Riyals (SR) viz:

Small Vehicles: SR25

Light Trucks and Small Buses: SR35

Large Buses: SR50

Trucks: SR5 per tonne
Water

There are passenger ferries running between Iran and Bahrain; the trip takes about 16 hours each way. There is a port tax of BD3.
Main port/s

Mina Salman, Mina Manama and Mina Muharraq.

Getting about
National transport
Road

Bahrain's road network is fairly good. There are good tarmac roads between centres, and six-lane highways form a ring road by-pass system for Manama and Muharraq.

Buses

A national bus company provides public transport throughout the populated areas of the country.

Rail

There are no railways in Bahrain.

Water

Dhow trips are arranged most weekends to sand bars and nearby islands from the old wharf (Mina Manama) on King Faisal Road. Boat trips to neighbouring islands are frequently arranged on Friday and publicised in the local press.

City transport

It is easy to cover both Manama and Muharraq on foot, though renting a car will make it easier to get to farther-flung locations.

Taxis

Taxis (with orange side wings and black-on-yellow number plates) are plentiful and fares are regulated. Fares are by meter and only vary when coming from the airport or when travelling by night.

Taxis are readily available for the 6.5km journey from Bahrain International airport to Manama, for which there is a charge in addition to the meter reading. Recommended fares from the airport are displayed outside the arrivals terminal.

Shared taxis or 'pick-ups' can be hailed from any bus stop. They do not use meters. Fares vary depending on the destination, but are lower than standard taxi fares. However, they can be very cramped and uncomfortable. The 'pick-ups' have white and orange number plates, and a yellow circle with the licence number in black painted on the driver's door.

Car hire

Insurance is compulsory and international driving licences must be validated at the Ministry of Interior Traffic Headquarters before use in Bahrain. Car hire firms are listed in the local telephone directory, and it is generally recommended to compare prices. Driving is on the right. Seatbelts are compulsory for both the driver and front seat passenger, and young children must be seated in the back. Road signs are in English and Arabic. The maximum speed limit on highways is 100kph, and on inner city roads it is generally between 50–80kph. If an accident occurs, the vehicle must not be moved until traffic police arrive.

Telephone area codes

The international direct dialling code (IDD) for Bahrain is +973 followed by subscriber's number.

Useful telephone numbers

Emergency service: 999

Directory enquiries: 181

International enquiries: 191

International bookings: 151

Operator: 100

Time in Arabic: 141

Time in English: 140

Telephone faults: 121

Useful addresses

Chambers of Commerce

Bahrain Chamber of Commerce and Industry, Bld 122, Road 1605, Block 216,

PO Box 248, Manama; tel: 17-229-555; internet: www.bahrainchamber. org.bh/english/index.htm)

Central bank

Central Bank of Bahrain (CBB), King Faisal Highway, Diplomatic Area, Block 317, Road 1702, Building 96, PO Box 27, Manama; tel: 17-535-535; web: www.cbb. gov.bh).

Travel information

Bahrain International Airport, PO Box 586, Manama; tel: 17-321-151.

Bahrain Tourism Company, PO Box 5831, Manama; tel: 17-534-321

Gulf Air, PO Box 138, Manama; tel: 17-228-820.

Ministry of tourism

Tourism Affairs, Ministry of Information, PO Box 26613, Manama; tel: 17-201-203; e-mail: btour@ bahraintourism.com).

Ministries

Ministry of Industry and Commerce, PO Box 5479, Manama; tel: 17-568-000, internet: www.commerce.gov.bh

Ministry of Defence, PO Box 245 Manama; tel: 17-766–666/17-653-333

Ministry of Education, PO Box 43 Manama; tel: 17-680-105, e-mail: moe@moe.gov.bh

Ministry of Foreign Affairs, PO Box 547, Manama; tel: 17-227-555, e-mail: contactus@mofa.gov.bh

Ministry of Health, PO Box 12, Manama, tel: 17-255-555, e-mail: info@health.gov.bh

Ministry of Housing and Urban Planning, PO Box 5802, Manama; tel: 17-533-000

Ministry of Industry and Commerce, PO Box 60667, Manama; tel: 17-574-777, e-mail: info@moic.gov.bh

Ministry of Information, PO Box 253, Manama; tel: 17-455-555, e-mail: info@iaa.gov.bh

Ministry of the Interior, PO Box 13, Manama; tel: 17-272-111, e-mail: dma@info.gov.bh

Ministry of Justice, Islamic Affairs and Waqf, PO Box 450, Manama; tel: 17-513-300, e-mail: info@moj.gov.bh

Ministry of Municipalities (general Directorate of Urban Planning) and Agriculture, PO Box 53, Manama; email: prinfo@mun.gov.bh

Ministry of Oil & Environment: PO Box 2, Manama; tel: 17-456-666, email: info@noga.gov.bh

Prime Minister's Office, PO Box 1000, Manama, tel: 17-200-000

Ministry of Social Development (formerly Labour and Social Affairs), PO Box 32333, Manama; tel: 17-873-777/ 17-687-800, e-mail: info@mlsd.gov.bh

Ministry of Transport & Telecommunications, PO Box 10325, Manama; tel: 17-534-534, e-mail info@mtt.gov.bh

Index

AB-4 Pipeline 302
ABN-Amro 171
ALBA 304
 defrauded 215
 lawsuit 304
ARAMCO 312
AWACS 313
 1982 cover extended to Bahrain 58
 US supplies to Saudi Arabia 58
Abadan 302
 refinery 60
Abbas, Mahmoud 302
Abdul-Karim, Ibrahim
 Minister of Finance 110, 133
Abdulkhaleq Abdullah
 denied entry to Bahrain to attend Gulf
  Development Forum on Water 264
abstinence 299
Abu Dhabi 302
Abu Dhabi Global Market 289
Abu Mazen 303
Abu Musa and The Tumbs
 annexed by Shah of Iran 36
Abu Safah oilfield 125, 303
 ARAMCO development 204
 Bahrain seeking increased
  production 156
 exported through Ras Tanurah 209
 King Faisal decision to divide revenue
  50/50 with Bahrain 39
 operated by Saudi ARAMCO 104, 172
 production maintained in 1984 102
 revenue shared by Saudi Arabia 11, 19, 61
 sales handled by BAPCO 209
Achaemenian Persians 35
Aden 303
al-Adha 299
Advisory Council appointed 1956 37
Afghanistan
 Soviet invasion 47, 54, 303
agitation for reform of social fields 37
agriculture 3
 hampered by lack of water 89
 land availability 10

land lost to urban development 159
 production 64
 subsidies 64
Al-Ahli Commercial Bank 133, 146, 166
 management contract with Bank of
  America 44
Ahli United Bank 303
Al-Ahlia Bank 25
Al-Ahlia Saudi Insurance 64, 304
aid
 2018 US$10 billion from Kuwait, Saudi
  Arabia and the UAE 279
Air Cargo Terminal 142
air-to-air missiles 58
Airborne Warning and Control System 304
Ajam 304
al-Ajmi, Sheikha bint Hassan
  al-Khrayyesh 304
Alaswad, Ali 278, 304
al-Alawi, Majid 304
al-Alawi, Sayed Mahmoud 304
 finance minister 25
Alcoa 305
 ALBA accuses of corruption 215
Alexandria 296
all-male suffrage 7
Allah 305
Almoayed, Tariq
 Minister of Information 160
alumina 305
 imported from Australia 171
 Western Australia source 11
aluminium
 1979 rise in spot price 40
 biggest export earner 165
 billets 306
 downstream projects 70
 exports 171
 GCC production 305
 government investment 208
 powder 3
 price drop 154
 price recession 92
 regional market growing 23

Aluminium Bahrain   62, 92, 117, 305
   1972 production began   11
   1979 government owned 77.9%   40
   1987 two-phase expansion   123
   1990 major expansion plans   147
   1993 expansion completed   158
   Alcoa court action   215
   Bahraini-isation of work force   70
   began industrialisation in Bahrain   69
   capacity increase planned for 1997   171
   consumes 40% natural gas
     production   11
   contributes 8% of GDP   209
   cost cutting exercise   40
   downstream expansion   85
   downstream industries   98
   expansion plans   40
   funding   22
   GCC first integrated industry   123
   government sold 20% to SABIC   40
   J/V government, SABIC, Kaiser Aluminium
     and Breton Investments   51
   July 1988 expansion finance
     finalised   134
   major employer   41, 270
   new potroom   23
   over-manned, redundancies   23
   plan to link power station to national
     grid   149
   plans to increase capacity   165
   Plant Council   12
   principal buyers   12
   production increase   154
   proposed expansion   23
   satellite industries   12
   shareholders   12, 22, 92
   smelter   3
     powered by natural gas   22
   spin-offs
     Bahrain Atomisers, BALEXCO,
       Midal Cables   41
   successful metallurgical industry   40
   supplying intermediate industries   123
   US$1.4 billion expansion agreed in
     2000   192
Alusuisse   12, 24, 93
Alwadaei, Sayed Ahmed
   Bahrain Institute for Rights and
     Democracy   261

Amalgamated Metal Co   23, 305
Amazon Web Services   291
American hostages in Tehran   47
Americans for Democracy and Human
   Rights in Bahrain   306
Amir   306
Amnesty International   164, 169, 237, 306
   report on human rights abuses   260
   reports Bahrain human rights crisis   235
   torture of Shi'ites documented   189
Anaizah tribe   270
Ancient Egypt   295 – 296
Anglo-Persian Oil Co   302, 307
Anno Domini   295
Anno Hegirae   295
Ansar Allah   354
anti-government activities   169
anti-government protests   237
   late-1984   163
Anti-Money Laundering/Countering
   Financing of Terrorism   286
anti-US sentiment   204
Appeal Court   169, 307
apprenticeship programmes   66
al-Aqsa Mosque   307
al-Arab, Ali   278, 307
Arab/African Summit Conference   308
Arab and Allied Military Forces   308
Arab Asian Bank   107, 116
Arab Bank   308
Arab Bank for Economic Development in
   Africa   308
Arab Banking Co   59, 63, 84, 104, 108, 116,
   155, 171, 181, 308
   growth through foreign acquisitions   108
Arab Boycott   308, 373
Arab Co-operation Council   308
Arab democracy
   developed early in Bahrain   208
Arab Free Trade Area   309
Arab Fund for Economic and Social
   Development   309
Arab Gulf University   129, 309
Arab Gulf states   309
Arab Insurance Group   59, 96, 309
   J/V Kuwait. Libya and UAE   64
Arab Investment Banking Co   309
The Arab Investment Co   84
Arab Iron and Steel Co   59, 98, 117, 171, 309

INDEX 433

Arab Iron and Steel Co (cont.)
 1986 closed 135
 British Steel report optimistic 124
 pelletising plant 61, 79
Arab Islamic state 68
Arab/Israeli war
 October 1973 310
 relations with US strained 2
Arab League 310
 Bahrain member of 1, 7, 67
Arab Light crude
 from Saudi Arabia refined by
 BANOCO 167
 preferential rates from Saudi Arabia 157
 price marker 310
 via pipeline from Saudi Arabia 209
Arab Maritime Petroleum Transport
 Co 310
Arab Mining Co 62, 95
Arab Monetary Fund 310
Arab nationalism 233
Arab Nationalist Movement 310
Arab News 311
Arab Petroleum Investments Co 22, 49, 311
Arab Shipbuilding and Repair Yard 41, 52,
 59, 135, 311
 1977 began operations 135
 1987 dry dock occupancy 90% 135
 1989 profit 148
 demand rising in 1994 161
 doubled revenue in 1988/89 143
 first downstream venture 12
 operated by Lisnave 41
 shareholders 62
 strategic position 41
 tanker war benefits 135
Arab Spring XI, 237, 249, 311
 Bahrain only Gulf monarchy unrest 278
Arab states
 failure of approach to Israel 54
Arab unity 269
Arab World
 no ties with Iron Curtain countries 8
Arabian Gulf 233, 311
Arabian Insurance Co 81
Arabian Light crude 311
Arabian Peninsula 312
Arabian Sea 312
Arabic nomenclature 301

Arafat, Yasser 312
Argus Sour Crude Index 312
Arlabank 116
Arlabank International 84
Armilla Patrol 130
Army 312
arrest of five Sunni Bahrainis 196
al-Asalah 256, 312
Ash Sharqiyah 340
Asharq al-Aswat 312
Ashburton, John 312
al-Asheeri, Ali Rashed 284
al-Ashtar Brigades 312, 390
Ashton, Catherine 244
Ashura 271, 298, 312
Asian community, attacks on 178
associated gas 313
 Awali oilfield 209
 feedstock for gas gathering facility 21
 vented 21
Atlantic Richfield 313
Augustus 297
Awali oilfield 3, 21, 313
 enhanced recovery 125
 natural gas reserves 226
 production increase 242
 residue gases for power generation 21
Ayatollah Khomeini 47

BAII Insurance Services 96
BP Statistical Review of World Energy
 2014 260, 329
Ba'ath 313
Ba'athists 314
Babylon 296
Babylonian ruler 295
Babylonians 35
Bacon, Roger 297
Baghdad 314
 Iran calls for overthrow of Ba'athist
 regime 55
Baghdad Pact 277, 314
Bahama 85
Bahrain
 background to independence 315
 building up defences 131
 close association with Saudi Arabia 130
 declined to join proposed federation 6
 financial aid to Palestinians 57

434 INDEX

Bahrain (contd.)
    independence supported by Saudi
        Arabia 97
    independence from Britain 67
    lay-offs in oil industry 77
    links with India and UK 276
    links to US 145
    majority population Shi'a 144
    military weakness 58
    pro-Iraqi policies
        friction with Iran 136
    pro-Western 130
    supported Saddam Hussein in
        private 54
Bahrain Agricultural Foods Storage and
    Security 314
Bahrain Aluminium Extrusion Co XIV, 24,
    69, 101, 154, 314
    Board approves modernisation plan 71
    diversification 143
    part privatisation planned 158
    plans to float on BSE 147
Bahrain Association of Banks 80, 314
Bahrain Atomisers International 24, 69, 93
Bahrain Aviation Fuel Co 314
Bahrain Bourse 315
Bahrain Centre for Human Rights 315
    Maryam al-Khawaja, Acting
        President 244
Bahrain Currency Board 5
Bahrain Defence Force 315
    Commander-in-Chief
        Hamad bin Isa al-Khalifa 67
Bahrain Development Bank 315
Bahrain-Dhahran air shuttle 45
Bahrain dinar 5, 316
Bahrain dissidents 316
Bahrain Family Planning Association 119
Bahrain Field 316
Bahrain FinTech Bay 316
Bahrain Fishing Co 3, 10, 65, 159, 316
Bahrain Forum for Human Rights 317
Bahrain Freedom Movement 317
Bahrain Hotels Co 1990 flotation 147
Bahrain Human Rights Monitor 317
Bahrain Human Rights Observatory 317
Bahrain Human Rights Society 317

Bahrain Independent Commission of Inquiry
    (aka Bassiouni Commission) 251,
    318, 376
    critical report 238
Bahrain Institute for Political
    Development 320
Bahrain Institute for Rights and
    Democracy 261, 320
Bahrain International Airport 60, 161, 320
    expansion 153
    first BA Concorde flight 46
    first with runway purpose-built for
        jumbo jets 15
Bahrain International Bank 107, 116, 155,
    320
    share issue oversubscribed 63
Bahrain International Circuit 235
Bahrain International Investment
    Centre 109, 117
Bahrain Iron and Steel Co 171
Bahrain Islamic Bank 80, 109, 175, 321
Bahrain Ispat Co 171, 321
Bahrain Justice and Development
    Movement 321
Bahrain and Kuwait Investment Co 116
    share issue oversubscribed 63
Bahrain-Kuwait Petrochemicals
    Industries Co 49
Bahrain Laughs, by Lewis Morland 377
Bahrain Light Industry Co 63
Bahrain Maritime and Mercantile
    International 321
Bahrain Middle East Bank 107, 116, 321
Bahrain Monetary Agency 15, 42, 50, 63,
    106, 116, 160, 321
    Abdulla Saif
        Director General 25
    central banking powers 80
    encouraging insurance and reinsurance
        companies 81
    Ibrahim Abdul-Karim
        Deputy Chairman 25
    investment banking licences 81
    Khalifa bin Sulman al-Khalifa
        Chaiman 25
    regulate domestic banking 25
    treasury bills 126
    well-regulated banking sector 175

INDEX   435

Bahrain National Cold Storage and
    Warehousing Co
    privatised   158
Bahrain National Gas Co   61, 91, 321
    1990 new gas plant commissioned   148
    expansion plan approved   125
    expansion plans   142
    gas-liquefaction plant expansion   135,
        140
    J/V with BANOCO, Caltex and APIC   49
Bahrain National Museum   141
Bahrain National Oil Co   39, 166, 322
    1978 government ownership 100%   21
    1979 took full control oil production   49
Bahrain Navy   131
Bahrain Oilfield   260, 322
    production declining   38
Bahrain Petroleum Co   3, 10, 20, 75, 125, 132,
        205, 322
    2005 under modernisation   205
    expatriate workforce   76
    first commercial discovery 1932   38
    formed 1999   187
    formed jointly by Standard Oil Co and
        Caltex   38
    modernisation programme   140
    modernisation of refinery   157
    production   77
    redundancies   76
    refinery   4
    second largest employer   11
    Sitra Refinery expansion   187
    Sitra Refinery modernisation
        postponed   147
    support services   77
    US$300 million expansion planned   167
    US$800 million to upgrade Sitra
        Refinery   192
    workforce   76
Bahrain Police Force fired tear gas   277
Bahrain Refinery   323
Bahrain Salam for Democracy and Human
        Rights   249, 323
Bahrain Saudi Aluminium Marketing
        Co   69, 154
Bahrain Ship Repairing and Engineering
        Co   323
Bahrain Slipway Co   323
    to cease operating   135

Bahrain Steel   324
Bahrain Stock Exchange   146, 155, 160, 184,
        324
    1987 established   126
    foreign shareholders   154
    non-Bahraini Gulf citizens allowed to
        trade   142
Bahrain Telecommunications Co   166, 324
    privatised   193
Bahrain Transparency Society   257, 324
Bahrain University   324
Bahrain Uprising   234, 324, 372, 376
Bahrain uprisings   XI
Bahrain Watch   257, 324
    blog   263
Bahraini Kuwaiti Investment Group   107,
        109
Bahraini Saudi Bank   95, 166, 324
Bahraini society becoming divided   253
Bahraini Women's Day   324
Bahraini workforce
    job cuts in unskilled   99
Bahraini-isation   149, 207, 325
    policy   177
    programme to discriminate in favour of
        locals   198
Bairam   299
balance of payments
    1992 deficit   151
Balfour Beatty   51
Ballast Nedam   88, 325
    causeway contract   72
Banco Atlántico   108
Banco do Comércio e Indústria de São
        Paulo   106
Banco di Roma   106
Banco de Vizcaya   106
Bandar Resort   141
Bank of America   25, 44, 106
bank assets   241
Bank of Bahrain and Kuwait   25, 43, 109, 116,
        133, 146, 166, 325
Bank of Bahrain and the Middle East   63
Bank of England   5
Bank Melli Iran   325, 347
    accused by US of financing Iran's nuclear
        programmes   216
Bank Negara Indonesia   106
Bank of Oman   105

Bankers Security Deposit Account   126
Bankers' Society of Bahrain   106
banking   104
banking centre   160
banking sector   126
   1988 signs of recovery   132
   includes gold dealing and commodity
     trading operations   64
   mainstay of economy   138
   prospects mixed 2012   241
   rationalisation   139
banking services   2
bankruptcy law   127, 280
Banoco Arab Medium   325
Banque Arabe Internationale
   d'Investissement   325
Banque Franco-Arabe d'Investissements
   Internationaux   326
Banque Paribas   109, 326
Barclays Bank   105, 133
Basel III   326
Basra   326
Bassiouni, Cherif
   Chairman BICI   238
Bassiouni Commission (aka Bahrain
   Independent Commission of
   Inquiry (BICI)   277
Bayt Siyadi   141, 326
Begin, Menachem   57, 326
Beirut   42
   eclipse of   82
Belgrave, Charles   37, 327
   Advisor   268
Bilad al-Qadeem
   tear gas fired   277
bi-lateral relations
   with Kuwait and Saudi Arabia   69
Bin Mahfouz family   107
birth rate differentials   232
bissextile   297
bitcoin   286
blockade   328
boat-building   3
bomb attack Sitra 2015   263
Bombay High crude   91
boom days   68
boycotts
   Israel and Rhodesia   5
Bramco Group   329

quarried rock contract   72
'brass plate' firms
   deterred by government   43
Breaking of the Fast   299
Brent crude   192, 282
   price fall   179
Breton Investments   24, 62, 92, 305, 329
   owned 5.1% ALBA   40
bridge Manama to Muharraq   148
Britain
   close political ties   227
   independence from   35
   maintains close ties   1
   treaty relationship   19
British   35
   administer defence and foreign affairs
     from Bahrain   36
   Foreign Office   330, 340
   government
     responsible for Bahrain defence and
      foreign affairs   1
   influence pre-1971   276
   military in Palestine   326
   naval presence   238
   political and military treaties with   1
   protectorate   315
   Residency   97
   role in Bahrain   330
British Airports International   52
British Bank of the Middle East   109, 329
British Broadcasting Co   330
British Empire   303
British Mandate for Palestine   308
British Overseas Airways Co (BOAC)   232
British Petroleum   330
British Political Resident   371
British Smelter Constructions   25
British troops called on to restore order   277
Brown and Root Marine   331
budget
   1973   4
   1975–76   19
   1976   15
   1983   68
     deficit   102
   1986–88   126
   1987   126
   1988   132
     one year only   131

INDEX

1989 146
1989–90 138
1992 151
1994 156
1998 179
1999 185
1999–2000
   public sector salaries
      60% current expenditure 192
2003–04 198
2004 202
2009 229
2011 240
2016 281
oil price break-even point 240
bureaucracy
   over-manned 127
   well entrenched 221
Bushire 268
business registration fees 20

CEIC Data 331
cabinet 100
Cable and Wireless 46, 194, 331
Caesar, Julius 297
Cairo 269, 331
calendars
   Christian 295
   Egyptian 296
   Hijri 295
   Islamic 295
   lunar 296
   Mesopotamian 296
   pre-Islamic Middle Eastern 296
   Roman Republican 297
   solar 296
calends 297
Caltex 20, 85, 331
   contracted to purchase propane, butane
     and naphtha 40
Caltex Petroleum Co 76, 91
Camp David Accords 47, 57, 331
Canadian Imperial Bank of Commerce 106
Canopus Decree 296
capital expenditure 185
   to rise in 1997 175
Capital Markets Group 106
capital punishment 174
cash support

Kuwait and Saudi Arabia 170
causeway to Saudi Arabia 14
   benefits for both countries 35
   bidding starts 51
   construction spin-offs 44
   effects on business 101
   financed by Saudi Arabia 51
   Gulf of Bahrain to al-Khobar 101
   link to trans-European system 14
   linking Bahrain to Saudi Arabia 18
   political signal to Tehran 137
   pre-qualification of tenderers 34
   strategic and economic link 144
   target opening 1986 71
   tourist revenue 72
   stimulus to business 134
census 332
   1965 69
   April 1971 2
   April 2010 416
Central Bank of Bahrain 229, 332
   2006 law 225
   committed to US$ peg 282
   fintech innovation unit 285
   key policy rate 241
Central Boycott Office 332
Central Statistics Bureau 140
Central Statistics Organisation 194
   import/export statistics 159
Chamber of Commerce 88
cheap energy 125
Chevron 332
   1998 offshore explorations 180
ChevronTexaco
   awarded exploration block 204
China 296, 332
   1988 Saudi Arabia only Gulf state without
     formal links 138
   1990 trade and technical co-operation
     agreement signed 146
   embassy in Bahrain opened 1990 146
   full diplomatic relations established in
     1988 138
Christian churches 271
Christian movable feasts 298
Citi Islamic Investment Bank 171, 333
Citibank Bahrain 106, 333
   Islamic subsidiary in Manama 175
Civil calendar 296

438 INDEX

civil service
  government aims to trim   99
civil unrest   253
Clark, Alan   145
Clinton, Hillary   333
  US Secretary of State   234
Cohen, William   333
  US Defence Secretary   188
commercial banking structure
  Bahrain best developed by 1970s   67
commercial banking
  mixed results in 1988   139
Commercial Companies Law   84, 333
  took effect 1 June 1987   127
commercial registration certificate   152
common currency   334
Common Market   334
Commonwealth of Independent States   335
communications key to service centre
  success   46
Compagnie Générale de Géophysique   90
Concorde   52, 84
  Bahrain first BA destination   6
constituencies   1, 68, 335
Constituent Assembly   335 – 336
  elections first held 1972   1
constitution
  1972   195
  1973   335
  1975 suspended   168
  2002   195, 335
    established two-chamber
      parliament   256
    protests   200
  December 1973 ratified by Emir   68
  draft   1
  draft approved by National
    Assembly   68
  first published June 1973   1, 7
  judicial power   68
  legislative powers   68
  modelled on Kuwait's 1962
    Constitution   68
Constitutional Courts   336
constitutional monarchy   220
constitutional reforms
  announced by Emir Hamad
    al-Khalifa   220
  demand lead by labour movement   100

construction sector
  principal borrower   26
  work declines in 1986/87   128
Consultative Assembly   336
Consultative Council   173, 336
  government appinted   178
consumer demand   2
consumer goods
  majority imported   186
consumer lending   211
consumption tax   202
container port
  plans for Hidd   148
Continental Illinois National Bank and
    Trust Co   106
Co-operation Council for the Arab States of
    the Gulf
  see Gulf Co-operation Council   228
corporate income tax   274, 290
corruption   233
cost of living   2
  rising sharply   9
costs of doing business   225
cottage-type industries   10
Council of Deputies
  2006 elections   228
Council of Ministers   86
  formerly Advisory Council   37
Council of Representatives   336
Council of State   7, 336
  formed January 1970
    executive powers   1
coup d'état
  1981 attempt   56, 85, 144, 336
Court of Cassation
  2019 upheld death sentences of al-Arab
    and al-Malali   278
Covid-19 pandemic   287
Creation   295
credit growth improvement   241
credit rating downgrade   240
Creditcorp International   108
crescent new moons   295
crowd-funding   336
Crown Prince
  Salman bin Hamad al-Khalifa   214
crude oil and refined petroleum products
  exports and imports   60
crypto-asset   337

INDEX

crypto-currency 286, 337
cultivated pearls 2
cultural heritage 141
Currency Board 337
currency devaluation
    aid required to avoid 282
current account 247, 252
    1999 deficit 186
    2011 surplus 240
current expenditure
    to be reduced from 1985 102
customs union
    2003 introduced by GCC 203

DHL
    distribution centre under
        construction 161
Daawa 337
Dahdaleh, Victor 215, 337
dairy farm 10
Daiwa Securities Co 133, 337
Damascus 337
Dammam oilfield
    Bahrain purchases oil from 204
al-Dar Island 141, 337
date palm trees 3
date-processing plant 64
Day of Rage XII
death sentence use 338
debt
    low levels 197
    manageable situation 201
    Management Office 274
    provisions 133
decem 297
decentralisation of power 198
declaration of independence 1
Decree No 41 198
defence budget 338
    1980s steady increase 137
democratic institutions
    1950s proposals declined by ruling
        family 269
democracy 233
    experiment 87
    promised by King Hamad 195
democratic system of government 68
deportation from London
    six Bahrainis 97

deposit insurance 107
desalination
    increasing capacity 60
    plants 338
    reverse osmosis plants 149
    Sitra plant 3
    to combat water crisis 103
detention without trial 189
development bonds 131, 338
    1977 launch 20
development loans
    from IDB, Saudi Arabia, Kuwait and
        UAE 170
Development Plan 338
    extended by two years to 1987 102
    five-year 128
Dhahran 338
Dhahran Air Base 145
dhow traffic 161
Dhu al-Hijjah 296, 298
diesel fuel
    reduction of sulphur content 187
Dilmun 339
Dilmun civilisation 35, 141
Dimashq 337
dinar 339
    pegged to US dollar 186, 202
diplomatic profile 144
direct aid
    from Arab countries falls in 1998 179
direct reduction steel plants 95
Directorate for Customs and Ports 73
Directorate of Civil Aviation Affairs
    open skies policy 153
Directorate of Election and
        Referendum 257, 339
dishdasha 270
disparities of wealth
    GCC aim to erode across region 69
disposable income relatively high 186
distillation unit 78
diversification
    economy 66
    industry 124
domestic banking 95, 109
domestic borrowing increase by
        government 180
domestic tensions 150
Dow Jones 241, 339

Dowar al-Lulu 384
downstream activities
targeted as part diversification
strategy 191
dry dock 4
Dubai 62
Dubai 5, 339
increasing competition from 205
offshore banking plans scuppered 42
Dubai International Financial Centre 209, 289
Dubai Islamic Bank 44
Dukhan oilfield 103, 189, 339
new recovery techniques
to extend life 104
Dulsais 339
duplication of industries 98

early-retirement scheme launched
2019 279
earth satellite station 52
1968 first station commissioned in
Bahrain 46
East India Co 339
East of Suez 340
British withdrawal policy 229
Easter 298
Eastern Bank 109
Eastern Province, Saudi Arabia 340
1987 population 66% Bahraini 123
Western expatriates 18
Eastern Region 340
Ecclestone, Bernie 235
Ecole 42 288
economic
2003 performance 205
activity returns to pre-turmoil
norms 240
climate uncertain in 1988 131
crisis avoided 253
crunch expected 68
diversification 144
policy 197
policy changes by Emir 184
reforms 187
schisms 168
stability due to oil price rise in 1997 177
strategy 246
uncertainty 144

Economic Development Board 286, 341
to attract FDI 206
GDP 2012 forecast 239
Mohammed bin Essa al-Khalifa,
CEO 214, 221
Economic Freedom Index
Wall Street Journal/Heritage
Foundation 239
Economic Vision 2030 271, 287, 341
McKinsey & Co 271
economy
1989 medium-term challenges 138
2000 government spending cutbacks 190
diversification 134
government plans to attract foreign
investment 140
government plans to diversify 140
growth in 2019 286
threat of instability 216
education
1929 girls' began 268
free for boys and girls 9
free in 1984 69
Gulf's highest level 2
vocational training 9
Egypt 124, 269
arms agreement with Soviet Union 277
retaining diplomatic ties with Israel 57
Egyptian Civil (or 'wandering') year 296
Eid al-Adha 298
Eid al-Fitr 298 – 299
elapsed time 295
elected legislature
1955 requested and rejected 276
Election Day
fixed as 7 December 68
election monitors
international 279
elections
Constituent Assembly first held 1972 1
municipal
2006 213, 228
first held 2002 195
municipal and national
2002
irregular turnout 196
national
2002 200

INDEX 441

boycotted by political
societies 195
Elections
won by Islamists and
conservatives 201
2006 213, 228
first woman elected 213
2010 233
2014
boycotted by opposition 256
monitors 257
electoral districts
distorted allocation 195
electoral roll
Sunnis added 232
electricity
generated by non-associated gas 22
generation fossil fuel fired 260
grid-sharing scheme 125
power grid connections 242
price rise 20
requirements reassessed 125
rising demand 171
state dominates generation 242
Electricity and Water Authority 242, 341
Emir 341
Emirates 341
employment
decisive issue 239
growth projections 94
opportunities 176
public sector 175
patterns 118
problem for middle class Bahrainis 9
EnCana Co 204, 342
Energy Information Administration 260,
342
energy sector
government role 242
Eni 273
entrepôt trade 5
epagomenal days 296 – 297
Ereli, J Adam 233
d'Estaing, Giscard
March 1980 successful Gulf tour 48
Etihad Airways 342
euro-zone 241
Eurobond

legislature votes against as
un-Islamic 196
Eurodollar 342
Eurofima 26
Europe-Arab Bank 342
European Bahrain Organisation for Human
Rights 342
European Central Bank 342
European Community 343
European Currency Unit 343
European Economic Community 58, 343
European Union 175, 244, 343
equity investment funds 165
US relations 251
European Union Institute for Security
Studies 245, 343
exchange control 5
exchange rate
peg against US dollar 223, 241, 274
executions 169, 270
exempt company 343
introduced 1979 43
status 81
exile 270
expatriate workers 118
40% of population 2001 194
1990 exodus 149
expatriates 99
exploration 90
Awali oilfield extent 21
plans for off-shore 39
export-substitution industries 94
exports 5
main customers 5
revenue 176
exports and imports,
gap widening 156
extra-budgetary operations 252

F-5 fighter jets 58
ordered from US 343
F-16 fighter jets 137, 343
ordered for delivery 1989 onwards 131
FALCO
ASRY site dredging 13
FRAB-Bank 346
Fakih, Lama 284
Farewell Pilgrimage 295
Farewell to Arabia, David Holden 269

Fasht al-Adham 344
  land reclamation scheme 128
Fasht Dibal 344
  occupied by Qatar 111
fasting 299
Fatah 344, 352
Fateel, Naji 244, 344
al-Fatih Coalition 256
feasibility study
  C E Lummus 78
  heavy oil conversion cracker 78
February 14 Coalition 344
federation proposed
  Bahrain opted out 36
female labour force participation 275
festivals of Islam 295
Field, Michael 268, 301
FinTech 345
FinTech Bay 346
Finance Ministry 344
financial
  policy 4
  services 191
financial centre 42
  competition from Dubai 180
Financial Centre of the Future award
  1995 Bahrain named winner 209
financial markets 95
financial sector 344
  16% of GDP 246
  2006 IMF report on 211
  competition from Dubai 197
  foreign ownership 192
  fund management 175
  future in doubt 144
  growth of Islamic services 197
  international capital markets 175
  Islamic banking 175
  long term viability questioned by 1990
    Kuwait invasion 145
  rationalisation 149
  recognised as regional hub 202
Financial Sector Assessment
    Programme 225, 345
  CBB efforts to implement 274
financial watchdog 220
First National Bank of Houston 106
fiscal
  deficit 247

  narrowed in 1999 185
  rising in 2013 252
  prudent policy 202
  reform 274
  transparency 274
  unsustainability 240
Fiscal Balance Programme 290, 346
fishing 3, 10, 65
Fitch Ratings
  2008 stable outlook 223
Five Pillars of the Islamic faith 299
food stockpile 346
Food and Agriculture Organisation 3
foreign assets 229
foreign banks
  questioning viability 105
foreign companies law 152, 346
foreign direct investment 193, 206, 216
foreign dumping 93
foreign interference
  investigation ordered by King
    Hamad 251
foreign investment
  boosted by 100% foreign ownership 160
  rules liberalised 177
  sluggish in 2000 190
foreign investors
  increasing incentives 156
foreign nationals
  permitted 100% ownership 216
  sizable proportion of workforce 170
foreign ownership 156, 280
foreign policy 88, 189
  in favour of GCC unity 175
  maturing throughout Gulf 138
  reassessed 48
foreign relations
  close ties with UK and USA 8
foreign reserves 197
foreign trade 159
foreign unskilled labour
  Indo-Pakistan, Afghans and Iranians 9
foreign workers
  gradual replacement 127
  job cuts 99
Formula One Grand Prix 222
  cancelled March 2011 235
Forum for the Future
  hosted by Bahrain in 2005 213

INDEX

Four Year Development Plan
1981–55 64
fourteenth Iranian province 233
fracking
US market leader 273
France
1980 agreement on supply of military
equipment 48
discussions on weaponary and training
facilities 48
relations warmed after Emir visit to
Paris 8
Fraser Institute 193, 238, 346
Economic Freedom Index 238
free education 249
free-enterprise economy encouraged 66
free medical care 249
free trade zone planned for Hidd 148
freedom of association under threat 245
freedom of religious belief 1
freedom of speech 1
fuel subsidies
threat to cut failed 253
Fund of Funds 403
fundamentalism, growth 100
Future Bank 216, 347

G-8 347
GARMCO 349
GCC
funded projects 290
unified customs levy on imports 73
gas
associated and non-associated
production rising 39
feedstock
for energy-intensive heavy
industry 98
reserves 4, 49, 125
gas-gathering 347
plant 104
Gateway Gulf Investor Forum 285
Gaza 57, 347
gemsbok 383
General Agreement on Trade in
Services 348
General Committee for Bahraini
Workers 87, 348
General Tenders Law 348

General Trade Union 371
Gilgamesh 36
global financial crisis challenge for GCC 222
Global Islamic and Sustainable Fintech
Center 288, 348
golf course planned for tourists 153
good governance 202
'good neighbour' policy 8
government
1966 annual income 276
bond issue over-subscribed 247
budgeted revenue
oil 57% in 1979 38
committed to linking economy to its
neighbours 34
crack down on peaceful dissent 284
debt 252, 289
external debt 252
grants and subsidies cut 163
house building project 44
housing bank 44
hyper-sensitive to criticism 257
intolerance of criticism 258
job eligibility 257
reluctance to raise taxes 179
revenues 20
services growth deceleration 287
stable 145
wages and allowances boost 175
zero tolerance policy 284
grants
from Arab countries fall in 1998 179
Kuwait and Saudi Arabia contributions
decreasing 165
Gray Mackenzie 348
Greater Arab Free Trade Area 309
Greek-Egyptian astronomers 296
Greeks 35
green coke 348
plan shelved 23
Gregorian calendar 295, 297–298
festivals 298
Pope Gregory 297
grievances against Royal Family
shared by Shi'a and Sunni 271
Grindlays Bank 95
gross domestic product 124, 157, 208, 228,
348
1993 156

444 INDEX

2013 growth 258
banking and insurance contribution
increase to 12% 166
consistently high 201
oil contribution drops to 17% 166
oil production contribution 197
Group of 8 347
growing problems with security 100
growth
IMF projects will decelerate 273
The Guardian daily newspaper 237, 349
guest workers
abuse reported 204
Gulf 349
Gulf Air 15, 215, 349
Boeing 777 order cancelled 167
Boeings, Airbuses and Lockheed
TriStars 154
competition from Oman Air and
Emirates 154
expanding fleet 142, 153
increased profits 52
loan managed by GIB 126
new HQ planned 148
plans to go public in 1995 153
regional airline 46
headquartered at Bahrain 46
Gulf Aluminium Rolling Mill Co 59, 71, 93,
117, 349
began operations January 1986 134
new plant at Sitra 171
shareholders 62
Gulf Aluminium Rolling Mill Co
to generate aluminium fabrication
industry 103
Gulf Aviation 350
Gulf of Bahrain 350
available for exploration 208
Gulf business activity
general revival 139
Gulf common market 59, 350
Gulf Consolidated Services and
Industries 109
Gulf Co-operation Council 58, 144, 174, 350
agency for integrating economic
activity 98
Bahrain benefits from 98
call for co-ordinated tax regimes 202
citizens of all member countries 228

collective defence clauses 234
condemned Israel invasion of
Lebanon 56
co-ordinated policies 59
ineffective against Iraq invasion of
Kuwait 145
Peninsula Shield Force
despatched to Bahrain via
Causeway XII
relations with Iran 137
support for UNSC call for Iran/Iraq
ceasefire 55
supported Bahrain measures to quell
dissent 164
Unified Economic Agreement 190
Gulf crisis 144, 350
Gulf currency assets
strong 43
Gulf Daily News 251
Gulf deployment force 58
Gulf Development Forum on Water
Security 350
Abdulkhaleq Abdullah denied entry to
attend 264
Gulf Finance House 350
Gulf Industrial Investment Co 171, 350
Gulf International Bank 22, 51, 59, 63, 70,
84, 104, 108, 115, 133, 350
'low risk, low reward' strategy 108
Gulf Investment Co 59, 351
Gulf Organisation for Industrial
Consulting 93, 351
Gulf Petrochemical Industries Co 59, 61, 95,
117, 165, 351
downstream industry 78
hopes for downstream petrochemical
industries 98
processes Khuff gas 158
urea plant 143
Gulf region instability 54
Gulf-Riyad Bank 351
Gulf states 351
Gulf Technical College
Business Administration faculty
added 14
Gulf University 102, 351
Gulf War 351

The Hague 351

INDEX

Haig, Alexander   351
  US Secretary of State
    resigns 1982   58
Hakim   351
Halcrow-Burns
  ASRY second dry dock   148
Hamad Town   271, 351
  1983 first residents move in   68
Hammurabi   295
Haq Movement for Liberty and
    Democracy   352
Harakat al-Muqawama al-Islamia   352
Harakat al-Tahir al-Watani al-Falistin   352
Hawar Islands   352
  Bahrain plans for causeway from   179
  closer to resolution in 2000   189
  dispute with Qatar   169
    prevents exploration   156
  International Court of Justice   164
  relations with Qatar worsen   179
health insurance   179
heavy industrial area   14
heavy industry   117
  cheap feedstock from gas   98
Heavy Oil Conversion Co   59, 61, 78, 95
  proposed by Ministry of Development
    and Industry   78
hereditary emirate   220
hereditary rule   68
Heritage Foundation report   193, 205, 353
  Index of Economic Freedom   227
Hezbollah   353
  GCC brands as terrorist organisation   263
Hezbollah-Bahrain   353
  backing from Iran   169
  Iran accused of plotting with   174
Hidd   353
  chosen for new container port and free
    trade zone   148
  container port and free trade zone
    delayed   180
  generating and desalination facilities
    planned   172
  port and industrial free zone plans   175
Higher Council for Economic
    Development   354
  government announced
    establishment   193
Al-Hijjah   298

Hijrah   295
Hijri
  calendar   295
  leap year   298
Hindu temples   271
Hitachi   79
Holden, David   269
  Farewell to Arabia   276
hospitality sector   246
hotel industry
  to benefit from Causeway   122
hotel market
  over-subscribed   72
hotel rooms
  from shortage to over-supply   45
hoteliers
  confident of long term prospects   45
hotels
  plans for 20 new   165
household debt   275
housing
  shortage   102
  shortage in Shi'a areas   279
  stock   19
Housing Bank   81
housing programmes   68
  1984 rents fixed at 25% of householder
    income   69
housing scheme   13
  accelerated by government   13
  BD40 million donated by Saudi Arabian
    King Khaled   13
Houthi   354
human rights   189
  abuses   178
Human Rights Watch   257, 376
  Annual Report 2019
    continued repression   284
Human Rights Watch report 2013
  Interfere, Restrict and Control   244
Hussein, Saddam   354
  President of Iraq   54
Huwar   354
hydraulic fracturing
  extraction of shale oil   272
  fracking   272
hydrocarbons   208
  2008 revenues   229
  construction of new facilities   61

Hydrocarbons (contd.)
foundation for refining and aluminium
smelter 208
government revenue 281
sector deminishing 254
sector rebounding 258
hydrocracker 78
hydrocracking
facilities at Sitra Refinery 205
unit investment 95
hydrofracking 354
Hyundai
1975 began work on ASRY in Bahrain 13

INVESTCORP
ABC managed facility 126
Ikhwan al-Muslimin 378
illiteracy quotient lowest in Gulf 66
immigrant labour
rise in cost of imported food 64
immigration 86, 232
Imperial Bank of Persia 355
import duties 17
form of state revenue 101
import substitution industries 102
import and export control 5
imports 5
68% of GDP in 1999 186
main suppliers 5
revenue 176
incendiary attacks 173
Indian crude 104
Indian fuel standards 209
Indian nationals
senior posts in Defence Force 183
Indian sub-continent 228
Indo-Pakistani unskilled labour 2
Indus Valley peoples 35
industrial area for the region
proposed for Bahrain, Saudi Arabia and
Qatar 71
industrial development 3, 355
foreign participation 5
Ministry of Trade and Development 140
industrial diversification 3, 85
industrial expansion 51
planned by government 139
industrial investment
private finance 103

industrial strategy 73
industrialisation 59
inequalities 233
inequality
exacerbated by economic crisis 279
inflation 3, 156, 197, 258
food price 240
low 201
Information Affairs Authority 237, 376
American journalists detained 264
Information and eGovernment
Authority 355
Infosamak 155
infrastructure, early investment 19
instability perceived 277
Institute for International Finance 239
institutional funds 20
insurance sector 64
well capitalised 211
'inter-generational equity' 202
inter-Gulf trade 73
regional stabilisation 123
intercalation 295–296
interest rates 180, 197
high in 1999 186
intermarriage 271
International Business Times 260
International Court of Justice 355
2001 resolution of Qatar dispute 204
dispute with Qatar 151
Hawar Islands dispute 169
Qatar takes Hawar Islands dispute
to ICJ 164
international criticism 237
international debt 143
international financial and commercial
institutions 205
International Herald Tribune 245, 355
International Labour Organisation 355
International Monetary Fund 239, 355
1983 Bahrain country report 71
2004 assessment of economy 209
2004 overview of economy 201
2006 report on financial sector 211
2014 assessment of economy 258
2018 overview of economy 273
challenges 202
fiscal sustainability concerns 241

INDEX 447

International Organisation of
    Migration 204
international telecommunications 15
Investcorp Bank 181, 356
investment
    1999 boost for non-oil sectors 187
    incentives 140
investment banking licences 109, 356
    introduced 1978 43
investment incentives 191
investment location 225
investor confidence 247
inward investment 206
Iran 356
    1970 agreed to relinquish claim to
        Bahrain 6
    1979 declaration of Islamic Republic 47
    1979 revolution
        threatens regional order 97
    2011 intervention feared 234
    actions against Baghdad 54
    alleged support for Shi'as in Bahrain 173
    ambassadors exchanged with
        Bahrain 174
    ambassadors withdrawn 262
    claim to sovereignty 36
    claimed Bahrain as part of Iran 54
    decision to relinquish islands 1
    diplomatic relations restored 179
    dispute with Iraq 59
    foreign policy 233
        Bahrain claimed as fourteenth
            province 233
    improved relations 189
    incite Shi'ite communities 121
    majority population Shi'a 144
    military superpower 229
    Mohammad Khatami
        President since May 1997 189
    no longer backing Hezbollah-
        Bahrain 169
    relations 229
    renewed claims to Bahrain 47
    revived sovereignty over Bahrain
        post-Pahlavi regime 136
    revolution 47
    revolutionary Islam 54
    Saudi Arabian embassy attacked 262
    sends troops to Iraq border 54

    tensions rise 262
Iranian
    aggression provokes concern 54
    chauvinism 36
    immigrants 85
    politics post-Ayatollah Khomeini 136
    regime exhorting Bahrain Shi'a to
        rebel 55
    significant influence 276
    sovereignty recognised by Bahrain 233
    threat 357
    unskilled labour 3
Iranian Revolution 37, 43
Iranians
    calling for overthrow of Gulf
        Monarchies 56
Iran/Iraq War 54, 357
    1980 outbreak 64
    1981 GCC Summit attempt to resolve 59
    1982 Iraq loses battle of Korramshahr 55
    1988 cease-fire 130, 136
    1988 end of hostilities 144
    Abadan refinery destroyed 60
    affect on Bahrain 121
    Bahrain on front line 82
    efforts to enlist aid of Egyptian troops
        fail 55
    post cease-fire optimism 136
Iraq 54, 204, 269, 358
    1990 invasion of Kuwait 144–145
        economic impact 150
    dispute with Iran 59
    Iran sends troops to Iraq border 54
    oil quota re-introduced 157
    regional ambitions 144
Iron Curtain countries trade 8
Isa Town low-cost housing 52
Isa Town Prison
    female human rights defenders
        attacked 284
Ishmael 299
Islamic
    banking 252
    calendar 296, 298
        Hijri 295
    day 298
    economics 171, 358
    finance 229
    finance sector fast growing 206

448 INDEX

Islamic (contd.)
    financial services 211
    financing 359
    insurance companies 229
    retail banks 252
    year 298
Islamic Action Association 195, 358
Islamic Bank 95
Islamic Daawa Party 337
Islamic Development Bank 358
Islamic Enlightenment Society 86
Islamic Front for the Liberation of
    Bahrain 359
Islamic Heritage Revival Society 359
Islamic Law 359
Islamic National Wefaq (Accord)
    Society 359
Islamic Resistance Movement 352
Islamic Revolution 85
    Persian claims to Bahrain revived 144
Islamic Revolutionary Guard Corps 357
Islamic State 359
Islamic State of Iraq and the Levant 359
Islamic Summit Conference
    1981 November, Riyadh 360
ism 300
Israel 296
    attacks on Lebanon 54
    attacks on Palestinians 54
    Gaza conflict 2008–14 360
    invasion of Lebanon 1982
        condemned by Bahrain 56
    Lebanon conflict 2006 360
    pro-Israeli Lobby 385
    Western supporters 56
    withdrawal from occupied territories
        called for 57
Istanbul 360

JGC Corporation 140, 148
Jakarta 361
al-Jamri, Abdel-Amir 361
    opposition leader 174
    Shi'a cleric 183
al-Jamri, Mansour 361
Japan Gasoline Co 49
    gas-gathering facility contract 21
Japanese cultured pearls 9
Jarallah, Ahmed 114

Jaw Prison 2015 riot 260
Jebel Ali Free Zone, Dubai 156
Jebel al-Dukhan oilfield
    first well spudded 1931 66
    production declining 49
Jerusalem 57
job market vibrant 280
job opportunities critical for social
    stability 127
job problems in creating 99
jobs
    labour minister promises to create
        40,000 68
joggers stoned by villagers 168
joint consultative committees 87
journalists
    Americans deported 263
    jailed 264
Jubail Industrial City 128
judicial system 246
    overhaul 237
judiciary
    instituted by King Hamad 195
Julian Calendar 296
Julius Caesar 296
junior technical college
    Saudi Arabia donated BD13 million 14

al-Kaaki family 107
Kaiser Aluminium Bahrain 62
Kaiser Aluminium 92, 305
    government buys Kaiser Aluminium's
        stake in ALBA 142
    owned 17% of ALBA 40
Kanoo
    merchant family 74
    Yusuf bin Ahmed 363
Kanoo Group 363
Keffiyeh 363
Khaleej al-Bahrain 363
khaleeji 334
al-Khalifa
    Dynasty 237
    family council 100
    regime supported by GCC troops 234
    Ruling Family
        divisions on economic policy 184
        favoured ties with Saudi Arabia
            and US 56

INDEX 449

grudges against 270
monopolise power 271
relatively benevolent policies 137
resistance to democracy 276
Sunni Muslim 144, 168
Sunni Muslims 54, 163, 214, 270
Abdullah bin Ahmed
Hakim 1796–1843 363
Abdullah bin Salman
Co-Regent 1825–34 363
Ahmed bin Mohammed
assumed sovereignty 1782/83 7
Hakim 1783–1795 1, 364
Ali bin Khalifa
Hakim 1868–69 364
Hamad bin Isa bin Ali 364
Hamad bin Isa bin Salman 183, 227
Commander-in-Chief Defence
Forces 67
constitutional reforms
announced 237, 246
Crown Prince 131, 174
King 364
King from February 2002 188
Minister of Defence 7
promise to introduce democracy 195
visit to Paris 288
Isa bin Abdullah 73
Ministry of Development and
Industry Under Secretary 72
Isa bin Ali
Hakim 1869–1932 365
Isa bin Ali House 141
Isa bin Salman bin Hamad 7
1961 became Hakim 277
died 6 March 1999 188
Hakim 1961–71, Emir 1971–99 1, 365
plan for National Assembly
announced 1992 153
political unrest 178
visit to Saudi King Faisal 1966 122
Khalifa bin Ahmed 366
Minister of Defence 131
Khalifa bin Salman 58
harsh treatment of Shi'ites 188
Prime Minister 7, 67, 86, 120, 174,
183–184, 188, 214, 245, 271, 366
Mohammed bin Essa 366
Chief Executive EDB 214

Mohammed bin Khalifa
Hakim 1834–42, 1849–68, 1869 366
Minister of Oil 281
Mohammed bin Mubarak
Foreign Minister and Deputy Prime
Minister 367
Minister of Foreign Affairs
visits Beijing 146
Sabrika bint Ibrahim
wife of King Hamad bin Isa bin
Salman al-Khalifa 367
Salman bin Ahmed
Co-Regent 1825–34 363
Salman bin Hamad bin Isa (1894–1961)
Hakim 1942–61 367
traditional paternalistic rule 100
Salman bin Hamad bin Isa (b. 1969)
Announced National Action Charter
2000 188
appointed First Deputy Prime
Minister 2013 253
appointed Prime Minister November
2020 367
continues reform process 221
introduced reforms 227
meeting with UK Prime Minister
Cameron 235
Khalij 367
Khalij al-Bahrain oilfield 367
Kharg Island 82
Khatami, Mohammed 367
al-Khawaja, Abdulhadi 244, 368
al-Khawaja, Maryam 244, 368
al-Khawaja, Zainab 244, 368
al-Khobar 368
Khomeini, Ruhollah 54
pro-Khomeini slogans
during Shi'a demonstrations 1980 55
Battle of Khorramshahr 55
Khuff Zone
development drilling 90
gas prodution raised 104
gas reserves 39
non-associated gas 61
production 22
production increasing 39
Khutbah 295
King Fahd Causeway 110, 122, 160, 232, 269,
369

450 INDEX

King Fahd Causeway (contd.)
   1978 bids invited   18
   Bahrain integration with Eastern
      Province markets   123
   costs   18
   custom duty payments   88
   economic benefits   123
   local constructors to benefit   63
   price reductions for Bahrain
      consumers   123
King Faisal Corniche   369
King Faisal II   19
King Faisal sea-front highway   128
King Hamad   251
King, Tom
   British Defence Secretary   145
Kleinwort Benson   106
Kobe Steel   61, 79, 369
   Gulf Aluminium Rolling Mill   70
Koran   295
Koran Revelation   298
Kroll Associates Bahrain
   uncovered corruption   215
kunya   300
Kuwait   2, 269
   1983 bombings   86
   goodwill   46
   Iraqi invasion of   369
   support for Iraq in Iran/Iraq War   82
   US Congress blocks arms sales   130
Kuwait Airways   370
Kuwait Asia Bank   84, 107–108, 116
Kuwait-Bahrain Chemical Co   394
Kuwait Desalination Plant Co   62
Kuwait Foreign Petroleum
      Exploration Co   112, 370
   subsidiary of KPC   103
Kuwait Foreign Trading, Contracting and
      Investment Co   62
Kuwait Investment Co   370
Kuwait Metal Pipes   62
Kuwaiti dinars   42

labour
   code   372
   force   37
   local expensive and not adequately
      trained   128
   movement   100, 371

national workforce
   women 55%   127
   organisations   245
   shortages   2
   technical expertise   2
labour market
   discrimination against Shi'a   189
   reforms   223, 275
Lailat al-Miraj   298
Lailat al-Qadr   298
laissez-faire administration   66
Lamb, Christina   249
land tenure system   89
laqab   300
laundering of drugs money   146
Law of Associations   245, 373
Lazard Fréres   106
Le Swave   288
League of Arab States   373
   Bahrain member of   67
Lebanon
   Israeli withdrawal   59
legal structure   66
legal system   193
Lent   298
Levey, Stuart   373
   US Treasury Secretary   216
Libya   56
light industrial projects   44
light industries   63
liquefied natural gas
   LNG terminal   255
Lisnave Shipyards SA   13, 52, 62
   ASRY managed by   94
   Portuguese shipyard   41
list of Islamist militant groups   263
livestock   65
living standards   200
   worsening   183
Lloyds Bank   133
Lloyds of London   64
loans   241
   business
      slow growth   241
   from Kuwait and Saudi Arabia   186
local plants   103
local producers
   legislation gives advantage over foreign
      suppliers   134

INDEX

local sponsor 216
localised strikes 37
low cost of doing business 289
low cost housing 44
low sulphur fuel oil 21, 373
Lummus 95
lunar calendar 296
lunar year 295
lunation 295

M-60 Tanks 374
macroeconomic performance 210
macroeconomic policies 224
Madinat Hamad 89, 102, 351
majlis 87
    weekly audience 100
Majlis al-Nuwab 336
Majlis al-Shura 100, 188, 213, 336, 374
    expanded role proposed by Emir 184
major projects held back 128
al-Malali, Ahmed 374
    2019 executed 278
Malinowski, Tom 250, 374
    declared *persona non grata* 250
    US Assistant Secretary of State for
        Democracy, Human Rights and
        Labour 250
Manama 2, 374
    business centre 205
    capital 205
    close relationship with Washington 137
    increasing contacts with Soviet
        Union 138
Manama Dialogue 374
    participants deported 264
Manama/Muharraq
    second causeway link planned 143
al-Manbar al-Islami 256, 375
manpower development 66
al-Maraj, Rasheed
    Central Bank of Bahrain Governor 285
Margaret Thatcher
    1981 visit to Bahrain 58
Marine Midland Bank 106
Marketing and Promotions Board 160
al-Marzouq, Khalil 250
matems 85
Mauddud Formation 157
Mawlid al-Nabi 298

McClaren Formula One 222
McKinsey & Co
    Economic Vision 2030 271
Mecca 295, 375
    departure from 295
medical services 69
Medina 295
Méndez, Juan E
    UN Special Rapporteur 245
merchant class 66
merchants
    Indian and Persian 268
Mesopotamia 35
Mesopotamian calendar 296
Mezzofiore, Gianluca 260
Midal Cables 24, 70, 93, 375
    expansion plans 71
    training and employing Bahrainis 71
Middle East 375
Middle East (Annual) Review 375
Middle East Economic Digest 145, 375
    Abdulla al-Saudi interview 126
Middle East Engineering Ltd 375
Middle East Financial Group 107
Middle East Review XI
Middle East and North Africa 375
Midland Bank 105, 132
migrant workers
    60% of workforce 198
military
    air base at Suman 128
    assistance from Saudi Arabia 97
    tribunals 237
    upheaval in the Gulf 144
military base 110
military court
    June 2011 tried doctors and nurses 235
Mina Salman 4, 60, 375
    causeway to Sitra Island 14
    container port 75
    effects of causeway 101
    efficiently run by 1980 46
    free port 5
    goods unloaded for Saudi Arabia 161
    industrial area 94
    industrial zone on reclaimed land 14
    port for container vessels planned 142
    sea port 84
    six futher berths 14

452 INDEX

Mina Salman (contd.)
trans-shipment traffic 75
Mina Salman Port Development
Scheme 113, 375
minimum wage 203
Ministry of Labour and Social Affairs 376
Abdel-Nabi al-Shoala, Minister 170
cost of work permits increased 177
Ministry of Commerce
exempt commercial companies
regulations 84
Ministry of Development and Engineering
Services 13
Ministry of Electricity and Water 172, 242
Hidd power and desalination
expansion 192
Ministry of Information Affairs 376
Ministry of Interior 257
denied Jaw Prison torture
allegations 261
Ministry of Justice
suspended al-Wefaq National Islamic
Society 249
Ministry for Offshore Exploration 273
Ministry of Social Development 245, 376
al-Moayyed, Dr Tawfeq
GPIC Chief Executive 78
Mohammed, Ibrahim Abdul-Karim
Minister of Finance and National
Economy 133
monarchical rule
instigated by al-Khalifa family 168
Monarchy 376
monetary policy 186, 241
Moody's 175, 281, 290, 377
2018 credit rating downgraded 282
2018 oil discovery to boost recovery 281
2019 credit profile 283
banking profits warning 180
Moore, Alan 25, 377
Morland, Lewis 377
mosques
King orders rebuilding 246
Most Favoured Nation 377
import tariff reduction 193
tariff on imports relatively low 190
al-Moumen, Qassim Abdullah Ali 377
Movement for the National Liberation of
Palestine 352

Mubarak, Hosni 57, 377
President of Egypt 55
Muharram 298, 377
Al-Muharraq 377
Muharraq Island 2, 52
municipal councils
elected members 1
Muntakalat 222, 377
Formula One Grand Prix 215
Muslim 378
Muslim Brotherhood 256, 378

Najadi, Hussain 107, 378
Najd 378
nasab 300
Nass, Sameer Abdulla 280
Nasser, Gamal Abdul 378
Nasserism 269
National Action Charter 188, 379
2001 referendum 220
commitment to respect for human
rights 189
National Assembly 1, 67, 87, 173, 379
1973 December first convened 7
1975 August dissolved by Emiri decree 7
1975 closed 68
1999 reactivated 214
authorised by Emiri Decree 1972 67
called for by Constituton 7
elected by universal suffrage 188
first elections 1
formed 16 December 1972 67
plans to appoint announced 153
prorogued 1975 100
ratified participation agreement
oil and natural gas production 10
Shi'a pressure for 67
Shi'a demands for reinstatement 178
suspended August 1975 37
to replace Majlis al-Shura 188
unwritten policy one-third Shi'a 67
National Bank of Abu Dhabi 109
National Bank of Bahrain 25, 43, 109, 146,
152, 166, 379
1977 year of consolidation 26
government plans to reduce
shareholding 158
National Bank of Kuwait
GCC Economic Report 239

INDEX 453

National Chemical Industries Co
    sulphur derivatives plant 159
National Commercial Bank 107
National Democratic Action Society 195, 379
National Institute for Human Rights 261
National Liberation Front 380
National Museum 380
National Oil Co 11
National Oil and Gas Authority (noga) 231, 380
    estimates demand to increase 3%
        on 2010 242
    regulatory and oversight of oil
        industry 231
National Union Committee 371, 380
National Westminster Bank 51
nationalism 269
Nationalist Democratic Rally 195, 380
nationality 270
natural gas 3
    Awali Oilfield reserves 226
    increased utilisation 167
    plans to import from Qatar 248
    plans to increase imports 260
    reserves 85, 209, 242
        over-estimated in 1975 13
    uses 157
natural gas liquids 381
    Bahrain Oilfield
        gas gathering and processing
            facility 39
        gas gathering facility 21
        March 1980 exports started 49
        plant opened 1979 61
        propane, butane, naphtha
            exports 61
Near East (aka Middle East) 381
Nejd 381
Nesom, Gayle 301
nest industries, labour intensive 74
net foreign exchange income 24
netback prices 112
new Arabia pipeline
    Abqaiq to Sitra 248
New Year 296
Night of Power or of the Decree 298
Nikko Securities Co 133, 381
Nimr al-Nimr 381

Nippon Denro Ispat 171
nisba 300
noga
nogaholding 381
nominated councils 1
Nomura Securities 106
non-associated gas 381
    Khuff Zone 49, 61
    reserves 22
non-hydrocarbon sector
    resilient 273
non-NATO ally of US 203
non-oil
    2013 activity slowed 258
    economic activity 252
        rebounded 247
    GDP 217, 240
        imports rise in 1992 151
        industry contracted in 1997 180
non-performing loans 252
non-Shia foreigners
    influx 271
North American Free Trade Area 175, 381
North Atlantic Treaty Organisation 381
North Islands
    1992 unsuccessful oil exploration 156
North Sitra 349
    industrial estate financed by Kuwait 103
Norwich Winterthur Insurance (Gulf) 81
Notzon, Beth 301
nuclear agreement reached 262
nuclear power 242
al-Nusra Front 381

OAPEC dry dock 381
OPEC quotas
    Bahrain not subject to 166
Occidental contract to double
        production 242
official reserves 247, 252
offshore banking 80
    BMA to issue licences 6
    caution in sector 50
    increased regional competition 139
Offshore Banking Unit/s 82, 382
    assets 63
    domestic economy contribution 139
    first in Middle East opened 1976 67
    launched in 1975 by BMA 16

454 INDEX

Offshore Banking Unit/s (contd.)
  major players 108
  moratorium on new licences 42
  recovered from 1990–91 Gulf crisis 151
oil
  1936 refinery in operation 38
  1998 price slump 185
  1999 revenue rise 185
  2013 fiscal breakeven price 252
  2018 Khalij al-Bahrain discovery
    announced 272
  concession awarded to Standard
    Oil Co 38
  continued dependence on revenues 128
  contribution to GDP 185
  dependency 197
  discovered 1932 2
  earnings 60
  exploration 166
    Hawar Islands 156
    North Islands 156
  export earnings 132
  export products 125
  export revenue 60
  exports 236
    down in 1982 75
    refined products 204
  first to export 19
  foreign currency earner 124
  GDP 242
  glut weathered by Bahrain 88
  imports from Saudi Arabia 75
  industry
    expansion 225
    largest employer 38
  Khalij al-Bahrain discovery
    announced 291
  main export markets 176
  market sluggish in 1989 138
  pipeline network 236
  policy
    Bahrain follows Saudi Arabia
      lead 44
  price
    2008 collapse 240
    2014 slump 259
    fall 54, 176
      financial constraints on
        region 178

    threatens regional order 97
    quadruples 11
  production 4, 132, 242
  production extended 230
  production and refining major
    industry 3
  refinery maintenance costs 20
  reserves 3, 156
    2011 236
    Awali oilfield 208
    declining 204
    Gulf of Bahrain 226
    Gulf of Bahrain potential 204
    limited to Awali and Abu Safah
      oilfields 190
    onshore 281
  revenue
    one third to Royal Family 232
    quadruples 11
  revenues 4, 19, 125
  stabilisation fund 202
  two-thirds government revenue 208
  value added 39
Oil & Gas Journal 236, 382
Olex Cables Co 24, 93
Oman (Sultanate of) 382
Oman Air 382
Oman and South Yemen dispute
  GCC move to resolve 59
Omanis 35
Ombudsman 261
one-off payment to every family by King
  Hamad 234
open economy 206
Operation Decisive Storm XII
opposition 284
  activists 249
  exiles encouraged to return 200
  Shi'ite-led 188
opposition groups
  target luxury hotels 176
Organisation of Arab Petroleum Exporting
  Countries
  ASRY first joint venture 12
  ASRY first major industrial venture 19
  Bahrain chosen for first OAPEC
    downstream operation 7
  Bahrain member 38, 157
  oil embargo on Western world 4

INDEX 455

Organisation of the Petroleum Exporting
  Countries 4, 7, 382
  Bahrain not a member 157
  March 1999 production cap 185
  non-members 38
  policies followed by Bahrain 48
  stabilised price of crude 126
organised protest 168
oryx 141, 383
Overseas Trust Bank 106

package of reforms 274
Pahlavi Régime 383
Pakistani nationals
  senior posts in Defence Force 183
Palestine 383
Palestine Liberation Organisation 8, 384
  mediation between Bahrain and Iran 47
Palestinian problem 56
  Bahrain diplomats working for
    solution 57
  Bahrain supports cause 2
  European initiative 57
  future of territories occupied by
    Israel 54
Palestinians 54
parastatals 177
pariah state 235
parliament
  1975 dissolved 163
  bicameral 200
  established by King Hamad 195
  lower chamber elected 256
  Shi'a majority 163
  upper chamber appointed 256
parliamentary experimentation 37
PayPal 288
peace talks between Iraq and Iran 136
pearl diving 384
  destroyed by Japanese cultivated
    pearls 2
  prosperity 249
pearl fishing 3
pearl fishing fleet 268
pearl industry
  Bahrain the centre of 268
  Japanese cultured pearls 85
  Manama and Muharraq prosperous
    communities 9

Pearl Investment 109
pearl market 268
Pearl Revolution 237
  Saudi Arabian-led forces intervene 237
Pearl Square/Roundabout 384
  2011 demonstrations response to 235
  Shi'a protesters killed 233
pearling banks 9
Pemex
  dinar bond issue 26
Peninsula Shield 384
Pentecost 298
Persian Gulf 233
Persian sovereignty 384
petrodollars 16, 83, 105, 385
petroleum
  products
    fall in demand 54
  provides half government revenue 2
petroleum coke
  price quadrupled 23
petroleum exploration
  1999 re-initiated by Texaco 187
Petroma and Hutchinson
  plans to build oil refinery 180
Petronas awarded exploration block 204
Philippine government
  dinar bond issue 26
pipeline 209
plot to overthrow the government
  77 Shi'a detained 1981 100
political
  ambitions of workforce XI
  conflict eased in 1997 173
  development 86
  freedom shrinks 279
  groups prohibited until 2001 245
  instability 240
  liberalisation 188
    encouraged by King Hamad 195
  reforms 189
  risk factors affect on banking 105
  tensions remain 199
Political Agent 227, 385
political influence
  Emir competes with Prime Minister 187
political organisations
  harassed by authorities 245

456 INDEX

political power
  dominated by al-Khalifa family   212
political prisoners   189, 270
  pardoned   220
  Red Cross estimates 1,400   173
  released   234
political and street unrest   253
political tensions
  aggrevated by uncertain regional
    situation   207
political uncertainty
  financial sector   176
political unrest
  1996–97   183
  persistent   247
  social tensions root cause   187
pomegranate cakes   271
Popular Front for the Liberation of the
    Arabian Gulf   86
population   19, 36
  1966   276
  60% Shi'a in 1986   100
  65% Shi'a   214
  89% in Manama and Muharraq   228
  indigenous increasing 10,000 a year   99
  lower growth expected   125
Portuguese   35
post-Suez situation   269
post-war reconstruction boom
  slow to materialise   136
potline   385
poultry farm   10
power
  generating capacity   13
  generation to increase   60, 103
  grid   242
  integration with gas   98
power station
  ALBA expansion link to national grid   149
power and water plan approved   149
Prakesh Industries
  new steel rolling mill   171
pre-Islamic
  Middle Eastern calendars   296
premier *entrepôt*   8
press censorship
  foreign journalists expelled   100
prime minister
  appointed by King   257

prison abuse allegations   284
private sector
  1999 investment slowdown   186
  employers   128
  government to encourage development
    and investment   202
  investment   128
  participation in industry   73
private wealth
  attempt to attract   133
privatisation   206
  limited   177, 198
  major programme planned   139
  plans   147
  WTO suggests step up   191
Pro-Israeli Lobby   385
promissory notes issue
  BMA responsibility   25
Prophet Mohammed   298
  left Mecca for Medina   295
Prophet's Birthday   298
prosperity
  based on pearling   8
  since oil   55
protests October 2010   233
Ptolemy First   296
Ptolomaic astronomers   297
public debt   274
public payroll   279
public sector
  government plans announced   175
  government to reduce role and size   202
  wages   210
public utilities
  privatisation welcomed by IMF   203
public wage bill   274

Qadi   299
al-Qaeda   386
Qajar, Ahmed Shah
  Shah of Persia   383
Qantas   232
Qatar   386
  dispute over islands   151
  long standing territorial and family
    disputes   8
  municipal elections 1999   184
  opted for single-state independence   36
  relations with improve   229

INDEX

territorial conflict with   110
trade links   2
al-Qauod, Lateefah   213, 386
Qit'at Jaradah   386
Quds Force   357
Quintilis   297

REDEC   388
Rabeea, Falah   387
Bahrain Salam   249
Rabi al-Awal   298
Rafsanjani, Hashemi
President of Iran   137
the Raj   269
Rajab   298
Rajab, Nabeel   244, 284, 387
Ramadan   298
ransom of a ram
Ishmael   299
Rapid Deployment Force (GCC)   59
Rapid Deployment Force (US)   59
Rapid Deployment Joint Task Force   387
Ras Tanura   387
re-exports   5
Reagan, Ronald   388
thanks Sheikh Isa bin Salman
al-Khalifa   130
real estate
GCC citizen ownership permitted   193
reclaimed land Manama expansion   14
reclamation scheme between Bahrain and
Qatar   103
reconciliation talks   249
recreational facilities   14
recurrent expenditure
politically imperative to maintain   185
Red Cross   173
referendum 2001
National Action Charter   220
refined petroleum products exports   242
refining   388
reform movements   87
reform process
2008 developments   221
Sheikh Salman bin Hamad
al-Khalifa   214
years to become apparent   196
refugee camps
Jordan   271

regional airline Gulf Air   269
regional aluminium industry   124
regional banking centre
Dubai   249
regional centre
development as   2
regional economy   122
regional recession concern   97
regional situation
uncertain post 2003 Gulf War   200
regional tyre plant
Bahrain hopes for funding   99
Rejectionist Front (States)   388
rejectionist states
objected to Fahd al-Saud Palestinian
proposals   57
reputation
damaged by 2011 demonstrations   235
reservoirs being depleted   149
residue gases   21, 388
Resistance Brigades   388
Reuters   246, 278, 388
revenue raising exercise   20
reverse osmosis desalination plant
planned by ALBA   158
Rezayat, Brown and Root   118
Riffa   389
Riffa Fort   153
Riffa power station   149
Riyadh   389
Robert Fleming & Co   106
Rohani, Sadiq   389
Roman Republican calendar   297
Ross Group   3
Ross Seafoods (Gulf) Ltd   10
Rouhani, Sadiq   54
Royal Air Force
Tornado strike aircraft sent to
Bahrain   145
Royal Navy   130

SABIC
plan for aluminium smelter in Jubail   40
Saad, Khalid
Bahrain FinTech Bay CEO   285
sabotage plot   144
Sadat, Anwar   47, 390
1981 assassination   57

al-Sadr, Mohammed Baqr
    1980 executed in Iraq 55
Safavid Persians 35
Salafism 256
al-Salam Bank-Bahrain 390
salinity 3
Salman, Ali 250, 284, 390
    called for return of parliament 163
Samaan, Alees 212, 390
al-Samahji Exchange Co 117
Sanabis tourist beach 128
Sanger, Richard 232, 390
Santa Fe International 90
Saraya al-Ashtar (SaA) 390
Sasanian Persians 35
al-Saud
    alarmed by spread of democracy in
        peninsula 100
    Crown Prince Faud al-Saud
        proposals for resolution of Palestinian
            problem 57
    Faisal bin Abdul-Aziz
        Abu Safah oilfield 19
al-Saudi, Abdulla
    ABC President 126
Saudi Arabia 2, 269, 391
    aid from 391
    bilateral assistance 89
    concerned by Bahrain Shi'a unrest 174
    Eastern Province 35
        Shi'a community 164
    economic problems 97
    National Guard 174
    relationship important to Bahrain 19
    special relationship 46
    sphere of influence 144
    troops to Bahrain 234, 262
    US Congress blocks arms sale 130
    underwrites Bahrain independence 97
    Western expatriates 18
    within US sphere of influence XI
Saudi Arabian Basic Industries Co 62, 391
Saudi Arabian crude 4
Saudi Arabian Monetary Authority 83
    restricted Bahrain OBUs 105
Saudi Arabian riyal 42
Saudi-Bahrain Causeway
    see King Fahd Causeway 88
Saudi Bank 391

Saudi Cables Co 93
Saudi currency revalued 50
Saudi Development Fund 392
Saudi entrepreneurs 101
Saudi-Kuwaiti Mediation Mission 1, 392
Saudi Research and Development Co 392
Schadenfreude 393
Schlumberger 393
school
    1919 first opened 268
    Bahrain had first in Arabian Gulf 66
school leavers 69
Schultz, George 393
    US Secretary of State 58
seasonal year 296
Second Ululu 296
Second World War
    British concerns on German presence in
        Middle East XI
    military base 232
sectarian conflict 261
sectarian politics 188
security courts
    dismantled by King Hamad 200
security forces
    predominantly Pakistani 169
security laws dismantled 195
Security Pacific Bank 105
security threats mostly Iranian 144
septem 297
service centre 18
    Bahrain role for Saudi Arabia 83
service sector
    50% of employment 190
    buoyant 252
Seven Sisters 185, 393
sewerage system 13
shades of colonialism XI
Shah 393
shale gas discoveries
    need foreign investment 275
shale oil
    extraction expertise 272
al-Shamil Bank 393
al-Shara, Farouk 393
    foreign minister of Syria 169
Sharia 393
Sharia-compliant procedures 288
Sharjah 393

INDEX 459

Shawaal 299
sheep rearing 10
Sheikh 394
Shell Fisheries 394
Shi'a majority ruled by a Sunni minority XI
Shi'a Muslim
    dispossessed by al-Khalifa family 99
Shi'a Muslims 55
    1994 disturbances 163
    2011 Shi'ite opposition failed
        uprising 278
    73 convicted after 1982 secret trial 56
    alienation 198
    boycotted 2002 elections 213
    community 183
    complain of discrimination 163
    complaints on exclusion from
        government jobs 214
    disaffection 97
    discontent 262
    dissidents 188
    five Cabinet ministers 67
    high population growth 189
    higher unemployment rate 163
    low profile maintained 121
    major branch of Islam 394
    majority in Bahrain 163
    migrations from Iran 99
    more than half the population 54
    political and economic discrimina-
        tion 168
    possible nucleus for dissent 162
    protests towards ruling family 163
    recruited into defence force 183
    rites 271
    still a majority in 2019 276
    unable to join police or armed
        forces 163
    villages with Sunni no-go areas 271
shipping business downturn 122
al-Shirawi, Yusuf 72, 86, 98, 102, 394
    BAPCO Chairman 112
    Minister of Industry and
        Development 67, 124
al-Shoala, Abdel-Nabi
    Minister of Labour and Social
        Affairs 394
show trials 169
shura 87

Sinai Accord 395
al-Sindi, Murtada Majid Ramadan
        Alawi 395
Singapore 42
single currency
    2010 to be introduced by GCC 203
Sitra Island 395
    desalination plant 3
    oil port 4
    power station 149
    hydrocarbon facility 61
Sitra Refinery 323, 395
    2005 capacity 204
    2018 pipeline to Abqaiq
        commissioned 294
    development scheme 125
    hydrocracking facilities 204, 209
    plans to expand by 2017 260
    Saudi Arabia cuts oil supply 125
    studies to modernise 132
    technical and management training 97
Sixtilis 297
Siyadi House 326
Smith Barney Harris Upham 106
Snamprogetti
    to build twin ammonia and methanol
        plant 78
social security contributions
    cut to encourge job creation 127
social services 52
social tension root causes 200
societies 228
socio-economic priorities 198
'soft loans'
    from Saudi Arabia, Kuwait and Abu
        Dhabi 8
    from Saudi Arabia and Kuwait 19
solar year 295–296
Sosigenes 297
Souk al-Manakh 84, 114, 126, 395
South Yemen dispute with Oman 59
sovereign wealth fund 232
Soviet Union 395
    discussions on diplomatic relations 131
    growing threat to area 48
Speakers Corner 233
Special Branch 37
special relationship
    Saudi Arabia/Bahrain 35

460 INDEX

Spot Metal aka Spot Price   395
Spring Equinox   297–298
Standard & Chartered Bank   109
Standard and Poor's
    2008 rating stable   223
    2017 Bahrain debt junk level   271
    predicts low oil price   396
    rate revised from negative to stable   247
Standard Oil Co   3, 395
State Council   396
State Department (US)   396
state of emergency
    15 March–1 June 2011   235
    proclaimed 1956   37
state income
    main sources   15
state-ownership   197
State Security Court   169, 173, 396
    abolished   220
State Security Law
    abolished   220
    dismantled by King Hamad   200
state sinecures   281
Station F   288
Statistical Bureau   332
statutory reserve requirement   107
steel plants
    direct-reduction method
        Saudi Arabia, Qatar and Iraq   124
steel works plan
    scaled back to pelletisation plant   98
Stinger anti-aircraft missiles   396
    1987 US Congress approves sale with
        stringent conditions   130
stock exchange
    delays in establishing   132
    increase in market capitalisation   180
    opened June 1989   139
stock exchanges
    Bahrain and Oman to link   166
stock market index   252
    declined in 2012   247
stress testing exercise   211
strike   371
strike by foreigners legalised by court   99
structural reform agenda   203
subsidies   274
    agriculture   64
    introduced   9

reduced on water and electricity   279
Suez Canal   396
    1956 invasion by Britain and France   277
Suez crisis   37
Suez War   372
sukuk   282
    Islamic bonds   396
sulphuric acid plant   103
Sumerians   35
Sumitomo Bank   106
Sun Hung Kai Bank   108
Sunday Times   249
Sunni Islamist parties
    free to operate   279
Sunni Muslim   396
    concerned by Iran ancient claim to
        Bahrain   100
    mosques   271
    outnumbered by Shi'a   85
    promoted to key government
        positions   99
    protestors   233
    rulers   232
    ruling sect   183
    ruling sect in Arabian Gulf   67
Sunni-Shi'a community tensions
    Iraq   214
Supreme Council for Oil   397
synodic cycle   296
Syria   56
Syrian Sunnis   271
system of government   68

Tahrir Square   233
Taif   397
    July 1982 GCC meeting   55
Taif Treaty   397
takaful   229
talks
    deadlocked between government and
        opposition   254
    regional alliance to prevent super-power
        influence   48
Tamkeen   280, 397
tanker escort operations   137
tanker-servicing industries   121
tanker war   135, 397
tariffs
    reduction on consumer goods   185

INDEX 461

Tashritu 296
Tatweer Petroleum 398
   deal to increase oilfield production 242
al-Taweel, Ali 261
tax-free income 69
taxation 5
   need to introduce 274
taxes 15
   no corporate or income 280
Technal 93
technical and professional skills
   incentives for 68
Tehran 398
   Islamic revolution 136
   1979 resignation of civilian
      government 47
   course of moderation 136
   Islamic regime 54
Tehran Radio
   inflammatory broadcasts during Iran/Iraq
      fighting 55
telecommunication
   second mobile network 198
   services 2
tele-density 194
tensions
   Sunni/Shi'a 269
Texaco 398
   oil exploration 184
Texas Commerce Bank 106
al-Thani, Khalifa bin Hamad
   deposed Emir of Qatar 174
Thatcher, Margaret 398
   visits to thank for assisting Royal
      Navy 130
The Arabian Peninsula by R Sanger 232
The Economist 270
The Merchants 268
   Michael Field 301
The Times
   describes Bahrain as pariah state 235
   Personal Column 269
thobe 270
Tiffany & Co 108
tight oil 398
Tornado GR.1 398
torture
   reports of 235
tourism 119, 160

affected by unrest 239
aimed at Gulf Arab market 197
archeological sites 119
becoming single biggest industry 160
government promoting 153
sensitive to political unrest 176
benefit from Causeway opening 123
trade balance 197
   1996 surplus 176
trade deficit
   1998 in red 181
   doubled in 1984 102
   problem 138
   widened in 1989 146
   widened in 1992 151
trade gap 5
   1992 rise 151
trade profile 186
trade surplus
   1999 5.1% of GDP 186
trades unions
   demands for rejected by Ruler 276
   permitted by King Hamed 195
   plans for shelved 100
trading community
   anxieties about causeway 101
trading nation
   historical role of Bahrain 66
trading opportunities
   with Soviet Union and China 138
traditional crafts 141
Trafco 158
Train 10,000 skills programme 127, 398
training programmes
   BAPCO, ALBA, Gulf Air, Cable and
      Wireless 14
training schemes for workers 53
training schools
   ASRY, State Electricity Dept, hotel and
      catering industry 14
Trans-Arabian Investment Bank 108
Transparency International 398
   Corruption Perceptions Index 245, 251
transport and communications facilities 52
Treasury bills 131
Treasury bonds
   funded budget deficit 126
Tree of Life 141
trilateral agreements 48

troop reinforcements 234
Trucial States 227, 268, 399
Turks 35
United Nations Special Commission 401
United Nations Special Rapporteur 401
US Army Corps of Engineers 401
   constructing air base 137
US Congress
   pro-Israel lobby deny arms sales 137
   Pro-Israeli Lobby 385
US dollar appreciation 2008–09 228
US Energy Information Administration 401
US Fifth Fleet 250, 344
   regional security umbrella 196
US Navy
   1971 took over Royal Navy
      installations in Bahrain 137
   Bahrain facilities 2, 8
   Fifth Fleet based in Bahrain 203, 234
   Gulf patrols from Bahrain 130
   major facility in Bahrain 145
US policy 196
USSR 399
Ultra large crude carriers (ULCCs) 399
Umm Nasan island
   causeway to cross 44
unemployment 177, 189, 258, 280
   25% of youth 207
   across all levels of population 206
   Bahrain facing threat of 140
   benefits 216
   chronic 183
   government concern 178
   high among Bahraini nationals 210
   high levels threaten instability 198
   high youth 216
   insurance 203
   low in 2014 252
   relatively high 170
Union des Banques Arabes et
      Françaises 399
Union of Soviet Socialist Republics 399
United Arab Emirates 399
   Bahrain opts out 1
   trade links 2
   troops to Bahrain 234
United Arab Shipping Co 399
United Gulf Bank 107, 116, 400
United Gulf Holding Co 400

United Gulf Investments 107
United Nations 400
   member of 1
United Nations Human Rights Council 400
United Nations Security Council 400
   called to enact sanctions against
      Israel 56
   Resolution 598 130, 401
      Iran accepts 18 July 1988 130
United States of America
   maintains close ties 1
universal suffrage 228
University of Bahrain 168, 401
unrest 1994 168
unrest continued into 1995 164
urbanisation 2, 9
Utub 402

value added tax 202, 279, 290, 402
Venerable Bede 297
very large crude carriers 402
visas
   7-day 120
   flexible 280
Vision 2030 291
vocational training 9, 203
Voluntary Retirement Scheme 290, 402

Wa'ad 379
   dissolved 278
al-Wadaei, Duaa 284
al-Wafa
   political umbrella of the Saraya
      al-Ashtar 403
wages in private sector below public
      sector 279
al-Waha Fund of Funds 289, 403
Wahabiyya 403
al-Wahdawi political society 257
   condemned air strikes on Yemen 403
Wahhabi 35, 269, 403
   strictures 276
Wall Street Journal 205, 215, 403
   Economic Freedom Index 239
Wandering Calendar 296
war on terrorism supported by Bahrain 203
Washington 2
   Manama links 58
   strong relationship with 137

INDEX 463

war-on-terrorism supported by
Bahrain 196
water
consumption 125, 159
cost to rise 125
resource problem acute 149
shortage
limiting agriculture
development 103
weapons sales
approved by US State Department 285
weaving 3
al-Wefaq National Islamic Society 403
Ali Salman charged with spying for
Qatar 278
boycotted 2002 elections 195
boycotted 2014 election 256
Ministry of Justice sought to suspend
activities 249
success in 2006 elections 213
welfare payments 253
Welfare State 269
Well Number One 404
West Bank 57, 404
West Texas Intermediate crude 282
western dress 270
Western Geophysical 90
Western naval escort operations 130
wet gas processed by BANAGAS 157
Whittaker Co 108
wholesale banks
recovery dependent on political
stability 241
Williams & Glyn 25

Wood Mackenzie 293, 404
work force
government determined to increase share
of nationals 152
work permits
cost increase 177
fees 280
government forced to re-issue 128
working weekends 42
World Trade Organisation 405
Bahrain founder member 205
stresses importance of speeding up
economy 190
full membership due 2003 192

Yamaichi Securities 106
Yemen 405
Bahrain sends fighter jets 257
Yom Kippur War 310
youth employment 127

Zaidi sect 354
Zallaq Beach project 114
al-Zamil Aluminium Factory 93
al-Zamil Group 74
A A Zayani 24, 405
Zayani Investments 93
Zubara Arab Rulers
ended Persian domination of Bahrain
in 1783 136
Zubara Fort
claimed by Bahrain 164
Zubara Island 405